ABRAHAM LINCOLN

From a photograph made at Springfield soon after his nomination for
President

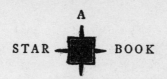

STAR BOOK

ABRAHAM LINCOLN

BY LORD CHARNWOOD

GARDEN CITY, NEW YORK

GARDEN CITY PUBLISHING CO., INC.

GENERAL EDITOR'S PREFACE

STATESMEN—even the greatest—have rarely won the same unquestioning recognition that falls to the great warriors or those supreme in science, art or literature. Not in their own lifetime and hardly to this day have the claims to supremacy of our own Oliver Cromwell, William III. and Lord Chatham rested on so sure a foundation as those of a Marlborough or a Nelson, a Newton, a Milton or a Hogarth. This is only natural. A warrior, a man of science, an artist or a poet are judged in the main by definite achievements, by the victories they have won over foreign enemies or over ignorance and prejudice, by the joy and enlightenment they have brought to the consciousness of their own and succeeding generations. For the statesman there is no such exact measure of greatness. The greater he is, the less likely is his work to be marked by decisive achievement which can be recalled by anniversaries or signalised by some outstanding event: the chief work of a great statesman rests in a gradual change of direction given to the policy of his people, still more in a change of the spirit within them. Again, the statesman must work with a rough and ready instrument. The soldier finds or makes his army ready to yield unhesitating obedience to his commands, the sailor animates his fleet with his own personal touch, and the great man in art, literature or science is master of his material, if he can master himself. The statesman cannot mould a heterogeneous people, as the men of a well-disciplined army or navy can be moulded, to respond to his call and his alone. He has to do all his work in a society of which a large part cannot see his object and another large part, as far as they do see it, oppose it. Hence his work at

the best is often incomplete and he has to be satisfied with a rough average rather than with his ideal.

Lincoln, one of the few supreme statesmen of the last three centuries, was no exception to this rule. He was misunderstood and underrated in his lifetime, and even yet has hardly come to his own. For his place is among the great men of the earth. To them he belongs by right of his immense power of hard work, his unfaltering pursuit of what seemed to him right, and above all by that childlike directness and simplicity of vision which none but the greatest carry beyond their earliest years. It is fit that the first considered attempt by an Englishman to give a picture of Lincoln, the great hero of America's struggle for the noblest cause, should come at a time when we in England are passing through as fiery a trial for a cause we feel to be as noble. It is a time when we may learn much from Lincoln's failures and success, from his patience, his modesty, his serene optimism and his eloquence, so simple and so magnificent.

BASIL WILLIAMS.

Biscot Camp,
Luton,
March, 1916.

CONTENTS

ABRAHAM LINCOLN

ABRAHAM LINCOLN

ABRAHAM LINCOLN

CHAPTER I

BOYHOOD OF LINCOLN

The subject of this memoir is revered by multitudes of his countrymen as the preserver of their commonwealth. This reverence has grown with the lapse of time and the accumulation of evidence. It is blended with a peculiar affection, seldom bestowed upon the memory of statesmen. It is shared to-day by many who remember with no less affection how their own fathers fought against him. He died with every circumstance of tragedy, yet it is not the accident of his death but the purpose of his life that is remembered.

Readers of history in another country cannot doubt that the praise so given is rightly given; yet any bare record of the American Civil War may leave them wondering why it has been so unquestioningly accorded. The position and task of the American President in that crisis cannot be understood from those of other historic rulers or historic leaders of a people; and it may seem as if, after that tremendous conflict in which there was no lack of heroes, some perverse whim had made men single out for glory the puzzled civil magistrate who sat by. Thus when an English writer tells again this tale, which has been well told already and in which there can remain no important new facts to disclose, he must endeavour to make clear to Englishmen circumstances and conditions which are familiar to Americans. He will incur the certainty that here and there his own perspective of American affairs and persons will be false, or his own touch unsympathetic. He had better do this than

chronicle sayings and doings which to him and to those for whom he writes have no significance. Nor should the writer shrink too timidly from the display of a partisanship which, on one side or the other, it would be insensate not to feel. The true obligation of impartiality is that he should conceal no fact which, in his own mind, tells against his views.

Abraham Lincoln, sixteenth President of the United States of America, was born on February 12, 1809, in a log cabin on a barren farm in the backwoods of Kentucky, about three miles west of a place called Hodgensville in what is now La Rue County.

Fifty years later when he had been nominated for the Presidency he was asked for material for an account of his early life. "Why," he said, "it is a great folly to attempt to make anything out of me or my early life. It can all be condensed into a single sentence; and that sentence you will find in Gray's 'Elegy':—

"'The short and simple annals of the poor.'

That's my life, and that's all you or anyone else can make out of it." His other references to early days were rare. He would repeat queer reminiscences of the backwoods to illustrate questions of state; but of his own part in that old life he spoke reluctantly and sadly. Nevertheless there was once extracted from him an awkward autobiographical fragment, and his friends have collected and recorded concerning his earlier years quite as much as is common in great men's biographies or can as a rule be reproduced with its true associations. Thus there are tales enough of the untaught student's perseverance, and of the boy giant's gentleness and prowess; tales, too, more than enough in proportion, of the fun which varied but did not pervade his existence, and of the young rustic's occasional and somewhat oafish pranks. But, in any conception we may form as to the growth of his mind and character, this fact must have its place, that to the man himself the thought of his early life was unattractive, void of self-content over the difficulties

which he had conquered, and void of romantic fondness for vanished joys of youth.

Much the same may be said of his ancestry and family connections. Contempt for lowly beginnings, abhorrent as it is to any honest mind, would to Lincoln's mind have probably been inconceivable, but he lacked that interest in ancestry which is generally marked in his countrymen, and from talk of his nearer progenitors he seems to have shrunk with a positive sadness of which some causes will soon be apparent. Since his death it has been ascertained that in 1638 one Samuel Lincoln of Norwich emigrated to Massachusetts. Descent from him could be claimed by a prosperous family in Virginia, several of whom fought on the Southern side in the Civil War. One Abraham Lincoln, grandfather of the President and apparently a grandson of Samuel, crossed the mountains from Virginia in 1780 and settled his family in Kentucky, of which the nearer portions had recently been explored. One morning four years later he was at work near his cabin with Mordecai, Josiah, and Thomas, his sons, when a shot from the bushes near by brought him down. Mordecai ran to the house, Josiah to a fort, which was close to them. Thomas, aged six, stayed by his father's body. Mordecai seized a gun and, looking through the window, saw an Indian in war paint stooping to pick up Thomas. He fired and killed the savage, and, when Thomas had run into the cabin, continued firing at others who appeared among the bushes. Shortly Josiah returned with soldiers from the fort, and the Indians ran off, leaving Abraham the elder dead. Mordecai, his heir-at-law, prospered. We hear of him long after as an old man of substance and repute in Western Illinois. He had decided views about Indians. The sight of a redskin would move him to strange excitement; he would disappear into the bushes with his gun, and his conscience as a son and a sportsman would not be satisfied till he had stalked and shot him. We are further informed that he was a " good old man." Josiah also moved to Illinois, and it is pleasant to learn that he also was a good old

man, and, as became a good old man, prospered pretty well. But President Lincoln and his sister knew neither these excellent elders nor any other of their father's kin.

And those with whom the story of his own first twenty-one years is bound up invite almost as summary treatment. Thomas Lincoln never prospered like Mordecai and Josiah, and never seems to have left the impress of his goodness or of anything else on any man. But, while learning to carpenter under one Joseph Hanks, he married his employer's niece Nancy, and by her became the father first of a daughter Sarah, and four years later, at the farm near Hodgensville aforesaid, of Abraham, the future President. In 1816, after several migrations, he transported his household down the Ohio to a spot on the Indiana shore, near which the village of Gentryville soon sprang up. There he abode till Abraham was nearly twenty-one. When the boy was eight his mother died, leaving him in his sister's care; but after a year or so Thomas went back alone to Kentucky and, after brief wooing, brought back a wife, Sarah, the widow of one Mr. Johnston, whom he had courted vainly before her first marriage. He brought with her some useful additions to his household gear, and her rather useless son John Johnston. Relatives of Abraham's mother and other old neighbours—in particular John and Dennis Hanks—accompanied all the family's migrations. Ultimately, in 1830, they all moved further west into Illinois. Meanwhile Abraham from an early age did such various tasks for his father or for neighbouring farmers as from time to time suited the father. When an older lad he was put for a while in charge of a ferry boat, and this led to the two great adventures of his early days, voyages with a cargo boat and two mates down by river to New Orleans. The second and more memorable of these voyages was just after the migration to Illinois. He returned from it to a place called New Salem, in Illinois, some distance from his father's new farm, in expectation of work in a store which was about to be opened.

Abraham, by this time, was of age, and in accordance with custom had been set free to shift for himself.

Each of these migrations was effected with great labour in transportation of baggage (sometimes in home-made boats), clearing of timber, and building; and Thomas Lincoln cannot have been wanting in the capacity for great exertions. But historians have been inclined to be hard on him. He seems to have been without sustained industry; in any case he had not much money sense and could not turn his industry to much account. Some hint that he drank, but it is admitted that most Kentucky men drank more. There are indications that he was a dutiful but ineffective father, chastising not too often or too much, but generally on the wrong occasion. He was no scholar and did not encourage his son that way; but he had a great liking for stories. He was of a peaceable and inoffensive temper, but on great provocation would turn on a bully with surprising and dire consequences. Old Thomas, after Abraham was turned loose, continued a migrant, always towards a supposed better farm further west, always with a mortgage on him. Abraham, when he was a struggling professional man, helped him with money as well as he could. We have his letter to the old man on his death-bed, a letter of genuine but mild affection with due words of piety. He explains that illness in his own household makes it impossible for him to pay a last visit to his father, and then, with that curious directness which is common in the families of the poor and has as a rule no sting, he remarks that an interview, if it had been possible, might have given more pain than pleasure to both. Everybody has insisted from the first how little Abraham took after his father, but more than one of the traits attributed to Thomas will certainly reappear.

Abraham, as a man, when for once he spoke of his mother, whom he very seldom mentioned, spoke with intense feeling for her motherly care. " I owe," he said, " everything that I am to her." It pleased him in this talk to explain by inheritance from her the mental quali-

ties which distinguished him from the house of Lincoln, and from others of the house of Hanks. She was, he said, the illegitimate daughter of a Virginian gentleman, whose name he did not know, but from whom as he guessed the peculiar gifts, of which he could not fail to be conscious, were derived.

Sarah his sister was married at Gentryville to one Mr. Grigsby. The Grigsbys were rather great people, as people went in Gentryville. It is said to have become fixed in the boy's mind that the Grigsbys had not treated Sarah well; and this was the beginning of certain woes.

Sarah Bush Lincoln, his stepmother, was good to him and he to her. Above all she encouraged him in his early studies, to which a fretful housewife could have opposed such terrible obstacles. She lived to hope that he might not be elected President for fear that enemies should kill him, and she lived to have her fear fulfilled. His affectionate care over her continued to the end. She lived latterly with her son John Johnston. Abraham's later letters to this companion of his youth deserve to be looked up in the eight large volumes called his Works, for it is hard to see how a man could speak or act better to an impecunious friend who would not face his own troubles squarely. It is sad that the " ever your affectionate brother " of the earlier letters declines to " yours sincerely " in the last; but it is an honest decline of affection, for the man had proved to be cheating his mother, and Abraham had had to stop it.

Two of the cousinhood, Dennis Hanks, a character of comedy, and John Hanks, the serious and steady character of the connection, deserve mention. They and John Johnston make momentary reappearances again. Otherwise the whole of Abraham Lincoln's kindred are now out of the story. They have been disposed of thus hastily at the outset, not because they were discreditable or slight people, but because Lincoln himself when he began to find his footing in the world seems to have felt sadly that his family was just so much to him and no more. The dearest of his recollections attached to pre-

mature death; the next to chronic failure. Rightly or wrongly (and we know enough about heredity now to expect any guess as to its working in a particular case to be wrong) he attributed the best that he had inherited to a licentious connection and a nameless progenitor. Quite early he must have been intensely ambitious, and discovered in himself intellectual power; but from his twelfth year to his twenty-first there was hardly a soul to comprehend that side of him. This chill upon his memory unmistakably influenced the particular complexion of his melancholy. Unmistakably too he early learnt to think that he was odd, that his oddity was connected with his strength, that he might be destined to stand alone and capable of so standing.

The life of the farming pioneer in what was then the Far West afforded a fair prospect of laborious independence. But at least till Lincoln was grown up, when a time of rapid growth and change set in, it offered no hope of quickly gotten wealth, and it imposed severe hardship on all. The country was thickly wooded; the settler had before him at the outset heavy toil in clearing the ground and in building some rude shelter,—a house or just a " half-faced camp," that is, a shed with one side open to the weather such as that in which the Lincoln family passed their first winter near Gentryville. The site once chosen and the clearing once made, there was no such ease of cultivation or such certain fertility as later settlers found yet further west when the development of railways, of agricultural machinery, and of Eastern or European markets had opened out to cultivation the enormous stretches of level grass plain beyond the Mississippi.

Till population had grown a good deal, pioneer families were largely occupied in producing for themselves with their own hands what, in their hardy if not always frugal view, were the necessities and comforts of life. They had no Eastern market for their produce, for railways did not begin to be made till 1840, and it was many years before they crossed the Eastern mountains. An occa-

sional cargo was taken on a flat-bottomed boat down the nearest creek, as a stream is called in America, into the Ohio and so by the innumerable windings of the Mississippi to New Orleans; but no return cargo could be brought up stream. Knives and axes were the most precious objects to be gained by trade; woollen fabrics were rare in the West, when Lincoln was born, and the white man and woman, like the red whom they had displaced, were chiefly dressed in deer skins. The woods abounded in game, and in the early stages of the development of the West a man could largely support himself by his gun. The cold of every winter is there great, and an occasional winter made itself long remembered, like the " winter of the deep snow " in Illinois, by the havoc of its sudden onset and the suffering of its long duration. The settling of a forest country was accompanied here as elsewhere by the occasional ravages of strange and destructive pestilences and the constant presence of malaria. Population was soon thick enough for occasional gatherings, convivial or religious, and in either case apt to be wild, but for long it was not thick enough for the life of most settlers to be other than lonely as well as hard.

Abraham Lincoln in his teens grew very fast, and by nineteen he was nearly six foot four. His weight was never quite proportionate to this. His ungainly figure, with long arms and large hands and relatively small development of chest, and the strange deep-cut lineaments of his face were perhaps the evidence of unfit (sometimes insufficient) food in these years of growth. But his muscular strength was great, and startling statistical tales are told of the weight he could lift and the force of his blows with a mallet or an axe. To a gentle and thoughtful boy with secret ambition in him such strength is a great gift, and in such surroundings most obviously so. Lincoln as a lad was a valuable workman at the varied tasks that came his way, without needing that intense application to manual pursuits which the bent of his mind made irksome to him. And he was a person

of high consideration among the lads of his age and company. The manners of the people then settling in Indiana and Illinois had not the extreme ferocity for which Kentucky had earlier been famous, and which crops up here and there in frontier life elsewhere. All the same, as might naturally be supposed, they shared Plato's opinion that youths and men in the prime of life should settle their differences with their fists. Young Lincoln's few serious combats were satisfactorily decisive, and neither they nor his friendly wrestling bouts ended in the quarrels which were too common among his neighbours. Thus, for all his originality and oddity, he early grew accustomed to mix in the sort of company he was likely to meet, without either inward shrinking or the need of conscious self-assertion.

In one thing he stood aloof from the sports of his fellows. Most backwoodsmen were bred to the gun; he has told us that he shot a turkey when he was eight and never afterwards shot at all. There is an early tale of his protests against an aimless slaughter of mud turtles; and it may be guessed that the dislike of all killing, which gave him sore trouble later, began when he was young. Tales survive of his kindness to helpless men and animals. It marks the real hardness of his surroundings, and their hardening effect on many, that his exertions in saving a drunken man from death in the snow are related with apparent surprise. Some tales of his helping a pig stuck in a bog or a dog on an ice floe and the like seem to indicate a curious and lasting trait. These things seem not to have been done spontaneously, but on mature reflection after he had passed unheeding by. He grew to be a man of prompt action in circumstances of certain kinds; but generally his impulse was slow and not very sure. Taste and the minor sensibilities were a little deficient in him. As a lady once candidly explained to him, he was not ready with little gracious acts. But rare occasions, such as can arouse a passionate sense of justice, would kindle his slow, kind nature with a sudden fire.

The total amount of his schooling, at the several brief periods for which there happened to have been a school accessible and facility to get to it, was afterwards computed by himself at something under twelve months. With this slight help distributed over the years from his eighth to his fifteenth birthday he taught himself to read, write, and do sums. The stories of the effort and painful shifts, by which great men accomplish this initial labour almost unhelped, have in all cases the same pathos, and have a certain sameness in detail. Having learnt to read he had the following books within his reach: the Bible, "Æsop's Fables," "Robinson Crusoe," the "Pilgrim's Progress," a "History of the United States," and Weems' "Life of Washington." Later on the fancy took him to learn the laws of his State, and he obtained the "Laws of Indiana." These books he did read, and read again, and pondered, not with any dreamy or purely intellectual interest, but like one who desires the weapon of learning for practical ends, and desires also to have patterns of what life should be. As already said, his service as a labourer could be considerable, and when something stirred his ambition to do a task quickly his energy could be prodigious. But "bone idle is what I called him," was the verdict long after of one, perhaps too critical, employer. "I found him," he said, "cocked up on a haystack with a book. 'What are you reading?' I said. 'I'm not reading, I'm studying,' says he. 'What are you studying?' says I. 'Law,' says he, as proud as Cicero. 'Great God Almighty!' said I." The boy's correction, "studying" for "reading," was impertinent, but probably sound. To be equally sound, we must reckon among his educational facilities the abundant stories which came his way in a community which, however unlettered, was certainly not dull-spirited; the occasional newspaper; the rare lectures or political meetings; the much more frequent religious meetings, with preachers who taught a grim doctrine, but who preached with vigour and sometimes with the deepest sincerity; the hymns often of great emotional power over a simple

congregation—Cowper's " There is a fountain filled with blood," is one recorded favourite among them; the songs, far other than hymns, which Dennis Hanks and his other mates would pick up or compose; and the practice in rhetoric and the art of exposition, which he unblushingly afforded himself before audiences of fellow labourers who welcomed the jest and the excuse for stopping work. The achievement of the self-taught man remains wonderful, but, if he surmounts his difficulties at all, some of his limitations may turn to sheer advantage. There is some advantage merely in being driven to make the most of few books; great advantage in having one's choice restricted by circumstances to good books; great advantage too in the consciousness of untrained faculty which leaves a man capable in mature life of deliberately undertaking mental discipline.

Along with the legends and authentic records of his self-training, signs of an ambition which showed itself early and which was from the first a clean and a high ambition, there are also other legends showing Lincoln as a naughty boy among naughty boys. The selection here made from these lacks refinement, and the reader must note that this was literally a big, naughty boy, not a man who had grown stiff in coarseness and ill-nature. First it must be recalled that Abraham bore a grudge against the Grigsbys, an honourable grudge in its origin and perhaps the only grudge he ever bore. There had arisen from this a combat, of which the details might displease the fastidious, but which was noble in so far that Abraham rescued a weaker combatant who was overmatched. But there ensued something more displeasing, a series of lampoons by Abraham, in prose and a kind of verse. These were gross and silly enough, though probably to the taste of the public which he then addressed, but it is the sequel that matters. In a work called " The First Chronicles of Reuben," it is related how Reuben and Josiah, the sons of Reuben Grigsby the elder, took to themselves wives on the same day. By local custom the bridal feast took place and the two

young couples began their married careers under the roof
of the bridegrooms' father. Moreover, it was the custom
that, at a certain stage in the celebrations, the brides
should be escorted to their chambers by hired attendants
who shortly after conducted the bridegrooms thither.
On this occasion some sense of mischief afoot disturbed
the heart of Mrs. Reuben Grigsby the elder, and, hasten-
ing upstairs, just after the attendants had returned, she
cried out in a loud voice and to the great consternation
of all concerned, "Why, Reuben, you're in bed with the
wrong wife!" The historian who, to the manifest
annoyance of Lincoln's other biographers, has preserved
this and much other priceless information, infers that
Abraham, who was not invited to the feast, had plotted
this domestic catastrophe and won over the attendants
to his evil purpose. This is not a certain inference, nor is
it absolutely beyond doubt that the event recorded in
"The First Chronicles of Reuben" ever happened at all.
What is certain is that these Chronicles themselves, composed in what purports to be the style of Scripture, were
circulated for the joint edification of the proud race of
Grigsby and of their envious neighbours in the hand-
writing of Abraham Lincoln, then between seventeen and
eighteen. Not without reason does an earlier manuscript
of the same author conclude, after several correct
exercises in compound subtraction, with the distich:—

> "Abraham Lincoln, his hand and pen,
> He will be good, but God knows when."

Not to be too solemn about a tale which has here been
told for the whimsical fancy of its unseemliness and
because it is probably the worst that there is to tell, we
may here look forward and face the well-known fact that
the unseemliness in talk of rough, rustic boys flavoured
the great President's conversation through life. It is
well to be plain about this. Lincoln was quite without
any elegant and sentimental dissoluteness, such as can be
attractively portrayed. His life was austere and seems
to have been so from the start. He had that shy

reverence for womanhood which is sometimes acquired as easily in rough as in polished surroundings and often quite as steadily maintained. The testimony of his early companions, along with some fragments of the boy's feeble but sincere attempts at verse, shows that he acquired it young. But a large part of the stories and pithy sayings for which he was famous wherever he went, but of which when their setting is lost it is impossible to recover the enjoyment, were undeniably coarse, and naturally enough this fact was jarring to some of those in America who most revered him. It should not really be hard, in any comprehensive view of his character and the circumstances in which it unfolded itself, to trace in this bent of his humour something not discordant with the widening sympathy and deepening tenderness of his nature. The words of his political associate in Illinois, Mr. Leonard Swett, afterwards Attorney-General of the United States, may suffice. He writes: "Almost any man, who will tell a very vulgar story, has, in a degree, a vulgar mind. But it was not so with him; with all his purity of character and exalted morality and sensibility, which no man can doubt, when hunting for wit he had no ability to discriminate between the vulgar and refined substances from which he extracted it. It was the wit he was after, the pure jewel, and he would pick it up out of the mud or dirt just as readily as from a parlour table." In any case his best remembered utterances of this order, when least fit for print, were both wise and incomparably witty, and in any case they did not prevent grave gentlemen, who marvelled at them rather uncomfortably, from receiving the deep impression of what they called his pure-mindedness.

One last recollection of Lincoln's boyhood has appealed, beyond any other, to some of his friends as prophetic of things to come. Mention has already been made of his two long trips down the Mississippi. With the novel responsibilities which they threw on him, and the novel sights and company which he met all the way to the strange, distant city of New Orleans, they must

have been great experiences. Only two incidents of
them are recorded. In the first voyage he and his mates
had been disturbed at night by a band of negro marauders
and had had a sharp fight in repelling them, but in the
second voyage he met with the negro in a way that to
him was more memorable. He and the young fellows
with him saw, among the sights of New Orleans, negroes
chained, maltreated, whipped and scourged; they came in
their rambles upon a slave auction where a fine mulatto
girl was being pinched and prodded and trotted up and
down the room like a horse to show how she moved,
that "bidders might satisfy themselves," as the auc-
tioneer said, of the soundness of the article to be sold.
John Johnston and John Hanks and Abraham Lincoln
saw these sights with the unsophisticated eyes of honest
country lads from a free State. In their home circle
it seems that slavery was always spoken of with horror.
One of them had a tenacious memory and a tenacious
will. " Lincoln saw it," John Hanks said long after, and
other men's recollections of Lincoln's talk confirmed him
—" Lincoln saw it; his heart bled; said nothing much,
was silent. I can say, knowing it, that it was on this
trip that he formed his opinion of slavery. It ran its
iron into him then and there, May, 1831. I have heard
him say so often." Perhaps in other talks old John
Hanks dramatised his early remembrances a little; he
related how at the slave auction Lincoln said, " By God,
boys, let's get away from this. If ever I get a chance to
hit that thing, I'll hit it hard."

The youth, who probably did not express his indignation in these prophetic words, was in fact chosen to deal
" that thing " a blow from which it seems unlikely to
recover as a permitted institution among civilised men,
and it is certain that from this early time the thought
of slavery never ceased to be hateful to him. Yet it is
not in the light of a crusader against this special evil
that we are to regard him. When he came back from
this voyage to his new home in Illinois he was simply a
youth ambitious of an honourable part in the life of the

young country of which he was proud. We may regard, and he himself regarded, the liberation of the slaves, which will always be associated with his name, as a part of a larger work, the restoration of his country to its earliest and noblest tradition, which alone gave permanence or worth to its existence as a nation.

CHAPTER II

THE GROWTH OF THE AMERICAN NATION

1. *The Formation of a National Government.*

IT is of course impossible to understand the life of a politician in another country without study of its conditions and its past. In the case of America this study is especially necessary, not only because the many points of comparison between that country and our own are apt to conceal profound differences of customs and institutions, but because the broader difference between a new country and an old is in many respects more important than we conceive. But in the case of Lincoln there is peculiar reason for carrying such a study far back. He himself appealed unceasingly to a tradition of the past. In tracing the causes which up to his time had tended to conjoin the United States more closely and the cause which more recently had begun to threaten them with disruption, we shall be examining the elements of the problem with which it was his work in life to deal.

The " Thirteen United States of America " which in 1776 declared their independence of Great Britain were so many distinct Colonies distributed unevenly along 1,300 miles of the Atlantic coast. These thirteen Colonies can easily be identified on the map when it is explained that Maine in the extreme north was then an unsettled forest tract claimed by the Colony of Massachusetts, that Florida in the extreme south belonged to Spain, and that Vermont, which soon after asserted its separate existence, was a part of the State of New York. Almost every one of these Colonies had its marked peculiarities and its points of antagonism as against its nearest neighbours; but they fell into three groups. We may broadly contrast the five southernmost, which included

16

those which were the richest and of which in many ways the leading State was Virginia, with the four (or later six) northernmost States known collectively as New England. Both groups had at first been colonised by the same class, the smaller landed gentry of England with a sprinkling of well-to-do traders, though the South received later a larger number of poor and shiftless immigrants than the North, and the North attracted a larger number of artisans. The physical conditions of the South led to the growth of large farms, or " plantations " as they were called, and of a class of large proprietors; negro slaves thrived there and were useful in the cultivation of tobacco, indigo, rice, and later of cotton. The North continued to be a country of small farms, but its people turned also to fishery and to commerce, and the sea carrying trade became early its predominant interest, yielding place later on to manufacturing industries. The South was attached in the main, though by no means altogether, to the Church of England; New England owed its origin to successive immigrations of Puritans often belonging to the Congregational or Independent body; with the honourable exception of Rhode Island these communities showed none of the liberal and tolerant spirit which the Independents of the old country often developed; they manifested, however, the frequent virtues as well as the occasional defects of the Puritan character. The middle group of Colonies were of more mixed origin; New York and New Jersey had been Dutch possessions, Delaware was partly Swedish, Pennsylvania had begun as a Quaker settlement but included many different elements; in physical and economic conditions they resembled on the whole New England, but they lacked, some of them conspicuously, the Puritan discipline, and had a certain cosmopolitan character. Though there were sharp antagonisms among the northern settlements, and the southern settlements were kept distinct by the great distances between them, the tendency of events was to soften these minor differences. But it greatly intensified one broad distinction which marked

off the southern group from the middle and the northern groups equally.

Nevertheless, before independence was thought of there were common characteristics distinguishing Americans from English people. They are the better worth an attempt to note them because, as a historian of America wrote some years ago, " the typical American of 1900 is on the whole more like his ancestor of 1775 than is the typical Englishman." In all the Colonies alike the conditions of life encouraged personal independence. In all alike they also encouraged a special kind of ability which may be called practical rather than thorough—that of a workman who must be competent at many tasks and has neither opportunity nor inducement to become perfect at one; that of the scientific man irresistibly drawn to inventions which shall make life less hard; that of the scholar or philosopher who must supply the new community's need of lawyers and politicians.

On the other hand, many of the colonists' forefathers had come to their new home with distinct aspirations for a better ordering of human life than the old world allowed, and it has frequently been noticed that Americans from the first have been more prone than their kinsmen in England to pay homage to large ideal conceptions. This is a disposition not entirely favourable to painstaking and sure-footed reform. The idealist American is perhaps too ready to pay himself with fine words, which the subtler and shyer Englishman avoids and rather too readily sets down as insincere in others. Moreover, this tendency is quite consistent with the peculiar conservatism characteristic of America. New conditions in which tradition gave no guidance called forth great inventive powers and bred a certain pride in novelty. An American economist has written in a sanguine humour, " The process of transplanting removes many of the shackles of custom and tradition which retard the progress of older countries. In a new country things cannot be done in the old way, and therefore they are probably done in the best way." But a new country is always apt to cling

with tenacity to those old things for which it still has use; and a remote and undeveloped country does not fully share the continual commerce in ideas which brings about change (and, in the main, advance) in the old world. The conservatism which these causes tend to produce has in any case been marked in America. Thus, as readers of Lowell are aware, in spite of the ceaseless efflorescence of the modern slang of America, the language of America is in many respects that of an older England than ours, and the like has all along been true of important literature, and still more of oratory, in America. Moreover, as the sentences which have just been quoted may suggest, the maxim that has once hit the occasion, or the new practice or expedient once necessitated by the conditions of the moment, has been readily hallowed as expressing the wisdom of the ages. An Englishman will quote Burke as he would quote Demosthenes or Plato, but Americans have been apt to quote their elder statesmen as they would quote the Bible. In like manner political practices of accidental origin—for instance, that a representative should be an inhabitant of the place he represents—acquire in America something like the force of constitutional law.

In this connection we must recall the period at which the earliest settlers came from England, and the political heritage which they consequently brought with them. This heritage included a certain aptitude for local government, which was fostered in the south by the rise of a class of large landowners and in the north by the Congregational Church system. It included also a great tenacity of the subject's rights as against the State—the spirit of Hampden refusing payment of ship-money— and a disposition to look on the law and the Courts as the bulwarks of such rights against Government. But it did not include—and this explains the real meaning of the War of Independence—any sort of feeling of allegiance to a Parliament which represented Great Britain only, and which had gained its position even in Great Britain since the fathers of Virginia and Massachusetts left home. Nor did it include—and this was of great im-

portance in its influence on the form of the Constitution—any real understanding of or any aptitude for the English Parliamentary Government, under which the leaders of the legislative body and the advisers of the Crown in its executive functions are the same men, and under which the elected persons, presumed for the moment to represent the people, are allowed for that moment an almost unfettered supremacy.

Thus there was much that made it easy for the Colonies to combine in the single act of repudiating British sovereignty, yet the characteristics which may be ascribed to them in common were not such as inclined them or fitted them to build up a great new unity.

The Colonies, however, backed up by the British Government with the vigour which Chatham imparted to it, had acted together against a common danger from the French. When the States, as we must now call them, acted together against the British Government they did so in name as " United States," and they shortly proceeded to draw up " Articles of Confederation and Perpetual Union." But it was union of a feeble kind. The separate government of each State, in its internal affairs, was easy to provide for; representative institutions always existed, and no more change was needed than to substitute elected officers for the Governors and Councillors formerly appointed by the Crown. For the Union a Congress was provided which was to represent all the States in dealings with the outside world, but it was a Government with no effective powers except such as each separate State might independently choose to lend it. It might wage war with England, but it could not effectually control or regularly pay the military service of its own citizens; it might make a treaty of peace with England, but it could not enforce on its citizens distasteful obligations of that treaty. Such an ill-devised machine would have worked well enough for a time, if the Union Government could have attached to itself popular sentiments of honour and loyalty. But the sentiments were not there; and it worked badly.

When once we were reconciled to a defeat which proved good for us, it became a tradition among English writers to venerate the American Revolution. Later English historians have revolted from this indiscriminate veneration. They insist on another side of the facts: on the hopelessness of the American cause but for the commanding genius of Washington and his moral authority, and for the command which France and Spain obtained of the seas; on the petty quarrelsomeness with which the rights of the Colonists were urged, and the meanly skilful agitation which forced on the final rupture; on the lack of sustained patriotic effort during the war; on the base cruelty and dishonesty with which the loyal minority were persecuted and the private rights guaranteed by the peace ignored. It does not concern us to ascertain the precise justice in this displeasing picture; no man now regrets the main result of the Revolution, and we know that a new country is a new country, and that there was much in the circumstances of the war to encourage indiscipline and ferocity. But the fact that there is cause for such an indictment bears in two ways upon our present subject.

In the first place, there has been a tendency both in England and in America to look at this history upside down. The epoch of the Revolution and the Constitution has been regarded as a heroic age—wherein lived the elder Brutus, Mucius Scævola, Clælia and the rest—to be followed by almost continuous disappointment, disillusionment and decline. A more pleasing and more bracing view is nearer to the historic truth. The faults of a later time were largely survivals, and the later history is largely that of growth though in the face of terrific obstacles and many influences that favoured decay. The nobility of the Revolution in the eighteenth century may be rated higher or lower, but in the Civil War, in which the elder brothers of so many men now living bore their part, the people of the North and of the South alike displayed far more heroic qualities.

In the second place, the War of Independence and of

the Revolution lacked some of the characteristics of other national uprisings. It was not a revolt against grievous oppression or against a wholly foreign domination, but against a political system which the people mildly resented and which only statesmen felt to be pernicious and found to be past cure. The cause appealed to far-seeing political aspiration and appealed also to turbulent and ambitious spirits and to whatever was present of a merely revolutionary temper, but the ordinary law-abiding man who minded his own business was not greatly moved one way or the other in his heart.

The subsequent movement which, in a few years after independence was secured, gave the United States a national and a working Constitution was altogether the work of a few, to which popular movement contributed nothing. Of popular aspiration for unity there was none. Statesmen knew that the new nation or group of nations lay helpless between pressing dangers from abroad and its own financial difficulties. They saw clearly that they must create a Government of the Union which could exercise directly upon the individual American citizen an authority like that of the Government of his own State. They did this, but with a reluctant and half-convinced public opinion behind them.

The makers of the Constitution earned in a manner the full praise that has ever since been bestowed on them. But they did not, as it has often been suggested they did, create a sort of archetype and pattern for all Governments that may hereafter partake of a federal character. Nor has the curious machine which they devised—with its balanced opposition between two legislative chambers, between the whole Legislature and the independent executive power of the President, between the governing power of the moment and the permanent expression of the people's will embodied in certain almost unalterable laws—worked conspicuously better than other political constitutions. The American Constitution owes its peculiarities partly to the form which the State Governments had naturally taken, and partly to sheer mis-

understanding of the British Constitution, but much more to the want at the time of any strong sense of national unity and to the existence of a good deal of dislike to all government whatsoever. The sufficient merit of its founders was that of patient and skilful diplomatists, who, undeterred by difficulties, found out the most satisfactory settlement that had a chance of being accepted by the States.

So the Colonies, which in 1776 had declared their independence of Great Britain under the name of the United States of America, entered in 1789 into the possession of machinery of government under which their unity and independence could be maintained.

It will be well at once to describe those features of the Constitution which it will be necessary for us later to bear in mind. It is generally known that the President of the United States is an elected officer—elected by what operates, though intended to act otherwise, as a popular vote. During the four years of his office he might roughly be said to combine the functions of the King in this country and those of a Prime Minister whose Cabinet is in due subjection to him. But that description needs one very important qualification. He wields, with certain slight restrictions, the whole executive power of government, but neither he nor any of his ministers can, like the ministers of our King, sit or speak in the Legislature, nor can he, like our King, dissolve that Legislature. He has indeed a veto on Acts of Congress, which can only be overridden by a large majority in both Houses. But the executive and the legislative powers in America were purposely so constituted as to be independent of each other to a degree which is unknown in this country.

It is perhaps not very commonly understood that President and Congress alike are as strictly fettered in their action by the Constitution as a limited liability company is by its Memorandum of Association. This Constitution, which defines both the form of government and certain liberties of the subject, is not unalterable,

but it can be altered only by a process which requires both the consent of a great majority in Congress or alternatively of a great majority of the legislatures of the distinct States composing the Union, and also ratification of amendments by three-fourths of the several States. Thus we shall have to notice later that a " Constitutional Amendment " abolishing slavery became a terror of the future to many people in the slave States, but remained all the time an impossibility in the view of most people in the free States.

We have, above all things, to dismiss from our minds any idea that the Legislature of a State is subordinate to the Congress of the United States, or that a State Governor is an officer under the President. The Constitution of the Union was the product of a half-developed sense of nationality. Under it the State authority (in the American sense of " State ") and the Union or Federal authority go on side by side working in separate spheres, each subject to Constitutional restrictions, but each in its own sphere supreme. Thus the State authority is powerless to make peace or war or to impose customs duties, for those are Federal matters. But the Union authority is equally powerless, wherever a State authority has been constituted, to punish ordinary crime, to promote education, or to regulate factories. In particular, by the Constitution as it stood till after the Civil War, the Union authority was able to prohibit the importation of slaves from abroad after the end of 1807, but had no power to abolish slavery itself in any of the States.

Further, Congress had to be constituted in such a manner as to be agreeable to the smaller States which did not wish to enter into a Union in which their influence would be swamped by their more populous neighbours. Their interest was secured by providing that in the Senate each State should have two members and no more, while in the House of Representatives the people of the whole Union are represented according to population. Thus legislation through Congress requires the concurrence of two forces which may easily be op-

posed, that of the majority of American citizens and that of the majority of the several States. Of the two chambers, the Senate, whose members are elected for six years, and to secure continuity do not all retire at the same time, became as time went on, though not at first, attractive to statesmen of position, and acquired therefore additional influence.

Lastly, the Union was and is still the possessor of Territories not included in any State, and in the Territories, whatever subordinate self-government they might be allowed, the Federal authority has always been supreme and uncontrolled in all matters. But as these Territories have become more settled and more populated, portions of them have steadily from the first been organised as States and admitted to the Union. It is for Congress to settle the time of their admission and to make any conditions in regard to their Constitutions as States. But when once admitted as States they have thenceforward the full rights of the original States. Within all the Territories, while they remained under its jurisdiction it lay with Congress to determine whether slavery should be lawful or not, and, when any portion of them was ripe for admission to the Union as a State, Congress could insist that the new State's Constitution should or should not prohibit slavery. When the Constitution of the Union was being settled, slavery was the subject of most careful compromise; but in any union formed between slave States and free, a bitter root of controversy must have remained, and the opening through which controversy actually returned was provided by the Territories.

On all other matters the makers of the Constitution had in the highest temper of statesmanship found a way round seemingly insuperable difficulties. The whole attitude of " the fathers " towards slavery is a question of some consequence to a biographer of Lincoln, and we shall return to it in a little while.

2. *Territorial Expansion.*

A machine of government had been created, and we are shortly to consider how it was got to work. But the large dominion to be governed had to be settled, and its area was about to undergo an enormous expansion. It will be convenient at this point to mark the stages of this development.

The thirteen Colonies had, when they first revolted, definite western boundaries, the westernmost of them reaching back from the sea-board to a frontier in the Alleghany Mountains. But at the close of the war Great Britain ceded to the United States the whole of the inland country up to the Mississippi River. Virginia had in the meantime effectively colonised Kentucky to the west of her, and for a time this was treated as within her borders. In a similar way Tennessee had been settled from North and South Carolina and was treated as part of the former. Virginia had also established claims by conquest north of the Ohio River in what was called the North-West Territory, but these claims and all similar claims of particular States in unsettled or half-settled territory were shortly before or shortly after the adoption of the Constitution ceded to the Union Government. But the dominions of that Government soon received a vast accession. In 1803, by a brave exercise of the Constitutional powers which he was otherwise disposed to restrict jealously, President Jefferson bought from Napoleon I. the great expanse of country west of the Mississippi called Louisiana. This region in the extreme south was no wider than the present State of Louisiana, but further north it widened out so as to take in the whole watershed of the Missouri and its tributaries, including in the extreme north nearly all the present State of Montana. In 1819 Florida was purchased from Spain, and that country at the same time abandoned its claims to a strip of coastland which now forms the sea-board of Alabama and Mississippi.

Such was the extent of the United States when Lincoln

began his political life. In the movement of population by which this domain was being settled up, different streams may be roughly distinguished. First, there was from 1780 onwards a constant movement of the poorer class and of younger sons of rich men from the great State of Virginia and to some extent from the Carolinas into Kentucky and Tennessee, whence they often shifted further north into Indiana and Illinois, or sometimes further west into Missouri. It was mainly a movement of single families or groups of families of adventurous pioneers, very sturdy, and very turbulent. Then there came the expansion of the great plantation interest in the further South, carrying with it as it spread, not occasional slaves as in Kentucky and Tennessee, but the whole plantation system. This movement went not only directly westward, but still more by the Gulf of Mexico and up the Mississippi, into the State of Louisiana, where a considerable French population had settled, the State of Mississippi, and later into Missouri. Later still came the westward movement from the Northern States. The energies of the people in these States had at first been to a great extent absorbed by sea-going pursuits and the subjugation of their own rugged soil, so that they reached western regions like Illinois rather later than did the settlers from States further south. Ultimately, as their manufactures grew, immigration from Europe began its steady flow to these States, and the great westward stream, which continuing in our days has filled up the rich lands of the far North-West, grew in volume. But want of natural timber and other causes hindered the development of the fertile prairie soil in the regions beyond the upper Mississippi, till the period of railway development, which began about 1840, was far advanced. Illinois was Far West in 1830, Iowa and Minnesota continued to be so in 1860. The Northerners, when they began to move westward, came in comparatively large numbers, bringing comparatively ordered habits and the full machinery of outward civilisation with them. Thus a great social change followed upon their arrival

in the regions to which only scattered pioneers such as the Lincolns had previously penetrated. In Illinois, with which so much of our story is bound up, the rapidity of that change may be estimated from the fact that the population of that State multiplied sevenfold between the time when Lincoln settled there and the day when he left it as President.

The concluding stages by which the dominions of the United States came to be as we know them were: the annexation by agreement in 1846 of the Republic of Texas, which had separated itself from Mexico and which claimed besides the great State of Texas a considerable territory reaching north-west to the upper portions of the Arkansas River; the apportionment to the Union by a delimitation treaty with Great Britain in 1846 of the Oregon Territory, including roughly the State of that name and the rest of the basin of the Columbia River up to the present frontier—British Columbia being at the same time apportioned to Great Britain; the conquest from Mexico in 1848 of California and a vast mountainous tract at the back of it; the purchase from Mexico of a small frontier strip in 1853; and the acquisition at several later times of various outlying dependencies which will in no way concern us.

3. *The Growth of the Practice and Traditions of the Union Government.*

We must turn back to the internal growth of the new united nation. When the Constitution had been formed and the question of its acceptance by the States had been at last settled, and when Washington had been inaugurated as the first President under it, a wholly new conflict arose between two parties, led by two Ministers in the President's Cabinet, Alexander Hamilton and Thomas Jefferson. Both were potent and remarkable men, Hamilton in all senses a great man. These two men, for all their antagonism, did services to their country, without which the vigorous growth of the new nation would not have been possible.

The figure of Alexander Hamilton, then Secretary of the Treasury (ranked by Talleyrand with Fox and Napoleon as one of the three great men he had known), must fascinate any English student of the period. If his name is not celebrated in the same way in the country which he so eminently served, it is perhaps because in his ideas, as in his origin, he was not strictly American. As a boy, half Scotch, half French Huguenot, from the English West Indian island of Nevis, he had been at school in New York when his speeches had some real effect in attaching that city to the cause of Independence. He had served brilliantly in the war, on Washington's staff and with his regiment. He had chivalrously defended, as an advocate and in other ways, the Englishmen and loyalists against whose cause he fought. He had induced the great central State of New York to accept the Constitution, when the strongest local party would have rejected it and made the Union impossible. As Washington's Secretary of the Treasury he organised the machinery of government, helped his chief to preserve a strong, upright and cautious foreign policy at the critical point of the young Republic's infancy, and performed perhaps the greatest and most difficult service of all in setting the disordered finances of the country upon a sound footing. In early middle age he ended a life, not flawless but admirable and lovable, in a duel, murderously forced upon him by one Aaron Burr. This man, who was an elegant profligate, with many graces but no public principle, was a claimant to the Presidency in opposition to Hamilton's greatest opponent, Jefferson; Hamilton knowingly incurred a feud which must at the best have been dangerous to him, by unhesitatingly throwing his weight upon the side of Jefferson, his own ungenerous rival. The details of his policy do not concern us, but the United States could hardly have endured for many years without the passionate sense of the need of government and the genius for actual administration with which Hamilton set the new nation on its way. Nevertheless—so do gifts differ—the general spirit which has on the

whole informed the American nation and held it together
was neither respected nor understood by him. His party,
called the Federalists, because they claimed to stand for
a strong and an efficient Federal Government, did not
survive him long. It is of interest to us here only because, with its early disappearance, there ceased for ever
to be in America any party whatsoever which in any
sense represented aristocratic principles or leanings.

The fate of Jefferson's party (at first called Republican
but by no means to be confused with the Republican
party which will concern us later) was far different, for
the Democratic party, represented by the President of
the United States at this moment, claims to descend from
it in unbroken apostolic succession. But we need not
pause to trace the connecting thread between them, real
as it is, for parties are not to be regarded as individuals.
Indeed the personality of Thomas Jefferson, Secretary of
State in Washington's Cabinet, impressed itself, during
his life and long after, upon all America more than that
of any other man. Democrats to-day have described Lincoln, who by no means belonged to their party, as Jefferson's spiritual heir; and Lincoln would have welcomed
the description.

No biographer has achieved an understanding presentment of Jefferson's curious character, which as presented
by unfriendly critics is an unpleasing combination of
contrasting elements. A tall and active fellow, a good
horseman and a good shot, living through seven years
of civil war, which he had himself heralded in, without
the inclination to strike a blow; a scholar, musician, and
mathematician, without delicacy, elevation, or precision
of thought or language; a man of intense ambition, without either administrative capacity or the courage to assert
himself in counsel or in debate; a dealer in philanthropic
sentiment, privately malignant and vindictive. This is
not as a whole a credible portrait; it cannot stand for the
man as his friends knew him; but there is evidence for
each feature of it, and it remains impossible for a
foreigner to think of Jefferson and not compare him to his

disadvantage with the antagonist whom he eclipsed. By pertinacious industry, however, working chiefly through private correspondence, he constructed a great party, dominated a nation, and dominated it mainly for good. For the rapid and complete triumph of Jefferson's party over its opponents signifies a very definite and lasting conversion of the main stream of American public opinion to what may be called the sane element in the principles of the French Revolution. At the time when he set himself to counterwork Hamilton, American statesmanship was likely to be directed only to making Government strong and to ensuring the stability of the business world; for reaction against the bloody absurdities that had happened in France was strong in America, and in English thought, which still had influence in America, it was all-powerful. Against this he asserted an intense belief in the value of freedom, in the equal claim of men of all conditions to the consideration of government, and in the supreme importance to government of the consenting mind of the governed. And he made this sense so definitely a part of the national stock of ideas that, while the older-established principles of strong and sound government were not lost to sight, they were consciously rated as subordinate to the principles of liberty.

It must not be supposed that the ascendency thus early acquired by what may be called liberal opinions in America was a matter merely of setting some fine phrases in circulation, or of adopting, as was early done in most States, a wide franchise and other external marks of democracy. We may dwell a little longer on the unusual but curiously popular figure of Jefferson, for it illustrates the spirit with which the commonwealth became imbued under his leadership. He has sometimes been presented as a man of flabby character whose historical part was that of intermediary between impracticable French " philosophes " and the ruffians and swindlers that Martin Chuzzlewit encountered, who were all "children of liberty," and whose "boastful answer to the Despot and the Tyrant was that their bright home was in the Settin'

Sun." He was nothing of the kind. His judgment was probably unsound on the questions of foreign policy on which as Secretary of State he differed from Washington, and he leaned, no doubt, to a jealous and too narrow insistence upon the limits set by the Constitution to the Government's power. But he and his party were emphatically right in the resistance which they offered to certain needless measures of coercion. As President, though he was not a great President, he suffered the sensible course of administration originated by his opponent to continue undisturbed, and America owed to one bold and far-seeing act of his the greatest of the steps by which her territory was enlarged. It is, however, in the field of domestic policy, which rested with the States and with which a President has often little to do, that the results of his principles must be sought. Jefferson was a man who had worked unwearyingly in Virginia at sound, and what we should now call conservative, reforms, establishing religious toleration, reforming a preposterous land law, seeking to provide education for the poor, striving unsuccessfully for a sensible scheme of gradual emancipation of the slaves. In like manner his disciples after him, in their several States, devoted themselves to the kind of work in removing manifest abuses and providing for manifest new social needs in which English reformers like Romilly and Bentham, and the leaders of the first reformed Parliament, were to be successful somewhat later. The Americans who so exasperated Dickens vainly supposed themselves to be far ahead of England in much that we now consider essential to a well-ordered nation. But there could have been no answer to Americans of Jefferson's generation if they had made the same claim.

It is with this fact in mind that we should approach the famous words of Jefferson which echoed so long with triumphant or reproachful sound in the ears of Americans and to which long after Lincoln was to make a memorable appeal. The propaganda which he carried on when the Constitution had been adopted was on behalf of a principle which he had enunciated as a younger man when

he drafted the Declaration of Independence. That document is mainly a rehearsal of the colonists' grievances,
and is as strictly lawyerlike and about as fair or unfair
as the arguments of a Parliamentarian under Charles I.
But the argumentation is prefaced with these sounding
words: " We hold these truths to be self-evident:—that
all men are created equal; that they are endowed by their
Creator with certain unalienable rights; that among these
are life, liberty and the pursuit of happiness. That to
secure these rights, governments are instituted among
men, deriving their just powers from the consent of the
governed." Few propositions outside the Bible have
offered so easy a mark to the shafts of unintelligently
clever criticism.

Jefferson, when he said that " all men are created
equal," and the Tory Dr. Johnson, when he spoke of
" the natural equality of man," used a curious eighteenth
century phrase, of which a Greek scholar can see the
origin; but it did not mean anything absurd, nor, on the
other hand, did it convey a mere platitude. It should
not be necessary to explain, as Lincoln did long after,
that Jefferson did not suppose all men to be of equal
height or weight or equally wise or equally good. He
did, however, contend for a principle of which one elementary application is the law which makes murder the
same crime whatever be the relative positions of the
murderer and the murdered man. Such a law was indeed
firmly rooted in England before Jefferson talked of
equality, but it amazed the rest of Europe when the
House of Lords hanged a peer for the murder of his
servant. There are indefinitely many further ways in
which men who are utterly unequal had best be treated
as creatures equally entitled to the consideration of government and of their neighbours. It is safer to carry
this principle too far than not to carry it far enough.
If Jefferson had expressed this and his cognate principle
of liberty with scientific precision, or with the full personal sincerity with which a greater man like Lincoln
expressed it, he would have said little from which any

Englishman to-day would dissent. None the less he would have enunciated a doctrine which most Governments then existing set at naught or proscribed, and for which Hamilton and the prosperous champions of independence who supported him had no use.

The Declaration of Independence was not a very candid State paper, and the popularity Jefferson afterwards created for its sentiments was not wholly free from humbug. Many men were more ready to think themselves the equals of Washington or Hamilton in the respects in which they were not so, than to think a negro their own equal in the respects in which he was. The boundless space and untrammelled conditions of the new world made liberty and equality in some directions highly attainable ideals, so much so that they seemed to demand little effort or discipline. The patriotic orators under whom Lincoln sat in his youth would ascribe to the political wisdom of their great democracy what was really the result of geography. They would regard the extent of forest and prairie as creditable to themselves, just as some few Englishmen have regarded our location upon an island.

This does not, however, do away with the value of that tradition of the new world which in its purest and sincerest form became part and parcel of Lincoln's mind. Jefferson was a great American patriot. In his case insistence on the rights of the several States sprang from no half-hearted desire for a great American nation; he regarded these provincial organisations as machinery by which government and the people could be brought nearer together; and he contributed that which was most needed for the evolution of a vigorous national life. He imparted to the very recent historical origin of his country, and his followers imparted to its material conditions, a certain element of poetry and the felt presence of a wholesome national ideal. The patriotism of an older country derives its glory and its pride from influences deep rooted in the past, creating a tradition of public and private action which needs no definite formula. The

man who did more than any other to supply this lack in a new country, by imbuing its national consciousness— even its national cant—with high aspiration, did—it may well be—more than any strong administrator or construc- tive statesman to create a Union which should thereafter seem worth preserving.

4. *The Missouri Compromise.*

No sober critic, applying to the American statesmen of the first generation the standards which he would apply to their English contemporaries, can blame them in the least because they framed their Constitution as best they could and were not deterred by the scruples which they felt about slavery from effecting a Union between States which, on all other grounds except their latent difference upon slavery, seemed meant to be one. But many of these men had set their hands in the Declara- tion of Independence to the most unqualified claim of liberty and equality for all men and proceeded, in the Constitution, to give nineteen years' grace to " that most detestable sum of all villainies," as Wesley called it, the African slave trade, and to impose on the States which thought slavery wrong the dirty work of restoring escaped slaves to captivity. "Why," Dr. Johnson had asked, " do the loudest yelps for liberty come from the drivers of slaves?" We are forced to recognise, upon any study of the facts, that they could not really have made the Union otherwise than as they did; yet a doubt presents itself as to the general soundness and sincerity of their boasted notions of liberty. Now, later on we shall have to understand the policy as to slavery on behalf of which Lincoln stepped forward as a leader. In his own con- stantly reiterated words it was a return to the position of " the fathers," and, though he was not a professional historian, it concerns us to know that there was sincerity at least in his intensely historical view of politics. We have, then, to see first how " the fathers "—that is, the most considerable men among those who won Independ-

ence and made the Constitution—set out with a very
honest view on the subject of slavery, but with a too
comfortable hope of its approaching end, which one or two
lived to see frustrated; secondly, how the men who succeeded them were led to abandon such hopes and content
themselves with a compromise as to slavery which they
trusted would at least keep the American nation in being.

Among those who signed the Declaration of Independence there were presumably some of Dr. Johnson's
"yelpers." It mattered more that there were sturdy
people who had no idea of giving up slavery and probably
did not relish having to join in protestations about
equality. Men like Jefferson ought to have known well
that their associates in South Carolina and Georgia in
particular did not share their aspirations—the people of
Georgia indeed were recent and ardent converts to the
slave system. But these sincere and insincere believers
in slavery were the exceptions; their views did not then
seem to prevail even in the greatest of the slave States,
Virginia. Broadly speaking, the American opinion on
this matter in 1775 or in 1789 had gone as far ahead of
English opinion, as English opinion had in turn gone
ahead of American, when, in 1833, the year after the
first Reform Bill, the English people put its hand into
its pocket and bought out its own slave owners in the
West Indies. The British Government had forced several of the American Colonies to permit slavery against
their will, and only in 1769 it had vetoed, in the interest
of British trade, a Colonial enactment for suppressing
the slave trade. This was sincerely felt as a part, though
a minor part, of the grievance against the mother country.
So far did such views prevail on the surface that a Convention of all the Colonies in 1774 unanimously voted
that "the abolition of domestic slavery is the greatest
object of desire in those Colonies where it was unhappily
introduced in their infant state. But previous to the
enfranchisement of the slaves in law, it is necessary to
exclude all further importation from Africa." It was
therefore very commonly assumed when, after an interval

of war which suspended such reforms, Independence was achieved, that slavery was a doomed institution.

Those among the "fathers" whose names are best known in England, Washington, John Adams, Jefferson, Madison, Franklin, and Hamilton, were all opponents of slavery. These include the first four Presidents, and the leaders of very different schools of thought. Some of them, Washington and Jefferson at least, had a few slaves of their own. Washington's attitude to his slaves is illustrated by a letter which he wrote to secure the return of a black attendant of Mrs. Washington's who had run away (a thing which he had boasted could never occur in his household); the runaway was to be brought back if she could be persuaded to return; her master's legal power to compel her was not to be used. She was in fact free, but had foolishly left a good place; and there is no reason to suppose that it was otherwise with Jefferson's slaves. Jefferson's theory was vehemently against slavery. In old age he gave up hope in the matter and was more solicitous for union than for liberty, but this was after the disappointment of many efforts. In these efforts he had no illusory notion of equality; he wrote in 1791, when he had been defeated in the attempt to carry a measure of gradual emancipation in Virginia: "Nobody wishes more than I do to see such proofs as you exhibit, that Nature has given to our black brothers talents equal to those of the other colours of men, and that the appearance of a want of them is owing mainly to the degraded condition of their existence, both in Africa and America. I can add with truth, that nobody wishes more ardently to see a good system commenced for raising the condition both of their body and mind to what it ought to be, as fast as the imbecility of their present existence and other circumstances, which cannot be neglected, will permit."

When he felt at last that freedom was not making way, his letters, by which his influence was chiefly exercised, abounded in passionate regrets. "I tremble for my country," he wrote, "when I think of the negro

and remember that God is just." But if he is judged not by his sentiments, or even by his efforts, but by what he accomplished, this rhetorical champion of freedom did accomplish one great act, the first link as it proved in the chain of events by which slavery was ultimately abolished. In 1784 the North-West Territory, as it was called, was ceded by Virginia to the old Congress of the days before the Union. Jefferson then endeavoured to pass an Ordinance by which slavery should be excluded from all territory that might ever belong to Congress. In this indeed he failed, for in part of the territory likely to be acquired slavery was already established, but the result was a famous Ordinance of 1787, by which slavery was for ever excluded from the soil of the North-West Territory itself, and thus, when they came into being, the States of Ohio, Indiana, Illinois, Michigan, and Wisconsin found themselves congenitally incapable of becoming slave States.

The further achievements of that generation in this matter were considerable. It must of course be understood that the holding of slaves and the slave trade from Africa were regarded as two distinct questions. The new Congress abolished the slave trade on the first day on which the Constitution allowed it to do so, that is, on January 1, 1808. The mother country abolished it just about the same time. But already all but three of the States had for themselves abolished the slave trade in their own borders. As to slavery itself, seven of the original thirteen States and Vermont, the first of the added States, had abolished that before 1805. These indeed were Northern States, where slavery was not of importance, but in Virginia there was, or had been till lately, a growing opinion that slavery was not economical, and, with the ignorance common in one part of a country of the true conditions in another part, it was natural to look upon emancipation as a policy which would spread of itself. At any rate it is certain fact that the chief among the men who had made the Constitution had at that time so regarded it, and continued to do so.

Under this belief and in the presence of many pressing subjects of interest the early movement for emancipation in America died down with its work half finished.

But before this happy belief expired an economic event had happened which riveted slavery upon the South. In 1793 Eli Whitney, a Yale student upon a holiday in the South, invented the first machine for cleaning cotton of its seeds. The export of cotton jumped from 192,000 lbs. in 1791 to 6,000,000 lbs. in 1795. Slave labour had been found, or was believed, to be especially economical in cotton growing. Slavery therefore rapidly became the mainstay of wealth and of the social system in South Carolina and throughout the far South; and in a little while the baser sort of planters in Virginia discovered that breeding slaves to sell down South was a very profitable form of stock-raising.

We may pass to the year 1820, when an enactment was passed by Congress which for thirty-four years thereafter might be regarded as hardly less fundamental than the Constitution itself. Up till then nine new States had been added to the original thirteen. It was repugnant to principles still strong in the North that these States should be admitted to the Union with State Constitutions which permitted slavery. On the other hand, it was for two reasons important to the chief slave States, that they should be. They would otherwise be closed to Southern planters who wished to migrate to unexhausted soil carrying with them the methods of industry and the ways of life which they understood. Furthermore, the North wa bound to have before long a great preponderance of population, and if this were not neutralised by keeping the number of States on one side and the other equal there would be a future political danger to slavery. Up to a certain point the North could with good conscience yield to the South in this matter, for the soil of four of the new slave States had been ceded to the Union by old slave States and slave-holders had settled freely upon it; and in a fifth, Louisiana, slavery had been safeguarded by the express stipulations of the treaty with France,

which applied to that portion, though no other, of the
territory then ceded.   Naturally, then, it had happened,
though without any definite agreement, that for years past
slave States and free States had been admitted to the
Union in pairs.   Now arose the question of a further
portion of the old French territory, the present State of
Missouri.   A few slave-holders with their slaves had in
fact settled there, but no distinct claims on behalf of
slavery could be alleged.   The Northern Senators and
members of Congress demanded therefore that the Constitution of Missouri should provide for the gradual extinction of slavery there.   Naturally there arose a controversy which sounded to the aged Jefferson like " a
fire-bell in the night " and revealed for the first time to
all America a deep rift in the Union.   The Representatives of the South eventually carried their main point
with the votes of several Northern men, known to history
as the " Dough-faces," who all lost their seats at the
next election.   Missouri was admitted as a slave State,
Maine about the same time as a free State; and it was
enacted that thereafter in the remainder of the territory
that had been bought from France slavery should be
unlawful north of latitude 36° 30', while by tacit agreement permitted south of it.

This was the Missouri Compromise.   The North regarded it at first as a humiliation, but learnt to point to
it later as a sort of Magna Carta for the Northern territories.   The adoption of it marks a point from which
it became for thirty-four years the express ambition of
the principal American statesmen and the tacit objec. of
every party manager to keep the slavery question from
ever becoming again a burning issue in politics.   The
collapse of it in 1854 was to prove the decisive event
in the career of Abraham Lincoln, aged 11 when it was
passed.

5. Leaders, Parties, and Tendencies in Lincoln's Youth.

Just about the year 1830, when Lincoln started life
in Illinois, several distinct movements in national life

began or culminated. They link themselves with several famous names.

The two leaders to whom, as a young politician, Lincoln owed some sort of allegiance were Webster and Clay, and they continued throughout his long political apprenticeship to be recognised in most of America as the great men of their time. Daniel Webster must have been nearly a great man. He was always passed over for the Presidency. That was not so much because of the private failings which marked his robust and generous character, as because in days of artificial party issues, when vital questions are dealt with by mere compromise, high office seems to belong of right to men of less originality. If he was never quite so great as all America took him to be, it was not for want of brains or of honesty, but because his consuming passion for the Union at all costs led him into the path of least apparent risk to it. Twice as Secretary of State (that is, chiefly, Foreign Minister) he showed himself a statesman, but above all he was an orator and one of those rare orators who accomplish a definite task by their oratory. In his style he carried on the tradition of English Parliamentary speaking, and developed its vices yet further; but the massive force of argument behind gave him his real power. That power he devoted to the education of the people in a feeling for the nation and for its greatness. As an advocate he had appeared in great cases in the Supreme Court. John Marshall, the Chief Justice from 1801 to 1835, brought a great legal mind of the higher type to the settlement of doubtful points in the Constitution, and his statesmanlike judgments did much both to strengthen the United States Government and to gain public confidence for it. It was a memorable work, for the power of the Union Government, under its new Constitution, lay in the grip of the Courts. The pleading of the young Webster contributed much to this. Later on Webster, and a school of followers, of whom perhaps we may take " our Elijah Pogram " to have been one, used ceremonial occasions, on which Englishmen only

suffer the speakers, for the purpose of inculcating their patriotic doctrine, and Webster at least was doing good. His greatest speech, upon an occasion to which we shall shortly come, was itself an event. Lincoln found in it as inspiring a political treatise as many Englishmen have discovered in the speeches and writings of Burke.

Henry Clay was a slighter but more attractive person. He was apparently the first American public man whom his countrymen styled " magnetic," but a sort of scheming instability caused him after one or two trials to be set down as an " impossible " candidate for the Presidency. As a dashing young man from the West he had the chief hand in forcing on the second war with Great Britain, from 1812 to 1814, which arose out of perhaps insufficient causes and ended in no clear result, but which, it is probable, marked a stage in the growth of loyalty to America. As an older man he was famed as an " architect of compromises," for though he strove for emancipation in his own State, Kentucky, and dreamed of a great scheme for colonising the slaves in Africa, he was supremely anxious to avert collision between North and South, and in this respect was typical of his generation. But about 1830 he was chiefly known as the apostle of what was called the " American policy." This was a policy which aimed at using the powers of the national Government for the development of the boundless resources of the country. Its methods comprised a national banking system, the use of the money of the Union on great public works, and a protective tariff, which it was hoped might chiefly operate to encourage promising but " infant " industries and to tax the luxuries of the rich. Whatever may have been the merits of this policy, which made some commotion for a few years, we can easily understand that it appealed to the imagination of young Lincoln at a time of keen political energy on his part of which we have but meagre details.

A third celebrity of this period, in his own locality a still more powerful man, was John Caldwell Calhoun, of South Carolina. He enjoyed beyond all his con-

temporaries the fame of an intellectual person. Lincoln conceded high admiration to his concise and penetrating phrases. An Englishwoman, Harriet Martineau, who knew him, has described him as "embodied intellect." He had undoubtedly in full measure those negative titles to respect which have gone far in America to ensure praise from the public and the historians; for he was correct and austere, and, which is more, kindly among his family and his slaves. He is credited, too, with an observance of high principle in public life, which it might be difficult to illustrate from his recorded actions. But the warmer-blooded Andrew Jackson set him down as "heartless, selfish, and a physical coward," and Jackson could speak generously of an opponent whom he really knew. His intellect must have been powerful enough, but it was that of a man who delights in arguing, and delights in elaborate deductions from principles which he is too proud to revise; a man, too, who is fearless in accepting conclusions which startle or repel the vulgar mind; who is undisturbed in his logical processes by good sense, healthy sentiment, or any vigorous appetite for truth. Such men have disciples who reap the disgrace which their masters are apt somehow to avoid; they give the prestige of wisdom and high thought to causes which could not otherwise earn them. A Northern soldier came back wounded in 1865 and described to the next soldier in the hospital Calhoun's monument at Charleston. The other said: "What you saw is not the real monument, but I have seen it. It is the desolated, ruined South. . . . That is Calhoun's real monument."

This man was a Radical, and known as the successor of Jefferson, but his Radicalism showed itself in drawing inspiration solely from the popular catchwords of his own locality. He adored the Union, but it was to be a Union directed by distinguished politicians from the South in a sectional Southern interest. He did not originate, but he secured the strength of orthodoxy and fashion to a tone of sentiment and opinion which for a generation held undisputed supremacy in the heart of

the South. Americans might have seemed at this time to be united in a curiously exultant national self-consciousness, but though there was no sharp division of sections, the boasted glory of the one America meant to many planters in the South the glory of their own settled and free life with their dignified equals round them and their often contented dependents under them. Plain men among them doubtless took things as they were, and, without any particular wish to change them, did not pretend they were perfect. But it is evident that in a widening circle of clever young men in the South the claim of some peculiar virtue for Southern institutions became habitual in the first half of the nineteenth century. Their way of life was beautiful in their eyes. It rested upon slavery. Therefore slavery was a good thing. It was wicked even to criticise it, and it was weak to apologise for it or to pretend that it needed reformation. It was easy and it became apparently universal for the different Churches of the South to prostitute the Word of God in this cause. Later on crude notions of evolution began to get about in a few circles of advanced thought, and these lent themselves as easily to the same purpose. Loose, floating thoughts of this kind might have mattered little. Calhoun, as the recognised wise man of the old South, concentrated them and fastened them upon its people as a creed. Glorification of " our institution at the South " became the main principle of Southern politicians, and any conception that there may ever have been of a task for constructive statesmanship, in solving the negro problem, passed into oblivion under the influence of his revered reasoning faculty.

But, of his dark and dangerous sort, Calhoun was an able man. He foresaw early that the best weapon of the common interest of the slave States lay in the rights which might be claimed for each individual State against the Union. The idea that a discontented State might secede from the Union was not novel—it had been mooted in New England, during the last war against Great Britain, and, curiously enough, among the rump of the

old Federalist party, but it was generally discounted. Calhoun first brought it into prominence, veiled in an elaborate form which some previous South Carolinian had devised. The occasion had nothing to do with slavery. It concerned Free Trade, a very respectable issue, but so clearly a minor issue that to break up a great country upon it would have gone beyond the limit of solemn frivolity, and Calhoun must be taken to have been forging an implement with which his own section of the States could claim and extort concessions from the Union. A protective tariff had been passed in 1828. The Southern States, which would have to pay the protective duties but did not profit by them, disliked it. Calhoun and others took the intelligible but too refined point, that the powers of Congress under the Constitution authorised a tariff for revenue but not a tariff for a protective purpose. Every State, Calhoun declared, must have the Constitutional right to protect itself against an Act of Congress which it deemed unconstitutional. Let such a State, in special Convention, "nullify" the Act of Congress. Let Congress then, unless it compromised the matter, submit its Act to the people in the form of an Amendment to the Constitution. It would then require a three fourths majority of all the States to pass the obnoxious Act. Last but not least, if the Act was passed, the protesting State had, Calhoun claimed, the right to secede from the Union.

Controversy over this tariff raged for fully four years, and had a memorable issue. In the course of 1830 the doctrine of "nullification" and "secession" was discussed in the Senate, and the view of Calhoun was expounded by one Senator Hayne. Webster answered him in a speech which he meant should become a popular classic, and which did become so. He set forth his own doctrine of the Union and appealed to national against State loyalty in the most influential oration that was perhaps ever made. "His utterance," writes President Wilson, "sent a thrill through all the East and North which was unmistakably a thrill of triumph. Men were

glad because of what he had said. He had touched
the national self-consciousness, awakened it, and pleased
it with a morning vision of its great tasks and certain
destiny." Later there came in the President, the redoubtable Andrew Jackson, the most memorable President between Jefferson and Lincoln. He said very little
—only, on Jefferson's birthday he gave the toast, " Our
Federal Union; it must be preserved." But when in
1832, in spite of concessions by Congress, a Convention
was summoned in South Carolina to " nullify " the tariff,
he issued the appropriate orders to the United States
Army, in case such action was carried out, and it is understood that he sent Calhoun private word that he would
be the first man to be hanged for treason. Nullification
quietly collapsed. The North was thrilled still more
than by Webster's oratory, and as not a single other State
showed signs of backing South Carolina, it became thenceforth the fixed belief of the North that the Union was
recognised as in law indissoluble, as Webster contended
it was. None the less the idea of secession had been
planted, and planted in a fertile soil.

General Andrew Jackson, whose other great achievements must now be told, was not an intellectual person,
but his ferocious and, in the literal sense, shocking character is refreshing to the student of this period. He
had been in his day the typical product of the West—
a far wilder West than that from which Lincoln later
came. Originally a lawyer, he had won martial fame
in fights with Indians and in the celebrated victory over
the British forces at New Orleans. He was a sincere
Puritan; and he had a courtly dignity of manner; but he
was of arbitrary and passionate temper, and he was a
sanguinary duellist. His most savage duels, it should
be added, concerned the honour of a lady whom he
married chivalrously, and loved devotedly to the end.
The case that can be made for his many arbitrary acts
shows them in some instances to have been justifiable, and
shows him in general to have been honest.

When in 1824 Jackson had expected to become

President, and, owing to proceedings which do not now matter, John Quincy Adams, son of a former President, and himself a remarkable man, was made President instead of him, Jackson resolved to overthrow the ruling class of Virginian country gentlemen and Boston city magnates which seemed to him to control Government, and to call into life a real democracy. To this end he created a new party, against which of course an opposition party arose.

Neither of the new parties was in any sense either aristocratic or democratic. " The Democracy," or Democratic party, has continued in existence ever since, and through most of Lincoln's life ruled America. In trying to fix the character of a party in a foreign country we cannot hope to be exact in our portraiture. At the first start, however, this party was engaged in combating certain tendencies to Government interference in business. It was more especially hostile to a National Bank, which Jackson himself regarded as a most dangerous form of alliance between the administration and the richest class. Of the growth of what may be called the money power in American politics he had an intense, indeed prophetic, dread. Martin Van Buren, his friend and successor, whatever else he may have been, was a sound economist of what is now called the old school, and on a financial issue he did what few men in his office have done, he deliberately sacrificed his popularity to his principles. Beyond this the party was and has continued prone, in a manner which we had better not too clearly define, to insist upon the restrictions of the Constitution, whether in the interest of individual liberty or of State rights. This tendency was disguised at the first by the arbitrary action of Jackson's own proceedings, for Jackson alone among Presidents displayed the sentiments of what may be called a popular despot. Its insistence upon State rights, aided perhaps by its dislike of Protection, attracted to it the leading politicians of the South, who in the main dominated its counsels, though later on they liked to do it through Northern instru-

ments. But it must not in the least be imagined that either party was Northern or Southern; for there were many Whigs in the South, and very many Democrats in the North. Moreover, it should be clearly grasped, though it is hard, that among Northern Democrats insistence on State rights did not involve the faintest leaning towards the doctrine of secession; on the contrary a typical Democrat would believe that these limitations to the power of the Union were the very things that gave it endurance and strength. Slavery, moreover, had friends and foes in both parties. If we boldly attempted to define the prevailing tone of the Democrats we might say that, while they and their opponents expressed loyalty to the Union and the Constitution, the Democrats would be prone to lay the emphasis upon the Constitution. Whatever might be the case with an average Whig, a man like Lincoln would be stirred in his heart by the general spirit of the country's institutions, while the typical Democrat of that time would dwell affectionately on the legal instruments and formal maxims in which that spirit was embodied.

Of the Whigs it is a little harder to speak definitely, nor is it very necessary, for in two only out of seven Presidential elections did they elect their candidate, and in each case that candidate then died, and in 1854 they perished as a party utterly and for ever. Just for a time they were identified with the " American policy " of Clay. When that passed out of favour they never really attempted to formulate any platform, or to take permanently any very definite stand. They nevertheless had the adherence of the ablest men of the country, and, as an opposition party to a party in power which furnished much ground for criticism, they possessed an attraction for generous youth.

The Democrats at once, and the Whigs not long after them, created elaborate party machines, on the need of which Jackson insisted as the only means of really giving influence to the common people. The prevailing system and habit of local self-government made such organisa-

tion easy. Men of one party in a township or in a
county assembled, formulated their opinions, and sent
delegates with instructions, more or less precise, to party
conventions for larger areas, these would send delegates
to the State Convention and these in turn to the National Convention of the Party. The party candidates
for the Presidency, as well as for all other elective positions, were and are thus chosen, and the party " platform " or declaration of policy was and is thus formulated. Such machinery, which in England is likely always
to play a less important part, has acquired an evil name.
At the best there has always been a risk that a " platform " designed to detach voters from the opposite party
will be an insincere and eviscerated document, by which
active public opinion is rather muzzled than expressed.
There has been a risk too that the " available " candidate
should be some blameless nonentity, to whom no one
objects, and whom therefore no one really wants. But it
must be observed that the rapidity with which such
organisation was taken up betokened the prevalence of
a widespread and keen interest in political affairs.

The days of really great moneyed interests and of
corruption of the gravest sort were as yet far distant,
but one demoralising influence was imposed upon the
new party system by its author at its birth. Jackson,
in his perpetual fury, believed that office holders under
the more or less imaginary ruling clique that had held
sway were a corrupt gang, and he began to turn them
out. He was encouraged to extend to the whole country
a system which had prevailed in New York and with
which Van Buren was too familiar. " To the victors
belong the spoils," exclaimed a certain respectable Mr.
Marcy. A wholesale dismissal of office holders large
and small, and replacement of them by sound Democrats, soon took place. Once started, the " spoils system "
could hardly be stopped. Thenceforward there was a
standing danger that the party machine would be in the
hands of a crew of jobbers and dingy hunters after
petty offices. England, of course, has had and now has

practices theoretically as indefensible, but none possessing any such sinister importance. It is hard, therefore, for us to conceive how little of really vicious intent was necessary to set this disastrous influence going. There was no trained Civil Service with its unpartisan traditions. In the case of offices corresponding to those of our permanent heads of departments it seemed reasonable that the official should, like his chief the Minister concerned, be a person in harmony with the President. As to the smaller offices—the thousands of village postmasterships and so forth—one man was likely to do the work as well as another; the dispossessed official could, in the then condition of the country, easily find another equally lucrative employment; "turn and turn about" seemed to be the rule of fair play.

There were now few genuine issues in politics. Compromise on vital questions was understood to be the highest statesmanship. The Constitution itself, with its curious system of checks and balances, rendered it difficult to bring anything to pass. Added to this was a party system with obvious natural weaknesses, infected from the first with a dangerous malady. The political life, which lay on the surface of the national life of America, thus began to assume an air of futility, and, it must be added, of squalor. Only, Englishmen, recollecting the feebleness and corruption which marked their aristocratic government through a great part of the eighteenth century, must not enlarge their phylacteries at the expense of American democracy. And it is yet more important to remember that the fittest machinery for popular government, the machinery through which the real judgment of the people will prevail, can only by degrees and after many failures be devised. Popular government was then young, and it is young still.

So much for the great world of politics in those days. But in or about 1830 a Quaker named Lundy had, as Quakers used to say, "a concern" to walk 125 miles through the snow of a New England winter and speak his mind to William Lloyd Garrison. Garrison was a

poor man who, like Franklin, had raised himself as a working printer, and was now occupied in philanthropy. Stirred up by Lundy, he succeeded after many painful experiences, in gaol and among mobs, in publishing in Boston on January 1, 1831, the first number of the *Liberator*. In it he said: "I shall strenuously contend for the immediate enfranchisement of our slave population. I will be as hard as truth and as uncompromising as justice. I will not equivocate; I will not excuse; I will not retreat a single inch; and I will be heard." This was the beginning of the new Abolitionist movement. The Abolitionists, in the main, were impracticable people; Garrison in the end proved otherwise. Under the existing Constitution, they had nothing to propose but that the free States should withdraw from "their covenant with death and agreement with hell"—in other words, from the Union,—whereby they would not have liberated one slave. They included possibly too many of that sort who would seek salvation by repenting of other men's sins. But even these did not indulge this propensity at their ease, for by this time the politicians, the polite world, the mass of the people, the churches (even in Boston), not merely avoided the dangerous topic; they angrily proscribed it. The Abolitionists took their lives in their hands, and sometimes lost them. Only two men of standing helped them: Channing, the great preacher, who sacrificed thereby a fashionable congregation; and Adams, the sour, upright, able ex-President, the only ex-President who ever made for himself an after-career in Congress. In 1852 a still more potent ally came to their help, a poor lady, Mrs. Beecher Stowe, who in that year published "Uncle Tom's Cabin," often said to have influenced opinion more than any other book of modern times. Broadly speaking, they accomplished two things. If they did not gain love in quarters where they might have looked for it, they gained the very valuable hatred of their enemies; for they goaded Southern politicians to fury and madness, of which the first symptom was their effort to suppress Abolitionist petitions to Con-

gress. But above all they educated in their labour of thirty years a school of opinion, not entirely in agreement with them but ready one day to revolt with decision from continued complicity in wrong.

6. *Slavery and Southern Society.*

In the midst of this growing America, a portion, by no means sharply marked off, and accustomed to the end to think itself intensely American, was distinguished by a peculiar institution. What was the character of that institution as it presented itself in 1830 and onwards?

Granting, as many slave holders did, though their leaders always denied it, that slavery originated in foul wrongs and rested legally upon a vile principle, what did it look like in its practical working? Most of us have received from two different sources two broad but vivid general impressions on this subject, which seem hard to reconcile but which are both in the main true. On the one hand, a visitor from England or the North, coming on a visit to the South, or in earlier days to the British West Indies, expecting perhaps to see all the horror of slavery at a glance, would be, as a young British officer once wrote home, "most agreeably undeceived as to the situation of these poor people." He would discern at once that a Southern gentleman had no more notion of using his legal privilege to be cruel to his slave than he himself had of overdriving his old horse. He might easily on the contrary find quite ordinary slave owners who had a very decided sense of responsibility in regard to their human chattels. Around his host's house, where the owner's children, petted by a black nurse, played with the little black children or with some beloved old negro, he might see that pretty aspect of "our institution at the South," which undoubtedly created in many young Southerners as they grew up a certain amount of genuine sentiment in favour of slavery. Riding wider afield he might be struck, as General Sherman was, with the contentment of the negroes whom he

met on the plantations. On enquiry he would learn that the slave in old age was sure of food and shelter and free from work, and that as he approached old age his task was systematically diminished. As to excessive toil at any time of life, he would perhaps conclude that it was no easy thing to drive a gang of Africans really hard. He would be assured, quite incorrectly, that the slave's food and comfort generally were greater than those of factory workers in the North, and, perhaps only too truly, that his privations were less than those of the English agricultural labourer at that time. A wide and careful survey of the subject was made by Frederick Law Olmsted, a New York farmer, who wrote what but for their gloomy subject would be among the best books of travel. He presents to us the picture of a prevailingly sullen, sapless, brutish life, but certainly not of acute misery or habitual oppression. A Southerner old enough to remember slavery would probably not question the accuracy of his details, but would insist, very likely with truth, that there was more human happiness there than an investigator on such a quest would readily discover. Even on large plantations in the extreme South, where the owner only lived part of the year, and most things had to be left to an almost always unsatisfactory overseer, the verdict of the observer was apt to be " not so bad as I expected."

On the other hand, many of us know Longfellow's grim poem of the Hunted Negro. It is a true picture of the life led in the Dismal Swamps of Virginia by numbers of skulking fugitives, till the industry of negro-hunting, conducted with hounds of considerable value, ultimately made their lairs untenable. The scenes in the auction room where, perhaps on the death or failure of their owner, husbands and wives, parents and children, were constantly being severed, and negresses were habitually puffed as brood mares; the gentleman who had lately sold his half-brother, to be sent far south, because he was impudent; the devilish cruelty with which almost the only recorded slave insurrection was stamped out; the chase

and capture and return in fetters of slaves who had
escaped north, or, it might be, of free negroes in their
place; the advertisements for such runaways, which
Dickens collected, and which described each by his scars
or mutilations; the systematic slave breeding, for the
supply of the cotton States, which had become a staple
industry of the once glorious Virginia; the demand arising for the restoration of the African slave trade—all
these were realities. The Southern people, in the phrase
of President Wilson, " knew that their lives were honourable, their relations with their slaves humane, their responsibility for the existence of slavery amongst them
remote "; they burned with indignation when the whole
South was held responsible for the occasional abuses
of slavery. But the harsh philanthropist, who denounced
them indiscriminately, merely dwelt on those aspects of
slavery which came to his knowledge or which he actually
saw on the border line. And the occasional abuses, however occasional, were made by the deliberate choice of
Southern statesmanship an essential part of the institution. Honourable and humane men in the South scorned
exceedingly the slave hunter and the slave dealer. A
candid slave owner, discussing " Uncle Tom's Cabin,"
found one detail flagrantly unfair; the ruined master
would have had to sell his slaves to the brute, Legree, but
for the world he would not have shaken hands with him.
" Your children," exclaimed Lincoln, " may play with
the little black children, but they must not play with
his "—the slave dealer's, or the slave driver's, or the
slave hunter's. By that fact alone, as he bitingly but
unanswerably insisted, the whole decent society of the
South condemned the foundation on which it rested.

It is needless to discuss just how dark or how fair
American slavery in its working should be painted. The
moderate conclusions which are quite sufficient for our
purpose are uncontested. First, this much must certainly
be conceded to those who would defend the slave system,
that in the case of the average slave it was very doubtful whether his happiness (apart from that of future

generations) could be increased by suddenly turning him
into a free man working for a wage; justice would certainly have demanded that the change should be accompanied by other provisions for his benefit. But,
secondly, on the refractory negro, more vicious, or sometimes, one may suspect, more manly than his fellows, the
system was likely to act barbarously. Thirdly, every slave
family was exposed to the risk, on such occasions as the
death or great impoverishment of its owner, of being
ruthlessly torn asunder, and the fact that negroes often
rebounded or seemed to rebound from sorrows of this
sort with surprising levity does not much lessen the horror
of it. Fourthly, it is inherent in slavery that its burden
should be most felt precisely by the best minds and
strongest characters among the slaves.. And, though the
capacity of the negroes for advancement could not then
and cannot yet be truly measured, yet it existed, and
the policy of the South shut the door upon it. Lastly,
the system abounded in brutalising influences upon a large
number of white people who were accessory to it, and
notoriously it degraded the poor or " mean whites," for
whom it left no industrial opening, and among whom it
caused work to be despised.

There is thus no escape from Lincoln's judgment:
" If slavery is not wrong, nothing is wrong."   It does
not follow that the way to right the wrong was simple,
or that instant and unmitigated emancipation was the
best way. But it does follow that, failing this, it was
for the statesmen of the South to devise a policy by which
the most flagrant evils should be stopped, and, however
cautiously and experimentally, the raising of the status
of the slave should be proceeded with. It does not
follow that the people who, on one pretext or another,
shut their eyes to the evil of the system, while they tried
to keep their personal dealing humane, can be sweepingly
condemned by any man. But it does follow that a
deliberate and sustained policy which, neglecting all reform, strove at all costs to perpetuate the system and
extend it to wider regions, was as criminal a policy as

ever lay at the door of any statesmen. And this, in fact, became the policy of the South.

"The South" meant, for political purposes, the owners of land and slaves in the greater part of the States in which slavery was lawful. The poor whites never acquired the political importance of the working classes in the North, and count for little in the story. Some of the more northerly slave States partook in a greater degree of the conditions and ideas of the North and were doubtfully to be reckoned with the South. Moreover, there is a tract of mountainous country, lying between the Atlantic sea-board and the basin of the Mississippi and extending southwards to the borders of Georgia and Alabama, of which the very vigorous and independent inhabitants were and are in many ways a people apart, often cherishing to this day family feuds which are prosecuted in the true spirit of the Icelandic Sagas.

The South, excluding these districts, was predominantly Democratic in politics, and its leaders owed some allegiance to the tradition of Radicals like Jefferson. But it was none the less proud of its aristocracy and of the permeating influence of aristocratic manners and traditions. A very large number of Southerners felt themselves to be ladies and gentlemen, and felt further that there were few or none like them among the "Yankee" traders of the North. A claim of that sort is likely to be aggressively made by those who have least title to make it, and, as strife between North and South grew hotter, the gentility of the latter infected with additional vulgarity the political controversy of private life and even of Congress. But, as observant Northerners were quite aware, these pretensions had a foundation of fact. An Englishman, then or now, in chance meetings with Americans of either section, would at once be aware of something indefinable in their bearing to which he was a stranger; but in the case of the Southerner the strangeness would often have a positive charm, such as may be found also among people of the Old World under south-

ern latitudes and relatively primitive conditions. Newly-
gotten and ill-carried wealth was in those days (Mr.
Olmsted, of New York State, assures us) as offensive in
the more recently developed and more prosperous parts
of the South as in New York City itself; and throughout
the South sound instruction and intellectual activity were
markedly lacking—indeed, there is no serious Southern
literature by which we can check these impressions of
his. Comparing the masses of moderately well-to-do
and educated people with whom he associated in the
North and in the South, he finds them both free from
the peculiar vulgarity which, we may be pained to know,
he had discovered among us in England; he finds honesty
and dishonesty in serious matters of conduct as prevalent
in one section as in the other; he finds the Northerner
better taught and more alert in mind; but he ascribes
to him an objectionable quality of "smartness," a determination to show you that he is a stirring and pushing
fellow, from which the Southerner is wholly free; and he
finds that the Southerner has derived from home influences and from boarding schools in which the influence
of many similar homes is concentrated, not indeed any
great refinement, but a manner which is "more true, more
quiet, more modestly self-assured, more dignified." This
advantage, we are to understand, is diffused over a comparatively larger class than in England. Beyond this he
discerns in a few parts of the South and notably in South
Carolina a somewhat inaccessible, select society, of which
the nucleus is formed by a few (incredibly few) old
Colonial families which have not gone under, and which
altogether is so small that some old gentlewomen can
enumerate all the members of it. Few as they are, these
form "unquestionably a wealthy and remarkably generous, refined, and accomplished first class, clinging with
some pertinacity, although with too evident an effort,
to the traditional manners and customs of an established
gentry."

No doubt the sense of high breeding, which was common in the South, went beyond mere manners; it played

its part in making the struggle of the Southern population, including the "mean whites," in the Civil War one of the most heroic, if one of the most mistaken, in which a whole population has ever been engaged; it went along with integrity and a high average of governing capacity among public men; and it fitted the gentry of the South to contribute, when they should choose, an element of great value to the common life of America. As it was, the South suffered to the full the political degeneration which threatens every powerful class which, with a distinct class interest of its own, is secluded from real contact with competing classes with other interests and other ideas. It is not to be assumed that all individual Southerners liked the policy which they learnt to support in docile masses. But their very qualities of loyalty made them the more ready, under accepted and respected leaders, to adopt political aims and methods which no man now recalls without regret.

The connection between slavery and politics was this: as population slowly grew in the South, and as the land in the older States became to some extent exhausted, the desire for fresh territory in which cultivation by slaves could flourish became stronger and stronger. This was the reason for which the South became increasingly aware of a sectional interest in politics. In all other respects the community of public interests, of business dealings, and of general intercourse was as great between North and South as between East and West. It is certain that throughout the South, with the doubtful exception of South Carolina, political instinct and patriotic pride would have made the idea of separation intolerable upon any ground except that of slavery. In regard to this matter of dispute a peculiar phenomenon is to be observed. The quarrel grew not out of any steady opposition between North and South, but out of the habitual domination of the country by the South and the long-continued submission of the North to that domination.

For the North had its full share of blame for the long course of proceedings which prepared the coming tragedy,

and the most impassioned writers on the side of the Union during the Civil War have put that blame highest. The South became arrogant and wrong-headed, and no defence is possible for the chief acts of Southern policy which will be recorded later; but the North was abject. To its own best sons it seemed to have lost both its conscience and its manhood, and to be stifled in the coils of its own miserable political apparatus. Certainly the prevailing attitude of the Northern to the Southern politicians was that of truckling. And Southerners who went to Washington had a further reason for acquiring a fatal sense of superiority to the North. The tradition of popular government which maintained itself in the South caused men who were respected, in private life, and were up to a point capable leaders, who were, in short, representative, to be sent to Congress and to be kept there. The childish perversion of popular government which took hold of the newer and more unsettled population in the North led them to send to Congress an ever-changing succession of unmeritable and sometimes shady people. The eventual stirring of the mind of the North which so closely concerns this biography was a thing hard to bring about, and to the South it brought a great shock of surprise.

7. Intellectual Development.

No survey of the political movements of this period should conclude without directing attention to something more important, which cannot be examined here. In the years from 1830 till some time after the death of Lincoln, America made those contributions to the literature of our common language which, though neither her first nor her last, seemed likely to be most permanently valued. The learning and literature of America at that time centred round Boston and Harvard University in the adjacent city of Cambridge, and no invidious comparison is intended or will be felt if they, with their poets and historians and men of letters at that time, with their peculiar atmosphere, instinct then and now with a life

athletic, learned, business-like and religious, are taken to
show the dawning capacities of the new nation. No places
in the United States exhibit more visibly the kinship of
America with England, yet in none certainly can a
stranger see more readily that America is independent of
the Old World in something more than politics. Many
of their streets and buildings would in England seem
redolent of the past, yet no cities of the Eastern States
played so large a part in the development, material and
mental, of the raw and vigorous West. The limitations
of their greatest writers are in a manner the sign of their
achievement. It would have been contrary to all human
analogy if a country, in such an early stage of creation
out of such a chaos, had put forth books marked strongly
as its own and yet as the products of a mature national
mind. It would also have been surprising if since the
Civil War the rush of still more appalling and more complex practical problems had not obstructed for a while
the flow of imaginative or scientific production. But the
growth of those relatively early years was great. Boston
had been the home of a loveless Christianity; its insurrection in the War of Independence had been soiled by
shifty dealing and mere acidity; but Boston from the
days of Emerson to those of Phillips Brooks radiated
a temper and a mental force that was manly, tender, and
clean. The man among these writers about whose exact
rank, neither low nor very high among poets, there can
be least dispute was Longfellow. He might seem from
his favourite subjects to be hardly American; it was his
deliberately chosen task to bring to the new country some
savour of things gentle and mellow caught from the literature of Europe. But, in the first place, no writer could
in the detail of his work have been more racy of that
New England countryside which lay round his home;
and, in the second place, no writer could have spoken
more unerringly to the ear of the whole wide America
of which his home was a little part. It seems strange to
couple the name of this mild and scholarly man with the
thought of that crude Western world to which we must

in a moment pass. But the connection is real and vital.
It is well shown in the appreciation written of him and
his fellows by the American writer who most violently
contrasts with him, Walt Whitman.

A student of American history may feel something like
the experience which is common among travellers in
America. When they come home they cannot tell their
friends what really interested them. Ugly things and
very dull things are prominent in their story, as in the
tales of American humorists. The general impression
they convey is of something tiresomely extensive, distract-
ingly miscellaneous, and yet insufferably monotonous.
But that is not what they mean. They had better not
seek to express themselves by too definite instances. They
will be understood and believed when they say that to
them America, with its vast spaces from ocean to ocean,
does present itself as one country, not less worthy than
any other of the love which it has actually inspired; a
country which is the home of distinctive types of manhood and womanhood, bringing their own addition to the
varying forms in which kindness and courage and truth
make themselves admirable to mankind. The soul of
a single people seems to be somewhere present in that
great mass, no less than in some tiny city State of antiquity. Only it has to struggle, submerged evermore by a
flood of newcomers, and defeated evermore by difficulties
quite unlike those of other lands; and it struggles seemingly with undaunted and with rational hope.

Americans are fond of discussing Americanism. Very
often they select as a pattern of it Abraham Lincoln, the
man who kept the North together but has been pronounced to have been a Southerner in his inherited character. Whether he was so typical or not, it is the central
fact of this biography that no man ever pondered more
deeply in his own way, or answered more firmly the question whether there was indeed an American nationality
worth preserving.

CHAPTER III

1. *Life at New Salem.*

FROM this talk of large political movements we have to recall ourselves to a young labouring man with hardly any schooling, naturally and incurably uncouth, but with a curious, quite modest, impulse to assert a kindly ascendency over the companions whom chance threw in his way, and with something of the gift, which odd, shy people often possess, for using their very oddity as a weapon in their struggles. In the conditions of real equality which still prevailed in a newly settled country it is not wonderful that he made his way into political life when he was twenty-five, but it was not till twenty years later that he played an important part in events of enduring significance.

Thus the many years of public activity with which we are concerned in this and the following chapter belong rather to his apprenticeship than to his life's work; and this apprenticeship at first sight contrasts more strongly with his fame afterwards than does his boyhood of poverty and comparatively romantic hardship. For many poor boys have lived to make a great mark on history, but as a rule they have entered early on a life either of learning or of adventure or of large business. But the affairs in which Lincoln early became immersed have an air of pettiness, and from the point of view of most educated men and women in the Eastern States or in Europe, many of the associates and competitors of his early manhood, to whom he had to look up as his superiors in knowledge, would certainly have seemed crude people with a narrow horizon. Indeed, till he was called upon to take supreme control of very great mat-

ters, Lincoln must have had singularly little intercourse either with men versed in great affairs or with men of approved intellectual distinction. But a mind too original to be subdued to its surroundings found much that was stimulating in this time when Illinois was beginning rapidly to fill up. There were plenty of men with shrewd wits and robust character to be met with, and the mental atmosphere which surrounded him was one of keen interest in life. Lincoln eventually stands out as a surprising figure from among the other lawyers and little politicians of Illinois, as any great man does from any crowd, but some tribute is due to the undistinguished and historically uninteresting men whose generous appreciation gave rapid way to the poor, queer youth, and ultimately pushed him into a greater arena as their selected champion.

In 1831, at the age of twenty-two, Lincoln, returning from his New Orleans voyage, settled in New Salem to await the arrival of his patron, Denton Offutt, with the goods for a new store in which Lincoln was to be his assistant. The village itself was three years old. It never got much beyond a population of one hundred, and like many similar little towns of the West it has long since perished off the earth. But it was a busy place for a while, and, contrary to what its name might suggest, it aspired to be rather fast. It was a cock-fighting and whisky-drinking society into which Lincoln was launched. He managed to combine strict abstinence from liquor with keen participation in all its other diversions. One departure from total abstinence stands alleged among the feats of strength for which he became noted. He hoisted a whisky barrel, of unspecified but evidently considerable content, on to his knees in a squatting posture and drank from the bunghole. But this very arduous potation stood alone. Offutt was some time before he arrived with his goods, and Lincoln lived by odd jobs. At the very beginning one Mentor Graham, a schoolmaster officiating in some election, employed him as a clerk, and the clerk seized the occasion to make

himself well known to New Salem as a story-teller. Then there was a heavy job at rail-splitting, and another job in navigating the Sangamon River. Offutt's store was at last set up, and for about a year the assistant in this important establishment had valuable opportunities of conversation with all New Salem. He had also leisure for study. He had mentioned to the aforesaid Mentor Graham his "notion to study English grammar," and had been introduced to a work called "Kirkham's Grammar," which by a walk of some miles he could borrow from a neighbour. This he would read, lying full length on the counter with his head on a parcel of calico. At other odd times he would work away at arithmetic. Offutt's kindly interest procured him distinction in another field. At Clary's Grove, near New Salem, lived a formidable set of young ruffians, over whose somewhat disguised chivalry of temper the staid historian of Lincoln's youth becomes rapturous. They were given to wrecking the store of any New Salem tradesman who offended them; so it shows some spirit in Mr. Denton Offutt that he backed his Abraham Lincoln to beat their Jack Armstrong in a wrestling match. He did beat him; moreover, some charm in the way he bore himself made him thenceforth not hated but beloved of Clary's Grove in general, and the Armstrongs in particular. Hannah Armstrong, Jack's wife, thereafter mended and patched his clothes for him, and, years later, he had the satisfaction, as their unfeed advocate, of securing the acquittal of their son from a charge of murder, of which there is some reason to hope he may not have been guilty. It is, by the way, a relief to tell that there once was a noted wrestling match in which Lincoln was beaten; it is characteristic of the country that his friends were sure there was foul play, and characteristic of him that he indignantly denied it.

Within a year Offutt's store, in the phrase of the time, "petered out," leaving Lincoln shiftless. But the victor of Clary's Grove, with his added mastery of " Kirk-

ham's Grammar," was now ripe for public life. Moreover, his experience as a waterman gave him ideas on the question, which then agitated his neighbours, whether the Sangamon River could be made navigable. He had a scheme of his own for doing this; and in the spring of 1832 he wrote to the local paper a boyish but modest and sensible statement of his views and ambitions, announcing that he would be a candidate in the autumn elections for the State Legislature.

Meanwhile he had his one experience of soldiering. The Indian chief, Black Hawk, who had agreed to abide west of the Mississippi, broke the treaty and led his warriors back into their former haunts in Northern Illinois. The Governor of the State called for volunteers, and Lincoln became one. He obtained the elective rank of captain of his company, and contrived to maintain some sort of order in that, doubtless brave, but undisciplined body. He saw no fighting, but he could earn his living for some months, and stored up material for effective chaff in Congress long afterwards about the military glory which General Cass's supporters for the Presidency wished to attach to their candidate. His most glorious exploit consisted in saving from his own men a poor old friendly Indian who had fallen among them. A letter of credentials, which the helpless creature produced, was pronounced a forgery and he was about to be hanged as a spy, when Lincoln appeared on the scene, " swarthy with resolution and rage," and somehow terrified his disorderly company into dropping their prey.

The war ended in time for a brief candidature, and a supporter of his at the time preserved a record of one of his speeches. His last important speech will hereafter be given in full for other reasons; this may be so given too, for it is not a hundred words long: " Fellow Citizens, I presume you all know who I am. I am humble Abraham Lincoln. I have been solicited by many friends to become a candidate for the Legislature. My politics are short and sweet like the old woman's dance. I am in favour of a national bank. I

am in favour of the internal improvement system and a high protective tariff. These are my sentiments and political principles. If elected, I shall be thankful; if not, it will be all the same."

To this succinct declaration of policy may be added from his earlier letter that he advocated a law against usury, and laws for the improvement of education. The principles of the speech are those which the new Whig party was upholding against the Democrats under Jackson (the President) and Van Buren. Lincoln's neighbours, like the people of Illinois generally, were almost entirely on the side of the Democrats. It is interesting that however he came by his views, they were early and permanently fixed on the side then unpopular in Illinois; and it is interesting that though, naturally, not elected, he secured very nearly the whole of the votes of his immediate neighbourhood.

The penniless Lincoln was now hankering to become a lawyer, though with some thoughts of the more practicable career of a blacksmith. Unexpectedly, however, he was tempted into his one venture, singularly unsuccessful, in business. Two gentlemen named Herndon, cousins of a biographer of Lincoln's, started a store in New Salem and got tired of it. One sold his share to a Mr. Berry, the other sold his to Lincoln. The latter sale was entirely on credit—no money passed at the time, because there was no money. The vendor explained afterwards that he relied solely on Lincoln's honesty. He had to wait a long while for full payment, but what is known of storekeeping in New Salem shows that he did very well for himself in getting out of his venture as he did. Messrs. Berry and Lincoln next acquired, likewise for credit, the stock and goodwill of two other storekeepers, one of them the victim of a raid from Clary's Grove. The senior partner then applied himself diligently to personal consumption of the firm's liquid goods; the junior member of the firm was devoted in part to intellectual and humorous converse with the male customers, but a fatal shyness prevented

him from talking to the ladies. For the rest, he walked long distances to borrow books, got through Gibbon and through Rollin's "History of the World," began his study of Blackstone, and acquired a settled habit of reading novels. So business languished. Early in 1833 Berry and Lincoln sold out to another adventurer. This also was a credit transaction. The purchaser without avoidable delay failed and disappeared. Berry then died of drink, leaving to Lincoln the sole responsibility for the debts of the partnership. Lincoln could with no difficulty and not much reproach have freed himself by bankruptcy. As a matter of fact, he ultimately paid everything, but it took him about fifteen years of striving and pinching himself.

Lincoln is one of the many public characters to whom the standing epithet "honest" became attached; in his case the claim to this rested originally on the only conclusive authority, that of his creditors. But there is equally good authority, that of his biographer, William Herndon, for many years his partner as a lawyer, that "he had no money sense." This must be understood with the large qualification that he meant to pay his way and, unlike the great statesmen of the eighteenth century in England, did pay it. But, though with much experience of poverty in his early career, he never developed even a reasonable desire to be rich. Wealth remained in his view "a superfluity of the things one does not want." He was always interested in mathematics, but mainly as a discipline in thinking, and partly, perhaps, in association with mechanical problems of which he was fond enough to have once in his life patented an invention. The interest never led him to take to accounts or to long-sighted financial provisions. In later days, when he received a payment for his fees, his partner's share would be paid then and there; and perhaps the rent would be paid, and the balance would be spent at once in groceries and other goods likely to be soon wanted, including at long intervals, when the need was very urgent, a new hat.

These are amiable personal traits, but they mark the limitations of his capacity as a statesman. The chief questions which agitated the Illinois Legislature were economic, and so at first were the issues between Whigs and Democrats in Federal policy. Lincoln, though he threw himself into these affairs with youthful fervour, would appear never to have had much grasp of such matters. " In this respect alone," writes an admirer, " I have always considered Mr. Lincoln a weak man." It is only when (rarely, at first) constitutional or moral issues emerge that his politics become interesting. We can guess the causes which attached him to the Whigs. As the party out of power, and in Illinois quite out of favour, they had doubtless some advantage in character. As we have seen, the greatest minds among American statesmen of that day, Webster and Clay, were Whigs. Lincoln's simple and quite reasonable, if inconclusive, argument for Protection, can be found among his speeches of some years later. And schemes of internal development certainly fired his imagination.

After his failure in business Lincoln subsisted for a while on odd jobs for farmers, but was soon employed as assistant surveyor by John Calhoun, then surveyor of the county. This gentleman, who had been educated as a lawyer but " taught school in preference," was a keen Democrat, and had to assure Lincoln that office as his assistant would not necessitate his desertion of his principles. He was a clever man, and Lincoln remembered him long after as the most formidable antagonist he ever met in debate. With the help, again, of Mentor Graham, Lincoln soon learned the surveyor's business. He continued at this work till he was able to start as a lawyer, and there is evidence that his surveys of property were done with extreme accuracy. Soon he further obtained the local Postmastership. This, the only position except the Presidency itself which he ever held in the Federal Government, was not onerous, for the mails were infrequent; he " carried the office around in his hat "; we are glad to be told that " his administration

gave satisfaction." Once calamity threatened him; a creditor distrained on the horse and the instruments necessary to his surveyorship; but Lincoln was reputed to be a helpful fellow, and friends were ready to help him; they bought the horse and instruments back for him. To this time belongs his first acquaintance with some writers of unsettling tendency, Tom Paine, Voltaire, and Volney, who was then recognised as one of the dangerous authors. Cock-fights, strange feats of strength, or of usefulness with axe or hammer or scythe, and a passion for mimicry continue. In 1834 he became a candidate again. " Can't the party raise any better material than that? " asked a bystander before a speech of his; after it, he exclaimed that the speaker knew more than all the other candidates put together. This time he was elected, being then twenty-five, and thereafter he was returned for three further terms of two years. Shortly before his second election in 1836 the State capital was removed to Springfield, in his own county. There in 1837 Lincoln fixed his home. He had long been reading law in his curious, spasmodically concentrated way, and he had practised a little as a " pettifogger," that is, an unlicensed practitioner in the inferior courts. He had now obtained his license and was very shortly taken into partnership by an old friend in Springfield.

2. *In the Illinois Legislature.*

Here his youth may be said to end. Springfield was a different place from New Salem. There were carriages in it, and ladies who studied poetry and the fashions. There were families from Virginia and Kentucky who were conscious of ancestry, while graver, possibly more pushing, people from the North-eastern States, soon to outnumber them, were a little inclined to ridicule what they called their " illusory ascendency." There was a brisk competition of churches, and mutual improvement societies such as the " Young Men's Lyceum " had a rival claim to attention with races and cock-fights.

And it was an altered Abraham Lincoln that came to inhabit Springfield. Arriving a day or two before his first law partnership was settled he came into the shop of a thriving young tradesman, Mr. Joshua Speed, to ask about the price of the cheapest bedding and other necessary articles. The sum for which Lincoln, who had not one cent, would have had to ask, and would have been readily allowed, credit, was only seventeen dollars. But this huge prospect of debt so visibly depressed him that Speed instantly proposed an arrangement which involved no money debt. He took him upstairs and installed him—Western domestic arrangements were and are still simple—as the joint occupant of his own large bed. " Well, Speed, I'm moved," was the terse acknowledgment. Speed was to move him later by more precious charity. We are concerned for the moment with what moved Speed. "I looked up at him," said he, long after, " and I thought then, as I think now, that I never saw so gloomy and melancholy a face in my life." The struggle of ambition and poverty may well have been telling on Lincoln; but besides that a tragical love story (shortly to be told) had left a deep and permanent mark; but these influences worked, we may suppose, upon a disposition quite as prone to sadness as to mirth. His exceedingly gregarious habit, drawing him to almost any assembly of his own sex, continued all his life; but it alternated from the first with a habit of solitude or abstraction, the abstraction of a man who, when he does wish to read, will read intently in the midst of crowd or noise, or walking along the street. He was what might unkindly be called almost a professional humorist, the master of a thousand startling stories, delightful to the hearer, but possibly tiresome in written reminiscences, but we know too well that gifts of this kind are as compatible with sadness as they certainly are with deadly seriousness.

The Legislature of Illinois in the eight years from 1834 to 1842, in which Lincoln belonged to it, was, though not a wise, a vigorous body. In the conditions

which then existed it was not likely to have been captured as the Legislatures of wilder and more thinly-peopled States have sometimes been by a disreputable element in the community, nor to have subsided into the hands of the dull mechanical class of professional politicians with which, rightly or wrongly, we have now been led to associate American State Government. The fact of Lincoln's own election suggests that dishonest adventurers might easily have got there, but equally suggests that a very different type of men prevailed. " The Legislature," we are told, " contained the youth and blood and fire of the frontier." Among the Democrats in the Legislature was Stephen Douglas, who was to become one of the most powerful men in the United States while Lincoln was still unknown; and several of Lincoln's Whig colleagues were afterwards to play distinguished or honourable parts in politics or war. We need not linger over them, but what we know of those with whom he had any special intimacy makes it entirely pleasant to associate him with them. After a short time in which, like any sensible young member of an assembly, he watched and hardly ever spoke, Lincoln soon made his way among these men, and in 1838 and 1840 the Whig members—though, being in a minority, they could not elect him—gave him their unanimous votes for the Speakership of the Assembly. The business which engrossed the Legislature, at least up to 1838, was the development of the natural resources of the State. These were great. It was natural that railways, canals and other public works to develop them should be pushed forward at the public cost. Other new countries since, with less excuse because with greater warning from experience, have plunged in this matter, and, though the Governor protested, the Illinois Legislature, Whigs and Democrats, Lincoln and every one else, plunged gaily, so that, during the collapse which followed, Illinois, though, like Lincoln himself, it paid its debts in the end, was driven in 1840 to suspend interest payments for several years.

Very little is recorded of Lincoln's legislative doings. What is related chiefly exhibits his delight in the game of negotiation and combination by which he and the other members for his county, together known as " the Long Nine," advanced the particular projects which pleased their constituents or struck their own fancy. Thus he early had a hand in the removal of the capital from Vandalia to Springfield in his own county. The map of Illinois suggests that Springfield was a better site for the purpose than Vandalia and at least as good as Jacksonville or Peoria or any of its other competitors. Of his few recorded speeches one concerns a proposed inquiry into some alleged impropriety in the allotment of shares in the State Bank. It is certainly the speech of a bold man; it argues with remarkable directness that whereas a committee of prominent citizens which had already inquired into this matter consisted of men of known honesty, the proposed committee of the Legislators, whom he was addressing, would consist of men who, for all he knew, might be honest, and, for all he knew, might not.

The Federal politics of this time, though Lincoln played an active local part in the campaigns of the Whig party, concern us little. The Whigs, to whom he did subordinate service, were, as has been said, an unlucky party. In 1840, in the reaction which extreme commercial depression created against the previously omnipotent Democrats, the Whig candidate for the Presidency was successful. This was General Harrison, a respected soldier of the last war, who was glorified as a sort of Cincinnatus and elected after an outburst of enthusiastic tomfoolery such as never before or since rejoiced the American people. But President Harrison had hardly been in office a month when he died. Some say he was worried to death by office seekers, but a more prosaic cause, pneumonia, can also be alleged. It is satisfactory that this good man's grandson worthily filled his office forty-eight years after, but his immediate successor was of course the Vice-President, Tyler, chosen as an influen-

tial opponent of the last Democrat Presidents, but not because he agreed with the Whigs. Cultivated but narrow-minded, highly independent and wholly perverse, he satisfied no aspiration of the Whigs and paved the way effectually for the Democrat who succeeded him.

Throughout these years Lincoln was of course working at law, which became, with the development of the country, a more arduous and a more learned profession. Sessions of the Legislature did not last long, and political canvasses were only occasional. If Lincoln was active in these matters he was in many other directions, too, a keen participator in the keen life of the society round him. Nevertheless politics as such, and apart from any large purpose to be achieved through them, had for many years a special fascination for him. For one thing he was argumentative in the best sense, with a passion for what the Greeks sometimes called " dialectic "; his rare capacity for solitary thought, the most marked and the greatest of his powers, went absolutely hand in hand with the desire to reduce his thoughts to a form which would carry logical conviction to others. Further, there can be no doubt—and such a combination of tastes, though it seems to be uncommon, is quite intelligible—that the somewhat unholy business of party management was at first attractive to him. To the end he showed no intuitive comprehension of individual men. His sincere friendly intention, the unanswerable force of an argument, the convincing analogy veiled in an unseemly story, must take their chance of suiting the particular taste of Senator Sherman or General McClellan; but any question of managing men in the mass—will a given candidate's influence with this section of people count for more than his unpopularity with that section? and so on—involved an element of subtle and longsighted calculation which was vastly congenial to him. We are to see him hereafter applying this sort of science on a grand scale and for a great end. His early discipline in it is a dull subject, interesting only where it displays, as it sometimes does, the perfect fairness with

which this ambitious man could treat his own claims as against those of a colleague and competitor.

In forming any judgment of Lincoln's career it must, further, be realised that, while he was growing up as a statesman, the prevailing conception of popular government was all the time becoming more unfavourable to leadership and to robust individuality. The new party machinery adopted by the Democrats under Jackson, as the proper mode of securing government by the people, induced a deadly uniformity of utterance; breach of that uniformity was not only rash, but improper. Once in early days it was demanded in a newspaper that " all candidates should show their hands." " Agreed," writes Lincoln, " here's mine "; and then follows a young man's avowal of advanced opinions; he would give the suffrage to " all whites who pay taxes or bear arms, by no means excluding females." Disraeli, who was Lincoln's contemporary, throve by exuberances quite as startling as this, nor has any English politician found it damaging to be bold. On this occasion indeed (in 1836) Lincoln was far from damaging himself; the Whigs had not till a few years later been induced, for self-preservation, to copy the Democratic machine. But it is striking that the admiring friend who reports this declaration, " too audacious and emphatic for the statesmen of a later day," must carefully explain how it could possibly suit the temper of a time which in a few years passed away. Very soon the question whether a proposal or even a sentiment was timely or premature came to bulk too large in the deliberations of Lincoln's friends. The reader will perhaps wonder later whether such considerations did not bulk too largely in Lincoln's own mind. Was there in his statesmanship, even in later days when he had great work to do, an element of that opportunism which, if not actually base, is at least cheap? Or did he come as near as a man with many human weaknesses could come to the wise and nobly calculated opportunism which is not merely the most beneficent statesmanship, but demands a heroic self-mastery?

The main interest of his doings in Illinois politics and in Congress is the help they may give in penetrating his later mind. On the one hand, it is certain that Lincoln trained himself to be a great student of the fitting opportunity. He evidently paid very serious attention to the counsels of friends who would check his rasher impulses. One of his closest associates insists that his impulsive judgment was bad, and he probably thought so himself. It will be seen later that the most momentous utterance he ever made was kept back through the whole space of two years of crisis at the instance of timid friends. It required not less courage and was certainly more effective when at last it did come out. The same great capacity for waiting marks any steps that he took for his own advancement. Indeed it was a happy thing for him and for his country that his character and the whole cast of his ideas and sympathies were of a kind to which the restraint imposed on an American politician was most congenial and to which therefore it could do least harm. He was to prove himself a patient man in other ways as well as this. On many things, perhaps on most, the thoughts he worked out in his own mind diverged very widely from those of his neighbours, but he was not in the least anxious either to conceal or to obtrude them. His social philosophy as he expressed it to his friends in these days was one which contemplated great future reforms—abolition of slavery and a strict temperance policy were among them. But he looked for them with a sort of fatalistic confidence in the ultimate victory of reason, and saw no use and a good deal of harm in premature political agitation for them. "All such questions," he is reported to have said, "must find lodgment with the most enlightened souls who stamp them with their approval. In God's own time they will be organised into law and thus woven into the fabric of our institutions." This seems a little cold-blooded, but perhaps we can already begin to recognise the man who, when the time had fully come, would be on the right side, and in whom the evil which he had deeply

but restrainedly hated would find an appallingly wary foe.

But there were crucial instances which test sufficiently whether this wary politician was a true man or not. The soil of Illinois was free soil by the Ordinance of 1787, and Congress would only admit it to the Union as a free State. But it had been largely peopled from the South. There had been much agitation against this restriction; prevailing sentiment to a late date strongly approved of slavery; it was at Alton in Illinois that, in 1836, Elijah Lovejoy, an Abolitionist publisher, had been martyred by the mob which had failed to intimidate him. In 1837, when the bold agitation of the Abolitionists was exciting much disapproval, the Illinois Legislature passed resolutions condemning that agitation and declaring in soothing tones the constitutional powerlessness of Congress to interfere with slavery in the Southern States. Now Lincoln himself—whether for good reasons or bad must be considered later—thoroughly disapproved of the actual agitation of the Abolitionists; and the resolutions in question, but for one merely theoretical point of law and for an unctuous misuse of the adjective "sacred," contained nothing which he could not literally have accepted. The objection to them lay in the motive which made it worth while to pass them. Lincoln drew up and placed on the records of the House a protest against these resolutions. He defines in it his own quite conservative opinions; he deprecates the promulgation of Abolition doctrines; but he does so because it "tends rather to increase than abate the evils" of slavery; and he lays down "that the institution of slavery is founded on both injustice and bad policy." One man alone could he induce to sign this protest with him, and that man was not seeking re-election.

By 1842 Lincoln had grown sensibly older, and a little less ready, we may take it, to provoke unnecessary antagonism. Probably very old members of Free Churches are the people best able to appreciate the

daring of the following utterance. Speaking on Washington's birthday in a Presbyterian church to a temperance society formed among the rougher people of the town and including former drunkards who desired to reform themselves, he broke out in protest against the doctrine that respectable persons should shun the company of people tempted to intemperance. "If," he said, "they believe as they profess that Omnipotence condescended to take upon Himself the form of sinful man, and as such die an ignominious death, surely they will not refuse submission to the infinitely lesser condescension, for the temporal and perhaps eternal salvation of a large, erring, and unfortunate class of their fellow creatures! Nor is the condescension very great. In my judgment such of us as have never fallen victims have been spared more from the absence of appetite than from any mental or moral superiority over those who have. Indeed, I believe, if we take habitual drunkards as a class, that their heads and their hearts will bear an advantageous comparison with those of any other class." It proved, at a later day, very lucky for America that the virtuous Lincoln, who did not drink strong drink— nor, it is sad to say, smoke, nor, which is all to the good, chew—did feel like that about drunkenness. But there was great and loud wrath. "It's a shame," said one, "that he should be permitted to abuse us so in the house of the Lord." It is certain that in this sort of way he did himself a good deal of injury as an aspiring politician. It is also the fact that he continued none the less persistently in a missionary work conceived in a spirit none the less Christian because it shocked many pious people.

3. *Marriage.*

The private life of Lincoln continued, and for many years increasingly, to be equally marked by indiscriminate sociability and brooding loneliness. Comfort and the various influences which may be associated with the old-

fashioned American word "elegance" seem never to enter into it. What is more, little can be discerned of positive happiness in the background of his life, as the freakish elasticity of his youth disappeared and, after a certain measure of marked success, the further objects of his ambition though not dropped became unlikely of attainment and seemed, we may guess, of doubtful value. All along he was being moulded for endurance rather than for enjoyment.

Nor, though his children evidently brought him happiness, does what we know of his domesticities and dearest affections weaken this general impression. When he married he had gone through a saddening experience. He started on manhood with a sound and chivalrous outlook on women in general, and a nervous terror of actual women when he met them. In New Salem days he absented himself from meals for the whole time that some ladies were staying at his boarding house. His clothes and his lack of upbringing must have weighed with him, besides his natural disposition. None the less, of course he fell in love. Miss Ann Rutledge, the daughter of a store and tavern keeper from Kentucky with whom Lincoln was boarding in 1833, has been described as of exquisite beauty; some say this is overstated, but speak strongly of her grace and charm. A lady who knew her gives these curiously collocated particulars: " Miss Rutledge had auburn hair, blue eyes, fair complexion. She was pretty, slightly slender, but in everything a good-hearted young woman. She was about five feet two inches high, and weighed in the neighbourhood of a hundred and twenty pounds. She was beloved by all who knew her. She died as it were of grief. In speaking of her death and her grave Lincoln once said to me, ' My heart lies buried there.' " The poor girl, when Lincoln first came courting to her, had passed through a grievous agitation. She had been engaged to a young man, who suddenly returned to his home in the Eastern States, after revealing to her, with some explanation which was more convincing to her than

to her friends, that he had been passing under an assumed name. It seems that his absence was strangely prolonged, that for a long time she did not hear from him, that his letters when they did come puzzled her, that she clung to him long, but yielded at last to her friends, who urged their very natural suspicions upon her. It is further suggested that there was some good explanation of his conduct all the while, and that she learnt this too late when actually engaged to Lincoln. However that may be, shortly after her engagement to Lincoln she fell seriously ill, insisted, as she lay ill, on a long interview with Lincoln alone, and a day or two later died. This was in 1835, when he was twenty-six. It is perhaps right to say that one biographer throws doubt on the significance of this story in Lincoln's life. The details as to Ann Rutledge's earlier lover are vague and uncertain. The main facts of Lincoln's first engagement and almost immediate loss of his betrothed are quite certain; the blow would have been staggering enough to any ordinary young lover and we know nothing of Lincoln which would discredit Mr. Herndon's judgment that its effect on him was both acute and permanent. There can be no real doubt that his spells of melancholy were ever afterwards more intense, and politer biographers should not have suppressed the testimony that for a time that melancholy seemed to his friends to verge upon insanity. He always found good friends, and, as was to happen again later, one of them, Mr. Bowline Greene, carried him off to his own secluded home and watched him carefully. He said " the thought that the snows and rains fell upon her grave filled him with indescribable grief." Two years later he told a fellow-legislator that " although he seemed to others to enjoy life rapturously, yet when alone he was so overcome by mental depression, he never dared to carry a pocket-knife." Later still Greene, who had helped him, died, and Lincoln was to speak over his grave. For once in his life he broke down entirely; " the tears ran down his yellow and shrivelled cheeks. . . . After re-

peated efforts he found it impossible to speak and strode
away sobbing."

The man whom a grief of this kind has affected not
only intensely, but morbidly, is almost sure, before its
influence has faded, to make love again, and is very
likely to do so foolishly. Miss Mary Owens was slightly
older than Lincoln. She was a handsome woman; commanding, but comfortable. In the tales of Lincoln's love
stories, much else is doubtfully related, but the lady's
weight is in each case stated with assurance, and when
she visited her sister in New Salem in 1836 Mary Owens
weighed one hundred and fifty pounds. There is nothing sad in her story; she was before long happily married—not to Lincoln—and she long outlived him. But
Lincoln, who had seen her on a previous visit and
partly remembered her, had been asked, perhaps in jest,
by her sister to marry her if she returned, and had
rashly announced half in jest that he would. Her sister
promptly fetched her, and he lingered for some time in
a half-engaged condition, writing her reasonable, conscientious, feeble letters, in which he put before her dispassionately the question whether she could patiently
bear "to see without sharing . . . a lot of flourishing
about in carriages, . . . to be poor without the means
of hiding your poverty," and assuring her that "I
should be much happier with you than the way I am,
provided I saw no signs of discontent in you." Whether
he rather wished to marry her but felt bound to hold
her free, or distinctly wished not to marry her but felt
bound not to hold himself free, he probably was never
sure. The lady very wisely decided that he could not
make her happy, and returned to Kentucky. She said
he was deficient in the little courteous attentions which
a woman's happiness requires of her husband. She gave
instances long after to prove her point; but she always
spoke of him with friendship and respect as "a man
with a heart full of human kindness and a head full of
common sense."

Rather unluckily, Lincoln, upon his rejection or re-

lease, relieved his feelings in a letter about Miss Owens
to one of the somewhat older married ladies who were
kind to him, the wife of one of his colleagues. She
ought to have burnt his letter, but she preserved it to
kindle mild gossip after his death. It is a burlesque
account of his whole adventure, describing, with touches
of very bad taste, his disillusionment with the now
maturer charms of Miss Owens when her sister brought
her back to New Salem, and making comedy of his own
honest bewilderment and his mingled relief and mortification when she at last refused him. We may take it
as evidence of the natural want of perception and right
instinctive judgment in minor matters which some who
knew and loved him attribute to him. But, besides that,
the man who found relief in this ill-conceived exercise
of humour was one in whom the prospect of marriage
caused some strange and pitiful perturbation of mind.

This was in 1838, and a year later Mary Todd came
from Kentucky to stay at Springfield with her brother-
in-law Ninian Edwards, a legislator of Illinois and a
close ally of Lincoln's. She was aged twenty-one, and
her weight was one hundred and thirty pounds. She was
well educated, and had family connections which were
highly esteemed. She was pleasant in company, but
somewhat imperious, and she was a vivacious talker.
When among the young men who now became attentive
in calling on the Edwards's Lincoln came and sat awkwardly gazing on Miss Todd, Mrs. Edwards appears to
have remarked that the two were not suited to each
other. But an engagement took place all the same.
As to the details of what followed, whether he or she
was the first to have doubts, and whether, as some say,
the great Stephen Douglas appeared on the scene as a
rival and withdrew rather generously but too late, is
uncertain. But Lincoln composed a letter to break off
his engagement. He showed it to Joshua Speed, who
told him that if he had the courage of a man he would
not write to her, but see her and speak. He did so.
She cried. He kissed and tried to comfort her. After

this Speed had to point out to him that he had really renewed his engagement. Again there may be some uncertainty whether on January 1, 1841, the bridal party had actually assembled and the bridegroom after long search was found by his friends wandering about in a state which made them watch day and night and keep knives from him. But it is quite certain from his letters that in some such way on " the fatal 1st of January, 1841," he broke down terribly. Some weeks later he wrote to his partner: " Whether I shall ever be better I cannot tell; I awfully forebode I shall not. To remain as I am is impossible. I must die or be better, as it appears to me." After a while Speed was able to remove him to his own parents' home in Kentucky, where he and his mother nursed him back to mental life.

Then in the course of 1841 Speed himself began to contemplate marriage, and Speed himself had painful searchings of heart, and Lincoln's turn came to show a sureness of perception in his friend's case that he wholly lacked in his own. " I know," he writes, " what the painful point with you is . . . it is an apprehension that you do not love her as you should. What nonsense! How came you to court her? But you say you reasoned yourself into it. What do you mean by that? Was it not that you found yourself unable to reason yourself out of it? Did you not think, and partly form the purpose, of courting her the first time you ever saw or heard of her? What had reason to do with it at that early stage?" A little later the lady of Speed's love falls ill. Lincoln writes: " I hope and believe that your present anxiety about her health and her life must and will for ever banish those horrid doubts which I know you sometimes felt as to the truth of your affection for her. . . . Perhaps this point is no longer a question with you, and my pertinacious dwelling upon it is a rude intrusion upon your feelings. If so, you must pardon me. You know the hell I have suffered upon that point, and how tender I am upon it." When he writes thus it is

no surprise to hear from him that he has lost his
hypochondria, but it may be that the keen recollection of
it gives him excessive anxieties for Speed. On the eve
of the wedding he writes: " You will always hereafter
be on ground that I have never occupied, and consequently, if advice were needed, I might advise wrong.
I do fondly hope, however, that you will never need
comfort from abroad. I incline to think it probable that
your nerves will occasionally fail you for a while; but
once you get them firmly graded now, that trouble is
over for ever. If you went through the ceremony
calmly or even with sufficient composure not to excite
alarm in any present, you are safe beyond question, and
in two or three months, to say the most, will be the
happiest of men." Soon he is reassured and can " feel
somewhat jealous of both of you now. You will be so
exclusively concerned with one another that I shall be
forgotten entirely. I shall feel very lonesome without
you." And a little later: " It cannot be told how it
thrills me with joy to hear you say you are far happier
than you ever expected to be. I know you too well to
suppose your expectations were not at least sometimes
extravagant, and if the reality exceeds them all, I say,
' Enough, dear Lord.' " And here follows what might
perhaps have been foreseen: " Your last letter gave me
more pleasure than the total sum of all that I have received since the fatal 1st of January, 1841. Since then
it seems to me I should have been entirely happy but
for the never absent idea that there is still one unhappy
whom I have contributed to make so. That kills my
soul. I cannot but reproach myself for even wishing to
be happy while she is otherwise." Very significantly he
has inquired of friends how that one enjoyed a trip on
the new railway cars to Jacksonville, and—not being
like Falkland in " The Rivals "—praises God that she
has enjoyed it exceedingly.

This was in the spring of 1842. Some three months
later he writes again to Speed: " I must gain confidence
in my own ability to keep my resolves when they are

made. In that ability I once prided myself as the only chief gem of my character. That gem I lost how and where you know too well. I have not regained it, and until I do I cannot trust myself in any matter of much importance. I believe now that, had you understood my case at the time as well as I understood yours afterwards, by the aid you would have given me I should have sailed through clear. . . . I always was superstitious. I believe God made me one of the instruments of bringing Fanny and you together, which union I have no doubt He had fore-ordained. Whatever He designs for me He will do. ' Stand still and see the salvation of the Lord,' is my text just now. If, as you say, you have told Fanny all, I should have no objection to her seeing this letter. I do not think I can come to Kentucky this season. I am so poor and make so little headway in the world that I drop back in a month of idleness as much as I gain in a year's sowing." At last in the autumn of that year Lincoln addresses to Speed a question at once so shrewd and so daringly intimate as perhaps no other man ever asked of his friend. "The immense sufferings you endured from the first days of September till the middle of February " (the date of Speed's wedding) " you never tried to conceal from me, and I well understood. You have now been the husband of a lovely woman nearly eight months. That you are happier now than the day you married her I well know. . . . But I want to ask a close question! ' Are you in *feeling* as well as in *judgment* glad you are married as you are? ' From anybody but me this would be an impudent question, not to be tolerated, but I know you will pardon it in me. Please answer it quickly, as I am impatient to know."

Speed remained in Kentucky; Lincoln was too poor for visits of pleasure; and Speed was not a man who cared for political life; but the memorials, from which the above quotations have been taken, of Lincoln's lasting friendship with Speed and his kind mother, who gave Lincoln a treasured Bible, and his kind young wife,

who made her husband's friend her own, and whose
violet, dropped into her husband's letter to him just as
he was sealing it, was among the few flowers that
Lincoln ever appreciated, throw the clearest light that
we can anywhere obtain on the inner mind of Lincoln.

As may have been foreseen, Mary Todd and he had
met again on a friendly footing. A managing lady is
credited with having brought about a meeting between
them, but evidently she did not do it till Lincoln was
at least getting desirous to be managed. He was much
absorbed at this time in law business, to which since his
breakdown he had applied himself more seriously. It
was at this period too that his notable address on temperance was given. Soon after his meetings with Miss
Todd began again he involved himself in a complication of a different kind. He had written, partly, it
seems, for the young lady's amusement, some innocent
if uninteresting political skits relating to some question
about taxes. This brought on him an unexpected challenge from a fiery but diminutive revenue official, one
Colonel Shields, a prominent Democratic politician.
Lincoln availed himself of the right of the challenged
to impose ridiculous conditions of combat, partly no
doubt in fun, but with the sensible object also of making
sure that he could disarm his antagonist with no risk
of harm to the little man. The tangled controversy
which ensued as to how and by whose fault the duel
eventually fell through has nothing in it now, but the
whole undignified business seems to have given Lincoln
lasting chagrin, and worried him greatly at a time when
it would have been well that he should be cheerful.
At last on November 4, 1842, when Lincoln was nearly
thirty-three, he was safely married. The wedding, held,
according to the prevailing custom, in a private house,
was an important function, for it was the first Episcopalian wedding that good society in Springfield had witnessed. Malicious fortune brought in a ludicrous incident at the last moment, for when in the lawyerlike
verbiage of the then American Prayer-Book the bride-

groom said, " With this ring I thee endow with all my
goods, chattels, lands and tenements," old Judge Brown
of the Illinois Supreme Court, who had never heard the
like, impatiently broke in, " God Almighty, Lincoln!
The statute fixes all that."

There is more than the conventional reason for
apology for pressing the subject a little further. Nothing very illuminating can be said as to the course of
Lincoln's married life, but much has already been made
public about it which, though it cannot be taken as reaching to the heart of the matter, is not properly to be dismissed as mere gossip. Mrs. Lincoln, it is clear, had a
high temper—the fact that, poor woman! after her husband had been murdered by her side, she developed
clear symptoms of insanity, may or may not, for all we
are entitled to know, be relevant in this regard. She
was much younger than her husband, and had gone
through a cruel experience for him. Moreover, she had
proper ambitions and was accustomed to proper conventional refinements; so her husband's exterior roughness
tried her sorely, not the less we may be sure because of
her real pride in him. Wife and tailor combined could
not, with any amount of money, have dressed him well.
Once, though they kept a servant then, Lincoln thought
it friendly to open the door himself in his shirt sleeves
when two most elegant ladies came to call. On such
occasions, and doubtless on other occasions of less
provocation, Mrs. Lincoln's high temper was let loose.
It seems pretty certain, too, that he met her with mere
forbearance, sad patience, and avoidance of conflict.
His fellow lawyers came to notice that he stayed away
from home on circuit when all the rest of them could
go home for a day or two. Fifteen years after his
wedding he himself confessed to his trouble, not dis-
loyally, but in a rather moving remonstrance with some
one who had felt intolerably provoked by Mrs. Lincoln.
There are slight indications that occasions of difficulty
and pain to Lincoln happened up to the end of his life.
On the other hand, there are slight indications that com-

mon love for their children helped to make the two happier, and there are no indications at all of any approach to a serious quarrel. All that is told us may be perfectly true and not by any means have justified the pity that some of Lincoln's friends were ready to feel for him. It is difficult to avoid suspecting that Lincoln's wife did not duly like his partner and biographer, Mr. Herndon, who felt it his duty to record so many painful facts and his own possibly too painful impression from them. On the other side, Mr. Herndon makes it clear that in some respects Mrs. Lincoln was an admirable wife for her husband. She faced the difficulties of their poverty with spirit and resolution. Testimony from other sources to her graceful hospitality abounds. More than this, from the very first she believed in his powers. It seems she had the discernment to know, when few others can have done so, how far greater he was than his rival Douglas. It was Herndon's belief, in days when he and Mrs. Lincoln were the two persons who saw most of him, that she sustained his just ambition, and that at the most critical moment of his personal career she had the courage to make him refuse an attractive appointment which must have ruined it. The worst that we are told with any certainty amounts to this, that like the very happily married writer of " Virginibus Puerisque," Lincoln discovered that marriage is " a field of battle and not a bed of roses "—a battle in which we are forced to suspect that he did not play his full part.

We should perhaps be right in associating his curious record, of right and high regard for women and inefficiency where a particular woman's happiness depended on him, with the belief in Woman Suffrage, which he early adopted and probably retained. Be that as it may, this part of his story points to something which runs through his whole character, something which perhaps may be expressed by saying that the natural bias of his qualities was towards the negative side. We hear, no doubt, of occasions when his vigour was instant and ter-

rible—like that of Hamlet on the ship for England; but these were occasions when the right or the necessity of the case was obvious. We have seen him also firm and absolutely independent where his conviction had already been thought out. Where there was room for further reflection, for patiently waiting on events, or for taking counsel of wise friends, manly decision had not come easily to him. He had let a third person almost engage him to Miss Owens. Once in this relation to her, he had let it be the woman's part and not the man's to have decision enough for the two. Speed had to tell him that he must face Miss Todd and speak to her, and Speed again had to make clear to him what the effect of his speaking had been. In time he decided what he thought his own feelings were, but it was by inference from the feelings of Speed. Lastly, it seems, the troubles of his married life were met by mere patience and avoidance. All this, of course, concerned a side of life's affairs in regard to which his mind had suffered painful shocks; but it shows the direction of his possible weakness and his possible strength in other things. It falls in with a trait which he himself noted in one of the letters to Speed: "I have no doubt," he writes, "it is the peculiar misfortune of both you and me to dream dreams of Elysium far exceeding all that anything earthly can realise." All such men have to go through deep waters; but they do not necessarily miss either success or happiness in the end. Lincoln's life may be said to have tested him by the test which Mr. Kipling states in his lines about Washington:—

" If you can dream—and not make dreams your master;
    If you can think—and not make thoughts your aim."

He was to prove that he could do this; it is for the following pages to show in how high a degree. Meanwhile one thing should already be clear about him. No shrewd judge of men could read his letters to Speed with care and not feel that, whatever mistakes this man might com-

mit, fundamentally he was worthy of entire trust. That, as a matter of fact, is what, to the end of his life, Speed and all the men who knew him and an ever widening circle of men who had to judge by more casual impressions did feel about Lincoln. Whatever was questionable in his private or public acts, his own explanation, if he happened to give one, would be taken by them as the full and naked truth, and, if there was no known explanation, it remained to them an irrebuttable presumption that his main intention was right.

CHAPTER IV

LINCOLN IN CONGRESS AND IN RETIREMENT

1. *The Mexican War and Lincoln's Work in Congress.*

LINCOLN had ceased before his marriage to sit in the Illinois Legislature. He had won sufficient standing for his ambition to aim higher; a former law partner of his was now in Congress, and he wished to follow. But he had to submit to a few years' delay of which the story is curious and honourable. His rivals for the representation of his own constituency were two fellow Whigs, Baker and Hardin, both of whom afterwards bore distinguished parts in the Mexican war and with both of whom he was friendly. Somewhat to his disgust at a party gathering in his own county in 1843, Baker was preferred to him. A letter of his gives a shrewd account of the manœuvres among members of various Churches which brought this about; it is curiously careful not to overstate the effect of these influences and characteristically denies that Baker had part in them. To make the thing harder, he was sent from this meeting to a convention, for the whole constituency, with which the nomination lay, and his duty, of course, was to work for Baker. Here it became obvious that Hardin would be chosen; nothing could be done for Baker at that time, but Lincoln, being against his will there in Baker's interests, took an opportunity in the bargaining that took place to advance Baker's claim, to the detriment of his own, to be Hardin's successor two years later.

By some perverse accident notes about details of party management fill a disproportionate space among those letters of Lincoln's which have been preserved, but these reveal that, with all his business-like attention

to the affairs of his very proper ambition, he was able throughout to illuminate dull matters of this order with action of singular disinterestedness. After being a second time postponed, no doubt to the advantage of his law business, he took his seat in the House of Representatives at Washington for two years in the spring of 1847. Two short sessions can hardly suffice for mastering the very complicated business of that body. He made hardly any mark. He probably learned much and was able to study at leisure the characters of his brother politicians. He earned the valuable esteem of some, and seems to have passed as a very pleasant, honest, plain specimen of the rough West. Like others of the younger Congressmen, he had the privilege of breakfasting with Webster. His brief career in the House seems to have disappointed him, and it certainly dissatisfied his constituents. The part that he played may impress us more favourably than it did them, but, slight as it was, it requires a historical explanation.

Mexico had detached itself from Spain in 1826, and in 1833 the province of Texas detached itself from Mexico. Texas was largely peopled by immigrants from the States, and these had grievances. One of them was that Mexico abolished slavery, but there was real misgovernment as well, and, among other cruel incidents of the rebellion which followed, the massacre of rebels at the Alamo stamped itself on American memory. The Republic of Texas began to seek annexation to the United States in 1839, but there was opposition in the States and there were difficulties with Mexico and other Governments. At last in 1845, at the very close of his term of office, President Tyler got the annexation pushed through in defiance of the Whigs who made him President. Mexico broke off diplomatic relations, but peace could no doubt have been preserved if peace had been any object with the new President Polk or with the Southern leaders whose views he represented. They had set their eyes upon a further acquisition, larger even than Texas—California, and the whole of the territories, still

belonging to Mexico, to the east of it. It is not contested, and would not have been contested then, that the
motive of their policy was the Southern desire to win
further soil for cultivation by slaves. But there was no
great difficulty in gaining some popularity for their
designs in the North. Talk about "our manifest destiny" to reach the Pacific may have been justly described
by Parson Wilbur as "half on it ign'ance and t'other
half rum," but it is easy to see how readily it might be
taken up, and indeed many Northerners at that moment
had a fancy of their own for expansion in the North-
West and were not over-well pleased with Polk when,
in 1846, he set the final seal upon the settlement with
Great Britain of the Oregon frontier.

When he did this Polk had already brought about
his own war. The judgment on that war expressed
at the time in the first "Biglow Papers" has seldom
been questioned since, and there seldom can have been
a war so sternly condemned by soldiers—Grant amongst
others—who fought in it gallantly. The facts seem to
have been just as Lincoln afterwards recited them in
Congress. The Rio Grande, which looks a reasonable
frontier on a map, was claimed by the United States
as the frontier of Texas. The territory occupied by
the American settlers of Texas reached admittedly up
to and beyond the River Nueces, east of the Rio
Grande. But in a sparsely settled country, where water
is not abundant, the actual border line, if there be any
clear line, between settlement from one side and settlement from the other will not for the convenience of
treaty-makers run along a river, but rather for the convenience of the settlers along the water-parting between
two rivers. So Mexico claimed both banks of the Rio
Grande and Spanish settlers inhabited both sides. Polk
ordered General Zachary Taylor, who was allowed no
discretion in the matter, to march troops right up to the
Rio Grande and occupy a position commanding the
encampment of the Mexican soldiers there. The Mexican commander, thus threatened, attacked. The Mex-

icans had thus begun the war. Polk could thus allege his duty to prosecute it. When the whole transaction was afterwards assailed his critics might be tempted to go, or represented as going, upon the false ground that only Congress can constitutionally declare war—that is, of course, sanction purely offensive operations. Long, however, before the dispute could come to a head, the brilliant successes of General Taylor and still more of General Scott, with a few trained troops against large undisciplined numbers, put all criticism at a disadvantage. The City of Mexico was occupied by Scott in September, 1847, and peace, with the cession of the vast domain that had been coveted, was concluded in May, 1848.

War having begun, the line of the Whig opposition was to vote supplies and protest as best they might against the language endorsing Polk's policy which, in the pettiest spirit of political manœuvre, was sometimes incorporated in the votes. In this Lincoln steadily supported them. One of his only two speeches of any length in Congress was made on the occasion of a vote of this kind in 1848. The subject was by that time so stale that his speech could hardly make much impression, but it appears to-day an extraordinarily clear, strong, upright presentment of the complex and unpopular case against the war. His other long speech is elevated above buffoonery by a brief, cogent, and earnest passage on the same theme, but it was a frank piece of clowning on a licensed occasion. It was the fashion for the House when its own dissolution and a Presidential election were both imminent to have a sort of rhetorical scrimmage in which members on both sides spoke for the edification of their own constituencies and that of Buncombe. The Whigs were now happy in having " diverted the war-thunder against the Democrats " by running for the Presidency General Taylor, a good soldier who did not know whether he was a Whig or a Democrat, but who, besides being a hero of the war, was inoffensive to the South, for he lived in Louisiana

and had slaves of his own. It is characteristic of the time that the Democrats, in whose counsels the Southern men prevailed, now began a practice of choosing Northern candidates, and nominated General Cass of Michigan, whose distinction had not been won in war. The Democratic Congressmen in this debate made game of the Whigs, with their war-hero, and seem to have carried a crude manner of pleasantry pretty far when Lincoln determined to show them that they could be beaten at that game. He seems to have succeeded admirably, with a burlesque comparison, too long to quote, of General Cass's martial exploits with his own, and other such-like matter enhanced by the most extravagant Western manner and delivery.

Anyone who reads much of the always grave and sometimes most moving orations of Lincoln's later years may do well to turn back to this agreeable piece of debating-society horse-play. But he should then turn a few pages further back to Lincoln's little Bill for the gradual and compensated extinction of slavery in the District of Columbia, where Washington stands. He introduced this of his own motion, without encouragement from Abolitionist or Non-Abolitionist, accompanying it with a brief statement that he had carefully ascertained that the representative people of the district privately approved of it, but had no right to commit them to public support of it. It perished, of course. With the views which he had long formed and continued to hold about slavery, very few opportunities could in these years come to him of proper and useful action against it. He seized upon these opportunities not less because in doing so he had to stand alone.

His career as a Congressman was soon over. There was no movement to re-elect him, and the Whigs now lost his constituency. His speeches and his votes against the Mexican war offended his friends. Even his partner, the Abolitionist, Mr. Herndon, whose further acquaintance we have to make, was too much infected with the popularity of a successful war to understand

Lincoln's plain position or to approve of his giving votes which might seem unpatriotic. Lincoln wrote back to him firmly but sadly. Persuaded as he was that political action in advance of public sentiment was idle, resigned and hardened as we might easily think him to many of the necessities of party discipline, it evidently caused him naïve surprise that, when he was called upon for a definite opinion, anybody should expect him, as he candidly puts it, to " tell a lie."

As a retiring Congressman he was invited to speak in several places in the East on behalf of Taylor's candidature; and after Taylor's election claimed his right as the proper person to be consulted, with certain others, about Government appointments in Illinois. Taylor carried out the " spoils system " with conscientious thoroughness; as he touchingly said, he had thought over the question from a soldier's point of view, and could not bear the thought that, while he as their chief enjoyed the Presidency, the private soldiers in the Whig ranks should not get whatever was going. Lincoln's attitude in the matter may be of interest. To take an example, he writes to the President, about the postmastership in some place, that he does not know whether the President desires to change the tenure of such offices on party grounds, and offers no advice; that A is a Whig whose appointment is much desired by the local Whigs, and a most respectable man; that B, also a Whig, would in Lincoln's judgment be a somewhat better but not so popular subject for appointment; that C, the present postmaster, is a Democrat, but is on every ground, save his political party, a proper person for the office. There was an office which he himself desired, it was that of " Commissioner of the General Land Office," a new office in Washington dealing with settlement on Government lands in the West. He was probably well suited to it; but his application was delayed by the fact that friends in Illinois wanted the post too; a certain Mr. Butterfield (a lawyer renowned for his jokes, which showed, it is said, " at least a well-marked humorous

intention ") got it; and then it fell to the lot of the disappointed Lincoln to have to defend Butterfield against some unfair attack. But a tempting offer was made him, that of the Governorship of Oregon Territory, and he wavered before refusing to take work which would, as it happened, have kept him far away when the opportunity of his life came. It was Mrs. Lincoln who would not let him cut himself off so completely from politics. As for himself, it is hard to resist the impression that he was at this time a tired man, disappointed as to the progress of his career and probably also disappointed and somewhat despondent about politics and the possibilities of good service that lay open to politicians. It may be that this was partly the reason why he was not at all aroused by the crisis in American politics which must now be related.

2. *California and the Compromise of 1850.*

It has been said that the motive for the conquests from Mexico was the desire for slave territory. The attractive part of the new dominion was of course California. Arizona and New Mexico are arid regions, and the mineral wealth of Nevada was unknown. The peacefully acquired region of Oregon, far north, need not concern us, but Oregon became a free State in 1859. Early in the war a struggle began between Northerners and Southerners (to a large extent independent of party) in the Senate and the House as to whether slavery should be allowed in the conquered land or not. David Wilmot, a Northern Democratic Congressman, proposed a proviso to the very first money grant connected with the war, that slavery should be forbidden in any territory to be annexed. The " Wilmot Proviso " was proposed again on every possible occasion; Lincoln, by the way, sturdily supported it while in Congress; it was always voted down. Cass proposed as a solution of all difficulties that the question of slavery should be left to the people of the new Territories or States them-

selves. The American public, apt as condensing an argument into a phrase, dismissed Cass's principle for the time being with the epithet "squatter sovereignty." Calhoun and his friends said it was contrary to the Constitution that an American citizen should not be free to move with his property, including his slaves, into territory won by the Union. The annexation was carried out, and the question of slavery was unsettled. Then events took a surprising turn.

In the winter of 1848 gold was discovered in California. Throughout 1849 gold-seekers came pouring in from every part of the world. This miscellaneous new people, whose rough ways have been more celebrated in literature than those of any similar crowd, lived at first in considerable anarchy, but they determined without delay to set up some regular system of government. In the course of 1849 they elected a Convention to draw up a State Constitution, and to the astonishment of all the States the Convention unanimously made the prohibition of slavery part of that Constitution. There was no likelihood that, with a further influx of settlers of the same sort, this decision of California would alter. Was California to be admitted as a State with this Constitution of its own choice, which the bulk of the people of America approved?

To politicians of the school now fully developed in the South there seemed nothing outrageous in saying that it should be refused admission. To them Calhoun's argument, which regarded a citizen's slave as his chattel in the same sense as his hat or walking-stick, seemed the ripe fruit of logic. It did not shock them in the least that they were forcing the slave system on an unwilling community, for were not the Northerners prepared to force the free system? A prominent Southern Senator, talking with a Northern colleague a little later, said triumphantly: "I see how it is. You may force freedom as much as you like, but we are to beware how we force slavery," and was surprised that the Northerner cheerfully accepted this position. It is necessary

to remember throughout the following years that, whatever ordinary Southerners thought in private, their
whole political action was now based on the assumption
that slavery, as it was, was an institution which no reasonable man could think wrong.

Zachary Taylor, unlike Harrison, the previous hero
of the Whigs, survived his inauguration by sixteen
months. He was no politician at all, but placed in the
position of President, for which fairness and firmness
were really the greatest qualifications, he was man
enough to rely on his own good sense. He had come
to Washington under the impression that the disputes
which raged there were due to the aggressiveness of the
North; a very little time there convinced him of the contrary. Slave-owner as he was, the claim of the South
to force slavery on California struck him as an arrogant
pretension, and so far as matters rested with him, he was
simply not to be moved by it. He sent a message to
Congress advising the admission of California with the
constitution of its own choice. When, as we shall
shortly see, the great men of the Senate thought the
case demanded conciliation and a great scheme of compromise, he resolutely disagreed; he used the whole of
his influence against their compromise, and it is believed
with good reason that he would have put his veto as
President on the chief measure in which the compromise
issued. If he had lived to carry out his policy, it seems
possible that there would have been an attempt to execute the threats of secession which were muttered—this
time in Virginia. But it is almost certain that at that
time, and with the position which he occupied, he would
have been able to quell the movement at once. There
is nothing to suggest that Taylor was a man of any
unusual gifts of intellect, but he had what we may call
character, and it was the one thing wanting in political
life at the time. The greatest minds in American
politics, as we shall see, viewed the occasion otherwise,
but, in the light of what followed, it seems a signal and
irreparable error that, when the spirit of aggression ris-

ing in the South had taken definite shape in a demand which was manifestly wrongful, it was bought off and not met with a straightforward refusal. Taylor died in the course of 1850 and Vice-President Millard Fillmore, of New York, succeeded him. Fillmore had an appearance of grave and benign wisdom which led a Frenchman to describe him as the ideal ruler of a Republic, but he was a pattern of that outwardly dignified, yet nerveless and heartless respectability, which was more dangerous to America at that period than political recklessness or want of scruple.

The actual issue of the crisis was that the admission of California was bought from the South by large concessions in other directions. This was the proposal of Henry Clay, who was now an old man anxious for the Union, but had been a lover of such compromises ever since he promoted the Missouri Compromise thirty years ago; but, to the savage indignation of some of his Boston admirers, Webster used the whole force of his influence and debating power in support of Clay. The chief concessions made to the South were two. In the first place Territorial Governments were set up in New Mexico and Utah (since then the home of the Mormons) without any restriction on slavery. This concession was defended in the North on the ground that it was a sham, because the physical character of those regions made successful slave plantations impossible there. But it was, of course, a surrender of the principle which had been struggled for in the Wilmot Proviso during the last four years; and the Southern leaders showed the clearness of their limited vision by valuing it just upon that ground. There had been reason for the territorial concessions to slavery in the past generation because it was established in the territories concerned; but there was no such reason now. The second concession was that of a new Federal law to ensure the return of fugitive slaves from the free States. The demand for this was partly factitious, for the States in the far South, which were not exposed to loss of slaves,

were the most insistent on it, and it would appear that the Southern leaders felt it politic to force the acceptance of the measure in a form which would humiliate their opponents. There is no escape from the contention, which Lincoln especially admitted without reserve, that the enactment of an effective Act of this sort was, if demanded, due under the provisions of the Constitution; but the measure actually passed was manifestly defiant of all principles of justice. It was so framed as almost to destroy the chance which a lawfully free negro might have of proving his freedom, if arrested by the professional slave-hunters as a runaway. It was the sort of Act which a President should have vetoed as a fraud upon the Constitution. Thus over and above the objection, now plain, to any compromise, the actual compromise proposed was marked by flagrant wrong. But it was put through by the weight of Webster and Clay.

This event marks the close of a period. It was the last achievement of Webster and Clay, both of whom passed away in 1852 in the hope that they had permanently pacified the Union. Calhoun, their great contemporary, had already died in 1850, gloomily presaging and lamenting the coming danger to the Union which was so largely his own creation. For a while the cheerful view of Webster and Clay seemed better justified. There had been angry protest in the North against the Fugitive Slave Law; there was some forcible resistance to arrests of negroes; and some States passed Protection of Liberty Acts of their own to impede the Federal law in its working. But the excitement, which had flared up suddenly, died down as suddenly. In the Presidential election of 1852 Northerners generally reflected that they wanted quiet and had an instinct, curiously falsified, that the Democratic party was the more likely to give it them. The Whigs again proposed a hero, General Scott, a greater soldier than Taylor, but a vainer man, who mistakenly broke with all precedent and went upon the stump for himself. The President who was elected, Franklin Pierce of New Hampshire, a friend of

Hawthorne, might perhaps claim the palm among the Presidents of those days, for sheer, deleterious insignificance. The favourite observation of his contemporaries upon him was that he was a gentleman, but his convivial nature made the social attractiveness of Southern circles in Washington overpowering to any brain or character that he may have possessed. A new generation of political personages now came to the front. Jefferson Davis of Mississippi, a man of force and considerable dignity, began to take the leading part in the powerful group of Southern Senators; Stephen Douglas, of Illinois, rapidly became the foremost man of the Democratic party generally; William Seward, late Governor of New York, and Salmon Chase, a Democrat, late Governor of Ohio, had played a manful part in the Senate in opposition to Webster and Clay and their compromise. From this time on we must look on these two, joined a little later by Charles Sumner, of Massachusetts, as the obvious leaders in the struggle against slavery which was shortly to be renewed, and in which Lincoln's part seemed likely to remain a humble one.

3. *Lincoln in Retirement.*

Whether Seward and Chase and the other opponents of the Compromise were right, as it now seems they were, or not, Lincoln was not the man who in the unlooked-for crisis of 1850 would have been likely to make an insurrectionary stand against his old party-leader Clay, and the revered constitutional authority of Webster. He had indeed little opportunity to do so in Illinois, but his one recorded speech of this period, an oration to a meeting of both parties on the death of Clay in 1852, expresses approval of the Compromise. This speech, which is significant of the trend of his thoughts at this time, does not lend itself to brief extracts because it is wanting in the frankness of his speeches before and after. A harsh reference to Abolitionists serves to disguise the fact that the whole speech

is animated by antagonism to slavery. The occasion and
the subject are used with rather disagreeable subtlety
to insinuate opposition to slavery into the minds of a
cautious audience. The speaker himself seems satisfied
with the mood of mere compromise which had governed
Clay in this matter, or rather perhaps he is twisting
Clay's attitude into one of more consistent opposition
to slavery than he really showed. In any case we can
be quite sure that the moderate and subtle but intensely
firm opinion with which a little later Lincoln returned
to political strife was the product of long and deep and
anxious thought during the years from 1849 to 1854.
On the surface it did not go far beyond the condemnation of slavery and acceptance of the Constitution which
had guided him earlier, nor did it seem to differ from
the wide-spread public opinion which in 1854 created a
new party; but there was this difference that Lincoln
had by then looked at the matter in all its bearings, and
prepared his mind for all eventualities. We shall find,
and need not be surprised to find, that he who now
hung back a little, and who later moved when public
opinion moved, later still continued to move when public opinion had receded.

What we know of these years of private life is mainly
due to Mr. William Herndon, the young lawyer already
quoted, whom he took into partnership in 1845, and
who kept on the business of the firm in Springfield till
Lincoln's death. This gentleman was, like Boswell, of
opinion that a great man is not best portrayed as a
figure in a stained-glass window. He had lived with
Lincoln, groaned under his odd ways, and loved them,
for sixteen years before his Presidency, and after his
death he devoted much research, in his own memory
and those of many others, to the task of substituting for
Lincoln's aureole the battered tall hat, with valuable
papers stuck in its lining, which he had long contemplated with reverent irritation. Mr. Herndon was not
endowed with Boswell's artistic gift for putting his
materials together, perhaps because he lacked that

delicacy and sureness of moral perception which more than redeemed Boswell's absurdities. He succeeded on the whole in his aim, for the figure that more or less distinctly emerges from the litter of his workshop is lovable; but in spite of all Lincoln's melancholy, the dreariness of his life, sitting with his feet on the table in his unswept and untidy office at Illinois, or riding on circuit or staying at ramshackle western inns with the Illinois bar, cannot have been so unrelieved as it is in Mr. Herndon's presentation. And Herndon overdid his part. He ferreted out petty incidents which he thought might display the acute Lincoln as slightly too acute, when for all that can be seen Lincoln acted just as any sensible man would have acted. But the result is that, in this part of his life especially, Lincoln's way of living was subjected to so close a scrutiny as few men have undergone.

Herndon's scrutiny does not reveal the current of his thoughts either on life generally or on the political problem which hereafter was to absorb him. It shows on the contrary, and the recollections of his Presidency confirm it, that his thought on any important topic though it might flash out without disguise in rare moments of intimacy, usually remained long unexpressed. His great sociability had perhaps even then a rather formidable side to it. He was not merely amusing himself and other people, when he chatted and exchanged anecdotes far into the night; there was an element, not ungenial, of purposeful study in it all. He was building up his knowledge of ordinary human nature, his insight into popular feeling, his rather slow but sure comprehension of the individual men whom he did know. It astonished the self-improving young Herndon that the serious books he read were few and that he seldom seemed to read the whole of them—though with the Bible, Shakespeare, and to a less extent Burns, he saturated his mind. The few books and the great many men were part of one study. In so far as his thought and study turned upon politics it seems to have led him

soon to the conclusion that he had for the present no part to play that was worth playing. By 1854, as he said himself, " his profession as a lawyer had almost superseded the thought of politics in his mind." But it does not seem that the melancholy sense of some great purpose unachieved or some great destiny awaiting him ever quite left him. He must have felt that his chance of political fame was in all appearance gone, and would have liked to win himself a considerable position and a little (very little) money as a lawyer; but the study, in the broadest sense, of which these years were full, evidently contemplated a larger education of himself as a man than professional keenness, or any such interest as he had in law, will explain. Middle-aged and from his own point of view a failure, he was set upon making himself a bigger man.

In some respects he let himself be. His exterior oddities never seem to have toned down much; he could not be taught to introduce tidiness or method into his office; nor did he make himself an exact lawyer; a rough and ready familiarity with practice and a firm grasp of larger principles of law contented him without any great apparatus of learning. His method of study was as odd as anything else about him; he could read hard and commit things to memory in the midst of bustle and noise; on the other hand, since reading aloud was his chosen way of impressing what he read on his own mind, he would do it at all sorts of times to the sore distraction of his partner. When his studies are spoken of, observation and thought on some plan concealed in his own mind must be taken to have formed the largest element in these studies. There was, however, one methodic discipline, highly commended of old but seldom perhaps seriously pursued with the like object by men of forty, even self-taught men, which he did pursue. Some time during these years he mastered the first six Books of Euclid. It would probably be no mere fancy if we were to trace certain definite effects of this discipline upon his mind and character.

The faculty which he had before shown of reducing his thought on any subject to the simplest and plainest terms possible, now grew so strong that few men can be compared with him in this. He was gaining, too, from some source, what the ancient geometers would themselves have claimed as partly the product of their study: the plain fact and its plain consequences were not only clear in calm hours of thought, but remained present to him, felt and instinctive, through seasons of confusion, passion, and dismay. His life in one sense was very full of companionship, but it is probable that in his real intellectual interests he was lonely. To Herndon, intelligently interested in many things, his master's mind, much as he held it in awe, seemed chillingly unpoetic—which is a curious view of a mind steeped in Shakespeare and Burns. The two partners had been separately to Niagara. Herndon was anxious to know what had been Lincoln's chief impression, and was pained by the reply, "I wondered where all that water came from," which he felt showed materialism and insensibility. Lincoln's thought had, very obviously, a sort of poetry of its own, but of a vast and rather awful kind. He had occasionally written verses of his own a little before this time; sad verses about a friend who had become a lunatic, wondering that he should be allowed to outlive his mind while happy young lives passed away, and sad verses about a visit to old familiar fields in Indiana, where he wandered brooding, as he says,

> " Till every sound appears a knell,
> And every spot a grave."

They are not great poetry; but they show a correct ear for verse, and they are not the verses of a man to whom any of the familiar forms of poetic association were unusual. They are those of a man in whom the habitual undercurrent of thought was melancholy.

Apart from these signs and the deep, humorous delight which he evidently took in his children, there

may be something slightly forbidding in this figure of a gaunt man, disappointed in ambition and not even happy at home, rubbing along through a rather rough crowd, with uniform rough geniality and perpetual jest; all the while in secret forging his own mind into an instrument for some vaguely foreshadowed end. But there are two or three facts which stand out certain and have to be taken account of in any image we may be tempted to form of him. In the first place, his was no forbidding figure at the time to those who knew him; a queer and a comic figure evidently, but liked, trusted, and by some loved; reputed for honest dealing and for kindly and gentle dealing; remarked too by some at that time, as before and ever after, for the melancholy of his face in repose; known by us beyond doubt to have gone through great pain; known lastly among his fellows in his profession for a fire of anger that flashed out only in the presence of cruelty and wrong.

His law practice, which he pursued with energy, and on which he was now, it seems, prepared to look as his sole business in life, fitted in none the less well with his deliberately adopted schemes of self-education. A great American lawyer, Mr. Choate, assures us that at the Illinois bar in those days Lincoln had to measure himself against very considerable men in suits of a class that required some intellect and training. And in his own way he held his own among these men. A lay-man may humbly conjecture that the combination in one person of the advocate and the solicitor must give opportunities of far truer intellectual training than the mere advocate can easily enjoy. The Illinois advocate was not all the time pleading the cause which he was employed to plead, and which if it was once offered to him it was his duty to accept; he was the personal adviser of the client whose cause he pleaded, and within certain limits he could determine whether the cause was brought at all, and if so whether he should take it up himself or leave it to another man. The rule in such matters was elastic and practice varied. Lin-

coln's practice went to the very limit of what is permissible in refusing legal aid to a cause he disapproved. Coming into court he discovered suddenly some fact about his case which was new to him but which would probably not have justified an English barrister in throwing up his brief. The case was called; he was absent; the judge sent to his hotel and got back a message: "Tell the judge I'm washing my hands." One client received advice much to this effect: "I can win your case; I can get you $600. I can also make an honest family miserable. But I shall not take your case, and I shall not take your fee. One piece of advice I will give you gratis: Go home and think seriously whether you cannot make $600 in some honest way." And this habit of mind was beyond his control. Colleagues whom he was engaged to assist in cases agreed that if a case lost his sympathy he became helpless and useless in it. This, of course, was not the way to make money; but he got along and won a considerable local position at the bar, for his perfect honesty in argument and in statement of fact was known to have won the confidence of the judges, and a difficult case which he thought was right elicited the full and curious powers of his mind. His invective upon occasion was by all accounts terrific. An advocate glanced at Lincoln's notes for his speech, when he was appearing against a very heartless swindler and saw that they concluded with the ominous words, "Skin Defendant." The vitriolic outburst which occurred at the point thus indicated seems to have been long remembered by the Illinois bar. To a young man who wished to be a lawyer yet shrunk from the profession lest it should necessarily involve some dishonesty Lincoln wrote earnestly and wisely, showing him how false his impression of the law was, but concluding with earnest entreaty that he would not enter the profession if he still had any fear of being led by it to become a knave.

One of his cases is interesting for its own sake, not for his part in it. He defended without fee the son

Stephen Douglas, who was four years younger than Lincoln, had come to Illinois from the Eastern States just about the time when Lincoln entered the Legislature. He had neither money nor friends to start with, but almost immediately secured, by his extraordinary address in pushing himself, a clerkship in the Assembly. He soon became, like Lincoln, a lawyer and a legislator, but was on the Democratic side. He rapidly soared into regions beyond the reach of Lincoln, and in 1847 became a Senator for Illinois, where he later became Chairman of the Committee on Territories, and as such had to consider the question of providing for the government of the districts called Kansas and Nebraska, which lay west and north-west of Missouri, and from which slavery was excluded by the Missouri Compromise. He was what in England is called a " Jingo," and was at one time eager to fight this country for the possession of what is now British Columbia. His short figure gave an impression of abounding strength and energy which obtained him the nickname of " the little Giant." With no assignable higher quality, and with the blustering, declamatory, shamelessly fallacious and evasive oratory of a common demagogue, he was nevertheless an accomplished Parliamentarian, and imposed himself as effectively upon the Senate as he did upon the people of Illinois and the North generally. He was, no doubt, a remarkable man, with the gift of attracting many people. A political opponent has described vividly how at first sight he was instantly repelled by the sinister and dangerous air of Douglas' scowl; a still stronger opponent, but a woman, Mrs. Beecher Stowe, seems on the contrary to have found it impossible to hate him. What he now did displayed at any rate a sporting quality.

In the course of 1854 Stephen Douglas while in charge of an inoffensive Bill dealing with the government of Kansas and Nebraska converted it into a form in which it empowered the people of Kansas at any time to decide for themselves whether they would permit

coln's practice went to the very limit of what is permissible in refusing legal aid to a cause he disapproved. Coming into court he discovered suddenly some fact about his case which was new to him but which would probably not have justified an English barrister in throwing up his brief. The case was called; he was absent; the judge sent to his hotel and got back a message: "Tell the judge I'm washing my hands." One client received advice much to this effect: "I can win your case; I can get you $600. I can also make an honest family miserable. But I shall not take your case, and I shall not take your fee. One piece of advice I will give you gratis: Go home and think seriously whether you cannot make $600 in some honest way." And this habit of mind was beyond his control. Colleagues whom he was engaged to assist in cases agreed that if a case lost his sympathy he became helpless and useless in it. This, of course, was not the way to make money; but he got along and won a considerable local position at the bar, for his perfect honesty in argument and in statement of fact was known to have won the confidence of the judges, and a difficult case which he thought was right elicited the full and curious powers of his mind. His invective upon occasion was by all accounts terrific. An advocate glanced at Lincoln's notes for his speech, when he was appearing against a very heartless swindler and saw that they concluded with the ominous words, "Skin Defendant." The vitriolic outburst which occurred at the point thus indicated seems to have been long remembered by the Illinois bar. To a young man who wished to be a lawyer yet shrunk from the profession lest it should necessarily involve some dishonesty Lincoln wrote earnestly and wisely, showing him how false his impression of the law was, but concluding with earnest entreaty that he would not enter the profession if he still had any fear of being led by it to become a knave.

One of his cases is interesting for its own sake, not for his part in it. He defended without fee the son

of his old foe and friend Jack Armstrong, and of
Hannah, who mended his breeches, on a charge of
murder. Six witnesses swore that they had seen him
do the deed about 11 P.M. on such and such a night.
Cross-examined: They saw it all quite clearly; they saw
it so clearly because of the moonlight. The only evidence for the defence was an almanac. There had been
no moon that night. Another case is interesting for his
sake. Two young men set up in a farm together,
bought a waggon and team from a poor old farmer,
Lincoln's client, did not pay him, and were sued. They
had both been just under twenty-one when they contracted the debt, and they were advised to plead
infancy. A stranger who was present in Court described
afterwards his own indignation as the rascally tale was
unfolded, and his greater indignation as he watched the
locally famous Mr. Lincoln, lying back in his seat, nodding complacently and saying, " I reckon that's so," as
each of the relevant facts was produced, and the relevant Statute read and expounded. At last, as the onlooker proceeded to relate, the time came for Lincoln
to address the jury, with whom, by Illinois law, the
issue still rested. Slowly he disengaged his long, lean
form from his seat, and before he had got it drawn out
to its height he had fixed a gaze of extraordinary
benevolence on the two disgraceful young defendants and
begun in this strain: " Gentlemen of the jury, are you
prepared that these two young men shall enter upon
life and go through life with the stain of a dishonourable transaction for ever affixed to them," and so forth
at just sufficient length and with just enough of Shakespearean padding about honour. The result with that
emotional and probably irregular Western court is obvious, and the story concludes with the quite credible
assertion that the defendants themselves were relieved.
Any good jury would, of course, have been steeled
against the appeal, which might have been expected, to
their compassion for a poor and honest old man. A
kind of innocent and benign cunning has been the most

engaging quality in not a few great characters. It is tempting, though at the risk of undue solemnity, to look for the secret of Lincoln's cunning in this instance. We know from copybooks and other sources that these two young men, starting on the down grade with the help of their blackguardly legal adviser, were objects for pity, more so than the man who was about to lose a certain number of dollars. Lincoln, as few other men would have done, felt a certain actual regret for them then and there; he felt it so naturally that he knew the same sympathy could be aroused, at least in twelve honest men who already wished they could find for the plaintiff. It has often been remarked that the cause of his later power was a knowledge of the people's mind which was curiously but vitally bound up with his own rectitude.

Any attempt that we may make to analyse a subtle character and in some respects to trace its growth is certain to miss the exact mark. But it is in any case plain that Abraham Lincoln left political life in 1849, a praiseworthy self-made man with good sound views but with nothing much to distinguish him above many other such, and at a sudden call returned to political life in 1854 with a touch of something quite uncommon added to those good sound views.

4. *The Repeal of the Missouri Compromise.*

The South had become captive to politicians, personally reputable and of some executive capacity, who had converted its natural prejudice into a definite doctrine which was paradoxical and almost inconceivably narrow, and who, as is common in such instances of perversion and fanaticism, knew hardly any scruple in the practical enforcement of their doctrine. In the North, on the other hand, though there were some few politicians who were clever and well-intentioned, public opinion had no very definite character, and public men generally speaking were flabby. At such a time the sheer adventurer has an excellent field before him and perhaps has his appointed use.

Stephen Douglas, who was four years younger than Lincoln, had come to Illinois from the Eastern States just about the time when Lincoln entered the Legislature. He had neither money nor friends to start with, but almost immediately secured, by his extraordinary address in pushing himself, a clerkship in the Assembly. He soon became, like Lincoln, a lawyer and a legislator, but was on the Democratic side. He rapidly soared into regions beyond the reach of Lincoln, and in 1847 became a Senator for Illinois, where he later became Chairman of the Committee on Territories, and as such had to consider the question of providing for the government of the districts called Kansas and Nebraska, which lay west and north-west of Missouri, and from which slavery was excluded by the Missouri Compromise. He was what in England is called a " Jingo," and was at one time eager to fight this country for the possession of what is now British Columbia. His short figure gave an impression of abounding strength and energy which obtained him the nickname of " the little Giant." With no assignable higher quality, and with the blustering, declamatory, shamelessly fallacious and evasive oratory of a common demagogue, he was nevertheless an accomplished Parliamentarian, and imposed himself as effectively upon the Senate as he did upon the people of Illinois and the North generally. He was, no doubt, a remarkable man, with the gift of attracting many people. A political opponent has described vividly how at first sight he was instantly repelled by the sinister and dangerous air of Douglas' scowl; a still stronger opponent, but a woman, Mrs. Beecher Stowe, seems on the contrary to have found it impossible to hate him. What he now did displayed at any rate a sporting quality.

In the course of 1854 Stephen Douglas while in charge of an inoffensive Bill dealing with the government of Kansas and Nebraska converted it into a form in which it empowered the people of Kansas at any time to decide for themselves whether they would permit

slavery or not, and in express terms repealed the Missouri Compromise. With the easy connivance of President Pierce and the enthusiastic support of the Southerners, and by some extraordinary exercise of his art as demagogue and Parliamentarian, he triumphantly ran this measure through.

Just how it came about seems to be rather obscure, but it is easy to conjecture his motives. Trained in a school in which scruple or principle were unknown and the man who arrives is the great man, Douglas, like other such adventurers, was accessible to visions of a sort. He cared nothing whether negroes were slaves or not, and doubtless despised Northern and Southern sentiment on that subject equally; as he frankly said once, on any question between white men and negroes he was on the side of the white men, and on any question between negroes and crocodiles he would be on the side of the negroes. But he did care for the development of the great national heritage in the West, that subject of an easy but perfectly wholesome patriotic pride with which we are familiar. It must have been a satisfaction to him to feel that North and South would now have an equal chance in that heritage, and also that the white settlers in the West would be relieved of any restriction on their freedom. None the less his action was to the last degree reckless. The North had shown itself ready in 1850 to put up with a great deal of quiet invasion of its former principle, but to lay hands upon the sacred letter of the Act in which that principle was enshrined was to invite exciting consequences.

The immediate consequences were two-fold. In the first place Southern settlers came pouring into Kansas and Northern settlers in still larger numbers (rendered larger still by the help of an emigration society formed in the North-East for that purpose) came pouring in too. It was at first a race to win Kansas for slavery or for freedom. When it became apparent that freedom was winning easily, the race turned into a civil war between these two classes of immigrants for the posses-

sion of the Territorial government, and this kept on its scandalous and bloody course for three or four years.

In the second place there was a revolution in the party system. The old Whig party, which, whatever its tendencies, had avoided having any principle in regard to slavery, now abruptly and opportunely expired. There had been an attempt once before, and that time mainly among the Democrats, to create a new " Free-soil Party," but it had come to very little. This time a permanent fusion was accomplished between the majority of the former Whigs in the North and a numerous secession from among the Northern Democrats. They created the great Republican party, of which the name and organisation have continued to this day, but of which the original principle was simply and solely that there should be no further extension of slavery upon territory present or future of the United States. It naturally consisted of Northerners only. This was of course an ominous fact, and caused people, who were too timid either to join the Republicans or turn Democrat, to take refuge in another strange party, formed about this time, which had no views about slavery. This was the " American " party, commonly called the " Know-Nothing " party from its ridiculous and objectionable secret organisation. Its principle was dislike of foreign immigrants, especially such as were Roman Catholics. To them ex-President Fillmore, protesting against " the madness of the times " when men ventured to say yes or no on a question relating to slavery, fled for comfort, and became their candidate for the Presidency at the next election.

It was in 1854 that Lincoln returned to political life as one of the founders of the Republican party. But it will be better at once to deal with one or two later events with which he was not specially concerned. The Republicans chose as their Presidential candidate in 1856 an attractive figure, John Frémont, a Southerner of French origin, who had conducted daring and successful explorations in Oregon, had some hand (perhaps a very

important hand) in conquering California from Mexico, and played a prominent part in securing California for freedom. The Southern Democrats again secured a Northern instrument in James Buchanan of Pennsylvania, an elderly and very respectable man, who was understood to be well versed in diplomatic and official life. He was a more memorable personage than Pierce. A great chorus of friendly witnesses to his character has united in ascribing all his actions to weakness.

Buchanan was elected; but for a brand-new party the Republicans had put up a very good fight, and they were in the highest of spirits when, shortly after Buchanan's Inauguration in 1857, a staggering blow fell upon them from an unexpected quarter. This was nothing less than a pronouncement by the Chief Justice and a majority of Justices in the Supreme Court of the United States, that the exclusion of slavery from any portion of the Territories, and therefore, of course, the whole aim and object of the Republicans, was, as Calhoun had contended eight or ten years before, unconstitutional.

Dred Scott was a Missouri slave whose misfortunes it is needless to compassionate, since, after giving his name to one of the most famous law cases in history, he was emancipated with his family by a new master into whose hands he had passed. Some time before the Missouri Compromise was repealed he had been taken by his master into Minnesota, as a result of which he claimed that he became, by virtue of the Missouri Compromise, a free man. His right to sue his master in a Federal Court rested on the allegation that he was now a citizen of Missouri, while his master was a citizen of another State. There was thus a preliminary question to be decided, Was he really a citizen, before the question, Was he a freeman, could arise at all. If the Supreme Court followed its established practice, and if it decided against his citizenship, it would not consider the question which interested the public, that of his freedom.

Chief Justice Roger Taney may be seen from the refined features of his portrait and the clear-cut literary

style of his famous judgment to have been a remarkable man. He was now eighty-three, but in unimpaired intellectual vigour. In a judgment, with which five of his colleagues entirely concurred and from which only two dissented, he decided that Dred Scott was not a citizen, and went on, contrary to practice, to pronounce, in what was probably to be considered as a mere *obiter dictum,* that Dred Scott was not free, because the Missouri Compromise had all along been unconstitutional and void. Justices McLean and Curtis, especially the latter, answered Taney's arguments in cogent judgments, which it seems generally to be thought were right. Many lawyers thought so then, and so did the prudent Fillmore. This is one of the rare cases where a layman may have an opinion on a point of law, for the argument of Taney was entirely historical and rested upon the opinion as to negroes and slavery which he ascribed to the makers of the Constitution and the authors of the Declaration of Independence. On the question of Scott's citizenship he laid down that these men had hardly counted Africans as human at all, and used words such as " men," " persons," " citizens " in a sense which necessarily excluded the negro. We have seen already that he was wrong—the Southern politician who called the words of the Declaration of Independence " a self-evident lie " was a sounder historian than Taney; but an amazing fact is to be added: the Constitution, whose authors, according to Taney, could not conceive of a negro as a citizen, was actually the act of a number of States in several of which negroes were exercising the full rights of citizens at the time. It would be easy to bring almost equally plain considerations to bear against the more elaborate argument of Taney that the Missouri Compromise was unconstitutional, but it is enough to say this much: the first four Presidents—that is, all the Presidents who were in public life when the Constitution was made—had all acted unhesitatingly upon the belief that Congress had the power to allow or forbid slavery in the Territories. The

fifth, John Quincy Adams, when he set his hand to Acts involving this principle, had consulted before doing so the whole of his Cabinet on this constitutional point and had signed such legislation with the full concurrence of them all. Even Polk had acted later upon the same view. The Dred Scott judgment would thus appear to show the penetrating power at that time of an altogether fantastic opinion.

The hope, which Taney is known to have entertained, that his judgment would compose excited public opinion, was by no means fulfilled. It raised fierce excitement. What practical effect would hereafter be given to the opinion of six out of the nine judges in that Court might depend on many things. But to the Republicans, who appealed much to antiquity, it was maddening to be thus assured that their whole " platform " was unconstitutional. In the long run, there seems to be no doubt that Taney helped the cause of freedom. He had tried to make evident the personal sense of compassion for " these unfortunate people " with which he contemplated the opinion that he ascribed to a past generation; but he failed to do this, and instead he succeeded in imparting to the supposed Constitutional view of the slave, as nothing but a chattel, a horror which went home to many thousands of the warm-hearted men and women of his country.

For the time, however, the Republicans were deeply depressed, and a further perplexity shortly befell them. An attempt, to which we must shortly return, was made to impose the slave system on Kansas against the now unmistakable will of the majority there. Against this attempt Douglas, in opposition to whom the Republican party had been formed, revolted to his lasting honour, and he now stood out for the occasion as the champion of freedom. It was at this late period of bewilderment and confusion that the life-story of Abraham Lincoln became one with the life-story of the American people.

CHAPTER V

THE RISE OF LINCOLN

1. *Lincoln's Return to Public Life.*

WE possess a single familiar letter in which Lincoln opened his heart about politics. It was written while old political ties were not yet quite broken and new ties not quite knit, and it was written to an old and a dear friend who was not his political associate. We may fittingly place it here, as a record of the strong and conflicting feelings out of which his consistent purpose in this crisis was formed.

"*24 August, 1855.*

"TO JOSHUA SPEED.

"You know what a poor correspondent I am. Ever since I received your very agreeable letter of the 22nd I have been intending to write you an answer to it. You suggest that in political action, now, you and I would differ. I suppose we would; not quite so much, however, as you may think. You know I dislike slavery, and you fully admit the abstract wrong of it. So far there is no cause of difference. But you say that sooner than yield your legal right to the slave, especially at the bidding of those who are not themselves interested, you would see the Union dissolved. I am not aware that any one is bidding you yield that right; very certainly I am not. I leave that matter entirely to yourself. I also acknowledge your rights and my obligations under the Constitution in regard to your slaves. I confess I hate to see the poor creatures hunted down and caught and carried back to their stripes and unrequited toil; but I bite my lips and keep quiet. In 1841 you and I had together a tedious low-water trip on a steamboat from Louisville to St. Louis. You may re-

member, as I well do, that from Louisville to the mouth
of the Ohio there were on board ten or a dozen slaves
shackled together with irons. That sight was a continual torment to me, and I see something like it every
time I touch the Ohio or any other slave border. It
is not fair for you to assume that I have no interest
in a thing which has, and continually exercises, the power
to make me miserable. You ought rather to appreciate
how much the great body of the Northern people do
crucify their feelings, in order to maintain their loyalty
to the Constitution and the Union. I do oppose the
extension of slavery because my judgment and feelings
so prompt me, and I am under no obligations to the
contrary. If for this you and I must differ, differ we
must. . . .

"You say that if Kansas fairly votes herself a free
State, as a Christian you will rejoice at it. All decent
slave holders talk that way and I do not doubt their
candour. But they never vote that way. Although in
a private letter or conversation you will express your
preference that Kansas shall be free, you will vote for
no man for Congress who would say the same thing
publicly. No such man could be elected from any district in a slave State. . . . The slave breeders and
slave traders are a small, odious and detested class
among you; and yet in politics they dictate the course
of all of you, and are as completely your masters as
you are the masters of your own negroes.

"You inquire where I now stand. That is a disputed
point. I think I am a Whig; but others say there are
no Whigs, and that I am an Abolitionist. When I was
at Washington I voted for the Wilmot Proviso as good
as forty times; and I never heard of any one attempting to un-Whig me for that. I now do no more than
oppose the extension of slavery. I am not a Know-
Nothing, that is certain. How could I be? How can
any one who abhors the oppression of negroes be in
favour of degrading classes of white people? Our
progress in degeneracy appears to me pretty rapid. As

a nation we began by declaring that ' all men are created equal.' We now practically read it, ' all men are created equal, except negroes.' When the Know-Nothings get control, it will read, ' all men are created equal, except negroes and foreigners and Catholics.' When it comes to this, I shall prefer emigrating to some country where they make no pretence of loving liberty—to Russia, for instance, where despotism can be taken pure, and without the base alloy of hypocrisy.

"Mary will probably pass a day or two in Louisville in October. My kindest regards to Mrs. Speed. On the leading subject of this letter I have more of her sympathy than I have of yours; and yet let me say I am

"Your friend forever,

"A. LINCOLN."

The shade of doubt which this letter suggests related really to the composition of political parties and the grouping of political forces, not in the least to the principles by which Lincoln's own actions would be guided. He has himself recorded that the repeal of the Missouri Compromise meant for him the sudden revival in a far stronger form of his interest in politics, and, we may add, of his political ambition. The opinions which he cherished most deeply demanded no longer patience but vehement action. The faculties of political organisation and of popular debate, of which he enjoyed the exercise, could now be used for a purpose which satisfied his understanding and his heart.

From 1854 onwards we find Lincoln almost incessantly occupied, at conventions, at public meetings, in correspondence, in secret consultation with those who looked to him for counsel, for the one object of strengthening the new Republican movement in his own State of Illinois, and, so far as opportunity offered, in the neighbouring States. Some of the best of his reported and the most effective of his unreported speeches were delivered between 1854 and 1858. Yet as large a part of his work in these years was done quietly in the back-

ground, and it continued to be his fate to be called upon
to efface himself.

It is unnecessary to follow in any detail the labours
by which he became a great leader in Illinois. It may
suffice to pick out two instances that illustrate the ways
of this astute, unselfish man. The first is very trifling
and shows him merely astute. A Springfield newspaper
called the *Conservative* was acquiring too much influence as the organ of moderate and decent opinion that
acquiesced in the extension of negro slavery. The
Abolitionist, Mr. Herndon, was a friend of the editor.
One day he showed Lincoln an article in a Southern
paper whch most boldly justified slavery whether the
slaves were black or white. Lincoln observed what a
good thing it would be if the pro-slavery papers of
Illinois could be led to go this length. Herndon ingeniously used his acquaintance with the editor to procure
that he should reprint this article with approval. Of
course that promising journalistic venture, the *Conservative,* was at once ruined by so gross an indiscretion.
This was hard on its confiding editor, and it is not to
Lincoln's credit that he suggested or connived at this
trick. But this trumpery tale happens to be a fair
illustration of two things. In the first place a large
part of Lincoln's activity went in the industrious and
watchful performance of services to his cause, very seldom as questionable but constantly as minute as this, and
in making himself as in this case confidant and adviser
to a number of less notable workers. In the second
place a biographer must set forth if he can the materials for the severest judgment on his subject, and in
the case of a man whose fame was built on his honesty, but who certainly had an aptitude for ingenious
tricks and took a humorous delight in them, this duty
might involve a tedious examination of many unimportant incidents. It may save such discussion hereafter to
say, as can safely be said upon a study of all the transactions in his life of which the circumstances are known,
that this trick on the editor of the *Conservative* marks

the limit of Lincoln's deviation from the straight path. Most of us might be very glad if we had really never done anything much more dishonest.

Our second tale of this period is much more memorable. In 1856 the term of office of one of the Senators for Illinois came to an end; and there was a chance of electing an opponent of Douglas. Those of the Republicans of Illinois who were former Whigs desired the election of Lincoln, but could only secure it by the adhesion of a sufficient number of former Democrats and waverers. United States Senators were elected by the Legislatures of their own States through a procedure similar to that of the Conclave of Cardinals which elects a Pope; if there were several candidates and no one of them had an absolute majority of the votes first cast, the candidate with most votes was not elected; the voting was repeated, perhaps many times, till some one had an absolute majority; the final result was brought about by a transfer of votes from one candidate to another in which the prompt and cunning wire-puller had sometimes a magnificent opportunity for his skill. In this particular contest there were many ballots, and Lincoln at first led. His supporters were full of eager hope. Lincoln, looking on, discerned before any of them the setting in of an under-current likely to result in the election of a supporter of Douglas. He discerned, too, that the surest way to prevent this was for the whole of his friends immediately to go over to the Democrat, Lyman Trumbull, who was a sound opponent of slavery. He sacrificed his own chance instantly by persuading his supporters to do this. They were very reluctant, but he overbore them; one, a very old friend, records that he never saw him more earnest and decided. The same friend records, what is necessary to the appreciation of Lincoln's conduct, that his personal disappointment and mortification at his failure were great. Lincoln, it will be remembered, had acted just in this way when he sought election to the House of Representatives; he was to repeat this line of conduct in a manner at least as

striking in the following year. Minute criticism of his action in many matters becomes pointless when we observe that his managing shrewdness was never more signally displayed than it was three times over in the sacrifice of his own personal chances.

For four years, it is to be remembered, the activity and influence of which we are speaking were of little importance beyond the boundaries of Illinois. It is true that at the Republican Convention in 1856 which chose Frémont as its candidate for the Presidency, Lincoln was exposed for a moment to the risk (for so it was to be regarded) of being nominated for the Vice-Presidency; but even his greatest speech was not noticed outside Illinois, and in the greater part of the Northern States his name was known to comparatively few and to them only as a local notability of the West. But in the course of 1858 he challenged the attention of the whole country. There was again a vacancy for a Senator for Illinois. Douglas was the sole and obvious candidate of the Democrats. Lincoln came forward as his opponent. The elections then pending of the State Legislature, which in its turn would elect a Senator, became a contest between Lincoln and Douglas. In the autumn of that year these rival champions held seven joint debates before mass meetings in the open air at important towns of Illinois, taking turns in the right of opening the debate and replying at its close; in addition each was speaking at meetings of his own at least once a day for three months. At the end of it all Douglas had won his seat in the Senate, and Lincoln had not yet gained recognition among the Republican leaders as one of themselves. Nevertheless the contest between Lincoln and Douglas was one of the decisive events in American history, partly from the mere fact that at that particular moment any one opposed Douglas at all; partly from the manner in which, in the hearing of all America, Lincoln formulated the issue between them; partly from the singular stroke by which he deliberately ensured his own defeat and certain further consequences.

2. *The Principles and the Oratory of Lincoln.*

We can best understand the causes which suddenly made him a man of national consequence by a somewhat close examination of the principles and the spirit which governed all his public activity from the moment of the repeal of the Missouri Compromise. The new Republican party which then began to form itself stood for what might seem a simple creed; slavery must be tolerated where it existed because the Constitution and the maintenance of the Union required it, but it must not be allowed to extend beyond its present limits because it was fundamentally wrong. This was what most Whigs and many Democrats in the North had always held, but the formulation of it as the platform of a party, and a party which must draw its members almost entirely from the North, was bound to raise in an acute form questions on which very few men had searched their hearts. Men who hated slavery were likely to falter and find excuses for yielding when confronted with the danger to the Union which would arise. Men who loved the Union might in the last resort be ready to sacrifice it if they could thereby be rid of complicity with slavery, or might be unwilling to maintain it at the cost of fratricidal war. The stress of conflicting emotions and the complications of the political situation were certain to try to the uttermost the faith of any Republican who was not very sure just how much he cared for the Union and how much for freedom, and what loyalty to either principle involved. It was the distinction of Lincoln—a man lacking in much of the knowledge which statesmen are supposed to possess, and capable of blundering and hesitation about details—first, that upon questions like these he was free from ambiguity of thought or faltering of will, and further, that upon his difficult path, amid bewildering and terrifying circumstances, he was able to take with him the minds of very many very ordinary men.

In a slightly conventional memorial oration upon

Clay, Lincoln had said of him that " he loved his country, partly because it was his own country, and mostly
because it was a free country." He might truly have
said the like of himself. To him the national unity of
America, with the Constitution which symbolised it, was
the subject of pride and of devotion just in so far as it
had embodied and could hereafter more fully embody
certain principles of permanent value to mankind. On
this he fully knew his own inner mind. For the preserva-
tion of an America which he could value more, say,
than men value the Argentine Republic, he was to show
himself better prepared than any other man to pay
any possible price. But he definitely refused to preserve
the Union by what in his estimation would have been
the real surrender of the principles which had made
Americans a distinct and self-respecting nation.

Those principles he found in the Declaration of Independence. Its rhetorical inexactitude gave him no trouble, and must not, now that its language is out of
fashion, blind us to the fact that the founders of the
United States did deliberately aspire to found a commonwealth in which common men and women should
count for more than elsewhere, and in which, as we
might now phrase it, all authority must defer somewhat
to the interests and to the sentiments of the under dog.
" Public opinion on any subject," he said, " always has
a ' central idea ' from which all its minor thoughts
radiate. The ' central idea ' in our public opinion at the
beginning was, and till recently has continued to be, ' the
equality of man '; and, although it has always submitted
patiently to whatever inequality seemed to be a matter
of actual necessity, its constant working has been a
steady and progressive effort towards the practical
equality of all men." The fathers, he said again, had
never intended any such obvious untruth as that
equality actually existed, or that any action of theirs
could immediately create it; but they had set up a
standard to which continual approximation could be
made.

So far as white men were concerned such approximation had actually taken place; the audiences Lincoln addressed were fully conscious that very many thousands
had found in the United States a scope to lead their
own lives which the traditions and institutions no less
than the physical conditions of their former countries
had denied them. There was no need for him to enlarge on this fact; but there are repeated indications of
the distaste and alarm with which he witnessed a
demand that newcomers from Europe, or some classes
of them, should be accorded lesser privileges than they
had enjoyed.

But notions of freedom and equality as applied to the
negroes presented a real difficulty. " There is," said
Lincoln, " a natural disgust in the minds of nearly all
white people at the idea of an indiscriminate amalgama-
tion of the white and black men." (We might perhaps
add that as the inferior race becomes educated and rises
in status it is likely itself to share the same disgust.)
Lincoln himself disliked the thought of intermarriage
between the races. He by no means took it for granted
that equality in political power must necessarily and
properly follow upon emancipation. Schemes for colonial
settlement of the negroes in Africa, or for gradual
emancipation accompanied by educational measures, appealed to his sympathy. It was not given him to take
a part in the settlement after the war, and it is impossible to guess what he would have achieved as a constructive statesman; but it is certain that he would have
proceeded with caution and with the patience of sure
faith; and he had that human sympathy with the white
people of the South, and no less with the slaves themselves, which taught him the difficulty of the problem.
But difficult as the problem was, one solution was certainly wrong, and that was the permanent acquiescence
in slavery. If we may judge from reiteration in his
speeches, no sophism angered him quite so much as the
very popular sophism which defended slavery by presenting a literal equality as the real alternative to it. " I

protest against the counterfeit logic which says that since I do not want a negro woman for my slave I must necessarily want her for my wife. I may want her for neither. I may simply let her alone. In some respects she is certainly not my equal. But in her natural right to eat the bread which she has earned by the sweat of her brow, she is my equal and the equal of any man."

The men who had made the Union had, as Lincoln contended, and in regard to most of them contended justly, been true to principle in their dealing with slavery. "They yielded to slavery," he insists, "what the necessity of the case required, and they yielded nothing more." It was, as we know, impossible for them in federating America, however much they might hope to inspire the new nation with just ideas, to take the power of legislating as to slavery within each existing State out of the hands of that State. Such power as they actually possessed of striking at slavery they used, as we have seen and as Lincoln recounted in detail, with all promptitude and almost to its fullest extent. They reasonably believed, though wrongly, that the natural tendency of opinion throughout the now freed Colonies with principles of freedom in the air would work steadily towards emancipation. "The fathers," Lincoln could fairly say, "place slavery, where the public mind could rest in the belief that it was in the course of ultimate extinction." The task for statesmen now was "to put slavery back where the fathers placed it."

Now this by no means implied that slavery in the States which now adhered to it should be exposed to attack from outside, or the slave owner be denied any right which he could claim under the Constitution, however odious and painful it might be, as in the case of the rendition of fugitive slaves, to yield him his rights. "We allow," says Lincoln, "slavery to exist in the slave States, not because it is right, but from the necessities of the Union. We grant a fugitive slave law because it is so 'nominated in the bond'; because our fathers so stipulated—had to—and we are bound to carry out

this agreement." And the obligations to the slave owners and the slave States, which this original agreement and the fundamental necessities of the Union involved, must be fulfilled unswervingly, in spirit as well as in the letter. Lincoln was ready to give the slave States any possible guarantee that the Constitution should not be altered so as to take away their existing right of self-government in the matter of slavery. He had remained in the past coldly aloof from the Abolitionist propaganda when Herndon and other friends tried to interest him in it, feeling, it seems, that agitation in the free States against laws which existed constitutionally in the slave States was not only futile but improper. With all his power he dissuaded his more impulsive friends from lending any aid to forcible and unlawful proceedings in defence of freedom in Kansas. "The battle of freedom," he exclaims in a vehement plea for what may be called moderate as against radical policy, "is to be fought out on principle. Slavery is violation of eternal right. We have temporised with it from the necessities of our condition; but as sure as God reigns and school children read, that black foul lie can never be consecrated into God's hallowed truth." In other words, the sure way and the only way to combat slavery lay in the firm and the scrupulous assertion of principles which would carry the reason and the conscience of the people with them; the repeal of the prohibition of slavery in the Territories was a defiance of such principles, but so too in its way was the disregard by Abolitionists of the rights covenanted to the slave States. This side of Lincoln's doctrine is apt to jar upon us. We feel with a great American historian that the North would have been depraved indeed if it had not bred Abolitionists, and it requires an effort to sympathise with Lincoln's rigidly correct feeling—sometimes harshly expressed and sometimes apparently cold. It is not possible to us, as it was to him a little later, to look on John Brown's adventure merely as a crime. Nor can we wonder that, when he was President and Civil

War was raging, many good men in the North mistook him and thought him half-hearted, because he persisted in his respect for the rights of the Slave States so long as there seemed to be a chance of saving the Union in that way. It was his primary business, he then said, to save the Union if he could; "if I could save the Union by emancipating all the slaves I would do so; if I could save it by emancipating none of them, I would do it; if I could save it by emancipating some and not others, I would do that too." But, as in the letter at the beginning of this chapter he called Speed to witness, his forbearance with slavery cost him real pain, and we shall misread both his policy as President and his character as a man if we fail to see that in the bottom of his mind he felt this forbearance to be required by the very same principles which roused him against the extension of the evil. Years before, he had written to an Abolitionist correspondent that respect for the rights of the slave States was due not only to the Constitution but, "as it seems to me, in a sense to freedom itself." Negro slavery was not the only important issue, nor was it an isolated issue. What really was in issue was the continuance of the nation "dedicated," as he said on a great occasion, "to the proposition that all men are equal," a nation founded by the Union of self-governing communities, some of which lagged far behind the others in applying in their own midst the elementary principles of freedom, but yet a nation actuated from its very foundation in some important respects by the acknowledgment of human rights.

The practical policy, then, on which his whole efforts were concentrated consisted in this single point—the express recognition of the essential evil of slavery by the enactment that it should not spread further in the Territories subject to the Union. If slavery were thus shut up within a ring fence and marked as a wrong thing which the Union as a whole might tolerate but would not be a party to, emancipation in the slave States would follow in course of time. It would come about,

Lincoln certainly thought, in a way far better for the slaves as well as for their masters, than any forced liberation. He was content to wait for it. " I do not mean that when it takes a turn towards ultimate extinction, it will be in a day, nor in a year, nor in two years. I do not suppose that in the most peaceful way ultimate extinction would occur in less than a hundred years at least, but that it will occur in the best way for both races in God's own good time I have no doubt." If we wonder whether this policy, if soon enough adopted by the Union as a whole, would really have brought on emancipation in the South, the best answer is that, when the policy did receive national sanction by the election of Lincoln, the principal slave States themselves instinctively recognised it as fatal to slavery.

For the extinction of slavery he would wait; for a decision on the principle of slavery he would not. It was idle to protest against agitation of the question. If politicians would be silent that would not get rid of " this same mighty deep-seated power that somehow operates on the minds of men, exciting them and stirring them up in every avenue of society—in politics, in religion, in literature, in morals, in all the manifold relations of life." The stand, temperate as it was, that he advocated against slavery should be taken at once and finally. The difference, of which people grown accustomed to slavery among their neighbours thought little, between letting it be in Missouri, which they could not help, and letting it cross the border into Kansas, which they could help, appeared to Lincoln the whole tremendous gulf between right and wrong, between a wise people's patience with ills they could not cure and a profligate people's acceptance of evil as their good. And here there was a distinction between Lincoln and many Republicans, which again may seem subtle, but which was really far wider than that which separated him from the Abolitionists. Slavery must be stopped from spreading into Kansas not because, as it turned out, the immigrants into Kansas mostly did not want it, but

because it was wrong, and the United States, where they were free to act, would not have it. The greatest evil in the repeal of the Missouri Compromise was the laxity of public tone which had made it possible. " Little by little, but steadily as man's march to the grave, we have been giving up the old faith for the new faith.'' Formerly some deference to the " central idea " of equality was general and in some sort of abstract sense slavery was admitted to be wrong. Now it was boldly claimed by the South that " slavery in the abstract was right." All the most powerful influences in the country, " Mammon " (for " the slave property is worth a billion dollars "), " fashion, philosophy," and even " the theology of the day," were enlisted in favour of this opinion. And it met with no resistance. " You yourself may detest slavery; but your neighbour has five or six slaves, and he is an excellent neighbour, or your son has married his daughter, and they beg you to help save their property, and you vote against your interests and principle to oblige a neighbour, hoping your vote will be on the losing side." And again " the party lash and the fear of ridicule will overawe justice and liberty; for it is a singular fact, but none the less a fact and well known by the most common experience, that men will do things under the terror of the party lash that they would not on any account or for any consideration do otherwise; while men, who will march up to the mouth of a loaded cannon without shrinking, will run from the terrible name of ' Abolitionist,' even when pronounced by a worthless creature whom they with good reason despise." And so people in the North, who could hardly stomach the doctrine that slavery was good, yet lapsed into the feeling that it was a thing indifferent, a thing for which they might rightly shuffle off their responsibility on to the immigrants into Kansas. This feeling that it was indifferent Lincoln pursued and chastised with special scorn. But the principle of freedom that they were surrendering was the principle of freedom for themselves as well as for the negro. The

sense of the negro's rights had been allowed to go back
till the prospect of emancipation for him looked immeasurably worse than it had a generation before. They
must recognise that when, by their connivance, they had
barred and bolted the door upon the negro, the spirit of
tyranny which they had evoked would then " turn and
rend them." The " central idea " which had now established itself in the intellect of the Southern was one
which favoured the enslavement of man by man " apart
from colour." A definite choice had to be made between
the principle of the fathers, which asserted certain rights
for all men, and that other principle against which the
fathers had rebelled and of which the " divine right of
kings " furnished Lincoln with his example. In what
particular manner the white people would be made to
feel the principle of tyranny when they had definitely
" denied freedom to others " and ceased to " deserve it
for themselves " Lincoln did not attempt to say, and
perhaps only dimly imagined. But he was as convinced
as any prophet that America stood at the parting of the
ways and must choose now the right principle or the
wrong with all its consequences.

The principle of tyranny presented itself for their
choice in a specious form in Douglas' " great patent,
everlasting principle of ' popular sovereignty.' " This
alleged principle was likely, so to say, to take upon their
blind side men who were sympathetic to the impatience
of control of any crowd resembling themselves but not
sympathetic to humanity of another race and colour. The
claim to some divine and indefeasible right of sovereignty
overriding all other considerations of the general good,
on the part of a majority greater or smaller at any given
time in any given area, is one which can generally be made
to bear a liberal semblance, though it certainly has no
necessary validity. Americans had never before thought
of granting it in the case of their outlying and unsettled
dominions; they would never, for instance, as Lincoln
remarked, have admitted the claim of settlers like the
Mormons to make polygamy lawful in the territory they

occupied. In the manner in which it was now employed the proposed principle could, as Lincoln contended, be reduced to this simple form "that, if one man chooses to enslave another, no third man shall have the right to object."

It is impossible to estimate how far Lincoln foresaw the strain to which a firm stand against slavery would subject the Union. It is likely enough that those worst forebodings for the Union, which events proved to be very true, were confined to timid men who made a practice of yielding to threats. Lincoln appreciated better than many of his fellows the sentiment of the South, but it is often hard for men, not in immediate contact with a school of thought which seems to them thoroughly perverse, to appreciate its pervasive power, and Lincoln was inclined to stake much upon the hope that reason will prevail. Moreover, he had a confidence in the strength of the Union which might have been justified if his predecessor in office had been a man of ordinary firmness. But it is not to be supposed that any undue hopefulness, if he felt it, influenced his judgment. He was of a temper which does not seek to forecast what the future has to show, and his melancholy prepared him well for any evil that might come. Two things we can say with certainty of his aim and purpose. On the one hand, as has already been said, whatever view he had taken of the peril to the Union he would never have sought to avoid the peril by what appeared to him a surrender of the principle which gave the Union its worth. On the other hand, he must always have been prepared to uphold the Union at whatever the cost might prove to be. To a man of deep and gentle nature war will always be hateful, but it can never, any more than an individual death, appear the worst of evils. And the claim of the Southern States to separate from a community which to him was venerable and to form a new nation, based on slavery and bound to live in discord with its neighbors, did not appeal to him at all, though in a certain literal sense it was a claim to liberty. His attitude to any possible movement for

secession was defined four years at least before secession came, in words such as it was not his habit to use without full sense of their possible effect or without much previous thought. They were quite simple: " We won't break up the Union, and you shan't."

Such were the main thoughts which would be found to animate the whole of Lincoln's notable campaign, beginning with his first encounter with Douglas in 1855 and culminating in his prolonged duel with him in the autumn of 1858. It is unnecessary here to follow the complexities, especially in regard to the Dred Scott judgments, through which the discussion wandered. It is now worth few men's while to do more than glance at two or three of his speeches at that period; his speeches in the formal Lincoln-Douglas debates, except the first, are not the best of them. A scientific student of rhetoric, as the art by which man do actually persuade crowds, might indeed do well to watch closely the use by Douglas and Lincoln of their respective weapons, but for most of us it is an unprofitable business to read reiterated argument, even though in beautiful language, upon points of doubt that no longer trouble us. Lincoln does not always show to advantage; later readers have found him inferior in urbanity to Douglas, of whom he disapproved, while Douglas probably disapproved of no man; his speeches are, of course, not free either from unsound arguments or from the rough and tumble of popular debate; occasionally he uses hackneyed phrases; but it is remarkable that a hackneyed or a falsely sentimental phrase in Lincoln comes always as a lapse and a surprise. Passages abound in these speeches which to almost any literate taste are arresting for the simple beauty of their English, a beauty characteristic of one who had learned to reason with Euclid and learned to feel and to speak with the authors of the Bible. And in their own kind they were a classic and probably unsurpassed achievement. Though Lincoln had to deal with a single issue demanding no great width of knowledge, it must be evident that the passions aroused by it and the confused and shifting

state of public sentiment made his problem very subtle, and it was a rare profundity and sincerity of thought which solved it in his own mind. In expressing the result of thought so far deeper than that of most men, he achieved a clearness of expression which very few writers, and those among the greatest, have excelled. He once during the Presidential election of 1856 wrote to a supporter of Fillmore to persuade him of a proposition which must seem paradoxical to anyone not deeply versed in American institutions, namely, that it was actually against Fillmore's interest to gain votes from Frémont in Illinois. He demonstrated his point, but he was not always judicious in his way of addressing solemn strangers, and in his rural manner he concludes his letter, " the whole thing is as simple as figuring out the weight of three small hogs," and this inelegant sentence conveys with little exaggeration one especial merit of his often austerely graceful language. Grave difficulties are handled in a style which could arouse all the interest of a boy and penetrate the understanding of a case-hardened party man.

But if in comparison with the acknowledged masterpieces of our prose we rank many passages in these speeches very high—and in fact the men who have appreciated them most highly have been fastidious scholars—we shall not yet have measured Lincoln's effort and performance. For these are not the compositions of a cloistered man of letters, they are the outpourings of an agitator upon the stump. The men who think hard are few; few of them can clothe their thought in apt and simple words; very, very few are those who in doing this could hold the attention of a miscellaneous and large crowd. Popular government owes that comparative failure, of which in recent times we have taken perhaps exaggerated notice, partly to the blindness of the polite world to the true difficulty and true value of work of this kind; and the importance which Roman education under the Empire gave to rhetoric was the mark not of deadness, but of the survival of a manly public spirit. Lin-

coln's wisdom had to utter itself in a voice which would reach the outskirts of a large and sometimes excited crowd in the open air. It was uttered in strenuous conflict with a man whose reputation quite overshadowed his; a person whose extraordinary and good-humoured vitality armed him with an external charm even for people who, like Mrs. Beecher Stowe, detested his principles; an orator whose mastery of popular appeal and of resourceful and evasive debate was quite unhampered by any weakness for the truth. The utterance had to be kept up day after day and night after night for a quarter of a year, by a man too poor to afford little comforts, travelling from one crowded inn to another, by slow trains on a railway whose officials paid little attention to him, while his more prosperous and distinguished rival could travel in comfort and comparative magnificence. The physical strain of electioneering, which is always considerable, its alternation of feverish excitement with a lassitude that, after a while, becomes prevailing and intense, were in this case far greater and more prolonged than in any other instance recorded of English or probably of American statesmen. If, upon his sudden elevation shortly afterwards, Lincoln was in a sense an obscure man raised up by chance, he was nevertheless a man who had accomplished a heroic labour.

On the whole the earthen vessel in which he carried his treasure of clear thought and clean feelings appears to have enhanced its flavour. There was at any rate nothing outward about him that aroused the passion of envy. A few peculiarly observant men were immediately impressed with his distinction, but there is no doubt that to the ordinary stranger he appeared as a very odd fish. "No portraits that I have ever seen," writes one, "do justice to the awkwardness and ungainliness of his figure." Its movements when he began to speak rather added to its ungainliness, and, though to a trained actor his elocution seemed perfect, his voice when he first opened his mouth surprised and jarred upon the hearers with a harsh note of curiously high pitch. But it was the sort

of oddity that arrests attention, and people's attention once caught was apt to be held by the man's transparent earnestness. Soon, as he lost thought of himself in his subject, his voice and manner changed; deeper notes, of which friends record the beauty, rang out, the sad eyes kindled, and the tall, gaunt figure, with the strange gesture of the long, uplifted arms, acquired even a certain majesty. Hearers recalled afterwards with evident sincerity the deep and instantaneous impression of some appeal to simple conscience, as when, " reaching his hands towards the stars of that still night," he proclaimed, " in some things she is certainly not my equal, but in her natural right to eat the bread that she has earned with the sweat of her brow, she is my equal, and the equal of Judge Douglas, and the equal of any man." Indeed, upon a sympathetic audience, already excited by the occasion, he could produce an effect which the reader of his recorded speeches would hardly believe. Of his speech at an early state convention of the Republican party there is no report except that after a few sentences every reporter laid down his pen for the opposite of the usual reason, and, as he proceeded, " the audience arose from their chairs and with pale faces and quivering lips pressed unconsciously towards him." And of his speech on another similar occasion several witnesses seem to have left descriptions hardly less incongruous with English experience of public meetings. If we credit him with these occasional manifestations of electric oratory—as to which it is certain that his quiet temperament did at times blaze out in a surprising fashion—it is not to be thought that he was ordinarily what could be called eloquent; some of his speeches are commonplace enough, and much of his debating with Douglas is of a drily argumentative kind that does honour to the mass meetings which heard it gladly. But the greatest gift of the orator he did possess; the personality behind the words was felt. " Beyond and above all skill," says the editor of a great paper who heard him at Peoria, " was the overwhelming conviction imposed upon the audience that the

speaker himself was charged with an irresistible and inspiring duty to his fellow men."

One fact about the method of his speaking is easily detected. In debate, at least, he had no use for perorations, and the reader who looks for them will often find that Lincoln just used up the last few minutes in clearing up some unimportant point which he wanted to explain only if there was time for it. We associate our older Parliamentary oratory with an art which keeps the hearer pleasedly expectant rather than dangerously attentive, through an argument which if dwelt upon might prove unsubstantial, secure that it all leads in the end to some great cadence of noble sound. But in Lincoln's argumentative speeches the employment of beautiful words is least sparing at the beginning or when he passes to a new subject. It seems as if he deliberately used up his rhetorical effects at the outset to put his audience in the temper in which they would earnestly follow him and to challenge their full attention to reasoning which was to satisfy their calmer judgment. He put himself in a position in which if his argument were not sound nothing could save his speech from failure as a speech. Perhaps no standing epithet of praise hangs with such a weight on a man's reputation as the epithet " honest." When the man is proved not to be a fraud, it suggests a very mediocre virtue. But the method by which Lincoln actually confirmed his early won and dangerous reputation of honesty was a positive and potent performance of rare distinction. It is no mean intellectual and spiritual achievement to be as honest in speech with a crowd as in the dearest intercourse of life. It is not, of course, pretended that he never used a fallacious argument or made an unfair score—he was entirely human. But this is the testimony of an Illinois political wire-puller to Lincoln: " He was one of the shrewdest politicians in the State. Nobody had more experience in that way. Nobody knew better what was passing in the minds of the people. Nobody knew better how to turn things to advantage politically." And then he goes on—and this

is really the sum of what is to be said of his oratory:
" He could not cheat people out of their votes any more
than he could out of their money."

3. *Lincoln against Douglas.*

It has now to be told how the contest with Douglas
which concluded Lincoln's labours in Illinois affected the
broad stream of political events in America as a whole.
Lincoln, as we know, was still only a local personage;
Illinois is a State bigger than Ireland, but it is only a
little part and was still a rather raw and provincial part
of the United States; but Douglas had for years been
a national personage, for a time the greatest man among
the Democrats, and now, for a reason which did him
honour, he was in disgrace with many of his party and
on the point of becoming the hero of all moderate
Republicans.

We need not follow in much detail the events of the
great political world. The repeal of the Missouri Compromise threw it into a ferment, which the continuing
disorders in Kansas were in themselves sufficient to keep
up. New great names were being made in debate in
the Senate; Seward, the most powerful opponent of the
repeal of the Missouri Compromise, kept his place as
the foremost man in the Republican party not by consistency in the stand that he made, but by his mastery
of New York political machinery; Sumner of Massachusetts, the friend of John Bright, kept up a continual protest for freedom in turgid, scholarly harangues, which
caught the spirit of Cicero's Philippics most successfully
in their personal offensiveness. Powerful voices in literature and the Press were heard upon the same side—the
New York Tribune, edited by Horace Greeley, acquired,
as far as a paper in so large a country can, a national
importance. Broadly it may be said that the stirring
intellect of America old and young was with the Republicans—it is a pleasant trifle to note that Longfellow
gave up a visit to Europe to vote for Frémont as Presi-

dent, and we know the views of Motley and of Lowell and of Darwin's fellow labourer Asa Gray. But fashion and that better and quite different influence, the tone of opinion prevailing in the pleasantest society, inclined always to the Southern view of every question, and these influences were nowhere more felt than among Washington politicians. A strong and respectable group of Southern Senators, of whom Jefferson Davis was the strongest, were the real driving power of the administration. Convivial President Pierce and doting President Buchanan after him were complaisant to their least scrupulous suggestions in a degree hardly credible of honourable men who were not themselves Southerners.

One famous incident of life in Congress must be told to explain the temper of the times. In 1856, during one of the many debates that arose out of Kansas, Sumner recited in the Senate a speech conscientiously calculated to sting the slave-owning Senators to madness. Sumner was a man with brains and with courage and rectitude beyond praise, set off by a powerful and noble frame, but he lacked every minor quality of greatness. He would not call his opponent in debate a skunk, but he would expend great verbal ingenuity in coupling his name with repeated references to that animal's attributes. On this occasion he used to the full both the finer and the most exquisitely tasteless qualities of his eloquence. This sort of thing passed the censorship of many excellent Northern men who would lament Lincoln's lack of refinement; and though from first to last the serious provocation in their disputes lay in the set policy of the Southern leaders, it ought to be realised that they, men who for the most part were quite kind to their slaves and had long ago argued themselves out of any compunction about slavery, were often exposed to intense verbal provocation. Nevertheless, what followed on Sumner's speech is terribly significant of the depravation of Southern honour.

Congressman Preston Brooks, of South Carolina, had an uncle in the Senate; South Carolina, and this Senator in particular, had been specially favoured with self-right-

eous insolence in Sumner's speech. A day or so later the
Senate had just risen and Sumner sat writing at his desk
in the Senate chamber in a position in which he could not
quickly rise. Brooks walked in, burning with piety
towards his State and his uncle, and in the presence, it
seems, of Southern Senators who could have stopped
him, beat Sumner on the head with a stick with all his
might. Sumner was incapacitated by injuries to his spine
for nearly five years. Brooks, with a virtuous air, explained in Congress that he had caught Sumner in a
helpless attitude because if Sumner had been free to
use his superior strength he, Brooks, would have had
to shoot him with his revolver. It seems to be hardly an
exaggeration to say that the whole South applauded
Brooks and exulted. Exuberant Southerners took to
challenging Northern men, knowing well that their principles compelled them to refuse duels, but that the refusal
would still be humiliating to the North. Brooks himself
challenged Burlingame, a distinguished Congressman afterwards sent by Lincoln as Minister to China, who had
denounced him. Burlingame accepted, and his second
arranged for a rifle duel at a wild spot across the frontier
at Niagara. Brooks then drew back; he alleged, perhaps
sincerely, that he would have been murdered on his way
through the Northern States, but Northern people were
a little solaced. The whole disgusting story contains only
one pleasant incident. Preston Brooks, who, after numbers of congratulations, testimonials, and presentations,
died within a year of his famous exploit, had first confessed himself tired of being a hero to every vulgar bully
in the South!

Now, though this dangerous temper burned steadily in
the South, and there were always sturdy Republicans
ready to provoke it, and questions arising out of slavery
would constantly recur to disturb high political circles, it
is not to be imagined that opinion in the North, the growing and bustling portion of the States, would remain for
years excited about the repeal of the Missouri Compromise. In 1857 men's minds were agitated by a great

commercial depression and collapse of credit, and in 1858 there took place one of the most curious (for it would seem to have deserved this cold description) of evanescent religious revivals. Meanwhile, by 1857 the actual bloodshed in Kansas had come to an end under the administration of an able Governor; the enormous majority of settlers in Kansas were now known to be against slavery and it was probably assumed that the legalisation of slavery could not be forced upon them. Prohibition of slavery there by Congress thus began to seem needless, and the Dred Scott judgments raised at least a grave doubt as to whether it was possible. Thus enthusiasm for the original platform of the Republicans was cooling down, and to the further embarrassment of that party, when towards the end of 1857 the Southern leaders attempted a legislative outrage, the great champion of the Northern protest was not a Republican, but Douglas himself.

A Convention had been elected in Kansas to frame a State Constitution. It represented only a fraction of the people, since, for some reason good or bad, the opponents of slavery did not vote in the election. But it was understood that whatever Constitution was framed would be submitted to the popular vote. The Convention framed a Constitution legalising slavery, and its proposals came before Congress backed by the influence of Buchanan. Under them the people of Kansas were to vote whether they would have this Constitution as it stood, or have it with the legalisation of slavery restricted to the slaves who had then been brought into the territory. No opportunity was to be given them of rejecting the Constitution altogether, though Governor Walker, himself in favor of slavery, assured the President that they wished to do so. Ultimately, by way of concession to vehement resistance, the majority in Congress passed an Act under which the people in Kansas were to vote simply for or against the slavery Constitution as it stood, only—if they voted for it, they as a State were to be rewarded with a large grant of public lands belonging to the Union in their territory. Eventually the Kansas people, unmoved by

this bribe, rejected the Constitution by a majority of
more than 11,000 to 1,800. Now, the Southern leaders,
three years before, had eagerly joined with Douglas to
claim a right of free choice for the Kansas people. The
shamelessness of this attempt to trick them out of it is
more significant even than the tale of Preston Brooks.
There was no hot blood there; the affair was quietly
plotted by respected leaders of the South. They were
men, in many ways of character and honour, understood
by weak men like Buchanan to represent the best traditions of American public life. But, as they showed also
in other instances that cannot be related here, slavery
had become for them a sacred cause which hallowed
almost any means. It is essential to remember this in
trying to understand the then political situation.

Douglas here behaved very honourably. He, with his
cause of popular sovereignty, could not have afforded to
identify himself with the fraud on Kansas, but he was
a good enough trickster to have made his protest safely
if he had cared to do so. As it was he braved the hatred
of Buchanan and the fury of his Southern friends by
instant, manly, courageous, and continued opposition. It
may therefore seem an ungracious thing that, immediately
after this, Lincoln should have accepted the invitation of
his friends to oppose Douglas' re-election. To most of
the leading Republicans out of Illinois it seemed altogether
unwise and undesirable that their party, which had seemed
to be losing ground, should do anything but welcome
Douglas as an ally. Of these Seward indeed went too
far for his friends, and in his sanguine hope that it would
work for freedom was ready to submit to the doctrine
of " popular sovereignty "; but, except the austere Chase,
now Governor of Ohio, who this once, but unfortunately
not again, was whole-heartedly with Lincoln, the Republican leaders in the East, and great Republican journals,
like the *Tribune,* declared their wish that Douglas
should be re-elected. Why, then, did Lincoln stand
against him?

It has often been suggested that his personal feelings

towards Douglas played some part in the matter,
though no one thinks they played the chief part. Probably they did play a part, and it is a relief to think that
Lincoln thoroughly gratified some minor feelings in this
contest. Lincoln no doubt enjoyed measuring himself
against other men; and it was galling to his ambition to
have been so completely outstripped by a man inferior
to him in every power except that of rapid success. He
had also the deepest distrust for Douglas as a politician,
thinking that he had neither principle nor scruple, though
Herndon, who knew, declares he neither distrusted nor
had cause to distrust Douglas in his professional dealings
as a lawyer. He had, by the way, one definite, if trifling,
score to wipe off. After their joint debate at Peoria in
1855 Douglas, finding him hard to tackle, suggested to
Lincoln that they should both undertake to make no more
speeches for the present. Lincoln oddly assented at once,
perhaps for no better reason than a ridiculous difficulty,
to which he once confessed, in refusing any request whatever. Lincoln of course had kept this agreement strictly,
while Douglas had availed himself of the first temptation
to break it. Thus on all grounds we may be sure that
Lincoln took pleasure in now opposing Douglas. But to
go further and say that the two men cordially hated each
other is probably to misread both. There is no necessary
connection between a keen desire to beat a man and any
sort of malignity towards him. That much at least may
be learned in English schools, and the whole history of
his dealing with men shows that in some school or other
Lincoln had learned it very thoroughly. Douglas, too,
though an unscrupulous, was not, we may guess, an ungenerous man.

But the main fact of the matter is that Lincoln would
have turned traitor to his rooted convictions if he had
not stood up and fought Douglas even at this moment
when Douglas was deserving of some sympathy.
Douglas, it must be observed, had simply acted on his
principle that the question between slavery and freedom
was to be settled by local, popular choice; he claimed

for the white men of Kansas the fair opportunity of voting; given that, he persistently declared, " I do not care whether slavery be voted up or voted down." In Lincoln's settled opinion this moral attitude of indifference to the wrongfulness of slavery, so long as respect was had to the liberties of the privileged race, was, so to say, treason to the basic principle of the American Commonwealth, a treason which had steadily been becoming rife and upon which it was time to stamp.

There can be no doubt of his earnestness about this. But the Republican leaders, honourably enough, regarded this as an unpractical line to take, and indeed to the political historian this is the most crucial question in American history. Nobody can say that civil war would or would not have occurred if this or that had been done a little differently, but Abraham Lincoln, at this crisis of his life, did, in pursuance of his peculiarly cherished principle, forge at least a link in the chain of events which actually precipitated the war. And he did it knowing better than any other man that he was doing something of great national importance, involving at least great national risk. Was he pursuing his principles, moderate as they were in the original conception, with fanaticism, or at the best preferring a solemn consistency of theory to the conscientious handling of facts not reducible to theory? As a question of practical statesmanship in the largest sense, how did matters really stand in regard to slavery and to the relations between South and North, and what was Lincoln's idea of " putting slavery back where the fathers placed it " really worth?

Herndon in these days went East to try to enlist the support of the great men for Lincoln. He found them friendly but immovable. Editor Horace Greeley said to him: " The Republican standard is too high; we want something practical." This, we may be pretty sure, stiffened Lincoln's back, as a man with a cause that he cared for, and, for that matter, as a really shrewd manager in a party which he thought stood for something. It reveals the flabbiness which the Northerners were in

danger of making a governing tradition of policy. The wrongfulness of any extension of slavery might be loudly asserted in 1854, but in 1858, when it no longer looked as if so great an extension of it was really imminent, there was no harm in shifting towards some less provocative principle on which more people at the moment might agree. Confronted with Northern politicians who would reason in this fashion stood a united South whose leaders were by now accustomed to make the Union Government go which way they chose and had no sort of disposition to compromise their principle in the least. "What," as Lincoln put it in an address given, not long after his contest with Douglas, at the Cooper Institute in New York, "what do you think will content the South?" "Nothing," he answered, "but an acknowledgment that slavery is right." "Holding as they do that slavery is morally right and socially elevating, they cannot cease to demand a full national recognition of it, as a legal right and a social blessing. Nor can we justifiably withhold this on any ground save our conviction that slavery is wrong." That being so, there was no use, he said, in "groping about for some middle ground between right and wrong," or in "a policy of 'don't care' on a question about which all true men do care." And there is ample evidence that he understood rightly the policy of the South. It is very doubtful whether any large extension of cultivation by slave labour was economically possible in Kansas or in regions yet further North, but we have seen to what lengths the Southern leaders would go in the attempt to secure even a limited recognition of slavery as lawful in a new State. They were not succeeding in the business of the Kansas Constitution. But they had a very good prospect of a far more important success. The celebrated dicta of Chief Justice Taney and other judges in the Dred Scott case had not amounted to an actual decision, nor if they had would a single decision have been irreversible. Whether the principle of them should become fixed in American Constitutional law depended (though this could not be openly said) on whether future

appointments to the Supreme Court were to be made by a President who shared Taney's views; whether the executive action of the President was governed by the same views; and on the subtle pressure which outside opinion does exercise, and in this case had surely exercised, upon judicial minds. If the simple principle that the right to a slave is just one form of the ordinary right to property once became firmly fixed in American jurisprudence it is hard to see how any laws prohibiting slavery could have continued to be held constitutional except in States which were free States when the Constitution was adopted. Of course, a State like New York where slaves were industrially useless would not therefore have been filled with slave plantations, but, among a loyally minded people, the tradition which reprobated slavery would have been greatly weakened. The South would have been freed from the sense that slavery was a doomed institution. If attempts to plant slavery further in the West with profit failed, there was Cuba and there was Central America, on which filibustering raids already found favour in the South, and in which the national Government might be led to adopt schemes of conquest or annexation. Moreover, it was avowed by leaders like Jefferson Davis that though it might be impracticable to hope for the repeal of the prohibition of the slave trade, at least some relaxation of its severity ought to be striven for, in the interest of Texas and New Mexico and of possible future Territories where there might be room for more slaves. Such were the views of the leaders whose influence preponderated with the present President and in the main with the present Congress. When Lincoln judged that a determined stand against their policy was required, and further that no such stand could be possible to a party which had embraced Douglas with his principle, " I care not whether slavery be voted up or voted down," there is no doubt now that he was right and the great body of Republican authority opposed to him wrong.

When Lincoln and his friends in Illinois determined

to fight Douglas, it became impossible for the Republican party as a whole to fall far behind them. This was in itself at that crisis an important thing. Lincoln added greatly to its importance by the opening words in the first speech of his campaign. They were the most carefully prepared words that he had yet spoken, and the most momentous that he had spoken till now or perhaps ever spoke. There is nothing in them for which what has been said of the situation and of his views will not have prepared us, and nothing which thousands of men might not have said to one another in private for a year or two before. But the first public avowal by a responsible man in trenchant phrase, that a grave issue has been joined upon which one party or the other must accept entire defeat, may be an event of great and perilous consequence.

He said: "If we could first know where we are and whither we are tending, we could better judge what to do and how to do it. We are now far into the fifth year since a policy was initiated with the avowed object, and confident promise, of putting an end to slavery agitation. Under the operation of that policy, that agitation has not only not ceased, but has constantly augmented. In my opinion it will not cease until a crisis shall have been reached and passed. 'A house divided against itself cannot stand.' I believe this Government cannot endure permanently half slave and half free. I do not expect the Union to be dissolved—I do not expect the house to fall—but I do expect that it will cease to be divided. It will become all one thing or all the other. Either the opponents of slavery will arrest the further spread of it and place it where the public mind shall rest in the belief that it is in course of ultimate extinction, or its advocates will push it forward till it shall become lawful alike in all the States, old as well as new—North as well as South."

It may perhaps be said that American public opinion has in the past been very timid in facing clear-cut issues. But, as has already been observed, an apt phrase crystal-

lising the unspoken thought of many is even more readily
caught up in America than anywhere else; so, though
but few people in States at a distance paid much attention
to the rest of the debates, or for a while again to Lincoln,
the comparison of the house divided against itself produced an effect in the country which did not wear out.
In this whole passage, moreover, Lincoln had certainly
formulated the question before the nation more boldly,
more clearly, more truly than any one before. It is impossible to estimate such influences precisely, but this was
among the speeches that rank as important actions, and
the story, most characteristic of the speaker, which lay
behind it, is worth relating in detail. Lincoln had actually
in a speech in 1856 declared that the United States could
not long endure half slave and half free. "What in
God's name," said some friend after the meeting, "could
induce you to promulgate such an opinion?" "Upon
my soul," he said, "I think it is true," and he could not
be argued out of this opinion. Finally the friend protested that, true or not, no good could come of spreading
this opinion abroad, and after grave reflection Lincoln
promised not to utter it again for the present. Now, in
1858, having prepared his speech he read it to Herndon.
Herndon questioned whether the passage on the divided
house was politic. Lincoln said: "I would rather be
defeated with this expression in my speech, and uphold
and discuss it before the people, than be victorious without it." Once more, just before he delivered it, he read
it over to a dozen or so of his closest supporters, for it
was his way to discuss his intentions fully with friends,
sometimes accepting their advice most submissively and
sometimes disregarding it wholly. One said it was
"ahead of its time," another that it was a "damned
fool utterance." All more or less strongly condemned
it, except this time Herndon, who, according to his
recollection, said, "It will make you President." He
listened to all and then addressed them, we are told, substantially as follows: "Friends, this thing has been retarded long enough. The time has come when these

sentiments should be uttered; and if it is decreed that I
should go down because of this speech, then let me go
down linked to the truth—let me die in the advocacy of
what is just and right." Rather a memorable pronouncement of a candidate to his committee; and the man who
records it is insistent upon every little illustration he can
find both of Lincoln's cunning and of his ambition.

Lincoln did go down in this particular contest. Many
friends wrote and reproved him after this " damned
fool utterance," but his defeat was not, after all, attributed to that. All the same he did himself assure his
defeat, and he did it with extraordinary skill, for the
purpose of ensuring that the next President should be a
Republican President, though it is impossible he should
at that time have counted upon being himself that Republican. Each candidate had undertaken to answer set
questions which his opponent might propound to him.
And great public attention was paid to the answers to
these interrogatories. The Dred Scott judgments created
a great difficulty for Douglas; he was bound to treat
them as right; but if they were right and Congress had
no power to prohibit slavery in a Territory, neither could
a Territorial Legislature with authority delegated by
Congress have that power; and, if this were made clear,
it would seem there was an end of that free choice of
the people in the Territories of which Douglas had been
the great advocate. Douglas would use all his evasive
skill in keeping away from this difficult point. If, however, he could be forced to face it Lincoln knew what
he would say. He would say that slavery would not be
actually unlawful in a Territory, but would never actually
exist in it if the Territorial Legislature chose to abstain,
as it could, from passing any of the laws which would
in practice be necessary to protect slave property. By
advocating this view Douglas would fully reassure those
of his former supporters in Illinois who puzzled themselves on the Dred Scott case, but he would infuriate the
South. Lincoln determined to force Douglas into this
position by the questions which he challenged him to

answer. When he told his friends of his ambition, they all told him he would lose his election. "Gentlemen," said Lincoln, "I am killing larger game; if Douglas answers, he can never be President, and the battle of 1860 is worth a hundred of this." The South was already angry with Douglas for his action over the Kansas Constitution, but he would have been an invincible candidate for the South to support in 1860, and it must have told in his favour that his offence then had been one of plain honesty. But in this fresh offence the Southern leaders had some cause to accuse him of double dealing, and they swore he should not be President.

A majority of the new Illinois Legislature returned Douglas to the Senate. Lincoln, however, had an actual majority of the votes of the whole State. Probably also he had gained a hold on Illinois for the future out of all proportion to the actual number of votes then given against the popular Douglas, and above all he had gathered to him a band of supporters who had unbounded belief in him. But his fall for the moment was little noticed or regretted outside Illinois, or at any rate in the great Eastern States, to which Illinois was, so to speak, the provinces and he a provincial attorney. His first words in the campaign had made a stir, but the rest of his speeches in these long debates could not be much noticed at a distance. Douglas had won, and the presumption was that he had proved himself the better man. Lincoln had performed what, apart from results, was a work of intellectual merit beyond the compass of any American statesman since Hamilton; moreover, as can now be seen, there had been great results; for, first, the young Republican party had not capitulated and collapsed, and, then, the great Democratic party, established in power, in indifference, and in complicity with wrong, was split clean in two. But these were not results that could be read yet awhile in election figures. Meanwhile the exhausted Lincoln reconciled himself for the moment to failure. As a private man he was thoroughly content that he could soon work off his debt for his election

expenses, could earn about £500 a year, and be secure
in the possession of the little house and the £2,000 capital
which was " as much as any man ought to have." As a
public man he was sadly proud that he had at least " said
some words which may bear fruit after I am forgotten."
Persistent melancholy and incurable elasticity can go together, and they make a very strong combination. The
tone of resignation had not passed away from his comparatively intimate letters when he was writing little
notes to one political acquaintance and another inciting
them to look forward to the fun of the next fight.

4. *John Brown.*

For the next few months the excitements of the great
political world concern this biography little. There was
strife between Davis and Douglas in the Senate. At a
meeting strong against slavery, Seward regained courage
from the occasion and roused the North with grave and
earnest words about the "irrepressible conflict." The
"underground railway," or chain of friendly houses by
which fugitive slaves were stealthily passed on to Canada,
became famous. Methodist professors riotously attempted to rescue an arrested fugitive at Oberlin. A
Southern grand jury threw out the bill of indictment
against a slave-trading crew caught red-handed. In California Democrats belonging to what was nicknamed
" the chivalry " forced upon Senator Broderick, a literally
democratic Irishman and the bravest of the Democrats
who stood out for fair treatment to Kansas, a duel in
which he might fairly be said to have been murdered.
The one event which demands more than allusion was
the raid and the death of John Brown.

John Brown, in whom Puritan religion, as strict as
that of his ancestors on the *Mayflower,* put forth gentler
beauties of character than his sanguinary mission may
suggest, had been somewhat of a failure as a scientific
farmer, but as a leader of fighting men in desperate adventure only such men as Drake or Garibaldi seem to
have excelled him. More particularly in the commotions

in Kansas he had led forays, slain ruthlessly, witnessed dry-eyed the deaths of several of his tall, strong sons, and as a rule earned success by cool judgment—all, as he was absolutely sure, at the clear call of God. In October, 1859—how and with whose help the stroke was prepared seems to be a question of some mystery—John Brown, gathering a little band of Abolitionists and negroes, invaded the slave States and seized the United States arsenal at Harper's Ferry in Virginia. In the details, which do not matter, of this tiny campaign, John Brown seems, for the first time in his life, to have blundered badly. This was the only thing that lay upon his conscience towards the last. What manner of success he can have expected does not appear; most likely he had neither care nor definite expectation as to the result. The United States troops under Robert Lee, soon to be famous, of course overcame him quickly. One of his prisoners describes how he held out to the last; a dead son beside him; one hand on the pulse of a dying son, his rifle in the other. He was captured, desperately wounded. Southerners could not believe the fact that Brown had not contemplated some hideous uprising of slaves against their wives and children, but he only wished to conquer them with the sword of the Lord and of Gideon, quietly freeing slaves as he went. So naturally there was talk of lynching, but the Virginian gentlemen concerned would not have that. Governor Wise, of Virginia, had some talk with him and justified his own high character rather than Brown's by the estimate he gave of him in a speech at Richmond. Brown was hanged. "Stonewall" Jackson, a brother fanatic, if that is the word, felt the spectacle "awful," as he never felt slaughter in battle, and "put up a prayer that if possible Brown might be saved." "So perish all foes of the human race," said the officer commanding on the occasion, and the South generally felt the like.

A little before his death Brown was asked: "How do you justify your acts?" He said: "I think, my friend, you are guilty of a great wrong against God and humanity

—I say it without wishing to be offensive—and it would be perfectly right for any one to interfere with you so far as to free those you wilfully and wickedly hold in bondage. I think I did right, and that others will do right who interfere with you at any time and at all times." In a conversation still later, he is reported to have concluded: " I wish to say furthermore that you had better—all you people at the South—prepare yourselves for a settlement of this question, that must come up for settlement sooner than you are prepared for it. You may dispose of me very easily. I am nearly disposed of now. But this question is still to be settled—this negro question I mean. The end of that is not yet." To a friend he wrote that he rejoiced like Paul because he knew like Paul that " if they killed him, it would greatly advance the cause of Christ."

Lincoln, who regarded lawlessness and slavery as twin evils, could only say of John Brown's raid: " That affair, in its philosophy, corresponds with the many attempts related in history at the assassination of kings and emperors. An enthusiast broods over the oppression of a people till he fancies himself commissioned by Heaven to liberate them. He ventures the attempt, which ends in little else than his own execution. Orsini's attempt on Louis Napoleon and John Brown's attempt at Harper's Ferry were, in their philosophy, precisely the same." Seward, it must be recorded, spoke far more sympathetically of him than Lincoln; and far more justly, for there is a flaw somewhere in this example, as his chief biographer regards it, of " Mr. Lincoln's common-sense judgment." John Brown had at least left to every healthy-minded Northern boy a memory worth much in the coming years of war and, one hopes, ever after. He had well deserved to be the subject of a song which, whatever may be its technical merits as literature, does stir. Emerson took the same view of him as the song writer, and Victor Hugo suggested as an epitaph for him: " Pro Christo sicut Christus." A calmer poet, Longfellow, wrote in his diary on Friday, December 2, 1859, the day

when Brown was hanged: " This will be a great day in
our history, the date of a new revolution, quite as much
needed as the old one. Even now, as I write, they are
leading old John Brown to execution in Virginia for
attempting to rescue slaves. This is sowing the wind to
reap the whirlwind, which will soon come."

Any one who is interested in Lincoln is almost forced
to linger over the contrasting though slighter character
who crossed the stage just before he suddenly took the
principal part upon it. Men like John Brown may be
fitly ranked with the equally rare men who, steering a
very different course, have consistently acted out the
principles of the Quakers, constraining no man whether
by violence or by law, yet going into the thick of life
prepared at all times to risk all. All such men are abnormal in the sense that most men literally could not put
life through on any similar plan and would be wrong and
foolish to try. The reason is that most men have a wider
range of sympathy and of intellect than they. But the
common sense of most of us revolts from any attitude of
condemnation or condescension towards them; for they
are more disinterested than most of us, more single-
minded, and in their own field often more successful.
With a very clear conscience we refuse to take example
from these men whose very defects have operated in them
as a special call; but undoubtedly most of us regard them
with a warmth of sympathy which we are slow to accord
to safer guides. We turn now from John Brown, who
saw in slavery a great oppression, and was very angry, and
went ahead slaying the nearest oppressor and liberating
—for some days at least—the nearest slave, to a patient
being, who, long ago in his youth, had boiled with anger
against slavery, but whose whole soul now expressed itself
in a policy of deadly moderation towards it: " Let us put
back slavery where the fathers placed it, and there let
it rest in peace." We are to study how he acted when
in power. In almost every department of policy we shall
see him watching and waiting while blood flows, suspending judgment, temporising, making trial of this expedient

and of that, adopting in the end, quite unthanked, the measure of which most men will say, when it succeeds, "That is what we always said should be done." Above all, in that point of policy which most interests us, we shall witness the long postponement of the blow that killed negro slavery, the steady subordination of this particular issue to what will not at once appeal to us as a larger and a higher issue. All this provoked at the time in many excellent and clever men dissatisfaction and deep suspicion; they longed for a leader whose heart visibly glowed with a sacred passion; they attributed his patience, the one quality of greatness which after a while everybody might have discerned in him, not to a self-mastery which almost passed belief, but to a tepid disposition and a mediocre if not a low level of desire. We who read of him to-day shall not escape our moments of lively sympathy with these grumblers of the time; we shall wish that this man could ever plunge, that he could ever see red, ever commit some passionate injustice; we shall suspect him of being, in the phrase of a great philosopher, "a disgustingly well-regulated person," lacking that indefinable quality akin to the honest passions of us ordinary men, but deeper and stronger, which alone could compel and could reward any true reverence for his memory. These moments will recur but they cannot last. A thousand little things, apparent on the surface but deeply significant; almost every trivial anecdote of his boyhood, his prime, or his closing years; his few recorded confidences; his equally few speeches made under strong emotion; the lineaments of his face described by observers whom photography corroborated; all these absolutely forbid any conception of Abraham Lincoln as a worthy commonplace person fortunately fitted to the requirements of his office at the moment, or as merely a "good man" in the negative and disparaging sense to which that term is often wrested. It is really evident that there were no frigid perfections about him at all; indeed the weakness of some parts of his conduct is so unlike what seems to be required of a successful ruler that it is certain some

almost unexampled quality of heart and mind went to the
doing of what he did. There is no need to define that
quality. The general wisdom of his statesmanship will
perhaps appear greater and its not infrequent errors less
the more fully the circumstances are appreciated. As to
the man, perhaps the sense will grow upon us that this
balanced and calculating person, with his finger on the
pulse of the electorate while he cracked his uncensored
jests with all comers, did of set purpose drink and refill
and drink again as full and fiery a cup of sacrifice as ever
was pressed to the lips of hero or of saint.

5. The Election of Lincoln.

Unlooked-for events were now raising Lincoln to the
highest place which his ambition could contemplate. His
own action in the months that followed his defeat by
Douglas cannot have contributed much to his surprising
elevation, yet it illustrates well his strength and his weakness, his real fitness, now and then startlingly revealed,
for the highest position, and the superficial unfitness which
long hid his capacity from many acute contemporaries.

In December, 1859, he made a number of speeches in
Kansas and elsewhere in the West, and in February, 1860,
he gave a memorable address in the Cooper Institute in
New York before as consciously intellectual an audience
as could be collected in that city, proceeding afterwards
to speak in several cities of New England. His appearance at the Cooper Institute, in particular, was a critical
venture, and he knew it. There was natural curiosity
about this untutored man from the West. An exaggerated report of his wit prepared the way for probable
disappointment. The surprise which awaited his hearers
was of a different kind; they were prepared for a florid
Western eloquence offensive to ears which were used to a
less spontaneous turgidity; they heard instead a speech
with no ornament at all, whose only beauty was that it
was true and that the speaker felt it. The single flaw
in the Cooper Institute speech has already been cited, the
narrow view of Western respectability as to John Brown.

For the rest, this speech, dry enough in a sense, is an incomparably masterly statement of the then political situation, reaching from its far back origin to the precise and definite question requiring decision at that moment. Mr. Choate, who as a young man was present, set down of late years his vivid recollection of that evening. " He appeared in every sense of the word like one of the plain people among whom he loved to be counted. At first sight there was nothing impressive or imposing about him; his clothes hung awkwardly on his giant frame; his face was of a dark pallor without the slightest tinge of colour; his seamed and rugged features bore the furrows of hardship and struggle; his deep-set eyes looked sad and anxious; his countenance in repose gave little evidence of the brilliant power which raised him from the lowest to the highest station among his countrymen; as he talked to me before the meeting he seemed ill at ease." We know, as a fact, that among his causes of apprehension, he was for the first time painfully conscious of those clothes. "When he spoke," proceeds Mr. Choate, " he was transformed; his eye kindled, his voice rang, his face shone and seemed to light up the whole assembly. For an hour and a half he held his audience in the hollow of his hand. His style of speech and manner of delivery were severely simple. What Lowell called ' the grand simplicities of the Bible,' with which he was so familiar, were reflected in his discourse. . . . It was marvellous to see how this untutored man, by mere self-discipline and the chastening of his own spirit, had outgrown all meretricious arts, and found his way to the grandeur and strength of absolute simplicity."

The newspapers of the day after this speech confirm these reverent reminiscences. On this, his first introduction to the cultivated world of the East, Lincoln's audience were at the moment and for the moment conscious of the power which he revealed. The Cooper Institute speech takes the plain principle that slavery is wrong, and draws the plain inference that it is idle to seek for common ground with men who say it is right. Strange but

tragically frequent examples show how rare it is for
statesmen in times of crisis to grasp the essential truth
so simply. It is creditable to the leading men of New
York that they recognised a speech which just at that
time urged this plain thing in sufficiently plain language
as a very great speech, and had an inkling of great and
simple qualities in the man who made it. It is not
specially discreditable that very soon and for a long while
part of them, or of those who were influenced by their
report, reverted to their former prejudices in regard to
Lincoln. When they saw him thrust by election managers
into the Presidency, very few indeed of what might
be called the better sort believed, or could easily learn,
that his great qualities were great enough to compensate
easily for the many things he lacked. This specially
grotesque specimen of the wild West was soon seen not
to be of the charlatan type; as a natural alternative he
was assumed to be something of a simpleton. Many
intelligent men retained this view of him throughout the
years of his trial, and, only when his triumph and tragic
death set going a sort of Lincoln myth, began to recollect
that " I came to love and trust him even before I knew
him," or the like. A single speech like this at the Cooper
Institute might be enough to show a later time that
Lincoln was a man of great intellect, but it could really
do little to prepare men in the East for what they next
heard of him.

Already a movement was afoot among his friends in
Illinois to secure his nomination for the Presidency at
the Convention of the Republican party which was to
be held in Chicago in May. Before that Convention
could assemble it had become fairly certain that whoever might be chosen as the Republican candidate would
be President of the United States, and signs were not
wanting that he would be faced with grave peril to the
Union. For the Democratic party, which had met in
Convention at Charleston in April, had proceeded to
split into two sections, Northern and Southern. This
memorable Convention was a dignified assembly gathered

in a serious mood in a city of some antiquity and social charm. From the first, however, a latent antipathy between the Northern and the Southern delegates made itself felt. The Northerners, predisposed to a certain deference towards the South and prepared to appreciate its graceful hospitality, experienced an uneasy sense that they were regarded as social inferiors. Worse trouble than this appeared when the Convention met for its first business, the framing of the party platform. Whether the position which Lincoln had forced Douglas to take up had precipitated this result or not, dissension between Northern and Southern Democrats on the subject of slavery had already manifested itself in Congress, and in the party Convention the division became irreparable. Douglas, it will be remembered, had started with the principle that slavery in the Territories formed a question for the people of each territory to decide; he had felt bound to accept the doctrine underlying the Dred Scott judgments, according to which slavery was by the Constitution lawful in all territories; pressed by Lincoln, he had tried to reconcile his original position with this doctrine by maintaining that while slavery was by the Constitution lawful in every Territory it was nevertheless lawful for a Territorial Legislature to make slave-owning practically impossible. In framing a declaration of the party principles as to slavery the Southern delegates in the Democratic Convention aimed at meeting this evasion. With considerable show of logic they asserted, in the party platform which they proposed, not merely the abstract rightfulness and lawfulness of slavery, but the duty of Congress itself to make any provision that might be necessary to protect it in the Territories. To this the Northern majority of the delegates could not consent; they carried an amendment declaring merely that they would abide by any decision of the Supreme Court as to slavery. Thereupon the delegates, not indeed of the whole South but of all the cotton-growing States except Georgia, withdrew from the Convention. The remaining delegates were, under the rules of the Con-

vention, too few to select a candidate for the Presidency, and the Convention adjourned, to re-assemble at Baltimore in June. Eventually, after attempts at reunion and further dissensions, two separate Democratic Conventions at Baltimore, a Northern and a Southern, nominated, as their respective candidates, Stephen Douglas, the obvious choice with whom, if the Southerners had cared to temporise further, a united Democratic party could have swept the polls, and John C. Breckinridge of Kentucky, a gentleman not otherwise known than as the standard bearer on this great occasion of the undisguised and unmitigated claims of the slave owners.

Thus it was that the American Democratic party forfeited power for twenty-four years, divided between the consistent maintenance of a paradox and the adroit maintenance of inconsistency. Another party in this election demands a moment's notice. A Convention of delegates, claiming to represent the old Whigs, met also at Baltimore and declared merely that it stood for " the Constitution of the country, the union of the States, and the enforcement of the laws." They nominated for the Presidency John Bell of Tennessee, and for the Vice-Presidency Edward Everett. This latter gentleman was afterwards chosen as the orator of the day at the ceremony on the battlefield of Gettysburg when Lincoln's most famous speech was spoken. He was a travelled man and a scholar; he was Secretary of State for a little while under Fillmore, and dealt honestly and firmly with the then troublous question of Cuba. His orations deserve to be looked at, for they are favourable examples of the eloquence which American taste applauded, and as such they help to show how original Lincoln was in the simpler beauty of his own simpler diction. In justice to the Whigs, let it be noted that they declared for the maintenance of the Union, committing themselves with decision on the question of the morrow; but it was a singular platform that resolutely and totally ignored the only issue of the day. Few politicians can really afford to despise either this conspicuously foolish attempt to over-

come a difficulty by shutting one's eyes to it, or the more plausible proposal of the Northern Democrats to continue temporising with a movement for slavery in which they were neither bold enough nor corrupted enough to join. The consequences, now known to us, of a determined stand against the advance of slavery were instinctively foreseen by these men, and they cannot be blamed for shrinking from them. Yet the historian now, knowing that those consequences exceeded in terror all that could have been foreseen, can only agree with the judgment expressed by Lincoln in one of his Kansas speeches: "We want and must have a national policy as to slavery which deals with it as being a wrong. Whoever would prevent slavery becoming national and perpetual yields all when he yields to a policy which treats it either as being right, or as being a matter of indifference." The Republican party had been founded upon just this opinion. Electoral victory was now being prepared for it, not because a majority was likely yet to take so resolute a view, but because its effective opponents were divided between those who had gone the length of calling slavery right and those who strove to treat it as indifferent. The fate of America may be said to have depended in the early months of 1860 on whether the nominee of the Republican party was a man who would maintain its principles with irresolution, or with obstinacy, or with firm moderation.

When it had first been suggested to Lincoln in the course of 1859 that he might be that nominee he said, "I do not think myself fit for the Presidency." This was probably his sincere opinion at the moment, though perhaps the moment was one of dejection. In any case his opinion soon changed, and though it is not clear whether he encouraged his friends to bring his name forward, we know in a general way that when they decided to do so he used every effort of his own to help them. We must accept without reserve Herndon's reiterated assertion that Lincoln was intensely ambitious; and, if ambition means the eager desire for great oppor-

tunities, the depreciation of it, which has long been a commonplace of literature, and which may be traced back to the Epicureans, is a piece of cant which ought to be withdrawn from currency, and ambition, commensurate with the powers which each man can discover in himself, should be frankly recognised as a part of Christian duty. In judging him to be the best man for the Presidency, Lincoln's Illinois friends and he himself formed a very sensible judgment, but they did so in flagrant contradiction to many superficial appearances. This candidate for the chief magistracy at a critical time of one of the great nations of the world had never administered any concern much larger than that post office that he once " carried around in his hat." Of the several other gentlemen whose names were before the party there was none who might not seem greatly to surpass him in experience of affairs. To one of them, Seward, the nomination seemed to belong almost of right. Chase and Seward both were known and dignified figures in that great assembly the Senate. Chase was of proved rectitude and courage, Seward of proved and very considerable ability. Chase had been Governor of Ohio, Seward of New York State; and the position of Governor in a State—a State it must be remembered is independent in almost the whole of what we call domestic politics—is strictly analogous to the position of President in the Union, and, especially in a great State, is the best training ground for the Presidency. But beyond this, Seward, between whom and Lincoln the real contest lay, had for some time filled a recognised though unofficial position as the leader of his party. He had failed, as has been seen in his dealings with Douglas, in stern insistence upon principle, but the failure was due rather to his sanguine and hopeful temper than to lack of courage. On the whole from the time when he first stood up against Webster in the discussions of 1850, when Lincoln was both silent and obscure, he had earned his position well. Hereafter, as Lincoln's subordinate, he was to do his country first-rate service, and to earn a pure fame as

the most generously loyal subordinate to a chief whom he had thought himself fit to command. We happen to have ample means of estimating now all Lincoln's Republican competitors; we know that none of the rest were equal to Seward; and we know that Seward himself, if he had had his way, would have brought the common cause to ruin. Looking back now at the comparison which Lincoln, when he entered into the contest, must have drawn between himself and Seward—for of the rest we need not take account—we can see that to himself at least and some few in Illinois he had now proved his capacities, and that in Seward's public record, more especially in his attitude towards Douglas, he had the means of measuring Seward. In spite of the far greater experience of the latter he may have thought himself to be his superior in that indefinable thing—the sheer strength of a man. Not only may he have thought this; he must have known it. He had shown his grasp of the essential facts when he forced the Republican party to do battle with Douglas and the party of indifference; he showed the same now when, after long years of patience and self-discipline, he pushed himself into Seward's place as the Republican leader.

All the same, what little we know of the methods by which he now helped his own promotion suggests that the people who then and long after set him down as a second-rate person may have had a good deal to go upon. A kind friend has produced a letter which he wrote in March, 1860, to a Kansas gentleman who desired to be a delegate to the Republican Convention, and who offered, upon condition, to persuade his fellow delegates from Kansas to support Lincoln. Here is the letter: "As to your kind wishes for myself, allow me to say I cannot enter the ring on the money basis—first because in the main it is wrong; and secondly I have not and cannot get the money. I say in the main the use of money is wrong; but for certain objects in a political contest the use of some is both right and indispensable. With me, as with yourself, this long struggle has been one

of great pecuniary loss. I now distinctly say this: If you shall be appointed a delegate to Chicago I will furnish one hundred dollars to bear the expenses of the trip." The Kansas gentleman failed to obtain the support of the Kansas delegates as a body for Lincoln. Lincoln none the less held to his promise of a hundred dollars if the man came to Chicago; and, having, we are assured, much confidence in him, took the earliest opportunity of appointing him to a lucrative office, besides consulting him as to other appointments in Kansas. This is all that we know of the affair, but our informant presents it as one of a number of instances in which Lincoln good-naturedly trusted a man too soon, and obstinately clung to his mistake. As to the appointment, the man had evidently begun by soliciting money in a way which would have marked him to most of us as a somewhat unsuitable candidate for any important post; and the payment of the hundred dollars plainly transgresses a code both of honour and of prudence which most politicians will recognise and which should not need definition. To say, as Lincoln probably said to himself, that there is nothing intrinsically wrong in a moderate payment for expenses to a fellow worker in a public cause, whom you believe to have sacrificed much, is to ignore the point, indeed several points. Lincoln, hungry now for some success in his own unrewarded career, was tempted to a small manœuvre by which he might pick up a little support; he was at the same time tempted, no less, to act generously (according to his means) towards a man who, he readily believed, had made sacrifices like his own. He was not the man to stand against this double temptation.

Petty lapses of this order, especially when the delinquent may be seen to hesitate and excuse himself, are more irritating than many larger and more brazen offences, for they give us the sense of not knowing where we are. When they are committed by a man of seemingly strong and high character, it is well to ask just what they signify. Some of the shrewdest observers of Lincoln,

friendly and unfriendly, concur in their description of
the weaknesses of which this incident may serve as the
example, weaknesses partly belonging to his temperament,
but partly such as a man risen from poverty, with little
variety of experience and with no background of home
training, stands small chance of escaping. For one thing
his judgment of men and how to treat them was as bad in
some ways as it was good in others. His own sure grasp
of the largest and commonest things in life, and his sober
and measured trust in human nature as a whole, gave him
a rare knowledge of the mind of the people in the mass.
So, too, when he had known a man long, or been with
him or against him in important transactions, he sometimes developed great insight and sureness of touch; and,
when the man was at bottom trustworthy, his robust confidence in him was sometimes of great public service. But
he had no gift of rapid perception and no instinctive tact
or prudence in regard to the very numerous and very
various men with whom he had slight dealings on which
he could bestow no thought. This is common with men
who have risen from poverty; if they have not become
hard and suspicious, they are generally obtuse to the
minor indications by which shrewd men of education know
the impostor, and they are perversely indulgent to little
meannesses in their fellows which they are incapable of
committing themselves. In Lincoln this was aggravated
by an immense good-nature—as he confessed, he could
hardly say " no ";—it was an obstinate good-nature,
which found a naughty pleasure in refusing to be corrected; and if it should happen that the object of his
weak benevolence had given him personal cause of offence, the good-nature became more incorrigible than
ever. Moreover, Lincoln's strength was a slow strength,
shown most in matters in which elementary principles of
right or the concentration of intense thought guided him.
Where minor and more subtle principles of conduct
should have come in, on questions which had not come
within the range of his reflection so far and to which,
amidst his heavy duties, he could not spare much cogi-

tation, he would not always show acute perception, and, which is far worse, he would often show weakness of will. The present instance may be ever so trifling, yet it does relate to the indistinct and dangerous borderland of political corruption. It need arouse no very serious suspicions. Mr. Herndon, whose pertinacious researches unearthed that Kansas gentleman's correspondence, and who is keenly censorious of Lincoln's fault, in the upshot trusts and reveres Lincoln. And the massive testimony of his keenest critics to his honesty quite decides the matter. But Lincoln had lived in a simple Western town, not in one of the already polluted great cities; he was a poor man himself and took the fact that wealth was used against him as a part of the inevitable drawbacks of his lot; and it is certain that he did not clearly take account of the whole business of corruption and jobbery as a hideous and growing peril to America. It is certain too that he lacked the delicate perception of propriety in such matters, or the strict resolution in adhering to it on small occasions, which might have been possessed by a far less honest man. The severest criticisms which Lincoln afterwards incurred were directed to the appointments which he made; we shall see hereafter that he had very solid reasons for his general conduct in such matters; but it cannot be said with conviction that he had that horror of appointment on other grounds than merit which enlightens, though it does not always govern, more educated statesmen. His administration would have been more successful, and the legacy he left to American public life more bountiful, if his traditions, or the length of his day's work, had allowed him to be more careful in these things. As it is he was not commended to the people of America and must not be commended to us by the absence of defects as a ruler or as a man, but by the qualities to which his defects belonged. An acute literary man wrote of Lincoln, when he had been three years in office, these remarkable words: " You can't help feeling an interest in him, a sympathy and a kind of pity; feeling, too, that he has some qualities of great value, yet

fearing that his weak points may wreck him or may wreck something. His life seems a series of wise, sound conclusions, slowly reached, oddly worked out, on great questions with constant failures in administration of detail and dealings with individuals." It was evidently a clever man who wrote this; he would have been a wise man if he had known that the praise he was bestowing on Lincoln was immeasurably greater than the blame.

So the natural prejudice of those who welcomed Lincoln as a prophet in the Cooper Institute but found his candidature for the Presidency ridiculous, was not wholly without justification. His partisans, however—also not unjustly—used his humble origin for all it was worth. The Republicans of Illinois were assembled at Decatur in preparation for the Chicago Convention, when, amid tumultuous cheers, there marched in old John Hanks and another pioneer bearing on their shoulders two long fence rails labelled: "Two rails from a lot made by Abraham Lincoln and John Hanks in the Sangamon Bottom in the year 1830." "Gentlemen," said Lincoln, in response to loud calls, "I suppose you want to know something about those things. Well, the truth is, John Hanks and I did make rails in the Sangamon Bottom. I don't know whether we made those rails or not; fact is, I don't think they are a credit to the makers. But I do know this: I made rails then, and I think I could make better ones than these now." It is unnecessary to tell of the part those rails were to play in the coming campaign. It is a contemptible trait in books like that able novel "Democracy," that they treat the sentiment which attached to the " Rail-splitter " as anything but honourable.

The Republican Convention met at Chicago in circumstances of far less dignity than the Democratic Convention at Charleston. Processions and brass bands, rough fellows collected by Lincoln's managers, rowdies imported from New York by Seward's, filled the streets with noise; and the saloon keepers did good business. Yet the actual Convention consisted of grave men in an earnest mood. Besides Seward and Chase and Lincoln, Messrs. Cameron

of Pennsylvania and Bates of Missouri, of whom we shall hear later, were proposed for the Presidency. So also were Messrs. Dayton and Collamer, politicians of some repute; and McLean, of the Supreme Court, had some supporters. The prevalent expectation in the States was that Seward would easily secure the nomination, but it very soon appeared in the Convention that his opponents were too strong for that. Several ballots took place; there were the usual conferences and bargainings, which probably affected the result but little; Lincoln's managers, especially Judge David Davis, afterwards of the Supreme Court, were shrewd people; Lincoln had written to them expressly that they could make no bargain binding on him, but when Cameron was clearly out of the running they did promise Cameron's supporters a place in Lincoln's Cabinet, and a similar promise was made for one Caleb Smith. The delegates from Pennsylvania went on to Lincoln; then those of Ohio; and before long his victory was assured. A Committee of the Convention, some of them sick at heart, was sent to bear the invitation to Lincoln. He received them in his little house with a simple dignity which one of them has recorded; and as they came away one said, " Well, we might have chosen a handsomer article, but I doubt whether a better."

On the whole, if we can put aside the illusion which besets us, who read the preceding history if at all in the light of Lincoln's speeches, and to whom his competitors are mere names, this was the most surprising nomination ever made in America. Other Presidential candidates have been born in poverty, but none ever wore the scars of poverty so plainly; others have been intrinsically more obscure, but these have usually been chosen as bearing the hall-mark of eminent prosperity or gentility. Lincoln had indeed at this time displayed brilliant ability in the debates with Douglas, and he had really shown a statesman's grasp of the situation more than any other Republican leader. The friends in Illinois who put him forward —men like David Davis, who was a man of distinction himself—did so from a true appreciation of his powers.

But this does not seem to have been the case with the bulk of the delegates from other States. The explanation given us of their action is curious. The choice was not the result of merit; on the other hand, it was not the work of the ordinary wicked wire-puller, for what may be called the machine was working for Seward. The choice was made by plain representative Americans who set to themselves this question: " With what candidate can we beat Douglas? " and who found the answer in the prevalence of a popular impression, concerning Lincoln and Seward, which was in fact wholly mistaken. There was, it happens, earnest opposition to Seward among some Eastern Republicans on the good ground that he was a clean man but with doubtful associates. This opposition could not by itself have defeated him. What did defeat him was his reputation at the moment as a very advanced Republican who would scare away the support of the weaker brethren. He was, for instance, the author of the alarming phrase about " irrepressible conflict," and he had spoken once, in a phrase that was misinterpreted, about " a higher law than the Constitution." Lincoln had in action taken a far stronger line than Seward; he was also the author of the phrase about the house divided against itself; but then, besides the fact that Lincoln was well regarded just where Douglas was most popular, Lincoln was a less noted man than Seward and his stronger words occasioned less wide alarm. So, to please those who liked compromise, the Convention rejected a man who would certainly have compromised, and chose one who would give all that moderation demanded and die before he yielded one further inch. Many Americans have been disposed to trace in the raising up of Lincoln the hand of a Providence protecting their country in its worst need. It would be affectation to set their idea altogether aside; it is, at any rate, a memorable incident in the history of a democracy, permeated with excellent intentions but often hopelessly subject to inferior influences, that at this critical moment the fit man was chosen on the very ground of his supposed unfitness.

The result of the contest between the four Presidential candidates was rendered almost a foregone conclusion by the decision of the Democrats. Lincoln in deference to the usual and seemly procedure took no part in the campaign, nor do his doings in the next months concern us. Seward, to his great honour, after privately expressing his bitter chagrin at the bestowal of what was his due upon "a little Illinois attorney," threw himself whole-heartedly into the contest, and went about making admirable speeches. On the night of November 6, Lincoln sat alone with the operator in the telegraph box at Springfield, receiving as they came in the results of the elections of Presidential electors in the various States. Long before the returns were complete his knowledge of such matters made him sure of his return, and before he left that box he had solved in principle, as he afterwards declared, the first and by no means least important problem of his Presidency, the choice of a Cabinet.

The victory was in one aspect far from complete. If we look not at the votes in the Electoral College with which the formal choice of President lay, but at the popular votes by which the electors were returned, we shall see that the new President was elected by a minority of the American people. He had a large majority over Douglas, but if Douglas had received the votes which were given for the Southern Democrat, Breckinridge, he would have had a considerable majority over Lincoln, though the odd machinery of the Electoral College would still have kept him out of the Presidency. In another aspect it was a fatally significant victory. Lincoln's votes were drawn only from the Northern States; he carried almost all the free States and he carried no others. For the first time in American history, the united North had used its superior numbers to outvote the South. This would in any case have caused great vexation, and the personality of the man chosen by the North aggravated it. The election of Lincoln was greeted throughout the South with a howl of derision.

CHAPTER VI

SECESSION

1. *The Case of the South against the Union.*

THE Republicans of the North had given their votes upon a very clear issue, but probably few of them had fully realised how grave a result would follow. Within a few days of the election of Lincoln the first step in the movement of Secession had been taken, and before the new President entered upon his duties it was plain that either the dissatisfied States must be allowed to leave the Union or the Union must be maintained by war.

Englishmen at that time and since have found a difficulty in grasping the precise cause of the war that followed. Of those who were inclined to sympathise with the North, some regarded the war as being simply about slavery, and, while unhesitatingly opposed to slavery, wondered whether it was right to make war upon it; others, regarding it as a war for the Union and not against slavery at all, wondered whether it was right to make war for a Union that could not be peaceably maintained. Now it is seldom possible to state the cause of a war quite candidly in a single sentence, because as a rule there are on each side people who concur in the final rupture for somewhat different reasons. But, in this case, forecasting a conclusion which must be examined in some detail, we can state the cause of war in a very few sentences. If we ask first what the South fought for, the answer is: the leaders of the South and the great mass of the Southern people had a single supreme and all-embracing object in view, namely, to ensure the permanence and, if need be, the extension of the slave system; they carried with them, however, a certain number of Southerners who were opposed or at least averse to slavery,

but who thought that the right of their States to leave the Union or remain in it as they chose must be maintained. If we ask what the North fought for, the answer is: A majority, by no means overwhelming, of the Northern people refused to purchase the adhesion of the South by conniving at any further extension of slavery, and an overwhelming majority refused to let the South dissolve the Union for slavery or for any other cause.

The issue about slavery, then, became merged in another issue, concerning the Union, which had so far remained in the background.

The first thing that must be grasped about it is the total difference of view which now existed between North and South in regard to the very nature of their connection. The divergence had taken place so completely and in the main so quietly that each side now realised with surprise and indignation that the other held an opposite opinion. In the North the Union was regarded as constituting a permanent and unquestionable national unity from which it was flat rebellion for a State or any other combination of persons to secede. In the South the Union appeared merely as a peculiarly venerable treaty of alliance, of which the dissolution would be very painful, but which left each State a sovereign body with an indefeasible right to secede if in the last resort it judged that the painful necessity had come. In a few border States there was division and doubt on this subject, a fact which must have helped to hide from each side the true strength of opinion on the other. But, setting aside these border States, there were in the North some who doubted whether it was expedient to fight for the Union, but none of any consequence who doubted that it was constitutionally correct; and there were in the South men who insisted that no occasion to secede had arisen, but these very men, when outvoted in their States, maintained most passionately the absolute right of secession.

The two sides contended for two contrary doctrines of constitutional law. It is natural when parties are disputing over a question of political wisdom and of

moral right that each should claim for its contention if possible the sanction of acknowledged legal principle. So it was with the parties to the English Civil War, and the tendency to regard matters from a legal point of view is to this day deeply engrained in the mental habits of America. But North and South were really divided by something other than legal opinion, a difference in the objects to which their feelings of loyalty and patriotism were directed. This difference found apt expression in the Cabinet of President Buchanan, who of course remained in office between the election of Lincoln in November and his inauguration in March. General Cass of Michigan had formerly stood for the Presidency with the support of the South, and he held Cabinet office now as a sympathiser with the South upon slavery, but he was a Northerner. "I see how it is," he said to two of his colleagues; "you are a Virginian, and you are a South Carolinian; I am not a Michigander, I am an American."

In a former chapter the creation of the Union and the beginnings of a common national life have been traced in outline. Obstacles to the Union had existed both in the North and in the South, and, after it had been carried, the tendency to threaten disruption upon some slight conflict of interest had shown itself in each. But a proud sense of single nationality had soon become prevalent in both, and in the North nothing whatever had happened to set back this growth, for the idea which Lowell had once attributed to his Hosea Biglow of abjuring Union with slave owners was a negligible force. Undivided allegiance to the Union was the natural sentiment of citizens of Ohio or Wisconsin, States created by the authority of the Union out of the common dominion of the Union. It had become, if anything, more deeply engrained in the original States of the North, for their predominant occupation in commerce would tend in this particular to give them larger views. The pride of a Boston man in the Commonwealth of Massachusetts was of the same order as his pride in the city of Boston; both were largely pride in the part which Boston and

Massachusetts had taken in making the United States of America. Such a man knew well that South Carolina had once threatened secession, but, for that matter, the so-called Federalists of New England had once threatened it. The argument of Webster in the case of South Carolina was a classic, and was taken as conclusive on the question of legal right. The terser and more resonant declaration of President Jackson, a Southerner, and the response to it which thrilled all States, South or North, outside South Carolina, had set the seal to Webster's doctrines. There had been loud and ominous talk of secession lately; it was certainly not mere bluster; Northerners in the main were cautious politicians and had been tempted to go far to conciliate it. But if the claim of Southern States were put in practice, the whole North would now regard it not as a respectable claim, but as an outrage.

It is important to notice that the disposition to take this view did not depend upon advanced opinions against slavery. Some of the most violent opponents of slavery would care relatively little about the Constitution or the Union; they would at first hesitate as to whether a peaceful separation between States which felt so differently on a moral question like slavery was not a more Christian solution of their difference than a fratricidal war. On the other hand, men who cared little about slavery, and would gladly have sacrificed any convictions they had upon that matter for the sake of the Union, were at first none the less vehement in their anger at an attack upon the Union. There is, moreover, a more subtle but still important point to be observed in this connection. Democrats in the North inclined as a party to stringent and perhaps pedantically legal views of State rights as against the rights of the Union; but this by no means necessarily meant that they sympathised more than Republicans with the claim to dissolve the Union. They laid emphasis on State rights merely because they believed that these would be a bulwark against any sort of government tyranny, and that the large power which was reserved

to the local or provincial authorities of the States made
the government of the nation as a whole more truly
expressive of the will of the whole people. They now
found themselves entangled (as we shall see) in curious
doubts as to what the Federal Government might do to
maintain the Union, but they had not the faintest doubt
that the Union was meant to be maintained. The point
which is now being emphasised must not be misappre-
hended; differences of sentiment in regard to slavery, in
regard to State rights, in regard to the authority of
Government, did, as the war went on and the price was
paid, gravely embarrass the North; but it was a solid
and unhesitating North which said that the South had
no right to secede.

Up to a certain point the sense of patriotic pride in
the Union had grown also in the South. It was fostered
at first by the predominant part which the South played
in the political life of the country. But for a generation
past the sense of a separate interest of the South had
been growing still more vigorously. The political predominance of the South had continued, but under a standing menace of downfall as the North grew more populous
and the patriotism which it at first encouraged had become perverted into an arrogantly unconscious feeling
that the Union was an excellent thing on condition that it
was subservient to the South. The common interest of
the Southern States was slavery; and, when the Northerners had become a majority which might one day
dominate the Federal Government, this common interest
of the slave States found a weapon at hand in the doctrine
of the inherent sovereignty of each individual State. This
doctrine of State sovereignty had come to be held as
universally in the South as the strict Unionist doctrine
in the North, and held with as quiet and unshakable a
confidence that it could not be questioned. It does not
seem at all strange that the State, as against the Union,
should have remained the supreme object of loyalty in
old communities like those of South Carolina and Virginia,
abounding as they did in conservative influences which

were lacking in the North. But this provincial loyalty
was not in the same sense a natural growth in States like
Alabama or Mississippi. These, no less than Indiana
and Illinois, were the creatures of the Federal Congress,
set up within the memory of living men, with arbitrary
boundaries that cut across any old lines of division.
There was, in fact, no spontaneous feeling of allegiance
attaching to these political units, and the doctrine of
their sovereignty had no use except as a screen for the
interest in slavery which the Southern States had in common. But Calhoun, in a manner characteristic of his
peculiar and dangerous type of intellect, had early seen
in a view of State sovereignty, which would otherwise
have been obsolete, the most serviceable weapon for the
joint interests of the Southern States. In a society where
intellectual life was restricted, his ascendency had been
great, though his disciples had, reasonably enough,
thrown aside the qualifications which his subtle mind
had attached to the right of secession. Thus in the
Southern States generally, even among men most strongly
opposed to the actual proposal to secede, the real or
alleged constitutional right of a State to secede if it chose
now passed unquestioned and was even regarded as a
precious liberty.

It is impossible to avoid asking whether on this question of constitutional law the Northern opinion or the
Southern opinion was correct. (The question was indeed
an important question in determining the proper course
of procedure for a President when confronted with secession, but it must be protested that the moral right and
political wisdom of neither party in the war depended
mainly, if at all, upon this legal point. It was a question
of the construction which a court of law should put upon
a document which was not drawn up with any view to
determining this point.) If we go behind the Constitution, which was then and is now in force, to the original
document of which it took the place, we shall find it entitled " Articles of Confederation and Perpetual Union,"
but we shall not find any such provisions as men desirous

of creating a stable and permanent federal government might have been expected to frame. If we read the actual Constitution we shall find no word distinctly implying that a State could or could not secede. As to the real intention of its chief authors, there can be no doubt that they hoped and trusted the Union would prove indissoluble, and equally little doubt that they did not wish to obtrude upon those whom they asked to enter into it the thought that this step would be irrevocable. For the view taken in the South there is one really powerful argument, on which Jefferson Davis insisted passionately in the argumentative memoirs with which he solaced himself in old age. It is that in several of the States, when the Constitution was accepted, public declarations were made to the citizens of those States by their own representatives that a State might withdraw from the Union. But this is far from conclusive. No man gets rid of the obligation of a bond by telling a witness that he does not mean to be bound; the question is not what he means, but what the party with whom he deals must naturally take him to mean. Now the Constitution of the United States upon the face of it purports to create a government able to take its place among the other governments of the world, able if it declares war to wield the whole force of its country in that war, and able if it makes peace to impose that peace upon all its subjects. This seems to imply that the authority of that government over part of the country should be legally indefeasible. It would have been ridiculous if, during a war with Great Britain, States on the Canadian border should have had the legal right to secede, and set up a neutral government with a view to subsequent reunion with Great Britain. The sound legal view of this matter would seem to be: that the doctrine of secession is so repugnant to the primary intention with which the national instrument of government was framed that it could only have been supported by an express reservation of the right to secede in the Constitution itself.

The Duke of Argyll, one of the few British statesmen

of the time who followed this struggle with intelligent interest, briefly summed up the question thus: " I know of no government in the world that could possibly have admitted the right of secession from its own allegiance." Oddly enough, President Buchanan, in his Message to Congress on December 4, put the same point not less forcibly.

But to say—as in a legal sense we may—that the Southern States rebelled is not necessarily to say that they were wrong. The deliberate endeavour of a people to separate themselves from the political sovereignty under which they live and set up a new political community, in which their national life shall develop itself more fully or more securely, must always command a certain respect. Whether it is entitled further to the full sympathy and to the support or at least acquiescence of others is a question which in particular cases involves considerations such as cannot be foreseen in any abstract discussion of political theory. But, speaking very generally, it is a question in the main of the worth which we attribute on the one hand to the common life to which it is sought to give freer scope, and on the other hand to the common life which may thereby be weakened or broken up. It sometimes seems to be held that when a decided majority of the people whose voices can be heard, in a more or less defined area, elect to live for the future under a particular government, all enlightened men elsewhere would wish them to have their way. If any such principle could be accepted without qualification, few movements for independence would ever have been more completely justified than the secession of the Southern States. If we set aside the highland region of which mention has already been made, in the six cotton-growing States which first seceded, and in several of those which followed as soon as it was clear that secession would be resisted, the preponderance of opinion in favour of the movement was overwhelming. This was not only so among the educated and governing portions of society, which were interested in slavery. While the negroes themselves were

unorganised and dumb and made no stir for freedom, the poorer class of white people, to whom the institution of slavery was in reality oppressive, were quite unconscious of this; the enslavement of the negro appeared to them a tribute to their own dignity, and their indiscriminating spirit of independence responded enthusiastically to the appeal that they should assert themselves against the real or fancied pretensions of the North. So large a statement would require some qualification if we were here concerned with the life of a Southern leader; and there was of course a brief space, to be dealt with in this chapter, in which the question of secession hung in the balance, and it is true in this, as in every case, that the men who gave the initial push were few. But, broadly speaking, it is certain that the movement for secession was begun with at least as general an enthusiasm and maintained with at least as loyal a devotion as any national movement with which it can be compared. And yet to-day, just fifty-one years after the consummation of its failure, it may be doubted whether one soul among the people concerned regrets that it failed.

English people from that time to this have found the statement incredible; but the fact is that this imposing movement, in which rich and poor, gentle and simple, astute men of state and pious clergymen, went hand in hand to the verge of ruin and beyond, was undertaken simply and solely in behalf of slavery. Northern writers of the time found it so surprising that they took refuge in the theory of conspiracy, alleging that a handful of schemers succeeded, by the help of fictitious popular clamour and intimidation of their opponents, in launching the South upon a course to which the real mind of the people was averse. Later and calmer historical survey of the facts has completely dispelled this view; and the English suspicion, that there must have been some cause beyond and above slavery for desiring independence, never had any facts to support it. Since 1830 no exponent of Southern views had ever hinted at secession on any other ground than slavery; every Southern leader de-

clared with undoubted truth that on every other ground
he prized the Union; outside South Carolina every Southern leader made an earnest attempt before he surrendered
the Union cause to secure the guarantees he thought sufficient for slavery within the Union. The Southern statesman (for the soldiers were not statesmen) whose
character most attracts sympathy now was Alexander
Stephens, the Vice-President of the Southern Confederacy, and though he was the man who persisted longest
in the view that slavery could be adequately secured without secession, he was none the less entitled to speak for
the South in his remarkable words on the Constitution
adopted by the Southern Confederacy: " The new Constitution has put at rest for ever all the agitating questions relating to our peculiar institution, African slavery.
This was the immediate cause of the late rupture and
present revolution. The prevailing ideas entertained by
Jefferson and most of the leading statesmen at the time of
the old Constitution were that the enslavement of the
African was wrong in principle socially, morally, and
politically. Our new government is founded upon exactly the opposite idea; its foundations are laid, its corner
stone rests, upon the great truth that the negro is not the
equal of the white man; that slavery—subordination to
the white man—is his natural and normal condition.
This, our new government, is the first in the history of
the world based upon this great physical, philosophical,
and moral truth. The great objects of humanity are best
attained when there is conformity to the Creator's laws
and decrees." Equally explicit and void of shame was
the Convention of the State of Mississippi. " Our position," they declared, " is thoroughly identified with
slavery."

It is common to reproach the Southern leaders with
reckless folly. They tried to destroy the Union, which
they really valued, for the sake of slavery, which they
valued more; they in fact destroyed slavery; and they
did this, it is said, in alarm at an imaginary danger. This
is not a true ground of reproach to them. It is true

that the danger to slavery from the election of Lincoln was not immediately pressing. He neither would have done nor could have done more than to prevent during his four years of office any new acquisition of territory in the slave-holding interest, and to impose his veto on any Bill extending slavery within the existing territory of the Union. His successor after four years might or might not have been like-minded. He did not seem to stand for any overwhelming force in American politics; there was a majority opposed to him in both Houses of Congress; a great majority of the Supreme Court, which might have an important part to play, held views of the Constitution opposed to his; he had been elected by a minority only of the whole American people. Why could not the Southern States have sat still, secure that no great harm would happen to their institution for the present, and hoping that their former ascendency would come back to them with the changing fortunes of party strife? This is an argument which might be expected to have weighed with Southern statesmen if each of them had been anxious merely to keep up the value of his own slave property for his own lifetime, but this was far from being their case. It is hard for us to put ourselves at the point of view of men who could sincerely speak of their property in negroes as theirs by the "decree of the Creator"; but it is certain that within the last two generations trouble of mind as to the rightfulness of slavery had died out in a large part of the South; the typical Southern leader valued the peculiar form of society under which he lived and wished to hand it on intact to his children's children. If their preposterous principle be granted, the most extreme among them deserve the credit of statesmanlike insight for having seen, the moment that Lincoln was elected, that they must strike for their institution now if they wished it to endure. The Convention of South Carolina justly observed that the majority in the North had voted that slavery was sinful; they had done little more than express this abstract opinion, but they had done all that. Lincoln's administration might have done

apparently little, and after it the pendulum would probably have swung back. But the much-talked-of swing of the pendulum is the most delusive of political phenomena; America was never going to return to where it was before this first explicit national assertion of the wrongfulness of slavery had been made. It would have been hard to forecast how the end would come, or how soon; but the end was certain if the Southern States had elected to remain the countrymen of a people who were coming to regard their fundamental institution with growing reprobation. Lincoln had said, " This government cannot endure permanently, half slave and half free." Lincoln was right, and so from their own point of view, that of men not brave or wise enough to take in hand a difficult social reform, were the leaders who declared immediately for secession:

In no other contest of history are those elements in human affairs on which tragic dramatists are prone to dwell so clearly marked as in the American Civil War. No unsophisticated person now, except in ignorance as to the cause of the war, can hesitate as to which side enlists his sympathy, or can regard the victory of the North otherwise than as the costly and imperfect triumph of the right. But the wrong side—emphatically wrong —is not lacking in dignity or human worth; the long-drawn agony of the struggle is not purely horrible to contemplate; there is nothing that in this case makes us reluctant to acknowledge the merits of the men who took arms in the evil cause. The experience as to the relations between superior and inferior races, which is now at the command of every intelligent Englishman, forbids us to think that the inferiority of the negro justified slavery, but it also forbids us to fancy that men to whom the relation of owner to slave had become natural must themselves have been altogether degraded. The men upon the Southern side who can claim any special admiration were simple soldiers who had no share in causing the war; among the political leaders whom they served, there was none who stands out now as a very

interesting personality, and their chosen chief is an unattractive figure; but we are not to think of these authors
of the war as a gang of hardened, unscrupulous, corrupted men. As a class they were reputable, public-
spirited, and religious men; they served their cause with
devotion and were not wholly to blame that they chose
it so ill. The responsibility for the actual secession does
not rest in an especial degree on any individual leader.
Secession began rather with the spontaneous movement
of the whole community of South Carolina, and in the
States which followed leading politicians expressed rather
than inspired the general will. The guilt which any of
us can venture to attribute for this action of a whole
deluded society must rest on men like Calhoun, who in
a previous generation, while opinion in the South was still
to some extent unformed, stifled all thought of reform
and gave the semblance of moral and intellectual justification to a system only susceptible of a historical excuse.

The South was neither base nor senseless, but it was
wrong. To some minds it may not seem to follow that
it was well to resist it by war, and indeed at the time, as
often happens, people took up arms with greater searchings of heart upon the right side than upon the wrong.
If the slave States had been suffered to depart in peace
they would have set up a new and peculiar political society,
more truly held together than the original Union by a
single avowed principle; a nation dedicated to the inequality of men. It is not really possible to think of the
free national life which they could thus have initiated as
a thing to be respected and preserved. Nor is it true
that their choice for themselves of this dingy freedom was
no concern of their neighbours. We have seen how the
slave interest hankered for enlarged dominion; and it
is certain that the Southern Confederacy, once firmly
established, would have been an aggressive and disturbing power upon the continent of America. The questions
of territorial and other rights between it and the old
Union might have been capable of satisfactory settlement for the moment, or they might have proved as

insoluble as Lincoln thought they were. But, at the best, if the States which adhered to the old Union had admitted the claim of the first seceding States to go, they could only have retained for themselves an insecure existence as a nation, threatened at each fresh conflict of interest or sentiment with a further disruption which could not upon any principle have been resisted. The preceding chapters have dwelt with iteration upon the sentiments which had operated to make Americans a people, and on the form and the degree in which those sentiments animated the mind of Lincoln. Only so perhaps can we fully appreciate for what the people of the North fought. It is inaccurate, though not gravely misleading, to say that they fought against slavery. It would be wholly false to say that they fought for mere dominion. They fought to preserve and complete a political unity nobly conceived by those who had done most to create it, and capable, as the sequel showed, of a permanent and a healthy continuance.

And it must never be forgotten, if we wish to enter into the spirit which sustained the North in its struggle, that loyalty for Union had a larger aspect than that of mere allegiance to a particular authority. Vividly present to the mind of some few, vaguely but honestly present to the mind of a great multitude, was the sense that even had slavery not entered into the question a larger cause than that of their recent Union was bound up with the issues of the war. The Government of the United States had been the first and most famous attempt in a great modern country to secure government by the will of the mass of the people. If in this crucial instance such a Government were seen to be intolerably weak, if it was found to be at the mercy of the first powerful minority which seized a worked-up occasion to rebel, what they had learnt to think the most hopeful agency for the uplifting of man everywhere would for ages to come have proved a failure. This feeling could not be stronger in any American than it was in Lincoln himself. " It has long been a question," he said, " whether any Government

which is not too strong for the liberties of the people can be strong enough to maintain itself." There is one marked feature of his patriotism, which could be illustrated by abundance of phrases from his speeches and letters, and which the people of several countries of Europe can appreciate to-day. His affection for his own country and its institutions is curiously dependent upon a wider cause of human good, and is not a whit the less intense for that. There is perhaps no better expression of this widespread feeling in the North than the unprepared speech which he delivered on his way to become President, in the Hall of Independence at Philadelphia, in which the Declaration of Independence had been signed. " I have never," he said, " had a feeling politically that did not spring from the sentiments embodied in the Declaration of Independence. I have often pondered over the dangers which were incurred by the men who assembled here and framed and adopted that Declaration of Independence. I have pondered over the toils that were endured by the officers and soldiers of the army who achieved that independence. I have often inquired of myself what great principle or idea it was that kept the Confederacy so long together. It was not the mere matter of separation of the colonies from the motherland, it was the sentiment in the Declaration of Independence which gave liberty, not alone to the people of this country, but I hope to the world, for all future time. It was that which gave promise that in due time the weight would be lifted from the shoulders of all men."

2. The Progress of Secession.

So much for the broad causes without which there could have been no Civil War in America. We have now to sketch the process by which the fuel was kindled. It will be remembered that the President elected in November does not enter upon his office for nearly four months. For that time, therefore, the conduct of government lay in the hands of President Buchanan, who, for all

his past subserviency to Southern interests, believed and said that secession was absolutely unlawful. Several members of his Cabinet were Southerners who favoured secession; but the only considerable man among them, Cobb of Georgia, soon declared that his loyalty to his own State was not compatible with his office and resigned; and, though others, including the Secretary for War, hung on to their position, it does not appear that they influenced Buchanan much, or that their somewhat dubious conduct while they remained was of great importance. Black, the Attorney-General, and Cass, the Secretary of State, who, however, resigned when his advice was disregarded, were not only loyal to the Union, but anxious that the Government should do everything that seemed necessary in its defence. Thus this administration, hitherto Southern in its sympathies, must be regarded for its remaining months as standing for the Union, so far as it stood for anything. Lincoln meanwhile had little that he could do but to watch events and prepare. There was, nevertheless, a point in the negotiations which took place between parties at which he took on himself a tremendous responsibility and at which his action was probably decisive of all that followed.

The Presidential election took place on November 6, 1860. On November 10 the Legislature of South Carolina, which had remained in session for this purpose, convened a specially elected Convention of the State to decide upon the question of secession. Slave owners and poor whites, young and old, street rabble, persons of fashion, politicians and clergy, the whole people of this peculiar State, distinguished in some marked respects even from its nearest neighbours, received the action of the Legislature with enthusiastic but grave approval. It was not till December 20 that the Convention could pass its formal "Ordinance of Secession," but there was never for a moment any doubt as to what it would do. The question was what other States would follow the example of South Carolina. There ensued in all the Southern States earnest discussion as to whether to secede or not,

and in the North, on which the action of South Carolina, however easily it might have been foretold, came as a shock, great bewilderment as to what was to be done. As has been said, there was in the South generally no disposition to give up Southern claims, no doubt as to the right of secession, and no fundamental and overriding loyalty to the Union, but there was a considerable reluctance to give up the Union and much doubt as to whether secession was really wise; there was in the North among those who then made themselves heard no doubt whatever as to the loyalty due to the Union, but there was, apart from previous differences about slavery, every possible variety and fluctuation of opinion as to the right way of dealing with States which should secede or rebel. In certain border States, few in number but likely to play an important part in civil war, Northern and Southern elements were mingled. Amid loud and distracted discussion, public and private, leaders of the several parties and of the two sections of the country conducted earnest negotiations in the hope of finding a peaceable settlement, and when Congress met, early in December, their debates took a formal shape in committees appointed by the Senate and by the House.

Meanwhile the President was called upon to deal with the problem presented for the Executive Government of the Union by the action of South Carolina. It may be observed that if he had given his mind to the military measures required to meet the possible future, the North, which in the end had his entire sympathy, would have begun the war with that advantage in preparation which, as it was, was gained by the South. In this respect he did nothing. But, apart from this, if he had taken up a clear and comprehensible attitude towards South Carolina and had given a lead to Unionist sympathy, he would have consolidated public opinion in the North, and he would have greatly strengthened those in the South who remained averse to secession. There would have been a considerable further secession, but in all likelihood it would not have become so formidable as it did. As it

was, the movement for secession proceeded with all the proud confidence that can be felt in a right which is not challenged, and the people of the South were not aware, though shrewd leaders like Jefferson Davis knew it well, of the risk they would encounter till they had committed themselves to defying it.

The problem before Buchanan was the same which, aggravated by his failure to deal with it, confronted Lincoln when he came into office, and it must be clearly understood. The secession of South Carolina was not a movement which could at once be quelled by prompt measures of repression. Even if sufficient military force and apt forms of law had existed for taking such measures they would have united the South in support of South Carolina, and alienated the North, which was anxious for conciliation. Yet it was possible for the Government of the Union, while patiently abstaining from violent or provocative action, to make plain that in the last resort it would maintain its rights in South Carolina with its full strength. The main dealings of the Union authorities with the people of a State came under a very few heads. There were local Federal Courts to try certain limited classes of issues; jurors, of course, could not be compelled to serve in these nor parties to appear. There was the postal service; the people of South Carolina did not at present interfere with this source of convenience to themselves and of revenue to the Union. There were customs duties to be collected at the ports, and there were forts at the entrance of the harbour in Charleston, South Carolina, as well as forts, dockyards and arsenals of the United States at a number of points in the Southern States; the Government should quietly but openly have taken steps to ensure that the collection should go on unmolested, and that the forts and the like should be made safe from attack, in South Carolina and everywhere else where they were likely to be threatened. Measures of this sort were early urged upon Buchanan by Scott, the Lieutenant-General (that is, Second in Command under the President) of the Army, who had been the officer

that carried out Jackson's military dispositions when secession was threatened in South Carolina thirty years before, and by other officers concerned, particularly by Major Anderson, a keen Southerner, but a keen soldier, commanding the forts at Charleston, and by Cass and Black in his Cabinet. Public opinion in the North demanded such measures.

If further action than the proper manning and supply of certain forts had been in contemplation, an embarrassing legal question would have arisen. In the opinion of the Attorney-General, of leading Democrats like Cass and Douglas, and apparently of most legal authorities of every party, there was an important distinction, puzzling to an English lawyer even if he is versed in the American Constitution, between the steps which the Government might justly take in self-protection, and measures which could be regarded as coercion of the State of South Carolina as such. These latter would be unlawful. Buchanan, instead of acting on or declaring his intentions, entertained Congress, which met early in December, with a Message, laying down very clearly the illegality of secession, but discussing at large this abstract question of the precise powers of the Executive in resisting secession. The legal question will not further concern us because the distinction which it was really intended to draw between lawful and unlawful measures against secession quite coincided, in its practical application, with what common sense and just feeling would in these peculiar circumstances have dictated. But, as a natural consequence of such discussion, an impression was spread abroad of the illegality of something vaguely called coercion, and of the shadowy nature of any power which the Government claimed.

Up to Lincoln's inauguration the story of the Charleston forts, of which one, lying on an island in the mouth of the harbour, was the famous Fort Sumter, is briefly this. Buchanan was early informed that if the Union Government desired to hold them, troops and ships of war should instantly be sent. Congressmen from South

Carolina remaining in Washington came to him and represented that their State regarded these forts upon its soil as their own; they gave assurances that there would be no attack on the forts if the existing military situation was not altered, and they tried to get a promise that the forts should not be reinforced. Buchanan would give them no promise, but he equally refused the entreaties of Scott and his own principal ministers that he should reinforce the forts, because he declared that this would precipitate a conflict. Towards the end of the year Major Anderson, not having men enough to hold all the forts if, as he expected, they were attacked, withdrew his whole force to Fort Sumter, which he thought the most defensible, dismantling the principal other fort. The Governor of South Carolina protested against this as a violation of a supposed understanding with the President, and seized upon the United States arsenal and the custom house, taking the revenue officers into State service. Commissioners had previously gone from South Carolina to Washington to request the surrender of the forts, upon terms of payment for property; they now declared that Anderson's withdrawal, as putting him in a better position for defence, was an act of war, and demanded that he should be ordered to retire to the mainland. Buchanan wavered; decided to yield to them on this last point; ultimately, on the last day of 1860, yielded instead to severe pressure from Black, and decided to reinforce Anderson on Fort Sumter. The actual attempt to reinforce him was bungled; a transport sent for this purpose was fired upon by the South Carolina forces, and returned idle. This first act of war, for some curious reason, caused no excitement. The people of the North were intensely relieved that Buchanan had not yielded to whatever South Carolina might demand, and, being prone to forgive and to applaud, seem for a time to have experienced a thrill of glory in the thought that the national administration had a mind. Dix, the Secretary of the Treasury, elated them yet further by telegraphing to a Treasury official at New Orleans, " If any one attempts

to haul down the American flag, shoot him on the spot."
But Anderson remained without reinforcements or
further provisions when Lincoln entered office; and
troops in the service first of South Carolina and afterwards of the Southern Confederacy, which was formed
in February, erected batteries and prepared to bombard
Fort Sumter.

No possible plea for President Buchanan can make
him rank among those who have held high office with
any credit at all, but he must at once be acquitted of
any intentional treachery to the Union. It is agreed
that he was a truthful and sincere man, and there is
something pleasant in the simple avowal he made to a
Southern negotiator who was pressing him for some
instant concession, that he always said his prayers before
deciding any important matter of State. His previous
dealings with Kansas would suggest to us robust unscru-
pulousness, but it seems that he had quite given his judgment over into the keeping of a little group of Southern
Senators. Now that he was deprived of this help, he had
only enough will left to be obstinate against other advice.
It is suggested that he had now but one motive, the desire
that the struggle should break out in his successor's time
rather than his own. Even this is perhaps to judge
Buchanan's notorious and calamitous laches unfairly.
Any action that he took must to a certain extent have
been provocative, and he knew it, and he may have
clung to the hope that by sheer inaction he would give
time for some possible forces of reason and conciliation
to work. If so, he was wrong, but similar and about
as foolish hopes paralysed Lincoln's Cabinet (and to a
less but still very dangerous degree Lincoln himself)
when they took up the problem which Buchanan's neglect
had made more urgent. Buchanan had in this instance
the advantage of far better advice, but this silly old man
must not be gibbeted and Lincoln left free from criticism
for his part in the same transaction. Both Presidents
hesitated where to us who look back the case seems clear.
The circumstances had altered in some respects when

Lincoln came in, but it is only upon a somewhat broad
survey of the governing tendencies of Lincoln's administration and of its mighty result in the mass that we discover what really distinguishes his slowness of action in
such cases as this from the hesitation of a man like
Buchanan. Buchanan waited in the hope of avoiding
action, Lincoln with the firm intention to see his path in
the fullest light he could get.

From an early date in November, 1860, every effort
was made, by men too numerous to mention, to devise
if possible such a settlement of what were now called
the grievances of the South as would prevent any other
State from following the example of South Carolina.
Apart from the intangible difference presented by much
disapprobation of slavery in the North and growing resentment in the South as this disapprobation grew louder,
the solid ground of dispute concerned the position of
slavery in the existing Territories and future acquisitions
of the United States Government; the quarrel arose from
the election of a President pledged to use whatever power
he had, though indeed that might prove little, to prevent
the further extension of slavery; and we may almost
confine our attention to this point. Other points came
into discussion. Several of the Northern States had
" Personal Liberty Laws " expressly devised to impede
the execution of the Federal law of 1850 as to fugitive
slaves. Some attention was devoted to these, especially
by Alexander Stephens, who, as the Southern leader most
opposed to immediate secession, wished to direct men's
minds to a grievance that could be remedied. Lincoln,
who had always said that, though the Fugitive Slave Law
should be made just and seemly, it ought in substance to
be enforced, made clear again that he thought such
" Personal Liberty Laws " should be amended, though
he protested that it was not for him as President-elect to
advise the State Legislatures on their own business. The
Republicans generally agreed. Some of the States concerned actually began amending their laws. Thus, if the
disquiet of the South had depended on this grievance, the

cause of disquiet would no doubt have been removed. Again the Republican leaders, including Lincoln in particular, let there be no ground for thinking that an attack was intended upon slavery in the States where it was established; they offered eventually to give the most solemn pledge possible in this matter by passing an Amendment of the Constitution declaring that it should never be altered so as to take away the independence of the existing slave States as to this portion of their democratic institutions. Lincoln indeed refused on several occasions to make any fresh public disclaimer of an intention to attack existing institutions. His views were "open to all who will read." " For the good men in the South," he writes privately, "—I regard the majority of them as such—I have no objection to repeat them seventy times seven. But I have bad men to deal with both North and South; men who are eager for something new upon which to base new misrepresentations; men who would like to frighten me, or at least fix upon me the character of timidity and cowardice." Nevertheless he endeavoured constantly in private correspondence to narrow and define the issue, which, as he insisted, concerned only the territorial extension of slavery.

The most serious of the negotiations that took place, and to which most hope was attached, consisted in the deliberations of a committee of thirteen appointed by the Senate in December, 1860, which took for its guidance a detailed scheme of compromise put forward by Senator Crittenden, of Kentucky. The efforts of this committee to come to an agreement broke down at the outset upon the question of the Territories, and the responsibility, for good or for evil, of bringing them to an end must probably be attributed to the advice of Lincoln. Crittenden's first proposal was that there should be a Constitutional Amendment declaring that slavery should be prohibited " in all the territory of the United States, now held or hereafter acquired, north of latitude 36 ° 30 ' "—(the limit fixed in the Missouri Compromise, but restricted then to the Louisiana purchase)—while in all

territory, now held or thereafter acquired south of that line, it should be permitted. Crittenden also proposed that when a Territory on either side of the line became a State, it should become free to decide the question for itself; but the discussion never reached this point. On the proposal as to the Territories there seemed at first to be a prospect that the Republicans would agree, in which case the South might very likely have agreed too. The desire for peace was intensely strong among the commercial men of New York and other cities, and it affected the great political managers and the statesmen who, like Seward himself, were in close touch with this commercial influence. Tenacious adherence to declared principle may have been as strong in country districts as the desire for accommodation was in these cities, but it was at any rate far less vocal, and on the whole it seems that compromise was then in the air. It seemed clear from the expressed opinions of his closest allies that Seward would support this compromise. Now Seward just at this time received Lincoln's offer of the office of Secretary of State, a great office and one in which Seward expected to rule Lincoln and the country, but in accepting which, as he did, he made it incumbent on himself not to part company at once with the man who would be nominally his chief. Then there occurred a visit paid on Seward's behalf by his friend Thurlow Weed, an astute political manager but also an able statesman, to Lincoln at Springfield. Weed brought back a written statement of Lincoln's views. Seward's support was not given to the compromise; nor naturally was that of the more radical Republicans, to use a term which now became common; and the Committee of Thirteen found itself unable to agree.

It is unnecessary to repeat what Lincoln's conviction on this, to him the one essential point of policy, was, or to quote from the numerous letters in which from the time of his nomination he tried to keep the minds of his friends firm on this single principle, and to show them that if there were the slightest further yielding as to

this, save indeed as to the peculiar case of New Mexico, which did not matter, and which perhaps he regarded as conceded already, the Southern policy of extending slavery and of " filibustering " against neighbouring counties for that purpose would revive in full force, and the whole labour of the Republican movement would have to begin over again. Since his election he had been writing also to Southern politicians who were personally friendly, to Gilmer of North Carolina, to whom he offered Cabinet office, and to Stephens, making absolutely plain that his difference with them lay in this one point, but making it no less plain that on this point he was, with entire respect to them, immovable. Now, on December 22, the *New York Tribune* was " enabled to state that Mr. Lincoln stands now as he stood in May last, square upon the Republican platform." The writing that Weed brought to Seward must have said, perhaps more elaborately, the same. If Lincoln had not stood square upon that platform there were others like Senator Wade of Ohio and Senator Grimes of Iowa who might have done so and might have been able to wreck the compromise. Lincoln, however, did wreck it, at a time when it seemed likely to succeed, and it is most probable that thereby he caused the Civil War. It cannot be said that he definitely expected the Civil War. Probably he avoided making any definite forecast; but he expressed no alarm, and he privately told a friend about this time that " he could not in his heart believe that the South designed the overthrow of the Government." But, if he had in his heart believed it, nothing in his life gives reason to think that he would have been more anxious to conciliate the South; on the contrary, it is in line with all we know of his feelings to suppose that he would have thought firmness all the more imperative. We cannot recall the solemnity of his long-considered speech about " a house divided against itself," with which all his words and acts accorded, without seeing that, if perhaps he speculated little about the risks, he was prepared to face them whatever they were. Doubtless he took a heavy responsibility, but

it is painful to find honourable historians, who heartily dislike the cause of slavery, capable to-day of wondering whether he was right to do so. "If he had not stood square" in December upon the same "platform" on which he had stood in May, if he had preferred to enroll himself among those statesmen of all countries whose strongest words are uttered for their own subsequent enjoyment in eating them, he might conceivably have saved much bloodshed, but he would not have left the United States a country of which any good man was proud to be a citizen.

Thus, by the end of 1860, the bottom was really out of the policy of compromise, and it is not worth while to examine the praiseworthy efforts that were still made for it while State after State in the South was deciding to secede. One interesting proposal, which was aired in January, 1861, deserves notice, namely, that the terms of compromise proposed by Crittenden should have been submitted to a vote of the whole people. It was not passed. Seward, whom many people now thought likely to catch at any and every proposal for a settlement, said afterwards with justice that it was "unconstitutional and ineffectual." Ineffectual it would have been in this sense: the compromise would in all probability have been carried by a majority consisting of men in the border States and of all those elsewhere who, though they feared war and desired good feeling, had no further definite opinion upon the chief questions at issue; but it would have left a local majority in many of the Southern States and a local majority in many of the Northern States as irreconcilable with each other as ever. It was opposed also to the spirit of the Constitution. In a great country where the people with infinitely varied interests and opinions can slowly make their predominant wishes appear, but cannot really take counsel together and give a firm decision upon any emergency, there may be exceptional cases when a popular vote on a defined issue would be valuable, significant, desired by the people themselves; but the machinery of representative government, however faulty,

is the only machinery by which the people can in some sense govern itself, instead of making itself ungovernable. Above all, in a serious crisis it is supremely repugnant to the spirit of popular government that the men chosen by a people to govern it should throw their responsibility back at the heads of the electors. It is well to be clear as to the kind of proceeding which the authors of this proposal were really advocating: a statesman has come before the ordinary citizen with a definite statement of the principle on which he would act, and an ordinary citizen has thereupon taken his part in entrusting him with power; then comes the moment for the statesman to carry out his principle, and the latent opposition becomes of necessity more alarming; the statesman is therefore to say to the ordinary citizen, " This is a more difficult matter than I thought; and if I am to act as I said I would, take on yourself the responsibility which I recently put myself forward to bear." The ordinary citizen will naturally as a rule decline a responsibility thus offered him, but he will not be grateful for the offer or glad to be a forced accomplice in this process of indecision.

If we could determine the prevailing sentiment in the North at some particular moment during the crisis, it would probably represent what very few individual men continued to think for six months together. Early in the crisis some strong opponents of slavery were for letting the South go, declaring, as did Horace Greeley of the *New York Tribune,* that " they would not be citizens of a Republic of which one part was pinned to the other part with bayonets "; but this sentiment seems soon to have given way when the same men began to consider, as Lincoln had considered, whether an agreement to sever the Union between the States, with the difficult adjustment of mutual interests which it would have involved, could be so effected as to secure a lasting peace. A blind rage on behalf of conciliation broke out later in prosperous business men in great towns—even in Boston it is related that " Beacon Street aristocrats " broke up a

meeting to commemorate John Brown on the anniversary of his death, and grave persons thought the meeting an outrage. Waves of eager desire for compromise passed over the Northern community. Observers at the time and historians after are easily mistaken as to popular feeling; the acute fluctuations of opinion inevitable among journalists, and in any sort of circle where men are constantly meeting and talking politics, may leave the great mass of quiet folk almost unaffected. We may be sure that there was a considerable body of steady opinion very much in accord with Lincoln; this should not be forgotten, but it must not be supposed that it prevailed constantly. On the contrary, it was inherent in the nature of the crisis that opinion wavered and swayed. We should miss the whole significance of Lincoln's story if we did not think of the North now and to the end of the war as exposed to disunion, hesitation, and quick reaction. If at this time a sufficiently authoritative leader with sufficiently determined timidity had inaugurated a policy of stampede, he might have had a vast and tumultuous following. Only his following would quickly, if too late, have repented. What was wanted, if the people of the North were to have what most justly might be called their way, was a leader who would not seem to hurry them along, nor yet be ever looking round to see if they followed, but just go groping forward among the innumerable obstacles, guided by such principles of good sense and of right as would perhaps on the whole and in the long run be approved by the maturer thought of most men; and Lincoln was such a leader.

When we turn to the South, where, as has been said, the movement for secession was making steady though not unopposed progress, we have indeed to make exceptions to any sweeping statement, but we must recognise a far more clearly defined and far more prevailing general opinion. We may set aside for the moment the border slave States of Maryland, Virginia, Kentucky, and Missouri, each of which has a distinct and an important history. Delaware belonged in effect to the North. In

Texas there were peculiar conditions, and Texas had an interesting history of its own in this matter, but may be treated as remote. There was also, as has been said, a highland region covering the west of Virginia and the east of Kentucky but reaching far south into the northern part of Alabama. Looking at the pathetic spectacle of enduring heroism in a mistaken cause which the South presented, many people have been ready to suppose that it was manœuvred and tricked into its folly by its politicians and might have recovered itself from it if the North and the Government had exercised greater patience and given it time. In support of this view instances are cited of strong Unionist feeling in the South. Such instances probably belong to the peculiar people of this highland country, or else to the mixed and more or less neutral population that might be found at New Orleans or trading along the Mississippi. There remains a solid and far larger South in which indeed (except for South Carolina) dominant Southern policy was briskly debated, but as a question of time, degree, and expediency. Three mental forces worked for the same end: the alarmed vested interest of the people of substance, aristocratic and otherwise; the racial sentiment of the poor whites, a sentiment often strongest in those who have no subject of worldly pride but their colour; and the philosophy of the clergy and other professional men who constituted what in some countries is called the intellectual class. These influences resulted in a rare uniformity of opinion that slavery was right and all attacks on it were monstrous, that the Southern States were free to secede and form, if they chose, a new Confederacy, and that they ought to do this if the moment should arrive when they could not otherwise safeguard their interests. Doubtless there were leading men who had thought over the matter in advance of the rest and taken counsel together long before, but the fact seems to be that such leaders now found their followers in advance of them. Jefferson Davis, by far the most commanding man among them, now found himself—certainly it served him right—

anxiously counselling delay, and spending nights in prayer before he made his farewell speech to the Senate in words of greater dignity and good feeling than seem to comport with the fanatical narrowness of his view and the progressive warping of his determined character to which it condemned him. Whatever fundamental loyalty to the Union existed in any man's heart there were months of debate in which it found no organised and hardly any audible expression. The most notable stand against actual secession was that which was made in Georgia by Stephens; he was determined and outspoken, but he proceeded wholly upon the ground that secession was premature. And this instance is significant of something further. It has been said that discussion and voting were not free, and it would be altogether unlikely that their freedom should in no cases be infringed, but there is no evidence that this charge was widely true. It is surely significant of the general temper of the South, and most honourable to it, that Stephens, who thus struggled against secession at that moment, was chosen Vice-President of the Southern Confederacy.

By February 4, 1861, the States of Mississippi, Florida, Alabama, Georgia, and Louisiana had followed South Carolina by passing Ordinances of Secession, and on that date representatives of these States met at Montgomery in Alabama to found a new Confederacy. Texas, where considerable resistance was offered by Governor Houston, the adventurous leader under whom that State had separated from Mexico, was in process of passing the like Ordinance. Virginia and North Carolina, which lie north of the region where cotton prevails, and with them their western neighbour Tennessee, and Arkansas, yet further west and separated from Tennessee by the Mississippi River, did not secede till after Lincoln's inauguration and the outbreak of war. But the position of Virginia (except for its western districts) admitted of very little doubt, and that of Tennessee and North Carolina was known to be much the same. Virginia took a historic pride in the Union, and its interest in slavery was not

quite the same as that of the cotton States, yet its strongest social ties were to the South. This State was now engaged in a last idle attempt to keep itself and other border States in the Union, with some hope also that the departed States might return; and on this same February 6, a "Peace Convention," invited by Virginia and attended by delegates from twenty-one States, met at Washington with ex-President Tyler in the chair; but for Virginia it was all along a condition of any terms of agreement that the right of any State to secede should be fully acknowledged.

The Congress of the seceding States, which met at Montgomery, was described by Stephens as, "taken all in all, the noblest, soberest, most intelligent, and most conservative body I was ever in." It has been remarked that Southern politicians of the agitator type were not sent to it. It adopted a provisional Constitution modelled largely upon that of the United States. Jefferson Davis, who had retired to his farm, was sent for to become President; Stephens, as already said, became Vice-President. The delegates there were to continue in session for the present as the regular Congress. Whether sobered by the thought that they were acting in the eyes of the world, or in accordance with their own prevailing sentiment, these men, some of whom had before urged the revival of the slave trade, now placed in their Constitution a perpetual prohibition of it, and when, as a regular legislature, they afterwards passed a penal statute which carried out this intention inadequately, President Davis conscientiously vetoed it and demanded a more satisfactory measure. At his inauguration the Southern President delivered an address, typical of that curious blending of propriety and insincerity, of which the politics of that period in America had offered many examples. It may seem incredible, but it contained no word of slavery, but recited in dignified terms how the South had been driven to separation by "wanton aggression on the part of others," and after it had "vainly endeavoured to secure tranquillity." The new Southern Congress now

resolved to take over the forts and other property in the seceded States that had belonged to the Union, and the first Confederate general, Beauregard, was sent to Charleston to hover over Fort Sumter.

3. *The Inauguration of Lincoln.*

The first necessary business of the President-elect, while he watched the gathering of what Emerson named " the hurricane in which he was called to the helm," was to construct a strong Cabinet, to which may be added the seemingly unnecessary business forced upon him of dealing with a horde of pilgrims who at once began visiting him to solicit some office or, in rarer cases, to press their disinterested opinions. His Cabinet, designed in principle, as has been said, while he was waiting in the telegraph office for election returns, was actually constructed with some delay and hesitation. Lincoln could not know personally all the men he invited to join him, but he proceeded with the view of conjoining in his administration representatives of the chief shades of opinion which in this critical time it would be his supreme duty to hold together. Not only different shades of opinion, but the local sentiment of different districts had to be considered; he once complained that if the twelve Apostles had to be chosen nowadays the principle of locality would have to be regarded; but at this time there was very solid reason why different States should be contented and why he should be advised as to their feelings. His own chief rivals for the Presidency offered a good choice from both these points of view. They were Seward of New York, Chase of Ohio, Bates of Missouri, Cameron of Pennsylvania. Seward and Chase were both able and outstanding men: the former was in a sense the old Republican leader, but was more and more coming to be regarded as the typical " Conservative," or cautious Republican; Chase on the other hand was a leader of the " Radicals," who were " stern and unbending " in their attitude towards slavery and towards the South.

These two must be got and kept together if possible. Bates was a good and capable man who moreover came from Missouri, a border slave State, where his influence was much to be desired. He became Attorney-General. Cameron, an unfortunate choice as it turned out, was a very wealthy business man of Pennsylvania, representative of the weighty Protectionist influence there. After he had been offered office, which had been without Lincoln's authority promised him in the Republican Convention, Lincoln was dismayed by representations that he was "a bad, corrupted man"; he wrote a curious letter asking Cameron to refuse his offer; Cameron instead produced evidence of the desire of Pennsylvania for him; Lincoln stuck to his offer; the old Whig element among Republicans, the Protectionist element, and above all, the friends of the indispensable Seward, would otherwise have been outweighted in the Cabinet. Cameron eventually became for a time Secretary of War. To these Lincoln, upon somebody's strong representations, tried, without much hope, to add some distinctly Southern politician. The effort, of course, failed. Ultimately the Cabinet was completed by the addition of Caleb Smith of Indiana as Secretary of the Interior, Gideon Welles of Connecticut as Secretary of the Navy, and Montgomery Blair of Maryland as Postmaster-General. Welles, with the guidance of a brilliant subordinate, Fox, served usefully, was very loyal to Lincoln, had an antipathy to England which was dangerous, and kept very diligently a diary for which we may be grateful now. Blair was a vehement, irresponsible person with an influential connection, and, which was important, his influence and that of his family lay in Maryland and other border slave States. Of all these men, Seward, Secretary of State—that is, Foreign Minister and something more—and Chase, Secretary of the Treasury, most concern us. Lincoln's offer to Seward was made and accepted in terms that did credit to both men, and Seward, still smarting at his own defeat, was admirably loyal. But his friends, though they had secured the appointment of

Cameron to support them, thought increasingly ill of the prospects of a Cabinet which included the Radical Chase. On the very night before his inauguration Lincoln received from Seward, who had just been helping to revise his Inaugural Address, a letter withdrawing his acceptance of office. By some not clearly recorded exercise of that great power over men, which, if with some failures, was generally at his command, he forced Seward to see that the unconditional withdrawal of this letter was his public duty. It must throughout what follows be remembered that Lincoln's first and most constant duty was to hold together the jarring elements in the North which these jarring elements in his own Cabinet represented; and it was one of his great achievements that he kept together, for as long as was needful, able but discordant public servants who could never have combined together without him.

On February 11, 1861, Lincoln, standing on the gallery at the end of a railway car, upon the instant of departure from the home to which he never returned, said to his old neighbours (according to the version of his speech which his private secretary got him to dictate immediately after): "My friends, no one, not in my situation, can appreciate my feeling of sadness at this parting. To this place, and the kindness of these people, I owe everything. Here I have lived for a quarter of a century, and have passed from a young to an old man. Here my children have been born and one is buried. I now leave, not knowing when or whether ever I may return, with a task before me greater than that which rested upon Washington. Without the assistance of that Divine Being who ever attended him, I cannot succeed. With that assistance, I cannot fail. Trusting in Him who can go with me, and remain with you, and be everywhere for good, let us confidently hope that all will yet be well. To His care commending you, as I hope in your prayers you will commend me, I bid you an affectionate farewell."

He was, indeed, going to a task not less great than Washington's, but he was going to it with a preparation

in many respects far inferior to his. For the last eight years he had laboured as a public speaker, and in a measure as a party leader, and had displayed and developed comprehension, perhaps unequalled, of some of the larger causes which mould public affairs. But, except in sheer moral discipline, those years had done nothing to supply the special training which he had previously lacked, for high executive office. In such office at such a time ready decision in an obscure and passing situation may often be a not less requisite than philosophic grasp either of the popular mind or of eternal laws. The powers which he had hitherto shown would still be needful to him, but so too would other powers which he had never practised in any comparable position, and which nature does not in a moment supply. Any attempt to judge of Lincoln's Presidency—and it can only be judged at all when it has gone on some way—must take account, not perhaps so much of his inexperience, as of his own reasonable consciousness of it and his great anxiety to use the advice of men who were in any way presumably more competent.

He deliberately delayed his arrival in Washington and availed himself of official invitations to stay at four great towns and five State capitals which he could conveniently pass on his way. The journey abounded in small incidents and speeches, some of which exposed him to a little ridicule in the press, though they probably created an undercurrent of sympathy for him. Near one station where the train stopped lived a little girl he knew, who had recently urged upon him to wear a beard or whiskers. To this dreadful young person, and to that persistent good nature of his which was now and then fatuous, was due the ill-designed hairy ornamentation which during his Presidency hid the really beautiful modelling of his jaw and chin. He enquired for her at the station, had her fetched from the crowd, claimed her praise for this supposed improvement, and kissed her in presence of the press. In New York he was guilty of a more sinister and tragic misfeasance. In that city, where,

if it may be said with respect, there has existed from of old a fashionable circle not convinced of its own gentility and insisting the more rigorously on minor decorum, Lincoln went to the opera, and history still deplores that this misguided man went there and sat there with his large hands in black kid gloves. Here perhaps it is well to say that the educated world of the Eastern States, including those who privately deplored Lincoln's supposed unfitness, treated its untried chief magistrate with that engrained good breeding to which it was utterly indifferent how plain a man he might be. His lesser speeches as he went were unstudied appeals to loyalty, with very simple avowals of inadequacy to his task, and expressions of reliance on the people's support when he tried to do his duty. To a man who can sometimes speak from the heart and to the heart as Lincoln did it is perhaps not given to be uniformly felicitous. Among these speeches was that delivered at Philadelphia, which has already been quoted, but most of them were not considered felicitous at the time. They were too unpretentious. Moreover, they contained sentences which seemed to understate the gravity of the crisis in a way which threw doubt on his own serious statesmanship. Whether they were felicitous or not, the intention of these much-criticised utterances was the best proof of his statesmanship. He would appeal to the steady loyalty of the North, but he was not going to arouse its passion. He assumed to the last that calm reflection might prevail in the South, which was menaced by nothing but " an artificial crisis." He referred to war as a possibility, but left no doubt of his own wish by all means to avoid it. " There will," he said, " be no bloodshed unless it be forced on the Government. The Government will not use force unless force is used against it."

Before he passed through Baltimore he received earnest communications from Seward and from General Scott. Each had received trustworthy information of a plot, which existed, to murder him in that city. Owing to their warnings he went through Baltimore secretly at

night, so that his arrival in Washington, on February 23, was unexpected. This was his obvious duty, and nobody who knew him was ever in doubt of his personal intrepidity; but of course it helped to damp the effect of what many people would have been glad to regard as a triumphal progress.

On March 4, 1861, old Buchanan came in his carriage to escort his successor to the inaugural ceremony, where it was the ironical fate of Chief Justice Taney to administer the oath to a President who had already gone far to undo his great work. Yet a third notable Democrat was there to do a pleasant little act. Douglas, Lincoln's defeated rival, placed himself with a fine ostentation by his side, and, observing that he was embarrassed as to where to put his new tall hat and preposterous goldknobbed cane, took charge of these encumbrances before the moment arrived for the most eagerly awaited of all his speeches. Lincoln had submitted his draft of his "First Inaugural" to Seward, and this draft with Seward's abundant suggestions of amendment has been preserved. It has considerable literary interest, and, by the readiness with which most of Seward's suggestions were adopted, and the decision with which some, and those not the least important, were set aside by Lincoln, it illustrates well the working relation which, after one short struggle, was to be established between these two men. By Seward's advice Lincoln added to an otherwise dry speech some concluding paragraphs of emotional appeal. The last sentence of the speech, which alone is much remembered, is Seward's in the first conception of it, Seward's in the slightly hackneyed phrase with which it ends, Lincoln's alone in the touch of haunting beauty which is on it.

His "First Inaugural" was by general confession an able state paper, setting forth simply and well a situation with which we are now familiar. It sets out dispassionately the state of the controversy on slavery, lays down with brief argument the position that the Union is indissoluble, and proceeds to define the duty of the Gov-

ernment in face of an attempt to dissolve it. "The power," he said, "confided to me will be used to hold, occupy, and possess the property and places belonging to the Government, and to collect the duties on imports; but beyond what may be necessary for these objects there will be no invasion, no using of force against or among the people anywhere. The mails, unless repelled, will continue to be furnished in all parts of the Union." He proceeded to set out what he conceived to be the impossibility of real separation; the intimate relations between the peoples of the several States must still continue; they would still remain for adjustment after any length of warfare; they could be far better adjusted in Union than in enmity. He concluded: "In your hands, my dissatisfied fellow-countrymen, and not in mine, is the momentous issue of civil war. The Government will not assail you. You can have no conflict without being yourselves the aggressors. I am loath to close. We are not enemies but friends. We must not be enemies. Though passion may have strained, it must not break our bonds of affection. The mystic chords of memory, stretching from every battlefield and patriot grave to every living heart and hearthstone all over this broad land, will yet swell the chorus of the Union, when again touched, as surely they will be, by the better angels of our nature."

4. *The Outbreak of War.*

Upon the newly-inaugurated President there now descended a swarm of office-seekers. The Republican party had never been in power before, and these patriotic people exceeded in number and voracity those that had assailed any American President before. To be accessible to all such was the normal duty of a President; it was perhaps additionally incumbent on him at this time. When in the course of nature the number of office-seekers abated, they were succeeded, as will be seen, by supplicants of another kind, whose petitions were often really harrowing. The horror of this enduring visitation has

been described by Artemus Ward in terms which Lincoln himself could not have improved upon. His classical treatment of the subject is worth serious reference; for it should be realised that Lincoln, who had both to learn his new trade of statecraft and to exercise it in a terrible emergency, did so with a large part of each day necessarily consumed by worrying and distasteful tasks of a much paltrier kind.

On the day after the Inauguration came word from Major Anderson at Fort Sumter that he could only hold out a few weeks longer unless reinforced and provisioned. With it came to Lincoln the opinion of General Scott, that to relieve Fort Sumter now would require a force of 20,000 men, which did not exist. The Cabinet was summoned with military and naval advisers. The sailors thought they could throw men and provisions into Fort Sumter; the soldiers said the ships would be destroyed by the Confederate batteries. Lincoln asked his Cabinet whether, assuming it to be feasible, it was politically advisable now to provision Fort Sumter. Blair said yes emphatically; Chase said yes in a qualified way. The other five members of the Cabinet said no; General Scott had given his opinion, as on a military question, that the fort should now be evacuated; they argued that the evacuation of this one fort would be recognised by the country as merely a military necessity arising from the neglect of the last administration. Lincoln reserved his decision.

Let us conceive the effect of a decision to evacuate Fort Sumter. South Carolina had for long claimed it as a due acknowledgment of its sovereign and independent rights, and for no other end; the Confederacy now claimed it and its first act had been to send Beauregard to threaten the fort. Even Buchanan had ended by withstanding these claims. The assertion that he would hold these forts had been the gist of Lincoln's Inaugural. This was the one fort that was in the eyes of the Northern public or the Southern public either; they probably never realised that there were other forts, Fort Pickens, for example, on the Gulf of Mexico, which the administra-

tion was prepared to defend. And now it was proposed
that Lincoln, who had put down his foot with a bang
yesterday, should take it up with a shuffle to-day. And
Lincoln reserved his judgment; and, which is much more,
went on reserving it till the question nearly settled itself
to his disgrace.

Lincoln lacked here, it would seem, not by any means
the qualities of the trained administrator, but just that
rough perception and vigour which untaught genius might
be supposed to possess. The passionate Jackson (who,
by the way, was a far more educated man in the respects
which count) would not have acted so. Lincoln, it is
true, had declared that he would take no provocative
step—" In your hands, my dissatisfied fellow-countrymen, and not in mine, is the momentous issue of civil
war," and the risk which he would have taken by over-
ruling that day the opinion of the bulk of his Cabinet
based on that of his chief military adviser is obvious, but
it seems to have been a lesser risk than he did take in
delaying so long to overrule his Cabinet. It is precisely
characteristic of his strength and of his weakness that
he did not at once yield to his advisers; that he long continued weighing the matter undisturbed by the danger
of delay; that he decided as soon as and no sooner than
he felt sure as to the political results, which alone here
mattered, for the military consequences amounted to
nothing.

This story was entangled from the first with another
difficult story. Commissioners from the Southern Confederacy came to Washington and sought interviews with
Seward; they came to treat for the recognition of the
Confederacy and the peaceful surrender of forts and the
like within its borders. Meanwhile the action of Virginia
was in the balance, and the " Peace Convention," summoned by Virginia, still " threshing again," as Lowell
said, " the already twice-threshed straw of debate." The
action of Virginia and of other border States, about which
Lincoln was intensely solicitous, would certainly depend
upon the action of the Government towards the States

that had already seceded. Might it not be well that the
Government should avoid immediate conflict with South
Carolina about Fort Sumter, though conflict with the
Confederacy about Fort Pickens and the rest would still
impend? Was it not possible that conflict could be staved
off till an agreement could be reached with Virginia and
the border States, which would induce the seceded States
to return? These questions were clearly absurd, but they
were as clearly natural, and they greatly exercised Seward.
Disappointed at not being President and equally disturbed at the prospect of civil war, but still inclined to
large and sanguine hopes, he was rather anxious to take
things out of Lincoln's hands and very anxious to serve
his country as the great peacemaker. Indirect negotiations now took place between him and the Southern Commissioners, who of course could not be officially recognised, through the medium of two Supreme Court
Judges, especially one Campbell, who was then in
Washington. Seward was quite loyal to Lincoln and
told him in a general way what he was doing; he was
also candid with Campbell and his friends, and explained
to them his lack of authority, but he talked freely and
rashly of what he hoped to bring about. Lincoln gave
Seward some proper cautions and left him all proper
freedom; but it is possible that he once told Douglas
that he intended, at that moment, to evacuate Fort Sumter. The upshot of the matter is that the decision of
the Government was delayed by negotiations which, as it
ought to have known, could come to nothing, and that
the Southern Government and the Commissioners, after
they had got home, thought they had been deceived in
these negotiations.

Discussions were still proceeding as to Fort Sumter
when a fresh difficulty arose for Lincoln, but one which
enabled him to become henceforth master in his Cabinet.
The strain of Seward's position upon a man inclined to
be vain and weak can easily be imagined, but the sudden
vagary in which it now resulted was surprising. Upon
April 1 he sent to Lincoln "Some Thoughts for the Presi-

dent's Consideration." In this paper, after deploring
what he described as the lack of any policy so far, and
defining, in a way that does not matter, his attitude as
to the forts in the South, he proceeded thus: " I would
demand explanations from Great Britain and Russia,
and send agents into Canada, Mexico, and Central
America, to raise a vigorous spirit of independence on
this continent against European intervention, and if
satisfactory explanations are not received from Spain and
France, would convene Congress and declare war
against them." In other words, Seward would seek to
end all domestic dissensions by suddenly creating out of
nothing a dazzling foreign policy. But this was not the
only point, even if it was the main point; he proceeded:
" Either the President must do it " (that is the sole conduct of this policy) " himself, or devolve it on some
member of his Cabinet. It is not my especial province.
But I neither seek to evade nor assume responsibility."
In other words, Seward put himself forward as the sole
director of the Government. In his brief reply Lincoln
made no reference whatever to Seward's amazing programme. He pointed out that the policy so far, as to
which Seward had complained, was one in which Seward
had entirely concurred. As to the concluding demand
that some one man, and that man Seward, should control
all policy, he wrote, " If this must be done, I must do it.
When a general line of policy is adopted, I apprehend
there is no danger of its being changed without good
reason, or continuing to be a subject of unnecessary debate; still, upon points arising in its progress I wish, and
suppose I am entitled to have, the advice of all the
Cabinet." Seward was not a fool, far from it; he was
one of the ablest men in America, only at that moment
strained and excited beyond the limits of his good sense.
Lincoln's quiet answer sobered him then and for ever
after. He showed a generous mind; he wrote to his
wife soon after: " Executive force and vigour are rare
qualities; the President is the best of us." And Lincoln's
generosity was no less; his private secretary, Nicolay,

saw these papers; but no other man knew anything of Seward's abortive rebellion against Lincoln till after they both were dead. The story needs no explanation, but the more attentively all the circumstances are considered, the more Lincoln's handling of this emergency, which threatened the ruin of his Government, throws into shade the weakness he had hitherto shown.

Lincoln was thus in a stronger position when he finally decided as to Fort Sumter. It is unnecessary to follow the repeated consultations that took place. There were preparations for possible expeditions both to Fort Sumter and to Fort Pickens, and various blunders about them, and Seward made some trouble by officious interference about them. An announcement was sent to the Governor of South Carolina that provisions would be sent to Fort Sumter and he was assured that if this was unopposed no further steps would be taken. What chiefly concerns us is that the eventual decision to send provisions but not troops to Fort Sumter was Lincoln's decision; but that it was not taken till after Senators and Congressmen had made clear to him that Northern opinion would support him. It was the right decision, for it conspicuously avoided the appearance of provocation, while it upheld the right of the Union; but it was taken perilously late, and the delay exposed the Government to the risk of a great humiliation.

An Alabama gentleman had urged Jefferson Davis that the impending struggle must not be delayed. "Unless," he said, "you sprinkle blood in the face of the people of Alabama, they will be back in the old Union in ten days." There is every reason to suppose that the gentleman's statement as to the probable collapse of the South was mere rhetoric, but it seems that his advice led to orders being sent to Beauregard to reduce Fort Sumter. Beauregard sent a summons to Anderson; Anderson, now all but starved out, replied that unless he received supplies or instructions he would surrender on April 15. Whether by Beauregard's orders or through some misunderstanding, the Confederate

batteries opened fire on Fort Sumter on April 12. Fort Sumter became untenable on the next day, when the relief ships, which Anderson had been led to expect sooner, but which could in no case really have helped him, were just appearing in the offing. Anderson very properly capitulated. On Sunday, April 14, 1861, he marched out with the honours of war. The Union flag had been fired upon in earnest by the Confederates, and, leaving Virginia and the States that went with it to join the Confederacy if they chose, the North sprang to arms.

In the events which had led up to the outbreak of war Abraham Lincoln had played a part more admirable and more decisive in its effect than his countrymen could have noted at the time or perhaps have appreciated since. He was confronted now with duties requiring mental gifts of a different kind from those which he had hitherto displayed, and with temptations to which he had not yet been exposed. In a general sense the greatness of mind and heart which he unfolded under fierce trial does not need to be demonstrated to-day. Yet in detail hardly an action of his Presidency is exempt from controversy; nor is his many-sided character one of those which men readily flatter themselves that they understand. There are always, moreover, those to whom it is a marvel how any great man came by his name. The particular tribute, which in the pages that follow it is desired to pay to him, consists in the careful examination of just those actions and just those qualities of his upon which candid detraction has in fact fastened, or on which candid admiration has pronounced with hesitancy.

CHAPTER VII

THE CONDITIONS OF THE WAR

In recounting the history of Lincoln's Presidency, it will be necessary to mark the course of the Civil War stage by stage as we proceed. There are, however, one or two general features of the contest with which it may be well to deal by way of preface.

It has seldom happened that a people entering upon a great war have understood at the outset what the character of that war would be. When the American Civil War broke out the North expected an easy victory, but, as disappointment came soon and was long maintained, many clever people adopted the opinion, which early prevailed in Europe, that there was no possibility of their success at all. At the first the difficulty of the task was unrecognised; under early and long-sustained disappointment the strength by which those difficulties could be overcome began to be despaired of without reason.

The North, after several slave States, which were at first doubtful, had adhered to it, had more than double the population of the South; of the Southern population a very large part were slaves, who, though industrially useful, could not be enlisted. In material resources the superiority of the North was no less marked, and its material wealth grew during the war to a greater extent than had perhaps ever happened to any other belligerent power. These advantages were likely to be decisive in the end, if the North could and would endure to the end. But at the very beginning these advantages simply did not tell at all, for the immediately available military force of the North was insignificant, and that of the South clearly superior to it; and even when they began to tell, it was bound to be very long before their full weight could be brought to bear. And the object which

214

was to be obtained was supremely difficult of attainment. It was not a defeat of the South which might result in the alteration of a frontier, the cession of some Colonies, the payment of an indemnity, and such like matters; it was a conquest of the South so complete that the Union could be restored on a firmer basis than before. Any less result than this would be failure in the war. And the country, to be thus completely conquered by an un-military people of nineteen millions, was of enormous extent: leaving out of account the huge outlying State of Texas, which is larger than Germany, the remaining Southern States which joined in the Confederacy have an area somewhat larger than that of Germany, Austria-Hungary, Holland, and Belgium put together; and this great region had no industrial centres or other points of such great strategic importance that by the occupation of them the remaining area could be dominated. The feat which the Northern people eventually achieved has been said by the English historians of the war (perhaps with some exaggeration) to have been " a greater one than that which Napoleon attempted to his own undoing when he invaded Russia in 1812."

On the other hand, the South was in some respects very favourably placed for resisting invasion from the North. The Southern forces during most of the war were, in the language of military writers, operating on interior lines; that is, the different portions of them lay nearer to one another than did the different portions of the Northern forces, and could be more quickly brought to converge on the same point; the country abounded in strong positions for defence which could be held by a relatively small force, while in every invading movement the invaders had to advance long distances from the base, thus exposing their lines of communication to at-tack. The advantage of this situation, if competent use were made of it, was bound to go very far towards com-pensating for inferiority of numbers; the North could not make its superior numbers on land tell in any rapidly decisive fashion without exposing itself to dangerous

counter-strokes. In naval strength its superiority was asserted almost from the first, and by cutting off foreign supplies caused the Southern armies to suffer severe privations before the war was half through; but its full effect could only be produced very slowly. Thus, if its people were brave and its leaders capable, the South was by no means in so hopeless a case as might at first have appeared; with good fortune it might hope to strike its powerful antagonist some deadly blow before that antagonist could bring its strength to bear; and even if this hope failed, a sufficiently tenacious defence might well wear down the patience of the North.

As soldiers the Southerners started with a superiority which the Northerners could only overtake slowly. If each people were taken in the mass, the proportion of Southerners bred to an outdoor life was higher. Generally speaking, if not exactly more frugal, they were far less used to living comfortably. Above all, all classes of people among them were still accustomed to think of fighting as a normal and suitable occupation for a man; while the prevailing temper of the North thought of man as meant for business, and its higher temper was apt to think of fighting as odious and war out of date. This, like the other advantages of the South, was transitory; before very long Northerners who became soldiers at a sacrifice of inclination, from the highest spirit of patriotism or in the methodic temper in which business has to be done, would become man for man as good soldiers as the Southerners; but the original superiority of the Southerners would continue to have a moral effect in their own ranks and on the mind of the enemy, more especially of the enemy's generals, even after its cause had ceased to exist; and herein the military advantage of the South was undoubtedly, through the first half of the war, considerable.

In the matter of leadership the South had certain very real and certain other apparent but probably delusive advantages. The United States had no large number of trained military officers, still capable of active service.

The armies of the North and South alike had to be commanded and staffed to a great extent by men who first studied their profession in that war; and the lack of ripe military judgment was likely to be felt most in the higher commands where the forces to be employed and co-ordinated were largest. The South secured what may be called its fair proportion of the comparatively few officers, but it was of tremendous moment that, among the officers who, when the war began, were recognised as competent, two, who sadly but in simple loyalty to the State of Virginia took the Southern side, were men of genius. The advantages of the South would have been no advantages without skill and resolution to make use of them. The main conditions of the war—the vast space, the difficulty in all parts of it of moving troops, the generally low level of military knowledge—were all such as greatly enhance the opportunities of the most gifted commander. Lee and " Stonewall " Jackson thus became, the former throughout the war, the latter till he was killed in the summer of 1863, factors of primary importance in the struggle. Wolseley, who had, besides studying their record, conversed both with Lee and with Moltke, thought Lee even greater than Moltke, and the military writers of our day speak of him as one of the great commanders of history. As to Jackson, Lee's belief in him is sufficient testimony to his value. And the good fortune of the South was not confined to these two signal instances. Most of the Southern generals who appeared early in the war could be retained in important commands to the end.

The South might have seemed at first equally fortunate in the character of the Administration at the back of the generals. An ascendency was at once conceded to Jefferson Davis, a tried political leader, to which Lincoln had to win his way, and the past experiences of the two men had been very different. The operations of war in which Lincoln had taken part were confined, according to his own romantic account in a speech in Congress, to stealing ducks and onions from the civil population; his

Ministers were as ignorant in the matter as he; their military adviser, Scott, was so infirm that he had soon to retire, and it proved most difficult to replace him. Jefferson Davis, on the other hand, started with knowledge of affairs, including military affairs; he had been Secretary of War in Pierce's Cabinet and Chairman of the Senate Committee on War since then; above all, he had been a soldier and had commanded a regiment with some distinction in the Mexican War. It is thought that he would have preferred a military command to the Presidency of the Confederacy, and as his own experience of actual war was as great as that of his generals, he can hardly be blamed for a disposition to interfere with them at the beginning. But military historians, while criticising (perhaps a little hastily) all Lincoln's interventions in the affairs of war up to the time when he found generals whom he trusted, insist that Davis' systematic interference was far more harmful to his cause; and Wolseley, who watched events closely from Canada and who visited the Southern Army in 1863, is most emphatic in this opinion. He interfered with Lee to an extent which nothing but Lee's devoted friendship and loyalty could have made tolerable. He put himself into relations of dire hostility with Joseph Johnston, and in 1864 suspended him in the most injudicious manner. Above all, when the military position of the South had begun to be acutely perilous, Jefferson Davis neither devised for himself, nor allowed his generals to devise, any bold policy by which the chance that still remained could be utilised. His energy of will showed itself in the end in nothing but a resolution to protract bloodshed after it had certainly become idle.

If we turn to the political conditions, on which, in any but a short war, so much depends, the South will appear to have had great advantages. Its people were more richly endowed than the mixed and crudely democratic multitude of the North, in the traditional aptitude for commanding or obeying which enables people to pull together in a crisis. And they were united in a cause

such as would secure the sustained loyalty of any ordinary people under any ordinary leader. For, though it was nothing but slavery that led to their assertion of independence, from the moment that they found themselves involved in war, they were fighting for a freedom to which they felt themselves entitled, and for nothing else whatever. A few successful encounters at the start tempted the ordinary Southerner to think himself a better man than the ordinary Northerner, even as the Southern Congressmen felt themselves superior to the persons whom the mistaken democracy of the North too frequently elected. This claim of independence soon acquired something of the fierce pride that might have been felt by an ancient nation. But it would have been impossible that the Northern people as a whole should be similarly possessed by the cause in which they fought. They did not seem to be fighting for their own liberty, and they would have hated to think that they were fighting for conquest. They were fighting for the maintenance of a national unity which they held dear. The question how far it was worth fighting a formidable enemy for the sake of eventual unity with him, was bound to present itself. Thus, far from wondering that the cause of the Union aroused no fuller devotion than it did in the whole lump of the Northern people, we may wonder that it inspired with so lofty a patriotism men and women in every rank of life who were able to leaven that lump. But the political element in this war was of such importance as to lead to a startling result; the North came nearest to yielding at a time when in a military sense its success had become sure. To preserve a united North was the greatest and one of the hardest of the duties of President Lincoln.

To a civilian reader the history of the war, in spite of the picturesque incidents of many battles, may easily be made dreary. Till far on in the lengthy process of subjecting the South, we might easily become immersed in some futile story of how General X. was superseded by General Y. in a command, for which neither discovered

any purpose but that of not co-operating with General Z. And this impression is not merely due to our failure to understand the difficulties which confronted these gallant officers. The dearth of trained military faculty, which was felt at the outset, could only be made good by the training which the war itself supplied. Such commanders as Grant and Sherman and Sheridan not only could not have been recognised at the beginning of the war; they were not then the soldiers that they afterwards become. And the want was necessarily very serious in the case of the higher commands which required the movement of large forces, the control of subordinates each of whom must have a wide discretion, and the energy of intellect and will necessary for resolving the more complex problems of strategy. We are called upon to admire upon both sides the devotion of forgotten thousands, and to admire upon the side of the South the brilliant and daring operations by which in so many battles Lee and Jackson defeated superior forces. On the Northern side, later on, great generals came to view, but it is in the main a different sort of achievement which we are called upon to appreciate. An Administration appointed to direct a stupendous operation of conquest was itself of necessity ill prepared for such a task; behind it were a Legislature and a public opinion equally ill prepared to support and to assist it. There were in its military service many intelligent and many enterprising men, but none, at first, so combining intelligence and enterprise that he could grapple with any great responsibility or that the civil power would have been warranted in reposing complete confidence in him. The history of the war has to be recounted in this volume chiefly with a view to these difficulties of the Administration.

One of the most interesting features of the war would, in any military study of it, be seen to be the character of the troops on both sides. On both sides their individual quality was high; on both, circumstances and the disposition of the people combined to make discipline weak. This character, common to the two armies, was conspicu-

ous in many battles of the war, but a larger interest attaches to the policy of the two administrations in raising and organising their civilian armies. The Southern Government, if its proceedings were studied in detail, would probably seem to have been better advised at the start on matters of military organisation; for instance, it had early and long retained a superiority in cavalry which was not a mere result of good fortune. But here, too, there was an inherent advantage in the very fact that the South had started upon a desperate venture. There can hardly be a more difficult problem of detail for statesmen than the co-ordination of military and civil requirements in the raising of an army. But in the South all civil considerations merged themselves in the paramount necessity of a military success for which all knew the utmost effort was needed. The several States of the South, claiming as they did a far larger independence than the Northern States, knew that they could only make that claim good by being efficient members of the Confederacy. Thus it was comparatively easy for the Confederate Government to adopt and maintain a consecutive policy in this matter, and though, from the conditions of a widely spread agricultural population, voluntary enlistment produced poor results at the beginning of the war, it appears to have been easy to introduce quite early an entirely compulsory system of a stringent kind.

The introduction of compulsory service in the North has its place in our subsequent story. The system that preceded it need not be dwelt upon here, because, full of instruction as a technical study of it (such as has been made by Colonel Henderson) must be, no brief survey by an amateur could be useful. It is necessary, however, to understand the position in which Lincoln's Administration was placed, without much experience in America, or perhaps elsewhere in the world, to guide it. It must not be contended, for it cannot be known that the problem was fully and duly envisaged by Lincoln on his Cabinet, but it would probably in any case have been impos-

sible for them to pursue from the first a consecutive and
well-thought-out policy for raising an army and keeping
up its strength. The position of the North differed fundamentally from that of the South; the North experienced
neither the ardour nor the throes of a revolution; it was
never in any fear of being conquered, only of not conquering. There was nothing, therefore, which at once
bestowed on the Government a moral power over the
country vastly in excess of that which it exercised in
normal times. This, however, was really necessary to
it if the problem of the Army was to be handled in the
way which was desirable from a military point of view.
Compulsory service could not at first be thought of. It
was never supposed that the tiny regular Army of the
United States Government could be raised to any very
great size by voluntary enlistment, and the limited increase of it which was attempted was not altogether successful. The existing militia system of the several States
was almost immediately found faulty and was discarded.
A great Volunteer Force had to be raised which should
be under the command of the President, who by the
Constitution is Commander-in-Chief of the forces of the
Union, but which must be raised in each State by the
State Governor (or, if he was utterly wanting, by leading local citizens). Now State Governors are not—it
must be recalled—officers under the President, but independent potentates acting usually in as much detachment
from him as the Vice-Chancellor of Oxford or Cambridge from the Board of Education or a Presbyterian
minister from a bishop. This group of men, for the
most part able, patriotic, and determined, were there to
be used and had to be consulted. It follows that the
policy of the North in raising and organising its armies
had at first to be a policy evolved between numerous
independent authorities which never met and were held
together by a somewhat ignorant public opinion, sometimes much depressed and sometimes, which was worse,
oversanguine. It is impossible to judge exactly how ill
or how well Lincoln, under such circumstances, grappled

with this particular problem, but many anomalies which seem to us preposterous—the raising of raw new regiments when fine seasoned regiments were short of half their strength, and so forth—were in these circumstances inevitable. The national system of recruiting, backed by compulsion, which was later set up, still required for its success the co-operation of State and local authorities of this wholly independent character.

Northern and Southern armies alike had necessarily to be commanded to a great extent by amateur officers; the number of officers, in the service or retired, who had been trained at West Point, was immeasurably too small for the needs of the armies. Amateurs had to be called in, and not only so, but they had in some cases to be given very important commands. The not altogether unwholesome tradition that a self-reliant man can turn his hand to anything was of course very strong in America, and the short military annals of the country had been thought to have added some illustrious instances to the roll of men of peace who have distinguished themselves in arms. So a political leader, no matter whether he was Democrat or Republican, who was a man of known general capacity, would sometimes at first seem suitable for an important command rather than the trained but unknown professional soldier who was the alternative. Moreover, it seemed foolish not to appoint him, when, as sometimes happened, he could bring thousands of recruits from his State. The Civil War turned out, however, to show the superiority of the duly trained military mind in a marked degree. Some West-Pointers of repute of course proved incapable, and a great many amateur colonels and generals, both North and South, attained a very fair level of competence in the service (the few conspicuous failures seem to have been quite exceptional); but, all the same, of the many clever and stirring men who then took up soldiering as novices and served for four years, not one achieved brilliant success; of the generals in the war whose names are remembered, some had indeed passed years in civil life, but every one had

received a thorough military training in the years of his early manhood. It certainly does not appear that the Administration was really neglectful of professional merit; it hungered to find it; but many appointments must at first have been made in a haphazard fashion, for there was no machinery for sifting claims. A zealous but unknown West-Pointer put under an outsider would be apt to write as Sherman did in early days: " Mr. Lincoln meant to insult me and the Army "; and a considerable jealousy evidently arose between West-Pointers and amateurs. It was aggravated by the rivalry between officers of the Eastern army and those of the, more largely amateur, Western army. The amateurs, too, had something to say on their side; they were apt to accuse West-Pointers as a class of a cringing belief that the South was invincible. There was nothing unnatural or very serious in all this, but political influences which arose later caused complaints of this nature to be made the most of, and a general charge to be made against Lincoln's Administration of appointing generals and removing them under improper political influences. This general charge, however, rests upon a limited number of alleged instances, and all of these which are of any importance will necessarily be examined in later chapters.

It may be useful to a reader who wishes to follow the main course of the war carefully, if the chief ways in which geographical facts affected it are here summarised —necessarily somewhat dryly. Minor operations at outlying points on the coast or in the Far West will be left out of account, so also will a serious political consideration, which we shall later see caused doubt for a time as to the proper strategy of the North.

It must be noted first, startling as it may be to Englishmen who remember the war partly by the exploits of the *Alabama,* that the naval superiority of the North was overwhelming. In spite of many gallant efforts by the Southern sailors, the North could blockade their coasts and could capture most of the Southern ports long before its superiority on land was established. Turning then

to land, we may treat the political frontier between the two powers, after a short preliminary stage of war, as being marked by the southern boundaries of Maryland, West Virginia, Kentucky, and Missouri, just as they are seen on the map to-day. In doing so, we must note that at the commencement of large operations parts of Kentucky and Missouri were occupied by Southern invading forces. This frontier is cut, not far from the Atlantic, by the parallel mountain chains which make up the Alleghanies or Appalachians. These in effect separated the field of operations into a narrow Eastern theatre of war, and an almost boundless Western theatre; and the operations in these two theatres were almost to the end independent of each other.

In the Eastern theatre of war lies Washington, the capital of the Union, a place of great importance to the North for obvious reasons, and especially because if it fell European powers would be likely to recognise the Confederacy. It lies, on the Potomac, right upon the frontier; and could be menaced also in the rear, for the broad and fertile trough between the mountain chains formed by the valley of the Shenandoah River, which flows northward to join the Potomac at a point north-west of Washington, was in Confederate hands and formed a sort of sally-port by which a force from Richmond could get almost behind Washington. A hundred miles south of Washington lay Richmond, which shortly became the capital of the Confederates, instead of Montgomery in Alabama. As a brand-new capital it mattered little to the Confederates, though at the very end of the war it became their last remaining stronghold. The intervening country, which was in Southern hands, was extraordinarily difficult. The reader may notice on the map the rivers with broad estuaries which are its most marked features, and with the names of which we shall become familiar. The rivers themselves were obstacles to an invading Northern army; their estuaries, on the other hand, soon afforded it safe communication by sea.

In the Western theatre of war we must remember first

the enormous length of frontier in proportion to the population on either side. This necessarily made the progress of Northern invasion slow, and its proper direction hard to determine, for diversions could be created by a counter-invasion elsewhere along the frontier or a stroke at the invaders' communications. The principal feature of the whole region is the great waterways, on which the same advantages which gave the sea to the North gave it also an immense superiority in the river warfare of flotillas of gunboats. When the North with its gunboats could get control of the Mississippi the South would be deprived of a considerable part of its territory and resources, and cut off from its last means of trading with Europe (save for the relief afforded by blockade-runners) by being cut off from Mexico and its ports. Further, when the North could control the tributaries of the Mississippi, especially the Cumberland and the Tennessee which flow into the great river through the Ohio, it would cut deep into the internal communications of the South. Against this menace the South could only contend by erecting powerful fortresses on the rivers, and the capture of some of them was the great object of the earlier Northern operations.

The railway system of the South must also be taken into account in connection with their waterways. This, of course, cannot be seen on a modern map. Perhaps the following may make the main points clear. The Southern railway system touched the Mississippi and the world beyond it at three points only: Memphis, Vicksburg, and New Orleans. A traveller wishing to go, say, from Richmond by rail towards the West could have, if distance were indifferent to him, a choice of three routes for part of the way. He could go through Knoxville in Tennessee to Chattanooga in that State, where he had a choice of routes further West, or he could take one of two alternative lines south into Georgia and thence go either to Atlanta or to Columbus in the west of that State. Arrived at Atlanta or Columbus, he could proceed further West either by making a detour northwards

through Chattanooga or by making a detour southwards through the seaport town of Mobile, crossing the harbour by boat. Thus the capture of Chattanooga from the South would go far towards cutting the whole Southern railway system in two, and the capture of Mobile would complete it. Lastly, we may notice two lines running north and south through the State of Mississippi, one through Corinth and Meridian, and the other nearer the great river. From this and the course of the rivers the strategic importance of some of the towns mentioned may be partly appreciated.

The subjugation of the South in fact began by a process, necessarily slow and much interrupted, whereby having been blockaded by sea it was surrounded by land, cut off from its Western territory, and deprived of its main internal lines of communication. Richmond, against which the North began to move within the first three months of the war, did not fall till nearly four years later, when the process just described had been completed, and when a Northern army had triumphantly progressed, wasting the resources of the country as it went, from Chattanooga to Atlanta, thence to the Atlantic coast of Georgia, and thence northward through the two Carolinas till it was about to join hands with the army assailing Richmond. Throughout this time the attention of a large part of the Northern public and of all those who watched the war from Europe was naturally fastened to a great extent upon the desperate fighting which occurred in the region of Washington and of Richmond and upon the ill success of the North in endeavours of unforeseen difficulty against the latter city. We shall see, however, that the long and humiliating failure of the North in this quarter was neither so unaccountable nor nearly so important as it appeared.

CHAPTER VIII

1. *Preliminary Stages.*

ON the morning after the bombardment of Fort Sumter there appeared a Proclamation by the President calling upon the Militia of the several States to furnish 75,000 men for the service of the United States in the suppression of an " unlawful combination." Their service, however, would expire by law thirty days after the next meeting of Congress, and, in compliance with a further requirement of law upon this subject, the President also summoned Congress to meet in extraordinary session upon July 4. The Army already in the service of the United States consisted of but 16,000 officers and men, and, though the men of this force, being less affected by State ties than their officers, remained, as did the men of the Navy, true almost without exception to their allegiance, all but 3,000 of them were unavailable and scattered in small frontier forts in the West. A few days later, when it became plain that the struggle might long outlast the three months of the Militia, the President called for Volunteers to enlist for three years' service, and perhaps (for the statements are conflicting) some 300,000 troops of one kind and another had been raised by June.

The affair of Fort Sumter and the President's Proclamation at once aroused and concentrated the whole public opinion of the free States in the North and, in an opposite sense, of the States which had already seceded. The border slave States had now to declare for the one side or for the other. Virginia as a whole joined the Southern Confederacy forthwith, but several Counties in the moun-

228

tainous region of the west of that State were strongly for the Union. These eventually succeeded with the support of Northern troops in separating from Virginia and forming the new State of West Virginia. Tennessee also joined the South, though in Eastern Tennessee the bulk of the people held out for the Union without such good fortune as their neighbours in West Virginia. Arkansas beyond the Mississippi followed the same example, though there were some doubt and division in all parts of that State. In Delaware, where the slaves were very few, the Governor did not formally comply with the President's Proclamation, but the people as a whole responded to it. The attitude of Maryland, which almost surrounds Washington, kept the Government at the capital in suspense and alarm for a while, for both the city of Baltimore and the existing State legislature were inclined to the South. In Kentucky and Missouri the State authorities were also for the South, and it was only after a struggle, and in Missouri much actual fighting, that the Unionist majority of the people in each State had its way.

The secession of Virginia had consequences even more important than the loss to the Union of a powerful State. General Robert E. Lee, a Virginian, then in Washington, was esteemed by General Scott to be the ablest officer in the service. Lincoln and his Secretary of War desired to confer on him the command of the Army. Lee's decision was made with much reluctance and, it seems, hesitation. He was not only opposed to the policy of secession, but denied the right of a State to secede; yet he believed that his absolute allegiance was due to Virginia. He resigned his commission in the United States Army, went to Richmond, and, in accordance with what Wolseley describes as the prevailing principle that had influenced most of the soldiers he met in the South, placed his sword at the disposal of his own State. The same loyalty to Virginia governed another great soldier, Thomas J. Jackson, whose historic nickname, " Stonewall," fails to convey the dashing celerity of his movements. While they both lived these two men were to be

linked together in the closest comradeship and mutual
trust. They sprang from different social conditions and
were of contrasting types. The epithet Cavalier has been
fitly enough applied to Lee, and Jackson, after conversion from the wild courses of his youth, was an austere
Puritan. To quote again from a soldier's memoirs,
Wolseley calls Lee "one of the few men who ever seriously impressed and awed me with their natural, their
inherent, greatness"; he speaks of his " majesty," and
of the " beauty," of his character, and of the " sweetness
of his smile and the impressive dignity of the old-fashioned style of his address"; " his greatness," he says,
" made me humble." " There was nothing," he tells us,
" of these refined characteristics in Stonewall Jackson,"
a man with " huge hands and feet." But he possessed
" an assured self-confidence, the outcome of his sure trust
in God. How simple, how humble-minded a man. As
his impressive eyes met yours unflinchingly, you knew that
his was an honest heart." To this he adds touches less
to be expected concerning a Puritan warrior, whose
Puritanism was in fact inclined to ferocity—how Jackson's " remarkable eyes lit up for the moment with a
look of real enthusiasm as he recalled the architectural
beauty of the seven lancet windows in York Minster,"
how " intense " was the " benignity " of his expression,
and how in him it seemed that " great strength of character and obstinate determination were united with extreme gentleness of disposition and with absolute tenderness towards all about him." Men such as these brought
to the Southern cause something besides their military.
capacity; but as to the greatness of that capacity, applied
in a war in which the scope was so great for individual
leaders of genius, there is no question. A civilian reader,
looking in the history of war chiefly for the evidences of
personal quality, can at least discern in these two famous
soldiers the moral daring which in doubtful circumstances
never flinches from the responsibility of a well-considered
risk, and, in both their cases as in those of some other
great commanders, can recognise in this rare and precious

attribute the outcome of their personal piety. We shall henceforth have to do with the Southern Confederacy and its armies, not in their inner history but with sole regard to the task which they imposed upon Lincoln and the North. But at this parting of the ways a tribute is due to the two men, pre-eminent among many devoted people, who, in their soldier-like and unreflecting loyalty to their cause, gave to it a lustre in which, so far as they can be judged, neither its statesmen nor its spiritual guides had a share.

There were Virginian officers who did not thus go with their State. Of these were Scott himself, and G. H. Thomas; and Farragut, the great sailor, was from Tennessee.

Throughout the free States of the North there took place a national uprising of which none who remember it have spoken without feeling anew its spontaneous ardour. Men flung off with delight the hesitancy of the preceding months, and recruiting went on with speed and enthusiasm. Party divisions for the moment disappeared. Old Buchanan made public his adhesion to the Government. Douglas called upon Lincoln to ask how best he could serve the public cause, and, at his request, went down to Illinois to guide opinion and advance recruiting there; so employed, the President's great rival, shortly after, fell ill and died, leaving the leadership of the Democrats to be filled thereafter by more scrupulous but less patriotic men. There was exultant confidence in the power of the nation to put down rebellion, and those who realised the peril in which for many days the capital and the administration were placed were only the more indignantly determined. Perhaps the most trustworthy record of popular emotions is to be found in popular humorists. Shortly after these days Artemus Ward, the author who almost vied with Shakespeare in Lincoln's affections, relates how the confiscation of his show in the South led him to have an interview with Jefferson Davis. " Even now," said Davis, in this pleasant fiction, " we have many frens in the North." " J. Davis," is the reply, " there's your grate mistaik. Many of us was your sincere frends,

and thought certin parties amung us was fussin' about you and meddlin' with your consarns intirely too much. But, J. Davis, the minit you fire a gun at the piece of dry goods called the Star-Spangled Banner, the North gits up and rises en massy, in defence of that banner. Not agin you as individooals—not agin the South even—but to save the flag. We should indeed be weak in the knees, unsound in the heart, milk-white in the liver, and soft in the hed, if we stood quietly by and saw this glorus Govyment smashed to pieces, either by a furrin or a intestine foe. The gentle-harted mother hates to take her naughty child across her knee, but she knows it is her dooty to do it. So we shall hate to whip the naughty South, but we must do it if you don't make back tracks at onct, and we shall wallup you out of your boots!" In the days which followed, when this prompt chastisement could not be effected and it seemed indeed as if the South would do most of the whipping, the discordant elements which mingled in this unanimity soon showed themselves. The minority that opposed the war was for a time silent and insignificant, but among the supporters of the war there were those who loved the Union and the Constitution and who, partly for this very reason, had hitherto cultivated the sympathies of the South. These—adherents mainly of the Democratic party—would desire that civil war should be waged with the least possible breach of the Constitution, and be concluded with the least possible social change; many of them would wish to fight not to a finish but to a compromise. On the other hand, there were those who loved liberty and hated alike the slave system of the South and the arrogance which it had engendered. These—the people distinguished within the Republican party as Radicals—would pay little heed to constitutional restraints in repelling an attack on the Constitution, and they would wish from the first to make avowed war upon that which caused the war—slavery. In the border States there was of course more active sympathy with the South, and in conflict with this the Radicalism of some of these States became more stalwart and

intractable. To such causes of dissension was added as time went on sheer fatigue of the war, and strangely enough this influence was as powerful with a few Radicals as it was with the ingrained Democratic partisans. They despaired of the result when success at last was imminent, and became sick of bloodshed when it passed what they presumably regarded as a reasonable amount.

It was the task of the Administration not only to conduct the war, but to preserve the unity of the North in spite of differences and its resolution in spite of disappointments. Lincoln was in more than one way well fitted for this task. Old experience in Illinois and Kentucky enabled him to understand very different points of view in regard to the cause of the South. The new question that was now to arise about slavery was but a particular form of the larger question of principle to which he had long thought out an answer as firm and as definite as it was moderate and in a sense subtle. He had, moreover, a quality of heart which, as it seemed to those near him, the protraction of the conflict, with its necessary strain upon him, only strengthened. In him a tenacity, which scarcely could falter in the cause which he judged to be right, was not merely pure from bitterness towards his antagonists, it was actually bound up with a deep-seated kindliness towards them. Whatever rank may be assigned to his services and to his deserts, it is first and foremost in these directions, though not in these directions alone, that the reader of his story must look for them. Upon attentive study he will probably appear as the embodiment, in a degree and manner which are alike rare, of the more constant and the higher judgment of his people. It is plainer still that he embodied the resolute purpose which underlay the fluctuations upon the surface of their political life. The English military historians, Wood and Edmonds, in their retrospect over the course of the war, well sum up its dramatic aspect when they say: "Against the great military genius of certain of the Southern leaders fate opposed the unbroken resolution and passionate devotion to the Union, which he

worshipped, of the great Northern President. As long as he lived, and ruled the people of the North, there could be no turning back."

There are plenty of indications in the literature of the time that Lincoln's determination soon began to be widely felt and to be appreciated by common people. Literally, crowds of people from all parts of the North saw him, exchanged a sentence or two, and carried home their impressions; and those who were near him record the constant fortitude of his bearing, noting as marked exceptions the unrestrained words of impatience and half-humorous despondency which did on rare occasions escape him. In a negative way, too, even the political world bore its testimony to this; his administration was charged with almost every other form of weakness, but there was never a suspicion that he would give in. Nor again, in the severest criticisms upon him by knowledgeable men that have been unearthed and collected, does the suggestion of petty personal aims or of anything but unselfish devotion ever find a place. The belief that he could be trusted spread itself among plain people, and, given this belief, plain people liked him the better because he was plain. But if at the distance at which we contemplate him, and at which from the moment of his death all America contemplated him, certain grand traits emerge, it is not for a moment to be supposed that in his life he stood out in front of the people as a great leader, or indeed as a leader at all, in the manner, say, of Chatham or even of Palmerston. Lincoln came to Washington doubtless with some deep thoughts which other men had not thought, doubtless also with some important knowledge, for instance of the border States, which many statesmen lacked, but he came there a man inexperienced in affairs. It was a part of his strength that he knew this very well, that he meant to learn, thought he could learn, did not mean to be hurried where he had not the knowledge to decide, entirely appreciated superior knowledge in others, and was entirely unawed by it. But Senators and Representatives in Congress and journalists of high

standing, as a rule, perceived the inexperience and not the strength. The deliberation with which he acted, patiently watching events, saying little, listening to all sides, conversing with a naïveté which was genuine but not quite artless, seemingly obdurate to the pressure of wise counsels on one side and on the other—all this struck many anxious observers as sheer incompetence, and when there was just and natural cause for their anxiety, there was no established presumption of his wisdom to set against it. And this effect was enhanced by what may be called his plainness, his awkwardness, and actual eccentricity in many minor matters. To many intelligent people who met him they were a grievous stumbling-block, and though some most cultivated men were not at all struck by them, and were pleased instead by his " seeming sincere, and honest, and steady," or the like, it is clear that no one in Washington was greatly impressed by him at first meeting. His oddities were real and incorrigible. Young John Hay, whom Nicolay, his private secretary, introduced as his assistant, a humorist like Lincoln himself, but with leanings to literary elegance and a keen eye for social distinctions, loved him all along and came to worship him, but irreverent amusement is to be traced in his recently published letters, and the glimpses which he gives us of " the Ancient " or " the Tycoon " when quite at home and quite at his ease fully justify him. Lincoln had great dignity and tact for use when he wanted them, but he did not always see the use of them. Senator Sherman was presented to the new President. " So you're John Sherman? " said Lincoln. " Let's see if you're as tall as I am. We'll measure." The grave politician, who was made to stand back to back with him before the company till this interesting question was settled, dimly perceived that the intention was friendly, but felt that there was a lack of ceremony. Lincoln's height was one of his subjects of harmless vanity; many tall men had to measure themselves against him in this manner, and probably felt like John Sherman. On all sorts of occasions and to all sorts of people he

would "tell a little story," which was often enough, in Lord Lyons' phrase, an "extreme" story. This was the way in which he had grown accustomed to be friendly in company; it served a purpose when intrusive questions had to be evaded, or reproofs or refusals to be given without offence. As his laborious and sorrowful task came to weigh heavier upon him, his capacity for play of this sort became a great resource to him. As his fame became established people recognised him as a humorist; the inevitable "little story" became to many an endearing form of eccentricity; but we may be sure it was not so always or to everybody.

"Those," says Carl Schurz, a political exile from Prussia, who did good service, military and political, to the Northern cause—"those who visited the White House—and the White House appeared to be open to whosoever wished to enter—saw there a man of unconventional manners, who, without the slightest effort to put on dignity, treated all men alike, much like old neighbours; whose speech had not seldom a rustic flavour about it; who always seemed to have time for a homely talk and never to be in a hurry to press business; and who occasionally spoke about important affairs of State with the same nonchalance—I might almost say irreverence—with which he might have discussed an every-day law case in his office at Springfield, Illinois."

Thus Lincoln was very far from inspiring general confidence in anything beyond his good intentions. He is remembered as a personality with a "something" about him—the vague phrase is John Bright's—which widely endeared him, but his was by no means that "magnetic" personality which we might be led to believe was indispensable in America. Indeed, it is remarkable that to some really good judges he remained always unimpressive. Charles Francis Adams, who during the Civil War served his country as well as Minister in London as his grandfather had done after the War of Independence, lamented to the end that Seward, his immediate chief, had to serve under an inferior man; and a more

sympathetic man, Lord Lyons, our representative at
Washington, refers to Lincoln with nothing more than
an amused kindliness. No detail of his policy has escaped
fierce criticism, and the man himself while he lived was
the subject of so much depreciation and condescending
approval, that we are forced to ask who discovered his
greatness till his death inclined them to idealise him.
The answer is that precisely those Americans of trained
intellect whose title to this description is clearest outside
America were the first who began to see beneath his
strange exterior. Lowell, watching the course of public
events with ceaseless scrutiny; Walt Whitman, sauntering
in Washington in the intervals of the labour among the
wounded by which he broke down his robust strength,
and seeing things as they passed with the sure observation of a poet; Motley, the historian of the Dutch Republic, studying affairs in the thick of them at the outset
of the war, and not less closely by correspondence when
he went as Minister to Vienna—such men when they
praised Lincoln after his death expressed a judgment
which they began to form from the first; a judgment
which started with the recognition of his honesty, traced
the evidence of his wisdom as it appeared, gradually and
not by repentant impulse learned his greatness. And it
is a judgment large enough to explain the lower estimate
of Lincoln which certainly had wide currency. Not to
multiply witnesses, Motley in June, 1861, having seen
him for the second time, writes: " I went and had an
hour's talk with Mr. Lincoln. I am very glad of it, for,
had I not done so, I should have left Washington with
a very inaccurate impression of the President. I am
now satisfied that he is a man of very considerable native
sagacity; and that he has an ingenuous, unsophisticated,
frank, and noble character. I believe him to be as
true as steel, and as courageous as true. At the same
time there is doubtless an ignorance about State matters,
and particularly about foreign affairs, which he does not
attempt to conceal, but which we must of necessity regret
in a man placed in such a position at such a crisis. Never-

requested that no more troops should pass through Baltimore. The Mayor of Baltimore and the railway authorities burned railway bridges and tore up railway lines, and the telegraph wires were cut. Thus for about five days the direct route to Washington from the North was barred. It seemed as if the boast of some Southern orator that the Confederate flag would float over the capital by May 1 might be fulfilled. Beauregard could have transported his now drilled troops by rail from South Carolina and would have found Washington isolated and hardly garrisoned. As a matter of fact, no such daring move was contemplated in the South, and the citizens of Richmond, Virginia, were themselves under a similar alarm; but the South had a real opportunity.

The fall of Washington at that moment would have had political consequences which no one realised better than Lincoln. It might well have led the Unionists in the border States to despair, and there is evidence that even then he so fully realised the task which lay before the North as to feel that the loss of Maryland, Kentucky, and Missouri would have made it impossible. He was at heart intensely anxious, and quaintly and injudiciously relieved his feelings by the remark to the " 6th Massachusetts " that he felt as if all other help were a dream, and they were " the only real thing." Yet those who were with him testify to his composure and to the vigour with which he concerted with his Cabinet the various measures of naval, military, financial, postal, and police preparation which the occasion required, but which need not here be detailed. Many of the measures of course lay outside the powers which Congress had conferred on the public departments, but the President had no hesitation in " availing himself," as he put it, " of the broader powers conferred by the Constitution in cases of insurrection," and looking for the sanction of Congress afterwards, rather than " let the Government at once fall into ruin." The difficulties of government were greatly aggravated by the uncertainty as to which of its servants,

sympathetic man, Lord Lyons, our representative at
Washington, refers to Lincoln with nothing more than
an amused kindliness. No detail of his policy has escaped
fierce criticism, and the man himself while he lived was
the subject of so much depreciation and condescending
approval, that we are forced to ask who discovered his
greatness till his death inclined them to idealise him.
The answer is that precisely those Americans of trained
intellect whose title to this description is clearest outside
America were the first who began to see beneath his
strange exterior. Lowell, watching the course of public
events with ceaseless scrutiny; Walt Whitman, sauntering
in Washington in the intervals of the labour among the
wounded by which he broke down his robust strength,
and seeing things as they passed with the sure observation of a poet; Motley, the historian of the Dutch Republic, studying affairs in the thick of them at the outset
of the war, and not less closely by correspondence when
he went as Minister to Vienna—such men when they
praised Lincoln after his death expressed a judgment
which they began to form from the first; a judgment
which started with the recognition of his honesty, traced
the evidence of his wisdom as it appeared, gradually and
not by repentant impulse learned his greatness. And it
is a judgment large enough to explain the lower estimate
of Lincoln which certainly had wide currency. Not to
multiply witnesses, Motley in June, 1861, having seen
him for the second time, writes: "I went and had an
hour's talk with Mr. Lincoln. I am very glad of it, for,
had I not done so, I should have left Washington with
a very inaccurate impression of the President. I am
now satisfied that he is a man of very considerable native
sagacity; and that he has an ingenuous, unsophisticated,
frank, and noble character. I believe him to be as
true as steel, and as courageous as true. At the same
time there is doubtless an ignorance about State matters,
and particularly about foreign affairs, which he does not
attempt to conceal, but which we must of necessity regret
in a man placed in such a position at such a crisis. Never-

theless his very modesty in this respect disarms criticism.
We parted very affectionately, and perhaps I shall never
set eyes on him again, but I feel that, so far as perfect
integrity and directness of purpose go, the country will
be safe in his hands." Three years had passed, and the
political world of America was in that storm of general
dissatisfaction in which not a member of Congress would
be known as " a Lincoln man," when Motley writes again
from Vienna to his mother, " I venerate Abraham Lincoln exactly because he is the true, honest type of American democracy. There is nothing of the shabby-genteel,
the would-be-but-couldn't-be fine gentleman; he is the
great American Demos, honest, shrewd, homely, wise,
humorous, cheerful, brave, blundering occasionally, but
through blunders struggling onwards towards what he
believes the right." In a later letter he observes, " His
mental abilities were large, and they became the more
robust as the more weight was imposed upon them."

This last sentence, especially if in Lincoln's mental
abilities the qualities of his character be included, probably indicates the chief point for remark in any estimate
of his presidency. It is true that he was judged at first
as a stranger among strangers. Walt Whitman has
described vividly a scene, with " a dash of comedy, almost
farce, such as Shakespeare puts in his blackest tragedies,"
outside the hotel in New York where Lincoln stayed on
his journey to Washington; " his look and gait, his perfect composure and coolness," to cut it short, the usually
noted marks of his eccentricity, " as he stood looking with
curiosity on that immense sea of faces, and the sea of
faces returned the look with similar curiosity, not a single
one " among the crowd " his personal friend." He was
not much otherwise situated when he came to Washington. It is true also that in the early days he was learning
his business. " Why, Mr. President," said some one
towards the end of his life, " you have changed your
mind." " Yes, I have," said he, " and I don't think much
of a man who isn't wiser to-day than he was yesterday."
But it seems to be above all true that the exercise of

power and the endurance of responsibility gave him new strength. This, of course, cannot be demonstrated, but Americans then living, who recall Abraham Lincoln, remark most frequently how the man grew to his task. And this perhaps is the main impression which the slight record here presented will convey, the impression of a man quite unlike the many statesmen whom power and the vexations attendant upon it have in some piteous way spoiled and marred, a man who started by being tough and shrewd and canny and became very strong and very wise, started with an inclination to honesty, courage, and kindness, and became, under a tremendous strain, honest, brave, and kind to an almost tremendous degree.

The North then started upon the struggle with an eagerness and unanimity from which the revulsion was to try all hearts, and the President's most of all; and not a man in the North guessed what the strain of that struggle was to be. At first indeed there was alarm in Washington for the immediate safety of the city. Confederate flags could be seen floating from the hotels in Alexandria across the river; Washington itself was full of rumours of plots and intended assassinations, and full of actual Southern spies; everything was disorganised; and Lincoln himself, walking round one night, found the arsenal with open doors, absolutely unguarded.

By April 20, first the Navy Yard at Gosport, in Virginia, had to be abandoned, then the Arsenal at Harper's Ferry, and on the day of this latter event Lee went over to the South. One regiment from Massachusetts, where the State authorities had prepared for war before the fall of Sumter, was already in Washington; but it had had to fight its way through a furious mob in Baltimore, with some loss of life on both sides. A deputation from many churches in that city came to the President, begging him to desist from his bloodthirsty preparations, but found him " constitutionally genial and jovial," and " wholly inaccessible to Christian appeals." It mattered more that a majority of the Maryland Legislature was for the South, and that the Governor temporised and

requested that no more troops should pass through Baltimore. The Mayor of Baltimore and the railway authorities burned railway bridges and tore up railway lines,
and the telegraph wires were cut. Thus for about five
days the direct route to Washington from the North was
barred. It seemed as if the boast of some Southern
orator that the Confederate flag would float over the
capital by May 1 might be fulfilled. Beauregard could
have transported his now drilled troops by rail from
South Carolina and would have found Washington isolated and hardly garrisoned. As a matter of fact, no
such daring move was contemplated in the South, and
the citizens of Richmond, Virginia, were themselves
under a similar alarm; but the South had a real opportunity.

The fall of Washington at that moment would have
had political consequences which no one realised better
than Lincoln. It might well have led the Unionists in
the border States to despair, and there is evidence that
even then he so fully realised the task which lay before
the North as to feel that the loss of Maryland, Kentucky,
and Missouri would have made it impossible. He was
at heart intensely anxious, and quaintly and injudiciously
relieved his feelings by the remark to the " 6th Massachusetts " that he felt as if all other help were a dream,
and they were " the only real thing." Yet those who
were with him testify to his composure and to the vigour
with which he concerted with his Cabinet the various
measures of naval, military, financial, postal, and police
preparation which the occasion required, but which need
not here be detailed. Many of the measures of course
lay outside the powers which Congress had conferred
on the public departments, but the President had no hesitation in " availing himself," as he put it, " of the broader
powers conferred by the Constitution in cases of insurrection," and looking for the sanction of Congress afterwards, rather than " let the Government at once fall
into ruin." The difficulties of government were greatly
aggravated by the uncertainty as to which of its servants,

civil, naval, or military, were loyal, and the need of rapidly filling the many posts left vacant by unexpected desertion. Meanwhile troops from New England, and also from New York, which had utterly disappointed some natural expectations in the South by the enthusiasm of its rally to the Union, quickly arrived near Baltimore. They repaired for themselves the interrupted railway tracks round the city, and by April 25 enough soldiers were in Washington to put an end to any present alarm. In case of need, the law of " habeas corpus " was suspended in Maryland. The President had no wish that unnecessary recourse should be had to martial law. Naturally, however, one of his generals summarily arrested a Southern recruiting agent in Baltimore. The ordinary law would probably have sufficed, and Lincoln is believed to have regretted this action, but it was obvious that he must support it when done. Hence arose an occasion for the old Chief Justice Taney to make a protest on behalf of legality, to which the President, who had armed force on his side, could not give way, and thus early began a controversy to which we must recur. It was gravely urged upon Lincoln that he should forcibly prevent the Legislature of Maryland from holding a formal sitting; he refused on the sensible ground that the legislators could assemble in some way and had better not assemble with a real grievance in constitutional law. Then a strange alteration came over Baltimore. Within three weeks all active demonstration in favour of the South had subsided; the disaffected Legislature resolved upon neutrality; the Governor, loyal at heart—if the brief epithet loyal may pass, as not begging any profound legal question—carried on affairs in the interest of the Union; postal communication and the passage of troops were free from interruption by the middle of May; and the pressing alarm about Maryland was over. These incidents of the first days of war have been recounted in some detail, because they may illustrate the gravity of the issue in the border States, in others of which the struggle, though further removed from observation,

lasted longer; and because, too, it is well to realise the stress of agitation under which the Government had to make far-reaching preparation for a larger struggle, while Lincoln, whose will was decisive in all these measures, carried on all the while that seemingly unimportant routine of a President's life which is in the quietest times exacting.

The alarm in Washington was only transitory, and it was generally supposed in the North that insurrection would be easily put down. Some even specified the number of days necessary, agreeably fixing upon a smaller number than the ninety days for which the militia were called out. Secretary Seward has been credited with language of this kind, and even General Scott, whose political judgment was feeble, though his military judgment was sound, seems at first to have rejected proposals, for example, for drilling irregular cavalry, made in the expectation of a war of some length. There is evidence that neither Lincoln nor Cameron, the Secretary of War, indulged in these pleasant fancies. Irresistible public opinion, in the East especially, demanded to see prompt activity. The North had arisen in its might; it was for the Administration to put forth that might, capture Richmond, to which the Confederate Government had moved, and therewith make an end of rebellion. The truth was that the North had to make its army before it could wisely advance into the assured territory of the South; the situation of the Southern Government in this respect was precisely the same. The North had enough to do meantime in making sure of the States which were still debatable ground. Such forces as were available must of necessity be used for this purpose, but for any larger operations of war military considerations, especially on the side which had the larger resources at its back, were in favour of waiting and perfecting the instrument which was to be used. But in the course of July the pressure of public opinion and of Congress, which had then assembled, overcame, not without some reason, the more cautious military view, and on the 21st of that month the

North received its first great lesson in adversity at the battle of Bull Run.

Before recounting this disaster we may proceed with the story of the struggle in the border States. At an early date the rising armies of the North had been organised into three commands, called the Department of the Potomac, on the front between Washington and Richmond, the Department of the Ohio, on the upper watershed of the river of that name, and the Department of the West. Of necessity the generals commanding in these two more Western Departments exercised a larger discretion than the general at Washington. The Department of the Ohio was under General McClellan, before the war a captain of Engineers, who had retired from active service and had been engaged as a railway manager, in which capacity he has already been noticed, but who had earned a good name in the Mexican War, had been keen enough in his profession to visit the Crimea, and was esteemed by General Scott. The people of West Virginia, who, as has been said, were trying to organise themselves as a new State, adhering to the Union, were invaded by forces despatched by the Governor of their old State. They lay mainly west of the mountains, and help could reach them up tributary valleys of the Ohio. They appealed to McClellan, and the successes quickly won by forces despatched by him, and afterwards under his direct command, secured West Virginia, and incidentally the reputation of McClellan. In Kentucky, further west, the Governor endeavoured to hold the field for the South with a body known as the State Guard, while Unionist leaders among the people were raising volunteer regiments for the North. Nothing, however, was determined by fighting between these forces. The State Legislature at first took up an attitude of neutrality, but a new Legislature, elected in June, was overwhelmingly for the Union. Ultimately the Confederate armies invaded Kentucky, and the Legislature thereupon invited the Union armies into the State to expel them, and placed 40,000 Kentucky volunteers at

the disposal of the President. Thenceforward, though Kentucky, stretching as it does for four hundred miles between the Mississippi and the Alleghanies, remained for long a battle-ground, the allegiance of its people to the Union was unshaken. But the uncertainty about their attitude continued till the autumn of 1861, and while it lasted was an important element in Lincoln's calculations. (It must be remembered that slavery existed in Kentucky, Maryland, and Missouri.) In Missouri the strife of factions was fierce. Already in January there had been reports of a conspiracy to seize the arsenal at St. Louis for the South when the time came, and General Scott had placed in command Captain Nathaniel Lyon, on whose loyalty he relied the more because he was an opponent of slavery. The Governor was in favour of the South—as was also the Legislature, and the Governor could count on some part of the State Militia; so Lincoln, when he called for volunteers, commissioned Lyon to raise them in Missouri. In this task a Union State Committee in St. Louis greatly helped him, and the large German population in that city was especially ready to enlist for the Union. Many of the German immigrants of those days had come to America partly for the sake of its free institutions. A State Convention was summoned by the Governor to pass an Ordinance of Secession, but its electors were minded otherwise, and the Convention voted against secession. In several encounters Lyon, who was an intrepid soldier, defeated the forces of the Governor; in June he took possession of the State capital, driving the Governor and Legislature away; the State Convention then again assembled and set up a Unionist Government for the State. This new State Government was not everywhere acknowledged; conspiracies in the Southern interest continued to exist in Missouri; and the State was repeatedly molested by invasions, of no great military consequence, from Arkansas. Indeed, in the autumn there was a serious recrudescence of trouble, in which Lyon lost his life. But substantially Missouri was secured for the Union. Nat-

urally enough, a great many of the citizens of Missouri who had combined to save their State to the Union became among the strongest of the " Radicals " who will later engage our attention. Many, however, of the leading men who had done most in this cause, including the friends of Blair, Lincoln's Postmaster-General, adhered no less emphatically to the " Conservative " section of the Republicans.

2. *Bull Run.*

Thus, in the autumn of 1861, North and South had become solidified into something like two countries. In the month of July, which now concerns us, this process was well on its way, but it is to be marked that the whole long tract of Kentucky still formed a neutral zone, which the Northern Government did not wish to harass, and which perhaps the South would have done well to let alone, while further west in Missouri the forces of the North were not even as fully organised as in the East. So the only possible direction in which any great blow could be struck was the direction of Richmond, now the capital, and it might seem, therefore, the heart, of the Confederacy. The Confederate Congress was to meet there on July 20. The *New York Tribune,* which was edited by Mr. Horace Greeley, a vigorous writer whose omniscience was unabated by the variation of his own opinion, was the one journal of far-reaching influence in the North; and it only gave exaggerated point to a general feeling when it declared that the Confederate Congress must not meet. The Senators and Congressmen now in Washington were not quite so exacting, but they had come there unanimous in their readiness to vote taxes and support the war in every way, and they wanted to see something done; and they wanted it all the more because the three months' service of the militia was running out. General Scott, still the chief military adviser of Government, was quite distinct in his preference for waiting and for perfecting the discipline and organisation of the volunteers, who had not yet

even been formed into brigades. On the militia he set
no value at all. For long he refused to countenance
any but minor movements preparatory to a later advance.
It is not quite certain, however, that Congress and public
opinion were wrong in clamouring for action. The
Southern troops were not much, if at all, more ready for
use than the Northerners; and Jefferson Davis and his
military adviser, Lee, desired time for their defensive
preparations. It was perhaps too much to expect that
the country after its great uprising should be content to
give supplies and men without end while nothing apparently happened; and the spirit of the troops themselves might suffer more from inaction than from defeat.
A further thought, while it made defeat seem more dangerous, made battle more tempting. There was fear
that European Powers might recognise the Southern Confederacy and enter into relations with it. Whether they
did so depended on whether they were confirmed in their
growing suspicion that the North could not conquer the
South. Balancing the military advice which was given
them as to the risk against this political importunity,
Lincoln and his Cabinet chose the risk, and Scott at
length withdrew his opposition. Lincoln was possibly
more sensitive to pressure than he afterwards became,
more prone to treat himself as a person under the orders
of the people, but there is no reason to doubt that he
acted on his own sober judgment as well as that of his
Cabinet. Whatever degree of confidence he reposed in
Scott, Scott was not very insistent; the risk was not overwhelming; the battle was very nearly won, would have
been won if the orders of Scott had been carried out.
No very great harm in fact followed the defeat of Bull
Run; and the danger of inaction was real. He was
probably then, as he certainly was afterwards, profoundly afraid that the excessive military caution which
he often encountered would destroy the cause of the
North by disheartening the people who supported the
war. That is no doubt a kind of fear to which many
statesmen are too prone, but Lincoln's sense of real pop-

ular feeling throughout the wide extent of the North is agreed to have been uncommonly sure. Definite judgment on such a question is impossible, but probably Lincoln and his Cabinet were wise.

However, they did not win their battle. The Southern army under Beauregard lay near the Bull Run river, some twenty miles from Washington, covering the railway junction of Manassas on the line to Richmond. The main Northern army, under General McDowell, a capable officer, lay south of the Potomac, where fortifications to guard Washington had already been erected on Virginian soil. In the Shenandoah Valley was another Southern force, under Joseph Johnston, watched by the Northern general Patterson at Harper's Ferry, which had been recovered by Scott's operations. Each of these Northern generals was in superior force to his opponent. McDowell was to attack the Confederate position at Manassas, while Patterson, whose numbers were nearly double Johnston's, was to keep him so seriously occupied that he could not join Beauregard. With whatever excuse of misunderstanding or the like, Patterson made hardly an attempt to carry out his part of Scott's orders, and Johnston, with the bulk of his force, succeeded in joining Beauregard the day before McDowell's attack, and without his gaining knowledge of this movement. The battle of Bull Run or Manassas (or rather the earlier and more famous of two battles so named) was an engagement of untrained troops in which up to a certain point the high individual quality of those troops supplied the place of discipline. McDowell handled with good judgment a very unhandy instrument. It was only since his advance had been contemplated that his army had been organised in brigades. The enemy, occupying high wooded banks on the south side of the Bull Run, a stream about as broad as the Thames at Oxford but fordable, was successfully pushed back to a high ridge beyond; but the stubborn attacks over difficult ground upon this further position failed from lack of co-ordination, and, when it already seemed doubtful

whether the tired soldiers of the North could renew them with any hope, they were themselves attacked on their right flank. It seems that from that moment their success upon that day was really hopeless, but some declare that the Northern soldiers with one accord became possessed of a belief that this flank attack by a comparatively small body was that of the whole force of Johnston, freshly arrived upon the scene. In any case they spontaneously retired in disorder; they were not effectively pursued, but McDowell was unable to rally them at Centreville, a mile or so behind the Bull Run. Among the camp followers the panic became extreme, and they pressed into Washington in wild alarm, accompanied by citizens and Congressmen who had come out to see a victory, and who left one or two of their number behind as prisoners of war. The result was a surprise to the Southern army. Johnston, who now took over the command, declared that it was as much disorganised by victory as the Northern army by defeat. With the full approval of his superiors in Richmond, he devoted himself to entrenching his position at Manassas. But in Washington, where rumours of victory had been arriving all through the day of battle, there prevailed for some time an impression that the city was exposed to immediate capture, and this impression was shared by McClellan, to whom universal opinion now turned as the appointed saviour, and who was forthwith summoned to Washington to take command of the army of the Potomac.

Within the circle of the Administration there was, of course, deep mortification. Old General Scott passionately declared himself to have been the greatest coward in America in having ever given way to the President's desire for action. Lincoln, who was often to prove his readiness to take blame on his own shoulders, evidently thought that the responsibility in this case was shared by Scott, and demanded to know whether Scott accused him of having overborne his judgment. The old general warmly, if a little ambiguously, replied that he had

served under many Presidents, but never known a kinder master. Plainly he felt that his better judgment had somehow been overpowered, and yet that there was nothing in their relations for which in his heart he could blame the President; and this trivial dialogue is worth remembering during the dreary and controversial tale of Lincoln's relations with Scott's successor. Lincoln, however bitterly disappointed, showed no signs of discomposure or hesitancy. The business of making the army of the Potomac quietly began over again. To the four days after Bull Run belongs one of the few records of the visits to the troops which Lincoln constantly paid when they were not too far from Washington, cheering them with little talks which served a good purpose without being notable. He was reviewing the brigade commanded at Bull Run by William Sherman, later, but not yet, one of the great figures in the war. He was open to all complaints, and a colonel of militia came to him with a grievance; he claimed that his term of service had already expired, that he had intended to go home, but that Sherman unlawfully threatened to shoot him if he did so. Lincoln had a good look at Sherman, and then advised the colonel to keep out of Sherman's way, as he looked like a man of his word. This was said in the hearing of many men, and Sherman records his lively gratitude for a simple jest which helped him greatly in keeping his brigade in existence.

Not one of the much more serious defeats suffered later in the war produced by itself so lively a sense of discomfiture in the North as this; thus none will equally claim our attention. But, except for the first false alarms in Washington, there was no disposition to mistake its military significance. The " second uprising of the North," which followed upon this bracing shock, left as vivid a memory as the little disaster of Bull Run. But there was of necessity a long pause while McClellan remodelled the army in the East, and the situation in the West was becoming ripe for important movements. The eagerness of the Northern people to make some progress

again asserted itself before long, but to their surprise,
and perhaps to that of a reader to-day, the last five
months of 1861 passed without notable military events.
Here then we may turn to the progress of other affairs,
departmental affairs, foreign affairs, and domestic policy,
which, it must not be forgotten, had pressed heavily upon
the Administration from the moment that war began.

3. Lincoln's Administration Generally.

Long before the Eastern public was very keenly aware
of Lincoln the members of his Cabinet had come to think
of the Administration as his Administration, some, like
Seward, of whom it could have been little expected, with
a loyal, and for America most fortunate, acceptance of
real subordination, and one at least, Chase, with indignant surprise that his own really great abilities were not
dominant. One Minister early told his friends that
there was but one vote in the Cabinet, the President's.
This must not be taken in the sense that Lincoln's personal guidance was present in every department. He
had his own department, concerned with the maintenance
of Northern unity and with that great underlying problem
of internal policy which will before long appear again,
and the business of the War Department was so immediately vital as to require his ceaseless attention; but in
other matters the degree and manner of his control of
course varied. Again, it is far from being the case that
the Cabinet had little influence on his action. He not
only consulted it much, but deferred to it much. His
wisdom seems to have shown itself in nothing more
strongly than in recognising when he wanted advice and
when he did not, when he needed support and when he
could stand alone. Sometimes he yielded to his Ministers because he valued their judgment, sometimes also
because he gauged by them the public support without
which his action must fail. Sometimes, when he was
sure of the necessity, he took grave steps without advice
from them or any one. More often he tried to arrive

with them at a real community of decision. It is often impossible to guess what acts of an Administration are rightly credited to its chief. The hidden merit or demerit of many statesmen has constantly lain in the power, or the lack of it, of guiding their colleagues and being guided in turn. If we tried to be exact in saying Lincoln, or Lincoln's Cabinet, or the North did this or that, it would be necessary to thresh out many bushels of tittle-tattle. The broad impression, however, remains that in the many things in which Lincoln did not directly rule he ruled through a group of capable men of whom he made the best use, and whom no other chief could have induced to serve so long in concord. As we proceed some authentic examples of his precise relations with them will appear, in which, unimportant as they seem, one test of his quality as a statesman and of his character should be sought.

The naval operations of the war afford many tales of daring on both sides which cannot here be noticed. They afford incidents of strange interest now, such as the exploit of the first submarine. (It belonged to the South; its submersion invariably resulted in the death of the whole crew; and, with full knowledge of this, a devoted crew went down and destroyed a valuable Northern iron-clad.) The ravages on commerce of the *Alabama* and some other Southern cruisers became only too famous in England, from whose ship-building yards they had escaped. The North failed too in some out of the fairly numerous combined naval and military expeditions, which were undertaken with a view to making the blockade more complete and less arduous by the occupation of Southern ports, and perhaps to more serious incursions into the South. Among those of them which will require no special notice, most succeeded. Thus by the spring of 1863 Florida was substantially in Northern hands, and by 1865 the South had but two ports left, Charleston and Wilmington; but the venture most attractive to Northern sentiment, an attack upon Charleston itself, proved a mere waste of military force. More-

over, till a strong military adviser was at last found in Grant there was some dissipation of military force in such expeditions. Nevertheless, the naval success of the North was so continuous and overwhelming that its history in detail need not be recounted in these pages. Almost from the first the ever-tightening grip of the blockade upon the Southern coasts made its power felt, and early in 1862 the inland waterways of the South were beginning to fall under the command of the Northern flotillas. Such a success needed, of course, the adoption of a decided policy from the outset; it needed great administrative ability to improvise a navy where hardly any existed, and where the conditions of its employment were in many respects novel; and it needed resourceful watching to meet the surprises of fresh naval invention by which the South, poor as were its possibilities for shipbuilding, might have rendered impotent, as once or twice it seemed likely to do, the Northern blockade. Gideon Welles, the responsible Cabinet Minister, was constant and would appear to have been capable at his task, but the inspiring mind of the Naval Department was found in Gustavus V. Fox, a retired naval officer, who at the beginning of Lincoln's administration was appointed Assistant Secretary of the Navy. The policy of blockade was begun by Lincoln's Proclamation on April 19, 1861. It was a hardy measure, certain to be a cause of friction with foreign Powers. The United States Government had contended in 1812 that a blockade which is to confer any rights against neutral commerce must be an effective blockade, and has not lately been inclined to take lax views upon such questions; but when it declared its blockade of the South it possessed only three steamships of war with which to make it effective. But the policy was stoutly maintained. The Naval Department at the very first set about buying merchant ships in Northern ports and adapting them to warlike use, and building ships of its own, in the design of which it shortly obtained the help of a Commission of Congress on the subject of ironclads. The Naval Department had at

least the fullest support and encouragement from Lincoln in the whole of its policy. Everything goes to show that he followed naval affairs carefully, but that, as he found them conducted on sound lines by men that he trusted, his intervention in them was of a modest kind. Welles continued throughout the member of his Cabinet with whom he had the least friction, and was probably one of those Ministers, common in England, who earn the confidence of their own departments without in any way impressing the imagination of the public; and a letter by Lincoln to Fox immediately after the affair of Fort Sumter shows the hearty esteem and confidence with which from the first he regarded Fox. Of the few slight records of his judgment in these matters one is significant. The unfortunate expedition against Charleston in the spring of 1863 was undertaken with high hopes by the Naval Department; but Lincoln, we happen to know, never believed it could succeed. He has, rightly or wrongly, been blamed for dealings with his military officers in which he may be said to have spurred them hard; he cannot reasonably be blamed for giving the rein to his expert subordinates, because his own judgment, which differed from theirs, turned out right. This is one of very many instances which suggest that at the time when his confidence in himself was full grown his disposition, if any, to interfere was well under control. It is also one of the indications that his attention was alert in many matters in which his hand was not seen.

He was no financier, and that important part of the history of the war, Northern finance, concerns us little. The real economic strength of the North was immense, for immigration and development were going on so fast, that, for all the strain of the war, production and exports increased. But the superficial disturbance caused by borrowing and the issue of paper money was great, and, though the North never bore the pinching that was endured in the South, it is an honourable thing that, for all the rise in the cost of living and for all the trouble

that occurred in business when the premium on gold often fluctuated between 40 and 60 and on one occasion rose to 185, neither the solid working class of the country generally nor the solid business class of New York were deeply affected by the grumbling at the duration of the war. The American verdict upon the financial policy of Chase, a man of intellect but new to such affairs, is one of high praise. Lincoln left him free in that policy. He had watched the acts and utterances of his chief contemporaries closely and early acquired a firm belief in Chase's ability. How much praise is due to the President, who for this reason kept Chase in his Cabinet, a later part of this story may show.

One function of Government was that of the President alone. An English statesman is alleged to have said upon becoming Prime Minister, " I had important and interesting business in my old office, but now my chief duty will be to create undeserving Peers." Lincoln, in the anxious days that followed his first inauguration, once looked especially harassed; a Senator said to him: " What is the matter, Mr. President? Is there bad news from Fort Sumter?" " Oh, no," he answered, " it's the Post Office at Baldinsville." The patronage of the President was enormous, including the most trifling offices under Government, such as village postmasterships. In the appointment to local offices, he was expected to consult the local Senators and Representatives of his own party, and of course to choose men who had worked for the party. In the vast majority of cases decent competence for the office in the people so recommended might be presumed. The established practice further required that a Republican President on coming in should replace with good Republicans most of the nominees of the late Democratic administration, which had done the like in its day. Lincoln's experience after a while led him to prophesy that the prevalence of office-seeking would be the ruin of American politics, but it certainly never occurred to him to try and break down then the accepted rule, of which no party yet complained. It would have

been unmeasured folly, even if he had thought of it, to have taken during such a crisis a new departure which would have vexed the Republicans far more than it would have pleased the Democrats. And at that time it was really of great consequence that public officials should be men of known loyalty to the Union, for obviously a postmaster of doubtful loyalty might do mischief. Lincoln, then, except in dealing with posts of special consequence, for which men with really special qualifications were to be found, frankly and without a question took as the great principle of his patronage the fairest possible distribution of favours among different classes and individuals among the supporters of the Government, whom it was his primary duty to keep together. His attitude in the whole business was perfectly understood and respected by scrupulous men who watched politics critically. It was the cause in one way of great worry to him, for, except when his indignation was kindled, he was abnormally reluctant to say " no,"—he once shuddered to think what would have happened to him if he had been a woman, but was consoled by the thought that his ugliness would have been a shield; and his private secretaries accuse him of carrying out his principle with needless and even ridiculous care. In appointments to which the party principle did not apply, but in which an ordinary man would have felt party prejudice, Lincoln's old opponents were often startled by his freedom from it. If jobbery be the right name for his persistent endeavour to keep the partisans of the Union pleased and united, his jobbery proved to have one shining attribute of virtue; later on, when, apart from the Democratic opposition which revived, there arose in the Republican party sections hostile to himself, the claims of personal adherence to him and the wavering prospects of his own reelection seem, from recorded instances, to have affected his choice remarkably little.

4. Foreign Policy and England.

The question, what was his influence upon foreign policy, is more difficult than the general praise bestowed upon it might lead us to expect; because, though he is known to have exercised a constant supervision over Seward, that influence was concealed from the diplomatic world.

For at least the first eighteen months of the war, apart from lesser points of quarrel, a real danger of foreign intervention hung over the North. The danger was increased by the ambitions of Napoleon III. in regard to Mexico, and by the loss and suffering caused to England, above all, not merely from the interruption of trade but from the suspension of cotton supplies by the blockade. From the first there was the fear that foreign powers would recognise the Southern Confederacy as an independent country; that they were then likely to offer mediation which it would at the best have been embarrassing for the President to reject; that they might ultimately, when their mediation had been rejected, be tempted to active intervention. It is curious that the one European Government which was recognised all along as friendly to the Republic was that of the Czar, Alexander II. of Russia, who in this same year, 1861, was accomplishing the project, bequeathed to him by his father, of emancipating the serfs. Mercier, the French Minister in Washington, advised his Government to recognise the South Confederacy as early as March, 1861. The Emperor of the French, though not the French people, inclined throughout to this policy; but he would not act apart from England, and the English Government, though Americans did not know it, had determined, and for the present was quite resolute, against any hasty action. Nevertheless an almost accidental cause very soon brought England and the North within sight of a war from which neither people was in appearance averse.

Neither the foreign policy of Lincoln's Government

nor, indeed, the relations of England and America from his day to our own can be understood without some study of the attitude of the two countries to each other during the war. If we could put aside any previous judgment on the cause as between North and South, there are still some marked features in the attitude of England during the war which every Englishman must now regret. It should emphatically be added that there were some upon which every Englishman should look back with satisfaction. Many of the expressions of English opinion at that time betray a powerlessness to comprehend another country and a self-sufficiency in judging it, which, it may humbly be claimed, were not always and are not now so characteristic of Englishmen as they were in that period of our history, in many ways so noble, which we associate with the rival influences of Palmerston and of Cobden. It is not at all surprising that ordinary English gentlemen started with a leaning towards the South; they liked Southerners and there was much in the manners of the North, and in the experiences of Englishmen trading with or investing in the North, which did not impress them favourably. Many Northerners discovered something snobbish and unsound in this preference, but they were not quite right. With this leaning, Englishmen readily accepted the plea of the South that it was threatened with intolerable interference; indeed to this day it is hardly credible to Englishmen that the grievance against which the South arose in such passionate revolt was so unsubstantial as it really was. On the other hand, the case of the North was not apprehended. How it came to pass, in the intricate and usually uninteresting play of American politics, that a business community, which had seemed pretty tolerant of slavery, was now at war on some point which was said to be and said not to be slavery, was a little hard to understand. Those of us who remember our parents' talk of the American Civil War did not hear from them the true and fairly simple explanation of the war, that the North fought because it refused to connive further in the extension of

slavery, and would not—could not decently—accept the disruption of a great country as the alternative. It is strictly true that the chivalrous South rose in blind passion for a cause at the bottom of which lay the narrowest of pecuniary interests, while the over-sharp Yankees, guided by a sort of comic backwoodsman, fought, whether wisely or not, for a cause as untainted as ever animated a nation in arms. But it seems a paradox even now, and there is no reproach in the fact, that our fathers, who had not followed the vacillating course of Northern politics hitherto, did not generally take it in. We shall see in a later chapter how Northern statesmanship added to their perplexity. But it is impossible not to be ashamed of some of the forms in which English feeling showed itself and was well known in the North to show itself. Not only the articles of some English newspapers, but the private letters of Americans who then found themselves in the politest circles in London, are unpleasant to read now. It is painful, too, that a leader of political thought like Cobden should even for a little while—and it was only a little while—have been swayed in such a matter by a sympathy relatively so petty as agreement with the Southern doctrine of Free Trade. We might now call it worthier of Prussia than of England that a great Englishman like Lord Salisbury (then Lord Robert Cecil) should have expressed friendship for the South as a good customer of ours, and antagonism for the North as a rival in our business. When such men as these said such things they were, of course, not brutally indifferent to right, they were merely blind to the fact that a very great and plain issue of right and wrong was really involved in the war. Gladstone, to take another instance, was not blind to that, but with irritating misapprehension he protested against the madness of plunging into war to propagate the cause of emancipation. Then came in his love of small states, and from his mouth, while he was a Cabinet Minister, came the impulsive pronouncement, bitterly regretted by him and bitterly resented in the North: " Jefferson Davis and

other leaders of the South have made an army; they are making, it appears, a navy; and they have made—what is more than either—they have made a nation." Many other Englishmen simply sympathised with the weaker side; many too, it should be confessed, with the apparently weaker side which they were really persuaded would win. ("Win the battles," said Lord Robert Cecil to a Northern lady, "and we Tories shall come round at once.") These things are recalled because their natural effect in America has to be understood. What is really lamentable is not that in this distant and debatable affair the sympathy of so many inclined to the South, but that, when at least there was a Northern side, there seemed at first to be hardly any capable of understanding or being stirred by it. Apart from politicians there were only two Englishmen of the first rank, Tennyson and Darwin, who, whether or not they understood the matter in detail, are known to have cared from their hearts for the Northern cause. It is pleasant to associate with these greater names that of the author of "Tom Brown." The names of those hostile to the North or apparently quite uninterested are numerous and surprising. Even Dickens, who had hated slavery, and who in "Martin Chuzzlewit" had appealed however bitterly to the higher national spirit which he thought latent in America, now, when that spirit had at last and in deed asserted itself, gave way in his letters to nothing but hatred of the whole country. And a disposition like this—explicable but odious—did no doubt exist in the England of those days.

There is, however, quite another aspect of this question besides that which has so painfully impressed many American memories. When the largest manufacturing industry of England was brought near to famine by the blockade, the voice of the stricken working population was loudly and persistently uttered on the side of the North. There has been no other demonstration so splendid of the spirit which remains widely diffused among individual English working men and which at one

time animated labour as a concentrated political force. John Bright, who completely grasped the situation in America, took a stand, in which J. S. Mill, W. E. Forster, and the Duke of Argyll share his credit, but which did peculiar and great honour to him as a Quaker who hated war. But there is something more that must be said. The conduct of the English Government, supported by the responsible leaders of the Opposition, was at that time, no less than now, the surest indication of the more deep-seated feelings of the real bulk of Englishmen on any great question affecting our international relations; and the attitude of the Government, in which Lord Palmerston was Prime Minister and Lord John Russell Foreign Secretary, and with which in this matter Conservative leaders like Disraeli and Sir Stafford Northcote entirely concurred, was at the very least free from grave reproach. Lord John Russell, and, there can be little doubt, his colleagues generally, regarded slavery as an "accursed institution," but they felt no anger with the people of the South for it, because, as he said, "we gave them that curse and ours were the hands from which they received that fatal gift"; in Lord John at least the one overmastering sentiment upon the outbreak of the war was that of sheer pain that "a great Republic, which has enjoyed institutions under which the people have been free and happy, is placed in jeopardy." Their insight into American affairs did not go deep; but the more seriously we rate "the strong antipathy to the North, the strong sympathy with the South, and the passionate wish to have cotton," of which a Minister, Lord Granville, wrote at the time, the greater is the credit due both to the Government as a whole and to Disraeli for having been conspicuously unmoved by these considerations; and "the general approval from Parliament, the press, and the public," which, as Lord Granville added, their policy received, is creditable too. It is perfectly true, as will be seen later, that at one dark moment in the fortunes of the North, the Government very cautiously considered the possibility of intervention.

But Disraeli, to whom a less patriotic course would have offered a party advantage, recalled to them their own better judgment; and it is impossible to read their correspondence on this question without perceiving that in this they were actuated by no hostility to the North, but by a sincere belief that the cause of the North was hopeless and that intervention, with a view to stopping bloodshed, might prove the course of honest friendship to all America. Englishmen of a later time have become deeply interested in America, and may wish that their fathers had better understood the great issue of the Civil War, but it is matter for pride, which in honesty should be here asserted, that with many selfish interests in this contest, of which they were most keenly aware, Englishmen, in their capacity as a nation, acted with complete integrity.

But for our immediate purpose the object of thus reviewing a subject on which American historians have lavished much research is to explain the effect produced in America by demonstrations of strong antipathy and sympathy in England. The effect in some ways has been long lasting. The South caught at every mark of sympathy with avidity, was led by its politicians to expect help, received none, and became resentful. It is surprising to be told, but may be true, that the embers of this resentment became dangerous to England in the autumn of 1914. In the North the memory of an antipathy which was almost instantly perceived has burnt deep—as many memoirs, for instance those recently published by Senator Lodge, show—into the minds of precisely those Americans to whom Englishmen have ever since been the readiest to accord their esteem. There were many men in the North with a ready-made dislike of England, but there were many also whose sensitiveness to English opinion, if in some ways difficult for us to appreciate, was intense. Republicans such as James Russell Lowell had writhed under the reproaches cast by Englishmen upon the acquiescence of all America in slavery; they felt that the North had suddenly cut off this reproach and staked

everything on the refusal to give way to slavery any further; they looked now for expressions of sympathy from many quarters in England; but in the English newspapers which they read and the reports of Americans in England they found evidence of nothing but dislike. There soon came evidence, as it seemed to the whole North, of actually hostile action on the part of the British Government. It issued a Proclamation enjoining neutrality upon British subjects. This was a matter of course on the outbreak of what was nothing less than war; but Northerners thought that at least some courteous explanation should first have been made to their Government, and there were other matters which they misinterpreted as signs of an agreement of England with France to go further and open diplomatic relations with the Confederate Government. Thus alike in the most prejudiced and in the most enlightened quarters in the North there arose an irritation which an Englishman must see to have been natural but can hardly think to have been warranted by the real facts.

Here came in the one clearly known and most certainly happy intervention of Lincoln's in foreign affairs. Early in May Seward brought to him the draft of a vehement despatch, telling the British Government peremptorily what the United States would not stand, and framed in a manner which must have frustrated any attempt by Adams in London to establish good relations with Lord John Russell. That draft now exists with the alterations made in Lincoln's own hand. With a few touches, some of them very minute, made with the skill of a master of language and of a life-long peacemaker, he changed the draft into a firm but entirely courteous despatch. In particular, instead of requiring Adams, as Seward would have done, to read the whole despatch to Russell and leave him with a copy of it, he left it to the man on the spot to convey its sense in what manner he judged best. Probably, as has been claimed for him, his few penstrokes made peaceful relations easy when Seward's despatch would have made them almost im-

possible; certainly a study of this document will prove both his strange, untutored diplomatic skill and the general soundness of his view of foreign affairs.

Now, however, followed a graver crisis in which his action requires some discussion. Messrs. Mason and Slidell were sent by the Confederate Government as their emissaries to England and France. They got to Havana and there took ship again on the British steamer *Trent*. A watchful Northern sea captain overhauled the *Trent*, took Mason and Slidell off her, and let her go. If he had taken the course, far more inconvenient to the *Trent*, of bringing her into a Northern harbour, where a Northern Prize Court might have adjudged these gentlemen to be bearers of enemy despatches, he would have been within the law. As it was he violated well-established usage, and no one has questioned the right and even the duty of the British Government to demand the release of the prisoners. This they did in a note of which the expression was made milder by the wish of the Queen (conveyed in almost the last letter of the Prince Consort), but which required compliance within a fortnight. Meanwhile Secretary Welles had approved the sea captain's action. The North was jubilant at the capture, the more so because Mason and Slidell were Southern statesmen of the lower type and held to be specially obnoxious; and the House of Representatives, to make matters worse, voted its approval of what had been done. Lincoln, on the very day when the news of the capture came, had seen and said privately that on the principles which America had itself upheld in the past the prisoners would have to be given up with an apology. But there is evidence that he now wavered, and that, bent as he was on maintaining a united North, he was still too distrustful of his own better judgment as against that of the public. At this very time he was already on other points in painful conflict with many friends. In any case he submitted to Seward a draft despatch making the ill-judged proposal of arbitration. He gave way to Seward, but at the Cabinet meeting on Christmas Eve, at which

Seward submitted a despatch yielding to the British demand, it is reported that Lincoln, as well as Chase and
others, was at first reluctant to agree, and that it was
Bates and Seward that persuaded the Cabinet to a just
and necessary surrender.

This was the last time that there was serious friction
in the actual intercourse of the two Governments. The
lapse of Great Britain in allowing the famous *Alabama*
to sail was due to delay and misadventure (" week-ends "
or the like) in the proceedings of subordinate officials,
and was never defended, and the numerous minor controversies that arose, as well as the standing disagree-
ment as to the law of blockade never reached the point
of danger. For all this great credit was due to Lord
Lyons and to C. F. Adams, and to Seward also, when
he had a little sobered down, but it might seem as if the
credit commonly given to Lincoln by Americans rested
on little but the single happy performance with the earlier
despatch which has been mentioned. Adams and Lyons
were not aware of his beneficent influence—the papers
of the latter contain little reference to him beyond a
kindly record of a trivial conversation, at the end of
which, as the Ambassador was going for a holiday to
England, the President said, " Tell the English people
I mean them no harm." Yet it is evident that Lincoln's
supporters in America, the writer of the Biglow Papers,
for instance, ascribed to him a wise, restraining power
in the *Trent* dispute. What is more, Lincoln later
claimed this for himself. Two or three years later, in
one of the confidences with which he often startled men
who were but slight acquaintances, but who generally
turned out worthy of confidence, he exclaimed with emphatic self-satisfaction, " Seward knows that I am his
master," and recalled with satisfaction how he had forced
Seward to yield to England in the *Trent* affair. It would
have been entirely unlike him to claim praise when it was
wholly undue to him; we find him, for example, writing
to Fox, of the Navy Department, about " a blunder
which was probably in part mine, and certainly was not

yours "; so that a puzzling question arises here. It is quite possible that Lincoln, who did not press his proposal of arbitration, really manœuvred Seward and the Cabinet into full acceptance of the British demands by making them see the consequences of any other action. It is also, however, likely enough that, being, as he was, interested in arbitration generally, he was too inexperienced to see the inappropriateness of the proposal in this case. If so, we may none the less credit him with having forced Seward to work for peace and friendly relations with Great Britain, and made that minister the agent, more skilful than himself, of a peaceful resolution which in its origin was his own.

5. *The Great Questions of Domestic Policy.*

The larger questions of civil policy which arose out of the fact of the war, and which weighed heavily on Lincoln before the end of 1861, can be related with less intricate detail if the fundamental point of difficulty is made clear.

Upon July 4 Congress met. In an able Message which was a skilful but simple appeal not only to Congress, but to the "plain people," the President set forth the nature of the struggle as he conceived it, putting perhaps in its most powerful form the contention that the Union was indissoluble, and declaring that the "experiment" of "our popular government" would have failed once for all if it did not prove that "when ballots have fairly and constitutionally decided, there can be no successful appeal back to bullets." He recounted the steps which he had taken since the bombardment of Fort Sumter, some of which might be held to exceed his constitutional authority as indeed they did, saying he would have been false to his trust if for fear of such illegality he had let the whole Constitution perish, and asking that, if necessary, Congress should ratify them. He appealed to Congress now to do its part, and especially he appealed for such prompt and adequate provision of money and men as would en-

able the war to be speedily brought to a close. Congress, with but a few dissentient voices, chiefly from the border States, approved all that he had done, and voted the supplies that he had asked. Then, by a resolution of both Houses, it defined the object of the war; the war was not for any purpose of conquest or subjugation, or of " overthrowing or interfering with the rights or established institutions " of the Southern States; it was solely " to preserve the Union with all the dignity, equality, and rights of the several States unimpaired."

In this resolution may be found the clue to the supreme political problem with which, side by side with the conduct of the war, Lincoln was called upon to grapple unceasingly for the rest of his life. That problem lay in the inevitable change, as the war dragged on, of the political object involved in it. The North as yet was not making war upon the institutions of Southern States, in other words upon slavery, and it would have been wrong to do so. It was simply asserting the supremacy of law by putting down what every man in the North regarded as rebellion. That rebellion, it seemed likely, would completely subside after a decisive defeat or two of the Southern forces. The law and the Union would then have been restored as before. A great victory would in fact have been won over slavery, for the policy of restricting its further spread would have prevailed, but the constitutional right of each Southern State to retain slavery within its borders was not to be denied by those who were fighting, as they claimed, for the Constitution.

Such at first was the position taken up by an unanimous Congress. It was obviously in accord with those political principles of Lincoln which have been examined in a former chapter. More than that, it was the position which, as he thought, his official duty as President imposed on him. It is exceedingly difficult for any Englishman to follow his course as the political situation developed. He was neither a dictator, nor an English Prime Minister. He was first and foremost an elected officer with powers and duties prescribed by a fixed Constitution

which he had sworn to obey. His oath was continually present to his mind.

He was there to uphold the Union and the laws, with just so much infraction of the letter of the law, and no more, as might be obviously necessary if the Union and the whole fabric of law were not to perish.

The mere duration of the war altered of necessity the policy of the North and of the President. Their task had presented itself as in theory the "suppression of an unlawful combination" within their country; it became in manifest fact the reabsorption of a country now hostile, with which reunion was possible only if slavery, the fundamental cause of difference, was uprooted.

As the hope of a speedy victory and an easy settlement vanished, wide differences of opinion appeared again in the North, and the lines on which this cleavage proceeded very soon showed themselves. There were those who gladly welcomed the idea of a crusade against slavery, and among them was an unreasonable section of so-called Radicals. These resented that delay in a policy of wholesale liberation which was enforced by legal and constitutional scruples, and by such practical considerations as the situation in the slave States which adhered to the North. There was, on the other hand, a Democratic party Opposition which before long began to revive. It combined many shades of opinion. There were supporters or actual agents of the South, few at first and very quiet, but ultimately developing a treasonable activity. There were those who constituted themselves the guardians of legality and jealously criticised all the measures of emergency which became more or less necessary. Of the bulk of the Democrats it would probably be fair to say that their conscious intention throughout was to be true to the Union, but that throughout they were beset by a respect for Southern rights which would have gone far to paralyse the arm of the Government. Lastly, there were Republicans, by no means in sympathy with the Democratic view, who became suspect to their Radical fellows and were vaguely classed together as Con-

servatives. This term may be taken to cover men simply of moderate and cautious, or in some cases, of variable disposition, but it included, too, some men who, while rigorous against the South, were half-hearted in their detestation of slavery.

So far as Lincoln's private opinions were concerned, it would have been impossible to rank him in any of these sections. He had as strong a sympathy with the Southern people as any Democrat, but he was for the restoration of the Union absolutely and without compromise. He was the most cautious of men, but his caution veiled a detestation of slavery of which he once said that he could not remember the time when he had not felt it. It was his business, so far as might be, to retain the support of all sections in the North to the Union. In the course, full of painful deliberation, which we shall see him pursuing, he tried to be guided by a two-fold principle which he constantly avowed. The Union was to be restored with as few departures from the ways of the Constitution as was possible; but such departures became his duty whenever he was thoroughly convinced that they were needful for the restoration of the Union.

Before the war was four months old, the inevitable subject of dispute between Northern parties had begun to trouble Lincoln. As soon as a Northern force set foot on Southern soil slaves were apt to escape to it, and the question arose, what should the Northern general do with them, for he was not there to make war on the private property of Southern citizens. General Butler —a newspaper character of some fame or notoriety throughout the war—commanded at Fort Monroe, a point on the coast of Virginia which was always held by the North. He learnt that the slaves who fled to him had been employed on making entrenchments for the Southern troops, so he adopted a view, which took the fancy of the North, that they were " contraband of war," and should be kept from their owners. The circumstances in which slaves could thus escape varied so much that great discretion must be left to the general on

the spot, and the practice of generals varied. Lincoln was well content to leave the matter so. Congress, however, passed an Act by which private property could be confiscated, if used in aid of the "insurrection" but not otherwise, and slaves were similarly dealt with. This moderate provision as to slaves met with a certain amount of opposition; it raised an alarming question in slave States like Missouri that had not seceded. Lincoln himself seems to have been averse to any legislation on the subject. He had deliberately concentrated his mind, or, as his critics would have said, narrowed it down to the sole question of maintaining the Union, and was resolved to treat all other questions as subordinate to this.

Shortly after, there reappeared upon the political scene a leader with what might seem a more sympathetic outlook. This was Frémont, Lincoln's predecessor as the Republican candidate for the Presidency. Frémont was one of those men who make brilliant and romantic figures in their earlier career, and later appear to have lost all solid qualities. It must be recalled that, though scarcely a professional soldier (for he had held a commission, but served only in the Ordnance Survey) he had conducted a great exploring expedition, had seen fighting as a free-lance in California, and, it is claimed, had with his handful of men done much to win that great State from Mexico. Add to this that he, a Southerner by birth, was known among the leaders who had made California a free State, and it is plain how appropriate it must have seemed when he was set to command the Western Department, which for the moment meant Missouri. Here by want of competence, and, which was more surprising, lethargy he had made a present of some successes to a Southern invading force, and had sacrificed the promising life of General Lyon. Lincoln, loath to remove him, had made a good effort at helping him out by tactfully persuading a more experienced general to serve as a subordinate on his staff. At the end of August Frémont suddenly issued a proclamation establishing martial law throughout Missouri. This contained other

dangerous provisions, but above all it liberated the slaves and confiscated the whole property of all persons proved (before Court Martial) to have taken active part with the enemy in the field. It is obvious that such a measure was liable to shocking abuse, that it was certain to infuriate many friends of the Union, and that it was in conflict with the law which Congress had just passed on the subject. To Lincoln's mind it presented the alarming prospect that it might turn the scale against the Union cause in the still pending deliberations in Kentucky. Lincoln's overpowering solicitude on such a point is among the proofs that his understanding of the military situation, however elementary, was sound. He wished, characteristically, that Frémont himself should withdraw his Proclamation. He invited him to withdraw it in private letters from which one sentence may be taken: " You speak of it as being the only means of saving the Government. On the contrary, it is itself the surrender of the Government. Can it be pretended that it is any longer the Government of the United States—any government of constitution and laws—wherein a general or a president may make permanent rules of property by proclamation?" Frémont preferred to make Lincoln publicly overrule him, which he did; and the inevitable consequence followed. When some months later, the utter military disorganisation, which Frémont let arise while he busied himself with politics, and the scandalous waste, out of which his flatterers enriched themselves, compelled the President to remove him from his command, Frémont became, for a time at least, to patriotic crowds and to many intelligent, upright and earnest men from St. Louis to Boston, the chivalrous and pure-hearted soldier of freedom, and Lincoln, the soulless politician, dead to the cause of liberty, who, to gratify a few wire-pulling friends, had struck this hero down on the eve of victory to his army—an army which, by the way, he had reduced almost to nonentity.

This salient instance explains well enough the nature of one half of the trial which Lincoln throughout the

war had to undergo. Pursuing the restoration of the Union with a thoroughness which must estrange from him the Democrats of the North, he was fated from the first to estrange also Radicals who were generally as devoted to the Union as himself and with whose over-mastering hatred of slavery he really sympathised. In the following chapter we are more concerned with the other half of his trial, the war itself. Of his minor political difficulties few instances need be given—only it must be remembered that they were many and involved, besides delicate questions of principle, the careful sifting of much confident hearsay; and, though the critics of public men are wont to forget it, that there are only twenty-four hours in the day.

But the year 1861 was to close with a further vexation that must be related. Secretary Cameron proved incapable on the business side of war administration. Waste and alleged corruption called down upon him a searching investigation by a committee of the House of Representatives. He had not added to his own considerable riches, but his political henchmen had grown fat. The displeasure with the whole Administration was the greater because the war was not progressing favourably, or at all. There were complaints of the Naval Department also, but politicians testified their belief in the honesty of Welles without saying a word for Cameron. There is every reason to think he was not personally dishonourable. Lincoln believed in his complete integrity, and so also did sterner critics, Chase, an apostle of economy and uprightness, and Senator Sumner. But he had to go. He opened the door for his removal by a circular to generals on the subject of slaves, which was comparable to Frémont's Proclamation and of which Lincoln had to forbid the issue. He accepted the appointment of Minister to Russia, and when, before long, he returned, he justified himself and Lincoln's judgment by his disinterested friendship and support. He was removed from the War Office at the end of December and a remarkable incident followed. While Lincoln's

heart was still set on his law practice, the prospect of appearing as something more than a backwoods attorney smiled for a single moment on him. He was briefed to appear in an important case outside Illinois with an eminent lawyer from the East, Edwin M. Stanton; but he was not allowed to open his mouth, for Stanton snuffed him out with supreme contempt, and he returned home crestfallen. Stanton before the war was a strong Democrat, but hated slavery. In the last days of Buchanan's Presidency he was made Attorney-General and helped much to restore the lost credit of that Administration. He was now in Washington, criticising the slow conduct of the war with that explosive fury and scorn which led him to commit frequent injustice (at the very end of the war he publicly and monstrously accused Sherman of being bribed into terms of peace by Southern gold), which concealed from most eyes his real kindness and a lurking tenderness of heart, but which made him a vigorous administrator intolerant of dishonesty and inefficiency. He was more contemptuous of Lincoln than ever, he would constantly be denouncing his imbecility, and it is incredible that kind friends were wanting to convey his opinion to Lincoln. Lincoln made him Secretary of War.

Since the summer, to the impatient bewilderment of the Northern people, of Congress, now again in session, and of the President himself, their armies in the field were accomplishing just nothing at all, and, as this agitating year, 1861, closed, a deep gloom settled on the North, to be broken after a while by the glare of recurrent disaster.

CHAPTER IX

THE DISASTERS OF THE NORTH

1. *Military Policy of the North.*

THE story of the war has here to be told from the point of view of the civilian administrator, the President; stirring incidents of combat and much else of interest must be neglected; episodes in the war which peculiarly concerned him, or have given rise to controversy about him, must be related lengthily. The President was an inexperienced man. It should be said, too—for respect requires perfect frankness—that he was one of an inexperienced people. The Americans had conquered their independence from Great Britain at the time when the ruling factions of our country had reached their utmost degree of inefficiency. They had fought an indecisive war with us in 1812-14, while our main business was to win at Salamanca and Vittoria. These experiences in some ways warped American ideas of war and politics, and their influence perhaps survives to this day. The extent of the President's authority and his position in regard to the advice he could obtain have been explained. An examination of the tangle in which military policy was first involved may make the chief incidents of the war throughout easier to follow.

Immediately after Bull Run McClellan had been summoned to Washington to command the army of the Potomac. In November, Scott, worn out by infirmity, and finding his authority slighted by "my ambitious junior," retired, and thereupon McClellan, while retaining his immediate command upon the Potomac, was made for the time General-in-Chief over all the armies of the North. There were, it should be repeated, two other principal armies besides that of the Potomac: the army

of the Ohio, of which General Buell was given command
in July; and that of the West, to which General Halleck
was appointed, though Frémont seems to have retained
independent command in Missouri.   All these armies
were in an early stage of formation and training, and
from a purely military point of view there could be no
haste to undertake a movement of invasion with any of
them.

Three distinct views of military policy were presented
to Lincoln in the early days.   Scott, as soon as it was
clear that the South meant real fighting, saw how serious
its resistance would be.   His military judgment was in
favour of a strictly defensive attitude before Washington; of training the volunteers for at least four months
in healthy camps; and of then pushing a large army right
down the Mississippi valley to New Orleans, making
the whole line of that river secure, and establishing a
pressure on the South between this Western army and
the naval blockade which must slowly have strangled
the Confederacy.   He was aware that public impatience
might not allow a rigid adherence to his policy, and in
fact, when his view was made public before Bull Run,
"Scott's Anaconda," coiling itself round the Confederacy, was the subject of general derision.   The view
of the Northern public and of the influential men in Congress was in favour of speedy and, as it was hoped,
decisive action, and this was understood as involving,
whatever else was done, an attempt soon to capture
Richmond.   In McClellan's view, as in Scott's, the first
object was the full preparation of the Army, but he
would have wished to wait till he had a fully trained
force of 273,000 men on the Potomac, and a powerful
fleet with many transports to support his movements;
and, when he had all this, to move southwards in irresistible force, both advancing direct into Virginia and
landing at points on the coast, subduing each of the
Atlantic States of the Confederacy in turn.   If the in-
definite delay and the overwhelming force which his fancy
pictured could have been granted him, it is plain, the

military critics have said, that "he could not have destroyed the Southern armies—they would have withdrawn inland, and the heart of the Confederacy would have remained untouched." But neither the time nor the force for which he wished could be allowed him. So he had to put aside his plan, but in some ways perhaps it still influenced him.

It would have been impossible to disregard the wishes of those, who in the last resort were masters, for a vigorous attempt on Richmond, and the continually unsuccessful attempts that were made did serve a military purpose, for they kept up a constant drain upon the resources of the South. In any well-thought-out policy the objects both of Scott's plan and of the popular plan would have been borne in mind. That no such policy was consistently followed from the first was partly a result of the long-continued difficulty in finding any younger man who could adequately take the place of Scott; it was not for a want of clear ideas, right or wrong, on Lincoln's part.

Only two days after the battle of Bull Run, he put on paper his own view as to the future employment of the three armies. He thought that one should "threaten" Richmond; that one should move from Cincinnati, in Ohio, by a pass called Cumberland Gap in Kentucky, upon Knoxville in Eastern Tennessee; and that the third, using Cairo on the Mississippi as its base, should advance upon Memphis, some 120 miles further south on that river. Apparently he did not at first wish to commit the army of the Potomac very deeply in its advance on Richmond, and he certainly wished throughout that it should cover Washington against any possible attack. Memphis was one of the three points at which the Southern railway system touched the great river and communicated with the States beyond—Vicksburg and New Orleans, much further south, were the others. Knoxville again is a point, by occupying which, the Northern forces would have cut the direct railway communication between Virginia and the West, but for this move into

Eastern Tennessee Lincoln had other reasons nearer his heart. The people of that region were strongly for the Union; they were invaded by the Confederates and held down by severe coercion, and distressing appeals from them for help kept arriving through the autumn; could they have been succoured and their mountainous country occupied by the North, a great stronghold of the Union would, it seemed to Lincoln, have been planted securely far into the midst of the Confederacy. Therefore he persistently urged this part of his scheme on the attention of his generals. The chief military objection raised by Buell was that his army would have to advance 150 miles from the nearest base of supply upon a railway; (for 200 miles to the west of the Alleghanies there were no railways running from north to south). To meet this Lincoln, in September, urged upon a meeting of important Senators and Representatives the construction of a railway line from Lexington in Kentucky southwards, but his hearers, with their minds narrowed down to an advance on Richmond, seem to have thought the relatively small cost in time and money of this work too great. Lincoln still thought an expedition to Eastern Tennessee practicable at once, and it has been argued from the circumstances in which one was made nearly two years later that he was right. It would, one may suppose, have been unwise to separate the armies of the Ohio and of the West so widely; for the main army of the Confederates in the West, under their most trusted general, Albert Sidney Johnston, was from September onwards in South-western Kentucky, and could have struck at either of these two Northern armies; and this was in Buell's mind. On the other hand, Lincoln's object was a wise one in itself and would have been worth some postponement of the advance along the Mississippi if thereby the army in the West could have been used in support of it. However this may be, the fact is that Lincoln's plan, as it stood, was backed up by McClellan; McClellan was perhaps unduly anxious for Buell to move on Eastern Tennessee, because this would have

supported the invasion of Virginia which he himself was
now contemplating, and he was probably forgetful of
the West; but he was Lincoln's highest military adviser
and his capacity was still trusted.   Buell's own view was
that, when he moved, it should be towards Western Tennessee.   He would have had a railway connection behind
him all his way, and Albert Johnston's army would have
lain before him.   He wished that Halleck meanwhile
should advance up the courses of the Tennessee and
Cumberland Rivers; Eastern Tennessee (he may have
thought) would be in the end more effectively succoured;
their two armies would thus have converged on Johnston's.   Halleck agreed with Buell to the extent of dis-
agreeing with Lincoln and McClellan, but no further.
He declined to move in concert with Buell.   Frémont
had disorganised the army of the West, and Halleck,
till he had repaired the mischief, permitted only certain
minor enterprises under his command.

Each of the three generals, including the General-in-
Chief, who was the Government's chief adviser, was set
upon his own immediate purpose, and indisposed to
understanding the situation of the others—Buell perhaps
the least so.   Each of them had at first a very sound
reason, the unreadiness of his army, for being in no hurry
to move, but then each of them soon appeared to be a
slow or unenterprising commander.   Buell was perhaps
unlucky in this, for his whole conduct is the subject of
some controversy; but he did appear slow, and the two
others, it is universally agreed, really were so.   As 1861
drew to a close, it became urgent that something should
be done somewhere, even if it were not done in the best
possible direction.   The political pressure upon the Administration became as great as before Bull Run.   The
army of the Potomac had rapidly become a fine army,
and its enemy, in no way superior, lay entrenching at
Manassas, twenty miles in front of it.   When Lincoln
grew despondent and declared that " if something was
not done soon, the bottom would drop out of the whole
concern," soldiers remark that the military situation was

really sound; but he was right, for a people can hardly
be kept up to the pitch of a high enterprise if it is forced
to think that nothing will happen. Before the end of
the year 1861 military reasons for waiting were no
longer being urged; McClellan had long been promising
immediate action, Buell and Halleck seemed merely unable to agree.

In later days when Lincoln had learnt much by experience it is hard to trace the signs of his influence in
military matters, because, though he followed them
closely, he was commonly in full agreement with his
chief general and he invariably and rightly left him free.
At this stage, when his position was more difficult, and
his guidance came from common sense and the military
books, of which, ever since Bull Run, he had been trying,
amidst all his work, to tear out the heart, there is evidence on which to judge the intelligence which he applied
to the war. Certainly he now and ever after looked at
the matter as a whole and formed a clear view of it,
which, for a civilian at any rate, was a reasonable view.
Certainly also at this time and for long after no military
adviser attempted, in correcting any error of his, to
supply him with a better opinion equally clear and comprehensive. This is probably why some Northern military critics, when they came to read his correspondence
with his generals, called him, as his chief biographers
were tempted to think him, " the ablest strategist of the
war." Grant and Sherman did not say this; they said,
what is another thing, that his was the greatest intellectual force that they had met with. Strictly speaking, he
could not be a strategist. If he were so judged, he
would certainly be found guilty of having, till Grant
came to Washington, unduly scattered his forces. He
could pick out the main objects; but as to how to econo-
mise effort, what force and how composed and equipped
was necessary for a particular enterprise, whether in
given conditions of roads, weather, supplies, and previous fatigue, a movement was practicable, and how
long it would take, any clever subaltern with actual ex-

perience of campaigning ought to have been a better judge than he. The test, which the reader must be asked to apply to his conduct of the war, is whether he followed duly or unduly his own imperfect judgment, whether, on the whole, he gave in whenever it was wise to the generals under him, and whether he did so without losing his broad view or surrendering his ultimate purpose. It is really no small proof of strength that, with the definite judgments which he constantly formed, he very rarely indeed gave imperative orders as Commander-in-Chief, which he was, to any general. The circumstances, all of which will soon appear, in which he was tempted or obliged to do so, are only the few marked exceptions to his habitual conduct. There are significant contrary instances in which he abstained even from seeking to know his general's precise intentions. At the time which has just been reviewed, when the scheme of the war was in the making, his correspondence with Buell and Halleck shows his fundamental intention. He emphatically abstains from forcing them; he lucidly, though not so tactfully as later, urges his own view upon the consideration of his general, begging him, not necessarily to act upon it, but at least to see the point, and if he will not do what is wished, to form and explain as clearly a plan for doing something better.

2. The War in the West Up to May, 1862.

The pressure upon McClellan to move grew stronger and indeed more justifiable month after month, and when at last, in March, 1862, McClellan did move, the story of the severest adversity to the North, of Lincoln's sorest trials, and, some still say, his gravest failures, began. Its details will concern us more than those of any other part of the war. But events in the West began earlier, proceeded faster, and should be told first. Buell could not obtain from McClellan permission to carry out his own scheme. He did, however, obtain permission for Halleck, if he consented, to send flotillas up the

Tennessee and Cumberland Rivers to make a diversion while Buell, as Lincoln had proposed and as McClellan had now ordered, marched upon Eastern Tennessee. Halleck would not move. Buell prepared to move alone, and in January, 1862, sent forward a small force under Thomas to meet an equally small Confederate force that had advanced through Cumberland Gap into Eastern Kentucky. Thomas won a complete victory, most welcome as the first success since the defeat of Bull Run, at a place called Mill Springs, far up the Cumberland River towards the mountains. But at the end of January, while Buell was following up with his forces rather widely dispersed because he expected no support from Halleck, he was brought to a stop, for Halleck, without warning, did make an important movement of his own, in which he would need Buell's support.

The Cumberland and the Tennessee are navigable rivers which in their lower course flow parallel in a northerly or north-westerly direction to join the Ohio not far above its junction with the Mississippi at Cairo. Fort Henry was a Confederate fort guarding the navigation of the Tennessee near the northern boundary of the State of that name, Fort Donelson was another on the Cumberland not far off. Ulysses Simpson Grant, who had served with real distinction in the Mexican War, had retired from the Army and had been more or less employed about his father's leather store in Illinois and in the gloomy pursuit of intoxication and of raising small sums from reluctant friends when he met them. On the outbreak of the Civil War he suddenly pulled himself together, and with some difficulty got employment from the Governor of Illinois as a Major-General in the State Militia (obtaining Army rank later). Since then, while serving under Halleck, he had shown sense and promptitude in seizing an important point on the Ohio, upon which the Confederates had designs. He had a quick eye for seeing important points. Grant was now ordered or obtained permission from Halleck to capture Fort Henry and Fort Donelson. By the sudden movements

of Grant and of the flotilla acting with him, the Confederates were forced to abandon Fort Henry on February 6, 1862. Ten days later Fort Donelson surrendered with nearly 10,000 prisoners, after a brilliant and nearly successful sortie by the garrison, in which Grant showed, further, tenacity and a collected mind under the pressure of imminent calamity. Halleck had given Grant little help. Buell was reluctant to detach any of his volunteer troops from their comrades to act with a strange army, and Halleck had not warned him of his intentions. Halleck soon applied to Lincoln for the supreme command over the two Western armies with Buell under him. This was given to him. Experience showed that one or the other must command now that concerted action was necessary. Nothing was known at Washington to set against Halleck's own claim of the credit for the late successes. So Lincoln gave him the command, though present knowledge shows clearly that Buell was the better man. Grant had been left before Fort Donelson in a position of some danger from the army under Albert Johnston; and, from needless fear of Beauregard with a Confederate force under him yet further West, Halleck let slip the chance of sending Grant in pursuit of Johnston, who was falling back up the Cumberland valley. As it was, Johnston for a time evacuated Nashville, further up the Cumberland, the chief town of Tennessee and a great railway centre, which Buell promptly occupied; Beauregard withdrew the Confederate troops from Columbus, a fortress of great reputed strength on the Mississippi not far below Cairo, to positions forty or fifty miles (as the crow flies) further down the stream. Thus, as it was, some important steps had been gained in securing that control of the navigation of the river which was one of the great military objects of the North. Furthermore, successful work was being done still further West by General Curtis in Missouri, who drove an invading force back into Arkansas and inflicted a crushing defeat upon them there in March. But a great stroke should now have been struck. Buell, it is said, saw

plainly that his forces and Halleck's should have been concentrated as far up the Tennessee as possible in an endeavour to seize upon the main railway system of the Confederacy in the West. Halleck preferred, it would seem, to concentrate upon nothing and to scatter his forces upon minor enterprises, provided he did not risk any important engagement. An important engagement with the hope of destroying an army of the enemy was the very thing which, as Johnston's forces now stood, he should have sought, but he appears to have been contented by the temporary retirement of an unscathed enemy who would return again reinforced. Buell was an unlucky man, and Halleck got quite all he deserved, so it is possible that events have been described to us without enough regard to Halleck's case as against Buell. But at any rate, while much should have been happening, nothing very definite did happen till April 6, when Albert Johnston, now strongly reinforced from the extreme South, came upon Grant, who (it is not clear why) had lain encamped, without entrenching, and not expecting immediate attack, near Shiloh, far up the Tennessee River in the extreme south of Tennessee State. Buell at the time, though without clear information as to Grant's danger, was on his way to join him. There seems to have been negligence both on Halleck's part and on Grant's. The battle of Shiloh is said to have been highly characteristic of the combats of partly disciplined armies, in which the individual qualities, good or bad, of the troops play a conspicuous part. Direction on the part of Johnston or Grant was not conspicuously seen, but the latter, whose troops were surprised and driven back some distance, was intensely determined. In the course of that afternoon Albert Johnston was killed. Rightly or wrongly Jefferson Davis and his other friends regarded his death as the greatest of calamities to the South. After the manner of many battles, more especially in this war, the battle of Shiloh was the subject of long subsequent dispute between friends of Grant and of Buell, and far more bitter dispute between friends of

Albert Johnston and Beauregard. But it seems that the South was on the point of winning, till late on the 6th the approach of the first reinforcements from Buell made it useless to attempt more. By the following morning further large reinforcements had come up; Grant in his turn attacked, and Beauregard had difficulty in turning a precipitate retirement into an orderly retreat upon Corinth, forty miles away, a junction upon the principal railway line to be defended. The next day General Pope, who had some time before been detached by Halleck for this purpose, after arduous work in canal cutting, captured, with 7,000 prisoners, the northernmost forts held by the Confederacy on the Mississippi. But Halleck's plans required that his further advance should be stopped. Halleck himself, in his own time, arrived at the front. In his own time, after being joined by Pope, he advanced, carefully entrenching himself every night. He covered in something over a month the forty miles route to Corinth, which, to his surprise, was bloodlessly evacuated before him. He was an engineer, and like some other engineers in the Civil War, was overmuch set upon a methodical and cautious procedure. But his mere advance to Corinth caused the Confederates to abandon yet another fort on the Mississippi, and on June 6 the Northern troops were able to occupy Memphis, for which Lincoln had long wished, while the flotilla accompanying them destroyed a Confederate flotilla. Meanwhile, on May 1, Admiral Farragut, daringly running up the Mississippi, had captured New Orleans, and a Northern force under Butler was able to establish itself in Louisiana. The North had now gained the command of most of the Mississippi, for only the hundred miles or so between Vicksburg far south and Port Hudson, between that and New Orleans, was still held by the South; and command by Northern gunboats of the chief tributaries of the great river was also established. The Confederate armies in the West were left intact, though with some severe losses, and would be able before long to strike northward in a well-chosen direction; for all that

these were great and permanent gains. Yet the North was not cheered. The great loss of life at Shiloh, the greatest battle in the war so far, created a horrible impression. Halleck, under whom all this progress had been made, properly enough received a credit, which critics later have found to be excessive, though it is plain that he had reorganised his army well; but Grant was felt to have been caught napping at Shiloh; there were other rumours about him, too, and he fell deep into general disfavour. The events of the Western war did not pause for long, but, till the end of this year 1862, the North made no further definite progress, and the South, though it was able to invade the North, achieved no important result. It will be well then here to take up the story of events in the East and to follow them continuously till May, 1863, when the dazzling fortune of the South in that theatre of the war reached its highest point.

3. The War in the East Up to May, 1863.

The interest of this part of the Civil War lies chiefly in the achievements of Lee and " Stonewall " Jackson. From the point of view of the North, it was not only disastrous but forms a dreary and controversial chapter. George McClellan came to Washington amid overwhelming demonstrations of public confidence. His comparative youth added to the interest taken in him; and he was spoken of as " the young Napoleon." This ridiculous name for a man already thirty-four was a sign that the people expected impossible things from him. Letters to his wife, which have been injudiciously published, show him to us delighting at first in the consideration paid to him by Lincoln and Scott, proudly confident in his own powers, rather elated than otherwise by a sense that the safety of the country rested on him alone. " I shall carry the thing *en grande,* and crush the rebels in one campaign." He soon had a magnificent army; he may be said to have made it himself. Before, as he thought, the time had come to use it, he had fallen from favour,

and a dead set was being made against him in Washington. A little later, at the crisis of his great venture, when, as he claimed, the Confederate capital could have been taken, his expedition was recalled. Then at a moment of deadly peril to the country his services were again called in. He warded off the danger. Yet a little while and his services were discarded for ever. This summary, which is the truth, but not the whole truth, must enlist a certain sympathy for him. The chief fact of his later life should at once be added. In 1864, when a Presidential election was approaching and despondency prevailed widely in the North, he was selected as the champion of a great party. The Democrats adopted a " platform " which expressed neither more nor less than a desire to end the war on any terms. In accordance with the invariable tradition of party opposition in war time, they chose a war hero as their candidate for the Presidency. McClellan publicly repudiated their principles, and no doubt he meant it, but he became their candidate—their master or their servant as it might prove. That he was Lincoln's opponent in the election of that year ensured that his merits and his misfortunes would be long remembered, but his action then may suggest to any one the doubtful point in his career all along.

Some estimate of his curious yet by no means uncommon type of character is necessary, if Lincoln's relations with him are to be understood at all. The devotion to him shown by his troops proves that he had great titles to confidence, besides, what he also had, a certain faculty of parade, with his handsome charger, his imposing staff and the rest. He was a great trainer of soldiers, and with some strange lapses, a good organiser. He was careful for the welfare of his men; and his almost tender carefulness of their lives contrasted afterwards with what appeared the ruthless carelessness of Grant. Unlike some of his successors, he could never be called an incapable commander. His great opponent, Lee, who had known him of old, was wont to calculate on his extraor-

dinary want of enterprise, but he spoke of him on the whole in terms of ample respect—also, by the way, he sympathised with him like a soldier when, as he naturally assumed, he became a victim to scheming politicians; and Lee confided this feeling to the ready ears of another great soldier, Wolseley. As he showed himself in civil life, McClellan was an attractive gentleman of genial address; it was voted that he was " magnetic," and his private life was so entirely irreproachable as to afford lively satisfaction. More than this, it may be conjectured that to a certain standard of honour, loyalty, and patriotism, which he set consciously before himself, he would always have been devotedly true. But if it be asked further whether McClellan was the desired instrument for Lincoln's and the country's needs, and whether, as the saying is, he was a man to go tiger-hunting with, something very much against him, though hard to define, appears in every part of his record (except indeed, one performance in his Peninsular Campaign). Did he ever do his best to beat the enemy? Did he ever, except for a moment, concentrate himself singly upon any great object? Were even his preparations thorough? Was his information ever accurate? Was his purpose in the war ever definite, and, if so, made plain to his Government? Was he often betrayed into marked frankness, or into marked generosity? No one would be ready to answer yes to any of these questions. McClellan fills so memorable a place in American history that he demands such a label as can be given to him. In the most moving and the most authentic of all Visions of Judgment, men were not set on the right hand or the left according as they were of irreproachable or reproachable character; they were divided into those who did and those who did not. In the provisional judgment which men, if they make it modestly, should at times make with decision, McClellan's place is clear. The quality, " spiacente a Dio ed ai nemici suoi," of the men who did not, ran through and through him.

Lincoln required first a general who would make no

fatal blunder, but he required too, when he could find
him, a general of undaunted enterprise; he did not wish
to expose the North to disaster, but he did mean to conquer the South. There was some security in employing
McClellan, though employing him did at one time throw
on Lincoln's unfit shoulders the task of defending Washington. It proved very hard to find another general
equally trustworthy. But, in the light of facts which
Lincoln came to perceive, it proved impossible to consider McClellan as the man to finish the war.

We need only notice the doings of the main armies in
this theatre of the war and take no account of various
minor affairs at outlying posts. From the battle of Bull
Run, which was on July 21, 1861, to March 5, 1862,
the Southern army under Joseph Johnston lay quietly
drilling at Manassas. It, of course, entrenched its position, but to add to the appearance of its strength, it constructed embrasures for more than its number of guns
and had dummy guns to show in them. At one moment
there was a prospect that it might move. Johnston and
the general with him had no idea of attacking the army
of the Potomac where it lay, but they did think that with
a further 50,000 or 60,000 they might successfully invade Maryland, crossing higher up the Potomac, and by
drawing McClellan away from his present position, get
a chance of defeating him. The Southern President
came to Manassas, at their invitation, on October 1, but
he did not think well to withdraw the trained men whom
he could have sent to Johnston from the various points
in the South at which they were stationed; he may have
had good reasons but it is likely that he sacrificed one
of the best chances of the South. McClellan's army was
soon in as good a state of preparation as Johnston's.
Early in October McClellan had, on his own statement,
over 147,000 men at his disposal; Joseph Johnston, on
his own statement, under 47,000. Johnston was well
informed as to McClellan's numbers—very likely he
could get information from Maryland more easily than
McClellan from Virginia. The two armies lay not

twenty-five miles apart. The weather and the roads were good to the end of December; the roads were practicable by March and they seem to have been so all the time. As spring approached, it appeared to the Southern generals that McClellan must soon advance. Johnston thought that his right flank was liable to be turned and the railway communications south of Manassas liable to be cut. In the course of February it was realised that his position was too dangerous; the large stores accumulated there were removed; and when, early in March, there were reports of unusual activity in the Northern camp, Johnston, still expecting attack from the same direction, began his retreat. On March 9 it was learned in Washington that Manassas had been completely evacuated. McClellan marched his whole army there, and marched it back. Johnston withdrew quietly behind the Rapidan River, some 30 miles further south, and to his surprise was left free from any pursuit.

For months past the incessant report in the papers, " all quiet upon the Potomac," had been getting upon the nerves of the North. The gradual conversion of their pride in an imposing army into puzzled rage at its inactivity has left a deeper impression on Northern memories than the shock of disappointment at Bull Run. Public men of weight had been pressing for an advance in November, and when the Joint Committee of Congress, an arbitrary and meddlesome, but able and perhaps on the whole useful body, was set up in December, it brought its full influence to bear on the President. Lincoln was already anxious enough; he wished to rouse McClellan himself to activity, while he screened him against excessive impatience or interference with his plans. It is impossible to say what was McClellan's real mind. Quite early he seems to have held out hopes to Lincoln that he would soon attack, but he was writing to his wife that he expected to be attacked by superior numbers. It is certain, however, that he was possessed now and always by a delusion as to the enemy's strength. For instance: Lincoln at last felt bound to work out for

himself definite prospects for a forward movement; it is
sufficient to say of this layman's effort that he proposed
substantially the line of advance which Johnston a little
later began to dread most; Lincoln's plan was submitted
for McClellan's consideration; McClellan rejected it,
and his reasons were based on his assertion that he would
have to meet nearly equal numbers. He, in fact, outnumbered the enemy by more than three to one. If we
find the President later setting aside the general's judgment on grounds that are not fully explained, we must
recall McClellan's vast and persistent miscalculations of
an enemy resident in his neighbourhood. And the distrust which he thus created was aggravated by another
propensity of his vague mind. His illusory fear was the
companion of an extravagant hope; the Confederate
army was invincible when all the world expected him to
attack it then and there, but the blow which he would
deal it in his own place and his own time was to have
decisive results, which were indeed impossible; the enemy
was to "pass beneath the Caudine Forks." The demands which he made on the Administration for men and
supplies seemed to have no finality about them; his tone
in regard to them seemed to degenerate into a chronic
grumble. The War Department certainly did not in-
tend to stint him in any way; but he was an unsatisfactory man to deal with in these matters. There was a
great mystery as to what became of the men sent to him.
In the idyllic phrase, which Lincoln once used of him
or of some other general, sending troops to him was
"like shifting fleas across a barn floor with a shovel—
not half of them ever get there." But his fault was
graver than this; utterly ignoring the needs of the West,
he tried, as General-in-Chief, to divert to his own army
the recruits and the stores required for the other armies.

The difficulty with him went yet further; McClellan
himself deliberately set to work to destroy personal harmony between himself and his Government. It counts
for little that in private he soon set down all the civil
authorities as the "greatest set of incapables," and so

forth, but it counts for more that he was personally insolent to the President. Lincoln had been in the habit, mistaken in this case but natural in a chief who desires to be friendly, of calling at McClellan's house rather than summoning him to his own. McClellan acquired a habit of avoiding him, he treated his enquiries as idle curiosity, and he probably thought, not without a grain of reason, that Lincoln's way of discussing matters with many people led him into indiscretion. So one evening when Lincoln and Seward were waiting at the general's house for his return, McClellan came in and went upstairs; a message was sent that the President would be glad to see him; he said he was tired and would rather be excused that night. Lincoln damped down his friends' indignation at this; he would, he once said, " hold General McClellan's stirrup for him if he will only win us victories." But he called no more at McClellan's, and a curious abruptness in some of his orders later marks his unsuccessful effort to deal with McClellan in another way. The slightly ridiculous light in which the story shows Lincoln would not obscure to any soldier the full gravity of such an incident. It was not merely foolish to treat a kind superior rudely; a general who thus drew down a curtain between his own mind and that of the Government evidently went a very long way to ensure failure in war.

Lincoln had failed to move McClellan early in December. For part of that month and January McClellan was very ill. Consultations were held with other generals, including McDowell, who could not be given the chief command because the troops did not trust him. McDowell and the rest were in agreement with Lincoln. Then McClellan suddenly recovered and was present at a renewed consultation. He snubbed McDowell; the inadequacy of his force to meet, in fact, less than a third of its number was " so plain that a blind man could see it "; he was severely and abruptly tackled as to his own plans by Secretary Chase; Lincoln intervened to shield him, got from him a distinct statement that he had in

his mind a definite time for moving, and adjourned the meeting. Stanton, one of the friends to whom McClellan had confided his grievances, was now at the War Department and was at one with the Joint Committee of Congress in his impatience that McClellan should move. At last, on January 27, Lincoln published a " General War Order " that a forward movement was to be made by the army of the Potomac and the Western armies on February 22. It seems a blundering step, but it roused McClellan. For a time he even thought of acting as Lincoln wished; he would move straight against Johnston, and " in ten days," he told Chase on February 13, " I shall be in Richmond." But he quickly returned to the plan which he seems to have been forming before but which he only now revealed to the Government, and it was a plan which involved further delay. When February 22 passed and nothing was done, the Joint Committee were indignant that Lincoln still stood by McClellan. But McClellan now was proposing definite action; apart from the difficulty of finding a better man, there was the fact that McClellan had made his army and was beloved by it; above all, Lincoln had not lost all the belief he had formed at first in McClellan's capacity; he believed that " if he could once get McClellan started " he would do well. Professional criticism, alive to McClellan's military faults, has justified Lincoln in this, and it was for something other than professional failure that Lincoln at last removed him.

McClellan had determined to move his army by sea to some point further down the coast of the Chesapeake Bay. The questions which Lincoln wrote to him requesting a written answer have never been adequately answered. Did McClellan's plan, he asked, require less time or money than Lincoln's? Did it make victory more certain? Did it make it more valuable? In case of disaster, did it make retreat more easy? The one point for consideration in McClellan's reply to him is that the enemy did not expect such a movement. This was quite true; but the enemy was able to meet it, and

McClellan was far too deliberate to reap any advantage from a surprise. His original plan was to land near a place called Urbana on the estuary of the Rappahannock, not fifty miles east of Richmond. When he heard that Johnston had retreated further south, he assumed, and ever after declared, that this was to anticipate his design upon Urbana, which, he said, must have reached the enemy's ears through the loose chattering of the Administration. As has been seen, this was quite untrue. His project of going to Urbana was now changed, by himself or the Government, upon the unanimous advice of his chief subordinate generals, into a movement to Fort Monroe, which he had even before regarded as preferable to a direct advance southwards. A few days after Johnston's retreat, the War Department began the embarkation of his troops for this point. Fort Monroe is at the end of the peninsula which lies between the estuaries of the York River on the north and the James on the south. Near the base of this projection of land, seventy-five miles from Fort Monroe, stands Richmond. On April 2, 1862, McClellan himself landed to begin the celebrated Peninsula Campaign which was to close in disappointment at the end of July.

Before the troops were sent to the Peninsula several things were to be done. An expedition to restore communication westward by the Baltimore and Ohio Railway involved bridging the Potomac with boats which were to be brought by canal. It collapsed because McClellan's boats were six inches too wide for the canal locks. Then Lincoln had insisted that the navigation of the lower Potomac should be made free from the menace of Confederate batteries which, if McClellan would have co-operated with the Navy Department, would have been cleared away long before. This was now done, and though a new peril to the transportation of McClellan's army suddenly and dramatically disclosed itself, it was as suddenly and dramatically removed. In the hasty abandonment of Norfolk harbour on the south of the James estuary by the North, a screw steamer called the

Merrimac had been partly burnt and scuttled by the North. On March 1 she steamed out of the harbour in sight of the North. The Confederates had raised her and converted her into an ironclad. Three wooden ships of the North gave gallant but useless fight to her and were destroyed that day; and the news spread consternation in every Northern port. On the very next morning there came into the mouth of the James the rival product of the Northern Navy Department and of the Swedish engineer Ericsson's invention. She was compared to a " cheesebox on a raft "; she was named the *Monitor,* and was the parent of a type of vessel so called which has been heard of much more recently. The *Merrimac* and the *Monitor* forthwith fought a three hours' duel; then each retired into harbour without fatal damage. But the *Merrimac* never came out again; she was destroyed by the Confederates when McClellan had advanced some way up the Peninsula; and it will be unnecessary to speak of the several similar efforts of the South, which nearly but not quite achieved very important successes later.

Before and after his arrival at the Peninsula, McClellan received several mortifications. Immediately after the humiliation of the enemy's escape from Manassas, he was without warning relieved of his command as General-in-Chief. This would in any case have followed naturally upon his expedition away from Washington; it was in public put on that ground alone; and he took it well. He had been urged to appoint corps commanders, for so large a force as his could not remain organised only in divisions; he preferred to wait till he had made trial of the generals under him; Lincoln would not have this delay, and appointed corps commanders chosen by himself because he believed them to be fighting men. The manner in which these and some other preparatory steps were taken were, without a doubt, intended to make McClellan feel the whip. They mark a departure, not quite happy at first, from Lincoln's formerly too gentle manner. A worse shock to Mc-

Clellan followed. The President had been emphatic in
his orders that a sufficient force should be left to make
Washington safe, and supposed that he had come to a
precise understanding on this point. He suddenly discovered that McClellan, who had now left for Fort
Monroe, had ordered McDowell to follow him with a
force so large that it would not leave the required number behind. Lincoln immediately ordered McDowell
and his whole corps to remain, though he subsequently
sent a part of it to McClellan. McClellan's story later
gives reason for thinking that he had intended no decep-
tion; but if so, he had expressed himself with unpar-
donable vagueness, and he had not in fact left Washington secure. Now and throughout this campaign
Lincoln took the line that Washington must be kept safe
—safe in the judgment of all the best military authorities
available.

McClellan's progress up the Peninsula was slow. He
had not informed himself correctly as to the geography;
he found the enemy not so unprepared as he had supposed; he wasted, it is agreed, a month in regular approaches to their thinly-manned fortifications at Yorktown, when he might have carried them by assault. He
was soon confronted by Joseph Johnston, and he seems
both to have exaggerated Johnston's numbers again and
to have been unprepared for his movements. The Administration does not seem to have spared any effort to
support him. In addition to the 100,000 troops he took
with him, 40,000 altogether were before long despatched
to him. He was operating in a very difficult country,
but he was opposed at first by not half his own number.
Lincoln, in friendly letters, urged upon him that delay
enabled the enemy to strengthen himself both in numbers
and in fortifications. The War Department did its best
for him. The whole of his incessant complaints on this
score are rendered unconvincing by the language of his
private letters about that " sink of iniquity, Washington," " those treacherous hounds," the civil authorities,
who were at least honest and intelligent men, and the

"Abolitionists and other scoundrels," who, he supposed, wished the destruction of his army. The criticism in Congress of himself and his generals was no doubt free, but so, as Lincoln reminded him, was the criticism of Lincoln himself. Justly or not, there were complaints of his relations with corps commanders. Lincoln gave no weight to them, but wrote him a manly and a kindly warning. The points of controversy which McClellan bequeathed to writers on the Civil War are innumerable, but no one can read his correspondence at this stage without concluding that he was almost impossible to deal with, and that the whole of his evidence in his own case was vitiated by a sheer hallucination that people wished him to fail. He had been nearly two months in the Peninsula when he was attacked at a disadvantage by Johnston, but defeated him on May 31 and June 1 in a battle which gave confidence and prestige to the Northern side, but which he did not follow up. A part of his army pursued the enemy to within four miles of Richmond, and it has been contended that if he had acted with energy he could at this time have taken that city. His delay, to whatever it was due, gave the enemy time to strengthen himself greatly both in men and in fortifications. The capable Johnston was severely wounded in the battle, and was replaced by the inspired Lee. According to McClellan's own account, which English writers have followed, his movements had been greatly embarrassed by the false hope given him that McDowell was now to march overland and join him. His statement that he was influenced by this is refuted by his own letters at the time. McClellan, however, suffered a great disappointment. The front of Washington was now clear of the enemy and Lincoln had determined to send McDowell when he was induced to keep him back by a diversion in the war which he had not expected, and which indeed McClellan had advised him not to expect.

"Stonewall" Jackson's most famous campaign happened at this juncture, and to save Washington, Lincoln and Stanton placed themselves, or were placed, in the

trying position of actually directing movements of troops. There were to the south and south-west of Washington, besides the troops under McDowell's command, two Northern forces respectively commanded by Generals Banks and Frémont. These two men were among the chief examples of those " political generals," the use of whom in this early and necessarily blundering stage of the war has been the subject of much comment. Banks was certainly a politician, a self-made man, who had worked in a factory and who had risen to be at one time Speaker of the House. He was now a general because as a powerful man in the patriotic State of Massachusetts he brought with him many men, and these were ready to obey him. On the other hand, he on several occasions showed good judgment both in military matters and in the questions of civil administration which came under him; his heart was in his duty; and, though he held high commands almost to the end of the war, want of competence was never imputed to him till the failure of a very difficult enterprise on which he was despatched in 1864. He was now in the lower valley of the Shenandoah, keeping a watch over a much smaller force under Jackson higher up the valley. Frémont was in some sense a soldier, but after his record in Missouri he should never have been employed. His new appointment was one of Lincoln's greatest mistakes, and it was a mistake of a characteristic kind. It will easily be understood that there were real political reasons for not leaving this popular champion of freedom unused and unrecognized. These reasons should not have, and probably would not have, prevailed. But Lincoln's personal reluctance to resist all entreaties on behalf of his own forerunner and his own rival was great; and then Frémont came to Lincoln and proposed to him a knight-errant's adventure to succour the oppressed Unionists of Tennessee by an expedition through West Virginia. So he was now to proceed there, but was kept for the present in the mountains near the Shenandoah valley. The way in which the forces under McDowell, Banks and Frémont were

scattered on various errands was unscientific; what could be done by Jackson, in correspondence with Lee, was certainly unforeseen. At the beginning of May, Jackson, who earlier in the spring had achieved some minor successes in the Shenandoah valley and had raided West Virginia, began a series of movements of which the brilliant skill and daring are recorded in Colonel Henderson's famous book. With a small force, surrounded by other forces, each of which, if concentrated, should have outnumbered him, he caught each in turn at a disadvantage, inflicted on them several damaging blows, and put the startled President and Secretary of War in fear for the safety of Washington. There seemed to be no one available who could immediately be charged with the supreme command of these three Northern forces, unless McDowell could have been spared from where he was; so Lincoln with Stanton's help took upon himself to ensure the co-operation of their three commanders by orders from Washington. His self-reliance had now begun to reach its full stature, his military good sense in comparison with McClellan's was proving greater than he had supposed, and he had probably not discovered its limitations. Presumably his plans now were, like an amateur's, too complicated, and it is not worth while to discuss them. But he was trying to cope with newly revealed military genius, and, so far as can be told, he was only prevented from crushing the adventurous Jackson by a piece of flat disobedience on the part of Frémont. Frémont, having thus appropriately punished Lincoln, was removed, this time finally, from command. Jackson, having successfully kept McDowell from McClellan, had before the end of June escaped safe southward. McClellan was nearing Richmond. Lee, by this time, had been set free from Jefferson Davis' office and had taken over the command of Joseph Johnston's army. Lincoln must have learnt a great deal, and he fully realised that the forces not under McClellan in the East should be under some single commander. Pope, an experienced soldier, had succeeded well in the West;

he was no longer necessary there, and there was no adverse criticism upon him. He was in all respects a proper choice, and he was now summoned to take command of what was to be called the army of Virginia. A few days later, upon the advice, as it seems, of Scott, Halleck himself was called from the West. His old command was left to Grant and he himself was made General-in-Chief and continued at Washington to the end of the war as an adviser of the Government. All the progress in the West had been made under Halleck's supervision, and his despatches had given an exaggerated impression of his own achievement at Corinth. He had not seen active service before the war, but he had a great name as an accomplished military writer; in after years he was well known as a writer on international law. He is not thought to have justified his appointment by showing sound judgment about war, and Lincoln upon some later emergency told him in his direct way that his military knowledge was useless if he could not give a definite decision in doubtful circumstances. But whether Halleck's abilities were great or small, Lincoln continued to use them, because he found him " wholly for the service," without personal favour or prejudice.

McClellan was slowly but steadily nearing Richmond. From June 26 to July 2 there took place a series of engagements between Lee and McClellan, or rather the commanders under him, known as the Seven Days' Battles. The fortunes of the fighting varied greatly, but the upshot is that, though the corps on McClellan's left won a strong position not far from Richmond, the sudden approach of Jackson's forces upon McClellan's right flank, which began on the 26th, placed him in what appears to have been, as he himself thought it, a situation of great danger. Lee is said to have " read McClellan like an open book," playing upon his caution, which made him, while his subordinates fought, more anxious to secure their retreat than to seize upon any advantage they gained. But Lee's reading deceived him in one respect. He had counted upon McClellan's retreating,

but thought he would retreat under difficulties right down the Peninsula to his original base and be thoroughly cut up on the way. But on July 2 McClellan with great skill withdrew his whole army to Harrison's Landing far up the James estuary, having effected with the Navy a complete transference of his base. Here his army lay in a position of security; they might yet threaten Richmond, and McClellan's soldiers still believed in him. But the South was led by a great commander and had now learned to give him unbounded confidence; there was some excuse for a panic in Wall Street, and every reason for dejection in the North.

On the third of the Seven Days, McClellan, much moved by the sight of dead and wounded comrades, sent a gloomy telegram to the Secretary of War, appealing with excessive eloquence for more men. " I only wish to say to the President," he remarked in it, " that I think he is wrong in regarding me as ungenerous when I said that my force was too weak." He concluded: " If I save the army now, I tell you plainly that I owe no thanks to you nor to any other persons in Washington. You have done your best to sacrifice this army." Stanton still expressed the extraordinary hope that Richmond would fall in a day or two. He had lately committed the folly of suspending enlistment, an act which, though of course there is an explanation of it, must rank as the one first-rate blunder of Lincoln's Administration. He was now negotiating through the astute Seward for offers from the State Governors of a levy of 300,000 men to follow up McClellan's success. Lincoln, as was his way, feared the worst. He seems at one moment to have had fears for McClellan's sanity. But he telegraphed, himself, an answer to him, which affords as fair an example as can be given of his characteristic manner. "Save your army at all events. Will send reinforcements as fast as we can. Of course they cannot reach you to-day or to-morrow, or next day. I have not said you were ungenerous for saying you needed reinforcements. I thought you were ungenerous in assuming that I did not

send them as fast as I could. I feel any misfortune to you and your army quite as keenly as you feel it yourself. If you have had a drawn battle or repulse, it is the price we pay for the enemy not being in Washington. We protected Washington and the enemy concentrated on you. Had we stripped Washington, he would have been upon us before the troops could have gotten to you. Less than a week ago you notified us reinforcements were leaving Richmond to come in front of us. It is the nature of the case, and neither you nor the Government are to blame. Please tell me at once the present condition and aspect of things."

Demands for an impossible number of reinforcements continued. Lincoln explained to McClellan a few days later that they were impossible, and added: " If in your frequent mention of responsibility you have the impression that I blame you for not doing more than you can, please be relieved of such an impression. I only beg that, in like manner, you will not ask impossibilities of me." Much argument upon Lincoln's next important act may be saved by the simple observations that the problem in regard to the defence of Washington was real, that McClellan's propensity to ask for the impossible was also real, and that Lincoln's patient and loyal attitude to him was real too.

Five days after his arrival at Harrison's Landing, McClellan wrote Lincoln a long letter. It was a treatise upon Lincoln's political duties. It was written as " on the brink of eternity." He was not then in fact in any danger, and possibly he had composed it seven days before as his political testament; and apprehensions, free from personal fear, excuse, without quite redeeming, its inappropriateness. The President is before all things not to abandon the cause. But the cause should be fought for upon Christian principles. Christian principles exclude warfare on private property. More especially do they exclude measures for emancipating slaves. And if the President gives way to radical views on slavery, he will get no soldiers. Then follows a mandate to the

President to appoint a Commander-in-Chief, not necessarily the writer. Such a summary does injustice to a certain elevation of tone in the letter, but that elevation is itself slightly strained. McClellan, whatever his private opinions, had not meddled with politics before he left Washington. The question why in this military crisis he should have written what a Democratic politician might have composed as a party manifesto must later have caused Lincoln some thought, but it apparently did not enter into the decision he next took. He arrived himself at Harrison's Landing next day. McClellan handed him the letter. Lincoln read it, and said that he was obliged to him. McClellan sent a copy to his wife as " a very important record."

Lincoln had come in order to learn the views of McClellan and all his corps commanders. They differed a good deal on important points, but a majority of them were naturally anxious to stay and fight there. Lincoln was left in some anxiety as to how the health of the troops would stand the climate of the coming months if they had to wait long where they were. He was also disturbed by McClellan's vagueness about the number of his men, for he now returned as present for duty a number which far exceeded that which some of his recent telegrams had given and yet fell short of the number sent him by an amount which no reasonable estimate of killed, wounded, and sick could explain. This added to Lincoln's doubt on the main question presented to him. McClellan believed that he could take Richmond, but he demanded for this very large reinforcements. Some part of them were already being collected, but the rest could by no means be given him without leaving Washington with far fewer troops to defend it than McClellan or anybody else had hitherto thought necessary.

On July 24, the day after his arrival at Washington, Halleck was sent to consult with McClellan and his generals. The record of their consultations sufficiently shows the intricacy of the problem to be decided. The question of the health of the climate in August weighed much

with Halleck, but the most striking feature of their conversation was the fluctuation of McClellan's own opinion
upon each important point—at one moment he even gave
Halleck the impression that he wished under all the circumstances to withdraw and to join Pope. When
Halleck returned to Washington McClellan telegraphed
in passionate anxiety to be left in the Peninsula and reinforced. On the other hand, some of the officers of
highest rank with him wrote strongly urging withdrawal. This latter was the course on which Lincoln
and Halleck decided. In the circumstances it was certainly the simplest course to concentrate all available
forces in an attack upon the enemy from the direction of
Washington which would keep that capital covered all
the while. It was in any case no hasty and no indefensible decision, nor is there any justification for the frequent
assertion that some malignant influence brought it about.
It is one of the steps taken by Lincoln which have been
the most often lamented. But if McClellan had had all
he demanded to take Richmond and had made good his
promise, what would Lee have done? Lee's own answer to a similar question later was, " We would swap
queens "; that is, he would have taken Washington. If
so the Confederacy would not have fallen, but in all
probability the North would have collapsed, and European Powers would at the least have recognised the Confederacy.

Lincoln indeed had acted as any prudent civilian Minister would then have acted. But disaster followed, or
rather there followed, with brief interruption, a succession of disasters which, after this long tale of hesitation,
can be quickly told. It would be easy to represent them
as a judgment upon the Administration which had rejected the guidance of McClellan. But in the true perspective of the war, the point which has now been reached
marks the final election by the North of the policy by
which it won the war. McClellan, even if he had taken
Richmond while Washington remained safe, would have
concentrated the efforts of the North upon a line of ad-

vance which gave little promise of finally reducing the
Confederacy. It is evident to-day that the right course
for the North was to keep the threatening of Richmond
and the recurrent hammering at the Southern forces on
that front duly related to that continual process by which
the vitals of the Southern country were being eaten into
from the west. This policy, it has been seen, was present
to Lincoln's mind from an early day; the temptation to
depart from it was now once for all rejected. On the
other hand, the three great Southern victories, the second battle of Bull Run, Fredericksburg, and Chancellorsville, which followed within the next nine months, had no
lasting influence. Jefferson Davis might perhaps have
done well if he had neglected all else and massed every
man he could gather to pursue the advantage which these
battles gave him. He did not—perhaps could not—do
this. But he concentrated his greatest resource of all,
the genius of Lee, upon a point at which the real danger
did not lie.

Pope had now set vigorously to work collecting and
pulling together his forces, which had previously been
scattered under different commanders in the north of
Virginia. He was guilty of a General Order which
shocked people by its boastfulness, insulted the Eastern
soldiers by a comparison with their Western comrades,
and threatened harsh and most unjust treatment of the
civil population of Virginia. But upon the whole he
created confidence, for he was an officer well trained in
his profession as well as an energetic man. The problem
was now to effect as quickly as possible the union of
Pope's troops and McClellan's in an overwhelming force.
Pope was anxious to keep McClellan unmolested while
he embarked his men. So, to occupy the enemy, he
pushed boldly into Virginia; he pushed too far, placed
himself in great danger from the lightning movements
which Lee now habitually employed Jackson to execute,
but extricated himself with much promptitude, though
with some considerable losses. McClellan had not been
deprived of command; he was in the curious and annoy-

ing position of having to transfer troops to Pope till, for a moment, not a man remained under him, but the process of embarking and transferring them gave full scope for energy and skill. McClellan, as it appeared to Lincoln, performed his task very slowly. This was not the judgment of impatience, for McClellan caused the delay by repeated and perverse disobedience to Halleck's orders. But the day drew near when 150,000 men might be concentrated under Pope against Lee's 55,000. The stroke which Lee now struck after earnest consultation with Jackson has been said to have been "perhaps the most daring in the history of warfare." He divided his army almost under the enemy's eyes and sent Jackson by a circuitous route to cut Pope's communications with Washington. Then followed an intricate tactical game, in which each side was bewildered as to the movements of the other. Pope became exasperated and abandoned his prudence. He turned on his enemy when he should and could have withdrawn to a safe position and waited. On August 29 and 30, in the ominous neighbourhood of the Bull Run and of Manassas, he sustained a heavy defeat. Then he abandoned hope before he need have done so, and, alleging that his men were demoralised, begged to be withdrawn within the defences of Washington, where he arrived on September 3, and, as was inevitable in the condition of his army, was relieved of his command. McClellan, in Lincoln's opinion, had now been guilty of the offence which that generous mind would find it hardest to forgive. He had not bestirred himself to get his men to Pope. In Lincoln's belief at the time he had wished Pope to fail. McClellan, who reached Washington at the crisis of Pope's difficulties, was consulted, and said to Lincoln that Pope must be left to get out of his scrape as best he could. It was perhaps only an awkward phrase, but it did not soften Lincoln.

Washington was now too strongly held to be attacked, but Lee determined to invade Maryland. At least this would keep Virginia safe during harvest time. It might

win him many recruits in Maryland. It would frighten the North, all the more because a Confederate force further west was at that same time invading Kentucky; it might accomplish there was no saying how much. This much, one may gather from the "Life of Lord John Russell," any great victory of the South on Northern soil would probably have accomplished: the Confederacy would have been recognised, as Jefferson Davis longed for it to be, by European Powers. Lincoln now acted in total disregard of his Cabinet and of all Washington, and in equal disregard of any false notions of dignity. By word of mouth he directed McClellan to take command of all the troops at Washington. His opinion of McClellan had not altered, but, as he said to his private secretaries, if McClellan could not fight himself, he excelled in making others ready to fight. No other step could have succeeded so quickly in restoring order and confidence to the Army. Few or no instructions were given to McClellan. He was simply allowed the freest possible hand, and was watched with keen solicitude as to how he would rise to his opportunity.

Lee, in his advance, expected his opponent to be slow. He actually again divided his small army, leaving Jackson with a part of it behind for a while to capture, as he did, the Northern fort at Harper's Ferry. A Northern private picked up a packet of cigars dropped by some Southern officer with a piece of paper round it. The paper was a copy of an order of Lee's which revealed to McClellan the opportunity now given him of crushing Lee in detail. But he did not rouse himself. He was somewhat hampered by lack of cavalry, and his greatest quality in the field was his care not to give chances to the enemy. His want of energy allowed Lee time to discover what had happened and fall back a little towards Harper's Ferry. Yet Lee dared, without having yet reunited his forces, to stop at a point where McClellan must be tempted to give him battle, and where, if he could only stand against McClellan, Jackson would be in a position to deliver a deadly counter-

stroke. Lee knew that for the South the chance of rapid success was worth any risk. McClellan, however, moved so slowly that Jackson was able to join Lee before the battle. The Northern army came up with them near the north bank of the Potomac on the Antietam Creek, a small tributary of that river, about sixty miles northeast of Washington. There, on September 17, 1862, McClellan ordered an attack, to which he did not attempt to give his personal direction. His corps commanders led assaults on Lee's position at different times and in so disconnected a manner that each was repulsed singly. But on the following morning Lee found himself in a situation which determined him to retreat.

As a military success the battle of Antietam demanded to be followed up. Reinforcements had now come to McClellan, and Lincoln telegraphed, " Please do not let him get off without being hurt." Lee was between the broad Potomac and a Northern army fully twice as large as his own, with other large forces near. McClellan's subordinates urged him to renew the attack and drive Lee into the river. But Lee was allowed to cross the river, and McClellan lay camped on the Antietam battlefield for a fortnight. He may have been dissatisfied with the condition of his army and its supplies. Some of his men wanted new boots; many of Lee's were limping barefoot. He certainly, as often before, exaggerated the strength of his enemy. Lee recrossed the Potomac little damaged. Lincoln, occupied in those days over the most momentous act of his political life, watched McClellan eagerly, and came to the Antietam to see things for himself. He came back in the full belief that McClellan would move at once. Once more undeceived, he pressed him with letters and telegrams from himself and Halleck. He was convinced that McClellan, if he tried, could cut off Lee from Richmond. Hearing of the fatigue of McClellan's horses, he telegraphed about the middle of October, " Will you pardon me for asking what your horses have done since the battle of Antietam that tires anything." This was unkind; McClellan in-

deed should have seen about cavalry in the days when he was organising in Washington, but at this moment the Southern horse had just raided right round his lines and got safe back, and his own much inferior cavalry was probably worn out with vain pursuit of them. On the same day Lincoln wrote more kindly, " My dear Sir, you remember my speaking to you of what I called your over-cautiousness. Are you not over-cautious when you assume that you cannot do what the enemy is constantly doing? Change positions with the enemy, and think you not, he would break your communications with Richmond within the next twenty-four hours." And after a brief analysis of the situation, which seems conclusive, he ends: " I say ' try '; if we never try we shall never succeed. . . . If we cannot beat him now when he bears the wastage of coming to us, we never can when we bear the wastage of going to him." His patience was nearing a limit which he had already fixed in his own mind. On October 28, more than five weeks after the battle, McClellan began to cross the Potomac, and took a week in the process. On November 5, McClellan was removed from his command, and General Burnside appointed in his place.

Lincoln had longed for the clear victory that he thought McClellan would win; he gloomily foreboded that he might not find a better man to put in his place; he felt sadly how he would be accused, as he has been ever since, of displacing McClellan because he was a Democrat. " In considering military merit," he wrote privately, " the world has abundant evidence that I disregard politics." A friend, a Republican general, wrote to him a week or so after McClellan had been removed to urge that all the generals ought to be men in thorough sympathy with the Administration. He received a crushing reply (to be followed in a day or two by a friendly invitation) indignantly proving that Democrats served as well in the field as Republicans. But in regard to McClellan himself we now know that a grave suspicion had entered Lincoln's mind. He might, per-

haps, in the fear of finding no one better, have tolerated his " over-cautiousness "; he did not care what line an officer who did his duty might in civil life take politically; but he would not take the risk of entrusting the war further to a general who let his politics govern his strategy, and who, as he put it simply, " did not want to hurt the enemy." This, he had begun to believe, was the cause of McClellan's lack of energy. He resolved to treat McClellan's conduct now, in fighting Lee or in letting him escape South, as the test of whether his own suspicion about him was justified or not. Lee did get clear away, and Lincoln dismissed McClellan in the full belief, right or wrong, that he was not sorry for Lee's escape.

It is not known exactly what further evidence Lincoln then had for his belief, but information which seems to have come later made him think afterwards that he had been right. The following story was told him by the Governor of Vermont, whose brother, a certain General Smith, served under McClellan and was long his intimate friend. Lincoln believed the story; so may we. The Mayor of New York, a shifty demagogue named Fernando Wood, had visited McClellan in the Peninsula with a proposal that he should become the Democratic candidate for the Presidency, and with a view to this should pledge himself to certain Democratic politicians to conduct the war in a way that should conciliate the South, which to Lincoln's mind meant an " inefficient " way. McClellan, after some days of unusual reserve, told Smith of this and showed him a letter which he had drafted giving the desired pledge. On Smith's earnest remonstrance that this " looked like treason," he did not send the letter then. But Wood came again after the battle of Antietam, and this time McClellan sent a letter in the same sense. This he afterwards confessed to Smith, showing him a copy of the letter. Smith and other generals asked, after this, to be relieved from service under him. If, as can hardly be doubted, McClellan did this, there can be no serious excuse for him, and no serious question that Lincoln was right when he

concluded it was unsafe to employ him. McClellan, according to all evidence except his own letters, was a nice man, and was not likely to harbour a thought of what to him seemed treason; it is honourable to him that he wished later to serve under Grant but was refused by him. But, to one of his views, the political situation before and after Antietam was alarming, and it is certain that to his inconclusive mind and character an attitude of half loyalty would be easy. He may not have wished that Lee should escape, but he had no ardent desire that he should not. Right or wrong, such was the ground of Lincoln's independent and conscientiously deliberate decision.

The result again did not reward him. His choice of Burnside was a mistake. There were corps commanders under McClellan who had earned special confidence, but they were all rather old. General Burnside, who was the senior among the rest, had lately succeeded in operations in connection with the Navy on the North Carolina coast, whereby certain harbours were permanently closed to the South. He had since served under McClellan at the Antietam, but had not earned much credit. He was a loyal friend to McClellan and very modest about his own capacity. Perhaps both these things prejudiced Lincoln in his favour. He continued in active service till nearly the end of the war, when a failure led to his retirement; and he was always popular and respected. At this juncture he failed disastrously. On December 11 and 12, 1862, Lee's army lay strongly posted on the south of the Rappahannock. Burnside, in spite, as it appears, of express warnings from Lincoln, attacked Lee at precisely the point, near the town of Fredericksburg, where his position was really impregnable. The defeat of the Northern army was bloody and overwhelming. Burnside's army became all but mutinous; his corps commanders, especially General Hooker, were loud in complaint. He was tempted to persist, in spite of all protests, in some further effort of rashness. Lincoln endeavoured to restrain him. Halleck, whom Lincoln

begged to give a definite military opinion, upholding or overriding Burnside's, had nothing more useful to offer than his own resignation. After discussions and re-criminations among all officers concerned, Burnside offered his resignation. Lincoln was by no means disposed to remove a general upon a first failure or to side with his subordinates against him, and refused to accept it. Burnside then offered the impossible alternative of the dismissal of all his corps commanders for disaffection to him, and on January 25, 1863, his resignation was accepted.

There was much discussion in the Cabinet as to the choice of his successor. It was thought unwise to give the Eastern army a commander from the West again. At Chase's instance the senior corps commander who was not too old, General Hooker, sometimes called "Fighting Joe Hooker," was appointed. He received a letter, often quoted as the letter of a man much altered from the Lincoln who had been groping a year earlier after the right way of treating McClellan: "I have placed you," wrote Lincoln, "at the head of the Army of the Potomac. Of course I have done this upon what appear to me to be sufficient reasons, and yet I think it best for you to know that there are some things in regard to which I am not quite satisfied with you. I believe you to be a brave and skilful soldier, which of course I like. I also believe that you do not mix politics with your profession, in which you are right. You have confidence in yourself, which is a valuable, if not indispensable, quality. You are ambitious, which, within reasonable bounds, does good rather than harm; but I think that during General Burnside's command of the army you have taken counsel of your ambition and thwarted him as much as you could, in which you did a great wrong to the country, and to a most meritorious and honourable brother officer. I have heard, in such a way as to believe it, of your recently saying that both the Army and the Government needed a dictator. Of course it was not for this, but in spite of it, that I gave

you the command. Only those generals who gain successes can set up dictators. What I now ask of you is military success, and I will risk the dictatorship. The Government will support you to the utmost of its ability, which is neither more nor less than it has done and will do for all commanders. I much fear that the spirit which you have aided to infuse into the army, of criticising their commander and withholding confidence from him, will now turn upon you. Neither you nor Napoleon, if he were alive again, could get any good out of an army while such a spirit prevails in it; and now beware of rashness. Beware of rashness, but with energy and sleepless vigilance go forward and give us victories."

" He talks to me like a father," exclaimed Hooker, enchanted with a rebuke such as this. He was a fine, frank, soldierly fellow, with a noble figure, with " a grand fighting head," fresh complexion and bright blue eyes. He was a good organiser; he put a stop to the constant desertions; he felt the need of improving the Northern cavalry; and he groaned at the spirit with which McClellan had infected his army, a curious collective inertness among men who individually were daring. He seems to have been highly strung; the very little wine that he drank perceptibly affected him; he gave it up altogether in his campaigns. And he cannot have been very clever, for the handsomest beating that Lee could give him left him unaware that Lee was a general. In the end of April he crossed the Rappahannock and the Rapidan, which still divided the two armies, and in the first week of May, 1863, a brief campaign, full of stirring incident, came to a close with the three days' battle of Chancellorsville, in which Hooker, hurt and dazed with pain, lost control and presence of mind, and, with heavy loss, drew back across the Rappahannock. The South had won another amazing victory; but " Stonewall " Jackson, at the age of thirty-nine, had fallen in the battle.

Abroad, this crowning disaster to the North seemed to presage the full triumph of the Confederacy; and it

was a gloomy time enough for Lincoln and his Ministers. A second and more serious invasion by Lee was impending, and the lingering progress of events in the West, of which the story must soon be resumed, caused protracted and deepening anxiety. But the tide turned soon. Moreover, Lincoln's military perplexities, which have demanded our detailed attention during these particular campaigns, were very nearly at an end. We have here to turn back to the political problem of his Presidency, for the bloody and inconclusive battle upon the Antietam, more than seven months before, had led strangely to political consequences which were great and memorable.

CHAPTER X

EMANCIPATION

WHEN the news of a second battle of Bull Run reached England it seemed at first to Lord John Russell that the failure of the North was certain, and he asked Palmerston and his colleagues to consider whether they must not soon recognise the Confederacy, and whether mediation in the interest of peace and humanity might not perhaps follow. But within two months all thoughts of recognising the Confederacy had been so completely put aside that even Fredericksburg and Chancellorsville caused no renewal of the suggestion, and an invitation from Louis Napoleon to joint action of this kind between England and France had once for all been rejected. The battle of Antietam had been fought in the meantime. This made men think that the South could no more win a speedy and decisive success than the North, and that victory must rest in the end with the side that could last. But that was not all; the battle of Antietam was followed within five days by an event which made it impossible for any Government of this country to take action unfriendly to the North.

On September 22, 1862, Abraham Lincoln set his hand to a Proclamation of which the principal words were these: "That, on the first day of January in the year of our Lord one thousand eight hundred and sixty-three, all persons held as slaves within any State, or designated part of a State, the people whereof shall then be in rebellion against the United States, shall be then, thenceforward and forever free."

The policy and the true effect of this act cannot be understood without some examination. Still less so can

the course of the man who will always be remembered as its author. First, in regard to the legal effect of the Proclamation; in normal times the President would of course not have had the power, which even the Legislature did not possess, to set free a single slave; the Proclamation was an act of war on his part, as Commander-in-Chief of the forces, by which slaves were to be taken from people at war with the United States, just as horses or carts might be taken, to subtract from their resources and add to those of the United States. In a curiously prophetic manner, ex-President John Quincy Adams had argued in Congress many years before that, if rebellion ever arose, this very thing might be done. Adams would probably have claimed that the command of the President became law in the States which took part in the rebellion. Lincoln only claimed legal force for his Proclamation in so far as it was an act of war based on sufficient necessity and plainly tending to help the Northern arms. If the legal question had ever been tried out, the Courts would no doubt have had to hold that at least those slaves who obtained actual freedom under the Proclamation became free in law; for it was certainly in good faith an act of war, and the military result justified it. A large amount of labour was withdrawn from the industry necessary to the South, and by the end of the war 180,000 coloured troops were in arms for the North, rendering services, especially in occupying conquered territory that was unhealthy for white troops, without which, in Lincoln's opinion, the war could never have been finished. The Proclamation had indeed an indirect effect more far-reaching than this; it committed the North to a course from which there could be no turning back, except by surrender; it made it a political certainty that by one means or another slavery would be ended if the North won. But in Lincoln's view of his duty as President, this ulterior consequence was not to determine his action. The fateful step by which the end of slavery was precipitated would not have taken the form it did take if it had not come to commend itself to him as a

military measure conducing to the suppression of rebellion.

On the broader grounds on which we naturally look at this measure, many people in the North had, as we have seen, been anxious from the beginning that he should adopt an active policy of freeing Southern slaves. It was intolerable to think that the war might end and leave slavery where it was. To convert the war into a crusade against slavery seemed to many the best way of arousing and uniting the North. This argument was reinforced by some of the American Ministers abroad. They were aware that people in Europe misunderstood and disliked the Constitutional propriety with which the Union government insisted that it was not attacking the domestic institutions of Southern States. English people did not know the American Constitution, and when told that the North did not threaten to abolish slavery would answer " Why not? " Many Englishmen, who might dislike the North and might have their doubts as to whether slavery was as bad as it was said to be, would none the less have respected men who would fight against it. They had no interest in the attempt of some of their own seceded Colonists to coerce, upon some metaphysical ground of law, others who in their turn wished to secede from them. Seward, with wonderful misjudgment, had instructed Ministers abroad to explain that no attack was threatened on slavery, for he was afraid that the purchasers of cotton in Europe would feel threatened in their selfish interests; the agents of the South were astute enough to take the same line and insist like him that the North was no more hostile to slavery than the South. If this misunderstanding were removed English hostility to the North would never again take a dangerous form. Lincoln, who knew less of affairs but more of men than Seward, was easily made to see this. Yet, with full knowledge of the reasons for adopting a decided policy against slavery, Lincoln waited through seventeen months of the war till the moment had come for him to strike his blow.

Some of his reasons for waiting were very plain. He was not going to take action on the alleged ground of military necessity till he was sure that the necessity existed. Nor was he going to take it till it would actually lead to the emancipation of a great number of slaves. Above all, he would not act till he felt that the North generally would sustain his action, for he knew, better than Congressmen who judged from their own friends in their own constituencies, how doubtful a large part of Northern opinion really was. We have seen how in the summer of 1861 he felt bound to disappoint the advanced opinion which supported Frémont. He continued for more than a year after in a course which alienated from himself the confidence of the men with whom he had most sympathy. He did this deliberately rather than imperil the unanimity with which the North supported the war. There was indeed grave danger of splitting the North in two if he appeared unnecessarily to change the issue from Union to Liberation. We have to remember that in all the Northern States the right of the Southern States to choose for themselves about slavery had been fully admitted, and that four of the Northern States were themselves slave States all this while.

But this is not the whole explanation of his delay. It is certain that apart from this danger he would at first rather not have played the historic part which he did play as the liberator of the slaves, if he could have succeeded in the more modest part of encouraging a process of gradual emancipation. In his Annual Message to Congress in December, 1861, he laid down the general principles of his policy in this matter. He gave warning in advance to the Democrats of the North, who were against all interference with Southern institutions, that " radical and extreme measures " might become indispensable to military success, and if indispensable would be taken; but he declared his anxiety that if possible the conflict with the South should not " degenerate into a violent and remorseless revolutionary struggle," for he looked forward with fear to a complete overturning of

the social system of the South. He feared it not only
for the white people but also for the black. "Gradual
and not sudden emancipation," he said, in a later Message, "is better for all." It is now probable that he
was right, and yet it is difficult not to sympathise with
the earnest Republicans who were impatient at his delay,
who were puzzled and pained by the free and easy way
in which in grave conversation he would allude to "the
nigger question," and who concluded that "the President is not with us; has no sound Anti-slavery sentiment."
Indeed, his sentiment did differ from theirs. Certainly, he
hated slavery, for he had contended more stubbornly
than any other man against any concession which seemed
to him to perpetuate slavery by stamping it with approval; but his hatred of it left him quite without the
passion of moral indignation against the slave owners,
in whose guilt the whole country, North and South,
seemed to him an accomplice. He would have classed
that very natural indignation under the head of "malice"
—"I shall do nothing in malice," he wrote to a citizen
of Louisiana; "what I deal with is too vast for malicious
dealing." But it was not, as we shall see before long,
too vast for an interest, as sympathetic as it was matter
of fact, in the welfare of the negroes. They were actual
human beings to him, and he knew that the mere abroga-
tion of the law of slavery was not the only thing necessary to their advancement. Looking back, with knowledge of what happened later, we cannot fail to be glad
that they were emancipated somehow, but we are forced
to regret that they could not have been emancipated by
some more considerate process. Lincoln, perhaps alone
among the Americans who were in earnest in this matter,
looked at it very much in the light in which all men look
at it to-day.

In the early part of 1862 the United States Government concluded a treaty with Great Britain for the more
effectual suppression of the African slave trade, and it
happened about the same time that the first white man
ever executed as a pirate under the American law against

the slave trade was hanged in New York. In those
months Lincoln was privately trying to bring about the
passing by the Legislature of Delaware of an Act for
emancipating, with fit provisions for their welfare, the
few slaves in that State, conditionally upon compensation
to be paid to the owners by the United States. He hoped
that if this example were set by Delaware, it would be
followed in Maryland, and would spread later. The
Delaware House were favourable to the scheme, but
the Senate of the State rejected it. Lincoln now made a
more public appeal in favour of his policy. In March,
1862, he sent a Message to Congress, which has already
been quoted, and in which he urged the two Houses to
pass Resolutions pledging the United States to give pecuniary help to any State which adopted gradual emancipation. It must be obvious that if the slave States of
the North could have been led to adopt this policy it
would have been a fitting preliminary to any action which
might be taken against slavery in the South; and the
policy might have been extended to those Southern States
which were first recovered for the Union. The point,
however, upon which Lincoln dwelt in his Message was
that, if slavery were once given up by the border States,
the South would abandon all hope that they would ever
join the Confederacy. In private letters to an editor of
a newspaper and others he pressed the consideration that
the cost of compensated abolition was small in proportion
to what might be gained by a quicker ending of the war.
During the discussion of his proposal in Congress and
again after the end of the Session he invited the Senators
and Representatives of the border States to private conference with him in which he besought of them " a calm
and enlarged consideration, ranging, if it may be, far
above, personal and partisan politics," of the opportunity of good now open to them. The hope of the Confederacy was, as he then conceived, fixed upon the sympathy which it might arouse in the border States,
two of which, Kentucky and Maryland, were in fact invaded that year with some hope of a rising among the

inhabitants. The " lever " which the Confederates hoped
to use in these States was the interest of the slave owners
there; " Break that lever before their eyes," he urged.
But the hundred and one reasons which can always be
found against action presented themselves at once to the
Representatives of the border States. Congress itself
so far accepted the President's view that both Houses
passed the Resolution which he had suggested. Indeed
it gladly did something more; a Bill, such as Lincoln himself had prepared as a Congressman fourteen years before, was passed for abolishing slavery in the District of
Columbia; compensation was paid to the owners; a sum
was set apart to help the settlement in Liberia of any of
the slaves who were willing to go; and at Lincoln's suggestion provision was added for the education of the
negro children. Nothing more was done at this time.

Throughout this matter Lincoln took counsel chiefly
with himself. He could not speak his full thought to the
public, and apparently he did not do so to any of his
Cabinet. Supposing that the border States had yielded
to his persuasion, it may still strike us as a very sanguine
calculation that their action would have had much effect
upon the resolution of the Confederates. But it must
be noted that when Lincoln first approached the Representatives of the border States, the highest expectations
were entertained of the victory that McClellan would
win in Virginia, and when he made his last, rather despair-
ing, appeal to them, the decision to withdraw the army
from the Peninsula had not yet been taken. If a really
heavy blow had been struck at the Confederates in Virginia, their chief hope of retrieving their military fortunes would certainly have lain in that invasion of Kentucky, which did shortly afterwards occur and which was
greatly encouraged by the hope of a rising of Kentucky
men who wished to join the Confederacy. This part of
Lincoln's calculations was therefore quite reasonable.
And it was further reasonable to suppose that, if the
South had then given in and Congress had acted in the
spirit of the Resolution which it had passed, the policy

of gradual emancipation, starting in the border States, would have spread steadily. The States which were disposed to hold out against the inducement that the cost of compensated emancipation, if they adopted it, would be borne by the whole Union, would have done so at a great risk; for each new free State would have been disposed before long to support a Constitutional Amendment to impose enfranchisement, possibly with no compensation, upon the States that still delayed. The force of example and the presence of this fear could not have been resisted long. Lincoln was not a man who could be accused of taking any course without a reason well thought out; we can safely conclude that in the summer of 1862 he nursed a hope, by no means visionary, of initiating a process of liberation free from certain evils in that upon which he was driven back.

Before, however, he had quite abandoned this hope he had already begun to see his way in case it failed. His last appeal to the border States was made on July 12, 1862, while McClellan's army still lay at Harrison's Landing. On the following day he privately told Seward and Bates that he had " about come to the conclusion that it was a military necessity, absolutely essential to the salvation of the nation, that we must free the slaves or be ourselves subdued." On July 22 he read to his Cabinet the first draft of his Proclamation of Emancipation; telling them before he consulted them that substantially his mind was made up. Various members of the Cabinet raised points on which he had already thought and had come to a conclusion, but, as he afterwards told a friend, Seward raised a point which had never struck him before. He said that, if issued at that time of depression, just after the failure in the Peninsula, the Proclamation would seem like " a cry of distress "; and that it would have a much better effect if it were issued after some military success.

Seward was certainly right. The danger of division in the North would have been increased and the prospect of a good effect abroad would have been diminished if

the Proclamation had been issued at a time of depression and manifest failure. Lincoln, who had been set on issuing it, instantly felt the force of this objection. He put aside his draft, and resolved not to issue the Proclamation till the right moment, and apparently resolved to keep the whole question open in his own mind till the time for action came.

Accordingly the two months which followed were not only full of anxiety about the war; they were full for him of a suspense painfully maintained. It troubled him perhaps comparatively little that he was driven into a position of greater aloofness from the support and sympathy of any party or school. He must now expect an opposition from the Democrats of the North, for they had declared themselves strongly against the Resolution which he had induced Congress to pass. And the strong Republicans for their part had acquiesced in it coldly, some of them contemptuously. In May of this year he had been forced for a second time publicly to repress a keen Republican general who tried to take this question of great policy into his own hands. General Hunter, commanding a small expedition which had seized Port Royal in South Carolina and some adjacent islands rich in cotton, had in a grand manner assumed to declare free all the slaves in South Carolina, Georgia and Florida. This, of course, could not be let pass. Congress, too, had been occupied in the summer with a new measure for confiscating rebel property; some Republicans in the West set great store on such confiscation; other Republicans saw in it the incidental advantage that more slaves might be liberated under it. It was learnt that the President might put his veto upon it. It seemed to purport, contrary to the Constitution, to attaint the property of rebels after their death, and Lincoln was unwilling that the Constitution should be stretched in the direction of revengeful harshness. The objectionable feature in the Bill was removed, and Lincoln accepted it. But the suspicion with which many Republicans were beginning to regard him was now reinforced by a certain jealousy of

Congressmen against the Executive power; they grumbled and sneered about having to " ascertain the Royal pleasure " before they could legislate. This was an able, energetic, and truly patriotic Congress, and must not be despised for its reluctance to be guided by Lincoln. But it was reluctant.

Throughout August and September he had to deal in the country with dread on the one side of any revolutionary action, and belief on the other side that he was timid and half-hearted. The precise state of his intentions could not with advantage be made public. To upholders of slavery he wrote plainly, " It may as well be understood once for all that I shall not surrender this game leaving any available card unplayed "; to its most zealous opponents he had to speak in an entirely different strain. While the second battle of Bull Run was impending, Horace Greeley published in the *New York Tribune* an " open letter " of angry complaint about Lincoln's supposed bias for slavery. Lincoln at once published a reply to his letter. " If there be in it," he said, "any statements or assumptions of fact which I may know to be erroneous, I do not now and here controvert them. If there be perceptible in it an impatient and dictatorial tone, I waive it in deference to an old friend whose heart I have always supposed to be right. My paramount object in this struggle is to save the Union. If I could save the Union without freeing any slaves I would do it; and if I could save it by freeing all the slaves I would do it; and if I could save it by freeing some and leaving others alone, I would also do that. I shall do less whenever I shall believe what I am doing hurts the cause, and I shall do more whenever I shall believe doing more will help the cause. I shall adopt new views so fast as they shall appear to be true views."

It was probably easy to him now to write these masterful generalities, but a week or two later, after Pope's defeat, he had to engage in a controversy which tried his feelings much more sorely. It had really grieved

him that clergymen in Illinois had opposed him as unorthodox, when he was fighting against the extension of
slavery. Now, a week or two after his correspondence
with Greeley, a deputation from a number of Churches in
Chicago waited upon him, and some of their members
spoke to him with assumed authority from on high, commanding him in God's name to emancipate the slaves.
He said, "I am approached with the most opposite
opinions and advice, and that by religious men who are
equally certain that they represent the divine will. I am
sure that either the one or the other class is mistaken
in that belief, and perhaps in some respects both. I hope
it will not be irreverent for me to say that, if it is probable that God would reveal His will to others, on a point
so connected with my duty, it might be supposed He
would reveal it directly to me. What good would a
proclamation of emancipation from me do especially as
we are now situated? I do not want to issue a document
that the whole world will see must necessarily be inoperative like the Pope's Bull against the comet. Do not
misunderstand me, because I have mentioned these ob-
jections. They indicate the difficulties that have thus far
prevented my acting in some such way as you desire. I
have not decided against a proclamation of liberty to the
slaves, but hold the matter under advisement. And I
can assure you that the subject is on my mind, by day and
night, more than any other. Whatever shall appear to be
God's will, I will do." The language of this speech,
especially when the touch is humorous, seems that of a
strained and slightly irritated man, but the solemnity
blended in it showed Lincoln's true mind.

In this month, September, 1862, he composed for his
own reading alone a sad and inconclusive fragment of
meditation which was found after his death. "The will
of God prevails," he wrote. "In great contests each
party claims to act in accordance with the will of God.
Both may be and one must be wrong. God cannot be
for and against the same thing at the same time. In the
present civil war it is quite possible that God's purpose

is something different from the purpose of either party,
and yet the human instrumentalities, working just as they
do, are of the best adaptation to effect His purpose. I
am almost ready to say that this is probably true, that
God wills this contest, and wills that it shall not end yet.
By His mere great power on the minds of the contestants,
He could have either saved or destroyed the Union
without a human contest. Yet the contest began, and,
having begun, He could give the final victory to either
side any day. Yet the contest proceeds." For Lincoln's
own part it seemed his plain duty to do what in the circumstances he thought safest for the Union, and yet he
was almost of a mind with the deputation which had
preached to him, that he must be doing God's will in
taking a great step towards emancipation. The solution,
that the great step must be taken at the first opportune
moment, was doubtless clear enough in principle, but it
must always remain arguable whether any particular
moment was opportune. He told soon afterwards how
his mind was finally made up.

On the day that he received the news of the battle of
Antietam, the draft Proclamation was taken from its
drawer and studied afresh; his visit to McClellan on the
battlefield intervened; but on the fifth day after the
battle the Cabinet was suddenly called together. When
the Ministers had assembled Lincoln first entertained
them by reading the short chapter of Artemus Ward
entitled " High-handed Outrage at Utica." It is less
amusing than most of Artemus Ward; but it had just
appeared; it pleased all the Ministers except Stanton,
to whom the frivolous reading he sometimes had to hear
from Lincoln was a standing vexation; and it was precisely that sort of relief to which Lincoln's mind when
overwrought could always turn. Having thus composed
himself for business, he reminded his Cabinet that he
had, as they were aware, thought a great deal about the
relation of the war to slavery, and had a few weeks before read them a draft Proclamation on this subject.
Ever since then, he said, his mind had been occupied

on the matter, and, though he wished it were a better
time, he thought the time had come now. "When the
rebel army was at Frederick," he is related to have continued, "I determined, as soon as it should be driven
out of Maryland, to issue a Proclamation of Emancipation such as I thought likely to be most useful. I said
nothing to any one, but I made the promise to myself
and "—here he hesitated a little—" to my Maker. The
rebel army is now driven out, and I am going to fulfil
that promise. I have got you together to hear what I
have written down. I do not wish your advice about the
main matter, for that I have determined for myself.
This I say without intending anything but respect for any
one of you." He then invited their suggestions upon the
expressions used in his draft and other minor matters,
and concluded: "One other observation I will make.
I know very well that many others might in this matter,
as in others, do better than I can; and if I was satisfied
that the public confidence was more fully possessed by
any one of them than by me, and knew of any constitutional way in which he could be put in my place, he
should have it. I would gladly yield it to him. But
though I believe I have not so much of the confidence
of the people as I had some time since, I do not know
that, all things considered, any other person has more;
and, however this may be, there is no way in which I
can have any other man put where I am. I am here;
I must do the best I can, and bear the responsibility of
taking the course which I feel I ought to take." Then
he read his draft, and in the long discussion which followed, and owing to which a few slight changes were
made in it, he told them further, without any false reserve, just how he came to his decision. In his great
perplexity he had gone on his knees, before the battle of
Antietam, and, like a child, he had promised that if a
victory was given which drove the enemy out of Maryland he would consider it as an indication that it was his
duty to move forward. "It might be thought strange,"
he said, "that he had in this way submitted the disposal

of matters, when the way was not clear to his mind what he should do. God had decided this question in favour of the slaves."

Such is the story of what we may now remember as one of the signal events in the chequered progress of Christianity. We have to follow its consequences a little further. These were not at first all that its author would have hoped. " Commendation in newspapers and by distinguished individuals is," he said in a private letter, " all that a vain man could wish," but recruits for the Army did not seem to come in faster. In October and November there were elections for Congress, and in a number of States the Democrats gained considerably, though it was noteworthy that the Republicans held their ground not only in New England and in the furthest Western States, but also in the border slave States. The Democrats, who from this time on became very formidable to Lincoln, had other matters of complaint, as will be seen later, but they chiefly denounced the President for trying to turn the war into one against slavery. " The Constitution as it is and the Union as it was" had been their election cry. The good hearing that they got, now as at a later time, was due to the fact that people were depressed about the war; and it is plain enough that Lincoln had been well advised in delaying his action till after a military success. As it was, there was much that seemed to show that public confidence in him was not strong, but public confidence in any man is hard to estimate, and the forces that in the end move opinion most are not quickly apparent. There are little indications that his power and character were slowly establishing their hold; it seems, for instance, to have been about this time that " old Abe " or " Uncle Abe " began to be widely known among common people by the significant name of " Father Abraham," and his secretaries say that he was becoming conscious that his official utterances had a deeper effect on public opinion than any immediate response to them in Congress showed.

In his Annual Message of December, 1862, Lincoln

put before Congress, probably with little hope of result, a comprehensive policy for dealing with slavery justly and finally. He proposed that a Constitutional Amendment should be submitted to the people providing: first, that compensation should be given in United States bonds to any State, whether now in rebellion or not, which should abolish slavery before the year 1900; secondly, that the slaves who had once enjoyed actual freedom through the chances of the war should be permanently free and that their owners should be compensated; thirdly, that Congress should have authority to spend money on colonisation for negroes. Even if the greater part of these objects could have been accomplished without a Constitutional Amendment, it is evident that such a procedure would have been more satisfactory in the eventual resettlement of the Union. He urged in his Message how desirable it was, as a part of the effort to restore the Union, that the whole North should be agreed in a concerted policy as to slavery, and that parties should for this purpose reconsider their positions. " The dogmas of the quiet past," he said, " are inadequate to the stormy present. The occasion is piled high with difficulty, and we must rise with the occasion. As our case is new, so we must think anew and act anew. We must disenthrall ourselves, and then we shall save our country. Fellow citizens, we cannot escape history. We of this Congress and this Administration will be remembered in spite of ourselves. No personal significance or insignificance can spare one or another of us. We say we are for the Union. The world will not forget that we say this. We know how to save the Union. The world knows we do know how to save it. In giving freedom to the slave we assure freedom to the free. We shall nobly save or meanly lose the last, best hope of earth. Other means may succeed, this could not fail." The last four words expressed too confident a hope as to what Northern policy apart from Northern arms could do towards ending the war, but it was impossible to exaggerate the value which a policy, concerted between parties in a spirit of

moderation, would have had in the settlement after victory. Every honest Democrat who then refused any
action against slavery must have regretted it before three
years were out, and many sensible Republicans who saw
no use in such moderation may have lived to regret their
part too. Nothing was done. It is thought that Lincoln
expected this; but the Proclamation of Emancipation
would begin to operate within a month; it would produce
by the end of the war a situation in which the country
would be compelled to decide on the principle of slavery,
and Lincoln had at least done his part in preparing men
to face the issue.

Before this, the nervous and irritable feeling of many
Northern politicians, who found in emancipation a good
subject for quarrel among themselves and in the slow
progress of the war a good subject of quarrel with the
Administration, led to a crisis in Lincoln's Cabinet. Radicals were inclined to think Seward's influence in the
Administration the cause of all public evils; some of
them had now got hold of a foolish private letter, which
he had written to Adams in England a few months before, denouncing the advocates of emancipation. Desiring his downfall, they induced a small " caucus " of Republican Senators to speak in the name of the party and
the nation and send the President a resolution demanding such changes in his Cabinet as would produce better
results in the war. Discontented men of opposite opinions could unite in demanding success in the war; and
Conservative Senators joined in this resolution hoping
that it would get rid not only of Seward, but also of
Chase and Stanton, the objects of their particular antipathy. Seward, on hearing of this, gave Lincoln his resignation, which was kept private. Though egotistic, he
was a clever man, and evidently a pleasant man to work
with; he was a useful Minister under a wise chief, though
he later proved a harmful one under a foolish chief.
Stanton was most loyal, and invaluable as head of the
War Department. Chase, as Lincoln said in private
afterwards, was " a pretty good fellow and a very able

man "; Lincoln had complete confidence in him as a
Finance Minister, and could not easily have replaced
him. But this handsome, dignified, and righteous person
was unhappily a sneak. Lincoln found as time went on
that, if he ever had to do what was disagreeable to some
important man, Chase would pay court to that important
man and hint how differently he himself would have done
as President. On this occasion he was evidently aware
that Chase had encouraged the Senators who attacked
Seward. Much as he wished to retain each of the two
for his own worth, he was above all determined that one
should not gain a victory over the other. Accordingly,
when a deputation of nine important Senators came to
Lincoln to present their grievances against Seward, they
found themselves, to their great annoyance, confronted
with all the Cabinet except Seward, who had resigned,
and they were invited by Lincoln to discuss the matter
in his presence with these Ministers. Chase, to his still
greater annoyance, found himself, as the principal Minister there, compelled for decency's sake to defend
Seward from the very attack which he had helped to
instigate. The deputation withdrew, not sure that, after
all, it wanted Seward removed. Chase next day tendered,
as was natural, his resignation. Lincoln was able, now
that he had the resignations of both men, to persuade
both of their joint duty to continue in the public service.
By this remarkable piece of riding he saved the Union
from a great danger. The Democratic opposition, not
actually to the prosecution of the war, but to any and
every measure essential for it, was now developing, and
a serious division, such as at this stage any important
resignation would have produced in the ranks of the
Republicans, or, as they now called themselves, the
" Union men," would have been perilous.

On the first day of January, 1863, the President signed
the further Proclamation needed to give effect to emancipation. The small portions of the South which were
not in rebellion were duly excepted; the naval and military authorities were ordered to maintain the freedom

of the slaves seeking their protection; the slaves were enjoined to abstain from violence and to " labour faithfully for reasonable wages " if opportunity were given them; all suitable slaves were to be taken into armed service, especially for garrison duties. Before the end of 1863, a hundred thousand coloured men were already serving, as combatants or as labourers, on military work in about equal number. They were needed, for volunteering was getting slack, and the work of guarding and repairing railway lines was specially repellent to Northern volunteers. The coloured regiments fought well; they behaved well in every way. Atrocious threats of vengeance on them and their white officers were officially uttered by Jefferson Davis, but, except for one hideous massacre wrought in the hottest of hot blood, only a few crimes by individuals were committed in execution of these threats. To Lincoln himself it was a stirring thought that when democratic government was finally vindicated and restored by the victory of the Union, " then there will be some black men who can remember that with silent tongue and clenched teeth and steady eye and well-poised bayonet they have helped mankind on to this great consummation." There was, however, prejudice at first among many Northern officers against negro enlistment. The greatest of the few great American artists, St. Gaudens, commemorated in sculpture (as the donor of the new playing fields at Harvard commemorated by his gift) the action of a brilliant and popular Massachusetts officer, Robert Gould Shaw, who set the example of leaving his own beloved regiment to take command of a coloured regiment, at the head of which he died, gallantly leading them and gallantly followed by them in a desperate fight.

It was easier to raise and train these negro soldiers than to arrange for the control, shelter, and employment of the other refugees who crowded especially to the protection of Grant's army in the West. The efforts made for their benefit cannot be related here, but the recollections of Army Chaplain John Eaton, whom Grant

selected to take charge of them in the West, throw a little more light on Lincoln and on the spirit of his dealing with " the nigger question." When Eaton after some time had to come to Washington, upon the business of his charge and to visit the President, he received that impression, of versatile power and of easy mastery over many details as well as over broad issues, which many who worked under Lincoln have described, but he was above all struck with the fact that from a very slight experience in early life Lincoln had gained a knowledge of negro character such as very few indeed in the North possessed. He was subjected to many seemingly trivial questions, of which he was quick enough to see the grave purpose, about all sorts of persons and things in the West, but he was also examined closely, in a way which commanded his fullest respect as an expert, about the ideas, understanding, and expectations of the ordinary negroes under his care, and more particularly as to the past history and the attainments of the few negroes who had become prominent men, and who therefore best illustrated the real capacities of their race. Later visits to the capital and to Lincoln deepened this impression, and convinced Eaton, though by trifling signs, of the rare quality of Lincoln's sympathy. Once, after Eaton's difficult business had been disposed of, the President turned to relating his own recent worries about a colony of negroes which he was trying to establish on a small island off Hayti. There flourishes in Southern latitudes a minute creature called *Dermatophilus penetrans,* or the jigger, which can inflict great pain on barefooted people by housing itself under their toe-nails. This Colony had a plague of jiggers, and every expedient for defeating them had failed. Lincoln was not merely giving the practical attention to this difficulty that might perhaps be expected; the Chaplain was amazed to find that at that moment, at the turning point of the war, a few days only after Vicksburg and Gettysburg, with his enormous pre-occupations, the President's mind had room for real and keen distress about the toes of the blacks in the Cow

Island. At the end of yet another interview Eaton was
startled by the question, put by the President with an air
of shyness, whether Frederick Douglass, a well-known
negro preacher, could be induced to visit him. Of course
he could. Frederick Douglass was then reputed to be
the ablest man ever born as a negro slave; he must have
met many of the best and kindest Northern friends of
the negro; and he went to Lincoln distressed at some
points in his policy, particularly at his failure to make
reprisals for murders of negro prisoners by Southern
troops. When he came away he was in a state little
short of ecstasy. It was not because he now understood,
as he did, Lincoln's policy. Lincoln had indeed won his
warm approval when he told him " with a quiver in his
voice " of his horror of killing men in cold blood for
what had been done by others, and his dread of what
might follow such a policy; but he had a deeper gratifi-
cation, the strangeness of which it is sad to realise. " He
treated me as a man," exclaimed Douglass. " He did
not let me feel for a moment that there was any difference in the colour of our skins."

Perhaps the hardest effort of speech that Lincoln ever
essayed was an address to negroes which had to do with
this very subject of colour. His audience were men who
had been free from birth or for some time and were
believed to be leaders among their community. It was
Lincoln's object to induce some of them to be pioneers
in an attempt at colonisation in some suitable climate, an
attempt which he felt must fail if it started with negroes
whose " intellects were clouded by slavery." He clung
to these projects of colonisation, as probably the best
among the various means by which the improvement of
the negro must be attempted, because their race, " suffering the greatest wrong ever inflicted on any people,"
would " yet be far removed from being on an equality
with the white race " when they ceased to be slaves; a
" physical difference broader than exists between almost
any other two races " and constituting " a greater disadvantage to us both," would always set a " ban " upon

the negroes even where they were best treated in America. This unpalatable fact he put before them with that total absence of pretence which was probably the only possible form of tact in such a discussion, with no affectation of a hope that progress would remove it or of a desire that the ordinary white man should lose the instinct that kept him apart from the black. But this only makes more apparent his simple recognition of an equality and fellowship which did exist between him and his hearers in a larger matter than that of social intercourse or political combination. His appeal to their capacity for taking large and unselfish views was as direct and as confident as in his addresses to his own people; it was made in the language of a man to whom the public spirit which might exist among black people was of the same quality as that which existed among white, in whose belief he and his hearers could equally find happiness in " being worthy of themselves " and in realising the " claim of kindred to the great God who made them."

It may be well here, without waiting to trace further the course of the war, in which at the point where we left it the slow but irresistible progress of conquest was about to set in, to recount briefly the later stages of the abolition of slavery in America. In 1863 it became apparent that popular feeling in Missouri and in Maryland was getting ripe for abolition. Bills were introduced into Congress to compensate their States if they did away with slavery; the compensation was to be larger if the abolition was immediate and not gradual. There was a majority in each House for these Bills, but the Democratic minority was able to kill them in the House of Representatives by the methods of " filibustering," or, as we call it, obstruction, to which the procedure of that body seems well adapted. The Republican majority had not been very zealous for the Bills; its members asked " why compensate for a wrong " which they had begun to feel would soon be abolished without compensation; but their leaders at least did their best for the Bills. It would have been idle after the failure of these pro-

posals to introduce the Bills that had been contemplated
for buying out the loyal slave owners in West Virginia,
Kentucky, and Tennessee, which was now fast being regained for the Union. Lincoln after his Message of
December, 1862, recognised it as useless for him to press
again the principles of gradual emancipation or of compensation, as to which it is worth remembrance that the
compensation which he proposed was for loyal and disloyal owners alike. His Administration, however, bought
every suitable slave in Delaware for service (service as
a free man) in the Army. In the course of 1864 a remarkable development of public opinion began to be
manifest in the States chiefly concerned. In the autumn
of that year Maryland, whose representatives had paid
so little attention to Lincoln two years before, passed an
Amendment to the State Constitution abolishing slavery
without compensation. A movement in the same direction was felt to be making progress in Kentucky and
Tennessee; and Missouri followed Maryland's example
in January, 1865. Meanwhile, Louisiana had been reconquered, and the Unionists in these States, constantly
encouraged and protected by Lincoln when Congress
looked upon them somewhat coldly or his generals showed
jealousy of their action, had banded themselves together
to form State Governments with Constitutions that forbade slavery. Lincoln, it may be noted, had suggested
to Louisiana that it would be well to frame some plan
by which the best educated of the negroes should be admitted to the franchise. Four years after his death a
Constitutional Amendment was passed by which any distinction as to franchise on the ground of race or colour
is forbidden in America. The policy of giving the vote
to negroes indiscriminately had commended itself to the
cold pedantry of some persons, including Chase, on the
ground of some natural right of all men to the suffrage;
but it was adopted as the most effective protection for
the negroes against laws, as to vagrancy and the like, by
which it was feared they might practically be enslaved
again. Whatever the excuse for it, it would seem to have

proved in fact a great obstacle to healthy relations between the two races. The true policy in such a matter
is doubtless that which Rhodes and other statesmen
adopted in the Cape Colony and which Lincoln had advocated in the case of Louisiana. It would be absurd
to imagine that the spirit which could champion the rights
of the negro and yet face fairly the abiding difficulty of
his case died in America with Lincoln, but it lost for many
a year to come its only great exponent.

But the question of overwhelming importance, between the principles of slavery and of freedom, was ready
for final decision when local opinion in six slave States
was already moving as we have seen. The Republican
Convention of 1864, which again chose Lincoln as its
candidate for the Presidency, declared itself in favour of
a Constitutional Amendment to abolish slavery once for
all throughout America. Whether the first suggestion
came from him or not, it is known that Lincoln's private
influence was energetically used to procure this resolution of the Convention. In his Message to Congress in
1864 he urged the initiation of this Amendment. Observation of elections made it all but certain that the
next Congress would be ready to take this action, but
Lincoln pleaded with the present doubtful Congress for
the advantage which would be gained by ready, and if
possible, unanimous concurrence in the North in the
course which would soon prevail. The necessary Resolution was passed in the Senate, but in the House of Representatives till within a few hours of the vote it was said
to be " the toss of a copper " whether the majority of
two-thirds, required for such a purpose, would be obtained. In the efforts made on either side to win over
the few doubtful voters Lincoln had taken his part. Right
or wrong, he was not the man to see a great and beneficent Act in danger of postponement without being
tempted to secure it if he could do so by terrifying some
unprincipled and white-livered opponents. With the
knowledge that he was always acquiring of the persons
in politics, he had been able to pick out two Democratic

Congressmen who were fit for his purpose—presumably they lay under suspicion of one of those treasonable practices which martial law under Lincoln treated very unceremoniously. He sent for them. He told them that the gaining of a certain number of doubtful votes would secure the Resolution. He told them that he was President of the United States. He told them that the President of the United States in war time exercised great and dreadful powers. And he told them that he looked to them personally to get him those votes. Whether this wrong manœuvre affected the result or not, on January 31, 1865, the Resolution was passed in the House by a two-thirds majority with a few votes to spare, and the great crowd in the galleries, defying all precedent, broke out in a demonstration of enthusiasm which some still recall as the most memorable scene in their lives. On December 18 of that year, when Lincoln had been eight months dead, William Seward, as Secretary of State, was able to certify that the requisite majority of States had passed the Thirteenth Amendment to the Constitution, and the cause of that " irrepressible conflict " which he had foretold, and in which he had played a weak but valuable part, was for ever extinguished.

At the present day, alike in the British Empire and in America, the unending difficulty of wholesome human relations between races of different and unequal development exercises many minds; but this difficulty cannot obscure the great service done by those who, first in England and later and more hardly in America, stamped out that cardinal principle of error that any race is without its human claim. Among these men William Lloyd Garrison lived to see the fruit of his labours, and to know and have friendly intercourse with Lincoln. There have been some comparable instances in which men with such different characters and methods have unconsciously conspired for a common end, as these two did when Garrison was projecting the " Liberator " and Lincoln began shaping himself for honourable public work in the vague. The part that Lincoln played in these events did not

seem to him a personal achievement of his own. He appeared to himself rather as an instrument. " I claim not," he once said in this connection, " to have controlled events, but confess plainly that events have controlled me." In 1864, when a petition was sent to him from some children that there should be no more child slaves, he wrote, " Please tell these little people that I am very glad their young hearts are so full of just and generous sympathy, and that, while I have not the power to grant all they ask, I trust they will remember that God has, and that, as it seems, He wills to do it." Yet, at least, he redeemed the boyish pledge that has been, fancifully perhaps, ascribed to him; each opportunity that to his judgment ever presented itself of striking some blow for human freedom was taken; the blows were timed and directed by the full force of his sagacity, and they were never restrained by private ambition or fear. It is probable that upon that cool review, which in the case of this singular figure is difficult, the sense of his potent accomplishment would not diminish, but increase.

CHAPTER XI

THE APPROACH OF VICTORY

1. *The War to the End of 1863.*

THE events of the Eastern theatre of war have been followed into the early summer of 1863, when Lee was for the second time about to invade the North. The Western theatre of war has been left unnoticed since the end of May, 1862. From that time to the end of the year no definite progress was made here by either side, but here also the perplexities of the military administration were considerable; and in Lincoln's life it must be noted that in these months the strain of anxiety about the Eastern army and about the policy of emancipation was accompanied by acute doubt in regard to the conduct of war in the West.

When Halleck had been summoned from the West, Lincoln had again a general by his side in Washington to exercise command under him of all the armies. Halleck was a man of some intellectual distinction who might be expected to take a broad view of the war as a whole; this and his freedom from petty feelings, as to which Lincoln's known opinion of him can be corroborated, doubtless made him useful as an adviser; nor for a considerable time was there any man with apparently better qualifications for his position. But Lincoln soon found, as has been seen, that Halleck lacked energy of will, and cannot have been long in discovering that his judgment was not very good. The President had thus to make the best use he could of expert advice upon which he would not have been justified in relying very fully.

When Halleck arrived at Corinth at the end of May, 1862, the whole of Western and Middle Tennessee was for the time clear of the enemy, and he turned his atten-

tion at once to the long delayed project of rescuing the
Unionists in Eastern Tennessee, which was occupied by
a Confederate army under General Kirby Smith. His
object was to seize Chattanooga, which lay about 150
miles to the east of him, and invade Eastern Tennessee
by way of the valley of the Tennessee River, which cuts
through the mountains behind Chattanooga. With this
in view he would doubtless have been wise if he had first
continued his advance with his whole force against the
Confederate army under Beauregard, which after evacu-
ating Corinth had fallen back to rest and recruit in a far
healthier situation 50 miles further south. Beauregard
would have been obliged either to fight him with inferior numbers or to shut himself up in the fortress of
Vicksburg. As it was, Halleck spent the month of June
merely in repairing the railway line which runs from
Corinth in the direction of Chattanooga. When he was
called to Washington he left Grant, who for several
months past had been kept idle as his second in command, in independent command of a force which was to
remain near the Mississippi confronting Beauregard, but
he restricted him to a merely defensive part by ordering
him to keep a part of his army ready to send to Buell
whenever that general needed it, as he soon did. Buell,
who again took over his former independent command,
was ordered by Halleck to advance on Chattanooga,
using Corinth as his base of supply. Buell had wished
that the base for the advance upon Chattanooga should
be transferred to Nashville, in the centre of Tennessee,
in which case the line of railway communication would
have been shorter and also less exposed to raids by the
Southern cavalry. After Halleck had gone, Buell obtained permission to effect this change of base. The
whole month of June had been wasted in repairing the
railway with a view to Halleck's faulty plan. When
Buell himself was allowed to proceed on his own lines and
was approaching Chattanooga, his communications with
Nashville were twice, in the middle of July and in the
middle of August, cut by Confederate cavalry raids, which

did such serious damage as to impose great delay upon him. In the end of August and beginning of September Kirby Smith, whose army had been strengthened by troops transferred from Beauregard, crossed the mountains from East Tennessee by passes some distance northeast of Chattanooga, and invaded Kentucky, sending detachments to threaten Louisville on the Indiana border of Kentucky and Cincinnati in Ohio. It was necessary for Buell to retreat, when, after a week or more of uncertainty, it became clear that Kirby Smith's main force was committed to this invasion. Meanwhile General Bragg, who, owing to the illness of Beauregard, had succeeded to his command, left part of his force to hold Grant in check, marched with the remainder to support Kirby Smith, and succeeded in placing himself between Buell's army and Louisville, to protect which from Kirby Smith had become Buell's first object. It seems that Bragg, who could easily have been reinforced by Kirby Smith, had now an opportunity of fighting Buell with great advantage. But the Confederate generals, who mistakenly believed that Kentucky was at heart with them, saw an imaginary political gain in occupying Frankfort, the State capital, and formally setting up a new State Government there. Bragg therefore marched on to join Kirby Smith at Frankfort, which was well to the east of Buell's line of retreat, and Buell was able to reach Louisville unopposed by September 25.

These events were watched in the North with all the more anxiety because the Confederate invasion of Kentucky began just about the time of the second battle of Bull Run, and Buell arrived at Louisville within a week after the battle of Antietam while people were wondering how that victory would be followed up. Men of intelligence and influence, especially in the Western States, were loud in their complaints of Buell's want of vigour. It is remarkable that the Unionists of Kentucky, who suffered the most through his supposed faults, expressed their confidence in him; but his own soldiers did not like him, for he was a strict disciplinarian without either tact or any

quality which much impressed them. Their reports to
their homes in Ohio, Indiana, and Illinois, from which
they mostly came, increased the feeling against him which
was arising in those States, and his relations with the
Governors of Ohio and Indiana, who were busy in sending him recruits and whose States were threatened with
invasion, seem, wherever the fault may have lain, to
have been unfortunate. Buell's most powerful friend had
been McClellan, and by an irrational but unavoidable
process of thought the real dilatoriness of McClellan became an argument for blaming Buell as well. Halleck
defended him loyally, but this by now probably seemed
to Lincoln the apology of one irresolute man for another.
Stanton, whose efficiency in the business of the War Department gave him great weight, had become eager for
the removal of Buell. Lincoln expected that as soon as
Buell could cover Louisville he would take the offensive
promptly. His army appears to have exceeded in numbers, though not very much, the combined forces of Bragg
and Kirby Smith, and except as to cavalry it was probably as good in quality. If energetically used by Halleck
some months before, the Western armies should have
been strong enough to accomplish great results; and if
the attempt had been made at first to raise much larger
armies, it seems likely that the difficulties of training and
organisation and command would have increased out of
proportion to any gain. Buell remained some days at
Louisville itself, receiving reinforcements which were
considerable, but consisted mainly of raw recruits. While
he was there orders arrived from Lincoln removing him
and appointing his second in command, the Virginian
Thomas, in his place. This was a wise choice; Thomas
was one of the four Northern generals who won abiding
distinction in the Civil War. But Thomas felt the injustice which was done to Buell, and he refused the command in a letter magnanimously defending him. The
fact was that Lincoln had rescinded his orders before
they were received, for he had issued them under the
belief that Buell was remaining on the defensive, but

learnt immediately that an offensive movement was in progress, and had no intention of changing commanders under those circumstances.

On October 8 a battle, which began in an accidental minor conflict, took place between Buell with 58,000 men and Bragg with considerably less than half that number of tried veterans. Buell made little use of his superior numbers, for which the fault may have lain with the corps commander who first became engaged and who did not report at once to him; the part of Buell's army which bore the brunt of the fighting suffered heavy losses, which made a painful impression in the North, and the public outcry against him, which had begun as soon as Kentucky was invaded by the Confederates, now increased. After the battle Bragg fell back and effected a junction with Kirby Smith. Their joint forces were not very far inferior to Buell's in numbers, but after a few more days Bragg determined to evacuate Kentucky, in which his hope of raising many recruits had been disappointed. Buell, on perceiving his intention, pursued him some distance, but, finding the roads bad for the movement of large bodies of troops, finally took up a position at Bowling Green, on the railway to the north of Nashville, intending later in the autumn to move a little south of Nashville and there to wait for the spring before again moving on Chattanooga. He was urged from Washington to press forward towards Chattanooga at once, but replied decidedly that he was unable to do so, and added that if a change of command was desired the present was a suitable time for it. At the end of October he was removed from command. In the meantime the Confederate forces that had been left to oppose Grant had attacked him and been signally defeated in two engagements, in each of which General Rosecrans, who was serving under Grant, was in immediate command on the Northern side. Rosecrans, who therefore began to be looked upon as a promising general, and indeed was one of those who, in the chatter of the time, were occasionally spoken of as suitable for a " military dictatorship,"

was now put in Buell's place, which Thomas had once refused. He advanced to Nashville, but was as firm as Buell in refusing to go further till he had accumulated rations enough to make him for a time independent of the railway. Ultimately he moved on Murfreesborough, some thirty miles further in the direction of Chattanooga. Here on December 31, 1862, Bragg, with somewhat inferior numbers, attacked him and gained an initial success, which Rosecrans and his subordinates, Thomas and Sheridan, were able to prevent him from making good. Bragg's losses were heavy, and, after waiting a few days in the hope that Rosecrans might retreat first, he fell back to a point near the Cumberland mountains a little in advance of Chattanooga. Thus the battle of Murfreesborough counted as a victory to the North, a slight set-off to the disaster at Fredericksburg a little while before. But it had no very striking consequences. For over six months Rosecrans proceeded no further. The Northern armies remained in more secure possession of all Tennessee west of the mountains than they had obtained in the first half of 1862; but the length of their communications and the great superiority of the South in cavalry, which could threaten those communications, suspended their further advance. Lincoln urged that their army could subsist on the country which it invaded, but Buell and Rosecrans treated the idea as impracticable; in fact, till a little later all Northern generals so regarded it.

Thus Chattanooga, which it was hoped would be occupied soon after Halleck had occupied Corinth, remained in Southern hands for more than a year after that, notwithstanding the removal of Buell, to whom this disappointment and the mortifying invasion of Kentucky were at first attributed. This was rightly felt to be unsatisfactory, but the chief blame that can now be imputed falls upon the mistakes of Halleck while he was still commanding in the West. There is no reason to suppose that Buell had any exceptional amount of intuition or of energy and it was right to demand that a general with both these qualities should be appointed if he could be found.

But he was at least a prudent officer, of fair capacity, doing his best. The criticisms upon him, of which the well informed were lavish, were uttered without appreciation of practical difficulties or of the standard by which he was really to be judged. So, with far more justice than McClellan, he has been numbered among the misused generals. Lincoln, there is no doubt, had watched his proceedings, as he watched those of Rosecrans after him, with a feeling of impatience, and set him down as unenterprising and obstinate. In one point his Administration was much to blame in its treatment of the Western commanders. It became common political talk that the way to get victories was to treat unsuccessful generals almost as harshly as the French in the Revolution were understood to have treated them. Lincoln did not go thus far, but it was probably with his authority that before Buell was removed Halleck, with reluctance on his own part, wrote a letter referring to this prevalent idea and calculated to put about among the Western commanders an expectation that whichever of them first did something notable would be put over his less successful colleagues. Later on, and, as we can hardly doubt, with Lincoln's consent, Grant and Rosecrans were each informed that the first of them to win a victory would get the vacant major-generalship in the United States Army in place of his present volunteer rank. This was not the way to handle men with proper professional pride, and it is one of those cases, which are strangely few, where Lincoln made the sort of mistake that might have been expected from his want of training and not from his native generosity. But in the main his treatment of this difficult question was sound. Sharing as he did the prevailing impatience with Buell, he had no intention of yielding to it till there was a real prospect that a change of generals would be a change for the better. When the appointment of Thomas was proposed there really was such a prospect. When Rosecrans was eventually put in Buell's place the result was disappointing to Lincoln, but it was evidently not a bad appointment, and a situation

had then arisen in which it would have been folly to retain Buell if any capable successor to him could be found; for the Governors of Indiana, Ohio and Illinois, of whom the first named was reputed the ablest of the " war Governors " in the West, and on whom his army depended for recruits, now combined in representations against him which could not be ignored. Lincoln, who could not have personal acquaintance with the generals of the Western armies as he had with those in the East, was, it should be observed, throughout unceasing in his efforts to get the fullest and clearest impression of them that he could; he was always, as it has been put, " taking measurements " of men, and a good deal of what seemed idle and gossipy talk with chance visitors, who could tell him little incidents or give him new impressions, seems to have had this serious purpose. For the first half of the war the choice of men for high commands was the most harassing of all the difficulties of his administration. There is no doubt of his constant watchfulness to discern and promote merit. He was certainly beset by the feeling that generals were apt to be wanting in the vigour and boldness which the conduct of the war demanded, but, though this in some cases probably misled him, upon the whole there was good reason for it. On the other hand, it must be considered that all this while he knew himself to be losing influence through his supposed want of energy in the war, and that he was under strong and unceasing pressure from every influential quarter to dismiss every general who caused disappointment. Newspapers and private letters of the time demonstrate that there was intense impatience against him for not producing victorious generals. This being so, his own patience in this matter and his resolution to give those under him a fair chance appear very remarkable and were certainly very wise.

We have come, however, to the end, not of all the clamour against Lincoln, but of his own worst perplexities. In passing to the operations further west we are passing to an instance in which Lincoln felt it right to

stand to the end by a decried commander, and that decried commander proved to possess the very qualities for
which he had vainly looked in others. The reverse side
of General Grant's fame is well enough known to the
world. Before the war he had been living under a cloud.
In the autumn of 1862, while his army lay between
Corinth and Memphis, the cloud still rested on his reputation. In spite of the glory he had won for a moment
at Fort Donelson, large circles were ready to speak of
him simply as an "incompetent and disagreeable man."
The crowning work of his life was accomplished with
terrible bloodshed which was often attributed to callous-
ness and incapacity on his part. The eight years of his
Presidency afterwards, which cannot properly be discussed here, added at the best no lustre to his memory.
Later still, when he visited Europe as a celebrity the general impression which he created seems to be contained
in the words "a rude man." Thus the Grant that we
discover in the recollections of a few loyal and loving
friends, and in the memoirs which he himself began when
late in life he lost his money and which he finished with
the pains of death upon him, is a surprising, in some ways
pathetic, figure. He had been a shy country boy, ready
enough at all the work of a farm and good with horses,
but with none of the business aptitude that make a successful farmer, when his father made him go to West
Point. Here he showed no great promise and made few
friends; his health became delicate, and he wanted to
leave the army and become a teacher of mathematics.
But the Mexican War, one of the most unjust in all history, as he afterwards said, broke out, and—so he later
thought—saved his life from consumption by keeping
him in the open air. After that he did retire, failed at
farming and other ventures, and at thirty-nine, when the
Civil War began, was, as has been seen, a shabby-look-
ing, shiftless fellow, pretty far gone in the habit of drink,
and more or less occupied about a leather business of his
father's. Rough in appearance and in manner he remained—the very opposite of smart- the very opposite

of versatile, the very opposite of expansive in speech or social intercourse. Unlike many rough people, he had a really simple character—truthful, modest, and kind; without varied interests, or complicated emotions, or much sense of fun, but thinking intensely on the problems that he did see before him, and in his silent way keenly sensitive on most of the points on which it is well to be sensitive. His friends reckoned up the very few occasions on which he was ever seen to be angry; only one could be recalled on which he was angry on his own account; the cruelty of a driver to animals in his supply train, heartless neglect in carrying out the arrangements he had made for the comfort of the sick and wounded, these were the sort of occasions which broke down Grant's habitual self-possession and good temper. "He was never too anxious," wrote Chaplain Eaton, who, having been set by him in charge of the negro refugees with his army, had excellent means of judging, "never too preoccupied with the great problems that beset him, to take a sincere and humane interest in the welfare of the most subordinate labourer dependent upon him." And he had delicacy of feeling in other ways. Once in the crowd at some hotel, in which he mingled an undistinguished figure, an old officer under him tried on a lecherous story for the entertainment of the General, who did not look the sort of man to resent it; Grant, who did not wish to set down an older man roughly, and had no ready phrases, but had, as it happens, a sensitive skin, was observed to blush to the roots of his hair in exquisite discomfort. It would be easy to multiply little recorded traits of this somewhat unexpected kind, which give grace to the memory of his determination in a duty which became very grim.

The simplicity of character as well as manner which endeared him to a few close associates was probably a very poor equipment for the Presidency, which, from that very simplicity, he afterwards treated as his due; and Grant presented in some ways as great a contrast as can be imagined to the large and complex mind of Lin-

coln. But he was the man that Lincoln had yearned for. Whatever degree of military skill may be ascribed to him, he had in the fullest measure the moral attributes of a commander. The sense that the war could be put through and must be put through possessed his soul. He was insusceptible to personal danger—at least, so observers said, though he himself told a different story—and he taught himself to keep a quiet mind in the presence of losses, rout in battle, or failure in a campaign. It was said that he never troubled himself with fancies as to what the enemy might be doing, and he confessed to having constantly told himself that the enemy was as much afraid of him as he of the enemy. His military talent was doubled in efficacy by his indomitable constancy. In one sense, moreover, and that a wholly good sense, he was a political general; for he had constantly before his mind the aims of the Government which employed him, perceiving early that there were only two possible ends to the war, the complete subjugation of the South or the complete failure of the Union; perceiving also that there was no danger of exhausting the resources of the North and great danger of discouraging its spirit, while the position of the South was in this respect the precise contrary. He was therefore the better able to serve the State as a soldier, because throughout he measured by a just standard the ulterior good or harm of success or failure in his enterprises.

The affectionate confidence which existed between Lee and "Stonewall" Jackson till the latter was killed at Chancellorsville had a parallel in the endearing friendship which sprung up between Grant and his principal subordinate, William T. Sherman, who was to bear a hardly less momentous part than his own in the conclusion of the war. Sherman was a man of quick wits and fancy, bright and mercurial disposition, capable of being a delightful companion to children, and capable of being sharp and inconsiderate to duller subordinates. It is a high tribute both to this brilliant soldier and to Grant himself that he always regarded Grant as hav-

ing made him, not only by his confidence but by his example.

As has been said, Grant was required to remain on the defensive between Memphis and Corinth, which mark the line of the Northern frontier at this period, while Buell was advancing on Chattanooga. Later, while the Confederates were invading Kentucky further east, attacks were also directed against Grant to keep him quiet. These were defeated, though Grant was unable to follow up his success at the time. When the invasion of Kentucky had collapsed and the Confederates under Bragg were retreating before Buell and his successor out of Middle Tennessee, it became possible for Grant and for Halleck and the Government at Washington to look to completing the conquest of the Mississippi River. The importance to the Confederates of a hold upon the Mississippi has been pointed out; if it were lost the whole of far South-West would manifestly be lost with it; in the North, on the other hand, public sentiment was strongly set upon freeing the navigation of the great river. The Confederacy now held the river from the fortress of Vicksburg, which after taking New Orleans Admiral Farragut had attacked in vain, down to Port Hudson, 120 miles further south, where the Confederate forces had since then seized and fortified another point of vantage. Vicksburg, it will be observed, lies 175 to 180 miles south of Memphis, or from Grand Junction, between Memphis and Corinth, the points in the occupation of the North which must serve Grant as a base. At Vicksburg itself, and for some distance south of it, a line of bluffs or steep-sided hills lying east of the Mississippi comes right up to the edge of the river. The river as it approaches these bluffs makes a sudden bend to the north-east and then again to the south-west, so that two successive reaches of the stream, each from three to four miles long, were commanded by the Vicksburg guns, 200 feet above the valley; the eastward or landward side of the fortress was also well situated for defence. To the north of Vicksburg the country on the east side of the

Mississippi is cut up by innumerable streams and "bayous" or marshy creeks, winding and intersecting amid a dense growth of cedars. The North, with a flotilla under Admiral Porter, commanded the Mississippi itself, and the Northern forces could freely move along its western shore to the impregnable river face of Vicksburg beyond. But the question of how to get safely to the assailable side of Vicksburg presented formidable difficulty to Grant and to the Government.

Grant's operations began in November, 1862. Advancing directly southward along the railway from Memphis with the bulk of his forces, he after a while detached Sherman with a force which proceeded down the Mississippi to the mouth of the Yazoo, a little north-west of Vicksburg. Here Sherman was to land, and, it was hoped, surprise the enemy at Vicksburg itself while the bulk of the enemy's forces were fully occupied by Grant's advance from the north. But Grant's lengthening communications were cut up by a cavalry raid, and he had to retreat, while Sherman came upon an enemy fully prepared and sustained a defeat a fortnight after Burnside's defeat at Fredericksburg. This was the first of a long series of failures during which Grant, who for his part was conspicuously frank and loyal in his relations with the Government, received upon the whole the fullest confidence and support from them. There occurred, however, about this time an incident which was trying to Grant, and of which the very simple facts must be stated, since it was the last of the occasions upon which severe criticism of Lincoln's military administration has been founded. General McClernand was an ambitious Illinois lawyer-politician of energy and courage; he was an old acquaintance of Lincoln's, and an old opponent; since the death of Douglas he and another lawyer-politician, Logan, had been the most powerful of the Democrats in Illinois; both were zealous in the war and had joined the Army upon its outbreak. Logan served as a general under Grant with confessed ability. It must be repeated that, North and South, former civilians had to be placed

in command for lack of enough soldiers of known capacity to go round, and that many of them, like Logan and like the Southern general, Polk, who was a bishop in the American Episcopal Church, did very good service. McClernand had early obtained high rank and had shown no sign as yet of having less aptitude for his new career than other men of similar antecedents. Grant, however, distrusted him, and proved to be right. In October, 1862, McClernand came to Lincoln with an offer of his personal services in raising troops from Illinois, Indiana, and Iowa, with a special view to clearing the Mississippi. He of course expected to be himself employed in this operation. Recruiting was at a low ebb, and it would have been folly to slight this offer. McClernand did in fact raise volunteers to the number of a whole army corps. He was placed under Grant in command of the expedition down the Mississippi which had already started under Sherman. Sherman's great promise had not yet been proved to any one but Grant; he appears at this time to have come under the disapproval of the Joint Committee of Congress on the War, and the newspaper Press had not long before announced, with affected regret, the news that he had become insane. McClernand, arriving just after Sherman's defeat near Vicksburg, fell in at once with a suggestion of his to attack the Post of Arkansas, a Confederate stronghold in the State of Arkansas and upon the river of that name, from the shelter of which Confederate gunboats had some chance of raiding the Mississippi above Vicksburg. The expedition succeeded in this early in January, 1863, and was then recalled to join Grant. This was a mortification to McClernand, who had hoped for a command independent of Grant. In his subsequent conduct he seems to have shown incapacity; he was certainly insubordinate to Grant, and he busied himself in intrigues against him, with such result as will soon be seen. As soon as Grant told the Administration that he was dissatisfied with McClernand, he was assured that he was at liberty to remove him from

command. This he eventually did after some months of trial.

In the first three months of 1863, while the army of the Potomac, shattered at Fredericksburg, was being pre-pared for the fresh attack upon Lee which ended at Chancellorsville, and while Bragg and Rosecrans lay con-fronting each other in Middle Tennessee, each content that the other was afraid to weaken himself by sending troops to the Mississippi, Grant was occupied in a series of enterprises apparently more cautious than that in which he eventually succeeded, but each in its turn futile. An attempt was made to render Vicksburg useless by a canal cutting across the bend of the Mississippi to the west of that fortress. Then Grant endeavoured with the able co-operation of Admiral Porter and his flotilla to secure a safe landing on the Yazoo, which enters the Mississippi a little above Vicksburg, so that he could move his army to the rear of Vicksburg by this route. Next Grant and Porter tried to establish a sure line of water communication from a point far up the Mississippi through an old canal, then somehow obstructed, into the upper waters of the Yazoo and so to a point on that river 30 or 40 miles to the north-east of Vicksburg, by which they would have turned the right of the main Con-federate force; but this was frustrated by the Confed-erates, who succeeded in establishing a strong fort further up the Yazoo. Yet a further effort was made to estab-lish a waterway by a canal quitting the Mississippi about 40 miles north of Vicksburg and communicating, through lakes, bayous, and smaller rivers, with its great tributary the Red River far to the south. This, like the first canal attempted, would have rendered Vicksburg useless.

Each of these projects failed in turn. The tedious engineering work which two of them involved was ren-dered more depressing by adverse conditions of weather and by ill-health among Grant's men. Natural grumbling among the troops was repeated and exaggerated in the North. McClernand employed the gift for intrigue, which perhaps had helped him to secure his command, in

an effort to get Grant removed. It is melancholy to add that a good many newspapers at this time began to print statements that Grant had again taken to drink. It is certain that he was at this time a total abstainer. It is said that he had offended the authors of this villainy by the restrictions which he had long before found necessary to put upon information to the Press. Some of the men freely confessed afterwards that they had been convinced of his sobriety, and added the marvellous apology that their business was to give the public " the news." Able and more honest journalists urged that Grant had proved his incompetence. Secretary Chase took up their complaints and pressed that Grant should be removed. Lincoln, before the outcry against Grant had risen to its height, had felt the need of closer information than he possessed about the situation on the Mississippi; and had hit upon the happy expedient of sending an able official of the War Department, who deserved and obtained the confidence of Grant and his officers, to accompany the Western army and report to him. Apart, however, from the reports he thus received, he had always treated the attacks on Grant with contempt. " I cannot spare this general; he fights," he said. In reply to complaints that Grant drank, he enquired (adapting, as he knew, George II.'s famous saying about Wolfe) what whisky he drank, explaining that he wished to send barrels of it to some of his other generals. His attitude is remarkable, because in his own mind he had not thought well of any of Grant's plans after his first failure in December; he had himself wished from an early day that Grant would take the very course by which he ultimately succeeded. He let him go his own way, as he afterwards told him, from " a general hope that you know better than I."

At the end of March Grant took a memorable determination to transfer his whole force to the south of Vicksburg and approach it from that direction. He was urged by Sherman to give up any further attempt to use the river, and, instead, to bring his whole army back to

Memphis and begin a necessarily slow approach on Vicksburg by the railway. He declared himself that on ordinary grounds of military prudence this would have been
the proper course, but he decided for himself that the
depressing effect of the retreat to Memphis would be
politically disastrous. At Grand Gulf, 30 miles south of
Vicksburg, the South possessed another fortified post on
the river; to reach this Grant required the help of the
Navy, not only in crossing from the western bank of the
river, but in transporting the supplies for which the roads
west of the river were inadequate. Admiral Porter, with
his gunboats and laden barges, successfully ran the gaunt-
let of the V_cksburg batteries by night without serious
damage. Grand Gulf was taken on May 3, and Grant's
army established at this new base.   A further doubt
now arose. General Banks in Louisiana was at this time
preparing to besiege Port Hudson. It might be well for
Grant to go south and join him, and, after reducing Port
Hudson, return with Banks' forces against Vicksburg.
This was what now commended itself to Lincoln. In
the letter of congratulation which some time later he was
able to send to Grant, after referring to his former
opinion which had been right, he confessed that he had
now been wrong. Banks was not yet ready to move, and
Vicksburg, now seriously threatened, might soon be reinforced. Orders to join Banks, though they were probably meant to be discretionary, were actually sent to
Grant, but too late. He had cut himself loose from his
base at Grand Gulf and marched his troops north, to live
with great hardship to themselves on the country and the
supplies they could take with them. He had with him
35,000 men. General Pemberton, to whom he had so
far been opposed, lay covering Vicksburg with 20,000
and a further force in the city; Joseph Johnston, whom
he afterwards described as the Southern general who in
all the war gave him most trouble, had been sent by
Jefferson Davis to take supreme command in the West,
and had collected 11,000 men at Jackson, the capital of
Mississippi, 45 miles east of Vicksburg. Grant was able

to take his enemy in detail. Having broken up Johnston's force he defeated Pemberton in a series of battles. His victory at Champion's Hill on May 16, not a fortnight after Chancellorsville, conveyed to his mind the assurance that the North would win the war. An assault on Vicksburg failed with heavy loss. Pemberton was at last closely invested in Vicksburg and Grant could establish safe communications with the North by way of the lower Yazoo and up the Mississippi above its mouth. There had been dissension between Pemberton and Johnston, who, seeing that gunboats proved able to pass Vicksburg in any case, thought that Pemberton, whom he could not at the moment hope to relieve, should abandon Vicksburg and try to save his army. Long before Johnston could be sufficiently reinforced to attack Grant, Grant's force had been raised to 71,000. On July 4, 1863, the day of the annual commemoration of national independence, Vicksburg was surrendered. Its garrison, who had suffered severely, were well victualled by Grant and allowed to go free on parole. Pemberton in his vexation treated Grant with peculiar insolence, which provoked a singular exhibition of the conqueror's good temper to him; and in his despatches to the President, Grant mentioned nothing with greater pride than the absence of a word or a sign on the part of his men which could hurt the feelings of the fallen. Johnston was forced to abandon the town of Jackson with its large stores to Sherman, but could not be pursued in his retreat. On July 9, five days later, the defender of Port Hudson, invested shortly before by Banks, who had not force enough for an assault, heard the news of Vicksburg and surrendered. Lincoln could now boast to the North that " the Father of Waters again goes unvexed to the sea."

At the very hour when Vicksburg was surrendered Lincoln had been issuing the news of another victory won in the preceding three days, which, along with the capture of Vicksburg, marked the turning point of the war. For more than a month after the battle of Chancellorsville the two opposing armies in the East had lain inac-

tive. The Conscription Law, with which we must deal later, had recently been passed, and various elements of discontent and disloyalty in the North showed a great deal of activity. It seems that Jefferson Davis at first saw no political advantage in the military risk of invading the North. Lee thought otherwise, and was eager to follow up his success. At last, early in June, 1863, he started northward. This time he aimed at the great industrial regions of Pennsylvania, hoping also while assailing them to draw Hooker further from Washington. Hooker, on first learning that Lee had crossed the Rappahannock, entertained the thought of himself going south of it and attacking Richmond. Lincoln dissuaded him, since he might be " entangled upon the river, like an ox jumped half over a fence "; he could not take Richmond for weeks, and his communications might be cut; besides, Lincoln added, his true objective point throughout was Lee's army and not Richmond. Hooker's later movements, in conformity with what he could gather of Lee's movements, were prudent and skilful. He rejected a later suggestion of Lincoln's that he should strike quickly at the most assailable point in Lee's lengthening line of communications, and he was wise, for Lee could live on the country he was traversing, and Hooker now aimed at covering Philadelphia or Baltimore and Washington, according to the direction which Lee might take, watching all the while for the moment to strike. He found himself hampered in some details by probably injudicious orders of his superior, Halleck, and became irritable and querulous; Lincoln had to exercise his simple arts to keep him to his duty and to soothe him, and was for the moment successful. Suddenly on June 27, with a battle in near prospect, Hooker sent in his resignation; probably he meant it, but there was no time to debate the matter. Probably he had lost confidence in himself, as he did before at Chancellorsville. Lincoln evidently judged that his state of mind made it wise to accept this resignation. He promptly appointed in Hooker's place one of his subordinates, General George

Meade, a lean, tall, studious, somewhat sharp-tongued man, not brilliant or popular or the choice that the army would have expected, but with a record in previous campaigns which made him seem to Lincoln trustworthy, as he was. A subordinate command in which he could really distinguish himself was later found for Hooker, who now took leave of his army in words of marked generosity towards Meade. All this while there was great excitement in the North. Urgent demands had been raised for the recall of McClellan, a course of which, Lincoln justly observed, no one could measure the inconvenience so well as he.

Lee was now feeling his way, somewhat in the dark as to his enemy's movements, because he had despatched most of his cavalry upon raiding expeditions towards the important industrial centre of Harrisburg. Meade continued on a parallel course to him, with his army spread out to guard against any movements of Lee's to the eastward. Each commander would have preferred to fight the other upon the defensive. Suddenly on July 1, three days after Meade had taken command, a chance collision took place north of the town of Gettysburg between the advance guards of the two armies. It developed into a general engagement, of which the result must partly depend on the speed with which each commander could bring up the remainder of his army. On the first day Lee achieved a decided success. The Northern troops were driven back upon steep heights just south of Gettysburg, of which the contour made it difficult for the enemy to co-ordinate his movements in any attack on them. Here Meade, who when the battle began was ten miles away and did not expect it, was able by the morning of the 2nd or during that day to bring up his full force; and here, contrary to his original choice of a position for bringing on a battle, he made his stand. The attack planned by Lee on the following day must, in his opinion, afterwards have been successful if " Stonewall " Jackson had been alive and with him. As it was, his most brilliant remaining subordinate, Longstreet, disapproved of any

assault, and on this and the following day obeyed his
orders reluctantly and too slowly. On July 3, 1863, Lee
renewed his attack. In previous battles the Northern
troops had been contending with invisible enemies in
woods; now, after a heavy cannonade, the whole Southern line could be seen advancing in the open to a desperate assault. This attack was crushed by the Northern
fire. First and last in the fighting round Gettysburg the
North lost 23,000 out of about 93,000 men, and the
South about an equal number out of 78,000. The net
result was that, after a day's delay, Lee felt compelled to
retreat. Nothing but an actual victory would have made
it wise for him to persist in his adventurous invasion.

The importance of this, which has been remembered as
the chief battle of the war, must be estimated rather by
the peril from which the North was delivered than by the
results it immediately reaped. Neither on July 3 nor
during Lee's subsequent retreat did Meade follow up his
advantage with the boldness to which Lincoln, in the
midst of his congratulations, exhorted him. On July 12
Lee recrossed the Potomac. Meade on the day before
had thought of attacking him, but desisted on the advice
of the majority in a council of war. That council of
war, as Lincoln said, should never have been held. Its
decision was demonstrably wrong, since it rested on the
hope that Lee would himself attack. Lincoln writhed
at a phrase in Meade's general orders about " driving the
invader from our soil." " Will our generals," he exclaimed in private, " never get that idea out of their
heads? The whole country is our soil." Meade, however, unlike McClellan, was only cautious, not lukewarm,
nor without a mind of his own. The army opposed to
him was much larger than that which McClellan failed
to overwhelm after Antietam. He had offered to resign
when he inferred Lincoln's dissatisfaction from a telegram. Lincoln refused this, and made it clear through
another officer that his strong opinion as to what might
have been done did not imply ingratitude or want of
confidence towards " a brave and skilful officer, and a

true man." Characteristically he relieved his sense of
Meade's omissions in a letter of most lucid criticism, and
characteristically he never sent it. Step by step Meade
moved on Lee's track into the enemy's country. Indecisive manœuvres on both sides continued over four
months. Lee was forced over the Rappahannock, then
over the Rapidan; Meade followed him, found his army
in peril, and prudently and promptly withdrew. In
December the two armies went into winter quarters on
the two sides of the Rappahannock to await the opening
of a very different campaign when the next spring was
far advanced.

The autumn months of 1863 witnessed in the Middle
West a varying conflict ending in a Northern victory
hardly less memorable than those of Gettysburg and
Vicksburg. At last, after the fall of Vicksburg, Rosecrans in Middle Tennessee found himself ready to advance. By skilful manœuvres, in the difficult country
where the Tennessee River cuts the Cumberland mountains and the parallel ranges which run from north-east
to south-west behind, he turned the flank of Bragg's position at Chattanooga and compelled him to evacuate that
town in the beginning of September. Bragg, as he retreated, succeeded in getting false reports as to his movements and the condition of his army conveyed to Rosecrans, who accordingly followed him up in an incautious
manner. By this time the bulk of the forces that had
been used against Vicksburg should have been brought
to support Rosecrans. Halleck, however, at first scattered them for purposes which he thought important in
the West. After a while, however, one part of the army
at Vicksburg was brought back to General Burnside in
Ohio, from whom it had been borrowed. Burnside accomplished the very advance by Lexington, in Kentucky,
over the mountains into Eastern Tennessee, which Lincoln had so long desired for the relief of the Unionists
there, and he was able to hold his ground, defeating at
Knoxville a little later an expedition under Longstreet
which was sent to dislodge him. Other portions of the

Western army were at last ordered to join Rosecrans, but did not reach him before he had met with disaster. For the Confederate authorities, eager to retrieve their losses, sent every available reinforcement to Bragg, and he was shortly able to turn back towards Chattanooga with over 71,000 men against the 57,000 with which Rosecrans, scattering his troops in false security, was pursuing him. The two armies came upon one another, without clear expectation, upon the Chicamauga Creek beyond the ridge which lies south-east of Chattanooga. The battle fought among the woods and hills by Chicamauga on September 19 and 20 surpassed any other in the war in the heaviness of the loss on each side. On the second day Bragg's manœuvres broke Rosecrans' line, and only an extraordinarily gallant stand by Thomas with a part of the line, in successive positions of retreat, prevented Bragg from turning the hasty retirement of the remainder into a disastrous rout. As it was, Rosecrans made good his retreat to Chattanooga, but there he was in danger of being completely cut off. A corps was promptly detached from Meade in Virginia, placed under Hooker, and sent to relieve him. Rosecrans, who in a situation of real difficulty seems to have had no resourcefulness, was replaced in his command by Thomas. Grant was appointed to supreme command of all the forces in the West and ordered to Chattanooga. There, after many intricate operations on either side, a great battle was eventually fought on November 24 and 25, 1863. Grant had about 60,000 men; Bragg, who had detached Longstreet for his vain attack on Burnside, had only 33,000, but he had one steep and entrenched ridge behind another on which to stand. The fight was marked by notable incidents—Hooker's " battle above the clouds "; and the impulse by which apparently with no word of command, Thomas' corps, tired of waiting while Sherman advanced upon the one flank and Hooker upon the other, arose and carried a ridge which the enemy and Grant himself had regarded as impregnable. It ended in a rout of the Confederates, which was ener-

getically followed up.   Bragg's army was broken and
driven right back into Georgia.   To sum up the events of
the year, the one serious invasion of the North by the
South had failed, and the dominion on which the Confederacy had any real hold was now restricted to the
Atlantic States, Alabama, and a part of the State of
Mississippi.

At this point, at which the issue of the war, if it were
only pursued, could not be doubted, and at which, as it
happens, the need of Lincoln's personal intervention in
military matters became greatly diminished, we may try
to obtain a general impression of his wisdom, or want of
it, in such affairs.   The closeness and keen intelligence
with which he followed the war is undoubted, but could
only be demonstrated by a lengthy accumulation of evidence.   The larger strategy of the North, sound in the
main, was of course the product of more than one co-
operating mind, but as his was undoubtedly the dominant
will of his Administration, so too it seems likely that,
with his early and sustained grasp of the general problem, he contributed not a little to the clearness and consistency of the strategical plans.   The amount of the
forces raised was for long, as we shall see later, beyond
his control, and, in the distribution of what he had to the
best effect, his own want of knowledge and the poor judgment of his earlier advisers seem to have caused some
errors.   He started with the evident desire to put himself almost unreservedly in the hands of the competent
military counsellors, and he was able in the end to do
so; but for a long intermediate period, as we have seen,
he was compelled as a responsible statesman to forego this
wish.   It was all that time his function first to pick out,
with very little to go by, the best officers he could find,
replacing them with better when he could; and secondly
to give them just so much direction, and no more, as his
wisdom at a distance and their more expert skill upon
the spot made proper.   In each of these respects his
occasional mistakes are plain enough, but the evidence,
upon which he has often been thought capable of setting

aside sound military considerations causelessly or in obedience to interested pressure, breaks down when the facts of any imputed instance are known. It is manifest that he gained rapidly both in knowledge of the men he dealt with and in the firm kindness with which he treated them. It is remarkable that, with his ever-burning desire to see vigour and ability displayed, he could watch so constantly as he did for the precise opportunity or the urgent necessity before he made changes in command. It is equally remarkable that, with his decided and often right views as to what should be done, his advice was always offered with equal deference and plainness. " Quite possibly I was wrong both then and now," he once wrote to Hooker, " but in the great responsibility resting upon me, I cannot be entirely silent. Now, all I ask is that you will be in such mood that we can get into action the best cordial judgment of yourself and General Halleck, with my poor mite added, if indeed he and you shall think it entitled to any consideration at all." The man whose habitual attitude was this, and who yet could upon the instant take his own decision, may be presumed to have been wise in many cases where we do not know his reasons. Few statesmen, perhaps, have so often stood waiting and refrained themselves from a firm will and not from the want of it, and for the sake of the rare moment of action.

The passing of the crisis in the war was fittingly commemorated by a number of State Governors who combined to institute a National Cemetery upon the field of Gettysburg. It was dedicated on November 19, 1863. The speech of the occasion was delivered by Edward Everett, the accomplished man once already mentioned as the orator of highest repute in his day. The President was bidden then to say a few words at the close. The oration with which for two hours Everett delighted his vast audience charms no longer, though it is full of graceful sentiment and contains a very reasonable survey of the rights and wrongs involved in the war, and of its progress till then. The few words of Abraham Lincoln were such as perhaps sank deep, but left his audience

unaware that a classic had been spoken which would endure with the English language. The most literary man present was also Lincoln's greatest admirer, young John Hay. To him it seemed that Mr. Everett spoke perfectly, and "the old man" gracefully for him. These were the few words: "Four score and seven years ago our fathers brought forth on this continent a new nation, conceived in liberty and dedicated to the proposition that all men are created equal. Now we are engaged in a great civil war, testing whether that nation, or any nation so conceived and so dedicated, can long endure. We are met on a great battlefield of that war. We have come to dedicate a portion of that field as a final resting place for those who here gave their lives that that nation might live. It is altogether fitting and proper that we should do this. But, in a larger sense, we cannot dedicate—we cannot consecrate—we cannot hallow—this ground. The brave men, living and dead, who struggled here have consecrated it far above our poor power to add or to detract. The world will little note nor long remember what we say here, but it can never forget what they did here. It is for us, the living, rather to be dedicated here to the unfinished work which they who fought here have thus far so nobly advanced. It is rather for us to be here dedicated to the great task remaining before us— that from these honoured dead we take increased devotion to that cause for which they gave the last full measure of devotion; that we here highly resolve that these dead shall not have died in vain; that this nation, under God, shall have a new birth of freedom; and that government of the people, by the people, for the people, shall not perish from the earth."

2. *Conscription and the Politics of 1863.*

The events of our day may tempt us to underestimate the magnitude of the American Civil War, not only in respect of its issues, but in respect of the efforts that were put forth. Impartial historians declare that "no pre-

vious war had ever in the same time entailed upon the
combatants such enormous sacrifices of life and wealth."
Even such battles as Malplaquet had not rivalled in
carnage the battles of this war, and in the space of these
four years there took place a number of engagements—
far more than can be recounted here—in many of which,
as at Gettysburg, the casualties amounted to a quarter
of the whole forces engaged. The Southern armies,
especially towards the end of the war, were continually
being pitted against vastly superior numbers; the Northern armies, whether we look at the whole war as one
vast enterprise of conquest or at almost any important
battle save that of Gettysburg, were as continually confronted with great obstacles in the matter of locality and
position. In this case, of a new and not much organised
country unprepared for war, exact or intelligible figures
as to losses or as to the forces raised must not be expected, but, according to what seems to be a fair estimate, the total deaths on the Northern and the Southern
side directly due to the war stood to the population of
the whole country at its beginning as at least 1 to 32. Of
these deaths about half occurred on the Northern and
half on the Southern side; this, however, implies that in
proportion to its population the South lost twice as heavily as the North.

Neither side obtained the levies of men that it needed
without resort to compulsion. The South, in which this
necessity either arose more quickly or was seen more
readily, had called up before the end of the war its whole
available manhood. In the North the proportion of
effort and sacrifice required was obviously less, and, at
least at one critical moment, it was disastrously under-
estimated. A system of compulsion, to be used in default
of volunteering, was brought into effect half-way through
the war. Under this system there were in arms at the
end of the war 980,000 white Northern soldiers, who
probably stood to the population at that time in as high
a proportion as 1 to 25, and everything was in readiness
for calling up a vastly greater number if necessary. After

twenty months of war, when the purely voluntary system still existed but was proving itself inadequate to make good the wastage of the armies, the number in arms for the North was 860,717, perhaps as much as 1 in 27 of the population then. It would be useless to evade the question which at once suggests itself, whether the results of voluntary enlistment in this country during the present war have surpassed to the extent to which they undoubtedly ought to have surpassed the standard set by the North in the Civil War. For these two cases furnish the only instances in which the institution of voluntary enlistment has been submitted to a severe test by Governments reluctant to abandon it. The two cases are of course not strictly comparable. Our own country in this matter had the advantages of riper organisation, political and social, and of the preparatory education given it by the Territorials and by Lord Roberts. The extremity of the need was in our case immediately apparent; and the cause at issue appealed with the utmost simplicity and intensity to every brave and to every gentle nature. In the Northern States, on the other hand, apart from all other considerations, there were certain to be sections, local, racial, and political, upon which the national cause could take no very firm hold. That this was so proves no unusual prevalence of selfishness or of stupidity; and the apathy of such sections of the people, like that of smaller sections in our own case, sets in a brighter light the devotion which made so many eager to give their all. Moreover, the general patriotism of the Northern people is not to be judged by the failure of the purely voluntary system, but rather, as will be seen later, by the success of the system which succeeded it. There is in our case no official statement of the exact number serving on any particular day, but the facts which are published make it safe to conclude that, at the end of fifteen months of war, when no compulsion was in force, the soldiers then in service and drawn from the United Kingdom alone amounted to 1 in 17 of the population. The population in this case is one of which a smaller proportion are of

military age than was the case in the Northern States, with their great number of immigrants. The apparent effect of these figures would be a good deal heightened if it were possible to make a correct addition in the case of each country for the numbers killed or disabled in war up to the dates in question and for the numbers serving afloat. Moreover, the North, when it was driven to abandon the purely voluntary system, had not reached the point at which the withdrawal of men from civil occupations could have been regarded among the people as itself a national danger, or at which the Government was compelled to deter some classes from enlisting; new industries unconnected with the war were all the while springing up, and the production and export of foodstuffs were increasing rapidly. For the reasons which have been stated, there is nothing invidious in thus answering an unavoidable question. Judged by any previous standard of voluntary national effort, the North answered the test well. Each of our related peoples must look upon the rally of its fathers and grandfathers in the one case, its brothers and sons in the other, with mingled feelings in which pride predominates, the most legitimate source of pride in our case being the unity of the Empire. To each the question must present itself whether the nations, democratic and otherwise, which have followed from the first, or, like the South, have rapidly adopted a different principle, have not, in this respect, a juster cause of pride. In some of these countries, by common and almost unquestioning consent, generation after generation of youths and men in their prime have held themselves at the instant disposal of their country if need should arise; and, in the absence of need and the absence of excitement, have contentedly borne the appreciable sacrifice of training. With this it is surely necessary to join a further question, whether the compulsion which, under conscription, the public imposes on individuals is comparable in its harshness to the sacrifice and the conflict of duties imposed by the voluntary system upon the best people in all classes as such.

From the manner in which the war arose it will easily be understood that the South was quicker than the North in shaping its policy for raising armies. Before a shot had been fired at Fort Sumter, and when only seven of the ten Southern States had yet seceded, President Jefferson Davis had at his command more than double the number of the United States Army as it then was. He had already lawful authority to raise that number to nearly three times as many. And, though there was protest in some States, and some friction between the Confederate War Department and the State militias, on the whole the seceding States, in theory jealous of their rights, submitted very readily in questions of defence to the Confederacy.

It is not clear how far the Southern people displayed their warlike temper by a sustained flow of voluntary enlistment; but their Congress showed the utmost promptitude in granting every necessary power to their President, and on April 16, 1862, a sweeping measure of compulsory service was passed. The President of the Confederacy could call into the service any white resident in the South between the ages of eighteen and thirty-five, with certain statutory exemptions. There was, of course, trouble about the difficult question of exemptions, and under conflicting pressure the Confederate Congress made and unmade various laws about them. After a time all statutory exemptions were done away, and it was left entirely in the discretion of the Southern President to say what men were required in various departments of civil life. The liability to serve was extended in September, 1862, to all between eighteen and forty-five, and finally in February, 1864, to all between seventeen and fifty. The rigorous conscription which necessity required could not be worked without much complaint. There was a party disposed to regard the law as unconstitutional. The existence of sovereign States within the Confederacy was very likely an obstacle to the local and largely voluntary organisation for deciding claims which can exist in a unified country. A Government so hard driven must,

even if liberally minded, have enforced the law with much actual hardship. A belief in the ruthlessness of the Southern conscription penetrated to the North. It was probably exaggerated from the temptation to suppose that secession was the work of a tyranny and not of the Southern people. Desertion and failure of the Conscription Law became common in the course of 1864, but this would seem to have been due not so much to resentment at the system as to the actual loss of a large part of the South, and the spread of a perception that the war was now hopelessly lost. In the last extremities of the Confederate Government the power of compulsion of course completely broke down. But, upon the surface at least, it seems plain that what has been called the military despotism of Jefferson Davis rested upon the determination rather than upon the submissiveness of the people.

In the North, where there was double the population to draw upon, the need for compulsion was not likely to be felt as soon. The various influences which would later depress enlistment had hardly begun to assert themselves, when the Government, as if to aggravate them in advance, committed a blunder which has never been surpassed in its own line. On April 3, 1862, recruiting was stopped dead; the central recruiting office at Washington was closed and its staff dispersed. Many writers agree in charging this error against Stanton. He must have been the prime author of it, but this does not exonerate Lincoln. It was no departmental matter, but a matter of supreme policy. Lincoln's knowledge of human nature and his appreciation of the larger bearings of every question might have been expected to set Stanton right, unless, indeed, the thing was done suddenly behind his back. In any case, this must be added to the indications seen in an earlier chapter, that Lincoln's calm strength and sure judgment had at that time not yet reached their full development. As for Stanton, a man of much narrower mind, but acute, devoted, and morally fearless, kept in the War Department as a sort of tame tiger to prey on abuses, negligences, pretensions, and

political influences, this was one among a hundred smaller erratic doings, which his critics have never thought of as outweighing his peculiar usefulness. His departmental point of view can easily be understood. Recruits, embarrassingly, presented themselves much faster than they could be organised or equipped, and an overdriven office did not pause to think out some scheme of enlistment for deferred service. Waste had been terrific, and Stanton did not dislike a petty economy which might shock people in Washington. McClellan clamoured for more men—let him do something with what he had got; Stanton, indeed, very readily became sanguine that McClellan, once in motion, would crush the Confederacy. Events conspired to make the mistake disastrous. In these very days the Confederacy was about to pass its own Conscription Act. McClellan, instead of pressing on to Richmond, sat down before Yorktown and let the Confederate conscripts come up. Halleck was crawling southward, when a rapid advance might have robbed the South of a large recruiting area. The reopening of enlistment came on the top of the huge disappointment at McClellan's failure in the peninsula. There was a creditable response to the call which was then made for volunteers. But the disappointment of the war continued throughout 1862; the second Bull Run; the inconclusive sequel to Antietam; Fredericksburg; and, side by side with these events, the long-drawn failure of Buell's and Rosecrans' operations. The spirit of voluntary service seems to have revived vigorously enough wherever and whenever the danger of Southern invasion became pressing, but under this protracted depressing influence it no longer rose to the task of subduing the South. It must be added that wages in civil employment were very high. Lincoln, it is evident, felt this apparent failure of patriotism sadly, but in calm retrospect it cannot seem surprising.

In the latter part of 1862 attempts were made to use the powers of compulsion which the several States possessed, under the antiquated laws as to militia which ex-

isted in all of them, in order to supplement recruiting. The number of men raised for short periods in this way is so small that the description of the Northern armies at this time as purely volunteer armies hardly needs qualification. It would probably be worth no one's while to investigate the makeshift system with which the Government, very properly, then tried to help itself out; for it speedily and completely failed. The Conscription Act, which became law on March 3, 1863, set up for the first time an organisation for recruiting which covered the whole country but was under the complete control of the Federal Government. It was placed under an officer of great ability, General J. B. Fry, formerly chief of staff to Buell, and now entitled Provost-Marshal-General. It was his business, through provost-marshals in a number of districts, each divisible into sub-districts as convenience might require, to enroll all male citizens between twenty and forty-five. He was to assign a quota, in other words a stated proportion of the number of troops for which the Government might at any time call, to each district, having regard to the number of previous enlistments from each district. The management of voluntary enlistment was placed in his hands, in order that the two methods of recruiting might be worked in harmony. The system as a whole was quite distinct from any such system of universal service as might have been set up beforehand in time of peace. Compulsion only came into force in default of sufficient volunteers from any district to provide its required number of the troops wanted. When it came into force the " drafts " of conscripts were chosen by lot from among those enrolled as liable for service. But there was a way of escape from actual service. It seems, from what Lincoln wrote, to have been looked upon as a time-honoured principle, established by precedent in all countries, that the man on whom the lot fell might provide a substitute if he could. The market price of a substitute (a commodity for the provision of which a class of " substitute brokers " came into being) proved to be about 1,000 dollars. Business

or professional men, who felt they could not be spared
from home but wished to act patriotically, did buy substitutes; but they need not have done so, for the law contained a provision intended, as Lincoln recorded, to safeguard poorer men against such a rise in prices. They
could escape by paying 300 dollars, or £60, not, in the
then state of wages, an extravagant penalty upon an able-
bodied man. The sums paid under this provision covered the cost of the recruiting business.

Most emphatically the Conscription Law operated
mainly as a stimulus to voluntary enlistment. The volunteer received, as the conscript did not, a bounty from
the Government; States, counties, and smaller localities,
when once a quota was assigned to them, vied with one
another in filling their quota with volunteers, and for that
purpose added to the Government bounty. It goes without saying that in a new country, with its scattered country population and its disorganised great new towns, there
were plenty of abuses. Substitute brokers provided the
wrong article; ingenious rascals invented the trade of
" bounty-jumping," and would enlist for a bounty, desert,
enlist for another bounty, and so on indefinitely; and the
number of men enrolled who were afterwards unac-
counted for was large. There was of course also grumbling of localities at the quotas assigned to them, though
no pains were spared to assign them fairly. There was
some opposition to the working of the law after it was
passed, but it was, not general, but partly the opposition
of rowdies in degraded neighbourhoods, partly factitious
political opposition, and partly seditious and openly
friendly to the South. In general the country accepted
the law as a manifest military necessity. The spirit and
manner of its acceptance may be judged from the results
of any of the calls for troops under this law. For example, in December, 1864, towards the end of the war,
211,752 men were brought up to the colours; of these it
seems that 194,715 were ordinary volunteers, 10,192
were substitutes provided by conscripts, and only 6,845
were actually compelled men. It is perhaps more signifi-

cant still that among those who did not serve there were only 460 who paid the 300-dollar penalty, as against the 10,192 who must have paid at least three times that sum for substitutes.   Behind the men who had been called up by the end of the war the North had, enrolled and ready to be called, over two million men.   The North had not to suffer as the South suffered, but unquestionably in this matter it rose to the occasion.

The constitutional validity of the law was much questioned by politicians, but never finally tried out on appeal to the Supreme Court.   There seems to be no room for doubt that Lincoln's own reasoning on this matter was sound.   The Constitution simply gave to Congress "power to raise and support armies," without a word as to the particular means to be used for the purpose; the new and extremely well-considered Constitution of the Confederacy was in this respect the same.   The Constitution, argued Lincoln, would not have given the power of raising armies without one word as to the mode in which it was to be exercised, if it had not meant Congress to be the sole judge as to the mode. "The principle," he wrote, " of the draft, which simply is involuntary or enforced service, is not new.   It has been practised in all ages of the world.   It was well known to the framers of our Constitution as one of the modes of raising armies.   . . . It had been used just before, in establishing our independence, and it was also used under the Constitution in 1812."   In fact, as we have seen, a certain power of compelling military service existed in each of the States and had existed in them from the first. Their ancestors had brought the principle with them from the old country, in which the system of the "militia ballot " had not fallen into desuetude when they became independent.   The traditional English jealousy, which the American Colonies had imbibed, against the military power of the Crown had never manifested itself in any objection to the means which might be taken to raise soldiers, but in establishing a strict control of the number which the Crown could at any moment maintain; and

this control had long been in England and had always been in America completely effective. We may therefore treat the protest which was raised against the law as unconstitutional, and the companion argument that it tended towards military despotism, as having belonged to the realm of political verbiage, and as neither founded in reason nor addressed to living popular emotions.

This is the way in which the Northern people, of whom a large part were, it must be remembered, Democrats, seem to have regarded these contentions, and a real sense, apart from these contentions, that conscription was unnecessary or produced avoidable hardship seems scarcely to have existed. It was probably for this reason that Lincoln never published the address to the people, or perhaps more particularly to the Democratic opposition, to which several references have already been made. In the course of it he said: "At the beginning of the war, and ever since, a variety of motives, pressing, some in one direction and some in the other, would be presented to the mind of each man physically fit to be a soldier, upon the combined effect of which motives he would, or would not, voluntarily enter the service. Among these motives would be patriotism, political bias, ambition, personal courage, love of adventure, want of employment, and convenience, or the opposite of some of these. We already have and have had in the service, as it appears, substantially all that can be obtained upon this voluntary weighing of motives. And yet we must somehow obtain more or relinquish the original object of the contest, together with all the blood and treasure already expended in the effort to secure it. To meet this necessity the law for the draft has been enacted. You who do not wish to be soldiers do not like this law. This is natural; nor does it imply want of patriotism. Nothing can be so just and necessary as to make us like it if it is disagreeable to us. We are prone, too, to find false arguments with which to excuse ourselves for opposing such disagreeable things." He proceeded to meet some of these arguments upon the

lines which have already been indicated. After speaking
of the precedents for conscription in America, he continued: " Wherein is the peculiar hardship now? Shall
we shrink from the necessary means to maintain our free
government, which our grandfathers employed to establish it and our fathers have already once employed to
maintain it? Are we degenerate? Has the manhood of
our race run out?" Unfair administration was apprehended. " This law," he said, " belongs to a class, which
class is composed of those laws whose object is to dis-
tribute burthens or benefits on the principle of equality.
No one of these laws can ever be practically administered
with that exactness which can be conceived of in the mind.
A tax law . . . will be a dead letter if no one will
be compelled to pay until it can be shown that every other
one will be compelled to pay in precisely the same proportion according to value; nay, even it will be a dead
letter if no one can be compelled to pay until it is certain
that every other one will pay at all. . . . This sort
of difficulty applies in full force to the practical administration of the draft law. In fact, the difficulty is greater
in the case of the draft law "; and he proceeded to state
the difficulties. " In all these points," he continued,
" errors will occur in spite of the utmost fidelity. The
Government is bound to administer the law with such an
approach to exactness as is usual in analogous cases, and
as entire good faith and fidelity will reach." Errors,
capable of correction, should, he promised, be corrected
when pointed out; but he concluded: " With these views
and on these principles, I feel bound to tell you it is my
purpose to see the draft law faithfully executed." It
was his way, as has been seen, sometimes to set his
thoughts very plainly on paper and to consider afterwards the wisdom of publishing them. This paper never
saw the light till after his death. It is said that some
scruple as to the custom in his office restrained him from
sending it out, but this scruple probably weighed with
him the more because he saw that the sincere people
whom he had thought of addressing needed no such ap-

peal. It was surely a wise man who, writing so wisely, could see the greater wisdom of silence.

The opposition to the Conscription Law may be treated simply as one element in the propaganda of the official Opposition to the Administration. The opposition to such a measure which we might possibly have expected to arise from churches, or from schools of thought independent of the ordinary parties, does not seem, as a matter of fact, to have arisen. The Democratic party had, as we have seen, revived in force in the latter part of 1862. Persons, ambitious, from whatever mixture of motives, of figuring as leaders of opposition during a war which they did not condemn, found a public to which to appeal, mainly because the war was not going well. They found a principle of opposition satisfactory to themselves in condemning the Proclamation of Emancipation. (It was significant that McClellan shortly after the Proclamation issued a General Order enjoining obedience to the Government and adding the hint that " the remedy for political errors, if any are committed, is to be found only in the action of the people at the polls.") In the curious creed which respectable men, with whom allegiance to an ancient party could be a powerful motive at such a time, were driven to construct for themselves, enforcement of the duty to defend the country and liberation of the enemy's slaves appeared as twin offences against the sacred principles of constitutional freedom. It would have been monstrous to say that most of the Democrats were opposed to the war. Though a considerable number had always disliked it and now found courage to speak loudly, the bulk were as loyal to the Union as those very strong Republicans like Greeley, who later on despaired of maintaining it. But there were naturally Democrats for whom a chance now appeared in politics, and who possessed that common type of political mind that meditates deeply on minor issues and is inflamed by zeal against minor evils. Such men began to debate with their consciences whether the wicked Government might not become more odious than the enemy.

governor or commander during great public peril is encouraged to consider what is right and necessary, not what is lawful, knowing that if necessary there will be enquiry into his conduct afterwards, but knowing also that, unless he acts quite unconscionably, he and his agents will be protected by an Act of Indemnity from the legal consequences of whatever they have done in good faith. The American Constitution would seem to render any such Act of Indemnity impossible. In a strictly legal sense, therefore, the power which Lincoln exercised must be said to have been usurped. The arguments by which he defended his own legality read now as good arguments on what the law should have been, but bad arguments on what the law was. He did not, perhaps, attach extreme importance to this legal contention, for he declared plainly that he was ready to break the law in minor matters rather than let the whole fabric of law go to ruin. This, however, does not prove that he was insincere when he pleaded legal as well as moral justification; he probably regarded the Constitution in a manner which modern lawyers find it difficult to realise; he probably applied in construing it a principle such as Hamilton laid down for the construction of statutes, that it was " qualified and controlled " by the Common Law and by considerations of " convenience " and of " reason " and of the policy which its framers, as wise and honest men, would have followed in present circumstances; he probably would have adapted to the occasion Hamilton's position that " construction may be made against the letter of the statute to render it agreeable to natural justice."

In the exercise of his supposed prerogative Lincoln sanctioned from beginning to end of the war the arrest of many suspected dangerous persons under what may be called " letters de cachet " from Seward and afterwards from Stanton. He publicly professed in 1863 his regret that he had not caused this to be done in cases, such as those of Lee and Joseph Johnston, where it had not been done. When agitation arose on the matter in

peal. It was surely a wise man who, writing so wisely, could see the greater wisdom of silence.

The opposition to the Conscription Law may be treated simply as one element in the propaganda of the official Opposition to the Administration. The opposition to such a measure which we might possibly have expected to arise from churches, or from schools of thought independent of the ordinary parties, does not seem, as a matter of fact, to have arisen. The Democratic party had, as we have seen, revived in force in the latter part of 1862. Persons, ambitious, from whatever mixture of motives, of figuring as leaders of opposition during a war which they did not condemn, found a public to which to appeal, mainly because the war was not going well. They found a principle of opposition satisfactory to themselves in condemning the Proclamation of Emancipation. (It was significant that McClellan shortly after the Proclamation issued a General Order enjoining obedience to the Government and adding the hint that "the remedy for political errors, if any are committed, is to be found only in the action of the people at the polls.") In the curious creed which respectable men, with whom allegiance to an ancient party could be a powerful motive at such a time, were driven to construct for themselves, enforcement of the duty to defend the country and liberation of the enemy's slaves appeared as twin offences against the sacred principles of constitutional freedom. It would have been monstrous to say that most of the Democrats were opposed to the war. Though a considerable number had always disliked it and now found courage to speak loudly, the bulk were as loyal to the Union as those very strong Republicans like Greeley, who later on despaired of maintaining it. But there were naturally Democrats for whom a chance now appeared in politics, and who possessed that common type of political mind that meditates deeply on minor issues and is inflamed by zeal against minor evils. Such men began to debate with their consciences whether the wicked Government might not become more odious than the enemy.

There arose, too, as there often arises in war time, a fraternal feeling between men who hated the war and men who reflected how much better they could have waged it themselves.

There was, of course, much in the conduct of the Government which called for criticism, and on that account it was a grievous pity that independence should have stultified itself by reviving in any form the root principle of party government, and recognising as the best critics of the Administration men who desired to take its place. More useful censure of the Government at that time might have come from men who, if they had axes to grind, would have publicly thrown them away. There were two points which especially called for criticism, apart from military administration, upon which, as it happened, Lincoln knew more than his critics knew and more than he could say. One of these points was extravagance and corruption in the matter of army contracts and the like; these evils were dangerously prevalent, but members of the Cabinet were as anxious to prevent them as any outside critic could be, and it was friendly help, not censure, that was required. The other point was the exercise of martial law, a difficult question, upon which a word must here be said, but upon which only those could usefully have spoken out whose general support of the Government was pronounced and sincere.

In almost every rebellion or civil war statesmen and the military officers under them are confronted with the need, for the sake of the public safety or even of ordinary justice, of rules and procedure which the law in peace time would abhor. In great conflicts, such as our own wars after the French Revolution and the American Civil War, statesmen such as Pitt and Lincoln, capable of handling such a problem well, have had their hands full of yet more urgent matters. The puzzling part of the problem does not lie in the neighbourhood of the actual fighting, where for the moment there can be no law but the will of the commander, but in the districts more dis tantly affected, or in the period when the war is smoulder-

ing out. Lincoln's Government had at first to guard itself against dangerous plots which could be scented but
not proved in Washington; later on it had to answer such
questions as this: What should be done when a suspected
agent of the enemy is vaguely seen to be working against
enlistment, when an attack by the civil mob upon the recruits is likely to result, and when the local magistrate
and police are not much to be trusted? There is no
doubt that Seward at the beginning, and Stanton persistently, and zealous local commanders now and then solved
such problems in a very hasty fashion, or that Lincoln
throughout was far more anxious to stand by vigorous
agents of the Government than to correct them.

Lincoln claimed that as Commander-in-Chief he had
during the continuance of civil war a lawful authority
over the lives and liberties of all citizens, whether loyal
or otherwise, such as any military commander exercises
in hostile country occupied by his troops. He held that
there was no proper legal remedy for persons injured
under this authority except by impeachment of himself.
He held, further, that this authority extended to every
place to which the action of the enemy in any form extended—that is, to the whole country. This he took to
be the doctrine of English Common Law, and he contended that the Constitution left this doctrine in full
force. Whatever may be said as to his view of the
Common Law doctrine, his construction of the Constitution would now be held by every one to have been
wrong. Plainly read, the Constitution swept away the
whole of that somewhat undefined doctrine of martial
law which may be found in some decisions of our Courts,
and it did much more. Every Legislature in the British
Empire can, subject to the veto of the Crown, enact
whatever exceptional measures of public safety it thinks
necessary in an emergency. The Constitution restricted
this legislative power within the very narrowest limits.
There is, moreover, a recognised British practice, initiated by Wellington and Castlereagh, by which all question as to the authority of martial law is avoided; a

governor or commander during great public peril is encouraged to consider what is right and necessary, not what is lawful, knowing that if necessary there will be enquiry into his conduct afterwards, but knowing also that, unless he acts quite unconscionably, he and his agents will be protected by an Act of Indemnity from the legal consequences of whatever they have done in good faith. The American Constitution would seem to render any such Act of Indemnity impossible. In a strictly legal sense, therefore, the power which Lincoln exercised must be said to have been usurped. The arguments by which he defended his own legality read now as good arguments on what the law should have been, but bad arguments on what the law was. He did not, perhaps, attach extreme importance to this legal contention, for he declared plainly that he was ready to break the law in minor matters rather than let the whole fabric of law go to ruin. This, however, does not prove that he was insincere when he pleaded legal as well as moral justification; he probably regarded the Constitution in a manner which modern lawyers find it difficult to realise; he probably applied in construing it a principle such as Hamilton laid down for the construction of statutes, that it was " qualified and controlled " by the Common Law and by considerations of " convenience " and of " reason " and of the policy which its framers, as wise and honest men, would have followed in present circumstances; he probably would have adapted to the occasion Hamilton's position that " construction may be made against the letter of the statute to render it agreeable to natural justice."

In the exercise of his supposed prerogative Lincoln sanctioned from beginning to end of the war the arrest of many suspected dangerous persons under what may be called " letters de cachet " from Seward and afterwards from Stanton. He publicly professed in 1863 his regret that he had not caused this to be done in cases, such as those of Lee and Joseph Johnston, where it had not been done. When agitation arose on the matter in

the end of 1862 many political prisoners were, no doubt wisely, released. Congress then proceeded, in 1863, to exercise such powers in the matter as the Constitution gave it by an Act suspending, where the President thought fit, the privilege of the writ of *habeas corpus*. A decision of the Supreme Court, delivered curiously enough by Lincoln's old friend David Davis, showed that the real effect of this Act, so far as valid under the Constitution, was ridiculously small (see *Ex parte Milligan,* 4 Russell, 2). In any case the Act was hedged about with many precautions. These were entirely disregarded by the Government, which proceeded avowedly upon Lincoln's theory of martial law. The whole country was eventually proclaimed to be under martial law, and many persons were at the orders of the local military commander tried and punished by court-martial for offences, such as the discouragement of enlistment or the encouragement of desertion, which might not have been punishable by the ordinary law, or of which the ordinary Courts might not have convicted them. This fresh outbreak of martial law must in large part be ascribed to Lincoln's determination that the Conscription Act should not be frustrated; but apart from offences relating to enlistment there was from 1863 onwards no lack of seditious plots fomented by the agents of the Confederacy in Canada, and there were several secret societies, " knights " of this, that, or the other. Lincoln, it is true, scoffed at these, but very often the general on the spot thought seriously of them, and the extreme Democratic leader, Vallandigham, boasted that there were half a million men in the North enrolled in such seditious organisations. Drastic as the Government proceedings were, the opposition to them died down before the popular conviction that strong measures were necessary, and the popular appreciation that the blood-thirsty despot " King Abraham I.," as some Democrats were pleased to call him, was not of the stuff of which despots were made and was among the least blood-thirsty men living. The civil Courts made no attempt to interfere; they said that, whatever the law, they

could not in fact resist generals commanding armies. British Courts would in many cases have declined to interfere, not on the ground that the general had the might, but on the ground that he had the right; yet, it seems, they would not quite have relinquished their hold on the matter, but would have held themselves free to consider whether the district in which martial law was exercised was materially affected by the state of war or not. The legal controversy ended in a manner hardly edifying to the layman; in the course of 1865 the Supreme Court solemnly tried out the question of the right of one Milligan to a writ of *habeas corpus*. At that time the war, the only ground on which the right could have been refused him, had for some months been ended; and nobody in court knew or cared whether Milligan was then living to enjoy his right or had been shot long before.

Save in a few cases of special public interest, Lincoln took no personal part in the actual administration of these coercive measures. So great a tax was put upon his time, and indeed his strength, by the personal consideration of cases of discipline in the army, that he could not possibly have undertaken a further labour of the sort. Moreover, he thought it more necessary for the public good to give steady support to his ministers and generals than to check their action in detail. He contended that no great injustice was likely to arise. Very likely he was wrong; not only Democrats, but men like Senator John Sherman, a strong and sensible Republican, thought him wrong. There are evil stories about the secret police under Stanton, and some records of the proceedings of the courts-martial, composed sometimes of the officers least useful at the front, are not creditable. Very likely, as John Sherman thought, the ordinary law would have met the needs of the case in many districts. The mere number of the political prisoners, who counted by thousands, proves nothing, for the least consideration of the circumstances will show that the active supporters of the Confederacy in the North must have been very numerous. Nor does it matter much that, to the horror of some

people, there were persons of station, culture, and respectability among the sufferers; persons of this kind were not likely to be exposed to charges of disloyal conduct if they were actively loyal. Obscure and ignorant men are much more likely to have become the innocent victims of spiteful accusers or vile agents of police. Doubtless this might happen; but that does not of itself condemn Lincoln for having maintained an extreme form of martial law. The particular kind of oppression that is likely to have occurred is one against which the normal procedure of justice and police in America is said to-day to provide no sufficient safeguard. It is almost certain that the regular course of law would have exposed the public weal to formidable dangers; but it by no means follows that it would have saved individuals from wrong. The risk that many individuals would be grievously wronged was at least not very great. The Government was not pursuing men for erroneous opinions, but for certain very definite kinds of action dangerous to the State. These were indeed kinds of action with which Lincoln thought ordinary Courts of justice " utterly incompetent " to deal, and he avowed that he aimed rather at preventing intended actions than at punishing them when done. To some minds this will seem to be an attitude dangerous to liberty, but he was surely justified when he said, " In such cases the purposes of men are much more easily understood than in cases of ordinary crime. The man who stands by and says nothing when the peril of his Government is discussed cannot be misunderstood. If not hindered, he is sure to help the enemy, much more if he talks ambiguously—talks for his country with ' buts ' and ' ifs ' and ' ands.' " In any case, Lincoln stood clearly and boldly for repressing speech or act, that could help the enemy, with extreme vigour and total disregard for the legalities of peace time. A little later on we shall see fully whether this imported on his part any touch whatever of the ferocity which it may seem to suggest.

The Democratic opposition which made some headway

in the first half of 1863 comprised a more extreme opposition prevailing in the West and led by Clement Vallandigham, a Congressman from Ohio, and a milder opposition led by Horatio Seymour, who from the end of 1862 to the end of 1864, when he failed of re-election, was Governor of New York State. The extreme section were often called "Copperheads," after a venomous snake of that name. Strictly, perhaps, this political term should be limited to the few who went so far as to desire the victory of the South; more loosely it was applied to a far larger number who went no further than to say that the war should be stopped. This demand, it must be observed, was based upon the change of policy shown in the Proclamation of Emancipation. "The war for the Union," said Vallandigham in Congress in January, 1863, "is in your hands a most bloody and costly failure. War for the Union was abandoned; war for the negro openly begun. With what success? Let the dead at Fredericksburg answer.—Ought this war to continue? I answer no—not a day, not an hour. What then? Shall we separate? Again I answer, no, no, no.—Stop fighting. Make an armistice. Accept at once friendly foreign mediation." And further: "The secret but real purpose of the war was to abolish slavery in the States, and with it the change of our present democratical form of government into an imperial despotism." This was in no sense treason; it was merely humbug. The alleged design to establish despotism, chiefly revealed at that moment by the liberation of slaves, had of course no existence. Equally false, as will be seen later, was the whole suggestion that any peace could have been had with the South except on the terms of separation. Vallandigham, a demagogue of real vigour, had perhaps so much honesty as is compatible with self-deception; at any rate, upon his subsequent visit to the South his intercourse with Southern leaders was conducted on the footing that the Union should be restored. But his character inspired no respect. Burnside, now commanding the troops in Ohio, held that violent denunciation of the Government in a

tone that tended to demoralise the troops was treason, since it certainly was not patriotism, and when in May, 1863, Vallandigham made a very violent and offensive speech in Ohio he had him arrested in his house at night, and sent him before a court-martial which imprisoned him. Loud protest was raised by every Democrat. This worry came upon Lincoln just after Chancellorsville. He regretted Burnside's action—later on he had to reverse the rash suppression of a newspaper by which Burnside provoked violent indignation—but on this occasion he would only say in public that he " regretted the necessity " of such action. Evidently he thought it his duty to support a well-intentioned general against a dangerous agitator. The course which after some consideration he took was of the nature of a practical joke, perhaps justified by its success. Vallandigham was indeed released; he was taken to the front and handed over to the Confederates as if he had been an exchanged prisoner of war. In reply to demands from the Democratic organisation in Ohio that Vallandigham might be allowed to return home, Lincoln offered to consent if their leaders would sign a pledge to support the war and promote the efficiency of the army. This they called an evasion. Vallandigham made his way to Canada and conducted intrigues from thence. In his absence he was put up for the governorship of Ohio in November, but defeated by a huge majority, doubtless the larger because of Gettysburg and Vicksburg. The next year he suddenly returned home, braving the chance of arrest, and, probably to his disappointment, Lincoln let him be. In reply to protests against Vallandigham's arrest which had been sent by meetings in Ohio and New York, Lincoln had written clear defences of his action, from which the foregoing account of his views on martial law has been taken. In one of them was a sentence which probably went further with the people of the North than any other : " Must I shoot a simple-minded soldier boy who deserts, while I must not touch a hair of a wily agitator who induces him to desert? " There may or may not be some fallacy

lurking here, but it must not be supposed that this sentence came from a pleader's ingenuity. It was the expression of a man really agonised by his weekly task of confirming sentences on deserters from the army.

Governor Seymour was a more presentable antagonist than Vallandigham. He did not propose to stop the war. On the contrary, his case was that the war could only be effectively carried on by a law-abiding Government, which would unite the people by maintaining the Constitution, not, as the Radicals argued, by the flagitious policy of freeing the slaves. It should be added that he was really concerned at the corruption which was becoming rife, for which war contracts gave some scope, and which, with a critic's obliviousness to the limitations of human force, he thought the most heavily-burdened Administration of its time could easily have put down. With a little imagination it is easy to understand the difficult position of the orthodox Democrats, who two years before had voted against restricting the extension of slavery, and were now asked for the sake of the Union to support a Government which was actually abolishing slavery by martial law. Also the attitude of the thoroughly self-righteous partisan is perfectly usual. Many of Governor Seymour's utterances were fair enough, and much of his conduct was patriotic enough. His main proceedings can be briefly summarised. His election as Governor in the end of 1862 was regarded as an important event, the appearance of a new leader holding an office of the greatest influence. Lincoln, assuming, as he had a right to do, the full willingness of Seymour to co-operate in prosecuting the war, did the simplest and best thing. He wrote and invited Seymour after his inauguration in March, 1863, to a personal conference with himself as to the ways in which, with their divergent views, they could best co-operate. The Governor waited three weeks before he acknowledged this letter. He then wrote and promised a full reply later. He never sent this reply. He protested energetically and firmly against the arrest of Vallandigham. In July, 1863, the Conscription Act

began to be put in force in New York city; then occurred the only serious trouble that ever did occur under the Act; and it was very serious. A mob of foreign immigrants, mainly Irish, put a forcible stop to the proceeding of the draft. It set fire to the houses of prominent Republicans, and prevented the fire brigade from saving them. It gave chase to all negroes that it met, beating some to death, stringing up others to trees and lamp-posts and burning them as they hung. It burned down an orphanage for coloured children after the police had with difficulty saved its helpless inmates. Four days of rioting prevailed throughout the city before the arrival of fresh troops restored order. After an interval of prudent length the draft was successfully carried out. Governor Seymour arrived in the city during the riots. He harangued this defiled mob in gentle terms, promising them, if they would be good, to help them in securing redress of the grievance to which he attributed their conduct. Thenceforward to the end of his term of office he persecuted Lincoln with complaints as to the unfairness of the quota imposed on certain districts under the Conscription Act. It is true that he also protested on presumably sincere constitutional grounds against the Act itself, begging Lincoln to suspend its enforcement till its validity had been determined by the Courts. As to this Lincoln most properly agreed to facilitate, if he could, an appeal to the Supreme Court, but declined, on the ground of urgent military necessity, to delay the drafts in the meantime. Seymour's obstructive conduct, however, was not confined to the intelligible ground of objection to the Act itself; it showed itself in the perpetual assertion that the quotas were unfair. No complaint as to this had been raised before the riots. It seems that a quite unintended error may in fact at first have been made. Lincoln, however, immediately reduced the quotas in question to the full extent which the alleged error would have required. Fresh complaints from Seymour followed, and so on to the end. Ultimately Seymour was invited to come to Washington and have out the

whole matter of his complaints in conference with Stanton. Like a prudent man, he again refused to face personal conference. It seems that Governor Seymour, who
was a great person in his day, was very decidedly, in the
common acceptance of the term, a gentleman. This has
been counted unto him for righteousness. It should
rather be treated as an aggravation of his very unmeritable conduct.

Thus, since the Proclamation of Emancipation the
North had again become possessed of what is sometimes
considered a necessity of good government, an organised
Opposition ready and anxious to take the place of the
existing Administration. It can well be understood that
honourable men entered into this combination, but it is
difficult to conceive on what common principle they could
hold together which would not have been disastrous in
its working. The more extreme leaders, who were likely
to prove the driving force among them, were not unfitly
satirised in a novel of the time called the " Man Without a Country." Their chance of success in fact depended
upon the ill-fortune of their country in the war and on
the irritation against the Government, which could be
aroused by that cause alone and not by such abuses as
they fairly criticised. In the latter part of 1863 the
war was going well. A great meeting of " Union men "
was summoned in August in Illinois. Lincoln was
tempted to go and speak to them, but he contented himself with a letter. Phrases in it might suggest the stump
orator, more than in fact his actual stump speeches usually
did. In it, however, he made plain in the simplest language the total fallacy of such talk of peace as had lately
become common; the Confederacy meant the Confederate
army and the men who controlled it; as a fact no suggestion of peace or compromise came from them; if it
ever came, the people should know it. In equally simple terms he sought to justify, even to supporters of the
Union who did not share his " wish that all men could
be free," his policy in regard to emancipation. In any
case, freedom had for the sake of the Union been prom-

ised to negroes who were now fighting or working for the North, " and the promise being made must be kept." As that most critical year of the war drew to a close there was a prevailing recognition that the rough but straight path along which the President groped his way was the right path, and upon the whole he enjoyed a degree of general favour which was not often his portion.

3. The War in 1864.

It is the general military opinion that before the war entered on its final stage Jefferson Davis should have concentrated all his forces for a larger invasion of the North than was ever in fact undertaken. In the Gettysburg campaign he might have strengthened Lee's army by 20,000 men if he could have withdrawn them from the forts at Charleston. Charleston, however, was threatened during 1863 by the sea and land forces of the North, in an expedition which was probably itself unwise, as Lincoln himself seems to have suspected, but which helped to divert a Confederate army. In the beginning of 1864 Davis still kept this force at Charleston; he persisted also in keeping a hold on his own State, Mississippi, with a further small army; while Longstreet still remained in the south-east corner of Tennessee, where a useful employment of his force was contemplated but none was made. The chief Southern armies with which we have to deal are that of Lee, lying south of the Rapidan, and that of Bragg, now superseded by Joseph Johnston, at Dalton, south of Chattanooga. The Confederacy, it is thought, was now in a position in which it might take long to reduce it, but the only military chance for it was concentration on one great counterstroke. This seems to have been the opinion of Lee and Longstreet. Jefferson Davis clung, even late in the year 1864, to the belief that disaster must somehow overtake any invading Northern army which pushed far. Possibly he reckoned also that the North would weary of the repeated checks in the process of conquest. Indeed, as

will be seen later, the North came near to doing so, while a serious invasion of the North, unless overwhelmingly successful, might really have revived its spirit. In any case Jefferson Davis, unlike Lincoln, had no desire to be guided by his best officers. He was for ever quarrelling with Joseph Johnston and often with Beauregard; the less capable Bragg, though removed from the West, was now installed as his chief adviser in Richmond; and the genius of Lee was not encouraged to apply itself to the larger strategy of the war.

At the beginning of 1864 an advance from Chatta-nooga southward into the heart of the Confederate country was in contemplation. Grant and Farragut wished that it should be supported by a joint military and naval attack upon Mobile, in Alabama, on the Gulf of Mexico. Other considerations on the part of the Government prevented this. In 1863 Marshal Bazaine had invaded Mexico to set up Louis Napoleon's ill-fated client the Archduke Maximilian as Emperor. As the so-called " Monroe Doctrine " (really attributable to the teaching of Hamilton and the action of John Quincy Adams, who was Secretary of State under President Monroe) declared, such an extension of European influence, more especially dynastic influence, on the American continent was highly unacceptable to the United States. Many in the North were much excited, so much so that during 1864 a preposterous resolution, which meant, if anything, war with France, was passed on the motion of one Henry Winter Davis. It was of course the business of Lincoln and of Seward, now moulded to his views, to avoid this disaster, and yet, with such dignity as the situation allowed, keep the French Government aware of the enmity which they might one day incur. They did this. But they apprehended that the French, with a footing for the moment in Mexico, had designs on Texas; and thus, though the Southern forces in Texas were cut off from the rest of the Confederacy and there was no haste for subduing them, it was thought expedient, with an eye on France, to assert the interest of

the Union in Texas. General Banks, in Louisiana, was sent to Texas with the forces which would otherwise have been sent to Mobile. His various endeavours ended in May, 1864, with the serious defeat of an expedition up the Red River. This defeat gave great annoyance to the North and made an end of Banks' reputation. It might conceivably have had a calamitous sequel in the capture by the South of Admiral Porter's river flotilla, which accompanied Banks, and the consequent undoing of the conquest of the Mississippi. As it was it wasted much force.

Before Grant could safely launch his forces southward from Chattanooga against Johnston, it was necessary to deal in some way with the Confederate force still at large in Mississippi. Grant determined to do this by the destruction of the railway system by which alone it could move eastward. For this purpose he left Thomas to hold Chattanooga, while Sherman was sent to Meridian, the chief railway centre in the Southern part of Mississippi. In February Sherman arrived there, and, though a subsidiary force, sent from Memphis on a similar but less important errand somewhat further north, met with a severe repulse, he was able unmolested to do such damage to the lines around Meridian as to secure Grant's purpose.

There was yet a further preliminary to the great final struggle. On March 1, 1864, pursuant to an Act of Congress which was necessary for this object, Lincoln conferred upon Grant the rank of Lieutenant-General, never held by any one else since Washington, for it was only brevet rank that was conferred on Scott. Therewith Grant took the command, under the President, of all the Northern armies. Grant came to Washington to receive his new honour. He had taken leave of Sherman in an interchange of letters which it is good to read; but he had intended to return to the West. Sherman, who might have desired the command in the West for himself, had unselfishly pressed him to return. He feared that the dreaded politicians would in some way hurt Grant,

and that he would be thwarted by them, become disgusted, and retire; they did hurt him, but not then, nor in the way that Sherman had expected. Grant, however, could trust Sherman to carry out the work he wanted done in the West, and he now saw that, as Lincoln might have told him and possibly did, the work he wanted done in the East must be done by him. He went West again for a few days only, to settle his plans with Sherman. Sherman with his army of 100,000 was to follow Johnston's army of about 60,000, wherever it went, till he destroyed it. Grant with his 120,000 was to keep up an equally unfaltering fight with Lee's army, also of 60,000. There was, of course, nothing original about this conception except the idea, fully present to both men's minds, of the risk and sacrifice with which it was worth while to carry it out. Lincoln and Grant had never met till this month. Grant at the first encounter was evidently somewhat on his guard. He was prepared to like Lincoln, but he was afraid of mistaken dictation from him, and determined to discourage it. Also Stanton had advised him that Lincoln, out of mere good nature, would talk unwisely of any plans discussed with him. This was probably quite unjust. Stanton, in order to keep politicians and officers in their places, was accustomed to bite off the noses of all comers. Lincoln, on the contrary, would talk to all sorts of people with a readiness which was sometimes astonishing, but there was a good deal of method in this—he learnt something from these people all the time—and he certainly had a very great power of keeping his own counsel when he chose. In any case, when Grant at the end of April left Washington for the front, he parted with Lincoln on terms of mutual trust which never afterwards varied. Lincoln in fact, satisfied as to his general purpose, had been happy to leave him to make his plans for himself. He wrote to Grant: " Not expecting to see you again before the spring campaign begins, I wish to express in this way my entire satisfaction with what you have done up to this time so far as I understand it. The particulars of your plan I neither

know nor seek to know. You are vigilant and self-reliant, and, pleased with this, I wish not to obtrude any constraints or restraints upon you. While I am very anxious that any great disaster or capture of our men in great numbers shall be avoided, I know these points are less likely to escape your attention than they would be mine. If there is anything wanting which is within my power to give, do not fail to let me know it. And now, with a brave army and a just cause, may God sustain you." Grant replied: "From my first entrance into the volunteer service of the country to the present day I have never had cause of complaint—have never expressed or implied a complaint against the Administration, or the Secretary of War, for throwing any embarrassment in the way of my vigorously prosecuting what appeared to me my duty. Indeed, since the promotion which placed me in command of all the armies, and in view of the great responsibility and importance of success, I have been astonished at the readiness with which everything asked for has been yielded, without even an explanation being asked. Should my success be less than I desire or expect, the least I can say is, the fault is not with you." At this point the real responsibility of Lincoln in regard to military events became comparatively small, and to the end of the war those events may be traced with even less detail than has hitherto been necessary.

Upon joining the Army of the Potomac Grant retained Meade, with whom he was pleased, in a somewhat anomalous position under him as commander of that army. "Wherever Lee goes," he told him, "there you will go too." His object of attack was, in agreement with the opinion which Lincoln had from an early date formed, Lee's army. If Lee could be compelled, or should choose, to shut himself up in Richmond, as did happen, then Richmond would become an object of attack, but not otherwise. Grant, however, hoped that he might force Lee to give him battle in the open. In the open or behind entrenchments, he meant to fight him, reckoning that if he lost double the number that Lee did, his own

loss could easily be made up, but Lee's would be irreparable. His hope was to a large extent disappointed. He
had to do with a greater general than himself, who, with
his men, knew every inch of a tangled country. In the
engagements which now followed, Grant's men were constantly being hurled against chosen positions, entrenched
and with the new device of wire entanglements in front
of them. "I mean," he wrote, "to fight it out on this
line if it takes all summer." It took summer, autumn,
winter, and the early spring. Once across the Rapidan
he was in the tract of scrubby jungle called the Wilder-
ness. He had hoped to escape out of this unopposed and
at the same time to turn Lee's right by a rapid march to
his own left. But he found Lee in his way. On May 5
and 6 there was stubborn and indecisive fighting, with a
loss to Grant of 17,660 and to Lee of perhaps over
10,000—from Grant's point of view something gained.
Then followed a further movement to the left to outflank Lee. Again Lee was to be found in the way in a
chosen position of his own near Spottsylvania Court
House. Here on the five days from May 8 to May 12
the heavy fighting was continued, with a total loss to
Grant of over 18,000 and probably a proportionate loss
to Lee. Another move by Grant to the left now caused
Lee to fall back to a position beyond the North Anna
River, on which an attack was made but speedily given
up. Further movements in the same general direction,
but without any such serious fighting—Grant still endeavouring to turn Lee's right, Lee still moving so as to
cover Richmond—brought Grant by the end of the month
to Cold Harbour, some ten miles east by north of Richmond, close upon the scene of McClellan's misadventures.
Meanwhile Grant had caused an expedition under General Butler to go by sea up the James, and to land a little
south of Richmond, which, with the connected fortress
of Petersburg, twenty-two miles to the south of it, had
only a weak garrison left. Butler was a man with remarkable powers of self-advertisement; he had now a
very good chance of taking Petersburg, but his expedition

failed totally. From June 1 to June 3 Grant was occupied on the most disastrous enterprise of his career, a hopeless attack upon a strong entrenched position, which, with the lesser encounters that took place within the next few days, cost the North 14,000 men, against a loss to the South which has been put as low as 1,700. It was the one battle which Grant regretted having fought. He gave up the hope of a fight with Lee on advantageous conditions outside Richmond. On June 12 he suddenly moved his army across the James to the neighbourhood of City Point, east of Petersburg. Lee must now stand siege in Richmond and Petersburg. Had he now marched north against Washington, Grant would have been after him and would have secured for his vastly larger force the battle in the open which he had so far vainly sought. Yet another disappointment followed. On July 30 an attempt was made to carry Petersburg by assault immediately after the explosion of an enormous mine. It failed with heavy loss, through the fault of the amiable but injudicious Burnside, who now passed into civil life, and of the officers under him. The siege was to be a long affair. In reality, for all the disappointment, and in spite of Grant's confessed mistake at Cold Harbour, his grim plan was progressing. The force which the South could ill spare was being worn down, and Grant was in a position in which, though he might have got there at less cost, and though the end would not be yet, the end was sure. His army was for the time a good deal shaken, and the estimation in which the West Point officers held him sank low. His own determination was quite unshaken, and, though Lincoln hinted somewhat mildly that these enormous losses ought not to recur, his confidence in Grant was unabated, too.

People in Washington who had watched all this with alternations of feeling that ended in dejection had had another trial to their nerves early in July. The Northern General Sigel, who commanded in the lower part of the Shenandoah Valley, protecting the Baltimore and Ohio Railway, had marched southward in June in pursuance

of a subsidiary part of Grant's scheme, but in a careless and rather purposeless manner. General Early, detached by Lee to deal with him, defeated him; outmanœuvred and defeated General Hunter, who was sent to supersede him; overwhelmed with superior force General Lew Wallace, who stood in his way further on; and upon July 11 appeared before Washington itself. The threat to Washington had been meant as no more than a threat, but the garrison was largely made up of recruits; reinforcements to it sent back by Grant arrived only on the same day as Early, and if that enterprising general had not wasted some previous days there might have been a chance that he could get into Washington, though not that he could hold it. As it was he attacked one of the Washington forts. Lincoln was present, exhibiting, till the officers there insisted on his retiring, the indifference to personal danger which he showed on other occasions too. The attack was soon given up, and in a few days Early had escaped back across the Potomac, leaving in Grant's mind a determination that the Shenandoah Valley should cease to be so useful to the South.

Sherman set out from Chattanooga on the day when Grant crossed the Rapidan. Joseph Johnston barred his way in one entrenched position after another. Sherman, with greater caution than Grant, or perhaps with greater facilities of ground, manœuvred him out of each position in turn, pushing him slowly back along the line of the railway towards Atlanta, the great manufacturing centre of Georgia, one hundred and twenty miles south by east from Chattanooga. Only once, towards the end of June at Kenesaw Mountain, some twenty miles north of Atlanta, did he attack Johnston's entrenchments, causing himself some unnecessary loss and failing in his direct attack on them, but probably thinking it necessary to show that he would attack whenever needed. Johnston has left a name as a master of defensive warfare, and doubtless delayed and hampered Sherman as much as he could. Jefferson Davis angrily and unwisely sent General Hood to supersede him. This less prudent officer gave

battle several times, bringing up the Confederate loss
before Atlanta fell to 34,000 against 30,000 on the other
side, and being, by great skill on Sherman's part, compelled to evacuate Atlanta on September 2.

By this time there had occurred the last and most
brilliant exploit of old Admiral Farragut, who on August
5 in a naval engagement of extraordinarily varied incident, had possessed himself of the harbour of Mobile,
with its forts, though the town remained as a stronghold
in Confederate hands and prevented a junction with Sherman which would have quite cut the Confederacy in two.

Nearer Washington, too, a memorable campaign was
in process. For three weeks after Early's unwelcome
visit, military mismanagement prevailed near Washington. Early was able to turn on his pursuers, and a further
raid, this time into Pennsylvania, took place. Grant was
too far off to exercise control except through a sufficiently
able subordinate, which Hunter was not. Halleck, as in
a former crisis, did not help matters. Lincoln, though
at this time he issued a large new call for recruits, was
unwilling any longer to give military orders. Just now
his political anxieties had reached their height. His judgment was never firmer, but friends thought his strength
was breaking under the strain. On this and on all
grounds he was certainly wise to decline direct interference in military affairs. On August 1 Grant ordered
General Philip H. Sheridan to the Shenandoah on temporary duty, expressing a wish that he should be put " in
command of all the troops in the field, with instructions
to put himself south of the enemy or follow him to the
death." Lincoln telegraphed to Grant, quoting this
despatch and adding, " This I think is exactly right; but
please look over the despatches you may have received
from here even since you made that order and see if there
is any idea in the head of any one here of putting our
army south of the enemy or following him to the death
in any direction. I repeat to you it will neither be done
nor attempted unless you watch it every day and hour and
force it." Grant now came to Hunter's army and gently

placed Sheridan in that general's place. The operations of that autumn, which established Sheridan's fame and culminated in his final defeat of Early at Cedar Creek on October 19, made him master of all the lower part of the valley. Before he retired into winter quarters he had so laid waste the resources of that unfortunate district that Richmond could no longer draw supplies from it, nor could it again support a Southern army in a sally against the North.

In the month of November Sherman began a new and extraordinary movement, of which the conception was all his own, sanctioned with reluctance by Grant, and viewed with anxiety by Lincoln, though he maintained his absolute resolve not to interfere. He had fortified himself in Atlanta, removing its civil inhabitants, in an entirely humane fashion, to places of safety, and he had secured a little rest for his army. But he lay far south in the heart of what he called "Jeff Davis' Empire," and Hood could continually harass him by attacks on his communications. Hood, now supervised by Beauregard, was gathering reinforcements, and Sherman learnt that he contemplated a diversion by invading Tennessee. Sherman determined to divide his forces, to send Thomas far back into Tennessee with sufficient men, as he calculated, to defend it, and himself with the rest of his army to set out for the eastern sea-coast, wasting no men on the maintenance of his communications, but living on the country and "making the people of Georgia feel the weight of the war." He set out for the East on November 15. Hood, at Beauregard's orders, shortly marched off for the North, where the cautious Thomas awaited events within the fortifications of Nashville. At Franklin, in the heart of Tennessee, about twenty miles south of Nashville, Hood's army suffered badly in an attack upon General Schofield, whom Thomas had left to check his advance while further reinforcements came to Nashville. Schofield fell back slowly on Thomas, Hood rashly pressing after him with a small but veteran army now numbering 44,000. Grant and the Washington author-

ities viewed with much concern an invasion which Thomas
had suffered to proceed so far. Grant had not shared
Sherman's faith in Thomas. He now repeatedly urged
him to act, but Thomas had his own views and obstinately
bided his time. Days followed when frozen sleet made
an advance impossible. Grant had already sent Logan
to supersede Thomas, and, growing still more anxious,
had started to come west himself, when the news reached
him of a battle on December 15 and 16 in which Thomas
had fallen on Hood, completely routing him, taking on
these days and in the pursuit that followed no less than
13,000 prisoners.

There was a song, "As we go marching through
Georgia," which was afterwards famous, and which Sherman could not endure. What his men most often sang,
while they actually were marching through Georgia, was
another, and of its kind a great song:—

> " John Brown's body lies amouldering in the grave,
> But his soul goes marching on.
> Glory, glory, Hallelujah."

Their progress was of the nature of a frolic, though in
one way a very stern frolic. They had little trouble from
the small and scattered Confederate forces that lay near
their route. They industriously and ingeniously destroyed
the railway track of the South, heating the rails and twisting them into knots; and the rich country of Georgia,
which had become the chief granary of the Confederates,
was devastated as they passed, for a space fifty or sixty
miles broad, by the destruction of all the produce they
could not consume. This was done under control by
organised forage parties. Reasonable measures were
taken to prevent private pillage of houses. No doubt it
happened. Sherman's able cavalry commander earned a
bad name, and " Uncle Billy," as they called him to his
face, clearly had a soft corner in his heart for the light-
hearted and light-fingered gentlemen called " bummers "
(a " bummer," says the Oxford Dictionary, " is one who
quits the ranks and goes on an independent foraging ex-

pedition on his own account"). They were, incidentally, Sherman found, good scouts. But the serious crimes committed were very few, judged by the standard of the ordinary civil population. The authentic complaints recorded relate to such matters as the smashing of a grand piano or the disappearance of some fine old Madeira. Thus the suffering caused to individuals was probably not extreme, and a long continuance of the war was rendered almost impossible. A little before Christmas Day, 1864, Sherman had captured, with slight opposition, the city of Savannah, on the Atlantic, with many guns and other spoils, and was soon ready to turn northwards on the last lap of his triumphant course. Lincoln's letter of thanks characteristically confessed his earlier unexpressed and unfulfilled fears.

Grant was proceeding all the time with his pressure on the single large fortress which Richmond and Petersburg together constituted. Its circuit was far too great for complete investment. His efforts were for a time directed to seizing the three railway lines which converged from the south on Petersburg and to that extent cutting off the supplies of the enemy. But he failed to get hold of the most important of these railways. He settled down to the slow process of entrenching his own lines securely and extending the entrenchment further and further round the south side of Petersburg. Lee was thus being forced to extend the position held by his own small army further and further. In time the lines would crack and the end come.

It need hardly be said that despair was invading the remnant of the Confederacy; supplies began to run short in Richmond, recruiting had ceased, desertion was increasing. Before the story of its long resistance closes it is better to face the gravest charge against the South. That charge relates to the misery inflicted upon many thousands of Northern prisoners in certain prisons or detention camps of the South. The alleged horrors were real and were great. The details should not be commemorated, but it is right to observe that the pitiable

condition in which the stricken survivors of this captivity returned, and the tale they had to tell, caused the bitterness which might be noted afterwards in some Northerners. The guilt lay mainly with a few subordinate but uncontrolled officials. In some degree it must have been shared by Jefferson Davis and his Administration, though a large allowance should be made for men so sorely driven. But it affords no ground whatever, as more fortunate prisoners taken by the Confederates have sometimes testified, for any general imputation of cruelty against the Southern officers, soldiers, or people. There is nothing in the record of the war which dishonours the South, nothing to restrain the tribute to its heroism which is due from a foreign writer, and which is irrepressible in the case of a writer who rejoices that the Confederacy failed.

4. *The Second Election of Lincoln:* 1864.

Having the general for whom he had long sought, Lincoln could now be in military matters little more than the most intelligent onlooker; he could maintain the attitude, congenial to him where he dealt with skilled men, that when he differed from them they probably knew better than he. This was well, for in 1864 his political anxieties became greater than they had been since war declared itself at Fort Sumter. Whole States which had belonged to the Confederacy were now securely held by the Union armies, and the difficult problem of their government was approaching its final settlement. It seemed that the war should soon end; so the question of peace was pressed urgently. Moreover, the election of a President was due in the autumn, and, strange as it is, the issue was to be whether, with victory in their grasp, the victors should themselves surrender.

It was not given to Lincoln after all to play a great part in the reconstruction of the South; that was reserved for much rougher and much weaker hands. But the lines on which he had moved from the first are of interest. West Virginia, with its solid Unionist population, was

simply allowed to form itself into an ordinary new State. But matters were not so simple where the Northern occupation was insecure, or where a tiny fraction of a State was held, or where a large part of the people leaned to the Confederacy. Military governors were of course appointed; in Tennessee this position was given to a strong Unionist, Andrew Johnson, who was already Senator for that State. In Louisiana and elsewhere Lincoln encouraged the citizens who would unreservedly accept the Union to organise State Governments for themselves. Where they did so there was friction between them and the Northern military governor who was still indispensable. There was also to the end triangular trouble between the factions in Missouri and the general commanding there. To these little difficulties, which were of course unceasing, Lincoln applied the firmness and tact which were no longer surprising in him, with a pleasing mixture of good temper and healthy irritation. But further difficulties lay in the attitude of Congress, which was concerned in the matter because each House could admit or reject the Senators or Representatives claiming to sit for a Southern State. There were questions about slavery in such States. Lincoln, as we have seen, had desired, if he could, to bring about the abolition of slavery through gradual and through local action, and he had wished to see the franchise given only to the few educated negroes. Nothing came of this, but it kept up the suspicion of Radicals in Congress that he was not sound on slavery; and, apart from slavery, the whole question of the terms on which people lately in arms against the country could be admitted as participators in the government of the country was one on which statesmen in Congress had their own very important point of view. Lincoln's main wish was that, with the greatest speed and the least heat spent on avoidable controversy, State government of spontaneous local growth should spring up in the reconquered South. " In all available ways," he had written to one of his military governors, " give the people a chance to express their wishes at these elections. Follow

forms of law as far as convenient, but at all events get
the expression of the largest number of people possible."
Above all he was afraid lest in the Southern elections to
Congress that very thing should happen which after his
death did happen. " To send a parcel of Northern men
here as representatives, elected, as would be understood
(and perhaps really so), at the point of the bayonet,
would be disgraceful and outrageous." For a time he and
Congress worked together well enough, but sharp dis-
agreement arose in 1864. He had propounded a particular plan for the reconstruction of Southern States. Senator Wade, the formidable Chairman of the Joint
Committee on the War, and Henry Winter Davis, a keen,
acrid, and fluent man who was powerful with the House,
carried a Bill under which a State could only be reconstructed on their own plan, which differed from Lincoln's.
The Bill came to Lincoln for signature in the last hours
of the session, and, amidst frightened protests from
friendly legislators then in his room, he let it lie there
unsigned, till it expired with the session, and went on with
his work. This was in July, 1864; his re-election was
at stake. The Democrats were gaining ground; he might
be giving extreme offence to the strongest Republican.
" If they choose," he said, " to make a point of this I do
not doubt that they can do harm " (indeed, those powerful men Wade and Davis now declared against his re-
election with ability and extraordinary bitterness) ; but
he continued: "At all events I must keep some consciousness of being somewhere near right. I must keep
some standard or principle fixed within myself." The
Bill would have repressed loyal efforts already made to
establish State Governments in the South. It contained
also a provision imposing the abolition of slavery on
every such reconstructed State. This was an attempt to
remedy any flaw in the constitutional effect of the Proclamation of Emancipation. But it was certainly in itself
flagrantly unconstitutional; and the only conclusive way
of abolishing slavery was the Constitutional Amendment,
for which Lincoln was now anxious. This was not a

pedantic point, for there might have been great trouble if the courts had later found a constitutional flaw in some negro's title to freedom. But the correctness of Lincoln's view hardly matters. In lots of little things, like a tired man who was careless by nature, Lincoln may perhaps have yielded to influence or acted for his political convenience in ways which may justly be censured, but it would be merely immoral to care whether he did so or did not, since at the crisis of his fate he could risk all for one scruple. In an earlier stage of his controversies with the parties he had written: "From time to time I have done and said what appeared to me proper to do and say. The public knows it all. It obliges nobody to follow me, and I trust it obliges me to follow nobody. The Radicals and Conservatives each agree with me in some things and disagree in others. I could wish both to agree with me in all things; for then they would agree with each other, and be too strong for any foe from any quarter. They, however, choose to do otherwise, and I do not question their right. I, too, shall do what seems to be my duty. I hold whoever commands in Missouri or elsewhere responsible to me and not to either Radicals or Conservatives. It is my duty to hear all; but at last I must, within my sphere, judge what to do and what to forbear."

In this same month of July, after the Confederate General Early's appearance before Washington had given Lincoln a pause from political cares, another trouble reached a point at which it is known to have tried his patience more than any other trouble of his Presidency. Peace after war is not always a matter of substituting the diplomatist for the soldier. When two sides were fighting, one for Union and the other for Independence, one or the other had to surrender the whole point at issue. In this case there might appear to have been a third possibility. The Southern States might have been invited to return to the Union on terms which admitted their right to secede again if they felt aggrieved. The invitation would in fact have been refused. But, if

it had been made and accepted, this would have been a worse surrender for the North than any mere acknowledgment that the South could not be reconquered; for national unity from that day to this would have existed on the sufferance of a factious or a foreign majority in any single State. Lincoln had faced this. He was there to restore the Union on a firm foundation. He meant to insist to the point of pedantry that, by not so much as a word or line from the President or any one seeming to act for him, should the lawful right of secession even appear to be acknowledged. Some men would have been glad to hang Jefferson Davis as a traitor, yet would have been ready to negotiate with him as with a foreign king. Lincoln, who would not have hurt one hair of his head, and would have talked things over with Mr. Davis quite pleasantly, would have died rather than treat with him on the footing that he was head of an independent Confederacy. The blood shed might have been shed for nothing if he had done so. But to many men, in the long agony of the war and its disappointments, the plain position became much obscured. The idea in various forms that by some sort of negotiation the issue could be evaded began to assert itself again and again. The delusion was freely propagated that the South was ready to give in if only Lincoln would encourage its approaches. It was sheer delusion. Jefferson Davis said frankly to the last that the Confederacy would have " independence or extermination," and though Stephens and many others spoke of peace to the electors in their own States, Jefferson Davis had his army with him, and the only result which agitation against him ever produced was that two months before the irreparable collapse the chief command under him was given to his most faithful servant Lee. But it was useless for Lincoln to expose the delusion in the plainest terms; it survived exposure and became a danger to Northern unity.

Lincoln therefore took a strange course, which generally succeeded. When honest men came to him and said that the South could be induced to yield, he proposed

to them that they should go to Jefferson Davis and see
for themselves. The Chairman of the Republican organisation ultimately approached Lincoln on this matter at
the request of a strong committee; but he was a sensible
man whom Lincoln at once converted by drafting the
precise message that would have to be sent to the Confederate President. On two earlier occasions such labourers for peace were allowed to go across the lines and talk
with Davis; it could be trusted to their honour to pretend to no authority; they had interesting talks with the
great enemy, and made religious appeals to him or entertained him with wild proposals for a joint war on
France over Mexico. They returned, converted also. But
in July Horace Greeley, the great editor, who was too
opinionated to be quite honest, was somehow convinced
that Southern agents at Niagara, who had really come
to hold intercourse with the disloyal group among the
Democrats, were " two ambassadors " from the Confederacy seeking an audience of Lincoln. He wrote to
Lincoln, begging him to receive them. Lincoln caused
Greeley to go to Niagara and see the supposed ambassadors himself. He gave him written authority to bring to
him any person with proper credentials, provided, as he
made plain in terms that perhaps were blunt, that the
basis of any negotiation should include the recognition
of the Union and the abolition of slavery. The persons
whom Greeley saw had no authority to treat about anything. Greeley in his irritation now urged Lincoln to
convey to Jefferson Davis through these mysterious men
his readiness to receive them if they were accredited. In
other words, the North was to begin suing for peace—a
thing clearly unwise, which Lincoln refused. Greeley
now involved Lincoln in a tangled controversy to which
he gave such a turn that, unless Lincoln would publish
the most passionately pacific of Greeley's letters, to the
great discouragement of the public with whom Greeley
counted, he must himself keep silent on what had passed.
He elected to keep silent while Greeley in his paper
criticised him as the person responsible for the continu-

ance of senseless bloodshed. This was publicly harmful; and, as for its private bearing, the reputation of obstinate blood-thirstiness was certain to be painful to Lincoln.

The history of Lincoln's Cabinet has a bearing upon what is to follow. He ruled his Ministers with undisputed authority, talked with them collectively upon the easiest terms, spoke to them as a headmaster to his school when they caballed against one another, kept them in some sort of unison in a manner which astonished all who knew them. Cameron had had to retire early; so did the little-known Caleb Smith, who was succeeded in his unimportant office as Secretary of the Interior by a Mr. Usher, who seems to have been well chosen. Bates, the Attorney-General, retired, weary of his work, towards the end of 1864, and Lincoln had the keen pleasure of appointing James Speed, the brother of that unforgotten and greatly honoured friend whom he honoured the more for his contentedness with private station. James Speed himself was in Lincoln's opinion " an honest man and a gentleman, and one of those well-poised men, not too common here, who are not spoiled by a big office."

Blair might be regarded as a delightful, or equally as an intolerable man. He attacked all manner of people causelessly and violently, and earned implacable dislike from the Radicals in his party. Then he frankly asked Lincoln to dismiss him whenever it was convenient. There came a time when Lincoln's re-election was in great peril, and he might, it was urged, have made it sure by dismissing Blair. It is significant that Lincoln then refused to promote his own cause by seeming to sacrifice Blair, but later on, when his own election was fairly certain, but a greater degree of unity in the Republican party was to be gained, did ask Blair to go; (Blair's quarrels, it should be added, had become more and more outrageous). So he went and immediately flung himself with enthusiasm into the advocacy of Lincoln's cause. All the men who left Lincoln remained his friends, except one who will shortly concern us. Of Lincoln's more important ministers Welles did his work for the Navy industriously but

unnoted. Stanton, on the other hand, and Lincoln's relations with Stanton are the subjects of many pages of literature. These two curious and seemingly incompatible men hit upon extraordinary methods of working together. It can be seen that Lincoln's chief care in dealing with his subordinates was to give support and to give free play to any man whose heart was in his work. In countless small matters he would let Stanton disobey him and flout him openly. ("Did Stanton tell you I was a damned fool? Then I expect I must be one, for he is almost always right and generally says what he means.") But every now and then, when he cared much about his own wish, he would step in and crush Stanton flat. Crowds of applicants to Lincoln with requests of a kind that must be granted sparingly were passed on to Stanton, pleased with the President, or mystified by his sadly observing that he had not much influence with this Administration but hoped to have more with the next. Stanton always refused them. He enjoyed doing it. Yet it seems a low trick to have thus indulged his taste for unpopularity, till one discovers that, when Stanton might have been blamed seriously and unfairly, Lincoln was very careful to shoulder the blame himself. The gist of their mutual dealings was that the hated Stanton received a thinly disguised, but quite unfailing support, and that hated or applauded, ill or well, wrong in this detail and right in that, he abode in his department and drove, and drove, and drove, and worshipped Lincoln. To Seward, who played first and last a notable part in history, and who all this time conducted foreign affairs under Lincoln without any mishap in the end, one tribute is due. When he had not a master it is said that his abilities were made useless by his egotism; yet it can be seen that, with his especial cause to be jealous of Lincoln, he could not even conceive how men let private jealousy divide them in the performance of duty.

It was otherwise with the ablest man in the Cabinet. Salmon P. Chase must really have been a good man in the days before he fell in love with his own goodness.

Lincoln and the country had confidence in his management of the Treasury, and Lincoln thought more highly
of his general ability than of that of any other man about
him.   He, for his part, distrusted and despised Lincoln.
Those who read Lincoln's important letters and speeches
see in him at once a great gentleman; there were but
few among the really well-educated men of America who
made much of his lacking some of the minor points of
gentility to which most of them were born; but of these
few Chase betrayed himself as one.   At the beginning of
1864 Chase was putting it about that he had himself no
wish to be President, but—; that of course he was loyal
to Mr. Lincoln, but—; and so forth.   He had, as indeed
he deserved, admirers who wished he should be President, and early in the year some of them expressed this
wish in a manifesto.   Chase wrote to Lincoln that this
was not his own doing; Lincoln replied that he himself
knew as little of these things " as my friends will allow
me to know."   To those who spoke to him of Chase's
intrigues he only said that Chase would in some ways
make a very good President, and he hoped they would
never have a worse President than he.   The movement in
favour of Chase collapsed very soon, and it evidently
had no effect on Lincoln.   Chase, however, was beginning to foster grievances of his own against Lincoln.
These related always to appointments in the service of
the Treasury.   He professed a horror of party influences
in appointments, and imputed corrupt motives to Lincoln
in such matters.   He shared the sound ideas of the later
civil service reformers, though he was far too easily managed by a low class of flatterers to have been of the
least use in carrying them out.   Lincoln would certainly
not at that crisis have permitted strife over civil service
reform, but some of his admirers have probably gone
too far in claiming him as a sturdy supporter of the old
school who would despise the reforming idea.   Letters
of his much earlier betray his doubts as to the old system, and he was exactly the man who in quieter times
could have improved matters with the least possible fuss

However that may be, all the tiresome circumstances of Chase's differences with him are well known, and in these instances Lincoln was clearly in the right, and Chase quarrelled only because he could not force upon him appointments that would have created fury. Once Chase was overruled and wrote his resignation. Lincoln went to him with the resignation in his hand, treated him with simple affection for a man whom he still liked, and made him take it back. Later on Chase got his own way on the whole, but was angry and sent another resignation. Some one heard of it and came to Lincoln to say that the loss of Chase would cause a financial panic. Lincoln's answer was to this effect: " Chase thinks he has become indispensable to the country; that his intimate friends know it, and he cannot comprehend why the country does not understand it. He also thinks he ought to be President; has no doubt whatever about that. It is inconceivable to him why people do not rise as one man and say so. He is a great statesman, and at the bottom a patriot. Ordinarily he discharges the duties of a public office with greater ability than any man I know. Mind, I say ' ordinarily,' but he has become irritable, uncomfortable, so that he is never perfectly happy unless he is thoroughly miserable and able to make everybody else just as uncomfortable as he is himself. He is either determined to annoy me, or that I shall pat him on the shoulder and coax him to stay. I don't think I ought to do it. I will not do it. I will take him at his word." So he did. This was at the end of June, 1864, when Lincoln's apprehensions about his own re-election were keen, and the resignation of Chase, along with the retention of Blair, seemed likely to provoke anger which was very dangerous to himself. An excellent successor to the indispensable man was soon found. Chase found more satisfaction than ever in insidious opposition to Lincoln. Lincoln's opportunity of requiting him was not yet.

The question of the Presidency loomed large from the beginning of the year to the election in November. At first, while the affairs of war seemed to be in good train,

the chief question was who should be the Republican candidate. It was obviously not a time when a President of even moderate ability and character, with all the threads in his hands, could wisely have been replaced except for overwhelming reasons. But since 1832, when Jackson had been re-elected, the practice of giving a President a second term had lapsed. It has been seen that there was friction, not wholly unnatural, between Lincoln and many of his party. The inner circles of politicians were considering what candidate could carry the country. They were doing so with great anxiety, for disaffection was growing serious in the North and the Democrats would make a good fight. They honestly doubted whether Lincoln was the best candidate, and attributed their own excited mood of criticism to the public at large. They forgot the leaning of ordinary men towards one who is already serving them honestly. Of the other possible candidates, including Chase, Frémont had the most energetic backers. Enough has been said already of his delusive attractiveness. General Butler had also some support. He was an impostor of a coarser but more useful stamp. A successful advocate in Massachusetts, he had commanded the militia of the State when they first appeared on the scene at Baltimore in 1861, and he had been in evidence ever since without sufficient opportunity till May, 1864, of proving that real military incapacity of which some of Lincoln's friends suspected him. He had a kind of resourceful impudence, coupled with executive vigour and a good deal of wit, which had made him useful in the less martial duties of his command. Generals in a war of this character were often so placed that they had little fighting to do and much civil government, and Butler, who had first treated slaves as " contraband " and had dealt with his difficulties about negroes with more heart and more sense than many generals, had to some extent earned his reputation among the Republicans. Thus of those volunteer generals who never became good soldiers he is said to have been the only one that escaped the constant process of weeding out. To the end he kept

confidently claiming higher rank in the Army, and when
he had signally failed under Grant at Petersburg he succeeded somehow in imposing himself upon that, at first
indignant, general. Nothing actually came of the danger
that the public might find a hero in this man, who was
neither scrupulous nor able, but he had so captivated experienced politicians that some continued even after Lincoln's re-election to think Butler the man whom the people would have preferred. Last but not least many were
anxious to nominate Grant. It was an innocent thought,
but Grant's merits were themselves the conclusive reason
why he should not be taken from the work he had already
in hand.

Through the early months of the year the active politicians earnestly collogued among themselves about possible candidates, and it seems there was little sign among
them of that general confidence in Lincoln which a little
while before had been recognised as prevailing in the
country. In May the small and light-headed section of
the so-called Radicals who favoured Frémont organised
for themselves a " national meeting " of some few people
at which they nominated him for the Presidency. They
had no chance of success, but they might have helped the
Democrats by carrying off some Republican votes. Besides, there are of course men who, having started as
extremists in one direction and failed, will go over to the
opposite extreme rather than moderate their aims.
Months later, when a Republican victory of some sort
became certain, unanimity among Republicans was secured; for some passions were appeased by the resignation of Blair, and Frémont was prevailed upon to withdraw. But in the meantime the Republican party had
sent its delegates to a Convention at Baltimore early in
June. This Convention met in a comparatively fortunate
hour. In spite of the open disaffection of small sections,
the Northern people had been in good spirits about the
war when Grant set out to overcome Lee. At first he was
felt to be progressing pretty well, and, though the reverse
at Cold Harbour had happened a few days before, the

size of that mishap was not yet appreciated. Ordinary citizens, called upon now and then to decide a broad and grave issue, often judge with greater calm than is possible to any but the best of the politicians and the journalists. Indeed, some serious politicians had been anxious to postpone the Convention, justly fearing that these ignorant delegates were not yet imbued with that contempt for Lincoln which they had worked up among themselves. At the Baltimore Convention the delegates of one State wanted Grant, but the nomination of Lincoln was immediate and almost unanimous. This same Convention declared for a Constitutional Amendment to abolish slavery. Lincoln would say nothing as to the choice of a candidate for the Vice-Presidency. He was right, but the result was most unhappy in the end. The Convention chose Andrew Johnson. Johnson, whom Lincoln could hardly endure, began life as a journeyman tailor. He had raised himself like Lincoln, and had performed a great part in rallying the Unionists of Tennessee. But—not to dwell upon the fact that he was drunk when he was sworn in as Vice-President—his political creed was that of bitter class-hatred, and his character degenerated into a weak and brutal obstinacy. This man was to succeed Lincoln. Lincoln, in his letter to accept the nomination, wrote modestly, refusing to take the decision of the Convention as a tribute to his peculiar fitness for his post, but was " reminded in this connection of a story of an old Dutch farmer, who remarked to a companion that it was not best to swap horses when crossing a stream."

It remained possible that the dissatisfied Republicans would revolt later and put another champion in the field. But now attention turned to the Democrats. Their Convention was to meet at Chicago at the end of August, and in the interval the North entered upon the period of deepest mental depression that came to it during the war. It is startling to learn now that in the course of that year, when the Confederacy lay like a nut in the nutcrackers, when the crushing of its resistance might indeed require a little stronger pressure than was ex-

pected, and the first splitting in its hard substance might not come on the side on which it was looked for, but when no wise man could have a doubt as to the end, the victorious people were inclined to think that the moment had come for giving in. " In this purpose to save the country and its liberties," said Lincoln, " no class of people seem so nearly unanimous as the soldiers in the field and the sailors afloat. Do they not have the hardest of it? Who should quail while they do not?" Yet there is conclusive authority for saying that there was now more quailing in the North than there had ever been before. When the war had gone on long, checks to the course of victory shook the nerves of people at home more than crushing defeats had shaken them in the first two years of the struggle, and men who would have wrapped the word " surrender " in periphrasis went about with surrender in their hearts. Thus the two months that went before the great rally of the Democrats at Chicago were months of good omen for a party which, however little the many honourable men in its ranks were willing to face the fact, must base its only hope upon the weakening of the national will. For public attention was turned away from other fields of war and fixed upon the Army of the Potomac. Sherman drove back Johnston, and routed Hood; Farragut at Mobile enriched the annals of the sea; but what told upon the imagination of the North was that Grant's earlier progress was followed by the definite failure of his original enterprise against Lee's army, by Northern defeats on the Shenandoah and an actual dash by the South against Washington, by the further failure of Grant's first assault upon Petersburg, and by hideous losses and some demoralisation in his army. The candidate that the Democrats would put forward and the general principle of their political strategy were well known many weeks before their Convention met; and the Republicans already despaired of defeating them. In the Chicago Convention there were men, apparently less reputable in character than their frank attitude suggests, who were outspoken against the war; their

leader was Vallandigham. There were men who spoke boldly for the war, but more boldly against emancipation and the faults of the Government; their leader was Seymour, talking with the accent of dignity and of patriotism. Seymour, for the war, presided over the Convention; Vallandigham, against the war, was the master spirit in its debates. It was hard for such men, with any saving of conscience, to combine. The mode of combination which they discovered is memorable in the history of faction. First they adopted a platform which meant peace; then they adopted a candidate intended to symbolise successful war. They resolved " that this Convention does explicitly declare, as the sense of the American people, that after four years of failure to restore the Union by the experiment of war . . . justice, humanity, liberty, and the public welfare demand that immediate efforts be made for a cessation of hostilities, with a view to an ultimate convention of the States or other peaceable means, to the end that at the earliest practicable moment peace may be restored on the basis of the Federal Union of the States." The fallacy which named the Union as the end while demanding as a means the immediate cessation of hostilities needs no demonstration. The resolution was thus translated: " Resolved that the war is a failure "; and the translation had that trenchant accuracy which is often found in American popular epigram. The candidate chosen was McClellan; McClellan in set terms repudiated the resolution that the war was a failure, and then accepted the candidature. He meant no harm to the cause of the Union, but he meant no definite and clearly conceived good. Electors might now vote Democratic because the party was peaceful or because the candidate was a warrior. The turn of fortune was about to arrest this combination in the really formidable progress of its crawling approach to power. Perhaps it was not only, as contemporary observers thought, events in the field that began within a few days to make havoc with the schemes of McClellan and his managers. Perhaps if the patience of the North had been tried a

but feel that the weal or woe of the nation will be de‹ cided in November. There is no proposal offered by any wing of the Democratic party but that must result in the permanent destruction of the Union." He would have been well content to make place for Grant if Grant had finished his work. But that work was delayed, and then Lincoln became greatly troubled by the movement to force Grant, the general whom he had at last found, into politics with his work undone; for all would have been lost if McClellan had come in with the war still progressing badly. Lincoln had been invited in June to a gathering in honour of Grant, got up with the thinly disguised object of putting the general forward as his rival. He wrote, with true diplomacy: " It is impossible for me to attend. I approve nevertheless of whatever may tend to strengthen and sustain General Grant and the noble armies now under his command. He and his brave soldiers are now in the midst of their great trial, and I trust that at your meeting you will so shape your good words that they may turn to men and guns, moving to his and their support." In August he told his mind plainly to Grant's friend Eaton. He never dreamed for a moment that Grant would willingly go off into politics with the military situation still insecure, and he believed that no possible pressure could force Grant to do so; but on this latter question he wished to make himself sure; with a view to future military measures he really needed to be sure of it. Eaton saw Grant, and in the course of conversation very tactfully brought to Grant's notice the designs of his would-be friends. " We had," writes Eaton, " been talking very quietly, but Grant's reply came in an instant and with a violence for which I was not prepared. He brought his clenched fists down hard on the strap arms of his camp chair, ' They can't do it. They can't compel me to do it.' Emphatic gesture was not a strong point with Grant. ' Have you said this to the President?' I asked. ' No,' said Grant. ' I have not thought it worth while to assure the President of my opinion. I consider it as important for the cause that

leader was Vallandigham. There were men who spoke boldly for the war, but more boldly against emancipation and the faults of the Government; their leader was Seymour, talking with the accent of dignity and of patriotism. Seymour, for the war, presided over the Convention; Vallandigham, against the war, was the master spirit in its debates. It was hard for such men, with any saving of conscience, to combine. The mode of combination which they discovered is memorable in the history of faction. First they adopted a platform which meant peace; then they adopted a candidate intended to symbolise successful war. They resolved " that this Convention does explicitly declare, as the sense of the American people, that after four years of failure to restore the Union by the experiment of war . . . justice, humanity, liberty, and the public welfare demand that immediate efforts be made for a cessation of hostilities, with a view to an ultimate convention of the States or other peaceable means, to the end that at the earliest practicable moment peace may be restored on the basis of the Federal Union of the States." The fallacy which named the Union as the end while demanding as a means the immediate cessation of hostilities needs no demonstration. The resolution was thus translated: " Resolved that the war is a failure "; and the translation had that trenchant accuracy which is often found in American popular epigram. The candidate chosen was McClellan; McClellan in set terms repudiated the resolution that the war was a failure, and then accepted the candidature. He meant no harm to the cause of the Union, but he meant no definite and clearly conceived good. Electors might now vote Democratic because the party was peaceful or because the candidate was a warrior. The turn of fortune was about to arrest this combination in the really formidable progress of its crawling approach to power. Perhaps it was not only, as contemporary observers thought, events in the field that began within a few days to make havoc with the schemes of McClellan and his managers. Perhaps if the patience of the North had been tried a

little longer the sense of the people would still have recoiled from the policy of the Democrats, which had now
been defined in hard outline. As a matter of fact it was
only in the months while the Chicago Convention was still
impending and for a few days or weeks after it had actually taken place that the panic of the Republicans lasted.
But during that time the alarm among them was very
great, whether it was wholly due to the discouragement
of the people about the war or originated among the
leaders and was communicated to their flock. Sagacious
party men reported from their own neighbourhoods that
there was no chance of winning the election. In one
quarter or another there was talk of setting aside Lincoln
and compelling Grant to be a candidate. About August
12 Lincoln was told by Thurlow Weed, the greatest of
party managers, that his election was hopeless. Ten days
later he received the same assurance from the central Republican Committee through their chairman, Raymond,
together with the advice that he should make overtures
for peace.

Supposing that in the following November McClellan
should have been elected, and that in the following March
he should have come into office with the war unfinished,
it seems now hardly credible that he would have returned
to slavery, or at least disbanded without protection the
150,000 negroes who were now serving the North. Lincoln, however, seriously believed that this was the course
to which McClellan's principles and those of his party
committed him, and that (policy and honour apart) this
would have been for military reasons fatal. McClellan
had repudiated the Peace Resolution, but his followers
and his character were to be reckoned with rather than
his words, and indeed his honest principles committed him
deeply to some attempt to reverse Lincoln's policy as to
slavery, and he clearly must have been driven into negotiations with the South. The confusion which must inevitably be created by attempts to satisfy the South, when
it was in no humour of moderation, and by the fury which
yielding would have provoked in half the people of the

North, was well and tersely described by Grant in a letter to a friend, which that friend published in support of Lincoln. At a fair at Philadelphia for the help of the wounded Lincoln said: "We accepted this war; we did not begin it. We accepted it for an object, and when that object is accomplished the war will end, and I hope to God that it will never end until that object is accomplished." Whatever the real mind of McClellan and of the average Democrat may have been, it was not this; and the posterity of Mr. Facing-both-ways may succeed in an election, but never in war or the making of lasting peace.

Lincoln looked forward with happiness, after he was actually re-elected, to the quieter pursuits of private life which might await him in four years' time. He looked forward not less happily to a period of peace administration first, and there can be no doubt that he would have prized as much as any man the highest honour that his countrymen could bestow, a second election to the Presidency. But, even in a smaller man who had passed through such an experience as he had and was not warped by power, these personal wishes might well have been merged in concern for the cause in hand. There is everything to indicate that they were completely so in his case. A President cannot wisely do much directly to promote his own re-election, but he appears to have done singularly little. At the beginning of 1864, when the end of the war seemed near, and the election of a Republican probable, he may well have thought that he would be the Republican candidate, but he had faced the possible choice of Chase very placidly, and of Grant he said, " If he takes Richmond let him have the Presidency." It was another matter when the war again seemed likely to drag on and a Democratic President might come in before the end of it. An editor who visited the over-burdened President in August told him that he needed some weeks of rest and seclusion. But he said, " I cannot fly from my thoughts. I do not think it is personal vanity or ambition, though I am not free from those infirmities, but I cannot

but feel that the weal or woe of the nation will be decided in November. There is no proposal offered by any
wing of the Democratic party but that must result in the
permanent destruction of the Union." He would have
been well content to make place for Grant if Grant had
finished his work. But that work was delayed, and then
Lincoln became greatly troubled by the movement to
force Grant, the general whom he had at last found, into
politics with his work undone; for all would have been
lost if McClellan had come in with the war still progressing badly. Lincoln had been invited in June to a gathering in honour of Grant, got up with the thinly disguised
object of putting the general forward as his rival. He
wrote, with true diplomacy: " It is impossible for me to
attend. I approve nevertheless of whatever may tend to
strengthen and sustain General Grant and the noble
armies now under his command. He and his brave soldiers are now in the midst of their great trial, and I trust
that at your meeting you will so shape your good words
that they may turn to men and guns, moving to his and
their support." In August he told his mind plainly to
Grant's friend Eaton. He never dreamed for a moment
that Grant would willingly go off into politics with the
military situation still insecure, and he believed that no
possible pressure could force Grant to do so; but on this
latter question he wished to make himself sure; with a
view to future military measures he really needed to be
sure of it. Eaton saw Grant, and in the course of conversation very tactfully brought to Grant's notice the
designs of his would-be friends. " We had," writes
Eaton, " been talking very quietly, but Grant's reply came
in an instant and with a violence for which I was not prepared. He brought his clenched fists down hard on the
strap arms of his camp chair, ' They can't do it. They
can't compel me to do it.' Emphatic gesture was not a
strong point with Grant. ' Have you said this to the
President?' I asked. ' No,' said Grant. ' I have not
thought it worth while to assure the President of my
opinion. I consider it as important for the cause that

he should be elected as that the army should be successful in the field.' "   " 1 told you," said Lincoln afterwards, " they could not get him to run till he had closed out the rebellion."   Since the great danger was now only that McClellan would become President in March, there was but one thing to do—to try and finish the war before then. Raymond's advice in favour of negotiations with the South now came, and Lincoln's mode of replying to this has been noticed.   Rumours were afloat that if McClellan won in November there would be an attempt to bring him irregularly into power at once.   Lincoln let it be known that he should stay at his post at all costs till the last lawful day.   On August 23, in that curious way in which deep emotion showed itself with him, he wrote a resolution upon a paper, which he folded and asked his ministers to endorse with their signatures without reading it. They all wrote their names on the back of it, ready, if that were possible, to commit themselves blindly to support of him in whatever he had resolved; a great tribute to him and to themselves.   He sealed it up and put it away.

How far in this dark time the confidence of the people had departed from Lincoln no one can tell.   It might be too sanguine a view of the world to suppose that they would have been proof against what may be called a conspiracy to run him down.   There were certainly quarters in which the perception of his worth came soon and remained.   Not all those who are poor or roughly brought up were among those plain men whose approval Lincoln desired and often expected; but at least the plain man does exist and the plain people did read Lincoln's words. The soldiers of the armies in the East by this time knew Lincoln well, and there were by now, as we shall see, in every part of the North, honest parents who had gone to Washington, and entered the White House very sad, and came out very happy, and taken their report of him home. No less could there be found, among those to whom America had given the greatest advantages that birth and upbringing can offer, families in which, when Lincoln died, a daughter could write to her father as Lady Harcourt

(then Miss Lily Motley) wrote: " I echo your ' thank God ' that we always appreciated him before he was taken from us." But if we look at the political world, we find indeed noble exceptions such as that of Charles Sumner among those who had been honestly perplexed by Lincoln's attitude on slavery; we have to allow for the feelings of some good State Governor who had come to him with a tiresome but serious proposition and been adroitly parried with an untactful and coarse apologue; yet it remains to be said that a thick veil, woven of self-conceit and half-education, blinded most politicians to any rare quality in Lincoln, and blinded them to what was due in decency to any man discharging his task. The evidence collected by Mr. Rhodes as to the tone prevailing in 1864 at Washington and among those in touch with Washington suggests that strictly political society was on the average as poor in brain and heart as the court of the most decadent European monarchy. It presents a stern picture of the isolation, on one side at least, in which Lincoln had to live and work.

A little before this crowning period of Lincoln's career Walt Whitman described him as a man in the streets of Washington could see him, if he chose. He has been speaking of the cavalry escort which the President's advisers insisted should go clanking about with him. " The party," he continues, " makes no great show in uniform or horses. Mr. Lincoln on the saddle generally rides a good-sized, easy-going grey horse, is dressed in plain black, somewhat rusty and dusty, and looks about as ordinary in attire, etc., as the commonest man. The entirely unornamental *cortège* arouses no sensation; only some curious stranger stops and gazes. I see very plainly Abraham Lincoln's dark brown face, with the deep-cut lines, the eyes always to me with a deep latent sadness in the expression. We have got so that we exchange bows, and very cordial ones. Sometimes the President goes and comes in an open barouche " (not, the poet intimates, a very smart turn-out). " Sometimes one of his sons, a boy of ten or twelve, accompanies him, riding at his right

on a pony. They passed me once very close, and I saw the President in the face fully as they were moving slowly, and his look, though abstracted, happened to be directed steadily in my eye. He bowed and smiled, but far beneath his smile I noticed well the expression I have alluded to. None of the artists or pictures has caught the deep though subtle and indirect expression of this man's face. There is something else there. One of the great portrait painters of two or three centuries ago is needed."

The little boy on the pony was Thomas, called "Tad," a constant companion of his father's little leisure, now dead. An elder boy, Robert, has lived to be welcomed as Ambassador in this country, and was at this time a student at Harvard. Willie, a clever and lovably mischievous child, "the chartered libertine of the White House" for a little while, had died at the age of twelve in the early days of 1862, when his father was getting so impatient to stir McClellan into action. These and a son who had long before died in infancy were the only children of Mr. and Mrs. Lincoln. Little has been made public concerning them, but enough to convey the impression of a wise and tender father, trusted by his children and delighting in them. John Nicolay, his loyal and capable secretary, and the delightful John Hay must be reckoned on the cheerful side—for there was one—of Lincoln's daily life. The life of the home at the White House, and sometimes in summer at the "Soldiers' Home" near Washington, was simple, and in his own case (not in that of his guests) regardless of the time, sufficiency, or quality of meals. He cannot have given people much trouble, but he gave some to the guard who watched him, themselves keenly watched by Stanton; for he loved, if he could, to walk alone from his midnight conferences at the War Department to the White House or the Soldiers' Home. The barest history of the events with which he dealt is proof enough of long and hard and anxious working days, which continued with hardly a break through four years. In that history many a complication has here been barely glanced at or clean left out;

in this year, for example, the difficulty about France and Mexico and the failure of the very estimable Banks in Texas have been but briefly noted. And there must be remembered, in addition, the duty of a President to be accessible to all people, a duty which Lincoln especially strove to fulfil.

Apart from formal receptions, the stream of callers on him must have given Lincoln many compensations for its huge monotony. Very odd, and sometimes attractive, samples of human nature would come under his keen eye. Now and then a visitor came neither with a troublesome request, nor for form's sake or for curiosity, but in simple honesty to pay a tribute of loyalty or speak a word of good cheer which Lincoln received with unfeigned gratitude.   Farmers and back-country folk, of the type he could best talk with, came and had more time than he ought to have spared bestowed on them. At long intervals there came a friend of very different days. Some ingenious men, for instance, fitted out Dennis Hanks in a new suit of clothes and sent him as their ambassador to plead for certain political offenders. It is much to be feared that they were more successful than they deserved, though Stanton intervened and Dennis, when he had seen him, favoured his old companion, the President, with advice to dismiss that minister. But the immense variety of puzzling requests to be dealt with in such interviews must have made heavy demands upon a conscientious and a kind man, especially if his conscience and his kindness were, in small matters, sometimes at variance. Lincoln sent a multitude away with that feeling, so grateful to poor people, that at least they had received such hearing as it was possible to give them; and in dealing with the applications which imposed the greatest strain on himself he made an ineffaceable impression upon the memory of his countrymen.

The American soldier did not take naturally to discipline. Death sentences, chiefly for desertion or for sleeping or other negligence on the part of sentries, were continually being passed by courts-martial. In some cases of

at some period these used to come before the President
on a stated day of the week, of which Lincoln would often
speak with horror. He was continually being appealed
to in relation to such sentences by the father or mother
of the culprit, or some friend. At one time, it may be, he
was too ready with pardon; " You do not know," he said,
" how hard it is to let a human being die, when you feel
that a stroke of your pen will save him." Butler used to
write to him that he was destroying the discipline of the
army. A letter of his to Meade shows clearly that, later
at least, he did not wish to exercise a merely cheap and
inconsiderate mercy. The import of the numberless pardon stories really is that he would spare himself no
trouble to enquire, and to intervene wherever he could
rightly give scope to his longing for clemency. A Congressman might force his way into his bedroom in the
middle of the night, rouse him from his sleep to bring to
his notice extenuating facts that had been overlooked, and
receive the decision, " Well, I don't see that it will do him
any good to be shot." It is related that William Scott, a
lad from a farm in Vermont, after a tremendous march
in the Peninsula campaign, volunteered to do double
guard duty to spare a sick comrade, slept at his post, was
caught, and was under sentence of death, when the President came to the army and heard of him. The President
visited him, chatted about his home, looked at his
mother's photograph, and so forth. Then he laid his
hands on the boy's shoulders and said with a trembling
voice, " My boy, you are not going to be shot. I believe
you when you tell me that you could not keep awake. I
am going to trust you and send you back to the regiment.
But I have been put to a great deal of trouble on your
account. . . . Now what I want to know is, how are
you going to pay my bill? " Scott told afterwards how
difficult it was to think, when his fixed expectation of death
was suddenly changed; but how he managed to master
himself, thank Mr. Lincoln and reckon up how, with his
pay and what his parents could raise by mortgage on their
farm and some help from his comrades, he might pay the

bill if it were not more than five or six hundred dollars.
" But it is a great deal more than that," said the President. " My bill is a very large one. Your friends cannot pay it, nor your bounty, nor the farm, nor all your comrades. There is only one man in the world who can pay it, and his name is William Scott. If from this day William Scott does his duty, so that, when he comes to die, he can look me in the face as he does now and say, ' I have kept my promise and I have done my duty as a soldier,' then my debt will be paid. Will you make the promise and try to keep it?" And William Scott did promise; and, not very long after, he was desperately wounded, and he died, but not before he could send a message to the President that he had tried to be a good soldier, and would have paid his debt in full if he had lived, and that he died thinking of Lincoln's kind face and thanking him for the chance he gave him to fall like a soldier in battle. If the story is not true—and there is no reason whatever to doubt it—still it is a remarkable man of whom people spin yarns of that kind.

When Lincoln's strength became visibly tried friends often sought to persuade him to spare himself the needless, and to him very often harrowing, labour of incessant interviews. They never succeeded. Lincoln told them he could not forget what he himself would feel in the place of the many poor souls who came to him desiring so little and with so little to get. But he owned to the severity of the strain. He was not too sensitive to the ridicule and reproach that surrounded him. " Give yourself no uneasiness," he had once said to some one who had sympathised with him over some such annoyance, " I have endured a great deal of ridicule without much malice, and have received a great deal of kindness not quite free from ridicule. I am used to it." But the gentle nature that such words express, and that made itself deeply felt by those that were nearest him, cannot but have suffered from want of appreciation. With all this added to the larger cares, which before the closing phases of the war opened had become so intense, Lincoln must

have been taxed near to the limit of what men have endured without loss of judgment, or loss of courage or loss of ordinary human feeling. There is no sign that any of these things happened to him; the study of his record rather shows a steady ripening of mind and character to the end. It has been seen how throughout his previous life the melancholy of his temperament impressed those who had the opportunity of observing it. A colleague of his at the Illinois bar has told how on circuit he sometimes came down in the morning and found Lincoln sitting alone over the embers of the fire, where he had sat all night in sad meditation, after an evening of jest apparently none the less hilarious for his total abstinence. There was no scope for this brooding now, and in a sense the time of his severest trial cannot have been the saddest time of Lincoln's life. It must have been a cause not of added depression but of added strength that he had long been accustomed to face the sternest aspect of the world. He had within his own mind two resources, often, perhaps normally, associated together, but seldom so fully combined as with him. In his most intimate circle he would draw upon his stores of poetry, particularly of tragedy; often, for instance, he would recite such speeches as Richard II.'s:

> " For God's sake let us sit upon the ground
> And tell sad stories of the death of kings.
> . . . . . All murdered."

Slighter acquaintances saw, day by day, another element in his thoughts, the companion to this; for the hardly interrupted play of humour in which he found relief continued to help him to the end. Whatever there was in it either of mannerism or of coarseness, no one can grudge it him; it is an oddity which endears. The humour of real life fades in reproduction, but Lincoln's, there is no doubt, was a vein of genuine comedy, deep, rich, and unsoured, of a larger human quality than marks the brilliant works of literary American humorists. It was, like the comedy of Shakespeare, plainly if unaccountably akin with the

graver and grander strain of thought and feeling that inspired the greatest of his speeches. Physically his splendid health does not seem to have been impaired beyond recovery. But it was manifestly near to breaking; and the " deep-cut lines " were cut still deeper, and the long legs were always cold.

The cloud over the North passed very suddenly. The North indeed paid the penalty of a nation which is spared the full strain of a war at the first, and begins to discover its seriousness when the hope of easy victory has been many times dashed down. It has been necessary to dwell upon the despondency which at one time prevailed; but it would be hard to rate too highly the military difficulty of the conquest undertaken by the North, or the trial involved to human nature by perseverance in such a task. If the depression during the summer was excessive, as it clearly was, at least the recovery which followed was fully adequate to the occasion which produced it. On September 2 Sherman telegraphed, "Atlanta is ours and fairly won." The strategic importance of earlier successes may have been greater, but the most ignorant man who looked at a map could see what it signified that the North could occupy an important city in the heart of Georgia. Then they recalled Farragut's victory of a month before. Then there followed, close to Washington, putting an end to a continual menace, stirring and picturesquely brilliant beyond other incidents of the war, Sheridan's repeated victories in the Shenandoah Valley. The war which had been " voted a failure " was evidently not a failure. At the same time men of high character conducted a vigorous campaign of speeches for Lincoln. General Schurz, the German revolutionary Liberal, who lived to tell Bismarck at his table that he still preferred democracy to his amused host's method of government, sacrificed his command in the Army—for Lincoln told him it could not be restored—to speak for Lincoln. Even Chase was carried away, and after months of insidious detraction, went for Lincoln on the stump. In the elections in November Lincoln was elected by an enormous popular majority,

giving him 212 out of the 233 votes in the electoral college, where in form the election is made. Three Northern States only, one of them his native State, had gone against him. He made some little speeches to parties which came to "serenade" him; some were not very formal speeches, for, as he said, he was now too old to "care much about the mode of doing things." But one was this: "It has long been a grave question whether any Government not too strong for the liberties of its people can be strong enough to maintain its existence in great emergencies. On this point the present rebellion brought our Government to a severe test, and a Presidential election occurring in regular course during the rebellion added not a little to the strain. But we cannot have a free Government without elections; and if the rebellion could force us to forego or postpone a national election it might fairly claim to have already conquered and ruined us. But the election along with its incidental and undesirable strife has done good too. It has demonstrated that a people's Government can sustain a national election in the midst of a great civil war. Until now it has not been known to the world that this was a possibility. But the rebellion continues, and now that the election is over may not all have a common interest to reunite in a common effort to save our common country? For my own part I have striven and shall strive to avoid placing any obstacle in the way. So long as I have been here I have not willingly planted a thorn in any man's bosom. While I am duly sensible to the high compliment of a re-election, and duly grateful as I trust to Almighty God for having directed my countrymen to a right conclusion, as I think, for their good, it adds nothing to my satisfaction that any man may be disappointed by the result. May I ask those who have not differed from me to join with me in this same spirit towards those who have? And now let me close by asking three hearty cheers for our brave soldiers and seamen, and their gallant and skilful commanders."

In the Cabinet he brought out the paper that he had

sealed up in the dark days of August; he reminded his ministers of how they had endorsed it unread, and he read it them. Its contents ran thus: " This morning, as for some days past, it seems exceedingly probable that this Administration will not be re-elected. Then it will be my duty to so co-operate with the President-elect as to save the Union between the election and the inauguration, as he will have secured his election on such ground that he cannot possibly save it afterwards." Lincoln explained what he had intended to do if McClellan had won. He would have gone to him and said, " General, this election shows that you are stronger, have more influence with the people of this country than I "; and he would have invited him to co-operate in saving the Union now, by using that great influence to secure from the people the willing enlistment of enough recruits. "And the general," said Seward, " would have said, ' Yes, yes '; and again the next day, when you spoke to him about it, ' Yes, yes '; and so on indefinitely, and he would have done nothing."

" Seldom in history," wrote Emerson in a letter after the election, " was so much staked upon a popular vote. I suppose never in history."

And to those Americans of all classes and in all districts of the North, who had set their hearts and were giving all they had to give to preserve the life of the nation, the political crisis of 1864 would seem to have been the most anxious moment of the war. It is impossible—it must be repeated—to guess how great the danger really was that their popular government might in the result betray the true and underlying will of the people; for in any country (and in America perhaps more than most) the average of politicians, whose voices are most loudly heard, can only in a rough and approximate fashion be representative. But there is in any case no cause for surprise that the North should at one time have trembled. Historic imagination is easily, though not one whit too deeply, moved by the heroic stand of the South. It is only after the effort to understand the light

in which the task of the North has presented itself to capable soldiers, that a civilian can perceive what sustained resolution was required if, though far the stronger, it was to make its strength tell.   Notwithstanding the somewhat painful impression which the political chronicle of this time at some points gives, it is the fact that the wisest Englishmen who were in those days in America and had means of observing what passed have retained a lasting sense of the constancy, under trial, of the North.

CHAPTER XII

THE END

ON December 6, 1864, Lincoln sent the last of his Annual Messages to Congress. He treated as matter for oblivion the "impugning of motives and heated controversy as to the proper means of advancing the Union cause," which had played so large a part in the Presidential election and the other elections of the autumn. For, as he said, " on the distinct issue of Union or no Union the politicians have shown their instinctive knowledge that there is no diversity among the people." This was accurate as well as generous, for though many Democrats had opposed the war, none had avowed that for the sake of peace he would give up the Union. Passing then to the means by which the Union could be made to prevail he wrote: " On careful consideration of all the evidence accessible it seems to me that no attempt at negotiation with the insurgent leader could result in any good. He would accept nothing short of severance of the Union—precisely what we will not and cannot give. Between him and us the issue is distinct, simple, and inflexible. It is an issue which can only be tried by war and decided by victory. The abandonment of armed resistance to the national authority on the part of the insurgents is the only indispensable condition to ending the war on the part of the Government." To avoid a possible misunderstanding he added that not a single person who was free by the terms of the Emancipation Proclamation or of any Act of Congress would be returned to slavery while he held the executive authority. " If the people should by whatever mode or means make it an executive duty to re-enslave such persons, another, and not I, must be their instrument to perform it." This last

sentence was no meaningless flourish; the Constitutional Amendment prohibiting slavery could not be passed for some time, and might conceivably be defeated; in the meantime the Courts might possibly have declared any negro in the Southern States a slave; Lincoln's words let it be seen that they would have found themselves without an arm to enforce their decision. But in fact there was no longer an issue with the South as to abolition. Jefferson Davis had himself declared that slavery was gone, for most slaves had now freed themselves, and that he for his part troubled very little over that. There remained, then, no issue between North and South except that between Independence and Union.

On the same day that he sent his annual message Lincoln gave himself a characteristic pleasure by another communication which he sent to the Senate. Old Roger Taney of the Dred Scott case had died in October; the Senate was now requested to confirm the President's nomination of a new Chief Justice to succeed him; and the President had nominated Chase. Chase's reputation as a lawyer had seemed to fit him for the position, but the well informed declared that, in spite of some appearances on the platform for Lincoln he still kept " going around peddling his griefs in private ears and sowing dissatisfaction against Lincoln." So in spite of Lincoln's pregnant remark on this subject that he " did not believe in keeping any man under," nobody supposed that Lincoln would appoint him. Sumner and Congressman Alley of Massachusetts had indeed gone to Lincoln to urge the appointment. " We found, to our dismay," Alley relates, " that the President had heard of the bitter criticisms of Mr. Chase upon himself and his Administration. Mr. Lincoln urged many of Chase's defects, to discover, as we afterwards learned, how his objection could be answered. We were both discouraged and made up our minds that the President did not mean to appoint Mr. Chase. It really seemed too much to expect of poor human nature." One morning Alley again saw the President. " I have something to tell you that will make you

happy," said Lincoln. " I have just sent Mr. Chase word
that he is to be appointed Chief Justice, and you are the
first man I have told of it." Alley said something natural
about Lincoln's magnanimity, but was told in reply what
the only real difficulty had been. Lincoln from his " convictions of duty to the Republican party and the country " had always meant to appoint Chase, subject to one
doubt which he had revolved in his mind till he had settled it. This doubt was simply whether Chase, beset as
he was by a craving for the Presidency which he could
never obtain, would ever really turn his attention with a
will to becoming the great Chief Justice that Lincoln
thought he could be. Lincoln's occasional failures of
tact had sometimes a noble side to them; he even thought
now of writing to Chase and telling him with simple
seriousness where he felt his temptation lay, and he with
difficulty came to see that this attempt at brotherly frankness would be misconstrued by a suspicious and jealous
man. Charles Sumner, Chase's advocate on this occasion, was all this time the most weighty and the most
pronounced of those Radicals who were beginning to
press for unrestricted negro suffrage in the South and in
general for a hard and inelastic scheme of " reconstruction," which they would have imposed on the conquered
South without an attempt to conciliate the feeling of the
vanquished or to invite their co-operation in building up
the new order. He was thus the chief opponent of that
more tentative, but as is now seen, more liberal and more
practical policy which lay very close to Lincoln's heart;
enough has been said of him to suggest too that this
grave person, bereft of any glimmering of fun, was in
one sense no congenial companion for Lincoln. But he
was stainlessly unselfish and sincere, and he was the
politician above all others in Washington with whom
Lincoln most gladly and most successfully maintained
easy social intercourse. And, to please him in little ways,
Lincoln would disentangle his long frame from the
" grotesque position of comfort " into which he had
twisted it in talk with some other friend, and would as-

sume in an instant a courtly demeanour when Sumner was about to enter his room.

On January 31, 1865, the resolution earlier passed by the Senate for a Constitutional Amendment to prohibit slavery was passed by the House of Representatives, as Lincoln had eagerly desired, so that the requisite voting of three quarters of the States in its favour could now begin. Before that time the Confederate Congress had, on March 13, 1865, closed its last, most anxious and distracted session by passing an Act for the enlistment of negro volunteers, who were to become free on enlistment. As a military measure it was belated and inoperative, but nothing could more eloquently have marked the practical extinction of slavery which the war had wrought than the consent of Southern legislators to convert the remaining slaves into soldiers.

The military operations of 1865 had proceeded but a very little way when the sense of what they portended was felt among the Southern leaders in Richmond. The fall of that capital itself might be hastened or be delayed; Lee's army if it escaped from Richmond might prolong resistance for a shorter or for a longer time, but Sherman's march to the sea, and the far harder achievements of the same kind which he was now beginning, made the South feel, as he knew it would feel, that not a port, not an arsenal, not a railway, not a corn district of the South lay any longer beyond the striking range of the North. Congressmen and public officials in Richmond knew that the people of the South now longed for peace and that the authority of the Confederacy was gone. They beset Jefferson Davis with demands that he should start negotiations. But none of them had determined what price they would pay for peace; and there was not among them any will that could really withstand their President. In one point indeed Jefferson Davis did wisely yield. On February 9, 1865, he consented to make Lee General-in-Chief of all the Southern armies. This belated delegation of larger authority to Lee had certain military results, but no political result whatever. Lee

could have been the dictator of the Confederacy if he had chosen, and no one then or since would have blamed him; but it was not in his mind to do anything but his duty as a soldier. The best beloved and most memorable by far of all the men who served that lost cause, he had done nothing to bring about secession at the beginning, nor now did he do anything but conform to the wishes of his political chief. As for that chief, Lincoln had interpreted Davis' simple position quite rightly. Having once embraced the cause of Southern independence and taken the oath as chief magistrate of an independent Confederacy, he would not yield up that cause while there was a man to obey his orders. Whether this attitude should be set down, as it usually has been set down, to a diseased pride or to a very real heroism on his part, he never faced the truth that the situation was desperate and the spirit of his people daunted at last. But it is probable that just like Lincoln he was ready that those who were in haste to make peace should see what peace involved; and it is probable too that, in his terrible position, he deluded himself with some vague and vain hopes as to the attitude of the North. Lincoln on the other hand would not enter into any proceedings in which the secession of the South was treated otherwise than as a rebellion which must cease; but this did not absolutely compel him to refuse every sort of informal communication with influential men in the South, which might help them to see where they stood and from which he too might learn something.

Old Mr. Francis Blair, the father of Lincoln's late Postmaster-General, was the last of the honest peacemakers whom Lincoln had allowed to see things for themselves by meeting Jefferson Davis. His visit took place in January, 1865, and from his determination to be a go-between and the curious and difficult position in which Lincoln and Davis both stood in this respect an odd result arose. The Confederate Vice-President Stephens, who had preached peace in the autumn without a quarrel with Davis, and two other Southern leaders presented themselves at Grant's headquarters with the pathetic mis-

representation that they were sent by Davis on a mission which Lincoln had undertaken to receive. What they could show was authority from Davis to negotiate with Lincoln on the footing of the independence of the Confederacy, and a politely turned intimation from Lincoln that he would at any time receive persons informally sent to talk with a view to the surrender of the rebel armies. Grant, however, was deeply impressed with the sincerity of their desire for peace, and he entreated Lincoln to receive them. Lincoln therefore decided to overlook the false pretence under which they came. He gave Grant strict orders not to delay his operations on this account, but he came himself with Seward and met Davis' three commissioners on a ship at Hampton Roads on February 3. He and Stephens had in old days been Whig Congressmen together, and Lincoln had once been moved to tears by a speech of Stephens. They met now as friends. Lincoln lost no time in making his position clear. The unhappy commissioners made every effort to lead him away from the plain ground he had chosen. It is evident that they and possible that Jefferson Davis had hoped that when face to face with them he would change his mind, and possibly Blair's talk had served to encourage this hope. They failed, but the conversation continued in a frank and friendly manner. Lincoln told them very freely his personal opinions as to how the North ought to treat the South when it did surrender, but was careful to point out that he could make no promise or bargain, except indeed this promise that so far as penalties for rebellion were concerned the executive power, which lay in his sole hands, would be liberally used. Slavery was discussed, and Seward told them of the Constitutional Amendment which Congress had now submitted to the people. One of the commissioners returning again to Lincoln's refusal to negotiate with armed rebels, as he considered them, cited the precedent of Charles I.'s conduct in this respect. " I do not profess," said Lincoln, " to be posted in history. On all such matters I turn you over to Seward. All I distinctly recollect about Charles I. is

that he lost his head in the end." Then he broke out into simple advice to Stephens as to the action he could now pursue. He had to report to Congress afterwards that the conference had had no result. He brought home, however, a personal compliment which he valued. " I understand, then," Stephens had said, " that you regard us as rebels, who are liable to be hanged for treason." " That is so," said Lincoln. " Well," said Stephens, " we supposed that would have to be your view. But, to tell you the truth, we have none of us been much afraid of being hanged with you as President." He brought home, besides the compliment, an idea of a kind which, if he could have had his way with his friends, might have been rich in good. He had discovered how hopeless the people of the South were, and he considered whether a friendly pronouncement might not lead them more read-ily to surrender. He deplored the suffering in which the South might now lie plunged, and it was a fixed part of his creed that slavery was the sin not of the South but of the nation. So he spent the day after his return in draft-ing a joint resolution which he hoped the two Houses of Congress might pass, and a Proclamation which he would in that case issue. In these he proposed to offer to the Southern States four hundred million dollars in United States bonds, being, as he calculated the cost to the North of two hundred days of war, to be allotted among those States in proportion to the property in slaves which each had lost. One half of this sum was to be paid at once if the war ended by April 1, and the other half upon the final adoption of the Constitutional Amendment. It would have been a happy thing if the work of restoring peace could have lain with a statesman whose rare aber-rations from the path of practical politics were of this kind. Yet, considering the natural passions which even in this least revengeful of civil wars could not quite be re-pressed, we should be judging the Congress of that day by a higher standard than we should apply in other coun-tries if we regarded this proposal as one that could have been hopefully submitted to them. Lincoln's illusions

were dispelled on the following day when he read what he had written to his Cabinet, and found that even among his own ministers not one man supported him. It would have been worse than useless to put forward his proposals and to fail. " You are all opposed to me," he said sadly; and he put his papers away. But the war had now so far progressed that it is necessary to turn back to the point at which we left it at the end of 1864.

Winter weather brought a brief pause to the operations of the armies. Sherman at Savannah was preparing to begin his northward march, a harder matter, owing to the rivers and marshes that lay in his way, than his triumphal progress from Atlanta. Efforts were made to concentrate all available forces against him at Augusta to his north-west. Making feints against Augusta on the one side, and against the city and port of Charleston on the other, he displayed the marvellous engineering capacity of his army by an advance of unlooked-for speed across the marshes to Columbia, due north of him, which is the State capital of South Carolina. He reached it on February 17, 1865. The intended concentration of the South at Augusta was broken up. The retreating Confederates set fire to great stores of cotton and the unfortunate city was burnt, a calamity for which the South, by a natural but most unjust mistake, blamed Sherman. The railway communications of Charleston were now certain to be severed; so the Confederates were forced to evacuate it, and on February 18, 1865, the North occupied the chief home of the misbegotten political ideals of the South and of its real culture and chivalry.

Admiral Porter (for age and ill-health had come upon Farragut) was ready at sea to co-operate with Sherman. Thomas' army in Tennessee had not been allowed by Grant to go into winter quarters. A part of it under Schofield was brought to Washington and there shipped for North Carolina, where, ever since Burnside's successful expedition in 1862, the Union Government had held the ports north of Wilmington. Wilmington itself was the only port left to the South, and Richmond had now come

to depend largely on the precarious and costly supplies which could still, notwithstanding the blockade, be run into that harbour. At the end of December, Butler, acting in flagrant disobedience to Grant, had achieved his crowning failure in a joint expedition with Porter against Wilmington. But Porter was not discouraged, nor was Grant, who from beginning to end of his career had worked well together with the Navy. On February 8, Porter, this time supported by an energetic general, Terry, effected a brilliant capture of Fort Fisher at the mouth of Wilmington harbour. The port was closed to the South. On the 22nd, the city itself fell to Schofield, and Sherman had now this sea base at hand if he needed it.

Meanwhile Grant's entrenchments on the east of Richmond and Petersburg were still extending southward, and Lee's defences had been stretched till they covered nearly forty miles. Grant's lines now cut the principal railway southward from the huge fortress, and he was able effectually to interrupt communication by road to the southwest. There could be little doubt that Richmond would fall soon, and the real question was coming to be whether Lee and his army could escape from Richmond and still carry on the war.

The appointment of Lee as General-in-Chief was not too late to bear one consequence which may have prolonged the war a little. Joseph Johnston, whose ability in a campaign of constant retirement before overwhelming force had been respected and redoubted by Sherman, had been discarded by Davis in the previous July. He was now put in command of the forces which it was hoped to concentrate against Sherman, with a view to holding up his northward advance and preventing him from joining hands with Grant before Richmond. There were altogether about 89,000 Confederate troops scattered in the Carolinas, Georgia, and Florida, and there would be about the same number under Sherman when Schofield in North Carolina could join him, but the number which Johnston could now collect together seems never to have

exceeded 33,000. It was Sherman's task by the rapidity
of his movements to prevent a very formidable concentration against him. Johnston on the other hand must
hinder if he could Sherman's junction with Schofield. Just
before that junction took place he narrowly missed dealing a considerable blow to Sherman's army at the battle
of Bentonville in the heart of North Carolina, but had in
the end to withdraw within an entrenched position where
Sherman would not attack him, but which upon the arrival of Schofield he was forced to abandon. On March
23, 1865, Sherman took possession of the town and railway junction of Goldsborough between Raleigh and New
Berne. From Savannah to Goldsborough he had led his
army 425 miles in fifty days, amid disadvantages of
ground and of weather which had called forth both extraordinary endurance and mechanical skill on the part of
his men. He lay now 140 miles south of Petersburg by
the railway. The port of New Berne to the east of him
on the estuary of the Neuse gave him a sure base of supplies, and would enable him quickly to move his army by
sea to Petersburg and Richmond if Grant should so decide. The direction in which Johnston would now fall
back lay inland up the Neuse Valley, also along a railway, towards Greensborough, some 150 miles south-west
of Petersburg; Greensborough was connected by another
railway with Petersburg and Richmond, and along this
line Lee might attempt to retire and join him.

All this time whatever designs Lee had of leaving
Richmond were suspended because the roads in that
weather were too bad for his transport; and, while of
necessity he waited, his possible openings narrowed.
Philip Sheridan had now received the coveted rank of
Major-General, which McClellan had resigned on the
day on which he was defeated for the Presidency. The
North delighted to find in his achievements the dashing
quality which appeals to civilian imagination, and Grant
now had in him, as well as in Sherman, a lieutenant who
would faithfully make his chief's purposes his own, and
who would execute them with independent decision. The

cold, in which his horses suffered, had driven Sheridan into winter quarters, but on February 27 he was able to start up the Shenandoah Valley again with 10,000 cavalry. Most of the Confederate cavalry under Early had now been dispersed, mainly for want of forage in the desolated valley; the rest were now dispersed by Sheridan, and the greater part of Early's small force of infantry with all his artillery were captured. There was a garrison in Lynchburg, 80 or 90 miles west of Richmond, which though strong enough to prevent Sheridan's cavalry from capturing that place was not otherwise of account; but there was no Confederate force in the field except Johnston's men near enough to co-operate with Lee; only some small and distant armies, hundreds of miles away with the railway communication between them and the East destroyed. Sheridan now broke up the railway and canal communication on the north-west side of Richmond. He was to have gone on south and eventually joined Sherman if he could; but, finding himself stopped for the time by floods in the upper valley of the James, he rode past the north of Richmond, and on March 19 joined Grant, to put his cavalry and brains at his service when Grant judged that the moment for his final effort had come.

On March 4, 1865, Abraham Lincoln took office for the second time as President of the United States. There was one new and striking feature in the simple ceremonial, the presence of a battalion of negro troops in his escort. This time, though he would say no sanguine word, it cannot have been a long continuance of war that filled his thoughts, but the scarcely less difficult though far happier task of restoring the fabric of peaceful society in the conquered South. His difficulties were now likely to come from the North no less than the South. Tentative proposals which he had once or twice made suggest the spirit in which he would have felt his way along this new path. In the inaugural address which he now delivered that spirit is none the less perceptible because he spoke of the past. The little speech at Gettysburg, with

its singular perfection of form, and the " Second Inaugural " are the chief outstanding examples of his peculiar oratorical power. The comparative rank of his oratory need not be discussed, for at any rate it was individual and unlike that of most other great speakers in history, though perhaps more like that of some great speeches in drama.

But there is a point of some moment in which the Second Inaugural does invite a comment, and a comment which should be quite explicit. Probably no other speech of a modern statesman uses so unreservedly the language of intense religious feeling. The occasion made it natural; neither the thought nor the words are in any way conventional; no sensible reader now could entertain a suspicion that the orator spoke to the heart of the people but did not speak from his own heart. But an old Illinois attorney, who thought he knew the real Lincoln behind the President, might have wondered whether the real Lincoln spoke here. For Lincoln's religion, like everything else in his character, became, when he was famous, a stock subject of discussion among his old associates. Many said " he was a Christian but did not know it." Some hinted, with an air of great sagacity, that " so far from his being a Christian or a religious man, the less said about it the better." In early manhood he broke away for ever from the scheme of Christian theology which was probably more or less common to the very various Churches which surrounded him. He had avowed this sweeping denial with a freedom which pained some friends, perhaps rather by its rashness than by its impiety, and he was apt to regard the procedure of theologians as a blasphemous twisting of the words of Christ. He rejected that belief in miracles and in the literally inspired accuracy of the Bible narrative which was no doubt held as fundamental by all these Churches. He rejected no less any attempt to substitute for this foundation the belief in any priestly authority or in the authority of any formal and earthly society called the Church. With this total independence of the expressed creeds of his neigh-

bours he still went and took his boys to Presbyterian public worship—their mother was an Episcopalian and his
own parents had been Baptists. He loved the Bible and
knew it intimately—he is said also by the way to have
stored in his memory a large number of hymns. In the
year before his death he wrote to Speed: " I am profit-
ably engaged in reading the Bible. Take all of this book
upon reason that you can and the balance upon faith and
you will live and die a better man." It was not so much
the Old Testament as the New Testament and what he
called " the true spirit of Christ " that he loved especially, and took with all possible seriousness as the rule
of life. His theology, in the narrower sense, may be
said to have been limited to an intense belief in a vast
and over-ruling Providence—the lighter forms of superstitious feelings which he is known to have had in common with most frontiersmen were apparently of no importance in his life. And this Providence, darkly spoken
of, was certainly conceived by him as intimately and
kindly related to his own life. In his Presidential candidature, when he owned to some one that the opposition
of clergymen hurt him deeply, he is said to have confessed
to being no Christian and to have continued, " I know that
there is a God and that He hates injustice and slavery. I
see the storm coming and I know that His hand is in it.
If He has a place and work for me, and I think He has,
I believe I am ready. I am nothing, but truth is everything; I know I am right because I know that liberty is
right, for Christ teaches it, and Christ is God. I have
told them that a house divided against itself cannot stand,
and Christ and reason say the same, and they will find it
so." When old acquaintances said that he had no religion
they based their opinion on such remarks as that the God,
of whom he had just been speaking solemnly, was " not
a person." It would be unprofitable to enquire what he,
and many others, meant by this expression, but, later at
any rate, this " impersonal " power was one with which
he could hold commune. His robust intellect, impatient
of unproved assertion, was unlikely to rest in the com-

mon assumption that things dimly seen may be treated as not being there. So humorous a man was also unlikely to be too conceited to say his prayers. At any rate he said them; said them intently; valued the fact that others prayed for him and for the nation; and, as in official Proclamations (concerning days of national religious observance) he could wield, like no other modern writer, the language of the Prayer Book, so he would speak of prayer without the smallest embarrassment in talk with a general or a statesman. It is possible that this was a development of later years. Lincoln did not, like most of us, arrest his growth. To Mrs. Lincoln it seemed that with the death of their child, Willie, a change came over his whole religious outlook. It well might; and since that grief, which came while his troubles were beginning, much else had come to Lincoln; and now through four years of unsurpassed trial his capacity had steadily grown, and his delicate fairness, his pitifulness, his patience, his modesty had grown therewith. Here is one of the few speeches ever delivered by a great man at the crisis of his fate on the sort of occasion which a tragedian telling his story would have devised for him. This man had stood alone in the dark. He had done justice; he had loved mercy; he had walked humbly with his God. The reader to whom religious utterance makes little appeal will not suppose that his imaginative words stand for no real experience. The reader whose piety knows no questions will not be pained to think that this man had professed no faith.

He said, "Fellow Countrymen: At this second appearance to take the oath of the Presidential office, there is less occasion for an extended address than there was at the first. Then a statement, somewhat in detail, of a course to be pursued, seemed fitting and proper. Now, at the expiration of four years, during which public declarations have been constantly called forth on every point and phase of the great contest which still absorbs the energies and engrosses the attention of the nation, little that is new could be presented. The progress of

our arms, upon which all else chiefly depends, is as well known to the public as to myself; and it is, I trust, reasonably satisfactory and encouraging to all. With high hope for the future, no prediction in regard to it is ventured.

" On the occasion corresponding to this four years ago, all thoughts were anxiously directed to an impending civil war. All dreaded it—all sought to avert it. While the inaugural address was being delivered from this place, devoted altogether to saving the Union without war, insurgent agents were in the city seeking to destroy it without war—seeking to dissolve the Union and divide effects, by negotiation. Both parties deprecated war; but one of them would make war rather than let the nation survive; and the other would accept war rather than let it perish. And the war came.

" One-eighth of the whole population were coloured slaves, not distributed generally over the Union, but localised in the Southern part of it. These slaves constituted a peculiar and powerful interest. All knew that this interest was, somehow, the cause of the war. To strengthen, perpetuate, and extend this interest was the object for which the insurgents would rend the Union, even by war; while the Government claimed no right to do more than to restrict the territorial enlargement of it. Neither party expected for the war the magnitude or the duration which it has already attained. Neither expected that the cause of the conflict might cease with, or even before, the conflict itself should cease. Each looked for an easier triumph, and a result less fundamental and astounding. Both read the same Bible, and pray to the same God; and each invokes His aid against the other. It may seem strange that any men should dare to ask a just God's assistance in wringing their bread from the sweat of other men's faces; but let us judge not, that we be not judged. The prayers of both could not be answered—that of neither has been answered fully. The Almighty has His own purposes. ' Woe unto the world because of offenses! for it must needs be that offenses come; but woe to that man by whom the offense cometh.'

If we shall suppose that American slavery is one of those offenses, which, in the providence of God, must needs come, but which, having continued through His appointed time, He now wills to remove, and that He gives to both North and South this terrible war, as the woe due to those by whom the offense came, shall we discern therein any departure from those divine attributes which the believers in a living God always ascribe to Him? Fondly do we hope—fervently do we pray—that this mighty scourge of war may speedily pass away. Yet, if God wills that it continue until all the wealth piled by the bondman's two hundred and fifty years of unrequited toil shall be sunk, and until every drop of blood drawn with the lash shall be paid with another drawn with the sword, as was said three thousand years ago, so still it must be said, 'The judgments of the Lord are true and righteous altogether.'

"With malice toward none; with charity for all; with firmness in the right, as God gives us to see the right, let us strive on to finish the work we are in; to bind up the nation's wounds, to care for him who shall have borne the battle, and for his widow, and his orphan—to do all which may achieve and cherish a just and lasting peace among ourselves, and with all nations."

Lincoln's own commentary may follow upon his speech: "March 15, 1865. Dear Mr. Weed,—Every one likes a little compliment. Thank you for yours on my little notification speech and on the recent inaugural address. I expect the latter to wear as well as—perhaps better than—anything I have produced; but I believe it is not immediately popular. Men are not flattered by being shown that there has been a difference of purpose between the Almighty and them. To deny it however in this case is to deny that there is a God governing the world. It is a truth which I thought needed to be told, and, as whatever of humiliation there is in it falls most directly on myself, I thought others might afford for me to tell it.

"Truly yours,
"A. LINCOLN."

On March 20, 1865, a period of bright sunshine seems to have begun in Lincoln's life. Robert Lincoln had some time before finished his course at Harvard, and his father had written to Grant modestly asking him if he could suggest the way, accordant with discipline and good example, in which the young man could best see something of military life. Grant immediately had him on to his staff, with a commission as captain, and now Grant invited Lincoln to come to his headquarters for a holiday visit. There was much in it besides holiday, for Grant was rapidly maturing his plans for the great event and wanted Lincoln near. Moreover Sheridan had just arrived, and while Lincoln was there Sherman came from Goldsborough with Admiral Porter for consultation as to Sherman's next move. Peremptory as he was in any necessary political instructions, Lincoln was now happy to say nothing of military matters, beyond expressing his earnest desire that the final overmastering of the Confederate armies should be accomplished with the least further bloodshed possible, and indulging the curiosity that any other guest might have shown. A letter home to Mrs. Lincoln betrays the interest with which he heard heavy firing quite near, which seemed to him a great battle, but did not excite those who knew. Then there were rides in the country with Grant's staff. Lincoln in his tall hat and frock coat was a marked and curious figure on a horse. He had once, by the way, insisted on riding with Butler, catechising him with remorseless chaff on engineering matters and forbidding his chief engineer to prompt him, along six miles of cheering Northern troops within easy sight and shot of the Confederate soldiers to whom his hat and coat identified him. But, however odd a figure, he impressed Grant's officers as a good and bold horseman. Then, after Sherman's arrival, there evidently was no end of talk. Sherman was at first amused by the President's anxiety as to whether his army was quite safe without him at Goldsborough; but that keen-witted soldier soon received, as he has said, an impression both of

goodness and of greatness such as no other man ever
gave him.

What especially remained on Sherman's and on
Porter's mind was the recollection of Lincoln's overpowering desire for mercy and for conciliation with the
conquered. Indeed Sherman blundered later in the terms
he first accepted from Johnston; for he did not see that
Lincoln's clemency for Southern leaders and desire for
the welfare of the South included no mercy at all for the
political principle of the Confederacy. Grant was not
exposed to any such mistake, for a week or two before
Lee had made overtures to him for some sort of conference and Lincoln had instantly forbidden him to confer
with Lee for any purpose but that of his unconditional
surrender. What, apart from the reconstruction of
Southern life and institutions, was in part weighing with
Lincoln was the question of punishments for rebellion.
By Act of Congress the holders of high political and military office in the South were liable as traitors, and there
was now talk of hanging in the North. Later events
showed that a very different sentiment would make itself
heard when the victory came; but Lincoln was much concerned. To some one who spoke to him of this matter
he exclaimed, " What have I to do with you, ye sons of
Zeruiah, that ye should this day be adversaries unto me?
Shall there any man be put to death this day in Israel? "
There can be no doubt that the prerogative of mercy
would have been vigorously used in his hands, but he did
not wish for a conflict on this matter at all; and Grant
was taught, in a parable about a teetotal Irishman who
forgave being served with liquor unbeknownst to himself,
that zeal in capturing Jefferson Davis and his colleagues
was not expected of him.

While Lincoln was at Grant's headquarters at City
Point, Lee, hoping to recover the use of the roads to the
south-west, endeavoured to cause a diversion of the besiegers' strength by a sortie on his east front. It failed
and gave the besiegers a further point of vantage. On
April 1 Sheridan was sent far round the south of Lee's

lines, and in a battle at a point called Five Forks established himself in possession of the railway running due
west from Petersburg. The defences were weakest on
this side, and to prevent the entrance of the enemy there
Lee was bound to withdraw troops from other quarters.
On the two following days Grant's army delivered
assaults at several points on the east side of the Petersburg defences, penetrating the outer lines and pushing on
against the inner fortifications of the town. On Sunday,
April 2, Jefferson Davis received in church word from
Lee to make instant preparation for departure, as Petersburg could not be held beyond that night and Richmond
must fall immediately. That night the Confederate Government left the capital, and Lee's evacuation of the
fortress began the next day. Lincoln was sent for. He
came by sea, and to the astonishment and alarm of the
naval officers made his way at once to Richmond with
entirely insufficient escort. There he strolled about, hand
in hand with his little son Tad, greeted by exultant negroes, and stared at by angry or curious Confederates,
while he visited the former prison of the Northern prisoners and other places of more pleasant attraction without receiving any annoyance from the inhabitants. He
had an interesting talk with Campbell, formerly a
Supreme Court judge, and a few weeks back one of
Davis' commissioners at Hampton Roads. Campbell
obtained permission to convene a meeting of the members
of the Virginia Legislature with a view to speedier surrender by Lee's army. But the permission was revoked,
for he somewhat clumsily mistook its terms, and, moreover, the object in view had meantime been accomplished.
    Jefferson Davis was then making his way with his min-
isters to Johnston's army. When they arrived he and
they held council with Johnston and Beauregard. He
would issue a Proclamation which would raise him many
soldiers and he would "whip them yet." No one answered him. At last he asked the opinion of Johnston,
who bluntly undeceived him as to facts, and told him that
further resistance would be a crime, and got his permis-

sion to treat with Sherman, while the fallen Confederate President escaped further south.

Lee's object was to make his way along the north side of the Appomattox River, which flows east through Petersburg to the James estuary, and at a certain point strike southwards towards Johnston's army. He fought for his escape with all his old daring and skill, while hardly less vigorous and skilful efforts were made not only to pursue, but to surround him. Grant in his pursuit sent letters of courteous entreaty that he would surrender and spare further slaughter. Northern cavalry got ahead of Lee, tearing up the railway lines he had hoped to use and blocking possible mountain passes; and his supply trains were being cut off. After a long running fight and one last fierce battle on April 6, at a place called Sailor's Creek, Lee found himself on April 9 at Appomattox Court House, some seventy miles west of Petersburg, surrounded beyond hope of escape. On that day he and Grant with their staffs met in a neighbouring farmhouse. Those present recalled afterwards the contrast of the stately Lee and the plain, ill-dressed Grant arriving mudsplashed in his haste. Lee greeted Meade as an old acquaintance and remarked how grey he had grown with years. Meade gracefully replied that Lee and not age was responsible for that. Grant had started " quite jubilant " on the news that Lee was ready to surrender, but in presence of " the downfall of a foe who had fought so long and valiantly " he fell into sadness. Pleasant " talk of old army times " followed, and he had almost forgotten, as he declares, the business in hand, when Lee asked him on what terms he would accept surrender. Grant sat down and wrote, not knowing when he began what he should go on to write. As he wrote he thought of the handsome sword Lee carried. Instantly he added to his terms permission for every Southern officer to keep his sword and his horse. Lee read the paper and when he came to that point was visibly moved. He gauged his man, and he ventured to ask something more. He thought, he said, Grant might not know that the Confed-

erate cavalry troopers owned their own horses. Grant said they would be badly wanted on the farms and added a further concession accordingly. " This will have the best possible effect on the men," said Lee. " It will do much towards conciliating our people." Grant included also in his written terms words of general pardon to Confederate officers for their treason. This was an inadvertent breach, perhaps, of Lincoln's orders, but it was one which met with no objection. Lee retired into civil life and devoted himself thereafter to his neighbours' service as head of a college in Virginia—much respected, very free with alms to old soldiers and not much caring whether they had fought for the South or for the North. Grant did not wait to set foot in the capital which he had conquered, but, the main business being over, posted off with all haste to see his son settled in at school.

Lincoln remained at City Point till April 8, when he started back by steamer. Those who were with him on the two days' voyage told afterwards of the happy talk, as of a quiet family party rejoicing in the return of peace. Somebody said that Jefferson Davis really ought to be hanged. The reply came in the quotation that he might almost have expected, "Judge not, that ye be not judged." On the second day, Sunday, the President read to them parts of " Macbeth." Sumner, who was one of them, recalled that he read twice over the lines,

> " Duncan is in his grave;
> After life's fitful fever he sleeps well;
> Treason has done his worst; nor steel, nor poison,
> Malice domestic, foreign levy, nothing
> Can touch him further."

On the Tuesday, April 11, a triumphant crowd came to the White House to greet Lincoln. He made them a speech, carefully prepared in substance rather than in form, dealing with the question of reconstruction in the South, with special reference to what was already in progress in Louisiana. The precise points of controversy that arose in this regard hardly matter now. Lincoln dis-

claimed any wish to insist pedantically upon any detailed plan of his; but he declared his wish equally to keep clear of any merely pedantic points of controversy with any in the South who were loyally striving to revive State Government with acceptance of the Union and without slavery; and he urged that genuine though small beginnings should be encouraged. He regretted that in Louisiana his wish for the enfranchisement of educated negroes and of negro soldiers had not been followed; but as the freedom of the negroes was unreservedly accepted, as provision was made for them in the public schools, and the new State constitution allowed the Legislature to enfranchise them, there was clear gain. " Concede that the new government of Louisiana is only to what it should be as the egg is to the fowl, we shall sooner have the fowl by hatching the egg than by smashing it. What has been said of Louisiana will apply generally to other States. So new and unprecedented," he ended, " is the whole case that no exclusive and inflexible plan can safely be prescribed as to details and collaterals. Such exclusive and inflexible plan would surely become a new entanglement. Important principles may and must be inflexible. In the present situation, as the phrase goes, it may be my duty to make some new announcement to the people of the South. I am considering, and shall not fail to act when satisfied that action will be proper." A full generation has had cause to lament that that announcement was never to be made.

On Good Friday, April 14, 1865, with solemn religious service the Union flag was hoisted again on Fort Sumter by General Anderson, its old defender. On that morning there was a Cabinet Council in Washington. Seward was absent, in bed with an injury from a carriage accident. Grant was there a little anxious to get news from Sherman. Lincoln was in a happy mood. He had earlier that morning enjoyed greatly a talk with Robert Lincoln about the young man's new experience of soldiering. He now told Grant and the Cabinet that good news was coming from Sherman. He knew it, he said, for last night he had

dreamed a dream, which had come to him several times before. In this dream, whenever it came, he was sailing in a ship of a peculiar build, indescribable but always the same, and being borne on it with great speed towards a dark and undefined shore. He had always dreamed this before victory. He dreamed it before Antietam, before Murfreesborough, before Gettysburg, before Vicksburg. Grant observed bluntly that Murfreesborough had not been a victory, or of any consequence anyway. Lincoln persisted on this topic undeterred. After some lesser business they discussed the reconstruction of the South. Lincoln rejoiced that Congress had adjourned and the " disturbing element " in it could not hinder the work. Before it met again, " if we are wise and discreet we shall re-animate the States and get their governments in successful operation, with order prevailing and the Union re-established." Lastly, there was talk of the treatment of rebels and of the demand that had been heard for " persecution " and " bloody work." " No one need expect me," said Lincoln, " to take any part in hanging or killing these men, even the worst of them. Frighten them out of the country, open the gates, let down the bars, scare them off." " Shoo," he added, throwing up his large hands like a man scaring sheep. " We must extinguish our resentments if we expect harmony and union. There is too much of the desire on the part of some of our very good friends to be masters, to interfere with and dictate to those States, to treat the people not as fellow citizens; there is too little respect for their rights. I do not sympathise in these feelings." Such was the tenor of his last recorded utterance on public affairs.

In the afternoon Mr. and Mrs. Lincoln drove together and he talked to her with keen pleasure of the life they would live when the Presidency was over. That night Mr. and Mrs. Lincoln went to the theatre, for the day was not observed as in England. The Grants were to have been with them, but changed their minds and left Washington that day, so a young officer, Major Rathbone, and the lady engaged to him, both of them there-

after ill-fated, came instead. The theatre was crowded; many officers returned from the war were there and eager to see Lincoln. The play was " Our American Cousin," a play in which the part of Lord Dundreary was afterwards developed and made famous. Some time after 10 o'clock, at a point in the play which it is said no person present could afterwards remember, a shot was heard in the theatre and Abraham Lincoln fell forward upon the front of the box unconscious and dying. A wild-looking man, who had entered the box unobserved and had done his work, was seen to strike with a knife at Major Rathbone, who tried to seize him. Then he jumped from the box to the stage; he caught a spur in the drapery and fell, breaking the small bone of his leg. He rose, shouted " Sic semper tyrannis," the motto of Virginia, disappeared behind the scenes, mounted a horse that was in waiting at the stage door, and rode away.

This was John Wilkes Booth, brother of a famous actor then playing " Hamlet " in Boston. He was an actor too, and an athletic and daring youth. In him that peculiarly ferocious political passion which occasionally showed itself among Southerners was further inflamed by brandy and by that ranting mode of thought which the stage develops in some few. He was the leader of a conspiracy which aimed at compassing the deaths of others besides Lincoln. Andrew Johnson, the Vice-President, was to die. So was Seward. That same night one of the conspirators, a gigantic boy of feeble mind, gained entrance to Seward's house and wounded three people, including Seward himself, who was lying already injured in bed and received four or five wounds. Neither he nor the others died. The weak-minded or mad boy, another man, whose offense consisted in having been asked to kill Johnson and refused to do so, and another alleged conspirator, a woman, were hanged after a court-martial whose proceedings did credit neither to the new President nor to others concerned. Booth himself, after many adventures, was shot in a barn in which he stood at bay and which had been set on fire by the soldiers pursuing

him. During his flight he is said to have felt much aggrieved that men did not praise him as they had praised Brutus and Cassius.

There were then in the South many broken and many permanently embittered men, indeed the temper which would be glad at Lincoln's death could be found here and there and notably among the partisans of the South in Washington. But, if it be wondered what measure of sympathy there was for Booth's dark deed, an answer lies in the fact that the murder of Lincoln would at no time have been difficult for a brave man. Fair blows were now as powerless as foul to arrest the end. On the very morning when Lincoln and Grant at the Cabinet had been telling of their hopes and fears for Sherman, Sherman himself at Raleigh in North Carolina had received and answered a letter from Johnston opening negotiations for a peaceful surrender. Three days later he was starting by rail for Greensborough when word came to him from the telegraph operator that an important message was upon the wire. He went to the telegraph box and heard it. Then he swore the telegraph operator to secrecy, for he feared that some provocation might lead to terrible disorders in Raleigh, if his army, flushed with triumph, were to learn, before his return in peace, the news that for many days after hushed their accustomed songs and shouts and cheering into a silence which was long remembered. He went off to meet Johnston and requested to be with him alone in a farmhouse near. There he told him of the murder of Lincoln. "The perspiration came out in large drops on Johnston's forehead," says Sherman, who watched him closely. He exclaimed that it was a disgrace to the age. Then he asked to know whether Sherman attributed the crime to the Confederate authorities. Sherman could assure him that no one dreamed of such a suspicion against men like him and General Lee; but he added that he was not so sure of " Jefferson Davis and men of that stripe." Then followed some delay, through a mistake of Sherman's which the authorities in Washington reversed, but in a few days all was settled

and the whole of the forces under Johnston's command laid down their arms. Twenty years later, as an old man and infirm, their leader left his Southern home to be present at Sherman's funeral, where he caught a chill from which he died soon after. Jefferson Davis was captured on May 10, near the borders of Florida. He was, not without plausible grounds but quite unjustly, suspected in regard to the murder, and he suffered imprisonment for some time till President Andrew Johnson released him when the evidence against him had been seen to be worthless. He lived many years in Mississippi and wrote memoirs, in which may be found the fullest legal argument for the great Secession, his own view of his quarrels with Joseph Johnston, and much besides. Amongst other things he tells how when they heard the news of Lincoln's murder some troops cheered, but he was truly sorry for the reason that Andrew Johnson was more hostile to the cause than Lincoln. It is disappointing to think, of one who played a memorable part in history with much determination, that in this reminiscence he sized his stature as a man fairly accurately. After several other surrenders of Southern towns and small scattered forces, the Confederate General Kirby Smith, in Texas, surrendered to General Canby, Banks' successor, on May 26, and after four years and forty-four days armed resistance to the Union was at an end.

On the night of Good Friday, Abraham Lincoln had been carried still unconscious to a house near the theatre. His sons and other friends were summoned. He never regained consciousness. "A look of unspeakable peace," say his secretaries who were there, " came over his worn features." At 7.22 on the morning of April 15, Stanton, watching him more closely than the rest, told them what had passed in the words, " Now he belongs to the ages."

The mourning of a nation, voiced to later times by some of the best lines of more than one of its poets, and deeper and more prevailing for the lack of comprehension which some had shown him before, followed his body in its slow progress—stopping at Baltimore, where once

his life had been threatened, for the homage of vast crowds; stopping at New York, where among the huge assembly old General Scott came to bid him affectionate farewell; stopping at other cities for the tribute of reverent multitudes—to Springfield, his home of so many years, where, on May 4, 1865, it was laid to rest. After the burial service the " Second Inaugural " was read over his grave, nor could better words than his own have been chosen to honour one who " with malice toward none, with charity toward all, with firmness in the right as God gave him to see the right, had striven on to finish the work that he was in." In England, apart from more formal tokens of a late-learnt regard and an unfeigned regret, *Punch* embodied in verse of rare felicity the manly contrition of its editor for ignorant derision in past years; and Queen Victoria symbolised best of all, and most acceptably to Americans, the feeling of her people when she wrote to Mrs. Lincoln " as a widow to a widow." Nor, though the transactions in which he bore his part were but little understood in this country till they were half forgotten, has tradition ever failed to give him, by just instinct, his rank with the greatest of our race.

Many great deeds had been done in the war. The greatest was the keeping of the North together in an enterprise so arduous, and an enterprise for objects so confusedly related as the Union and freedom. Abraham Lincoln did this; nobody else could have done it; to do it he bore on his sole shoulders such a weight of care and pain as few other men have borne. When it was over it seemed to the people that he had all along been thinking their real thoughts for them; but they knew that this was because he had fearlessly thought for himself. He had been able to save the nation, partly because he saw that unity was not to be sought by the way of base concession. He had been able to free the slaves, partly because he would not hasten to this object at the sacrifice of what he thought a larger purpose. This most unrelenting enemy to the project of the Confederacy was the one man who had quite purged his heart and mind from

hatred or even anger towards his fellow-countrymen of the South. That fact came to be seen in the South too, and generations in America are likely to remember it when all other features of his statecraft have grown indistinct. A thousand reminiscences ludicrous or pathetic, passing into myth but enshrining hard fact, will prove to them that this great feature of his policy was a matter of more than policy. They will remember it as adding a peculiar lustre to the renovation of their national existence; as no small part of the glory, surpassing that of former wars, which has become the common heritage of North and South. For perhaps not many conquerors, and certainly few successful statesmen, have escaped the tendency of power to harden or at least to narrow their human sympathies; but in this man a natural wealth of tender compassion became richer and more tender while in the stress of deadly conflict he developed an astounding strength.

Beyond his own country some of us recall his name as the greatest among those associated with the cause of popular government. He would have liked this tribute, and the element of truth in it is plain enough, yet it demands one final consideration. He accepted the institutions to which he was born, and he enjoyed them. His own intense experience of the weakness of democracy did not sour him, nor would any similar experience of later times have been likely to do so. Yet if he reflected much on forms of government it was with a dominant interest in something beyond them. For he was a citizen of that far country where there is neither aristocrat nor democrat. No political theory stands out from his words or actions; but they show a most unusual sense of the possible dignity of common men and common things. His humour rioted in comparisons between potent personages and Jim Jett's brother or old Judge Brown's drunken coachman, for the reason for which the rarely jesting Wordsworth found a hero in the " Leech-Gatherer " or in Nelson and a villain in Napoleon or in Peter Bell. He could use and respect and pardon and overrule his far

more accomplished ministers because he stood up to them with no more fear or cringing, with no more dislike or envy or disrespect than he had felt when he stood up long before to Jack Armstrong. He faced the difficulties and terrors of his high office with that same mind with which he had paid his way as a poor man or navigated a boat in rapids or in floods. If he had a theory of democracy it was contained in this condensed note which he wrote, perhaps as an autograph, a year or two before his Presidency: "As I would not be a slave, so I would not be a master. This expresses my idea of democracy. Whatever differs from this, to the extent of the difference, is no democracy.—A. LINCOLN."

APPENDIX

APPENDIX

BIBLIOGRAPHICAL NOTE

A COMPLETE bibliography of books dealing specially with Lincoln, and of books throwing important light upon his life or upon the history of the American Civil War, cannot be attempted here. The author aims only at mentioning the books which have been of greatest use to him and a few others to which reference ought obviously to be made.

The chief authorities for the life of Lincoln are:—
"Abraham Lincoln: A History," by John G. Nicolay and John Hay (his private secretaries), in ten volumes: The Century Company, New York, and T. Fisher Unwin, London; "The Works of Abraham Lincoln" (*i. e.*, speeches, letters, and State papers), in eight volumes: G. Putnam's Sons, London and New York; and, for his early life, "The Life of Abraham Lincoln," by Herndon and Weik: Appleton, London and New York.

There are numerous short biographies of Lincoln, but among these it is not invidious to mention as the best (expressing as it does the mature judgment of the highest authority) "A Short Life of Abraham Lincoln," by John G. Nicolay: The Century Company, New York.

The author may be allowed to refer, moreover, to the interest aroused in him as a boy by "Abraham Lincoln," by C. G. Leland, in the "New Plutarch Series": Marcus Ward & Co., London; and to the light he has much later derived from "Abraham Lincoln," by John T. Morse, Junior: Houghton Mifflin Company, Boston, U.S.A.

Among studies of Lincoln, containing a wealth of illustrative stories, a very high place is due to "The True Abraham Lincoln," by William Eleroy Curtis: The J. B. Lippincott Company, Philadelphia and London.

For the history of America at the period concerned the reader may be most confidently referred to a work, which

by plentiful extracts and citations enables its writer's judgment to be checked, without detracting from the interest and power of his narrative, namely, " History of the United States, 1850—1877," by James Ford Rhodes, in seven volumes: The Macmillan Company, London and New York.

Among the shorter complete histories of the United States are: " The United States: an Outline of Political History," by Goldwin Smith: The Macmillan Company, London and New York; the article " United States of America " (section " History ") in the " Encyclopædia Britannica " (see also the many excellent articles on American biography in the " Encyclopædia Britannica "); " The Cambridge Modern History: Vol. VII., United States of America ": Cambridge University Press, and The Macmillan Company, New York.

Two volumes of special interest in regard to the early days of the United States, in some ways complementary to each other in their different points of view, are: "Alexander Hamilton," by F. G. Oliver: Constable & Co., and " Historical Essays," by John Fitch.

Almost every point in regard to American institutions and political practice is fully treated in " The American Commonwealth," by Viscount Bryce, O.M., two volumes: The Macmillan Company, London and New York.

For the attitude of the British Government during the war the conclusive authority is the correspondence to be found in " The Life of Lord John Russell," by Sir Spencer Walpole, K.C.B., two volumes: Longmans, Green & Co., London and New York; and light on the attitude of the English people is thrown by " The Life of John Bright," by G. M. Trevelyan: Constable, London, and Houghton Mifflin Company, Boston, U.S.A.

With respect to the military history of the Civil War the author is specially indebted to " The Civil War in the United States," by W. Birkbeck Wood and Major J. E. Edmonds, R.E., with an introduction by Spenser Wilkinson: Methuen & Co., London, and Putnam, New York, which is the only concise and complete history of the war

written with full knowledge of all recent works bearing on the subject. Mr. Nicolay's chapters in the "Cambridge Modern History" give a very lucid narrative of the war.

Among works of special interest bearing on the war, though not much concerning the subject of this book, it is only necessary to mention "'Stonewall' Jackson," by Colonel Henderson, C.B., two volumes: Longmans, London and New York; "Battles and Leaders of the Civil War" (a book of monographs by several authors, many of them actors in the war), four volumes: T. Fisher Unwin, London, and Century Company, New York, and "Story of the Civil War," by J. C. Ropes: Putnam, London and New York.

It may be added that a life of General Robert E. Lee had been projected, as a companion volume to this in the same series, by Brigadier-General Frederick Maurice, C.B., and it is to be hoped that, though suspended by the present war, this book may still be written. Existing biographies of Lee are disappointing. It has been (especially in view of this intended book on Lee) outside the scope of this volume to present the history of the Civil War with special reference to the Southern actors in it, but "Memoirs of Jefferson Davis" must be here referred to as in some sense an authoritative, though not a very attractive or interesting, exposition of the views of Southern statesmen at the time.

An interesting sidelight on the war may be found in "Life with the Confederate Army," by Watson, being the experiences of a Scotchman who for a time served under the Confederacy.

In regard to slavery and to Southern society before the war the author has made much use of "Our Slave States," by Frederick Law Olmsted: Dix and Edwards, New York, 1856, and other works of the same author. Mr. Olmsted was a Northerner, but his very full observations can be checked by the numerous quotations on the same subject collected by Mr. Rhodes in his history.

For the history of the South since the war and the present position of the negroes, see the chapters on this

subject in Bryce's "American Commonwealth," second or any later edition, two volumes: Macmillan, London and New York.

Mr. Owen Wister's novel, " Lady Baltimore ": Macmillan, London and New York, embraces a most interesting study of the survivals of the old Southern society at the present time and of the present relations between it and the North.

The treatment of the negroes freed during the war is the main subject of " Grant, Lincoln and the Freedmen," by John Eaton and E. O. Mason: Longmans, Green & Co., London and New York, a book to which the author is also indebted for other interesting matter.

The personal memoirs, and especially the autobiographies dealing with the Civil War, are very numerous, and the author therefore would only wish to mention those which seem to him of altogether unusual interest. " Personal Memoirs of General U. S. Grant ": Century Company, New York, is a book of very high order (Sherman's memoirs: Appleton, New York, and his correspondence with his brother: Scribner, New York, have also been quoted in these pages).

Great interest both in regard to Lincoln personally and to the history of the United States after his death attaches to " Reminiscences," by Carl Schurz, three volumes (Vol. I. being concerned with Germany in 1848): John Murray, London, and Doubleday Page, New York, and to " The Life of John Hay," by W. R. Thayer, two volumes: Constable & Co., London, and Houghton Mifflin Company, Boston, U.S.A.

The author has derived much light from " Specimen Days, and Collect," by Walt Whitman: Wilson and McCormick, Glasgow, and McKay, U.S.A.

He may be allowed, in conclusion, to mention the encouragement given to him in beginning his work by the late Mr. Henry James, O.M., whose vivid and enthusiastic judgment of Lincoln he had the privilege of receiving.

CHRONOLOGICAL TABLE

Some events in History of United States.

1759. Capture of Quebec.

1765. Stamp Act passed.
1776. Declaration of Independence.

1783. American Independence recognised.
1787. Constitution framed.
North West Territory ceded by States to Congress and slavery excluded from it.
1789. Constitution comes into force.
1793. Eli Whitney invents cotton gin.

1799. Death of Washington.

1803. Louisiana purchase.
1804. Death of Hamilton.

1807. Fulton's steam-boat on Hudson.
1808. Slave Trade abolished by U. S. A.

1809. Abraham Lincoln born.

1812—1814. War with Great Britain.

1820. Missouri Compromise.
1823. Monroe doctrine declared.

Some events in English and General History.

1759. Capture of Quebec.
1757—60. Ministry of Chatham (William Pitt).
1760. *Contrat Social* published.
1764—76. Great inventions in spinning industries.
1765. Watt's steam engine.
1776. Publication of "Wealth of Nations."
1778. Death of Chatham.
1782. Rodney's victory.

1789. Meeting of States General.
1793. England at war with French Republic.
1794. Slave Trade abolished by French Convention.

1802. Peace of Amiens.
1803. England at war with Napoleon.
1805. Trafalgar.
1806. The American Fulton's steam-boat on Seine.
1807. Slave Trade abolished by Great Britain.
1808. Battle of Vimiera. Convention of Cintra.
Wordsworth's literary activity about at its culmination.
1809. Darwin, Tennyson, and Gladstone born.

1815. Waterloo.

1825. First railway opened in England.

461

Some events in History of United States.	Some events in English and General History.
1826. Death of Jefferson.	1826. Independence of Mexico and Spanish Colonies in South America recognised by Canning. 1827. Navarino.
1828. Commencement of "nullification" movement. Election of Jackson.	
	1829. Catholic emancipation.
1830. Hayne-Webster debate. 1831. Garrison publishes first number of *Liberator*. Lincoln starts life in New Salem. First railway opened in America.	1831. Mazzini founds Young Italy. 1832. First Reform Bill. 1833. Slavery abolished in British Colonies.
1834. Lincoln elected to Illinois legislature. 1837. End of Jackson's second presidency.	1836—40. Great Boer Trek. 1837. Queen Victoria's accession. First steam-boat from England to America. 1838. First telegraph line in England. 1839. Lord Durham's report on Canada.
1841. First telegraph in America. 1842. Lincoln leaves Illinois legislature, and (Nov.) is married.	1844. "Martin Chuzzlewit" published.
1845. Annexation of Texas. 1846. Boundary of Oregon and British Columbia settled with Great Britain. 1846-7. Mexican War. 1847-8. Lincoln in Congress. 1848. Gold discovery in California. 1850. Clay's compromise adopted. Death of Calham. 1852. Deaths of Clay and Webster. 1854. Missouri Compromise repealed. Republican Party formed.	1846. Boundary of Oregon and British Columbia settled with U. S. A. 1846-7. Irish famine. 1848. Revolution in France and in many parts of Europe. 1850. Constitution Act for Australian colonies. 1852. Constitution Act for New Zealand. 1854-5. Gold rush to Australia. Crimean War. 1854-6. Abolition of slavery in various Portuguese Dominions.

Some events in History of United States.	*Some events in English and General History.*
1856. Defeat of Frémont by Buchanan.	
1857. Dred Scott case.	1857-8. Indian Mutiny.
1858. Kansas. Lincoln-Douglas debate.	
1859. John Brown's raid.	1859. Publication of " Origin of Species."
	1859-60. Kingdom of Italy formed.
1860. Nov. Lincoln elected President.	1860. Slavery abolished in Dutch East Indies.
Dec. Secession carried in South Carolina.	
1861. Feb. 4. Southern Confederacy formed.	1861. Emancipation of Russian serfs.
Mar. 4. Lincoln inaugurated.	
Ap. 12—14. Bombardment of Fort Sumter.	
Ap. War begins. Further secessions.	
July. First Battle of Bull Run.	
Dec. Claim of Great Britain as to *Trent* accepted.	
1862. Ap.—Aug. McClellan in Peninsula.	1862. *Alabama* escapes from the Mersey (July).
Ap. Shiloh.	
May. Jackson in Shenandoah Valley.	
Aug.—Oct. Confederates in Kentucky.	
Aug. Second Battle of Bull Run.	
Sept. Antietam. Proclamation of emancipation.	
Nov. McClellan removed.	
Dec. Fredericksburg. Murfreesborough.	
1863. Mar. 1. Conscription Act.	1863. Revolution in Poland.
May. Chancellorsville. Jackson killed.	Maximilian proclaimed Emperor of Mexico.
July. Gettysburg, Vicksburg. New York riots.	
Sept. Chickamauga.	
Nov. Gettysburg speech. Chattanooga.	
1864. May. Beginning of Grant's and Sherman's great campaigns.	1864. Prussia and Austria invade Denmark.

Some events in History of United States.	*Some events in English and General History.*
1864. June. Cold Harbour. Baltimore Convention. July. Early's raid reaches Washington. Aug. Mobile. Chicago Convention. Sept. Sherman at Atlanta. Sheridan in Shenandoah Valley. Nov. Lincoln re-elected President. Dec. Nashville. Sherman at Savannah.	
1865. Jan. Congress passes 13th Amendment. Feb. Further progress of Sherman and Sheridan. Mar. 4. Second inauguration of Lincoln. Ap. 2—9. Richmond falls, and Lee surrenders. Ap. 14—15. Lincoln assassinated and dies. Dec. 13. Amendment ratified.	
1866. Atlantic cable successfully laid.	**1866.** Atlantic cable successfully laid. War between Austria and Prussia.
	1867. British North America Act. Slave children emancipated in Brazil. Fall and execution of Maximilian in Mexico.
1868. Rise of acute disorder in " reconstructed " South.	**1868.** Mikado resumes government in Japan.
1870. Amendment securing negro suffrage.	**1870.** Papal infallibility. Franco-German War.
1872. *Alabama* arbitration with Great Britain.	**1872.** *Alabama* arbitration with U. S. A. Responsible Government in Cape Colony.
1876. Admitted failure of Reconstruction. Election of Hayes.	
1877. Federal troops withdrawn from South.	
	1878. Slavery abolished in Cuba (last of Spanish Colonies).

INDEX

ABOLITION and Abolitionists: Early movement dies down, 36-9; rise of later movement, 50-2; persecuted, 51, 76; Lincoln's attitude, 76, 101, 116, 126-7, 151; their position in view of civil war, 172. *See* Slavery and Garrison.

Adams, Charles Francis: 236, 262, 264, 328.

Adams, John: 37, 236.

Adams, John Quincy: 47, 51, 115, 314, 388.

Aesop: 10.

Alabama, the: 224, 251, 264.

Alabama State: 175, 199, 212, 361, 388.

Alamo, the: 91.

Alexander II. of Russia: 256.

Alleghany (or Appalachian) Mountains: 26, 225, 244; distinct character of people in them, 56, 198.

Alley: 429.

Alton: 76.

Amendment of Constitution: how carried, 24; suggested amendment to conciliate South, 192; Thirteenth Amendment prohibiting slavery, 335-7, 431, 433; Fifteenth Amendment requiring negro suffrage, 334-5.

America, United States of, and American: Diverse character of Colonies, resemblances to and differences from England, 16-20; first attempt at Union, 20; independence and making of Constitution, 21-3; features of Constitution, 23-5; expansion, 26-8; Union Government brought into effect, 28-30, 41; rise of national tradition, 30-5; compromise on main cause of disunion, slavery, 35-40; parties and tendencies in the first half of nineteenth century, 40-52; triumph of Union sentiment, 45-6; growth of separate interest and sentiment in South, 43-5, 52-9; intellectual development and foundations of American patriotism, 59-61; further compromise on slavery, 96-101; political cleavage of North and South becomes definite, 109-12; "a house divided against itself," 143-7; for further developments, *see* North and South; *see also* Lincoln; Lincoln's position as to enforcement of union, 143-4; common heritage of America from Civil War, 455.

American Party, or Know-Nothings: 112, 117-8.

American Policy (so-called): 42-8.

Anderson, Major: 189-90, 208, 212-3, 449.

Appalachians. *See* Alleghany Mountains.

Appomattox River and Court House: 447.

Arbitration: 263-4.

465

INDEX

473

Inaugural Ceremony: Lincoln's first, 206; Lincoln's second, 438.

Independence. *See* Declaration of Independence.

Independents. *See* Congregationalists.

Indiana: 4, 9, 27, 38, 345.

Indians, North American: 3, 65.

Iowa: 27, 194.

Ironclads: 252.

JACKSON, Andrew: his opinion of Calhoun, 43; frustrates movement for
nullification, 46; his character, 46; revives party and promotes
growth of party machinery, and adopts "spoils system," 46-49;
other references, 66, 173, 209, 409.

Jackson, Thomas J., called "Stonewall," General: his acknowledged
genius, 217, 220; goes with State of Virginia, 229; his character,
230; Shenandoah Valley campaign and movement to outflank Mc-
Clellan, 295-8; Antietam campaign, 305; killed during victory of
Chancellorsville, 311; Lee's estimate of his loss, 357.

James, Henry: 461.

James River: 292, 298, 392-3, 438, 447.

Jefferson, Thomas: curious and displeasing character, 30; great and lasting influence on American life, 30-2; practical achievements in
statesmanship, 32; real sense and value of his doctrine, 32-5;
opinion and action as to slavery, 37-8; other references, 28, 46,
56, 179.

Jiggers: 331.

Johnson, Andrew: 400, 411, 451, 453.

Johnson, Samuel: 33, 35.

Johnston, Albert Sidney, General: 276-7, 281-2.

Johnston, John: 4, 6, 14.

Johnston, Joseph, General: 218, 247-8, 287-8, 295, 354-5, 378, 387, 390,
394, 436-7, 452.

KANSAS: 110-2, 115, 117, 126, 128, 139-40, 162-3.

Kentucky: 2-5, 9, 26, 81, 192, 197, 225, 229, 270, 334, 339-43.

Kipling, Rudyard: 88.

Kirkham's Grammar: 63.

"Know-Nothings." *See* American Party.

Knoxville: 226, 275, 359.

LAW, Lincoln's law study and practice, 10, 67, 68, 106-8, 271-2, 423.

Lee, Robert E., General: his acknowledged genius, 217, 220; goes with
State of Virginia, 229, 239, 376; his character, 230; cautious military advice at first, 246; opinion of McClellan, 285; operations
against McClellan, Pope, Burnside, and Hooker, 297, 311; invasion of Pennsylvania and retreat, 355-8, 386-7; resistance to Grant,
see Grant, 391-2, 398; appointed General in Chief, 431; abstains
always from political action, 431-2; final effort, surrender and
later life, 445-6.

La Couronne du Sacre de Louis XV

THE BOURBON
KINGS OF FRANCE

DESMOND SEWARD

BARNES & NOBLE
BOOKS
10 East 53d St., New York 10022
(a division of Harper & Row Publishers, Inc.)

Published in the U.S.A. 1976 by
HARPER & ROW PUBLISHERS, INC.
BARNES & NOBLE IMPORT DIVISION

ISBN 0–06–496185–0
Printed in Great Britain

CONTENTS

ILLUSTRATIONS

A genealogical tree appears at the beginning of each relevant chapter

ACKNOWLEDGEMENTS

I would like to thank the Hon John Jolliffe and Mrs Prudence Fay for their advice and helpful criticism. In addition, I am grateful to Mr Reresby Sitwell, the Hon Julian Guest, Mr Michael Thomas, Mr Hubert Witheford and Mr and Mrs Michael Dormer, who also gave me advice and encouragement, and above all to Mr Christopher Manning who read the typescript and the proofs. I have to acknowledge a special debt to Elisabeth, Viscountess Pollington for telling me of a seventeenth century English life of Louis XIII (see p 67).

Once again, I must thank Mr Richard Bancroft of the British Museum Reading Room and the members of his staff for their courteous and patient assistance.

For

EILEEN SEWARD

'Licentious or bigoted, noble or ignoble, there has seldom been a dull Bourbon. They were nearly all odd, original men of strong passions, unaccountable in their behaviour.'

Nancy Mitford

Foreword

'THAT ANCIENT LOYALTY'

This is a study of the Kings who reigned over France from 1589 until 1830. Eight monarchs are involved: Henri IV, Louis XIII, Louis XIV, Louis XV, Louis XVI, Louis XVII, Louis XVIII and Charles X; and also a pretender, Henri V.

Surprisingly, until now there has never been a straightforward narrative account of them written for the general reader, although there are many such studies of the Romanovs, Habsburgs and Hohenzollerns. Yet the Bourbons have been royal since 1548, when Antoine de Bourbon married the future Queen of Navarre. They have occupied the thrones of France and Navarre, of Spain, of the two Sicilies, of Parma and Piacenza, and of Lucca. Today there is again a Bourbon King in Spain, while a Bourbon Grand Duke reigns in Luxembourg. They are best known, however, as the mighty dynasty which once ruled France.

The Bourbons ruled their homeland for over two centuries, making it the greatest power in Europe, and taming and uniting a people who are arguably the most individualist and ungovernable in the world. The France of Louis XIV overawed even her most jealous neighbours, while the France of his successors, her predominance gone, charmed and inspired them by her civilization. The Bourbon Kings were the personification of both this grandeur and this seduction.

As Nancy Mitford said, there has seldom been a dull Bourbon. They emerge from a shadowy line of medieval princes of the blood—sons of St Louis but very far from the throne—with Henri IV. The founder of the dynasty, with his infectious gaiety and his sixty-four mistresses, is still a folk hero to the French, a mighty fighter and drinker. His enigmatic son Louis XIII was in complete contrast—lonely, morose and neurotic yet brilliantly successful in his partnership with Cardinal Richelieu. Louis XIV, the *Grand Monarque* with his 'red heels and his

xiii

golden snuff-box and his towering periwig', was worshipped at Versailles almost as a living idol and was one of the strangest and most remarkable kings who ever lived. Louis XV remains the most baffling of all French monarchs, intensely secretive and solitary; to at least one historian he is the most evil man ever to sit on a throne, directly responsible for the French Revolution; to another a seriously underestimated ruler who, had he lived longer, might have saved the monarchy.

Louis XVI came nearest to being a dull Bourbon, though with a consort, Marie Antoinette, who more than compensated for any dullness. But during the Revolution even Louis XVI became a figure of compelling interest, with his refusal to save himself by shedding his people's blood and then the martyrdom in which he was soon joined by his beautiful Queen. They were followed by their son, the pitiful Louis XVII who died in prison as a lonely, diseased little boy.

The Bourbons did not come to an end with the Revolution, but the Kings of the French Restoration are practically unknown to the general reader. Yet Louis XVIII, who gave France her first workable Parliamentary regime, is probably the most unappreciated of all French rulers. His brother, the charming but inept Charles X, who finally lost the throne, was also the King who commissioned six operas from Rossini, including *William Tell*, and refused to ban Victor Hugo's *Hernani*. Nor is it generally realized that a hundred years ago it seemed not merely possible but inevitable that the French would restore the Bourbon monarchy in the person of Charles X's grandson, Henri V; in the early 1870s both the President of France and the majority in the National Assembly were united in wishing to summon home the last member of the dynasty to be their King.

Alexis de Tocqueville wrote of the French under the *Ancien Régime*: 'Their feeling for the King was unlike that of any modern nation for its monarch, even the most absolute; indeed that ancient loyalty which was so thoroughly eradicated by the Revolution has become almost incomprehensible to the modern mind. The King's subjects felt towards him both the natural love of children for their father and the awe properly due to God alone.' The winning of that loyalty, the loss of it and the failure to regain it, are the theme of this book.

Prologue

PRINCES OF THE BLOOD (1276–1589)

The Bourbon claim to the throne of France

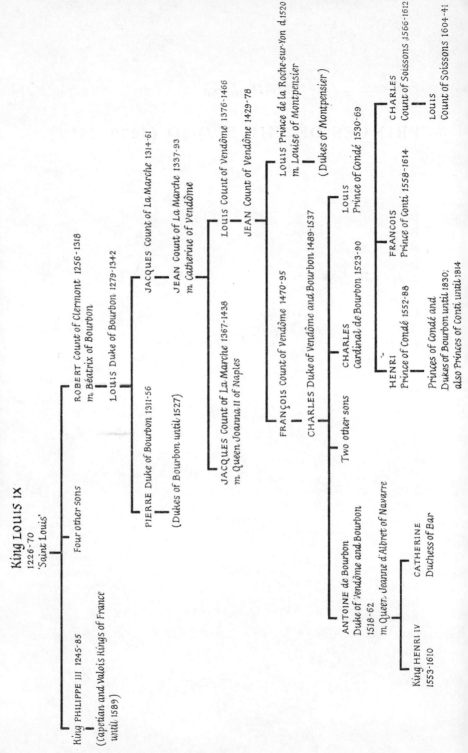

King LOUIS IX
1226-70
'Saint Louis'

King PHILIPPE III 1245-85
(Capetian and Valois Kings of France until 1589)

Four other sons

ROBERT Count of Clermont 1256-1318
m. Béatrix of Bourbon

LOUIS Duke of Bourbon 1279-1342

PIERRE Duke of Bourbon 1311-56
(Dukes of Bourbon until 1527)

JACQUES Count of La Marche 1314-61

JEAN Count of La Marche 1337-93
m. Catherine of Vendôme

JACQUES Count of La Marche 1367-1438
m. Queen Joanna II of Naples

LOUIS Count of Vendôme 1376-1466

JEAN Count of Vendôme 1429-78

FRANÇOIS Count of Vendôme 1470-95

CHARLES Duke of Vendôme and Bourbon 1489-1537

LOUIS Prince de la Roche-sur-Yon d.1520
m. Louise of Montpensier
(Dukes of Montpensier)

ANTOINE de Bourbon
Duke of Vendôme and Bourbon
1518-62
m. Queen Jeanne d'Albret of Navarre

CHARLES
Cardinal de Bourbon 1523-90

Two other sons

LOUIS
Prince of Condé 1530-69

King HENRI IV
1553-1610

CATHERINE
Duchess of Bar

HENRI
Prince of Condé 1552-88
Princes of Condé and
Dukes of Bourbon until 1830;
also Princes of Conti until 1814

FRANÇOIS
Prince of Conti 1558-1614

CHARLES
Count of Soissons 1566-1612

LOUIS
Count of Soissons 1604-41

In 1276 Robert, Count of Clermont, married Béatrix of Burgundy. Béatrix was a very great heiress indeed, her mother being the daughter of Archembault VIII, Lord of Bourbon and last of his line, who had died on Crusade in 1249. Although her mother was still alive and had married again, King Philippe III ordained that the lordship must pass to Béatrix. Bourbon l'Archembault (near Moulins in the modern *département* of Allier) took its name from some hot springs which the ancient Gauls had dedicated to the god Borvo. Since the ninth century its château had been the centre of a great *seigneurie* holding sway over a vast area of central France—the Bourbonnais. The descendants of Robert and Béatrix were to become the royal house of Bourbon.

Count Robert came of an even greater line than his wife. He was a Capetian, being the sixth son of King Louis IX, whose ancestor, Hugues Capet, Count of Paris, had seized the crown in 987 from the last Carolingians. Hugues took his name of Capet through being lay Abbot of Saint-Martin at Tours, where the cloak of the patron saint of France was venerated. As King, he was little more than feudal lord of about sixty dukes and counts, his effective realm reaching from just north of Paris to just south of Orleans. But with Philippe Auguste, who ascended the throne in 1180, the Capetian kings began to make real their authority. Louis IX (1226–70), who was Count Robert's father, inherited a realm which stretched from the North Sea to the Mediterranean. This crowned monk, who washed the feet of the poor and kissed lepers, was a strong, practical ruler. Unfortunately he was so much a product of his age as to lead two disastrous Crusades, to Syria and to North Africa, dying on the second; he was canonized in 1297. St Louis, who made the

3

monarchy almost sacred, was always present for his successors in the Sainte-Chapelle—which he built to house the Crown of Thorns—and in a charming life written by his friend, the Sieur of Joinville. (Of his reign, Joinville wrote, 'The throne shone like the sun which sheds its rays far and wide'.) Until the end, *Fils de Saint Louis* remained one of the proudest titles of a king of France.

Louis arranged rich marriages for all his sons. However when Robert of Clermont entered into the Bourbon inheritance in 1283, he was unable to take much pleasure in it. Five years before, during a tournament, Robert had received a blow on the head which rendered him permanently insane. He lived in quiet retirement until his death in 1318 at the age of sixty-two. He was succeeded by his son, and in 1327 King Charles IV made the *Seigneurie* of Bourbon into a Duchy.

When Charles died in 1328 the main line of the Capetians came to an end. However, it was (and is) almost impossible for the Capetian dynasty to fail, because of a provision in the Salic Law of the ancient Franks which forbids inheritance in the female line. Philippe of Valois, Charles IV's cousin, ascended the throne as Philippe VI. In 1346 he led his chivalry to disaster at Crécy, His one achievement was to purchase Vienne: the Counts of Vienne had styled themselves *Dauphin* (from the dolphin in their coat of arms), and from 1349 until 1830 the eldest son of the King of France was known as the Dauphin. Splendid and unlucky, Philippe personified the house which was to rule France for the next two centuries.

The Counts of Vendôme, who descended from a younger grandson of Robert de Clermont, were only distant cousins of the Valois, yet they were destined to inherit the throne as well as the Duchy of Bourbon. Charles, Comte de Vendôme, born in 1489, became one of the greatest lords in the kingdom, being made a Duke and Peer in his own right and Grand Huntsman of France. He played an important part in public life throughout the reign of François (1515–47): he performed the duties of the Count of Flanders at the King's Coronation, and in 1517 was one of three Princes who held the crown over the Queen's head at her coronation. The chroniclers give glimpses of the new Duke, gorgeously appareled, jousting at the Field of Cloth of Gold. In 1521 he commanded the rearguard of the royal army

during the King's campaign in Flanders; the year after, as the King's Lieutenant in Picardy, he conducted his own energetic campaign against the Imperial troops. However, in 1523 after the conspiracy of his cousin, the Constable de Bourbon, he was relieved of his command. Vendôme vindicated himself when King François was a prisoner in Spain, serving faithfully as President of the Council; he dismissed some Councillors of the Paris Parlement who had urged him to seize power, with the words 'Obey the King!' After the Constable's death, François rewarded Vendôme by recognizing him as first Prince of the Blood and head of the House of Bourbon. In his latter years the Duke seems to have spent most of his time away from court, devoting himself to his thirteen children. He had married Françoise d'Alençon, sister of the King's brother-in-law.

Vendôme died in 1547, aged forty-seven, and was succeeded by his son, Antoine de Bourbon. The Abbé de Brantôme remembered him: 'He was high-born, brave and valiant—men of the Bourbon race are never otherwise—and of a most handsome appearance (well-built, and much taller than my lords his brothers) and altogether regal in manner, very fine and eloquent in his speech'. But for all his courage and charm, Antoine was wildly unstable, to the point of insanity.

In 1548, when he was thirty, Antoine married Jeanne d'Albret, daughter of King Henri d'Albret of Navarre and Marguerite d'Angoulême, sister of François I. Her father died in 1555 and, as Jeanne III, she inherited Navarre. This ancient Kingdom had been reduced to a little strip of territory north of the Pyrenees—since 1512 most of the realm, on the far side of the mountains, had been occupied by the Spaniards. King Consort of this minute state, Antoine ranked as a European sovereign; the title, King of Navarre, was to be born by the Bourbons until 1830. As Jeanne's husband, Antoine was also lord of the d'Albret lands, a vast area of south-western France which included Béarn, Foix and Armagnac. He was the greatest magnate in France. But he was not satisfied, and dreamt feverishly of recovering his wife's lost domains.

After Henri II's death in a tournament in 1559, the French magnates saw the regency of his widow, Catherine de Medici, as an opportunity for a feudal revival. In his capacity of Governor of Guyenne, Antoine at once tried to recover

southern Navarre, in a notably foolhardy and unsuccessful expedition. But there were prizes to be won at home. Calvinism, with its aggressive ideology and para-military organization— each church had a captain as well as a minister—was sweeping France. Great nobles exploited the Reformation in the way they had the Hundred Years War. At the end of 1559 King Antoine adopted the Calvinist faith, Queen Jeanne already being an enthusiastic convert who corresponded with Calvin himself. However, Antoine's notorious fondness for loose women soon earned him a rebuke from the great Reformer. His marriage had begun as a love match; later Jeanne referred sadly to his many infidelities as 'a sharp thorn, not in my foot but in my heart'. In 1561 Antoine returned to the Roman Church: as Lieutenant-General he held the greatest office in the realm and was subordinate only to the Regent, Catherine de Medici.

The first War of Religion had now broken out. In October 1562, Antoine directed the siege of Rouen which was held by the Huguenots. He behaved with crazy bravado, dining in the trenches. Eventually he was shot while relieving himself in full view of the enemy. Mortally wounded, King Antoine expired a month later, in the arms of his latest mistress, having become a convert to Lutheranism on his deathbed. This futile weather-cock can never have suspected that his only son was to become King of France and found a new dynasty.

'That Man from Béarn'

HENRI IV (1589 — 1610)

_____

'I rule with my arse in the saddle and my gun in my fist'

The children of Henri IV

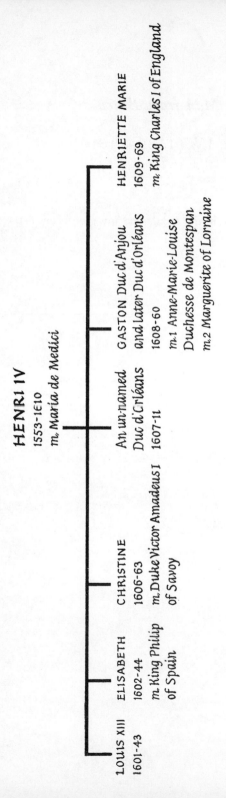

HENRI IV
1553-1610
m. Maria de Medici

LOUIS XIII
1601-43

ELISABETH
1602-44
m. King Philip
of Spain

CHRISTINE
1606-63
m. Duke Victor Amadeus I
of Savoy

An un-named
Duc d'Orléans
1607-11

GASTON Duc d'Anjou
and later Duc d'Orléans
1608-60
m.1 Anne-Marie-Louise
Duchesse de Montespan
m.2 Marguerite of Lorraine

HENRIETTE MARIE
1609-69
m. King Charles I of England

Henri's children by Gabrielle d'Estrées

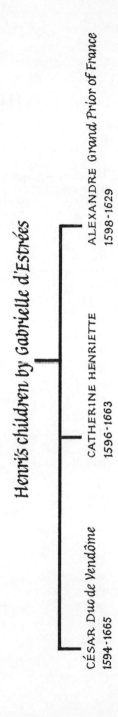

CÉSAR Duc de Vendôme
1594-1665

CATHERINE HENRIETTE
1596-1663

ALEXANDRE Grand Prior of France
1598-1629

Henri IV is certainly the most colourful of French Kings. The *Vert Galant* killed mountain bears with a knife, fought on foot with a pike at the head of his men, ate and drank enough for ten, had sixty-four mistresses, and wished every peasant to have a chicken in the pot on Sundays. At first sight this laughing, swaggering little hero seems quite different from the Bourbons who followed him. In fact he bequeathed a surprising number of his qualities to his descendants.

Henri of Navarre was born at Pau in Béarn, on 13 December 1553. At his christening the Navarrese King, Henri d'Albret, rubbed his grandson's lips with garlic and made him sip some wine. He enjoyed it and the old King, laughing, said, 'You're going to be a real Béarnais!' Philip II always referred to Henri as 'That Man from Béarn'. The baby was taken to a remote castle in the Pyrenees where he grew up with the local peasant children on a diet of bread, cheese and garlic, running barefoot in the mountains. He kept his southern accent—and his common touch—throughout his life. Of all the Kings of France he was the only Southerner.

His mother brought him up in the faith of Geneva. When, in 1561, Henri was taken to Paris on his father's orders and given a Catholic tutor, he refused to go to Mass. After his father's death, Jeanne reinstated the Protestant tutor; by the time he was ten Henri had changed his religion twice. He remained in Paris, attending classes at the Collège de Navarre. Eventually he was able to speak as well as write Latin and Greek with some fluency; he also acquired a knowledge of Spanish and Italian. In addition he learnt to write very beautiful French (Proust credits the Duchesse de Guermantes with writing '*le français exquis de Henri IV*'.) In 1567 he rejoined his mother and his sister Catherine at Pau. His education continued, including no doubt

instruction in fencing and the military arts. Relaxations were tennis—there was a magnificent court at Pau—swimming, hawking and, above all, hunting, which was one of the great passions of his life. He also learnt to dance, though, so his earliest biographer informs us, 'with more spirit than grace'.

The First War of Religion had come to an end in 1563 but the Second broke out in 1567, to be followed by the Third in 1568. There were between half a million and a million Huguenots in France, including a large number of experienced soldiers. But the vast majority of Frenchmen were Papists and when the Counter-Reformation began, a new, fanatical Catholicism came into fashion. Apart from a few rare eccentrics who were known as the *Politiques*, most people thought that the only solution was conversion or extermination.

The situation was made worse by the lack of any proper royal authority. From 1559 until 1589 France had inadequate Kings—François II (the husband of Mary, Queen of Scots), Charles IX and Henri III. These three decadent sons of Henri II left the government of the realm to their mother, Catherine de Medici, whose intrigues earned her a sinister name. Years later, when she and her brood were dead, Henri had some kind words: 'I ask you, what could she have done, poor woman, left at her husband's death with five small children and two families in France—ours and the Guises—who hoped to get the Crown for themselves? Wasn't it necessary for her to play some strange games, to deceive everybody, in order to protect her sons who reigned only because of her cunning? You may say she did harm to France—the marvel is she didn't do worse!'

When the Third War of Religion broke out, King Charles threatened to invade Béarn, and Queen Jeanne and her two children had to take refuge at La Rochelle. Jeanne's brother-in-law, Louis, Prince de Condé, commanded the Huguenot army; in March 1569 he was taken prisoner at Jarnac and shot. Although Condé's real successor was the Admiral de Coligny, the Huguenots hailed Henri as their champion; the fifteen-year-old boy and his mother were presented to the Protestant host who cheered them heartily. However, in 1570, when both sides had fought each other to a standstill, the Huguenots' right of public worship was restored, in a settlement guaranteed by four *places de sûreté*—towns with Huguenot garrisons.

Later, as a further guarantee, a marriage was arranged between Henri and the King's sister, Marguerite de Valois. Queen Jeanne died in June 1572, before it could take place (probably of tuberculosis, though it was rumoured that she had been poisoned by Catherine de Medici's perfumer, with gloves whose scent entered the brain).

Everyone believed that the marriage would bring peace and the great nobles of the realm, Protestant and Catholic, assembled in the capital. Henri's bride, Marguerite de Valois, was nineteen. Brantôme wrote, 'If in all the world there has ever been anyone perfect in beauty, it is the Queen of Navarre . . . and I think that all women who were, who are and who shall be are ugly next to her.' Portraits are less flattering. None the less, 'Margot' danced exquisitely, spoke Greek with astonishing fluency and was an excellent theologian. She was also a byword for promiscuity. The couple did not take to each other. On 18 August they were married at Nôtre-Dame, Marguerite wearing a royal crown and an ermine cape, with a long train of royal blue borne by three princesses. The marriage was the prelude to one of the most ghastly crimes in European history.

During the wedding, Catherine de Medici was deeply distracted by matters of state. Admiral de Coligny had persuaded Charles IX to attack Spain, a war which could only be disastrous. Catherine was in despair; Catholic nobles urged the Queen to agree to Coligny's assassination; reluctantly she yielded. The Guises, who had a father's murder to avenge, arranged the details. On 22 August one of their henchmen shot at the Admiral from a window, but only wounded him. The Huguenots were enraged. Catherine, terrified, accepted that a general massacre was the only solution. After much browbeating, King Charles, unbalanced at the best of times, agreed, screaming, 'Kill them all'. It was the eve of the feast of St Bartholomew.

Before dawn on Sunday 24 August 1572, the Duc de Guise's swordsmen broke into Coligny's bedroom. He was skewered with a pike, then his corpse was thrown out of the window to be hanged by its heels from the public gibbet. The tocsin sounded and the Paris mob was unleashed. Neither children nor pregnant women were spared—whole families had their throats cut. The Louvre was turned into a slaughterhouse, its floors and

11

staircases strewn with dead or dying Protestants. Henri and his cousin Condé were spared only because of their royal blood; they passed a terrifying night listening to the screams of their friends. The butchery continued for several days, at least 4,000 dying in Paris. Similar massacres took place in the provinces, 10,000 more Huguenots being killed by the end of September. But their strongholds held out and the Catholic 'final solution' merely precipitated the Fourth War of Religion.

Henri was forced to change his faith for a third time. He remained a prisoner at court for nearly four years. During this time he played the part of a simple, self-indulgent squire, hunting and whoring. Among those of other mistresses, he enjoyed the favours of Charlotte de Sauve, a beautiful blonde whom the Queen Mother had ordered to spy on him.

In 1575 a Venetian diplomat wrote a detailed description of the young King of Navarre. Henri was 'of medium height but very well built, with no beard as yet, brown skinned, and zestful and lively as his mother was; he is pleasant, affable and friendly in manner, and generous too, so people say. He is obsessed by hunting in which he spends all his time.'

In May 1574 Charles IX died in agony, of pulmonary tuberculosis—blood vessels burst all over his body. He was succeeded by his brother, Henri III, who for a few months had been a reluctant King of Poland. The last Valois monarch was an extraordinary figure; intelligent, cultivated and brave, he was also a homosexual and a religious maniac—transvestist orgies alternated with flagellant processions. This epicene psychopath surrounded himself with catamite *'mignons'* whose shrill quarrels often ended in lethal duels. On the whole he left government to his adored mother.

Two attempts at escape by the King of Navarre failed. A third scheme, in February 1576, was more carefully planned, but at the end of a day's hunting near Saint-Germain, news came to Henri that he had again been betrayed. Changing his plans, he galloped into the forest with only a few friends, though it was a freezing winter's night. They hardly drew rein for three weeks, until they reached Protestant Saumur and safety.

In May 1576 Henri III made peace with the Huguenots of the 'Calvinist Union'. They were given freedom of worship everywhere save Paris. A popular reaction saw the foundation of the

'Catholic League'; *La Ligue* mobilized the Faithful by parishes just as the Huguenots were by presbyteries. Between these two armed camps France sank into bloody anarchy.

Henri of Navarre, now the acknowledged leader of the Huguenots, ruled almost all south-western France. However, he seldom ruled it in peace, for there were five more 'wars of religion'. His armies were the Protestant lords and squirearchy on horseback. Until the fall of La Rochelle in 1628 these *'razats'* rode out to do battle for the soul of France, their cropped heads and Biblical speech (the 'patois of Canaan') anticipating the Roundheads of the English Civil War.

Henri held his court mainly at Nérac in Armagnac—the setting of *Love's Labour's Lost*, 'a park with a palace in it'. According to that dour Puritan, Agrippa d'Aubigné, the entire Huguenot court gave itself up to the pleasures of love. Henri could hardly be expected to remain content with one mistress. Mlle d'Ayelle, a Cypriot refugee, was succeeded by Mlle de Rebours and then by Xainte, one of Margot's women of the bedchamber. There were also tales of a girl who starved herself and her baby to death because of Henri's desertion, of another unreasonable lady who threw herself out of a window, and of a baker's daughter who drowned herself. In addition there was a charcoal burner's wife, and his groom's doxy whom he surprised in the stable (and who gave him a mild dose of gonorrhoea). Undoubtedly there was a pathological element in his insatiable sexuality. His chief passion at Nérac, Françoise de Montmorency-Fosseuse, was only fourteen when she became his mistress in 1579, and the honour went to her head when she found herself with child. But her baby died. In 1583 Marguerite left Henri for good.

By now Henri was fully mature, a stocky, jaunty little man with a fan-shaped black beard, upturned moustaches, hair *en brosse* and a tanned face with a great hooked nose and an invariable grin. His clothes were stained and shabby, he spoke broad Gascon and swore horribly, and he looked altogether more like a common soldier than a King. Ebullient, mercurial, laughing or weeping as the mood took him, he joked unceasingly, relying on charm rather than majesty. During the unending cavalry raids and sieges which occupied this period of his life, he developed remarkable powers of leadership. Yet in

13

some ways he had inherited the lack of balance of his father, King Antoine. His moods of melancholy were so extreme as to be pathological; he may well have been a manic depressive.

In January 1583 Henri at last met a woman worthy of him— Diane de Gramont, Comtesse de Guiche, known to history as '*la grande Corisande*'. A widow, she was twenty-six years old, a brunette with black eyes and a high forehead. Her friend, Montaigne, said there were few ladies in France who were a better judge of poetry. Corisande gave Henri intellectual as well as physical companionship. To her he wrote his most delightful letters, written as André Maurois says 'with a mixture of country warmth and Gascon poetry'. Sometimes he describes the landscape and the birds, sometimes he descends to the price of fish. He sent her passionate messages, 'loving nothing in the world so much as you . . . my soul, I kiss a million times those beautiful eyes which all my life I shall hold dearer than anything else in the world . . . I will live as your faithful slave. Good-night my soul.' He also wrote revealingly of his savage melancholia: 'all the Gehennas where a spirit can go are busy with mine', or 'until the tomb which is nearer than perhaps I realize'. He was incapable of being faithful, despite assurances that 'believe me, my fidelity is pure and stainless— there was never its like'. Corisande can hardly have relished his sorrow at losing little Gédéon, his son by Esther Imbert (daughter of a Protestant pastor)—'Think what it would have been like had he been legitimate.' With his letters he sent gifts —bird's feathers, fawns and wild boar piglets. The sheer number of his letters to Corisande shows how often he was away on campaign.

On 27 October 1587, at Coutras, Henri was forced to give battle to a greatly superior Catholic army. Henri III's favourite, Anne, Duc de Joyeuse, had 2,500 horse and 5,000 foot—the Huguenots numbered 2,000 horse and 4,000 foot. Navarre with a river at his back could not retreat. The two armies made a strange contrast; the Catholics in gilded armour and nodding plumes; the crop-headed Huguenots in leather jerkins and plain steel. Joyeuse launched a headlong frontal attack, his glittering cavalry only two deep. Henri had mixed musketeers with his cavalry and sited his three cannon where they could do most damage. The enemy were mown down, then three Huguenot

squadrons, each six deep, rolled them back. Henri, with his white plume and white scarf, led one squadron—his sword was red with blood. His followers were not so merciful; 5,000 Catholics were slain, including Joyeuse himself. The victory cost Henri only forty casualties.

He at once galloped off to present Corisande with the captured standards, disappearing for three weeks. He then informed his horrified followers that he had promised to marry her. Fortunately his gentleman-in-waiting, Agrippa d'Aubigné, made him realize that such a match would destroy any chance of inheriting the throne. Henri agreed not to see Corisande for two years. In the event he never saw her again. It was one of the very few occasions when Henri brought himself to resist a mistress.

After losing his army at Coutras, Henri III was at the mercy of the Catholic League. The *Seize*, a junta of fanatic Catholic bourgeois, controlled Paris. Against the King's express orders, Henri, Duc de Guise, made a triumphant entry into Paris in May 1588. The Duke was the hero of the Catholic mob—among the League it was openly argued that he would make a better King than the Valois, that he had a better right to the throne by virtue of his descent from Charlemagne. Henri III fled to Blois. He saw only one solution: at dawn on 23 December 1583, Henri de Guise was stabbed to death in the royal bedchamber, by the King's personal bodyguard, the Forty-five; the following day his brother, the Cardinal de Guise, was hacked to death by halberdiers. The League reacted with fury, mobs howling for revenge. King Henri discovered that he had alienated the greater part of his subjects and now ruled only a few towns in the Loire valley.

Inevitably he turned to his cousin of Navarre. They joined forces, after a public reconciliation and soon controlled the entire area between the Loire and the Seine. On 30 July they besieged Paris, with an army of 40,000 men. But on 1 August a Dominican friar, Jacques Clément, obtained an audience of the King and then stabbed him in the stomach, with a knife which he had concealed in his sleeve. The wound did not at first seem mortal. However, the King died during the night, after ordering his followers to take an oath of allegiance to Henri of Navarre.

Henri was King of France, but only in name. Most of the country was ruled by warlords, and everywhere the nobles robbed the bourgeois and harried the peasants, while the countryside swarmed with bandits. The League proclaimed as king Henri's uncle, the aged Cardinal de Bourbon, and struck coins in the name of 'Charles X'; but their real champion was the Duc de Mayenne (Guise's brother) who secretly hoped for the throne. A mere sixth of France supported Henri. His army dwindled every day—not many Catholics would fight for a heretic King who had been excommunicated. His only chance was to be a *Politique*, to appeal to those who preferred peace to religious war. Some years before, he had written to a friend, 'those who follow their conscience belong to my religion—my religion is that of everyone who is brave and true.' But while the Baron de Givry might fling himself at Henri's feet, crying, 'You are the King for real men—only cowards will desert you', there were not many men like Givry.

Meanwhile, Henri withdrew to Normandy with 7,000 troops, from where he could control the districts on which Paris depended for food, setting up his headquarters at Dieppe. Here he could obtain supplies and munitions from England. Mayenne pursued him, with 33,000 men. The odds were nearly five to one, and Henri's staff advised him to sail for England. Instead the King prepared an impregnable position. The road from Paris approached Dieppe through a marshy gap between two hills—on one side was the castle of Arques, on the other earthworks and trenches. Henri placed his *arquebusiers* and Swiss pikemen in the trenches and drew up his cavalry behind them; heavy *cuirassiers* armed with pistols but accustomed to charging home with the sword.

The Catholic cavalry were old-fashioned lancers who charged in widely spaced lines. Their commander, the Duc de Mayenne, was a strange figure, enormously fat, too fond of food and wine, gouty and tortured by venereal disease, who passed his days in a sluggish torpor, frequently retiring to bed. His staff were as idle and unbusinesslike as their commander. None the less, he lacked neither ambition nor courage.

The morning of 21 September 1589 was misty. When Mayenne attacked the trenches in the Arques defile, the mist prevented the castle's guns from firing. The Catholic pikemen

overran Henri's first line of trenches and the Catholic cavalry attacked on both flanks. When his front was on the point of disintegrating, Henri galloped up, shouting 'Are there not fifty noblemen of France who will come and die with their King?' His cavalry held the enemy—the Royalist foot rallied. Then the mist lifted and the castle batteries opened fire. The Leaguers withdrew hastily and Henri retook all the lost ground. Mayenne realized that he was facing a most formidable general. Some days later, news came that reinforcements were on their way to Henri—more Huguenot troops and an English expeditionary force. After another halfhearted engagement, the Duke withdrew.

Having taken the measure of his opponent, Henri was anxious to bring him to battle again. As bait he laid siege to Dreux. Mayenne advanced to its relief with 15,000 foot and 4,000 horse, and on 14 March 1590 engaged the King at Ivry. Henri had 8,000 infantry and 3,000 *cuirassiers*. A white plume in his helmet and a white scarf round his armour, he prayed before his troops—then he told them that, whatever happened, they must follow his white scarf. In the centre, he led his *cuirassiers* to crash into Mayenne's lancers, through whom they hacked and pistolled their way. All along the line the Royalists hurled back the enemy cavalry until they disintegrated, fleeing, abandoning their infantry to be shot down by Henri's *arquebusiers*. In his flight, Mayenne ordered the bridge at Ivry to be broken down behind him, cutting off many of his men from any hope of escape. The King ordered his exultant followers to spare Frenchmen but to give foreigners no quarter. Three thousand Leaguer foot and 800 cavalry died—nearly a hundred standards were taken.

In May he besieged Paris with 15,000 men, but the capital remained fanatically Catholic—even monks and friars took up arms. Rather than shed Parisian blood, Henri decided to starve the city into submission. (He is said to have passed his time debauching two young nuns, whom he afterwards made abbesses.) By July Paris was starving, horribly. There were cases of cannibalism—children were chased through the streets. People ate dead dogs, even the skins of dogs, together with rats and garbage. Some made flour from bones; those who ate it died. Thirteen thousand perished of hunger. At midnight on

17

27 July the King launched a general assault on the suburbs, but it was beaten back; despite its sufferings, Leaguer Paris was not prepared to surrender to a heretic King. Early in September it was relieved by the Duke of Parma, who ferried food across the Seine to the stricken city. Disconsolately the King withdrew, to winter in northern France. Many Royalist squires rode home.

It was in these gloomy days that Henri met Gabrielle d'Estrées. She was seventeen (Henri was thirty-seven), the daughter of a Picard nobleman, a plump, round-faced pink and white blonde who liked to dress in green. Gabrielle already had a lover, the sallow-faced Duc de Bellegarde (known as *feuille morte*—dead leaf). Rivalry drove the King into a frenzy. He showered letters on his *'belle ange'*—'My beautiful love, you are indeed to be admired, yet why should *I* praise you? Triumph at knowing how much I love you makes you unfaithful. Those fine words—spoken so sweetly by the side of your bed, on Tuesday when night was falling—have shattered all my illusions! Yet sorrow at leaving you so tore my heart that all night long I thought I would die—I am still in pain.' He wrote a poem, *Charmante Gabrielle*, and had it set to music. Eventually the affair went more smoothly. In the autumn of 1593 Gabrielle found herself *enceinte* with the King's child, the future Duc de Vendôme.

Meanwhile, after the setback at Paris, Henri's star had begun to rise again. In the summer of 1591 he was reinforced by English troops. For a time these were commanded by Queen Elizabeth's young favourite, the Earl of Essex, to whom Henri showed himself especially amiable. Sometimes relations were strained: Sir Roger Williams, being rebuked for his men's slow marching pace, snapped back that their ancestors had conquered France at that same pace. Even so, many Englishmen took a strong liking to Henri IV. In 1591 Sir Henry Unton, the English ambassador, wrote of him: 'He is a most noble, brave King, of great patience and magnanimity; not ceremonious, affable, familiar, and only followed for his true valour.'

Sully tells us that Henri's life on campaign was so exhausting that sometimes the King slept in his boots. Unton grumbled, 'we never rest, but are on horseback almost night and day.' None the less, Henri continued to hunt whenever possible.

The League was splitting into many factions. The Cardinal King, 'Charles X' had died in 1590, since when they had been unable to agree upon even a nominal candidate for the throne. The most formidable Catholic contender was the Infanta Isabella, daughter of Philip II of Spain—Guise, son of the murdered Duke, was to be her consort.

In November 1591 the Royalists beseiged Rouen. Henri, hearing that Parma was on his way to its rescue, galloped off with 7,000 cavalry to stop him. On 3 February 1592, at Aumâle, he unexpectedly made contact with the Spaniards and had to beat a hasty retreat after being wounded by a bullet in the loins; he was carried in a litter for several days. Unton commented gloomily, 'We all wish he were less valiant.' Parma relieved Rouen in April. However, he and Mayenne were trapped by Henri at Yvetot. When all seemed lost for them, Parma—who had been wounded—rose from his bed and evacuated his troops over the Seine by night. This great general then returned to the Low Countries where he died at the end of the year, his wound proving mortal.

One must admit that Henri IV lacked calibre as a soldier, compared with Parma. Though capable of fighting a defensive battle, as at Arques, the King was primarily a cavalry man—all his victories were won by the charge. His instincts as a captain of horse always came before his duty as a commander.

During 1592 Henri, the League and Philip II accepted a stalemate. The *Tiers Parti*, a combination of *Politiques* and moderate Leaguers, now asserted itself. Their solution was that Henri should turn Catholic. More and more Huguenots were willing to settle for a *Politique* monarchy—many urged the King to let himself be converted. After carefully counting his followers' reactions, Henri, in white satin from head to foot, was received into the Roman fold at Saint-Denis, on 23 July 1593. This conversion has too often been seen as an act of cynical statesmanship, summed up in the phrase '*Paris vaut bien une messe*' (there is no proof that he ever said it). In fact Henri wept over the gravity of the step. Since childhood his personal beliefs had been fought over by the kingdom's most persuasive theologians, and he must have become hopelessly confused. Within a fortnight, towns all over France were declaring for Henri, and on 25 February 1594 he was crowned King in

Chartres Cathedral. The impact upon France was extra-ordinary—Henri's putting on the Crown was accepted as both sacramental confirmation and seal of legality.

On 18 March Henri entered Paris, sold to him by its governor, the Comte de Cossé-Brissac. The same afternoon the Spanish troops marched out of Paris. Henri watched them, saying, 'My compliments to your King—go away and don't come back.'

The warlords still controlled most of France—Mayenne Burgundy, Joyeuse the upper Languedoc, Nemours the Lyonnais, Epernon Provence, and Mercoeur Brittany. But the bourgeoisie rallied to Henri. Town after town rebelled against the magnates; at Dijon, led by their mayor, armed citizens overcame Mayenne's troops and handed the town over to the Royalists.

Paris was still dangerous. Early in 1595, a young scholar, Jean Chastel, attacked Henri with a knife. Always agile, Henri recoiled so quickly that he escaped with only a cleft lip and a broken tooth.

At the beginning of 1595 Henri formally declared war on Spain. He had not done so before, to avoid the onslaught of Philip II's full military might, which was still directed against the Dutch. Soon the Spaniards were invading France on five fronts. In June Henri, operating in Burgundy, nearly lost his life in a cavalry skirmish at Fontenay-le-Français. With a small force of cavalry he found himself surrounded by the entire Spanish army. An enemy trooper slashed at him and was shot down only just in time by one of Henri's gentlemen. Luckily, reinforcements came up and the Spaniards withdrew. Henri wrote to his sister Catherine, 'You were very near becoming my heiress.'

In September 1595 Clement VIII at last agreed to give Henri absolution (officially he was still excommunicated). Six days later Mayenne negotiated a truce with Henri; in return for his submission he received three million livres and the governship of the Ile de France. Soon, of the warlords, the Duc de Mercoeur in Brittany alone remained. Elsewhere every important French city had recognized Henry IV by the summer of 1596.

But Philip II continued the war implacably. Henri was

desperate for money: in April 1596 he wrote to Rosny (the future Duc de Sully) that he had not a horse on which to fight nor a suit of armour. 'My shirts are all torn, my doublets out at elbow, my saucepan often empty. For two days I have been eating where I can—my quartermasters say they have nothing to serve at my table.' The King summoned the old feudal *Assemblée de Notables* to meet at Rouen in October 1596— nineteen from the nobility, nine from the clergy and fifty-two from the bourgeoisie. He invited them to share the task of saving France, in a tactful and flattering speech, and the necessary supplies were voted. Even so the war was far from won. In 1597 Amiens, capital of Picardy, was captured by the Spaniards. It was a severe loss, as not only was the town the centre of Franco–Flemish trade, but also a supply depot filled with munitions. Henri in person led an army to recapture it. 'I will have that town back or die,' he promised. 'I have been King of France long enough—I must become King of Navarre again.'

During his siege of Amiens, Henri reorganized the army. He placed the three veteran corps of Picardy, Champagne and Navarre (also known as Gascony) on a permanent basis, together with that of Piedmont and new regiments from the northern provinces, each of 1,200 picked musketeers and pikemen. There were also the Royal Guards and the various regiments of mercenaries, Swiss and German. His 4,000 Gendarmes d'Ordonnance provided the heavy cavalry.

Amiens surrendered on 25 September. Elsewhere the Spaniards were failing. The Dutch, still fighting the Spanish, were increasingly successful. Another Spanish Armada, destined for Ireland, was destroyed by storms. In March even Mercoeur surrendered. King Philip, in failing health, despaired and, on 2 May 1598 a treaty was signed at Vervins, by which France retained the frontiers of 1559 and regained any towns occupied by the Spaniards. (Queen Elizabeth of England was so furious that she called Henri the Anti-Christ of ingratitude.)

Henri had also taken steps to ensure peace at home. The Edict of Nantes, promulgated in April 1598, gave the Huguenots liberty of conscience and guaranteed their safety with 200 fortified towns maintained at the Crown's expense, though defended by their own Protestant garrisons. The Edict was not quite the triumph of common sense over bigotry that it seems

to modern eyes. In reality it was little more than an armed truce. Protestant France could muster 25,000 troops led by 3,500 noblemen who constituted an experienced and highly professional officer corps. An English observer, Sir Robert Dallington, noted: 'But as for warring any longer for religion, the Frenchman utterly disclaims it; he is at last grown wise— marry, he hath bought it somewhat dear!' France could simply not afford another civil war. Even so Henri had to bully the Parlements into registering the Edict.

Henri IV was now undisputed King of a France which was at peace for the first time for nearly half a century. At last he was able to enjoy Paris. He acquired new friends, like the fabulously rich tax farmer, Sebastien Zamet, an Italian from Lucca, who had begun his career as Catherine de Medici's shoemaker and then made his fortune as court money-lender. The King often dined and gambled or gave little supper parties for his mistresses in Zamet's hôtel in the Marais. Gabrielle became a familiar figure in the capital. She accompanied the King every-where; they rode together hand in hand, she riding astride like a man, resplendent in her favourite green, her golden hair studded with diamonds; she presided over the court like a Queen. As tactful and kindly in manners as she was warm-hearted and generous by nature, Gabrielle had the miraculous gift of making no enemies. She had born Henri several children, notably César whom the King made Duc de Vendôme. Gabrielle was given increasingly greater rank, eventually becoming a Peeress of France. Henri's love deepened every day. Eventually he decided to marry her. In token of betrothal he gave her his coronation ring, a great square-cut diamond.

Henri left her briefly in April 1598, when she was again big with child. Her labour began on Maundy Thursday, accom-panied by convulsions. On Good Friday, her stillborn child was cut out of her; she suffered such agony that her face turned black. She died the following day, of puerperal fever. Henri buried her with the obsequies of a Queen of France—for a week he wore black, and then the violet of half-mourning. He wrote to his sister, 'The roots of love are dead within me and will never revive.'

Perhaps fortunately for his sanity, he was soon busy with Savoy. Its Duke, Charles Emmanuel, who dreamt of restoring

the ancient Kingdom of Arles, delayed the surrender of Saluzzo and intrigued with Henri's courtiers; there was even a plot to poison the King. In late 1600 Henri invaded the Duchy. Snow made it a difficult campaign and Henri complained of the hardship—'France owes a lot to me, for what I suffer on her behalf.' By the peace of Lyons, signed in January 1601, Henri gained Savoyard territories on the Rhône which all but blocked communications between the Spanish Netherlands and Spain's possessions in northern Italy. It was the end of Henri's career as a soldier. Few monarchs have handled a pike or pistolled their way through a cavalry mêlée with such gusto.

He now had the task of rebuilding his ruined kingdom, a land of deserted villages and overgrown fields, of roads infested by highwaymen. Henri has been criticized for not giving France a new system of government and for restoring the traditional structure, the *Ancien Régime* which went down in 1789. But this is to ask that he should have been a man before his time. His education and outlook were those of the later Renaissance, not of the Enlightenment, and the Renaissance always looked to the past.

His chief minister was Maximilien de Béthune, Baron de Rosny, whom he made Duc de Sully and a Peer of France. Born in 1560, Sully belonged to the lesser nobility of Picardy and was a Huguenot. Bald, with a long beard like a patriarch, eccentric, avaricious and ill-mannered, he was also tireless in his master's service. He and he alone was able to work the archaic taxation system.

Henri's first concern was to tame the nobility, and he waged merciless war on the robber barons who plagued France. It took a full scale cavalry battle to defeat 'Captain Guillery's' band of outlaw noblemen in 1604. In 1607 the King lent cannon to a gentleman whose daughter had been abducted by a neighbour, so that he could batter down the walls of her kidnapper's château. He forbade nobles to ride over ripening crops. Formerly, provincial governorships had been tantamount to semi-independent fiefs, but Henri insisted on appointing every town governor and garrison commander. To the Duc d'Epernon who objected he wrote, 'Your letter is that of an angry man—I am not so yet and I pray you don't make me.' Fear of the overmighty subject also dictated his harsh treatment of his sister,

Catherine, now an eccentric old maid who had clung stubbornly to her Protestant faith, and still hoped to marry her cousin, the Comte de Soissons. Henri forced her to marry the Duke of Lorraine, who refused to allow her to practise her religion. Poor Catherine died three years later, 'of sadness and melancholy'.

In 1599, he met the last of his three great concubines, Henriette d'Entragues, daughter of the Governor of Orléans. A slim brunette, with a disturbing bosom and flashing black eyes, she at once infatuated Henri with her provoking airs and savage wit. She was a girl who knew just how to exploit the King's wild jealousies. He had been ready to marry Gabrielle d'Estrées, so she saw no reason why he should not make her his Queen instead. She blew hot and cold until at last Henri, frantic with lust, literally bought her from her father with the title of Marshal (although the man had never seen a battle), a large down payment in cash and a written promise that, should Henriette have a son by him, he would marry her as soon as he was divorced. A furious Sully sent the money in silver—it took many cartloads to deliver it.

However, Henri was just as capable of playing a double game in love as in war. When Rome obligingly annulled his marriage to Marguerite, he sought the hand of Marie de Medici, the twenty-seven-year-old daughter of the late Grand Duke Francesco I of Tuscany. In June 1600, Henriette, far gone with child, was resting in her bedchamber at Fontainebleau when the room was struck by lightning which actually passed under her bed. Terror made her miscarry. The King now regarded his promise as invalid, even if Mme de Verneuil (he had made Henriette a Marquise) did not. In October 1600 he married Marie by proxy.

From a political point of view Marie de Medici was thoroughly desirable—her uncle Grand Duke Ferdinand, was anti-Spanish and fabulously rich. Personally she was less desirable, a large, fat, stupid blonde with a vile temper. However, during the consummation of the marriage at Lyons she performed so well that afterwards the King boasted of her prowess. After a month's marital bliss he lovingly rejoined Henriette in Paris. When his wife arrived at the capital, the King insisted on presenting Henriette to her, saying, 'She has been my

mistress—now she is going to be your most biddable and obedient servant.' Henriette refused to curtsey and the King had to push her on to her knees before the infuriated Queen. He continued to sleep with both. On 27 September 1601 the Queen gave birth to a Dauphin.

Meanwhile Sully laboured tirelessly. When he became Superintendent of Finances he found the Crown in debt to the sum of £3 million. By 1608 he had paid off nearly half the debt, by redeeming mortgaged Crown revenues and increasing the yield from taxation. The principal direct tax was the *taille*, an arbitrarily assessed percentage of farm income or a specified percentage of a man's actual property. The chief indirect tax was the *gabelle*, an exorbitant duty on salt which caused much resentment. There were also duties on wine, besides customs levied at internal as well as external frontiers. Much of Sully's success was due to his reduction of profiteering by the tax farmers and of corruption in general.

As the nobility and clergy were exempt from taxation and many bourgeois purchased exemption, the taxes fell mainly on the peasantry, causing much hardship. Yet Henri cared for his peasants. In 1600 he told the Duke of Savoy, 'Should God let me live longer I will see that no peasant in my realm is without the means to have a chicken in his pot.' This wish for a chicken in every pot every Sunday is one of the most enduring of the legends about him. In the eighteenth century Henri IV was described as the only French King whose memory was kept green by the poor.

Another source of revenue was the *paulette* (named after a lawyer called Paulet). This was the sale of offices and titles in return for an annual payment of one-sixtieth of the purchase price. An office conferred nobility, including tax exemption, and in consequence a new aristocracy was created to balance the old feudal nobility. Before the Revolution almost every rich self-made man bought a title.

Henri knew that if France was to prosper, something more was needed than efficient methods of taxation. The country's chief source of wealth was crops and livestock, so he encouraged new methods of agriculture. Companies were founded to improve arable land, and Dutch experts were brought in to drain fen land. But peaceful conditions were quite sufficient for

the French peasant and by 1608 France was exporting grain. Waterways and canals were dug and roads repaired. In 1601 a Chamber of Commerce was founded, which investigated and encouraged horse breeding, linen manufacture, ship building, glass blowing and many other industries. The silk industry was revived, mulberry trees and skilled weavers being imported from Italy. Other luxury industries were founded, notably the Gobelin tapestry looms, and the Savonnerie carpet factory. Mineral resources were scientifically investigated, Henri creating the office of Grand Master of the Mines. Abroad, a spectacularly profitable treaty with Turkey obtained valuable facilities in the Levant for French merchants, while there were commercial treaties with England and the German Hansa. In Canada Samuel de Champlain established a tiny but enduring settlement of fur traders at Quebec. New edicts directed at increasing the country's prosperity were promulgated every month, edicts which the King not only read but helped to draft. Despite his hunting and whoring, Henri IV was his own first minister.

Sully, who combined the functions of Minister of Finance, Minister of the Interior, Minister of Transport and Minister of Works, was responsible for implementing all these reforms. But one must not underestimate Henri's contribution. He did far more than merely encourage his Minister, who lacked his enthusiastic response to new ideas. It was Henri who preached agricultural revolution, whose interest was largely responsible for the re-establishment of the silk industry, who supported the Canadian enterprise.

Henri's employment of Sully enabled him to avoid much of the odium incurred by unpopular policies. Sully's committees of privilege examined the nobles' rights to pensions and exemptions, to Crown lands and revenues, demanding full restitution where these had been usurped. These, together with his harshness and gauche arrogance, made him the most hated man in France. Soissons tried to dispose of him by a duel but backed down when Henri announced that he would act as Sully's second.

By 1602 the French nobility was thoroughly disenchanted. The hub of the opposition was the Maréchal de Biron, an old comrade-in-arms of Henri. During the Savoy campaign he

intrigued with the enemy, plotting the King's murder. An atheist and a student of witchcraft, there was something Satanic about Biron. He plotted a general uprising; Spain and Savoy were to invade while the Marshal and his friends would raise disaffected areas of the kingdom. Henri discovered the plot, but was reluctant to destroy such an old friend; three times he offered Biron a pardon if he would confess his treason, but was rebuffed. During his trial Biron raved and ranted, shrieking that Henri owed his throne to him. At his execution he had to be dragged to the block. The King commented, 'I would have given 200,000 crowns for him to have made it possible to pardon him; he did me good service though I saved his life three times.'

Then there was the conspiracy between Biron's friend, the Comte d'Auvergne, and Henriette's family, the d'Entragues, in 1604. Henriette had resolved to avenge herself when in the summer of 1604 her father had been ordered to surrender the Promise of Marriage (which he had concealed in a bottle). Henriette and her children were to flee to Spain, whereupon Philip III would recognize her son as King of France as soon as Henri had been assassinated. Two attempts were made on Henri's life but failed, then her sister informed the authorities. Henriette was confined to a convent. However, the King soon forgave her, though she never quite recovered her former influence.

Potentially the most dangerous conspirator of all was the Protestant Duc de Bouillon, who tried to stir up the Huguenots. However, Henri outmanœuvred him, sending Sully to the General Assembly of the Reformed Church in 1605, where he persuaded them to accept the status quo. The King then marched into Bouillon's lands in the Limousin, blowing up his château. In 1606 he arrived before the Duke's stronghold of Sedan with an army and cannon, and forced him to submit.

The court of Henri IV has been described as a cross between a barracks and a bawdy house. It was certainly informal. When the court wine taster drained Henri's glass to the last drop, instead of merely sipping it, the King complained, 'You might have left some for me.' He was on good terms with the Parisians, roaming the streets of his capital with little or no escort. He preferred to dress plainly, in grey satin without lace or embroidery, and was careless about washing: Henriette once

27

told him, 'You smell like carrion.' (However, the legend of Henri's chewing garlic like fruit, so that his breath felled an ox at twenty paces, is apocryphal.) His teeth were bad, stopped with lead and gold, and in later years he had to wear spectacles. He was so small that he always used a mounting block. Yet, for all these inelegancies, the English ambassador noted that the great lords of France trembled in King Henri's presence. He could be stately enough, receiving embassies seated on his throne, surrounded by Princes of the Blood; on such occasions he dressed magnificently, wearing diamonds in his hat. Indeed, during his reign the Louvre and the Tuileries lacked neither grace nor splendour.

Henri was a great builder, notably at Paris, Saint-Germain-en-Laye, Fontainebleau and Monceaux. His most notable enterprise was the gallery connecting the Louvre with the Tuileries, which an English visitor described as 'unspeakably fair'. At the Tuileries he created, in the opinion of the same visitor, 'the fairest garden for length of delectable walks that ever I saw'. At Saint-Germain-en-Laye he built a series of terraces which overlooked the Seine. (Here he installed hidden water jets which drenched the unwary courtiers who trod on them, to the King's joy.) There was a project to build an enormous new palace at Blois, but this came to nothing. Henri was also interested in public building. Work on the Pont Neuf commenced in 1604, and the next year the Place Royale (now the Place Vendôme) was begun, with its *pavillons* and arcades. There was also the Place Dauphine and the uncompleted '*Porte et Place de France*' which was intended to rehouse the Parisian poor.

Henri has never received his due as a patron of the arts. He was responsible for the second 'School of Fontainebleau'. (The first school, a product of the inspired patronage of François I, had lost its momentum under the last Valois.) At Henri's request, Toussaint Dubreuil executed a large number of frescoes at Fontainebleau and at the King's new château of Saint-Germain. Dubreuil also worked on the *petite galerie* of the Louvre, together with Jacob Bunel. Amboise Dubois probably painted the portraits in the great gallery, which so impressed an English tourist; Thomas Coryate refers to 'many goodly pictures of some of the Kings and Queens of France, made most

exactly in wainscot, and drawn out very lively in oil works upon the same'. Dubois also painted a portrait of Marie de Medici as Minerva. Both Henri and Marie were painted by Frans Pourbus in 1608; Henri, in formal black and wearing the Saint Esprit, looks every inch the soldier King, grizzled but still vigorous. Another artist who worked for him at Fontainebleau was Martin Fréminet, who decorated the Chapelle Royale.

One can hardly claim that Henri IV was an intellectual. The news that James I of England had written a book horrified him. (It was he who called James 'the wisest fool in Christendom'.) None the less, Henri was well aware that writers could play a useful political role in the presentation of the restored monarchy. The historian Jacques Auguste de Thou, who wrote a Latin *History of My Own Time*, was made Grand Master of the King's library, while a Historiographer Royal was appointed, Pierre Matthieu. There was an acknowledged Poet Laureate, François de Malherbe, who was made a Gentleman of the Bedchamber. Even a Huguenot scholar, the great Isaac Casaubon, received a court appointment.

The King sought to weaken the Huguenots, not by persecution but by encouraging a Catholic revival. The Jesuits were allowed to set up schools. He encouraged public disputations between theologians of the two persuasions. He even tried, unsuccessfully, to persuade Saint François de Sales to leave Savoy and accept a French diocese; he commented, 'A saint. And furthermore a gentleman too.' Throughout his reign, Catholic reform gathered momentum.

Despite these edifying preoccupations, the King continued to keep his *ménage à trois*. Henriette insisted she ought to be Queen and that the Dauphin Louis was a bastard, referring to Marie as 'your fat Florentine banker'. At the same time the Queen nagged Henri so viciously that often he had to flee from the marital bed, where he 'found thorns'. (Yet Sully tells engagingly how, when he brought the King and Queen presents at daybreak on New Year's Day 1606, the King told Marie, 'Awake, you dormouse, give me a kiss, and groan no more, for I have forgotten all our little quarrels; I am anxious to keep your mind easy, lest your health should suffer during your pregnancy.') To make life even more difficult, Marie acquired

two deplorable favourites, Concino and Leonora Concini. The latter, half maid, half lady-in-waiting, was the Queen's foster sister, who had married a foppish Florentine homosexual. Sully wrote that they deliberately worked on the Queen to make her dissatisfied with the King.

Henri had his bastards brought up at Saint-Germain-en-Laye with his children by Marie. The Queen had two more sons, a Duc d'Orléans who died in infancy, and Gaston, Duc d'Anjou; and two daughters—Elisabeth who married Philip IV of Spain, and Henriette Marie who married Charles I of England. Henriette's children were Gaston Henri, who was made Bishop of Metz and Abbot of Saint Germain when he was seven, and Gabrielle—both legitimized. Henri was devoted to them all. The Spanish ambassador entered an official audience to find him crawling on all fours round the throne room with children on his back.

The King's diversions continued to be hunting and gambling. At the latter he was a bad loser, paying his card debts grudgingly. His cronies now included François de Bassompierre, a high-spirited young soldier, while a somewhat surprising new friend was his confessor, a suave, saintly Jesuit. Henri liked Père Cotton so much that courtiers joked that the King had 'cotton in his ears'.

In 1605 Queen Marguerite—Henri had allowed her to retain the title—returned to Paris. She was enormously fat and wore a golden wig, employing blond English footmen for their hair. With her vast skirts she could block an entire doorway. She built an hôtel near the Louvre, filling it with gigolos and savants for she retained her conflicting tastes for vice and piety. (St Vincent de Paul was one of her chaplains.) She made fast friends with Henri's children whom she loaded with presents— they called her Aunt.

In 1609 Sir George Carew reported of Henri: 'His health and strength he hath in a great proportion, his body being not only able for all exercises, but even for excesses and distempers, both in intemperance and incontinency. And though he be sometimes bitten by the gout yet ever he findeth means suddenly to shake it off. And in the four years, that I served in that court, I found him little decayed in his countenance, or other disposition of his body, but he rather grew to look younger every day than

other.' Henri's good health may have owed something to good wine. Although he is celebrated for drinking enough for four, in fact he seems to have indulged in quality rather than quantity. A rousing traditional song is attributed to him in praise of 'my old Arbois', that rare and almost legendary wine from the Jura. Above all he enjoyed the still grey wine of Champagne, sometimes boasting that he was 'King of Ay', a noted Champenois vineyard.

Yet Henri was increasingly plagued by melancholy. Sometimes he blurted it out—'I wish I were dead'—at others he was known to dance and whistle by himself. He regretted his vices but had a pathological need of sex. To some extent his melancholy was soothed by religion. His skilled confessor, Père Cotton, realized that he was not altogether responsible for his sins.

As late as the end of 1609, true to the tradition of British diplomacy, Carew believed that Henri was anxious to avoid war. In fact Henri had been preparing for it for many years. When Sir George wrote, Henri had an army of 37,000 men under arms, all (save 1,000 mounted noblemen) being regular troops receiving pay. The arsenal in Paris was well stocked, and money had been set aside for a war chest. The artillery had been reorganized by Sully, as Grand Master of the Ordnance, and a corps of engineers had been formed. Although the army continued to be officered by noblemen, they now served on a professional instead of a feudal basis. Two military academies were instituted as well as a hospital for veterans. If necessary the King could muster 100,000 troops.

Henri was determined to break the encirclement of the Habsburgs, who among them ruled most of Europe. In Spain he intrigued with the persecuted Muslims and Philip III was so alarmed that in 1609 he ordered the expulsion of two million Moriscos. But it was in Germany that Henri saw most opportunity: he intended to enlist the Protestant Princes against the Emperor. His opportunity came with the death of the Duke of Cleves-Julich-Berg in March 1609; the succession was disputed and the Emperor occupied the duchies, to the alarm of the Princes. By August Henri was preparing for war.

The King seems to have referred to his ultimate objectives as 'a Grand Design', and in the past many historians credited him

with an inspired plan for European peace. The earliest account occurs in Sully's memoirs, the alleged project taking a more definite shape in the revised eighteenth-century version of Sully's memoirs. The supposed scheme aimed at guaranteeing nations and creeds by the collective agreement of a great European League led by France. Modern historians agree that the Grand Design was in large part invented by Sully, though possibly a few ideas may be ascribed to Henri. D'Aubigné limited it to confining Spain between the Pyrenees and the sea. Henri's real foreign policy was identical with that of Cardinal Richelieu—to make France the greatest power in Europe by breaking the Habsburg hegemony.

There now occurred Henri's last love affair, with the fifteen-year-old Charlotte de Montmorency. He first saw her at a ballet rehearsal at the Louvre, dressed as a nymph. She raised her spear as if to stab him, whereupon the King, in his own words, 'almost swooned away'. The King made himself a laughing-stock, dressed in scented ruffs and sleeves of Chinese satin. Sighing, he told Bassompierre, to whom she was engaged, 'I want to talk to you as a friend. I have just fallen in love, I am bewitched and worse by Mlle de Montmorency. If you marry her and she loves you I will hate you; if she loves me, you will hate me.' He explained that he was going to marry her to his nephew Condé, 'as a comfort for my old age'. When the worldly-wise Bassompierre said he would break off his engagement because it gave him an opportunity of showing how fond he was of the King, Henri burst into tears and said he would make his fortune as though he were one of his own bastards.

Condé, first Prince of the Blood, was a reserved, awkward youth of twenty, dissolute and reputed to have caught the pox. His favourite pastime was drinking in low taverns. He and Charlotte were married in May 1609. By now Henri had sunk to spying on Mme la Princesse, wearing a false beard and even hiding behind a tapestry to watch her through a hole. He persuaded her parents to petition for the annulment of her marriage. Unexpectedly Condé refused to bring his wife to court; at the end of 1609 the young couple fled to Brussels, where there was a last abortive attempt to procure Charlotte by kidnapping her and lowering her from a window by a rope.

But by then the King had greater matters to engage him.

For in August 1609 France began to arm. By the spring of 1\
40,000 men were massed in Champagne, Cleves-Julich-B\
was to be invaded in May. Instead of fighting for his own throne,
Henri would take the field as ruler of a great European power.

Yet he was in a strange mood, haunted by the fear of death.
'By God! I'm going to die in this city, I'll never get out of it,'
he told Sully. He expected to be murdered at Marie's belated
coronation which took place on 13 May, upsetting his intimates
by constant gloomy outbursts. His fears were grounded on
more than melancholy. Catholic fanatics were outraged that he
should seek alliances with Protestant Germany—Leaguer
France was far from dead. Undoubtedly there were many plots
on his life in 1610.

A demented out-of-work schoolmaster, François Ravaillac,
who had no connection with any of these plots, dreamt that he
had been summoned by God to kill Henri. The day after the
coronation, gloomier than ever, the King decided to visit Sully
at the Arsenal. After saying farewell three times to the Queen,
he set off in his carriage. As it slowed down at the corner of the
rue de la Ferronnerie, Ravaillac jumped up from the road, leant
through the window and stabbed him with a broken table-knife.
The King gasped, 'I'm wounded', whereupon Ravaillac stabbed
him again. Henri fell back, dead.

France was overwhelmed with grief. Sully feared a rebellion
but his fears were groundless. Ravaillac was executed with
fiendishly ingenious tortures in the Place de Grèves, amid the
applause of a revengeful mob.

Perhaps it was as well that Henri died when he did. Despite
his preparations, France was not ready for a war against the
combined might of Spain and the Empire; while the squalid
affair with Mme la Princesse, and the paranoiac terrors which
he experienced in Paris, indicate a mind on the edge of a severe
breakdown. None the less, Henri Quatre was a great King; even
today *'le Vert Galant'* is still one of France's heroes. As Mme
de Staël wrote, 'He was the most French of all French Kings.'

'That Idiot'

LOUIS XIII (1610–1643)

———————————

'God knows I never liked life'

The children of Louis XIII

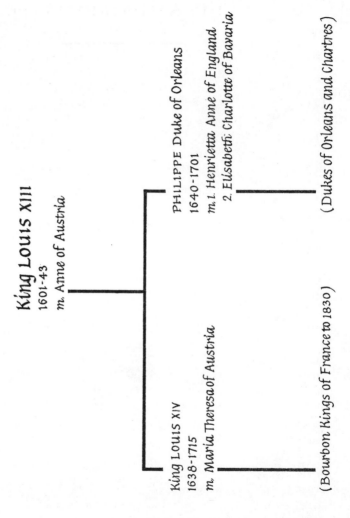

King LOUIS XIII
1601-43
m. Anne of Austria

King LOUIS XIV
1638-1715
m. Maria Theresa of Austria

PHILIPPE Duke of Orleans
1640-1701
m.1. Henrietta Anne of England
2. Elisabeth Charlotte of Bavaria

(Bourbon Kings of France to 1830)

(Dukes of Orleans and Chartres)

Louis XIII was born at Fontainebleau on 27 September 1602. It was a difficult birth, which may have been the original cause of his mother's dislike. Through Marie, he was a quarter Italian and a quarter Habsburg. Certainly no son was ever more different from his father.

Louis had a miserable childhood. He was a timid, unattractive little boy, and Henri tried to beat his timidity out of him. (He none the less adored his father; years later his greatest compliment about anyone was the odd remark, 'I'm near my father—I can smell his armpit.') Queen Marie, who seems to have lacked any maternal feeling, had him whipped every morning. He grew up neurotic and distrustful, one of the strangest and most enigmatic of all French Kings.

The news of Henri IV's assassination so shocked France that even the great princes rallied to the throne. The Parlement of Paris was summoned, in its capacity as first court of the realm, and the eight-year-old King presided over a *lit de justice*, a special Royal session of Parlement. The Duc d'Epernon, who commanded the infantry in Paris, entered the great hall of the Palais Royal where the Parlement sat. He was wearing his sword. 'My sword is still in its scabbard,' he shouted, 'but if the Queen is not made Regent at once I shall draw it.' The Parlement hastily declared that Marie's regency was according to the wishes of both the late and the present King. Louis was crowned at Rheims on 17 October 1610. The ceremony must have been a frightening experience for a boy of eight. Four day later, at Saint-Marcoul, he touched no less than 900 persons for the Evil.

Marie de Medici, who was as stupid as she was heartless, was quite confident that she could govern France. Her favourites,

the Concini, became all-powerful. Leonora slept next to the Queen's bedchamber, being consulted on all matters of state; her advice was partly dictated by astrologers, but mainly by her husband's insatiable thirst for money and titles. For the time being Marie and this ignoble pair had the sense to retain Henri's old ministers, although Sully soon resigned (he lived on in obscurity until 1641). Abroad, Henri's foreign policy was reversed—French troops were withdrawn from Cleves-Julich and an alliance was sought with Spain. At home, Concini had a programme of sorts; to keep the nobles in their place and to make Lorraine part of France. In the meantime he acquired a huge fortune by peddling favours—Leonora's speciality was selling pardons. He bought the marquisate of Ancres and then, although he had never seen a battle, took the title of Marshal.

Rebellion was inevitable. First Bouillon tried to raise the Huguenots: Marie bought him off with an enormous bribe. But the Huguenots were not the only threat. '*Les Grands*'—the Great Ones—considered that with Henri's IV's death, 'the day of Kings has passed and the day of great lords and princes has come.' They remained almost as formidable as they had been during the Wars of Religion. Each had a large 'household' —a retinue of armed noblemen amounting to a private army. Some had provincial governorships which provided them with fortresses—Epernon, Governor of Metz, seized its citadel as soon as Henri died, referring to his province as 'my kingdom of Austrasia'. Condé, First Prince of the Blood, had secret hopes of the throne itself. Early in 1614 he left court, raised an army and seized the fortress of Mézières. He publicly accused the government of squandering the realm's wealth, and inflicting hardship on the entire country. His manifesto concluded with an ultimatum that the States General (the representative body of the French nation) be summoned. He was joined by the Dukes of Mayenne, Longueville, Nevers and Vendôme, but as neither the bourgeois nor the Huguenots would support them, they allowed themselves to be bought off with the last of Sully's treasure.

The States General—140 clergy, 132 nobles and 192 bourgeois—met in the old Hôtel de Bourbon (opposite the Louvre) in October 1614. It was to be their last formal meeting until the fateful year of 1789. King Louis, who was now twelve,

presided, a sulky, pale-faced little figure in white satin. T
three estates squabbled furiously. The clergy imperiousiy
demanded the implementation of the Council of Trent. The
bourgeois countered—by urging that the French Church be
reformed; they also asked for an end to pensions paid to great
lords, the suppression of high military offices and the prohibition of duelling. As for the nobles, they did not want 'the
children of cordwainers and soap-boilers to call them brother',
demanding that anyone who called a bourgeois 'Monsieur'
should be fined. The assembly, having achieved nothing,
dispersed in March 1615 when royal officials summarily closed
the hall where it met. However preposterous Marie's regime
may have been, seventeenth-century France had no practicable
alternative to absolute monarchy.

During the assembly, the loyal address by the spokesman
of the clergy had been a brilliant analysis of the problems
confronting the state, couched in graceful terms which compli-
mented the Regent. The spokesman was the twenty-eight-year-
old Bishop of Luçon, Armand du Plessis de Richelieu. Marie,
delighted by such flattery, marked out the fascinating young
prelate for preferment.

In autumn 1615, just as the Regent and her son were setting
out for Bordeaux, Condé rose again. The Duc de Rohan formed
an alliance with him, leading the Huguenots into revolt. It was
a return to the bad days of the Valois; even worse, for now
Catholics and Protestants were banding together against the
Crown. Fortunately Condé lost his nerve, allowing himself to
be bought off once more, in May 1616. He received a million
and a half livres—he had already had four and a half million—
while a further six million was divided among his followers.

In October 1615 Louis was married at Bordeaux to Anne of
Austria, an ash-blonde, pink-faced Infanta of Spain. The new
Spanish alliance was doubly cemented by the marriage of
Madame Elisabeth, Enfant de France, to the Infante Don
Philip (the future Philip IV). The new Queen of France was
only thirteen. However, in November Louis consummated the
marriage—probably his mother told him that it was his duty.
The experience proved disastrous and gave the King a lifelong
aversion to physical love.

Marie intended to remain Regent for as long as possible.

When Louis was fifteen she slapped his face in front of the entire court; he tried to attend a meeting of the Royal Council, whereupon she took him by the shoulders and threw him out of the chamber. Saint-Simon says that according to his father, a friend of Louis, 'The Regent wanted a son who was only King in name and who would not interfere with her favourites. He was therefore brought up in a way as harmful as possible for his character. He was left completely idle, receiving no education whatsoever. He frequently complained about it to my father, and in later years often referred to the fact that he had not even been taught to read.' (Louis may have been indulging in a certain amount of self-pity; not only could he write elegant and economical French, but he spoke excellent Italian and Spanish.)

By now Louis was a very strange boy indeed, nervous and awkward, a King who stammered when he spoke, who was frequently tongue-tied. Yet he was not without kindly impulses. From an early age he disliked any derogatory remarks about his Huguenot subjects. As a boy of eleven he intervened passionately in a case where a girl was unjustly accused of murdering her baby.

His chief delight was falconry. His other favourite diversion was hunting—mainly stag, fox and wolf. He killed his first stag when he was only twelve. If possible he hawked or hunted every day and he is said to have ridden horses to death. He certainly achieved the notable feat of killing six wolves in one day. When it was too wet to go out, he flew hawks at tame finches which he kept in his room, chasing them all over the Louvre. Sometimes the solitary boy made teams of dogs run through the palace dragging cannon. At other times he cooked omelettes and made sweets in the palace kitchens. He had his own smithy. Another amusement was a little carriage—a kind of dog-cart—which he drove himself. He did not have a single friend, until the emergence of Charles d'Albert de Luynes, a rather dim falconer.

Voltaire says that Luynes ingratiated himself by teaching grey shrikes to fly at sparrows. In fact Luynes's job was to fly falcons at red kites, the most prized of all quarry. He was a big tall man, goodlooking rather than handsome, with curly hair and a pleasant expression. In his late thirties, he was the son of a Provençal hedge squire who farmed with his own hands the

family's manor near Marseilles. A gentle, unselfconfident soul, he was far from aggressive—once when challenged to a duel he sent his brother.

While hunting he frequently found himself alone in the forest with the King. The lonely, stuttering boy began to confide in this big man with the reassuring manner. Luynes was a very limited personality but he had the gift of sympathy. For the first time in his life the young King had met a human being whom he trusted: he became so dependent on his falconer that in his sleep he was heard to mutter 'Luynes! Luynes!' Marie, informed, thought of dismissing the man; she decided on bribery instead, making him Captain of the Tuileries and then Governor of Amboise with its great château.

Ancres, who had dismissed all Henri IV's old ministers, was only too aware of the hatred which his ignoble government inspired. Condé was cheered in the Paris taverns and in his cups spoke of seizing the throne. Everywhere obscene songs about the Regent were sung with enthusiasm. So frightened was Ancres that he and Leonora considered flying to Italy in disguise. But he would not leave his treasure. In September 1616 he managed to arrest Condé, besides sending troops into the provinces to cow *les Grands*. His regime acquired a most useful new servant when the Bishop of Luçon was given a post equivalent to Foreign Minister. The Marshal did not suspect that his greatest danger was the King whom he treated with the utmost contempt; he remained seated in his presence without doffing his hat; sometimes he even ignored him. The tongue-tied boy felt an overpowering sense of injustice—about this time he suffered a nervous fit of such violence that doctors suspected epilepsy.

It was Luynes of all people who organized the plot which brought Ancres down. When one of the conspirators asked the young King what they should do if the Marshal resisted arrest, Louis remained silent. Someone said, 'The King wishes that he should be killed'—Louis still kept silence.

On the morning of 24 April 1617 the Marshal d'Ancres strutted across the drawbridge of the Louvre. He stopped in the courtyard to read a petition. Suddenly the captain of the royal guard, the Marquis de Vitry, accompanied by twenty-five guardsmen, pushed through the crowd and, seizing him by the

arm, shouted 'In the King's name!' Ancres shrieked in Italian *'A me!'* and tried to draw his sword. Vitry's men drew pistols from beneath their cloaks—the Marshal fell to the ground, shot three times in the face. Kicking the body, Vitry cried, *'Vive le Roi!'*

Louis was waiting for the news with a sword in one hand and a pistol in the other. Climbing on to a billiard table he cried, *'Merci! Grand merci à vous! A cette heure je suis roi!'*

His mother was given the news by a lady-in-waiting. 'All I can hope for is a crown in heaven,' screamed the Regent, who ran up and down her chamber, wringing her hands. When asked who would tell Mme la Maréchale that her husband had been killed, Marie shrieked, 'I have myself to think about, leave me alone! if you don't want to *tell* her, *sing* it to her! Don't speak to me about them—I warned them long ago that they ought to escape to Italy.' Ignoring frantic appeals to see him, Louis sent word to his mother to stay in her chamber and not to meddle with affairs of state.

Ancres's body was secretly buried in the church of Saint-Germain-l'Auxerrois, but the mob dug it up, hung it on the Pont Neuf and then tore it to shreds. Royal guards burst into Leonora's room. Pulling her out of bed they found that she had already hidden some of her treasures beneath her mattress—it was rumoured that Crown jewels were among them. She was imprisoned in the Bastille, accused of plotting against the state and of black magic. Torture did not break her spirit. Asked at her trial what spells she had used to bewitch the Queen, she replied, 'Only the power of a strong mind over a weak one.' She was burnt at the stake in the Place de Grève.

The new ruler of France was Luynes, however much Louis might proclaim himself King. His government was scarcely more effective than Ancres's. The petty noble set about transforming himself into a great lord; he became the Duc de Luynes, Constable of France and Governor of Picardy. He also acquired a Rohan heiress for his bride. His two brothers, equally amiable and undistinguished, became Duc de Chaulnes and Duc de Piney-Luxemburg; they too were provided with heiresses.

What might be called the opposition was based on Blois, where the indignant Marie de Medici had been confined. In February 1619, aided by the Duc d'Epernon, she escaped from Blois after being lowered from the château by ropes. Dissatisfied nobles gathered round her at Angers and it looked as though the entire south would rise. Louis wanted to attack at once, but Luynes preferred to negotiate. In May 1619 Marie was given the government of Anjou, with three strongholds garrisoned by her supporters. There was a public reconciliation between mother and son—both wept, while continuing to loathe each other. But in the summer of 1620 rebel armies again began to gather, one at Rouen, the other at Poitiers. When the Royal Council met, Luynes had no idea how to deal with the crisis.

Louis intervened angrily. He had never spoken in public before. 'With so many dangers to face, we march against the most serious and the nearest, which is Normandy. We march now.' In a wet and windy July he led his little army to Rouen. The rebels were prepared to face Luynes but not the King—they fled. Louis's advisers were nervous about marching on to Caen, also held by rebels, whereupon the eighteen-year-old monarch, newly courageous, cried, '*Péril de ça, péril de là! Péril sur terre, péril sur mer. Allons droit à Caen!*' Caen surrendered. Louis then marched south to Anjou with 12,000 men. Marie's 4,000 followers met him at Ponts-de-Cé, two bridges over the Loire near Angers. Louis behaved just as his father would have done, charging with his men. Seeing the enemy weaken, he led a charge which drove them back to the bridge. After losing 700 men, the rebels broke and the bridge was taken, cutting Marie off from any hope of escape. However, there was another reconciliation and the Queen Mother was allowed to keep Anjou. The settlement was ably negotiated by her adviser, Richelieu.

In 1617 an edict had re-established the Church's right to its former lands in Protestant Béarn, but commissioners who attempted to enforce the edict were roughly handled. After his triumph at Ponts-de-Cé, Louis and his army paid a swift visit to Béarn and implemented the edict at gun-point before returning to Paris. As a result the Huguenot Assembly met at La Rochelle and swore to support their persecuted co-religionists.

They began to raise troops and gather munitions. Condé, now a loyal subject, convinced Luynes that war was inevitable.

The royal army marched south again, occupying Saumur where Louis was cheered so enthusiastically that he shouted back, *'Vive le peuple'*, and waved his hat to the crowd. (Later he showed his less warm side. Seeing among the throng a certain M d'Arsilemont, who was a famous highwayman, the King cried, *'Ah! Vous voilà!'* and had him arrested—within three days the man had been tried and broken on the wheel.) Montauban, an important Huguenot stronghold, was besieged in August 1621. A friar prophesied its speedy fall, but Montauban held out. Luynes showed himself to be hopelessly incompetent—in November the approach of a Protestant army under the Duc de Rohan forced him to raise the siege. Louis, by now completely disillusioned with his favourite, returned to Paris. Luynes continued the campaign despite terrible weather. He became depressed, then took to his bed. On 15 December 1621 he died of scarlet fever, abandoned even by his servants.

Louis had no intention of persecuting his Protestant subjects for their religion, but he was not going to tolerate separatism. For by now the Huguenots had set up something very like a republic on the Dutch model and a new state was emerging, which included most of the western seaboard together with a large area of southern France. In the Duc de Rohan and his brother, the Comte de Soubise, it had formidable leaders. The Royal Council tried to dissuade Louis from continuing the campaign but he knew how great was the danger.

He went to war again in April 1622, besieging the Ile de Riez, Soubise's marshy stronghold on the west coast, which could only be reached at low tide. On 16 April the King rose from his straw pallet and led a midnight attack, riding through the water at the head of his men. Soubise was completely taken by surprise and routed, losing 4,000 troops. Louis spent the following months storming Huguenot towns and blowing up their fortifications; Nègrepelisse was burnt to the ground for having murdered 400 royal soldiers. In October Rohan sued for peace—Protestant France had become a land of famine and corpses, of abandoned villages and ruined châteaux. At the peace of Montpelier the Huguenots gave up all their strongholds save La Rochelle and Montauban.

It had been a gruelling campaign in an exceptionally hot summer. The King had many times spent whole days in the saddle, sleeping in his clothes and dining on bread and cheese. In June, at Toulouse he was struck down by a mysterious fever which attacked him several times, forcing him to travel in a litter. Eventually he recovered and enjoyed himself at Marseilles, attending bull fights and fishing for tuna fish. The fever had been tuberculosis which would eventually kill him. In addition he suffered from a chronic gastric disorder which never left him, and he was further weakened by the ministrations of his doctors (in one year alone he was bled forty-seven times, purged 212 times and endured 215 enemas).

None the less, Louis usually had sufficient energy to hunt, dance and campaign. At twenty, he was a thin young man of medium height, elegant and athletic in build, who sat a horse particularly well. He wore a moustache, but as yet his long, tanned face was beardless. He had mastered his earlier awkwardness, save for stammering when angry, and had acquired a most dignified presence—what Saint-Simon calls *'l'allure royale'*. He had an intense dislike of luxury. Although on state occasions he wore a white satin suit and a black hat and cloak, he liked best to dress as a soldier and was fond of wearing armour. Indeed, he thoroughly enjoyed military life and spent much time on parades and drilling his troops.

Hunting remained his great passion. He talked of little else and even took his hounds to bed with him. Of all the Bourbons, every one of whom was remarkable for an almost fanatical devotion to the chase, Louis XIII was the greatest huntsman.

In character he was upright to the point of harshness. He had an exalted concept of kingship—Joinville's life of St Louis was a favourite book—and could be merciless to himself, always ready to sacrifice his own happiness. He once said, 'I should not be King if I had the feelings of an ordinary man.' His devotion to business was remarkable, considering that he detested reading and preferred carpentry and gardening (his peas were sold in the Paris market), let alone hunting, to administration. Yet he never missed a Council meeting and impressed ambassadors by his grasp of affairs. Extremely pious, he enjoyed the ceremonies of the Church and was scrupulous in confession. His religion verged on the puritanical;

a characteristic remark was 'Please God, adultery shall never enter into my house'.

In Paris Louis lived at the Louvre and the Tuileries, though he much preferred Saint-Germain-en-Laye. Summer and winter he rose at six am. His rising was divided into the *Petit Lever* and the *Grand Lever*, the latter being shortened, as Louis liked to take long baths. (Unlike most of his contemporaries he was extremely clean in his person; later he cropped his head and wore a long brown wig for the sake of cleanliness.) The day began with a Council meeting, after which the King went to Mass. There followed private and public audiences. Then he paid a formal visit to the Queen, before dining publicly. The afternoon was spent hunting or in military exercises. After supper there was sometimes a concert or a ballet. Louis composed some of these ballets himself and occasionally danced in them.

By 1619 Louis was deeply in love with Anne of Austria, but not physically. Both his confessor, Père Cotton, and Luynes tried to make him sleep with her; the Papal Nuncio urged that Heaven needed an heir to the throne of France; the Spanish ambassador considered the King's failure to beget a child an insult to Spanish honour. Eventually Luynes forced him to lie with Anne—he was in tears when he went to her bed, but from then on he slept with her regularly for some years.

To govern France a stronger hand was needed than that of a nervous and unsure young man, and Louis knew it. In 1622, much against his will, his mother persuaded him to obtain a Cardinal's hat for Richelieu. Marie, who had been reconciled yet again with her son after Luynes's death, owed her return to Paris to Richelieu's shrewd counsel. Unwillingly Louis recognized that here was a man who could save France, and in January 1624 he was admitted to the Council. La Vieuville, the aged mediocrity who was its President, tried to discredit him but was dismissed and arrested for his pains. On 13 August 1624 Cardinal Richelieu became head of the Council with the title 'Secretary of State for Commerce and the Marine'. In 1629 the King named him 'Principal Minister of State'.

Armand du Plessis had been born in 1585, the third son of a family of poor Poitevin nobles. Originally he had intended

to become a soldier but his elder brother, for whom the Bishopric of Luçon had been reserved—the appointment was in the gift of the family—died, and Armand entered the Church. In 1608, only twenty-one, he was consecrated Bishop of Luçon where he proved himself an exemplary pastor. He was burningly ambitious but his first step towards power, when Ancres gave him a post, turned out to be a serious set-back when the Marshal fell—the King shouted at him, 'I have escaped your tyranny, Luçon!' It took him years to vindicate himself, through the unlikely path of acting as adviser to Marie de Medici. His chief ally was the mysterious Capuchin friar, Père Joseph (better known as 'the Grey Eminence').

Richelieu's masterful, fastidious face with its high nose and prominent cheekbones, was the mask of a man who lived on the verge of total nervous breakdown, racked by headaches and indigestion, weakened by bad circulation. The Cardinal was agonizingly prone to depression and discouragement, terrified by bad news and by threats of violence, even by loud noises; he was frequently in tears—on occasion he even hid under his bed from whence he had to be coaxed by his valet. Greedy, avaricious, he was also coldly arrogant and lacked charm. Women in particular disliked him. Yet he was un-doubtedly one of the greatest of all Frenchmen; of seventeenth-century Englishmen, only Oliver Cromwell was of the same stature.

Of his aims he later wrote, 'I promised Your Majesty to use all my industry and all the authority which it pleased you to give me to ruin the Huguenot party, to bring down the pride of the great lords, to bring back all your subjects to their duty, and to restore your name to its rightful place among foreign nations.' Richelieu's determination to make his country the leading power of Europe at the expense of the Catholic Habsburgs conflicted in no way with his Catholicism; he believed that a strong France was essential for the health of the Church; that Rome could not be allowed to remain a mere tool of Spain. He quickly made Protestant alliances, with England and the Dutch.

The English alliance was soon jeopardized by the Duke of Buckingham. This magnificent creature visited France in May

1625 to assist at the marriage (by proxy) of Mme Henriette Marie to King Charles at Nôtre-Dame. For a week's visit he brought twenty-seven suits—one, of white velvet embroidered with diamonds and shedding loosely-sewn pearls as he walked, was valued at £24,000. His beauty and elegance took Paris by storm.

He was soon embroiled in a plot to seduce the Queen of France, by the Duchesse de Chevreuse, Luynes's widow, who was the evil genius of Louis XIII's marriage. In 1618 she had become Mistress of the Queen's Household. Richelieu wrote of her, 'She was the ruin of the Queen, whose wholesome outlook was corrupted by her example; she swayed the Queen's heart, ruined her, set her against the King and her duties.' It was her horseplay in the spring of 1622, when she persuaded the pregnant Queen to run down a gallery, which made Anne lose a Dauphin. Born in 1600, a tiny blonde with a delicate face and unforgettable eyes, Marie de Chevreuse was a woman of innumerable conquests. An enemy described her as the matchmaker behind every court love affair. Startlingly unconventional (in London she swam the Thames, to the horror of the English), she and her antics were a perennial scandal. Next to love affairs she enjoyed political intrigue, and nursed a real hatred of Louis, whom she referred to as 'that idiot'.

'La Chevrette's' latest lover was Lord Holland, one of Buckingham's suite. She swiftly enchanted the Duke with the prospect of cuckolding a King. At Amiens, where the court took official leave of the English embassy, Buckingham climbed into a private garden where the Queen was taking an evening walk; he may even have tried to rape her. Anne's shrieks summoned her attendants. Later, during less private interviews, he wept and spoke with such passion that he terrified her. Louis was so affronted that henceforward he refused to think seriously of an English alliance.

Despite his dealings with Protestant powers abroad, nothing could deflect Richelieu from his determination to break *Messieurs les prétendus réformés*. He wrote, 'So long as the Protestants in France are a state within a state, the King cannot be master of his realm or achieve great things abroad.' The capital of French Protestantism was still La Rochelle. In July 1627 an English fleet commanded by Buckingham put in at the Isle of

Ré opposite the port. Immediately the Rochellois rose, while throughout the south Rohan raised the Huguenot squirearchy. Luckily the royal garrison on Ré prevented Buckingham from consolidating his position and when they were relieved by Louis in November, the English hastily evacuated the island. La Rochelle was besieged. However, it was still possible for the English to relieve it as the French King did not possess a navy.

Richelieu, who never left the siege and wore a gilded cuirass over his purple soutane, had a solution. A breakwater was built across the mouth of the port, consisting of sunken ships on top of which a stone dyke was constructed; there were forts at each end and floating batteries were moored along it. Frantically, soldiers and peasants worked waist deep in the water. Louis and the Cardinal never left the dyke—the King had to be prevented from taking up a pick himself. On the landward side, the city was isolated by three lines of royal fortifications including thirteen forts. But the Rochellois, commanded by the fiery Duchesse de Rohan and by its mayor, the brave Jean Guiton, supported by eight fanatic pastors, resisted heroically. It was a dreadful winter and the besiegers suffered accordingly. Louis grew bored and went off to hunt. The Cardinal had a nervous collapse, though in March he none the less led an abortive night attack through a sewer.

By the spring the Rochellois were starving. When the English fleet returned, it found the dyke impregnable and sailed home. A second English expedition in September 1628 also turned back. Mme de Rohan boiled her leather armchair to make soup—others ate their shoes. On a single day 400 Rochellois died of hunger. Those who tried to escape were hanged by the besiegers. (However, Louis spared a young lady who had written to an officer saying she would marry him and turn Catholic if he would save her—the royal army celebrated their wedding in splendid style.) On 28 October 1628 La Rochelle surrendered. The King, wearing an armour damascened with golden fleurs-de-lis, rode into the city on All Saints' Day. He wept when he saw the misery caused by the siege—the unburied corpses and the scarcely less ghastly survivors. (Wagon-loads of food were brought in, whereupon a hundred Rochellois died of over-eating.) A triumphant

Richelieu said Mass in the city's principal church, giving Communion to Louis and his captains. La Rochelle's fortifications were razed to the ground and every church had to be returned to the Catholics. The Rochellois kept only the right to worship as Protestants.

The Duc de Rohan still held out in Languedoc, so in the spring of 1629 Louis launched a final campaign. Whole towns were demolished—in some places the King's officers hanged all males or sent them to the galleys. Eventually Rohan surrendered and was banished. The Huguenots were ordered to summon their Assembly for Louis to dictate his terms. Peace was signed at Alais in June 1629; the Protestants lost their *places de sûretés* but the Edict of Nantes was confirmed. Even though a Huguenot rising took place as late as 1752, Alais was the end of the Wars of Religion.

There was another focus of rebellion, in the person of the heir to the throne, 'Monsieur'. Born in 1608, Gaston, Duc d'Anjou, was not quite so useless as he has been painted; his fat face and bulging eyes give a misleading impression. He was both kind-natured and intelligent, a patron of the arts who collected paintings and gem stones. But he was also weak, and easily influenced. When in 1626 Richelieu wanted him to marry a Bourbon cousin, Mlle de Montpensier who was the richest heiress in France, Mme de Chevreuse put it into Monsieur's head that he did not want the marriage. A confused plot emerged in which the chief schemers were Gaston's bastard half-brothers, the Duc de Vendôme and the Grand Prior, his tutor the Marshal d'Ornano, and of course Mme de Chevreuse and her latest lover, the Comte de Chalais. Undoubtedly there was talk of murdering Richelieu and possibly Louis too—Gaston was to be made King and married to Anne of Austria. (Louis always thought that Anne had been in the conspiracy and never quite forgave her, saying on his deathbed, 'In my condition I have to forgive her but I don't have to believe her.') The plot came to light when Chalais lost his nerve and made a partial confession to Richelieu. The Vendôme brothers were sent to prison where the Grand Prior died. Chalais paid with his life; his execution was so bungled that it took thirty-four blows to sever his head. Mme de Chevreuse was banished to Poitou but escaped to Lorraine. Gaston con-

Henri IV in 1605

SOCIOS, QVI FORTIBVS ARMIS
LÆ SAUVE IVRA DEI

Louis XIII by Philippe de Champaigne

fessed everything with gusto, implicating everybody, and then tamely married Mlle de Montpensier—the ceremony was performed by Richelieu. As a reward Gaston was made Duke of Orleans.

The Cardinal was determined to show the nobility that they were not above the law. A royal edict was therefore issued which forbade duelling under pain of death. In 1627 the Comte des Chapelles and the Comte de Bouteville fought a duel in the Place Royale, ignoring the edict. Bouteville had taken part in no less than twenty-two affairs of honour. Within a month they had been arrested, tried, condemned and beheaded in the Place de Grève. It was well known that the Cardinal persuaded Louis that the executions were necessary. Richelieu attacked the nobility in other ways too. In 1628 he was responsible for an edict ordering the demolition of fortified châteaux, and for another which abolished the offices of Constable and Grand Admiral. By 1634 a tribunal in Poitiers was condemning over 200 noblemen for robbery and other crimes. In 1635 he instituted the office of *Intendant*—a royal representative in each province who kept an eye on the governor and on any other source of opposition. Such measures earned the Cardinal much hatred. One can only wonder at his courage; Gaston remained heir to the throne until 1638, and in the event of Louis's death Richelieu would probably have lost not only his place but his life as well.

Sometimes even Louis found Richelieu irritating. There is a story that on one occasion the King growled at him, 'You go first, since you are the real King.' Richelieu replied smoothly, 'Only to light the way,' and, picking up a torch, preceded Louis like a lackey. In reality the King seems to have been fond of the Cardinal rather than otherwise. His letters to him were often almost excessively affectionate; he could write, 'Be assured that I shall love you until my last breath', signing himself *'Louis de très bon coeur'*. Richelieu took care to let the King know exactly what he was doing. Besides a daily correspondence, the two men spent long hours together, discussing plans and projects. Louis once said of Richelieu, 'He is the greatest servant that France has ever had.' The Cardinal wrote gratefully, 'The capacity to permit his ministers to serve him is not the least of qualities in a great King.'

In the autumn of 1630 Louis fell so ill that he was not expected to live; he received the Last Sacraments, asking pardon for any wrong he might have done. The doctors thought he was suffering from dysentery but in fact he had an internal abscess: fortunately it burst, and he made a slow recovery, during which he was nursed by his wife and by his mother. The latter had now turned against the Cardinal. When Louis was at his weakest they insisted that he must dismiss Richelieu. Rumours of the Cardinal's imminent disgrace circulated, and appeared to be confirmed by Louis's curious coldness when Richelieu visited him. On his return to Paris, the King stayed with his mother at her new palace of the Luxembourg. On 10 November Marie took Louis into her chamber and again demanded that he dismiss the Cardinal. As she was speaking, Richelieu, who had been warned, burst into her room through a back door, to be met with a torrent of abuse from the Queen Mother. He knelt before the King begging for mercy, at which Marie screamed at Louis, 'Do you prefer a lackey to your own mother?' The King, who must have found the scene intolerable, told Richelieu to rise, bowed to his mother and left for his hunting-lodge at Versailles. Marie thought she had won: courtiers flocked to her, including the Marshal de Marillac and his brother, the Garde des Sceaux, as well as Bassompierre.

Richelieu made preparations for flight. Suddenly one of the King's young cronies, Claude de Saint-Simon, appeared with a message from Louis summoning him to Versailles. There he again knelt before the King, and in an emotional scene Louis told him, 'I have in you the most faithful, the most affectionate servant in the world. I have seen the respect and the attention which you have always paid the Queen my mother. If you had failed in your duty to her I would have cast you off. But she has no cause whatever to complain of you. She has let herself be prejudiced by a cabal whom I know very well how to destroy. Serve me as you have so far served me and I will defend you against every enemy.' The Marshal de Marillac was arrested at the head of his troops, accused of embezzlement and beheaded; his brother, the Garde des Sceaux, died in prison; Bassompierre was sent to the Bastille, where he spent twelve years. Louis, not the Cardinal, was responsible

for these measures. The Queen Mother was confined at Compiègne, from where in 1631 she fled to the Spanish Netherlands, dying in exile a decade later. Her attempt to overthrow Richelieu is known as 'The Day of Dupes'.

Gaston too left France. From Lorraine he appealed to all Frenchmen to revolt against the Cardinal. He won a valuable recruit in the rich and popular Duc de Montmorency, who was angry at not being given the great office of Constable which his father and grandfather had held. In autumn 1632 Gaston invaded France and was joined by Montmorency, but their little army was easily defeated at Castelnaudry. Monsieur fled at the first charge. Poor Montmorency, a paragon of knightly virtue, was beheaded at Toulouse. Gaston swore to relinquish evil companions and be 'especially fond of his cousin the Cardinal de Richelieu'. He soon fled again, to join his mother.

Louis was busy abroad, with the war of the Mantuan Succession, which broke out in 1629. (Mantua was important because it controlled one of the roads between Spanish Italy and the Empire.) The Duke of Mantua, a Gonzaga but also a Frenchman, defended his Ducal throne to the point of selling his Titians and Mantegnas. In the campaign's early stages Richelieu took the King's place, clad as a cavalier in clothes of *'feuille morte'* edged with gold, wearing a cuirass of polished steel, white jackboots, a plumed hat and a rapier. In March 1630 Louis stormed the Savoyard fortress of Pignerolo, having first forced the pass of Susa where he smashed his way through three lines of fortifications. The old Duke of Savoy knelt in the snow to kiss Louis's boots in token of submission, the war ending in April 1631 with the peace of Cherasco. Savoy ceded Pignerolo to France—with it went control of a pass over the Alps which guaranteed France access to Italy.

An incident during the campaign shows Louis's fatalism. The mistress of the house where he lodged fell ill with the plague. His staff were terrified but Louis, dismissing them, said simply, 'Withdraw and pray God that your own hostesses are not stricken, but first draw my bed curtains. I shall try to get some sleep and then we will leave to-morrow morning, early and without panic.'

During Gaston's revolt, the Parlement of Paris had refused to ratify a royal edict condemning the rebellion. Louis soon

forced them into a humiliating ratification. For the Parlement were not exempt from the revolution in government, their functions and privileges being constantly under attack. In 1641 Louis savagely told the senior President of the Paris Parlement, 'You have been created only to judge between Maître Pierre and Maître Jean and if you continue your plots I will clip your claws so close that your flesh will suffer.'

Culturally, the later years of Louis XIII's reign were a period of some distinction. In 1636 Corneille's *Le Cid* was triumphantly performed for the first time. Next year Descartes's *Discours de la Méthode* was published. The Academie Française was set up, charged with producing a dictionary which would preserve the purity of the French language. A natural history museum, the Jardin des Plantes, was founded for the instruction of medical students. In the *chambre bleue* of her hôtel near the Louvre, Mme de Rambouillet created the salon, holding receptions at which great lords and bourgeois intellectuals could meet on equal terms. Life was becoming altogether more graceful; the forerunners of the *boulevardiers* learnt to stroll through the elegant arcades of the Place Royale as well as to strut and bow at court. There were many new buildings in which they were able to parade, notably Louis's extension of the west wing of the Louvre and Richelieu's Palais Cardinal. Most of the hôtels of the Marais date from this period. At Fontainebleau and at Saint-Germain the King employed Simon Vouet, one of the best painters of the day; he also commissioned Philippe de Champaigne to paint an allegory of the royal triumph over heresy at La Rochelle. However, though Louis enjoyed plays, he had no deep interest in the arts and cancelled all literary pensions when Richelieu died.

A field in which Louis and Richelieu were less than successful was finance. Their government lived from hand to mouth, selling offices or confiscating the property of rebellious noblemen. The Cardinal increased taxes, but unlike Sully, relied on tax farmers. There were riots in Paris, peasant risings in Guyenne and Normandy—tax collectors were murdered and châteaux sacked until troops had to be sent in to restore order. One concrete achievement was a standard gold coinage, the famous *Louis d'or*, which made its appearance in 1640, bearing a most impressive portrait of the King.

In 1631 Théophraste Renaudot, a Paris doctor, published his *Gazette*, and was immediately given a royal pension. His journal, the first modern newspaper, was made to print royal edicts. It also published news bulletins which gave details of military campaigns—when they were successful—and of attempts to lighten taxes. Some of these bulletins were written by Louis himself, who had at once grasped their importance as a means of shaping public opinion.

Fully mature and bearded, the King had lost none of his neuroses. Scrupulously correct and owing something to fashionable Stoicism (he had probably read Epictetus), he still gave way to moods of hysterical depression during which he was quite unapproachable. Though an introvert, he was fond of such extrovert amusements as cards and parade grounds. His tastes were eccentric in their simplicity. When the axle of his carriage broke, the King, taking an axe, walked into the forest and returned with a sapling which he had trimmed. On campaign he could be found in a kitchen morosely cooking his supper. Like most Bourbons he had little time for intellectuals; Mme de Rambouillet's *précieuses* were not much in evidence at the court of Louis XIII.

In any case he detested court life. Probably Louis's ideal of paradise was the seventeenth century equivalent of a good London club. He tried to create his own world at Versailles—it is ironical that that monstrous edifice should have begun as a sanctuary of the simple life. The place was a small, lonely village outside Paris in a flat landscape of sandy soil and marshes. Its dreariness explained its isolation, an isolation which in turn explains its attraction for Louis. He had first visited Versailles-au-Val-de-Galie when he was a boy of six, on a hawking expedition in 1607. He began to hawk and hunt there again regularly in 1621. The long ride back to Paris irked him, so in 1624 he bought a little estate of hardly more than a hundred acres, and built a hunting-lodge. This first château of Versailles consisted of twenty-six rooms in a centre block with two wings, constructed in red brick and white stone, and roofed with blue slate. The bright colours are the reason for Saint-Simon's description, 'a card castle'. By 1636 it had been enlarged by the architect Philibert le Roy and consisted of three blocks around a courtyard, the fourth side

being closed by an arcade; there was a small pavilion at each angle. The park and hunting grounds were also extended. None the less a contemporary described it as 'a house fit for a gentleman with an income of only ten to twelve thousand livres'; Bassompierre even called it 'the miserable little house of Versailles'.

Versailles was meant for relaxation. The food, like the furniture, was plain and uncomplicated. Besides hunting the King played cards, billiards, backgammon, chess and spillikins with his boon companions (and also such long forgotten games as *renarde, moine, oie, tourniquet* and *trou-madame*). He liked to drill a small company of musketeers in the courtyard. Sometimes in his little carriage he inspected young trees he had planted; at others he lounged in his bedroom in a green velvet dressing-gown lined with squirrel fur. Very occasionally the Queen or the Queen Mother visited Versailles with their ladies, but they never stayed the night. '*Ce Prince si farouche pour les dames*', as Mme de Motteville terms him, gave it as his opinion that too many women would spoil everything. Versailles was essentially a bachelor paradise.

The King yearned for friendship. He sought ceaselessly a kindred spirit to whom he could unburden himself, someone who could dispel his overwhelming sense of isolation and desperate loneliness. The poor man was too suspicious and too inarticulate to have much chance of success. Mme de Motteville says of Louis, 'Among so many sombre mists and weird fancies the tender passion could find no place in his heart. He did not love as other men do, to take pleasure in it. His spirit had grown accustomed to bitterness and he loved only to be hurt.' Another person who knew the court of Louis XIII, M de Montglat, explains that, 'The King's love was not like that of other men, because he loved a girl without any thought of enjoying her favours, behaving to her as he would to a friend; even though it is perfectly possible for a man to have a mistress and a friend in one and the same person, that was not what he wanted, because his mistress was no more than his friend, a confidante to whom he could reveal the secrets of his heart.'

Louis had several mistresses, but as M de Montglat says, the relationship was invariably platonic. When Mlle de

Hautefort coyly dropped a letter into her bosom, the King retrieved it with a pair of tongs. She lasted longest of all his loves, holding sway for nearly a decade. He first met her in 1631 when she was a seventeen-year-old Maid of Honour to the Queen. Nicknamed 'Aurora' by the court, Marie de Hautefort was a big, bouncing, Gascon blonde with an aquiline nose. High-spirited, imperious and a little hard, she inflicted upon Louis all the miseries which he expected; their affair was a business of jealous quarrels and grudging reconciliations. He suspected her of making fun of him to the Queen, but loved her in spite of himself. One day he confided his love to Saint-Simon, whereupon that earthy young man suggested that he act as Louis's ambassador to Marie, hinting that if he did, the King would very soon find himself in bed with her. Louis was horrified. 'It is quite true that I'm in love with her,' he admitted, 'that I look for her everywhere, that I enjoy talking about her and that I dream about her even more. But it is also true that this happens in spite of myself, as I'm a man and weak in that way. Being King makes it no easier for me than for anyone else to indulge my feelings, because I have to be always on my guard against sin and giving scandal.' The astonished Saint-Simon concluded that Louis's passion was real enough, but kept in check by religious scruples. Mlle de Hautefort's influence was not altogether beneficial; as a loyal friend of Anne of Austria she disliked Richelieu and was pro-Spanish. On the other hand, she did her best to bring together the King and Queen, between whom there was now little love. Also, according to *la Grande Mademoiselle* (Gaston's daughter), she made the court more agreeable. As a *précieuse* with literary tastes, Marie complained that the King only talked to her about hounds and hunting (though she occasionally hunted herself). No doubt she preferred the music parties which took place three times a week.

Louis's other mistress, Mlle de La Fayette—who interrupted the Hautefort's tyranny—also tried to reconcile the royal couple. The King first met this timid little Maid of Honour with brown ringlets and blue eyes in the autumn of 1635, when she was only sixteen. A deeply pious girl, she refused and made the Sign of the Cross when Louis paid her the

unheard-of compliment of asking her to come and live with him at Versailles. She too hunted with the King and, entirely disinterested, seems to have genuinely loved him for himself. But she also detested Richelieu and his 'wicked policies'. Ruthlessly, the Cardinal ordered her confessor to encourage her leaning towards the religious life, and in May 1637 Louise de La Fayette entered a Carmelite convent in Paris, in the rue Saint-Antoine. The King was in tears. So was Louise. 'I shall never see him again,' she wept. Her confessor told the King that her decision could be postponed, but Louis replied that if he kept her from her vocation he would regret it all his life. For a few months he visited her at her convent, though he was only able to speak to her through a grille (her somewhat worldly abbess said that the King ought to exercise his royal prerogative and come inside, but he was shocked by this suggestion). Marie de Hautefort soon returned, to make his life a torment again.

During her brief reign, Louise had formed a friendship with Louis's confessor, a Jesuit called Nicolas Caussin. Potentially it was the most serious opposition which Richelieu ever encountered. Caussin held strict views on the nature of true repentance; he believed that absolution should only be given if the penitent felt real *contrition*, which included a strict resolve never to commit the sin again. (This was in contrast to the more normal view that *attrition*, a resolve to try not to sin again, was sufficient.) In addition Caussin believed that any alliance with a Protestant Prince was sacrilegious and a sin. He remonstrated in the confessional with Louis who, always scrupulous and fearful of damnation, began to have grim doubts about his eternal salvation. Finally Caussin actually dared to hector the King outside the confessional, vilifying Richelieu; he also made the terrible mistake of giving his penitent a letter from Marie de Medici. The Cardinal then managed to have Caussin dismissed and banished. He made sure that royal confessors were more tractable in future.

It is often said that Louis's favourite companions were grooms. But these grooms were noblemen, even if not of very high rank. Admittedly, Baradas, his favourite of the mid-1620s, was an uncouth brute who grew insufferably arrogant and

joined his betters in conspiring against the Cardinal. However, Claude de Rouvroy, Seigneur de Saint-Simon, was a very different type. Richelieu introduced him into the royal household as a page in 1626, when he was only nineteen. Saint-Simon speedily recommended himself by holding a second horse during the hunt in such a way that Louis was able to change mounts without touching the ground. Small, ugly, unlettered, Saint-Simon, apart from an ancient lineage, was not exactly distinguished; he had a wretched, mean appearance; Bassompierre called him 'the little insect'. He was none the less shrewd and honourable and, during the ten years in which he was the King's inseparable companion, had the sense to be grateful to Richelieu. So close were Louis and Saint-Simon that they could communicate without speaking—a mere glance between them was sufficient—while they had a secret language which only they could understand. The King appointed his friend Captain of Versailles, First Gentleman of the Bedchamber and Master of the Wolfhounds; in 1630 he made him Governor of Meulan and of Blaye, in 1635 a Duke and Peer of France. But in the end even Saint-Simon grew spoilt; by 1635 Louis was writing to Richelieu to complain of the new Duke's *'mauvaises humeurs'* and of how he always seems irritated with the King. Ironically, it was the loyalty and generosity which Louis so valued in him that brought about his downfall in 1636. The King decided to arrest and charge with treason an old friend of Saint-Simon, and Saint-Simon at once warned him. Louis would not tolerate such a betrayal of his confidence and, regardless of his own anguished feelings, banished Saint-Simon to Blaye.

Probably the Cardinal was Louis's truest friend. The King's letters to him are full of curiously intimate little details; how many times he has taken medicine, how many animals his hounds have killed, how cruel his favourites have been. He is also human enough to tell Richelieu not to be depressed because he knows how bad it is for his health.

The Cardinal did not waver in his determination to bring down the Habsburgs. Nevertheless, during the first decade of the Thirty Years War which convulsed Germany, it seemed that the Emperor Ferdinand II might impose his rule not only on Bohemia but upon all Germany. France was too weak

to challenge him openly. The Imperial troops were formidable, while the allied army of Spain was considered to be the best in Europe. As yet French troops were neither sufficiently numerous nor sufficiently disciplined to take on such opponents. Richelieu therefore waged a kind of Cold War, subsidizing the Emperor's Protestant enemies with French money. This policy proved almost too effective when King Gustav Adolf of Sweden all but destroyed the Imperial army; the 'Lion of the North' was a fanatic Lutheran, who aimed at establishing a great Protestant empire in place of that of the Habsburgs. Fortunately King Gustav was slain at Lutzen in 1632.

Throughout, Louis accepted the dangerous gamble of Richelieu's brinkmanship. He took a keen interest in expanding his army and in improving its equipment. By the end of his reign Louis possessed a standing army of nearly 200,000 men, compared with 100,000 in 1622. Among new types of cavalry which he introduced were mounted infantry (the Black Musketeers and the Grey Musketeers, destined to be among the *Ancien Régime*'s most famous regiments). The principal corps remained those of Henri IV—the Guards, with the Regiments of Picardy, Navarre, Champagne and Piedmont. There were also regiments of Swiss, German and Italian mercenaries together with about a hundred small regiments raised by their colonels. The élite troops were excellent, but the rest were still too much of a feudal rabble.

A navy was also built up. Coastal rights were resumed by the Crown and a *Conseil de la Marine* was established. Bases were set up at Atlantic ports, and there was a regular programme of shipbuilding (the largest vessel, *La Couronne*, was 2,000 tons, 500 more than Charles I's famous *Royal Sovereign*, and mounting 72 guns). By 1636 there was an Atlantic Fleet and a Mediterranean Fleet. The Archbishop of Bordeaux, Mgr Henri de Sourdis, proved a most capable Admiral of the Atlantic Fleet, who recruited officers from French Knights of Malta and from among merchant captains and privateers.

In 1635 Richelieu and Louis decided to bring the war into the open. A French herald, wearing his tabard and accompanied by a trumpeter, rode into Brussels to read out a formal declaration of war in the Grande Place. French troops were then sent to aid the Dutch and to invade Milan, but bad organization

brought these operations to a halt. An attempt to overrun Franche Comté also failed. The French army seemed hardly adequate for a full-scale war on three fronts.

The Habsburgs retaliated swiftly. In the summer of 1636, Imperial troops invaded Burgundy while a Spanish army commanded by the Cardinal Infante, Philip IV's viceroy in the Low Countries, invaded Picardy. He advanced across the Somme, to find only 10,000 French troops between him and Paris. The capital's walls had been dismantled and there were no troops for its defence; thousands of Parisians had fled. Richelieu, whose bodyguard was being hissed in the street and who was suffering from migraine, lost his nerve badly. At a meeting of the Council he advised the King to abandon Paris. Everyone present agreed with the Cardinal, with the exception of Louis, who for once overruled his great servant. To leave Paris, said the King, would demoralize the entire country. After promulgating a series of edicts tantamount to a general mobilization, Louis rode out to Senlis to join what troops were available. As he rode out, he was cheered. Somehow reinforcements, untrained but sufficient, were brought up. Meanwhile the Cardinal Infante took Corbie, the last fortress before Paris, which was now only eighty miles away; his forward troops reached Pontoise. But the Parisians rose to the occasion in the same way that they did at the battle of the Marne in 1914. Soon Louis had an army of 40,000 men and the Cardinal Infante withdrew, the French regaining Corbie on 14 November. For long afterwards 1636 was known as the Year of Corbie.

In 1637 France began to win victories, capturing towns on the Flemish frontier. The new navy won a significant triumph in an action with the Spaniards off Lerins; the following year it won its first major battle, off Fuentarrabia, sinking twenty Spanish ships. Also in 1638, France's Protestant ally, Duke Bernhardt of Saxe-Weimar, smashed the Imperial army at Rheinfelden and conquered most of Alsace; he died unexpectedly in 1639, whereupon the French took over his conquests. Ill-health prevented Louis from playing as active a part as he would have wished in military operations. In any case he had problems at home.

In 1636 Gaston d'Orléans was involved in yet another plot

against Richelieu, who only just escaped assassination. The Comte de Soissons, a Prince of the Blood, who had been connected with the plot, hatched a further conspiracy in which Gaston also joined. Both plots were discovered, but no really harsh measures could be taken against members of the Blood Royal. Gaston was bought off with a large sum of money (part of which paid for the Mansard wing at Blois) and Soissons fled to Sedan.

Louis's support for the Cardinal in the face of opposition from the entire nobility shows real moral courage. None the less Richelieu was always fearful of losing his favour—he considered the four square feet of the King's cabinet 'more difficult to conquer than all the battlefields of Europe'. During Louis's reign, twenty-six persons were beheaded for plotting against the Cardinal, and more died in prison (they included four Dukes and a Marshal of France). The King gave his support at terrible personal cost. Estrangements with his mother and his brother were inevitable, but surely not with his Queen. When war was declared on Spain, Mme de Chevreuse persuaded Anne to send details of any French military operations which she could discover to her brother, the Cardinal Infante. For four years the Queen of France was a spy for Spain. Eventually in August 1637 one of her messengers, M de La Porte, was intercepted. Marie de Hautefort saved Anne by boldly entering the Bastille, disguised as a man, and smuggling a letter to La Porte so that he was able to make his story tally with that of the Queen. As for Mme de Chevreuse, still youthful and slightly-built, she disguised herself as a page and galloped down lanes and byways until she reached Spain. It is likely that Anne had convinced herself that she was aiding the enemies of the Cardinal and not those of France.

One day in December 1637 Louis left Versailles to stay with Condé at Saint Maur. Passing through Paris, he decided to visit Soeur Angélique (the former Louise de La Fayette) at her convent in the rue Saint-Antoine. Their conversation continued until nightfall, by which time heavy rain was falling; the wind was so violent that it blew out the candles in the lanterns of the royal escort. Their captain, M de Guitaut, who was on familiar terms with the King and who was also devoted to the Queen, said that it would be impossible to reach Saint Maur in such a

violent storm; he advised the King to stay at the Louvre. Louis replied that his apartments were not ready, whereupon Guitaut suggested that he stay with the Queen. The night grew blacker than ever, the rain falling in torrents. Reluctantly, the King agreed. He had supper with the Queen and then spent the night in her bed. A little before midday on Sunday 5 September 1638, at Saint-Germain-en-Laye, Anne of Austria gave birth to a son, Louis Dieudonné—the God-given. Mlle de Hautefort persuaded Louis to go to the Queen's bedside and kiss her. Te Deums were sung throughout France.

The news was not welcomed by everyone; Gaston was no longer heir to the throne—Richelieu was safe. The Cardinal's enemies suggested that the King was not the father; indeed it was somewhat surprising that Anne should bear her first child in the twenty-third year of their marriage. But there was no doubt about the birth, which took place in poor Gaston's presence; to console him the King gave him a large sum of money.

The King continued to sleep with Anne. In his grim way he considered it his duty, though he now neither liked nor trusted her. Flirtatious, still goodlooking if a little plump, with her fair hair in ringlets, Anne was very conscious of her looks. (Mme de Motteville says that her only imperfections were too big a nose and wearing too much rouge.) Her voice was not attractive, a shrill falsetto—she yapped like a terrier. In character she was scatter-brained, lazy, a glutton, everything that Louis was not. He knew very well that she corresponded with Mme de Chevreuse, who was now in England.

Marie de Hautefort—'the creature' as Louis calls her in his letters to Richelieu—was not much solace. She had a stinging wit and bullied him unmercifully, demanding places at court for her family. In 1638 he wrote pathetically to the Cardinal, *'la créature est toujours en mauvaise humeur contre moi.'* He was driven to distraction by her love for a Captain in the Royal Guard, the Marquis de Gesvres, even writing to the young man's father to tell him how angry he was with his son. In the end she made herself so disagreeable that the King was thoroughly disenchanted with *all* women. Mlle de Hautefort could not believe it when she was finally asked to leave the court in November 1639.

Richelieu was uneasy. He knew that in his loneliness, Louis

might find some new favourite who might oppose the Cardinal. To protect himself, he had introduced the son of an old friend into the royal household—Henri d' Effiat, Marquis de Cinq Mars, who was appointed Master of the King's Wardrobe on 27 March 1638. It was the eighteenth birthday of this strikingly handsome young nobleman. The first thing he did was to add to his own wardrobe (which eventually included fifty-two suits). Louis soon took a passionate liking to him. Here was another long-sought friend. In the summer of 1639 he made him Grand Master of the Horse, and henceforward Cinq Mars was known as *Monsieur le Grand*. The King fawned on his new favourite, loading him with presents.

A thoroughly shallow creature, Cinq Mars, although intoxicated by his good fortune, was entirely without gratitude. He was bored by Louis, who spent more and more time hunting; digging out foxes and flying sparrowhawks at blackbirds were small consolation to a young man who loved Paris and had a beautiful mistress. He turned sulky and was continually slipping away. There were constant scenes in which Richelieu acted as peacemaker. Sometimes *Monsieur le Grand's hauteurs* were so insufferable that the King was unable to sleep from rage. It is often said that the relationship was homosexual, and Louis's behaviour was certainly abnormal. But there is no evidence whatsoever of homosexual behaviour on his part, even if he undoubtedly admired beauty in both sexes. The only hint of perversion is Tallemant des Réaux's squalid gossip, which includes a story of the King, wearing a bride's nightdress, sharing a bed with his favourite and kissing his hands. Tallemant is not noted for reliability. In fact, throughout the association with Cinq Mars, Louis continued to sleep with the Queen—in the late summer of 1640 she gave birth to another son, Philippe (the future 'Monsieur'). Anne did not show the slightest jealousy of Cinq Mars, though she had resented Mlle de Hautefort. Nor was the King any less assiduous at his devotions. He would hardly have written his pitiful complaints to Richelieu about the favourite's cruelty if he had thought the relationship a sin. What is particularly significant are the childish certificates which the pair signed after quarrels and sent to the Cardinal, stating that they were on good terms again. Basically the association was an adolescent friendship, even if

Louis was twenty years older than Cinq Mars; the King was not perverted but retarded—he had the emotional age of a boy of fifteen.

While these puerile quarrels were taking place, France was winning victory after victory. In 1640 the French conquered Artois, while across the Alps the Comte d'Harcourt routed the Habsburg armies three times and captured Turin. The Duke of Savoy hastily negotiated for peace with France.

Yet the French nobility were determined to overthrow Richelieu. The Comte de Soissons gathered a Spanish army at Sedan and began to invade France; luckily he was killed by a stray pistol bullet during the first skirmish. Next year the Duc de Bouillon revived the plan; he intended to invade France with a French army from Italy and raise the Huguenots of the Cévennes, while Gaston was to attack from the north. They were joined by no less a personage than Cinq Mars who signed their treaty with Spain; he hoped that if the plot were successful he might marry Marie de Gonzaga and obtain her fabulous wealth. In his conceit he had come to resent the Cardinal's admonitions; by now Louis was so irritated by his favourite that on one occasion he shouted '*Je le vomis!*' But Richelieu's spies soon discovered the plot.

In June 1642, at Narbonne, an agent of the Cardinal showed the King documents which gave irrefutable proof of Cinq Mars's treachery. Louis at once gave orders for his arrest and, after a brief attempt to hide in the back streets of Narbonne, the former favourite was incarcerated in the fortress of Montpelier. In September he was tried at Lyons, hopelessly compromised by the confessions of Gaston and Bouillon. The wretched young man broke down and admitted his guilt; he also incriminated his best friend, François-Auguste de Thou. Arrogant to the last, he protested at sharing a scaffold with de Thou because the latter was a commoner. On the day of Cinq Mars's execution, the King, who was playing chess, looked up at the clock and said, 'Aha, this morning at this very moment our dear friend is having a bad time [*un mauvais moment*].'

Ill-health—gout, rheumatism and fever striking at a constitution which was now dangerously undermined by pneumo-intestinal tuberculosis—together with the miseries of his private life had brought Louis to the verge of collapse. Unable

to hunt, he turned to music, being particularly soothed by the *airs de cour* composed and sung to the lute by Pierre de Nyert, whom he rewarded by appointing him *Premier Valet de la Garde Robe*. (He left him a considerable sum of money in his will.)

Spain was falling apart. In 1641 Portugal, which had been under Spanish rule since 1580, declared itself independent. Catalonia also rebelled, proclaiming Louis as sovereign Count of Barcelona. In 1642 the King added Roussillon and Cerdagne to France, whose frontier now extended along the entire length of the Pyrenees. Although Louis had personally directed the siege of Perpignan, his growing weakness had made it impossible to take much part in the campaign.

Meanwhile Richelieu lay dying. A skeleton, eaten by ulcers which paralysed him, he had to be carried in a litter; he was rowed up the Rhône in a gilded barge, his cabin hung with gold and crimson velvet. Although in agony as he lay on his bed of violet taffetas, the Cardinal's mind retained its icy clarity. But by the end of 1642 he was spitting blood, and his physicians diagnosed pleurisy—he offered his resignation. However, Louis answered that Richelieu must die as he had lived, First Minister of France, and came to his bedside to feed him spoonfuls of egg yolk with his own hand. The 'torment and ornament of his age' died on 4 December 1642. He had made France the greatest country in Europe; his achievements are the measure of Louis XIII's judgement. On his advice Louis appointed Mazarin to be his successor, with instructions to continue all the Cardinal's policies.

Louis himself was dying. At the end of March 1643 he told his doctor, Bouvard, 'I see from your silence that I am going to die.' He added, 'God knows I never liked life and that I shall be overjoyed to go to Him.' They brought the Dauphin to see him. When the King asked him his name the little boy replied, 'Louis XIV, *mon Papa*.' His father smiled and answered, 'Not yet, my son.' After receiving the Last Sacraments at the end of April, Louis diverted himself by ordering his gentlemen to sing psalms and hymns in which he sometimes joined. He died on 14 May 1643. His last word was 'Jesus'. He was only forty-one.

Acting on his instructions, an attendant removed the crucifix, which Louis wore on a cord round his neck, and took it to Soeur Angélique (Mlle de La Fayette) at her convent.

The day before he died the King had said to the old foe of his childhood, Condé, 'Monsieur, I know that the enemy is advancing towards our frontiers with a great and powerful army.' No one in Paris had heard of any enemy invasion. Louis added faintly, 'Your son will rout it and win a great victory.' They thought the dying man's mind was wandering. A week later, a strong Spanish force laid siege to Rocroi, a French fortress in the Ardennes. Condé's son, the Duc d'Enghien who was only twenty-two, led an army of 20,000 men to its relief. A brilliant, unorthodox commander, he marched straight at the Spaniards, positioning his troops too quickly for the enemy to manœuvre. Next day the Duke routed them with successive charges until only the famous Spanish infantry remained, commanded from a litter by the aged Count Fuentes. Enghien charged them three times until Fuentes was killed. Another final charge destroyed them; 8,000 Spaniards were killed and 7,000 taken prisoner, the cream of their army. It was the end of a military domination of Europe which had lasted since their victory at Pavia in 1525.

To his contemporaries, Louis XIII seemed a most effective monarch. James Howell,* writing in 1646, regarded him as an inspiration to English royalists: 'A successful and triumphant King both at home and abroad throughout the whole course of his reign,' wrote Howell, 'and that in so constant degree as if Fortune herself had been his companion and Victory his handmaid.'

Saint-Simon outlived his friend and master by fifty years, dying in 1693. He had known Louis XIII better than anyone. It is worth remembering that he and his son—the diarist—never ceased to venerate Louis's memory. To the end of his life the diarist wore on his finger a miniature of the King set in diamonds, while a lamp burnt perpetually before a bust of Louis in the family chapel. Father and son faithfully attended Mass at Saint-Denis on every anniversary of his death. Few Kings have inspired such gratitude and affection in their favourites.

---

* LVSTRA LVDOVICI OR THE Life of the late Victorious King of France, LEWIS the XIII (And of his Cardinal de Richelieu.) by Iames Howell, Esq, London 1646.

'The Love of Glory'

LOUIS XIV (1643–1715)

'The love of glory has all the same subtle shades and, may I
say, all the same questionings as the tender passions'

The children, grand-children and great grand-children of Louis XIV

LOUIS XIV
1638–1715
m. Maria Theresa of Austria

- Five other children, died in infancy

LOUIS, the 'Grand Dauphin'
1661–1711
m. Maria Anne of Bavaria

PHILIPPE Duc d'Anjou
King Philip V of Spain from 1700
1683–1746

CHARLES Duc de Berry
1686–1714

LOUIS Duc de Bourgogne and later Dauphin 1682–1712
m. Maria-Adelaide of Savoy

Louis Duc de Bretagne
1707–12

LOUIS XV
1710–74

An un-named Duc de Bretagne
1704–05

Louis's children by Mme de Montespan

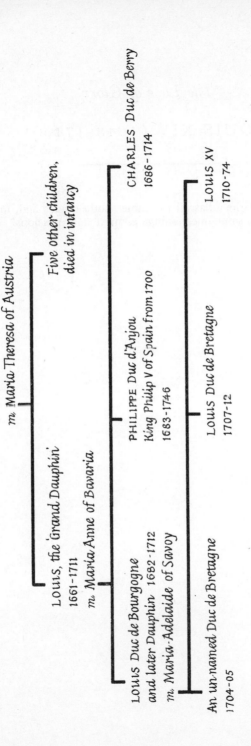
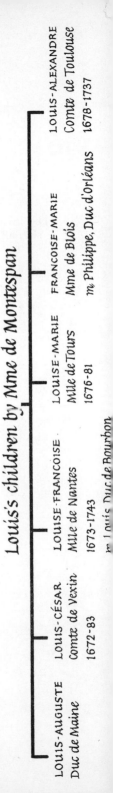

LOUIS-AUGUSTE
Duc de Maine

LOUIS-CÉSAR
Comte de Vexin
1672–83

LOUISE-FRANÇOISE
Mlle de Nantes
1673–1743
m. Louis Duc de Bourbon

LOUISE-MARIE
Mlle de Tours
1676–81

FRANÇOISE-MARIE
Mme de Blois
m. Philippe, Duc d'Orléans

LOUIS-ALEXANDRE
Comte de Toulouse
1678–1737

So much has been written about Louis XIV that it is impossible to think of him without prejudice. Many have admired him extravagantly, and as many have detested him no less fervently. It is not easy to distinguish the man from the King. He lived so completely in public that he almost ceased to exist as a private individual.

Louis ascended the throne in 1643, at the age of four and a half. He was already conscious of his superiority to other mortals; when Cinq Mars had presumptuously picked him up in his nursery, Louis had kicked and screamed till he was set down again. Even as a child he possessed a marked sense of theatre and must have relished his presentation to the Parlement in their red robes and bonnets. Their President, M Omar Talon, went on his knees before the boy to tell him that, to the lawyers, his chair of state represented 'the throne of the Living God', and that 'the realm's estates pay you honour and duty as they would to a God who can be seen'.

Anne of Austria swiftly persuaded the Parlement to set aside the late King's will, which had left her only the title of Regent while giving the substance of power to a council of advisers. Like Marie de Medici, she meant to be all-powerful, and like Marie de Medici, real power lay with an Italian favourite. But there was little resemblance between the Concini and Giulio Mazzarini, better known as Cardinal Mazarin. This low-born adventurer, who was reputed to be the grandson of a Sicilian fisherman, had combined the careers of soldier, diplomat and cleric, first in the Papal service and then in the French, winning the approval of Louis XIII and Richelieu who obtained the Red Hat for him (though he only took minor orders and was never a priest). Where Richelieu had been nervous and harsh,

Mazarin was suave and charming. His character was subtler, more accommodating. Never discouraged or depressed, his motto was 'Time is on my side'. Tall, fair-haired and handsome —Richelieu said he looked like Buckingham—he knew how to please women. Anne of Austria was completely captivated: as Voltaire put it, 'He had such dominion over her as a clever man may well have over a woman born with sufficient weakness to be ruled and sufficient obstinacy to persist in her choice.' Even so, the court was taken by surprise when the Regent confirmed him in his post of First Minister.

No one expected Mazarin to continue in office for very long. The opposition which had plagued Richelieu descended on the court; they had suffered either on behalf of, or with, the Queen and they expected to be rewarded. This *Cabale des Importants* included the Duc de Vendôme, Henri IV's son, and Vendôme's own son, the gallant Duc de Beaufort; the Bishop of Beauvais (whom a fellow prelate described as a 'mitred beast'); Marie de Hautefort, and, of course, Mme de Chevreuse. The latter shrilly insisted that Anne must return everything which Louis XIII had stolen from the great lords. After four months the Regent grew tired of her former friends, the last straw being a plot to murder Mazarin, and banished them.

Anne was a strong, vigorous woman, still goodlooking if somewhat full-blown. She ate enormously at all meals, and when angry screamed at those who displeased her. She was unconventional; during the torrid summer of 1646 she and her ladies, accompanied by little Louis, disported themselves in the Seine, clad in grey nightdresses. While the Regent may well have been in love with her First Minister, it is certain that she never lived with him; Anne was a devout Spanish Catholic and it would have been impossible for her to sleep with the Cardinal without her ladies knowing of such a spectacular liaison, as they themselves slept at the foot of her bed every night. None the less, she trusted Mazarin almost as a second husband.

In the long run it was fortunate for France that she did. Mazarin continued all Richelieu's policies and abroad the benefits were quickly evident. The Thirty Years War came to an end in 1648 when Sweden, France and the Empire made a peace by which France gained Alsace (even if it was still nominally subject to the Emperor). The negotiations were con-

ducted in French, the beginning of its long sway as the language of diplomacy. France remained at war with Spain, but the latter was now too weak to be of much danger.

Louis was an attractive little boy, bright, high-spirited and unusually goodlooking, though he lost some of his looks after catching smallpox in 1647. His education was designed to give him an ineradicable sense of the dignity of kingship; he had to copy out texts such as 'Homage is owed to Kings; they do what they wish'. He was told to model himself on Saint Louis and on his grandfather. Henri IV was now referred to as *'Henri le Grand'* in official documents, while one of Louis's tutors, Bishop Péréfixe, compiled a eulogistic life for the young monarch's edification. Anne is said to have told the boy not to copy his father because 'People wept at the death of Henri IV, but laughed at that of Louis XIII'. However, Louis always remembered his father with affection.

Each night the Queen's valet read him extracts from Eudes de Mezeray's *History of France*, though Louis himself much preferred fairy-tales. He was taught riding, fencing and deportment, how to carry himself as a King; he also learnt the lute and the guitar, and how to sing and dance. He could speak good Italian and passable Spanish. Apart from basic arithmetic, he was given little instruction in mathematics and remained more or less ignorant of geography, economics and modern history.

His tutors were so obsequious that he christened one— Marshal de Villeroy—*'Maréchal Oui-Sire'*, but it cannot be said that Louis was spoilt. Although fond of him, his mother regretted not having a daughter and preferred his delicate brother, Philippe, whom she called her little girl. If the King had his own household from the age of seven, his stockings were often in holes, while he never had enough sheets (for the rest of his life he slept with the bed clothes wrapped round his waist, and nothing over his chest and shoulders save a nightshirt). He was so much left to his own devices that once when he fell into the big fountain in the Palais Royal garden, he was not rescued until evening. On state occasions, however, he was paraded in a coat of cloth of gold and a plumed cavalier hat with a diamond buckle. He had toy soldiers of silver and toy cannon of gold, but his favourite possession was a miniature arquebus made by his father. Years later the King told Mme de Maintenon how he and

his brother had roamed happily through the Louvre, teasing the maids and stealing omelettes from the kitchens. They used to play with a servant's little girl—she pretended to be Queen and they acted as her footmen. But in 1648 life assumed an air so menacing that even children could not fail to notice it.

The Fronde was an expression of general discontent. Years of frustration and irritation had at last reached boiling point. But it was not an attempt at revolution in the contemporary English manner. There was an odd note of frivolity in its name, which meant catapulting—or even pea-shooting. A popular song ran:

> *Un vent de Fronde*
> *S'est levé ce matin*
> *Je crois qu'il gronde*
> *Contre le Mazarin.*

The attitude of the Frondeurs may have been negative and unconstructive, but they included the majority of articulate Frenchmen. There were to be two Frondes—the Fronde of the Parlement, and the Fronde of the Princes.

In five years, Mazarin had made himself even more hated than Richelieu. His financial methods—such as manipulating the *Rentes* (or government annuities) by withholding interest and then buying them cheap when the price fell—caused widespread bankruptcies among the bourgeois. Taxes were collected with such savagery that in 1646 over 20,000 Frenchmen were in prison for fiscal offences. At the same time the Cardinal displayed both avarice and ostentatious luxury—he was famous for his Titians and Correggios, his collection of gems and his exquisite library, notorious for hoarding bullion. Surrounded by a bevy of black-eyed nieces, always fondling some scented marmoset or lap-dog, speaking with a strong Italian accent, and embarrassingly obsequious, Mazarin aroused instinctive dislike in the Frenchmen of his time.

The office-holding *noblesse de la robe* was both alarmed and angered by the increasing power of the *Intendants* throughout the realm, which detracted from their prestige and diminished their influence. The Paris Parlement was finally infuriated beyond endurance by an edict of 1646 which made them pay

duty on fruit and vegetables sent up from their country houses. They began to refuse any edicts which increased taxation, winning considerable popularity. In May 1648 they announced their intention of serving the public and rooting out abuses of state. They even developed a presumptuous theory that the will of the King was not law—events across the Channel had not gone unnoticed. Mazarin smelt danger and in July agreed to reforms suggested by the Parlement. Then news came of another triumphant victory by Condé (Enghien, who had now succeeded his father) at Lens, and the Cardinal felt strong enough to arrest the three noisiest lawyers. An attempt to rescue one of them, the demagogue Broussel, turned into a riot and then into a revolt; 200 barricades blocked the narrow streets. A deputation went to the Queen to demand Broussel's release, and when it returned empty-handed it was nearly murdered by an armed mob. Despite the Queen's tearful opposition—she threatened to strangle Broussel with her own hands—Mazarin released the lawyers. Shortly after, the Regent signed a Declaration of Reform.

In January 1649 Condé and a royalist army surrounded Paris, whereupon Anne and the King fled to Saint-Germain. The siege continued for three months. During this time Louis and his mother slept on truckle beds at a Saint-Germain denuded of furniture. Ladies had to make do with straw palliasses, while gentlemen lay on the floor. There were ballets and banquets, but the royal coffers were soon empty—Louis dismissed his pages because he could not feed them. The royal party can hardly have been cheered by the news from England; Charles I had been beheaded. Anne groaned, 'This is a blow to make Kings tremble!' However, the first Fronde came to an end when the Regent grudgingly confirmed her Declaration. The court returned to Paris in August 1649.

Mazarin and the Regent were now threatened by 'Le Grand Condé'. The young warlord was an insufferably haughty little man with an overbred face like a bird of prey, who could never forget that he was First Prince of the Blood and possessed six dukedoms. He thought himself all-powerful, insulting both Anne and the Cardinal—on one occasion he pulled the latter's beard. To his own astonishment Condé was arrested and imprisoned at Vincennes in January 1650. His friends soon raised the standard

of revolt, beginning the Fronde of the Princes. All over France nobles rose, but at first the royal troops were successful (during one of these engagements, Louis was shot at). Meanwhile, behind Mazarin's back, a debauched little abbé, Paul de Gondi (the future Cardinal de Retz), who was the co-adjutor to the Archbishop of Paris, was plotting to unite the two Frondes; he was able to do so because his office gave him a seat in the Parlement, where he ostentatiously wore a dagger known as the breviary of M de Retz. He intrigued to such effect that the lawyers allied with the Princes, and Parlement asked the Regent to release Condé and dismiss Mazarin.

Mazarin fled to Cologne, disguised as a musketeer, with Anne's diamonds in his pocket. Gaston d'Orléans was proclaimed Lieutenant-General of France. Suspecting that the Queen was about to flee from Paris to join Mazarin, a Frondeur mob broke into the Louvre and demanded to see the King. Anne, who was on the point of leaving, hastily changed into a nightdress, while Louis leapt into bed—still wearing his boots—and pretended to be asleep. In single file the rabble of Paris shuffled past his bed, some daring to peer behind the curtains to see if he really were inside. Condé was released from Vincennes.

Gaston d'Orléans said that during these years the political scene changed so often and so swiftly that he was in a state of almost perpetual bewilderment. In September 1651 Louis was crowned at Rheims (during the celebrations he danced in a court ballet, wearing the costume of a 'Sun King'). The 'Eighth Sacrament' confirmed him in his extraordinary and precocious self-confidence. Furthermore, he had achieved his legal majority and Mazarin, feeling secure again, returned. It was too soon. Condé, during his absence, had quarrelled with the Parlement and had left Paris, but he now advanced on the capital with an army—he may even have hoped to seize the throne. In the battles which followed Condé very nearly captured Louis. Anne was only persuaded to stay in Paris by her confidence in that great soldier, Turennes, the son of Henri IV's old enemy, who had rallied to the Royalist party—she told him gratefully, 'Without you every town in France would have shut its gates on the King.' But Condé continued to advance. In July 1652 he fought a battle in the Faubourg Saint-Antoine, during which *La Grande Mademoiselle* (Gaston's daughter) trained the guns of the Bastille on

Turennes's troops and opened the gates to Condé. The royal forces withdrew, leaving Condé in occupation of the capital, and a massacre of Mazarin's supporters ensued; law and order broke down, to such an extent that the Parisians began to starve. Shrewdly Mazarin left France for a second time. Finally Condé lost his nerve and retreated to Flanders.

The Fronde collapsed. Peasants and bourgeois alike were desperate for peace; mercenary armies were devastating France and famine was widespread—there were cases of cannibalism. Both the nobles and the lawyers were disillusioned; their challenge to Absolutism had failed utterly. In October 1652 Louis XIV entered Paris to the cheers of its fickle inhabitants. The exiled Charles II of England rode beside him. In December the fourteen-year-old monarch showed both courage and dissimulation in effecting the arrest of Cardinal de Retz (Gondi). The latter was still dangerous in his residence at Nôtre-Dame, guarded by a mob who idolized him. When he visited the young King at the Louvre, he was greeted effusively by Louis, who spoke enthusiastically of a play which he had just seen, his last words as he left the room being, 'and above all when no one is on the stage'. The words were the signal for his Guards to arrest de Retz, who speedily found himself in Vincennes. Condé, who had fled to Spain, was condemned to death. The Parlement was humiliated by an edict that it must henceforward register all decrees of the royal council. In February 1653 Mazarin returned —he had triumphed, though his hair had turned white. The Fronde was over.

Mazarin was now undisputed master of France. He took pains to train the young King in statecraft; in 1654 he started to hold special sessions of the Council at which business was simplified so that the boy could follow; soon Louis was attending daily. Of this time he wrote in his memoirs how he never ceased to test himself in secret—'I was delighted and encouraged when I sometimes learnt that my youthful ideas had been adopted by able experienced men.' His already phenomenal self-confidence was growing. One day in March 1655, while hunting, he learnt that the Parlement had met without authorization to reconsider recent edicts; booted and spurred, Louis strode into the Parlement and told the Président, 'I forbid you to allow these meetings and any one of you to ask for them.' He began to impress

ambassadors with his knowledge of foreign policy. By 1657 he was visiting Mazarin every morning to discuss matters of state.

The one matter in which the Cardinal did not indulge the King was finance, which he never discussed. While he himself was amassing a vast fortune, Mazarin kept Louis short of ready cash. Voltaire says that he administered the royal finances like the steward of some bankrupt nobleman—the King often had to borrow money. Yet when Mazarin shrewdly presented Louis with all his own enormous wealth, in a specially drawn-up deed, Louis promptly returned it. Until the end he deferred to the Cardinal.

Mazarin's foreign policy was imaginative. Spain, for whom Condé was now fighting, had recaptured all the French gains, so the Cardinal made an alliance with Cromwell, after which the Spaniards were defeated on both sea and land. In 1658 Turennes won a great victory, the Battle of the Dunes, capturing Dunkirk, the key to Flanders. Louis made a grand entrance into the port, though by the terms of the treaty it soon had to be surrendered to the English. When the Protector died, the French court went into mourning. It was in 1658, too, that Spain made peace, France retaining Artois, Cerdagne and Roussillon and remaining in occupation of the Duchy of Lorraine; Condé received a full pardon. The peace was sealed by Louis's betrothal to a Spanish princess.

The King was no stranger to the pleasures of the bed. He was said to have been initiated, on his mother's instructions, by Mme de Beauvais, who was the chief lady-in-waiting and known as 'One-eyed Cateau'; she lay in wait for him as he returned from his bath. From her he went on to various chambermaids and laundresses, contracting gonorrhea to his shame and self-disgust.

In 1657 he had fallen head over heels in love with Mazarin's niece, Marie Mancini, who was only seventeen. Mme de Motteville describes her as sallow and scraggy, but in fact she was pretty enough, and interesting too—an intense bluestocking with huge brown eyes. She refused to become his mistress, the affair being highly intellectual; they exchanged verses and read favourite books to each other. Louis gave her his little dog, Friponne, and bought her Henrietta Maria's pearls (poverty had forced the English Queen to sell them). By

1658 the King wanted to marry Marie and was encouraged by
the exiled Queen Christina of Sweden. Mazarin was horrified
when Louis asked him for his niece in marriage; he told the
King that he would stab Marie rather than allow her to disgrace
the throne. The lovers parted tearfully in the courtyard of the
Louvre, Marie crying, 'You are King and you are weeping and
yet I have to leave!' A long, sad farewell lasted until the
autumn of 1659 when Marie begged Louis to stop writing to
her. (She became the wife of the Roman Prince Colonna, in
whose father's household Mazarin's father had been a servant;
it turned out an unhappy marriage.)

In June 1660 like his father before him, Louis married an
Infanta of Spain. At the nuptial blessing in the church at Saint-
Jean-de-Luz, near the Spanish border, Maria Theresa wore a
dress of silver brocade with a forty-foot train of blue velvet; she
was small and stout, almost a dwarf, with a long, fat face partly
redeemed by wonderfully curly hair of brilliant gold, and bright
blue eyes. Her husband, whom she was meeting for the first
time—they had been married by proxy—was in gold brocade;
she was alarmed by his insistence on consummating their marriage the same night. The following year Maria Theresa
presented him with a Dauphin (Louis—known to history as
le Grand Dauphin, to his contemporaries as *Monseigneur*), but
the six other children who followed all died in infancy. Amiable,
good-natured, but unintelligent, always chattering in bad
French, she bored Louis. The poor young woman solaced
herself with prayer and by indulging her passion for rich food,
especially chocolate, and garlic sauces.

At twenty-two Louis XIV was a handsome, well-built little
man of five feet four inches, dark-skinned, with long brown hair.
His face was round, with a firm yet sensual mouth, and was
dominated by a great Bourbon nose; at this time he wore a
pencil-thin moustache. His eyes are sometimes described as
grey, sometimes as hazel, being of that changeable hue which
the French call *chatoyant*. Despite his small size—he wore six-
inch heels to offset it—he had broad shoulders and was unusually muscular. He possessed an unmistakably regal presence
and what contemporaries describe as an almost god-like way of
carrying himself. He was already a man of overwhelmingly
strong personality, with a rather grave charm, which was

enhanced by beautiful manners; he seldom joked for fear of hurting people's feelings.

Louis was highly intelligent, with a marked sense of justice and fair play. (Lord Acton considered him 'by far the ablest man who was born in modern times on the steps of a throne'.) Although sensitive and emotional, he displayed almost complete self-control from a very early age—he never showed signs of pain, never gave way to weariness before his courtiers; in some ways he resembled an actor perpetually on stage. Like his grandfather he had voracious appetites, being a gargantuan eater and an insatiable womanizer, and like all Bourbons he loved hunting. A need for constant exercise was evident in long walks, in tennis and pall-mall, and in his enjoyment of dancing in court ballets.

So far the reign of Louis XIV had been very like that of Louis XIII. There had been a long minority under a tactless Queen Regent, who governed through an Italian favourite. The turbulence of the great nobles and the lawyers had plunged France into civil wars of just the same sort as those of the early years of the preceding reign. Finally, order had been established by a strong and ruthless First Minister.

From 1660, however, the Cardinal was ailing—he had cancer. Early on the morning of 9 March 1661 Pierrette, Louis's old nurse who still slept in his bedchamber, woke the King to tell him that Mazarin was dead. Louis rose, dressed, and locked himself in the Cardinal's room, weeping. When he emerged he ordered the court to go into mourning as if for a member of the royal family—he had been fond of the old man, almost as a second father (in his memoirs he wrote that he had loved him).

Next day Louis summoned the Council to meet at the Louvre, at seven o'clock in the morning. Each of its members hoped to be the new First Minister and all were astonished when the King told them, 'It is time for me to govern. You will help me with advice when I ask for it . . . Secretaries of State, I order you to sign nothing without my command, not even a passport or a safe conduct.' From his memoirs it is evident that Louis was amused by the Council's astonishment—he saw that they expected him to grow bored. He wrote, 'A man reigns by work and it is ungrateful and presumptuous to God, unjust and

tyrannical to men, to wish to reign without working.' He himself often worked a full eight-hour day, reading every document which bore his name.

Even at this early age he had evolved the principles which governed his reign. Mazarin had assured him that he could be the greatest King the world had ever known. He wrote proudly, 'A ruling and over-riding passion for greatness and glory obliterates all others'; and that for a King 'the love of glory has all the same subtle shades and, may I say, all the same questionings as the tender passions.' Louis considered himself not only master of his subjects but also owner of their goods; this belief was not his own invention, but was derived from the place of the Emperor in Roman Law. Nor was it a concept without dignity, for Louis also believed that it was his duty to consider the welfare of his subjects rather than his own. 'If God gives me grace to do all I hope to, I will bring happiness during my reign, to such an extent that . . . nobody, however poor he may be, shall be uncertain of his daily bread, either from his own labour or from public assistance by the state.'

Louis XIV set out to be a great King at a moment when France had decided that she wanted to be a great nation. He threatened Spain, and even the Papacy, with war merely because of trivial insults to his ambassadors. The French applauded, and welcomed his early campaigns. Their attitude was a little like that of the Germans in 1933—they wanted a ruler who would give them self-respect. After the remote Louis XIII, the country was delighted to find itself with a charming and accessible young King. Their adulation affected even *les Grands*, in the same way that Hitler's popularity cowed the German ruling classes. The upper ranks of the French nobility had been badly shaken by the débâcle of the Fronde. If Richelieu could bring them to heel, an able King who governed for himself, and was a popular idol, could easily exploit their lack of self-confidence.

Louis had the hypnotic charisma later possessed by Napoleon and by Hitler. Saint-Simon writes of his 'terrifying majesty'. His all-seeing glance could make the haughtiest duke tremble— he could make even Condé shake with fear. Fascist writers of the 1920s and 1930s saw him as a precursor of the Dictators—a ruler who embodied the National Will, the Warrior King of

Action Française. But, unlike Hitler and Mussolini, and indeed unlike Napoleon, Louis put his office before himself; he was the anointed King of France rather than Louis XIV. Voltaire has a revealing story, that when a sycophant proposed that the Académie should debate which was the King's greatest virtue, Louis actually blushed.

The Dauphin was born in June 1662. The King held a fête in celebration, in an enclosure between the Louvre and the Tuileries (which is still known as the Place de Carrousel—or 'Tournament Place'). Three Queens were watching from a dais —Anne of Austria, Maria Theresa and Henrietta Maria of England. The court celebrated just as the Valois would have done, with jousts and a trot-past to music of five companies of horsemen in fantastic costumes—Romans, Persians, Turks, Indians and Americans. Louis was at their head in the role of King of the Romans, clad in flame-colour.

It was about this time that he adopted the sun in splendour as his emblem (Louis XIII had chosen the device of a sun appearing from behind a cloud to symbolize his son's birth). Many other French Kings had used emblems—Louis XII the porcupine, François I the salamander—but none to such effect. For Louis XIV, the sun in splendour was a personal declaration of policy; he wrote in his memoirs, 'I chose the sun because of the unique quality of its radiance . . . the good it does everywhere, end- lessly creating joy and activity on all sides . . . Certainly the brightest, most beautiful image of a great King.'

His determination to be master was quickly shown. The *Surintendant des Finances*, Nicolas Fouquet, had plundered the royal treasury, exaggerating statements of government ex- penditure, and was parading his insolent and ostentatious luxury. He had prepared a refuge against disgrace by fortifying the island of Belle-Ile with cannon and armed retainers. He possessed a stranglehold over the treasury and the King feared him as a dangerous obstacle to financial reform. In August 1661 the unsuspecting Fouquet invited Louis to his magnificent château at Vaux-le-Vicomte (which was reputed to have cost eighteen million livres, about £750,000 in English money of the period); where he was giving a splendid housewarming party with a firework display and a play by Molière. Amid the bursting rockets, Louis grew angrier and angrier; he was

Louis XIV and his heirs, attributed to Largillière

Louis XIV, wax bust by Benoist

particularly incensed by Fouquet's arms, a climbing squirrel, and his motto, 'What heights shall I not reach', which were depicted everywhere. On the way home the King said to his mother, 'Madame, he is going to disgorge our money!' Within three weeks, Fouquet was in the Bastille (having been arrested by M d'Artagnan) and Louis made sure that he stayed in prison until his death nearly twenty years later.

To take Fouquet's place, the King appointed Colbert Controller-General. Mazarin had once said to Louis, 'I owe you everything, but I think I've repaid some of the debt by giving you Colbert.' Jean Baptiste Colbert was the son of a draper of Rheims, who had studied the law and then spent some time in banking before entering Mazarin's service. His worth was speedily recognized by the King, who preferred ministers of humble origin (no Prince of the Blood held ministerial office under Louis XIV, and only one Duke). Colbert did the work of many ministers—of finance, public works, trade and industry, agriculture, the colonies, the navy and even the arts. Although bemused by mercantilist economics—he believed that the more gold and silver a country possessed the more powerful it would be—this frowning, beetle-browed 'man of marble' was the most businesslike of all the ministers of the *Ancien Régime*. In 1661 the treasury received thirty-one million livres in revenue, while the tax farmers took more than double that amount. Colbert retrieved a good deal of it, introducing some measure of honesty into the public accounts. He then reduced direct taxation—the *taille*—by nearly a half; he did so by raising indirect taxation, with a luxury tax on coffee, tobacco and certain wines. However, he reduced the salt duty because salt was essential, and he exempted large families from the *taille*. A sense of social justice was also evident in the revocation of patents of nobility granted in the last thirty years; thousands of rich men were forced to bear a fair share of taxation. By 1667 he had more than doubled the royal revenues.

Tirelessly the Controller-General encouraged the establishment of new industries and the expansion of existing ones. He bought technical secrets from abroad, imported skilled labour, and employed inspectors to enforce uniform standards of quality. State factories were set up. Steel, tin-plate, glass, pottery, mirrors, furniture, clocks, velvet, silk, lace and linen,

all began to be manufactured in France on a large scale. It was now that the Gobelin tapestry looms came to Paris, that the carpets of Savonnerie became famous. Colbert was determined that nothing should be imported. He raised external customs duties, forbidding the export of corn to ensure a cheap supply. To aid the home market, he tried to abolish internal customs duties and began a nation-wide programme of canal-digging and road-building.

Colbert admired the Dutch for making their little country a European power solely through trade. He therefore set up five great trading companies, sent new colonists to Canada, now known officially as New France, established trading posts at Pondicherry and other ports in India and even Madagascar, and bought a dozen islands in the Caribbean. A navy was needed, not only for war, but to protect French merchantmen. As Minister of Marine, he increased the French navy from twenty ships to over 250, based on depots at Brest and Toulon, and manned by over 60,000 sailors; and founded a school for naval officers.

For all his good intentions, Colbert lacked human feeling. It was brutally evident in his otherwise admirable plans for New France. Sending out a cargo of '150 girls together with stallions, mares and ewes', he ordered the garrison to marry the girls on their arrival, and get them with child by the end of the year.

Modern research has shown that 'Colbertism' had many shortcomings. Though he attempted to moderate the ferocious exactions of the tax farmers, they were never properly restrained during bad harvests; it was this, not Louis's wars, which reduced French peasants to the misery later depicted by Bruyère. Nor was there any machinery to regulate the grain, trade and wheat prices, despite Colbert's belief in controls; so that both peasants and urban poor suffered unnecessarily. Colbert also failed to attract sufficient capital to his new trading companies. Undoubtedly his administration benefited the economy, and the royal finances in particular, but he was not quite the genius of popular legend.

Louis worked beside Colbert for several hours each day, examining every project and helping to draft the edicts. In the early years of the reign, when the treasury was almost bankrupt, he made many self-sacrificing economies, and gave his Controller-General enthusiastic support.

Louis's reform of the law has been described as the greatest legal work between Justinian and Napoleon. In 1667 the *Code Louis* was promulgated, simplifying and unifying all French legal procedure. Five more codes followed; a new code of criminal law, which limited the use of torture; a commercial code; a marine code; a code for woods and waters; and even a code for negro slaves in the colonies. The King worked with his ministers—notably the Chancellor Seguier—on these revisions, acquiring a comprehensive knowledge of the realm's two great legal traditions; the *Loi Coutumier* or Common Law of northern France, and the *Loi Ecrit* or Roman Law of France south of the Loire. From the former he derived his deep respect for his subjects' privileges, from the latter reasoned justification for his Absolutism. Few attempts to understand Louis's concept of kingship have paid attention to the impression which must have been made upon him by familiarity with the Roman Law and with the God-like rôle which it accords to the Emperor.

The King was much concerned with the enforcement of his new laws. In 1667 he appointed a special magistrate to administer the Paris police. M de la Reynie, who was his Lieutenant of Police for thirty years, trebled the force and introduced night patrols. In addition, street lighting was introduced; every street in Paris was provided with a lamp at each end and in the middle. Generally admired for his honesty and humanity, La Reynie was none the less responsible for what was later called the *cabinet noir*—censorship of the post and supplying the government with a weekly report on public opinion—and for operating a widespread network of police spies. He also enforced the *lettres de cachet* or 'sealed letters'; these were special warrants for arbitrary arrest without trial, which usually meant confinement in the Bastille, though surprisingly few were issued.

During Maria Theresa's first pregnancy, Louis's fancy was taken by a seventeen-year-old lady-in-waiting, Louise de la Baume le Blanc, Demoiselle de la Vallière. She was a country girl from Touraine, daughter of an impoverished captain of horse, who had taught her to shoot with a pistol and to use a boar spear. Her skill as a horsewoman and her fondness for hunting attracted Louis. She was an ash-blonde, thin and flat-chested, with a slight limp, rather shy and awkward but noted for her sweet nature. The early days together were spent in

hunting expeditions during which the King conducted an idyllic courtship. Louise became his mistress in June 1661, at Fontainebleau, but her ascendancy was not finally established until the affair of Madame, Monsieur's English wife in the following summer.

The second man in the kingdom, and the one closest to Louis, was his brother, Philippe, whom he made Duc d'Orléans after the unmourned Gaston's death in 1660. Small, goodlooking, 'Monsieur' had features which recalled those of Louis XIII. From his father he inherited a curious sexual makeup, which in his own case became homosexual. Early leanings in this direction were unwittingly indulged by Anne of Austria, who— with Gaston's unfortunate example in mind—kept the boy in petticoats for far longer than was customary, in the hope of making him more tractable (though tales of perverted practices being deliberately encouraged are nonsense). Like Louis XIII, Monsieur was a natural soldier who showed bravery on several occasions; unlike his father he was cheerful and garrulous—he was said to talk more than several women together. Although Louis loathed sodomites, the two brothers were devoted to each other. Unfortunately, while Louis was able to tolerate Philippe's eccentricities—ribbons, jewelled bracelets, drenching himself in feminine scents, painting his face, dancing at balls in female costume—he could not approve of a circle of vicious favourites which included the beautiful and malicious Chevalier de Lorraine and the no less evil Comte de Guiche.

To detach Monsieur from these unsavoury catamites, he was married in 1660 to Henrietta of England, Charles II's favourite sister. Monsieur was not entirely satisfactory as a husband and 'Madame', a lively, flirtatious brunette, was unhappy. The King seems to have thought of consoling her himself. So did the insolent and bisexual M de Guiche, who tried unsuccessfully to seduce her in the summer of 1662. Madame remained entirely innocent, but the affair annoyed Louis.

Mlle Louise knew something about the affair—she was a friend of one of Madame's messengers—but, always loyal, refused to tell the King. He became so angry that she fled to the convent at Chaillot; it was rumoured that she had taken the veil. Louis, horrified, rode hastily to Chaillot where he found her in tears lying on the guest-room floor. She was taken home by a

repentant King after an ecstatic reconciliation, and retained possession of his heart for the next five years, presenting him with three children. However, La Vallière was not recognized as *maîtresse en titre* until his mother's death in 1666, for fear of shocking Anne of Austria. The King was also considerate enough to spend part of every night in Maria Theresa's bed. The person who suffered most was Louise, whom Mme de Sevigné called 'the little violet hiding beneath the grass, ashamed to be a mistress, a mother'.

Louis joined with enthusiasm in Colbert's encouragement of the arts. His patronage was on a massive scale and was not limited to a mere distribution of pensions. The Academie Française made good its position as supreme arbiter of the language and of letters. Other academies were established—Inscriptions and Belles Lettres in 1663, Science in 1666, Architecture in 1671. The Academy of Painting and Sculpture was reconstituted, to make a much-needed distinction between artists and house-painters, between sculptors and masons. Mazarin's great library was opened to the public, the Jardin des Plantes extended.

The King's feeling for style is evident in the polished prose of his memoirs—even Voltaire admired his gift for graceful expression, and considered that his taste had been formed by reading Corneille. Certainly Louis loved the theatre and had the plays of Molière and Racine produced at court. It was the King who decided that the former's true bent was comedy and not tragedy; Louis was personally responsible for the production of *Les Précieuses Ridicules* (a play which made startlingly unconventional fun of the period's fashionable intellectuals); he also helped with *Le Bourgeois Gentilhomme*, arranging for Molière's introduction to his First Musician, Lully. He had a genuine passion for the French language and undoubtedly enjoyed writers' company. He was on close terms with Molière, whom he even asked to sit down, an honour rarely accorded to Princes of the Blood, and he was godfather to Molière's first child. (When Molière died without the Sacraments, Louis saw that he was given Christian burial despite the opposition of the Archbishop of Paris.) He was often read to by Racine and Boileau—the Dr Johnson of the age—whom he made his historiographers. Hearing Boileau in an argument shout, 'I

know more about poetry than the King,' he commented, 'Boileau is right—he *does* know more.'

Louis was fond of all the arts. His agents bought so many statues in Rome that the Pope forbade any further export of works of art. From Lully the King commissioned marches and ballet music, operas and motets, tolerating his dirtiness and his drinking. On Lully's death he appointed François Couperin as his new First Musician (the music of this virtuoso of the clavichord can still convey much of the atmosphere of Louis's court). An Academy of Music was founded in 1666. The following year a school of painting for Frenchmen was established in Rome. Although the country's greatest painter, Poussin, refused all invitations to come home, his most important follower, Charles Le Brun, became the King's First Painter, in which capacity he advised him on almost every aspect of decoration. Besides employing portrait painters like Pierre Mignard and Hyacinthe Rigau, Louis was directly responsible for the rise of a new school of engraving; he ordered that France's great buildings and treasures should be perpetuated in the *Cabinet des Médailles*, a national collection of engravings, while he himself posed for such engravers as Nanteuil. He also sat to sculptors, notably Antoine Coysevax.

It was Voltaire who first observed that while the earlier part of Louis XIV's reign abounded with men of literary genius, the end was a cultural desert, a verdict which has since been repeated *ad nauseam*. But the decline was hardly the King's fault; if he could encourage great artists he could hardly be expected to create them. Although Voltaire was not aware of it, one of the greatest of all French writers was secretly at work throughout the later years of the reign; the Duc de Saint-Simon's memoirs rank with the novels of Proust and Balzac, a masterpiece encapsulating an entire world. And Montesquieu, Buffon and Voltaire himself emerged only just after the reign was over.

Versailles was the supreme expression of Louis's love of beauty. This palace is often seen as a monument to megalomania, something 'un-French'. If it is a monument, it was meant as one to the Bourbon dynasty as a whole, intended to outshine the beautiful châteaux of the Valois; even the bluff Henri IV had had plans drawn up for a palace almost as large to

be built at Blois. Nor was the choice of Versailles a 'rejection of Paris'. The Valois had always lived away from the capital, in the Loire valley, and the move was quite in keeping with French tradition. Throughout his reign, Louis continued to beautify Paris; he built the Champs-Elysées, the first boulevards, the Observatory, the Place des Victoires, the Pont Royal, the Louvre Colonnade, the Invalides, the Place Vendôme, and the chapel of the Salpêtrière. He laid out the new street plan for the Faubourgs Saint-Germain and Saint-Honoré and extended the Tuileries. Even after he had moved out to Versailles, the King visited his capital regularly.

Louis's predilection for Versailles owed something to his father's memory, and something to his visits there with La Vallière. He began to enlarge it in 1661, though until 1668 the little palace was merely extended. In 1664 he gave an open-air fête at Versailles for Louise, which lasted for seven days and far outshone the Carrousel; its theme was *Les Plaisirs de l'Ile Enchanté* (a tale taken from Ariosto's *Orlando Furioso*). Amid the pageants and the tableaux, supper was served by 200 nymphs and shepherds at tables lit by 4,000 flaring torches. Another part of the entertainment was the first production of Molière's greatest play, *Tartuffe*.

Versailles in these early days was not yet sufficiently theatrical for the King's taste. Bernini visited him in 1665 and while his bust of Louis conveys both his good looks and his majesty, the face is as much that of a great actor as of a great King. Louis XIV needed a stage.

The second phase of rebuilding began in 1669. Louis had a complete new palace in mind, but would not allow his architects to demolish Louis XIII's 'house of cards'; he told them, 'If you pull it down I will have it rebuilt brick by brick.' It had to be included in the new building, enclosed on three sides by an *'envelope'* of red brick and white stone designed by Le Vau. He soon decided that this second palace was not big enough for anything other than a holiday residence, and a third rebuilding began. Thousands of workmen toiled for years, and so many millions were spent that the sum was made a state secret, but the palace was not fully complete until 1710. It was basically a three-sided building, so big that the garden front had 375 windows. Louis himself, advised by Le Brun, approved every

detail of its design and decoration—the gilding and the tiles, the chimneys and the terraces, the marble and the mirrors, the silver furniture and silken tapestries, the urns and sconces.

Although Le Vau designed the original plan, the architect who built Versailles was Jules Hardouin-Mansart—'a tall, well-built, handsome man of very humble origin but possessing a great deal of natural intelligence', says Saint-Simon. Louis was not concerned with 'the vulgarity of his origin' and became very fond of Mansart, whom he ennobled. On one occasion the King told his courtiers, in the architect's presence, 'I can make a score of dukes and peers in a quarter of an hour, but it would take centuries to make a Mansart.'

Of all the mistresses of the French Kings, Françoise-Athénaïs de Montespan was the most formidable. Born in 1640, a daughter of the Duc de Mortemart—his family, the Roche-chouart, was one of the oldest and grandest in Poitou—she had married an impoverished rake, the Marquis de Montespan. Like her mother in the previous reign, she became a lady-in-waiting, pleasing the Queen by her apparent piety. She soon endeared herself to Louise de la Vallière as a reassuring confidante. However, as early as 1666 she was having diabolical prayers said by witches to help her seduce the King. At first Louis did not seem interested—perhaps he realized that she was dangerous. While Athénais was very beautiful, dark and sensuous, with violet eyes, scarlet lips and an adorable figure (despite a tendency to plumpness), she was also both wild and arrogant, a compulsive gambler who was heavily in debt; and she combined a savage wit with a vile temper. In any case, she had two children and her proud and fiery husband would not be a willing cuckold. Athénais hid her ambition, biding her time, confident not only of her prayers but also of her charms. For Athénais was not only beautiful, she was interesting. Sophisticated, with a discerning taste in luxury, she dressed delightfully; even more important, she was extremely well-read and spoke exquisite French with a turn of phrase which was admired by Saint-Simon.

In the summer of 1667, during the invasion of Flanders, the King finally became her lover. La Vallière, who had recently been made a Duchess, and who was always trustful, suspected nothing. M de Montespan was furious and beat his wife; dressed in mourning, he drove to court with two great cuckold's

horns waving from the roof of his carriage. The King banished him. Louise was deserted, but to preserve the proprieties was forced to stay at court and retain the title of *maitresse en titre*— she still travelled in Louis's carriage with the Queen and Athénais. (These could be dreadful journeys for the ladies-in-waiting, as the King would not let them stop the carriage when they wished to relieve themselves.) Louise was allowed to depart in 1674, whereupon she entered a notoriously strict Carmelite convent where she remained—as Soeur Marie de la Miséricorde—until her death in 1710. When told that her son, the Duc de Vermandois, had died, she commented, 'I mourn his birth even more than his death.'

Athénais held the King for twelve years. She worked hard to do so, dyeing her hair blonde because he liked it better than brown; dieting (Mme de Sévigné once noted that she came back after an absence from court half her size) and having herself rubbed down with scent; patriotically, she dressed in French silks and velvets. To begin with, her life with Louis was an exuberant idyll. Voracious in bed, she satisfied his once in-satiable sexual appetite. She accompanied him when he inspec-ted the frontiers in 1678, even though she was pregnant. He adored children, so she presented him with seven (who were put in the care of her dear friend, Mme Scarron). He rewarded her richly, making her father Governor of Paris, paying her gambling debts and buying her wonderful jewels. He built her a fabulous château, Clagny (specially designed by Mansart) where to please him she made a garden filled with jonquils and jasmine, his favourite flowers. (The King was so fond of jasmine that sometimes the entire floor of his bedroom was covered with it.) Everybody else loathed her. Success made her intolerably haughty and unbridled her vicious tongue. Not even the King was spared, and he almost abandoned her in 1672 and again in 1674. To keep him, so it was later alleged, she commissioned blasphemous spells and gave him toad excrement as an aphro-disiac; she was even accused of having a Black Mass, during which a baby was sacrificed, said over her naked body. By the mid-1670s the King was tiring of her. Totally unsubmissive, she reacted violently to his many infidelities. He ceased to sleep with her in 1678, though the final breach did not come till later.

Military glory remained for Louis infinitely desirable. In the brutal Marquis de Louvois, the King had a wonderful Minister of War, whose reforms served France until the Revolution. Louvois introduced regimental uniforms, badges of rank, portable pontoon bridges and standardized artillery. For the first time the ordinary French soldier was regularly paid, well fed from field kitchens and had a chance of rising from the ranks. Louvois was responsible for the foundation of the Hôtel des Invalides—in its day the best old soldiers' home in the world—and of three schools of artillery, together with cadet companies for training young officers. He introduced grenadiers and hussars, replaced the pike by the musket and plug bayonet, and made the troops march in step to airs on the fife and drums specially composed by Lully. Hitherto the French had considered cavalry as the only soldiering fit for gentlemen; now Louis forbade anyone to join the cavalry without having first served in the infantry. A Corps of Engineers was set up to assist the great Vauban, who in 1663 had deeply impressed the King by his fortifications at Dunkirk, Vauban's principle being that the lower defences were, the less likely they were to be hit by enemy artillery.

The King restrained himself until this army had begun to take shape—and until Colbert had amassed sufficient funds. By 1667 he was ready. Philip IV of Spain had died in 1665, succeeded by the child Charles II. In May Louis suddenly overran southern Flanders, claiming that the province belonged to his wife as the child of Philip IV's first marriage, Charles being only the child of the second (the pretext gave the campaign its name, the 'War of Devolution'). In February 1668 Louis also invaded Franche Comté. England, Sweden and the United Provinces, who had been watching with considerable apprehension, quickly formed a Triple Alliance. In May he was forced to withdraw from Franche Comté, though he kept the towns he had won in Flanders.

The Triple Alliance infuriated Louis. The Dutch, who were its real architects, had already affronted him by responding to Colbert's tariffs with surcharges on all French wines, spirits and manufactured goods, while the activities of the Bank of Amsterdam were seriously depleting French currency. By the spring of 1672 he had isolated them from their allies, paying Sweden a

large annual subsidy and sending Charles II of England a secret pension; in the latter case Louis's agent was Madame, who, just before her death in 1670, persuaded her brother to ally with France.

The French army was now stronger than it had ever been, with nearly 120,000 highly trained soldiers. Voltaire describes Louis's newly formed household troops: 'There were four companies of life-guards, each comprising three hundred gentlemen, among whom were many young cadets, unpaid, but subject like everyone else to the strict rules of the service; there were also two hundred guardsmen, two hundred light horse, five hundred musketeers, all of gentle birth, young and of good appearance; twelve companies of men-at-arms, afterwards increased to sixteen; the hundred Swiss guards accompanied the King, and his regiments of French and Swiss guards mounted guard in front of his house and tent.' These troops, the *Maison du Roi*, whose uniforms were covered with gold and silver, became the crack troops of the *Ancien Régime*.

Besides Condé, the King had the services of another great captain, Turennes. Although the Dutch possessed the most formidable navy in the world, they had pitifully few troops. France declared war in April 1672, and in June the French cavalry swam the Rhine, Louis and the infantry following over their new pontoon bridge. The King, in jack-boots, a leather coat and a red-plumed hat, shared his men's rations but insisted on full ceremonial and used his tent as an audience chamber. By the end of the month Turennes had turned the Dutch line of defence, and Amsterdam was only twenty miles away. The Dutch fell back on their last resource, breaking down the dykes and flooding all the country around Amsterdam. Then they begged for peace.

Louis's terms were too much—a crushing indemnity and a large slice of territory. On hearing them, the Dutch overthrew the government of de Witt—he and his brother were torn to pieces by a mob—and replaced them with the young Prince of Orange who was appointed Stadtholder. By now all Europe went in fear of Louis, and the Dutch found new allies—Brandenburg and the Empire at the end of 1672, Spain and Lorraine in 1673, Denmark and the Rhine Palatinate in 1674.

Withdrawing from Holland, Louis struck swiftly at the

Spanish and conquered Franche Comté in six weeks, this time for good. Turennes laid waste to the Palatinate, burning two towns and twenty villages, and destroying vineyards, crops and livestock so that the enemy would be without supplies. When the Germans invaded Alsace at the end of 1674, Turennes drove them back in a terrible winter campaign, inflicting 40,000 casualties; while Condé repelled a Dutch and Spanish invasion. Next year the French were not so successful. A stray cannon-ball killed Turennes (Louis buried him in the royal sepulchre at Saint-Denis). Condé drove the Germans out of Alsace for a second time, but France was growing tired. Despite Colbert's striving, taxes had risen to enormous heights—the war was costing France something like £30 million a year—and there were sporadic risings among the Breton peasants.

The war dragged on for three more weary years, during which the French won some slight victories—Monsieur, painted and powdered as always, defeated the Prince of Orange at Mont Cassel by a courageous gamble, much to the King's jealousy. Meanwhile Louis was waging a most skilful diplomatic campaign; setting the Dutch against the Spanish and attacking the latter in Italy; stirring up rebellion in Hungary; he even managed to foment quarrels between the Dutch republicans and the Stadtholder's supporters. Louis's enemies grew even wearier of the war than the French. A peace conference met at Nijmegen in the summer of 1678 and was brilliantly handled by Louis's diplomats. A treaty signed in August gave him Franche Comté and twelve towns in Flanders—the latter constituting a valuable reinforcement to France's weak northern frontier—and Nancy. A separate treaty with Holland reduced the French tariffs, though it did not abolish them entirely. Nijmegen was an undoubted triumph for Louis and his policy of aggression.

The years which followed Nijmegen were the zenith of Louis's glory. In 1680 the Parlement of Paris bestowed upon him the title of 'The Great'. When the poor Queen died in 1683 Bossuet, in his funeral oration, spoke not only of her *'piété incomparable'* but also of *'les imortelles actions de Louis le Grand'*. Versailles was a fitting shrine. The King moved in permanently in May 1682. The following year Mme de Sévigné, visiting it for the first time, wrote ecstatically, *'Tout est grand, tout est magnifique.'* The King's chief joy was the vast garden

created by André le Nôtre. Louis loved to stroll through geo-
metrically-arranged terraces, down countless avenues, over the
lawns (or 'green carpets') shaded by carefully planted groves,
along great canals and lakes. There were a thousand fountains
and innumerable statues. He enjoyed chatting with the charming
Le Nôtre or with M de la Quintinie, the amiable kitchen
gardener, or visiting the orangery to see his beloved orange
trees (he was so fond of these trees that he even had them in his
rooms, in silver tubs). The King wrote a little guide to the
gardens, so that sightseers would know the correct sequence in
which to visit them. Louis spent nearly as much time in his
gardens as he did hunting.

His Versailles was a return to the Dijon of the medieval
Dukes of Burgundy, to the Fontainebleau of François I. Far
from being a Spanish importation, its ceremony was essentially
French, with rules laid down by Henri III in 1585. Louis
merely brought them up to date. There had to be more func-
tionaries because the court now numbered thousands instead of
hundreds. The ritual quality of life at Versailles was due not so
much to the ceremonies as to Louis's own awe-inspiring
personality.

To his subjects no King could have seemed less remote.
Every day thousands of Parisians rode out in special public con-
veyances to see him eating or walking at his new palace. (It was
rather as though Queen Elizabeth II lunched daily in public at
Hampton Court.) Anyone dressed like a gentleman and wearing
a sword was admitted to the gardens—swords could be hired at
the gates for a small fee—while the royal apartments were
frequently open to the public. Louis greeted everyone politely.
This gift of living gracefully in public was largely responsible
for the extraordinary popularity which he enjoyed during the
greater part of his reign.

He was awakened at about eight in the morning. Having
greeted the few courtiers privileged to have the *grande entrée*,
he said the Office of the Holy Spirit. He then dressed, each
garment being handed to him with ceremony after which he
wiped his face and hands on a napkin soaked in spirits of wine;
on alternate mornings he was shaved. (He seldom took baths
but changed his clothes, including his linen, three times a day.)
His breakfast consisted of white bread, and hot wine and water

or sage tea. He then said more prayers and completed his dressing. The *Lever* was now over. After giving orders for the day, he heard Mass. There followed a meeting of the Council or audiences. The King dined at one o'clock, alone and in public at a square table. He ate a comparatively light meal with plenty of fruit and vegetables, which he washed down with the still, grey champagne of Bouzy. (The fizzy variety was not yet known at court, though Dom Perignon had just invented it.) In the afternoon Louis either slept with his current mistress or took some other exercise. Often he hunted or went shooting on foot, being an excellent shot. After breaking his arm in 1683, he took to following hounds in a fast wagonette which he drove himself, or spent more time walking in his beloved gardens. When he returned, he recommenced work in his study. Supper was often served as late as eleven-thirty pm. It was Louis's main meal, and he ate enormously; in the old-fashioned way he never used a fork, eating with his fingers. Finally there was an entertainment—music, dancing, cards or billiards or some other gambling game. He usually went to bed at about one in the morning, with no less ceremony than at his rising.

Versailles was the instrument by which Louis tamed the upper nobility. He drew them to court with an unending series of entertainments and also by the lure of titles and pensions; these were of vital importance to an aristocracy which was to a large extent impoverished. Versailles was the only road to preferment and promotion; there were posts to be had in the royal household and in the Dauphin's household, commissions in the army, bishoprics, abbeys, canonries. Once at court, noblemen grew still poorer, from gambling or from having to buy splendid clothes. If they would not come, Louis ordered the *Intendant* in their province to make life difficult for them. Within a few years the dangerous war-lords, who only recently had terrorized France, were transformed into foppish courtiers, grateful for gifts to relieve their debt-ridden lives. There was only one plot against his government during the entire reign.

Louis has frequently been accused of destroying the French ruling class, but it will have been seen in the preceding chapters that he had good reason for doing so. Nor did he only make fops of his nobles: the courtiers of Versailles were moulded into an

officer corps—each one could be called to the colours at a moment's notice. In addition they frequently acted as commission agents, who for a given fee would procure an audience of the King to interest him in some commercial or scientific project, rather like modern public relations men.

If Louis was often responsible for financially ruining his nobles, he could show great kindness in individual cases. Mme de Sévigné tells us that when Marshal de Bellefonds came to the King in 1672 to resign his post at court, Louis took him aside and asked, '*Monsieur le Maréchal*, why do you want to leave me? Has it to do with religion? Or do you simply want to retire? Is it your heavy debts? If it is the latter, I will settle them and must know more about your affairs.' The Marshal replied, 'Sire, it is my debts. I am ruined. I cannot let my friends, who have helped me, suffer because I'm unable to pay them.' 'In that case,' said the King, 'their debts must be made good. I'm going to give you 100,000 francs for your house at Versailles and a guarantee of 400,000 francs which will serve as a surety should you die. You can pay off what you owe with the 100,000 francs—and then you can stay in my service.'

To read the memoirs of Saint-Simon—who hated him—is to experience something of Louis XIV's strange fascination. 'Never did a man use his words, his smiles, even his mere glances, with more grace,' wrote the Duke grudgingly; 'no man was ever more polite by instinct or more correct, or knew better how to honour age, merit or rank . . . his smallest gesture, his walk, his bearing, were all most fitting and becoming, being noble, grand and majestic, and yet perfectly natural.' Louis knew not only how to overawe, but also how to charm. When an old courtier asked him for permission to leave Versailles, the King answered, 'We have known each other for too long to say good-bye at our age, when we cannot hope to find new friends—don't desert me!' The compliment he paid to the aged Condé, who was having difficulty in climbing the stairs at Versailles, is legendary: 'One who carries such a weight of laurels can only move slowly.' These compliments were paid in a voice which was at once dignified and charming. He was elegant even in his rages; having been grossly insulted by a certain nobleman, the King threw his cane out of the window, saying, 'I should be sorry to strike a man of quality.' Above all, says Saint-Simon,

'he had no equal with women'. He had an ineffable way of half-raising himself at supper for each lady who arrived at table. He never passed the humblest petticoat without raising his hat, not even chambermaids. (The *honnête homme*, or French gentleman, of the period could be surprisingly polite to servants—the Duc de Beauvilliers apologized to his coachman if he kept him waiting.)

Louis's chief fault was his ferocious *amour propre*. The ambassador of the Elector of Brandenburg, Ezekiel Spannheim, noted in 1690 that the King was 'jealous to the smallest detail of his authority, excessively touchy about everything which concerns it or could harm it'. All the same, says Herr Spannheim, 'he is easily influenced by advisers and adopts their policies.' Nothing could be further from the truth than the claim (which he never made) *'l'état, c'est moi'*. The 'state' of Louis XIV was the bureaucracy which he created—his Council of a few all-powerful ministers, and the *Intendants*, each of whom was supreme in his province, overriding the Governor, the Parlement and the municipalities. These chosen servants often acted without their master realizing fully what they were about. As the years went by, however, Louis paid more and more attention to business, working as much as ten hours a day.

By the 1680s Louis was middle-aged and running to fat. His face was lined and sagging; because of the removal of several teeth from his upper jaw—the doctors broke it, smashing his palate—his mouth was shrunken, with pursed lips. He had shaved off his moustache and in place of his own long hair wore a full-bottomed periwig. Sometimes his eyes looked tired, even in official portraits. In 1686 his health was cruelly tested by a terrible operation for an anal fistula; on two occasions, fully conscious, he bore being cut many times, without a sound. Also he probably weakened himself by excessive purges (usually camomile or rhubarb). Yet he kept his huge appetite for food and women, and his love of exercise. At this period he dressed plainly, in a neat brown coat, with a waistcoat of red, green or blue, and the *Cordon Bleu* of the Saint-Esprit. Maturity made him more imposing than ever.

He was not only adored by his subjects, but was the most admired man in Christendom; as Voltaire says, 'Louis was looked on as the *only* King in Europe.' Every European sovereign

built his own Versailles, copied its etiquette and furniture and learnt to speak French. Schönbrunn in Austria, Het Loo in Holland, the garden façade of Hampton Court, still bear witness to their admiration. Foreigners flocked in crowds to see King Louis.

There were now new personalities at court. 'Monseigneur', as the Dauphin was known, was very tall, fat and yellow-haired. Dull, lazy, but unusually good-natured, he bore little resemblance to his father, who overawed him. Having been beaten and crammed by his tutors, Monseigneur detested books, although he collected pictures and furniture in his exquisite flat at Versailles and enjoyed good music. He lacked any aptitude for soldiering, but loved wolf-hunting above all else, exterminating wolves in the Ile de France. A shy man, he preferred to live quietly at Meudon with his ugly Bavarian wife, to whom he was devoted, until she succumbed to melancholia. They had three sons—the Dukes of Burgundy, Anjou and Berry. When his wife died in 1690, he married a certain Mlle de Choin, whose greatest charm, in the Dauphin's eyes, was her enormous bosom. If he had little influence, Monseigneur was none the less often to be seen at court, for his father was fond of him.

Louis liked all his children, including his bastards whom he legitimized, though they did not rank as Princes of the Blood. Of these the most important was his eldest son by Athénais—Louis-Auguste, whom the King made Duc du Maine. Sickly, limping and ineffectual, he failed miserably in his ambition to be a great soldier; he turned out both cowardly and boastful. (Even so, Saint-Simon's portrait of him is a spiteful caricature.) Louis married him to one of Condé's granddaughters. His brother, the Comte de Toulouse, was also a dull creature, but proved reasonably successful as a naval officer. He too was found a wealthy wife, one of the Noailles.

There was a nasty little scandal in 1682, when a homosexual clique was discovered at Versailles. It included Louis's son by La Vallière, the fifteen-year-old Duc de Vermandois, who had been corrupted by the Chevalier de Lorraine. Vermandois was treated with such contempt by the King that he left court of his own accord and joined the army. A sickly boy, he died the following year.

The most colourful arrival at court was Monsieur's second

wife (Madame had died in 1670), Liselotte von der Pfalz—the Princess-Palatine. This ugly German blonde with the figure of a Swiss Guard, was a convert from Protestantism, fat and red-faced, fond of dogs, beer and sausages, and much disliked by the court—a dislike which she heartily reciprocated. If unintellectual, Liselotte was brutally shrewd and observant, and her letters give a vivid picture of life at Versailles. Neither she nor Monsieur, now grown pot-bellied and stilted, but still festooned with diamonds and obsessed with his complexion, were exactly in love but they did their duty; after many failures Philippe managed to beget a son by—so he believed, according to his wife—rubbing his manhood with a holy medal.

The most formidable member of the King's new circle was his own second wife. Queen Maria Theresa died in 1683, her health undermined by pregnancies, killed by the excessive bleeding ordered by the doctors. (Colbert died the same year, sad and disillusioned.) Louis, to the court's astonishment, wept bitterly. He had been faithful to her for the last two years, even after being badly shaken by the death of a young mistress, Marie Angélique de Fontanges, in 1681. Among the friends of Mme de Montespan was a dark, statuesque widow in her forties, Mme Françoise Scarron. She was the granddaughter of Agrippa d'Aubigné, Henri IV's old henchman. Her father was a ne'er-do-well who had murdered his first wife, and Françoise had been born in prison, her mother being the governor's daughter. Since then her life had been as unusual as it was poverty-stricken. As a young girl, having been abandoned by her parents after a sojourn in Martinique where her father died, she was converted to Catholicism. At sixteen she married a crippled and disreputable poet, Paul Scarron, partly from pity, partly from poverty. Although the marriage could not be consummated, she was happy enough, gathering a little salon around her in their house in the Marais. However, Scarron died when she was twenty-four, leaving her almost penniless. Luckily, the Queen Mother, who had been one of Scarron's patrons, took pity on the pretty young widow and gave her a pension. Pious, yet none the less fond of the *beau monde*, Mme Scarron took up residence in a fashionable convent where she filled her time with good works and embroidery. She knew many people at court and was recommended to Athénais as a suitable person to

bring up her children. One of nature's governesses, she did this so efficiently and showed such discretion that the King rewarded her with a marquisate and the little estate of Maintenon.

Louis first began to know her well during their mutual concern over the health of the little Duc de Maine. He had started by disliking her, but eventually he came to admire her strong mysterious character and Junoesque figure. With her fine eyes and sober, enigmatic charm, dressed in elegant black with a becoming widow's cap, she was far from unattractive. Eventually he fell in love with her, but to his amazement the former widow Scarron refused to sleep with him; it was she who persuaded him to return to the Queen's bed. When Maria Theresa died, the King married Mme de Maintenon in secret—the date has never been discovered, but it was probably some time in 1684. He needed her: 'When a man leaves his youth behind him, he nearly always requires the companionship of a woman of even temper', is Voltaire's comment. Françoise did not find her exalted position one of unalloyed enjoyment—Louis, still voracious, must have been an exhausting husband for a middle-aged woman who was probably still a virgin. It is the measure of her remarkable personality that this new, morganatic wife was accepted without demur by the royal family and by the court.

For over thirty years the King showed an unwavering taste for domesticity. Although Mme de Maintenon complained of his unflagging virility, he was never once unfaithful. She rarely ventured out of her apartments, so her bedroom became his office; their two chairs were on each side of the fireplace, separated by Louis's table where he worked at his state papers. She set up a little theatre next door to her flat; here courtiers performed carefully chosen plays. Under her sober influence Louis grew pious. Operas were forbidden during Lent, and everyone had to communicate at Easter—people were rebuked for talking during Mass. Saint-Simon says that the court, in its efforts to please, 'sweated hypocrisy'. There was something a little sanctimonious about Mme de Maintenon. She favoured people one moment, only to cast them off the next. None the less she kept her place by her piety and won her 'battle for the King's soul'.

Although Mme de Montespan had finally lost the King, she

lingered on at court for several years, growing enormously fat (an Italian observer says that her thigh became as thick as a man's waist). She had finally been discredited in Louis's eyes by the great Poisoning Scandal, of which details first began to emerge in 1679, when the arrest of the mass murderess, Mme de Brinvilliers, led to the discovery of a vast network of professional poisoners and witches. During the panic which followed, the King established the *Chambre Ardente* (or 'Council for Burning') which accused some of the highest personages in France of murder and black magic, among them Marshal Luxembourg. Over 400 suspects were arrested and more than 200 were found guilty, thirty-six being executed (some were actually burnt). The court was abruptly dissolved in 1682 when Louis realized that Athénais might be involved—there were rumours of love philtres to secure his affections, of poisoned phials to remove rivals. Louis had the evidence destroyed. Eventually 'dreadful and ignominious Maintenon' harried 'thundering and incomparable Montespan' into leaving court. Like La Vallière, Athénais ended in a convent, where she died with decorous piety.

Mme de Maintenon has been blamed for the Revocation of the Edict of Nantes, but the King would have revoked the edict in any case. At the beginning of the reign, despite the loss of its military privileges, French Protestantism still remained something of a state within a state. Meanwhile the Gallican Church, laity as well as clergy, was increasingly critical—the Huguenots' privileged position made a striking contrast with the hysterical persecution of Catholics in the three kingdoms across the Channel. As early as 1669 measures were taken to make life difficult for French Protestants. In 1681 they were forbidden to enter government service. In 1682 when risings began in areas where the Reformed Faith was strong, dragoons were billeted in their houses with orders to behave as badly as possible (behaviour which included rape and torture). In 1685 the King at last revoked the Edict, orders being given for the destruction of all Protestant 'Temples' and for all ministers to leave France within a fortnight, or be sent to the galleys.

Out of two million Huguenots, probably 300,000 left France. Many were skilled artisans so it is often said that the Revocation of the Edict of Nantes postponed the French Industrial

Revolution by a century. In addition, more than 600 officers left the army for foreign service. In fact the exodus had surprisingly little effect on the French economy (except in a few specialized crafts such as watchmaking, though even here for hardly more than a decade). The loss of army officers was soon made good by Irish Catholics fleeing from the persecution of the Williamite government. From his own special point of view, Louis was amply repaid by the thunderous applause of the greater part of his subjects.

Paradoxically, he himself was inclined to be tolerant. At one moment he had even hoped that Rome would make doctrinal concessions to the Protestant Churches. The real motive for his persecution of the Huguenots was an anxiety to demonstrate that he was the true leader of the Catholic world; here a certain jealousy may be discerned, of the Emperor and the Polish King who were winning spectacular victories over the Turks. His natural tolerance was shown in 1670 when he took the Jews of Metz under his personal protection, and when he ordered that any criminal charges against Jews must be brought before the Royal Council. In 1687 he told a Siamese embassy that God had given men religions of slightly different hue—'as the green leaves of a tree subtly vary in colour'.

To the King, the Jansenists, with their fierce criticism of fellow Catholics, seemed just as troublesome as the Huguenots. This austere and noble sect took its name from Bishop Cornelius Jansen, a theologian who had died in 1640 and whose writings were taken up by French admirers; the basis of his teaching was that most men were damned and that only those few whom God had predestined would be saved. In practice Jansenism, with its terrifying consciousness of sin and the fruitlessness of human effort, led its followers to practise a harsh and uncompromising personal religion. The movement centred round a small community of devout gentlemen who settled near the Jansenist convent of Port Royal outside Paris. It soon attracted a distinguished following, including Pascal and later Racine. When in 1653 the Pope condemned five propositions which had been attributed to Jansen, the Jansenists said that they were not to be found in his book. Then the Jansenists attacked the Jesuits for their emphasis on Free Will. Louis, no theologian, could not grasp the finer points of the interminable quarrel. However,

many prominent Jansenists had been enthusiastic Frondeurs and he discerned the same rebellious note in their attitude towards the Papacy. As an inveterate optimist himself, he must have found their extreme pessimism distasteful. In 1679 he forbade Port Royal to take novices, and at the end of his reign had the remaining nuns evicted and the convent demolished. In 1713, at the King's request, Rome categorically condemned Jansenist beliefs.

Once Louis decided that any institution or belief was divisive, he was merciless. A new form of Quietism—the ancient doctrine that all that is necessary for salvation is a passive love of God—was propagated by a certain Mme Guyon, an unbalanced mystic who went in for ecstasies. When Mme Guyon's lectures to the girls of the school at Saint-Cyr, founded by Mme de Maintenon, resulted in outbreaks of mass hysteria, the King quickly came to the conclusion that her beliefs were a threat to public morality. However, she had a powerful ally in the elegant and saintly Fénelon, Archbishop of Cambrai, who published a partial defence of her views, his *Maximes des Saints*. The book was attacked by Bossuet and ultimately condemned by the Pope. Fénelon was banished to his diocese, while Mme Guyon was shut up in a convent.

Fénelon had been tutor to the Duke of Burgundy, the Dauphin's eldest son. Born in 1682, Louis de Bourgogne had grown up learned and hard-working; he stooped from too much study and was thin from fasting. Devout and a would-be philosopher, he was genuinely charitable, and on one occasion sold his mother's jewels to provide assistance for impoverished army officers. The Brandenburger Spannheim thought 'there was never a Prince of such promise'. What particularly struck him was the contrast between the Duke's cheerful, vivacious nature and the fact that he spoke little. The King found Bourgogne far more congenial than the Dauphin, despite the Duke's admiration for Fénelon.

Jacques-Bénigne Bossuet (1627–1704), Bishop of Meaux, was in many ways the reign's most representative churchman. In his writings, this pillar of Gallican orthodoxy expressed the religious attitude of most Frenchmen of his time. The 'Eagle of Meaux' was loud in his praise when Louis revoked the Edict of Nantes, but from a dislike of extremism and dissension rather

than from intolerance. His own religion was a balanced and generous French Catholicism which was all but anti-Roman; he drew up the 'Four Articles' which re-affirmed the independence of the Church of France from that of Rome; the 'Pope of Gallicanism' even showed a certain interest in the Church of England. Tall, white-haired, majestic, he was a familiar figure at Versailles. He moved courtiers to tears with his beautiful sermons, making an art form of the funeral oration (his *oraisons funèbres*, particularly those on the deaths of Queen Henrietta Maria and Madame, have something of the sad and stately measures of Purcell's 'Music for the Death of Queen Mary').

It says a good deal for the French Church of Louis XIV that it could produce men of the calibre of Bossuet and Fénelon. There were many other great churchmen—notably Dom Rancé, the 'Thundering Abbot' of the Trappists.

Bossuet was the classical exponent of French Absolutism. He claimed to discern a *'loi fondamental'* by which the King and his subjects accepted each other's rights and privileges as immutable and unchallengeable (this acceptance was the ultimate basis of the *Ancien Régime*). The King was indeed God's image on earth, the only source of law, yet if he acted immorally or ignored his subjects' rights he ceased to be an absolute monarch and became a mere despot. The distinction was one which Louis XIV undoubtedly recognized.

In his foreign policy, however, Louis showed less respect for other peoples' rights. Between 1679 and 1686, he bloodlessly acquired the remainder of Alsace, the Saar and much of Lorraine by means of the *Chambres de Réunion*—special legal tribunals who disinterred ancient treaties to justify French occupation. His new towns were made into strongholds by Vauban; Strasbourg (which had been entered by a combination of bribery and intimidation) becoming the strongest fortress in Europe. The King also laid claim to towns in the United Provinces and in the Spanish Netherlands. This aggressive foreign policy, together with an ostentatious build-up of the French army and navy, alarmed all Europe. In the summer of 1686, the League of Augsburg was formed against France— eventually it included the Emperor, most of the German Princes, Spain, Sweden, the Dutch and England. The Nine Years War opened early in 1689. Louis's greatest enemy was

the new Dutch Stadtholder, William of Orange, whom the Glorious Revolution had just made King of England. Louis's main objective was to break the Dutch and turn William III out of England, even if it meant fighting on five fronts.

Poor James II had been driven out of his kingdom but was not without supporters among his former subjects. Although he used James as a political tool and was well aware of his faults, Louis had a genuine affection for a brother monarch whom he had known since he was a small boy. A magnificent welcome awaited the exiled court at Saint-Germain, which was put at James's disposal. Mary of Modena was waited on as if she were Queen of France and given presents of gold and silver plate, jewellery, silks and velvets; a purse of 10,000 golden *louis* was on her dressing-table. King James received a pension large enough for him to keep his entire household. The French navy soon drove the English off the sea, routing their main fleet at Beachy Head. A French Armada took James and a Jacobite army to Ireland, which had remained loyal. As anticipated, this second front caused William III the utmost alarm. Unfortunately King James had lost his nerve; without enough experienced troops, he was easily defeated at the Boyne and fled to France once more. The Irish fought on bravely for two more years but the Jacobite cause was doomed.

In Germany the French at first conquered all before them. In February 1689, determined to knock the Elector Palatine out of the war, Louis issued an order to his troops to reduce the Palatinate to ashes. The real author of the order was Louvois, who, as Voltaire said, 'had become less humane through that hardening of sensibilities which a lengthy ministry produces.' The beautiful Rhineland went up in flames and Mannheim and Heidelberg were gutted; any Germans remaining in their ruined houses were butchered; 100,000 refugees fled north and east. German hatred of the French is often said to date from this campaign. In Italy, after several bloody reverses, the French conquered all Savoy save Turin.

Louis had excellent commanders in Marshals Catinat and Luxembourg. It was Catinat who conquered Savoy, while Luxembourg became known as the *'tapissier de Nôtre-Dame'*, so many were the enemy flags and standards which he brought home in triumph. In 1690 near Fleurus in Flanders he killed

6,000 of the enemy, taking 8,000 prisoners; in 1691 he took
Mons; in 1692 Namur, the strongest fortress in the Low
Countries, the King being present. At Steinkirk and Neerwinden (1692 and 1693), two more glorious victories were won,
though the casualties were so frightful that people said *De
Profundis* ought to be sung, rather than *Te Deum*. Unfortunately
Luxembourg died in 1695, just when the Dutch were beginning
to recover. The French also did well in Spain where the Duc de
Vendôme captured Barcelona. The French navy ruled the waves
after a brief reverse and French privateers harried English
ships and raided Jamaica and Newfoundland. Newfoundland was
almost conquered by the Comte de Frontenac and his *Canadiens*
(though at that date the entire population of New France was
only 11,000 souls). But for all the bloody battles, all the
marching and counter-marching, neither France nor her enemies
could win.

Louis was anxious to break up the League of Augsburg
before the question of the Spanish Succession would have to be
settled. He therefore bought off the Duke of Savoy by returning
his Duchy. The League dissolved. At the Treaty of Ryswick,
signed at the end of 1697, France gave up Lorraine and most of
her conquests in Germany and the Low Countries, besides
recognizing William III as King of England. Colbert's tariffs
were abolished. But she retained Strasbourg and other strong-
points on the Rhine frontier, and in America gained the Hudson
Bay and most of Newfoundland.

Louis took advantage of the peace to redecorate Marly. For
Louis XIV, this château—twelve little pavilions flanking a tiny
palace—was what the original Versailles had been for his father.
Here he relaxed among the people he liked best, etiquette being
much less formal than elsewhere, and picnicked with parties of
ladies in the woods. At Marly he indulged his passion for tulips;
four million a year were imported from Holland. The château's
new decorations, by Pierre Lepautre, are an early example of
rococo.

The treaty with Savoy brought to France the last of Louis's
great loves. This was Marie Adelaide, 'The Rose of Savoy', not
yet twelve years old, who arrived in 1696 to marry the King's
grandson, the Duc de Bourgogne. The King went to meet her.
He wrote enthusiastically to Mme de Maintenon, 'She is very

graceful and has the most perfect figure I have ever seen, dressed as if ready to sit for her portrait, with bright, beautiful eyes, admirable black eyelashes, as clear a pink and white complexion as could be desired, and the loveliest flaxen hair and plenty of it . . . ' Louis continued, 'I find her exactly what I would wish and should be sorry if she were more beautiful.' Until her marriage was consummated in 1699, Marie Adelaide lived with the King and Mme de Maintenon as a daughter, attending the school at Saint-Cyr. According to Saint-Simon, Mme de Maintenon, whom she called 'Aunt', treated her as a little doll. Louis adored the child; he took her for walks every day and let her sit on his lap and rumple his wig. She remained his favourite when she grew up plain but still vivacious. Marie Adelaide was the idol of the court—even Saint-Simon admired her. Giddy and flighty, hopelessly lacking in decorum, she had many flirtations though they were innocent enough, and was fond of rather coarse practical jokes. The King never scolded her and allowed her to run into his office at any moment of the day and rummage through his papers—she was the one person who was never frightened of him. At first her husband bored her, but then she fell in love and became a devoted wife. They had three children; a short-lived Duc de Bretagne, another Bretagne and the Duc d'Anjou (the future Louis XV).

As early as 1680 Colbert had warned the King of terrible poverty in the provinces. War was exhausting the country, and when the Controller-General died a broken man in 1683, the budget was in deficit to the tune of sixteen million livres (over £1,500,000 in contemporary English money). By 1689 Louis was in even worse difficulties and had to sell the silver furniture at Versailles. By the end of the Nine Years War the deficit was 138 million livres. Yet direct taxation and internal customs had already been increased, while a new tax, the *capitation* (a graduated poll tax) had been introduced in 1695; it was the first French taxation to be based on personal wealth. Titles and offices were being sold at an unheard-of extent; 500 bourgeois bought titles in 1696 alone (the price was 2,000 crowns). Apart from further loans from abroad at crippling interest, more cash could only be found by issuing paper money and then devaluing it, by a carefully contrived state bankruptcy, by forced loans and by lotteries. The need for money to pay for the war had coin-

cided with a depression; corn prices were low, wine producers
were cut off from their foreign markets and the shortage of raw
materials from abroad caused unemployment. In 1694 Fénelon,
addressing the King, wrote, 'Your people are dying of hunger
. . . France is nothing but a vast hospital.'

La Bruyère's famous description of French peasants at this
time still appalls. 'Sullen beasts, male and female, who, black
with dirt and white with hunger, live on black bread, grapes
and water in lairs.' But modern research shows that their
misery was due to a phenomenal succession of bad harvests
rather than to conscription or to money squandered on the
King's wars. The savagely inequitable tax system harried them
in bad years as in good, so that even prosperous *roturiers* dressed
in rags to conceal any appearance of wealth.

Louis no longer possessed ministers of the same calibre as
Colbert and Louvois. Instead he had men like Chamillart (a
protégé of Mme de Maintenon), who was excellent at billiards,
but no good as an administrator, and who allowed himself to be
bribed by contractors and even sold military decorations.
Saint-Simon believed that Chamillart only kept his post
because the King felt sorry for him and enjoyed correcting his
mistakes.

However, Louis was still his own First Minister. Contrary
to what has been alleged, he showed both realism and flexibility during the latter part of his reign. Recent research has
considerably altered the old picture of his last years as a
period of stagnation and decline. At home Louis was so active
in encouraging French commerce that the period after 1697 has
even been described as a second era of economic reform comparable with that under Colbert. In fact he was far more
imaginative than Colbert had ever been. Monopolies were
attacked, with other obstacles to trade; there was an attempt to
simplify internal customs barriers; a scheme for a uniform
system of weights and measures. The King tried to raise the
social status of French merchants, encouraging noblemen to
take part not only in overseas but also—and vainly—in domestic
trade. No one, not even nobles, was exempt from the *capitation*;
later the nobility also had to pay another tax, the *dixième*. Not
until 1789 would there be such an onslaught on privilege.
Louis's innovations were blocked by vested interests at almost

every level. None the less, he deserves full credit for his imagination. He saw the Canadians as more than mere producers of fur —there was a glut of beaver pelts—and encouraged new settlements, notably Louisiana in 1699; he had a vision of a New France which would stretch up the valley of the St Lawrence and down the Mississippi, from Hudson Bay to the Gulf of Mexico; he even created American titles of nobility. Further afield, he set up a new company to trade with China, in 1698, very much in Colbert's manner.

Louis was equally realistic in his foreign policy. He knew that war was inevitable over the Spanish Succession. France had to fight. It was a unique opportunity of ending the Habsburg encirclement. In addition, as he pointed out after the conflict had begun, 'The present war is a struggle for the commerce of the Spanish Indies and the wealth which they produce.' Crippled and half insane, so afflicted that his subjects called him 'The Bewitched', the childless Charles II of Spain was near death for several years. Who would inherit his vast domains—his Austrian cousins or the Bourbons? In 1700, after earlier negotiations, France unwillingly agreed to a treaty which would give Spain and Milan to the Archduke Charles (the Emperor's younger son) and Naples, Sicily, Tuscany and Guipuzcoa to the Dauphin. Then Louis was unexpectedly helped by Charles II who, angry that his Empire's fate had been decided without consulting him, suddenly made a will leaving everything to the Dauphin's second son, Philippe, Duc d'Anjou. Four weeks later Charles died. Louis hesitated before accepting the inheritance for his grandson. He told some great ladies, 'Whichever side I take I am well aware that I shall be blamed for it.' On 6 November he presented the Duc d'Anjou to the court, saying, 'Messieurs, the King of Spain!' As Saint-Simon comments, 'The eighteenth century opened for the House of France with a blaze of glory.'

When poor old James II died at Saint-Germain in September 1701, Louis recognized the Prince of Wales as King James III of England, Scotland and Ireland. It seemed an act of remarkable generosity, in the face of apocalyptic warnings from his ministers; in fact Louis knew that William III had already decided on war—the Grand Alliance against France by the Empire, the Dutch and the English had been signed at The

Hague a week previously. France's one ally was Bavaria. Spain was merely a corpse to be fought over. The enemy had two commanders of genius, Prince Eugène of Savoy and John Churchill, Duke of Marlborough. The first had a fanatical hatred of Louis (who had once refused him a commission in the French army). Churchill, although a greedy and ambitious time-server, was in war a master of organization and surprise. To oppose them the King had Catinat, Boufflers, Tallard, Vendôme and Villars. The last two were quite as colourful, if not so gifted, as Eugène and Churchill. The Duc de Vendôme was the grand-son of Henri IV, whom he much resembled, being wildly brave, a great trencherman and adored by his men. Unfortunately he never rose before four in the afternoon—but once out of bed, he could be an extremely formidable commander. Despite his notorious homosexuality, his slovenliness, his drinking and his syphilis—which cost him his nose—he was a favourite with the King. (Once when Vendôme was leaving court for a cure, the King asked him to return 'in a state in which one might kiss him with safety'. When the Duke came back without his nose, Louis told the court to pretend not to notice.) The Duc de Villars was described by Saint-Simon as 'the most fortunate man in the world'; a plump, amiable, unpolished Gascon, he owed his career to Louis, who had noticed his bravery during one of the Dutch campaigns. Although undoubtedly the best general that Louis now possessed, Villars had his own faults—boastful optimism and an odd manner, half blunt, half theatrical.

An unattractive side of Louis was his treatment of any promising Prince of the Blood. He refused military employment to Condé's young nephew, the Prince de Conti, who was a gifted soldier, and ruined his career.

Monsieur's brilliant son, the Duc de Chartres, was put off with equal shabbiness. 'Treading the galleries of Versailles,' as Saint-Simon described it, was not good for a young man with such a father and whose tutor had been the unsavoury Abbé Dubois. Philippe de Chartres had many gifts—he painted, sang, composed music (his opera *Panthée* was performed before the King) and was sufficiently interested in science and mechanics to have his own laboratory. He was above the other Princes of the Blood by his rank as a 'Grandson of France'—being a grandson of Louis XIII. He had married a daughter of Mme de

ontespan, Mlle de Blois, Monsieur's agreement to such a *mésalliance* having been bought by the bestowal of the *Cordon Bleu* of the Saint-Esprit on his beloved Chevalier de Lorraine. (Saint-Simon says that M de Chartres's mother, Madame, looked 'like Ceres after the rape of her daughter Proserpine', so horrified was she by the disgrace.) M de Chartres took solace in the bottle and in women; he was reputed to have naked harlots served up on silver dishes at his dinner parties. A notorious free thinker, he held orgies on Good Friday, read Rabelais bound like a missal during Mass, and tried to raise the Devil. Though these vices were not yet in full bloom in 1700, his life was already scandalous enough.

Since childhood, Monsieur had been accustomed to defer to the King. However, Louis's steady refusal to give a command to his son angered him beyond endurance. In June 1701 when Louis complained of M de Chartres's debauched life, Monsieur, flushed, his eyes red with rage, reminded the King of his own mistresses—soon both brothers were shouting at each other at the top of their voices. Monsieur, gluttonous, purple-faced and short of breath, had already been warned of apoplexy by a plain-spoken confessor. That night he had a fit during dinner, and he died the following day. Louis wept a good deal. Despite his absurdity, everyone had liked Monsieur; Saint-Simon admits, 'It was he who set all pleasure a-going and when he left us, life and merriment seemed to have departed.' A certain sense of guilt was evident in the King's sudden generosity to M de Chartres, who was given all his father's pensions and honours together with the Duchy of Orleans.

The war opened at the end of 1701, on three fronts. At first things did not go badly for the French. For two years Vendôme waged a surprisingly successful campaign against Eugène and the Imperial armies. In Germany, Villars won a glorious victory in the Black Forest near Friedlingen, and was rewarded with a Marshal's baton. Next year he won more victories, while Tallard defeated the Imperialists near Spiers. Unfortunately the Bavarians refused to join in an advance on Vienna and Villars resigned in disgust. France had lost her one chance of winning the war.

At home the Huguenot mountaineers of the Cévennes rose in revolt. They were known as *Camisards*, from the white shirts

they wore over their clothes to distinguish each other in the dark. The government used the most savage measures, perpetrating a kind of French Massacre of Glencoe when they burnt out mountain villages in mid-winter. Villars brought the rising to an end in 1704 by the imaginative expedient of offering its leader, Jean Cavalier, a colonelcy and persuading him to form his followers into a regiment which would fight for France. Cavalier also insisted on being taken to Versailles to see the King, but the young peasant was so humiliated when Louis passed him without saying a word that he took service with the English. It is said that nearly 100,000 men, women and children died during this rising, either *Camisards* or victims of their reprisals.

Abroad, a series of disasters began in 1704. At Blenheim, Marlborough killed 12,000 Frenchmen and captured even more, including the shortsighted Marshal Tallard, together with their entire artillery. The French were driven out of Germany, Bavaria was invaded and the Elector fled. In Spain, the English took Gibraltar while the Archduke Charles captured Barcelona —soon poor Philip V thought of taking refuge in America. In 1706 the elegant Villeroy, who was the son of Louis's old tutor, was routed by Marlborough at Ramillies (near Waterloo); when he returned to Versailles, the King greeted him with the words, '*M le Maréchal*, at our age one can no longer expect to be lucky.' The defeat cost France the Low Countries. Vendôme was recalled to hold off Marlborough, whereupon Prince Eugène drove the French out of Italy, killing the French commander in the process; next year Eugène invaded Provence, besieging Toulon, though he was driven out with heavy casualties. In 1708 even Vendôme was defeated, at Oudenarde by Marlborough, and the French army was almost destroyed in the ensuing retreat. Luckily the allies baulked at a full-scale invasion, though a small Dutch force actually penetrated as far as Versailles and captured one of the King's equerries.

It was the nadir of Louis's fortunes. The winter of 1708–9 was a terrible one. The cold was such that at Versailles wine froze in the glasses and ink on the pens. An iron-hard frost lasted until the end of March; animals froze to death in their barns, game birds in the trees, rabbits in their burrows; the spring wheat and barley perished, whole vineyards died and in the

south the entire olive crop was destroyed. Famine set in everywhere. Even at Versailles, royal servants were seen begging at the gates and Mme de Maintenon ate oatmeal bread ostentatiously; in Burgundy bracken was used to make flour, and throughout the countryside the peasants were reduced to nettles and boiled grass. Louis did what he could, imposing a special tax to feed the hungry, from which not even he himself was exempted; he forbade the baking of white bread, abolished transport dues and tariffs; he had his gold plate melted down, eating off silver gilt instead. All this did little to abate the famine. Even the troops starved, selling their muskets to buy bread.

France, bankrupt, starving, her industries and trade in ruins, her armies beaten and demoralized, and faced by triumphant and revengeful enemies, was now in a position very like that of Germany at the beginning of 1945. At a council meeting, the Duc de Beauvilliers drew such a miserable picture of France's condition that the Duc de Bourgogne burst into tears, followed by the entire council. This ruinous situation is often depicted by historians as the just reward of Louis's folly. Whatever the cause, it showed him at his greatest. He was not a Hitler who would sacrifice his country; humbling himself, he sued abjectly for peace, sending the Marquis de Torcy to obtain it on any terms. But the allies insisted that Louis must himself drive his grandson, Philip V, out of Spain. The King would accept anything but this. 'If I have to make war,' he said, 'I prefer to fight my enemies rather than my children.'

It was Louis's finest moment. He sent a circular letter to every provincial governor, to every bishop and to every municipality, explaining why France had to fight on; he admitted that all sources of revenue were virtually exhausted, and asked for advice and for help. Recruits flocked to the colours, while the rich handed in their plate and valuables; in 1710 the French even accepted the *dixième*, a ten per cent tax on all incomes. The tide began to turn. Marlborough defeated Villars at Malplaquet in late 1709, but only just; the French losing 8,000 men compared to the allies' 21,000. Next year Vendôme, 'happiest and haughtiest of men', utterly destroyed the Austrian army of Spain, hitherto victorious, at Villaviciosa. The allies were astonished by the French will to resist. In England the Tories

gained power and removed Marlborough from his command. But the situation still seemed desperate for France.

Meanwhile in April 1711, the first of a series of terrible personal blows struck Louis. The Dauphin, 'drowned in fat and sloth' though he was, had always seemed healthy enough. Suddenly he fell ill and died of smallpox, within little more than a week. The Duc de Bourgogne was now Dauphin, and impressed everyone by his sense of responsibility, attending all Council meetings and listening carefully to what ministers and generals had to say. Even Marie Adelaide became more serious. Then early in February 1712, when she was pregnant, she developed a fever; a rash appeared and she was dead within a few days. Louis wrote to Philip of Spain, 'There will never be a moment in my life when I shall not regret her.' Less than a week after his wife's death, the Duc de Bourgogne developed the mysterious rash. 'He was extraordinarily fond of his wife, and sorrow for her death gave him his fever.' He died three days later, perhaps the worst blow of all to Louis.

His mind formed by Fénelon, Bourgogne, had he lived, might have saved the *Ancien Régime*. He recognized and lamented the gulf between monarch and subject. He intended to introduce changes in taxation—which would have ended the privileged position of the nobility—and generally to broaden the entire basis of government. Few men have been mourned so deeply.

Early in March the Bourgognes' two surviving children sickened, and the elder, the five-year-old Duc de Bretagne, soon died. The younger, the Duc d'Anjou, was saved by his governess, the Duchesse de Ventadour, who said that he was too small to be bled, and had him breast-fed in her own room until the rash went. So mysterious were these deaths—probably a rare form of measles—that it was rumoured that the Duc de Bourgogne and his family had been poisoned by the Duc d'Orléans whose interest in chemistry was well known; the Duke was hissed in the streets. The Duc du Maine seems to have been largely responsible for spreading the slander. But the King had too much sense to believe such rumours. He showed incredible fortitude; Saint-Simon said that he truly merited the title of 'the Great' by his behaviour.

It was at this time that France was in most danger. Prince Eugène prepared to invade France from Flanders with 130,000

men. In April Louis entrusted Villars with his last army. In tears, his voice shaking, he told Villars, 'You see the condition I am in, *M le Maréchal*. Few people have known, as I have, what it is to lose a grandson, a grand-daughter and their son, all of great promise and deeply loved, within a few weeks. God is punishing me and I deserve it: I shall suffer less in the world to come.' The King went on to discuss what he should do if Villars failed. 'Most of my courtiers want me to go to Blois without waiting for the enemy to advance on Paris, as they may well do if our army is defeated.' But Louis thought that even if the worst happened, sufficient French troops would hold out on the north bank of the Somme. 'I shall go to Péronne or Saint-Quentin, collect all the troops I can muster and make a last stand with you, in which we will either die together or save the kingdom.'

But in July Villars captured the fortified town of Denain and cut the allied army in half. Eugène was forced to retreat, the French advancing steadily and capturing town after town. Within less than two months, Prince Eugène had lost over fifty battalions; fifty-three enemy standards were sent to Versailles. At the Treaty of Utrecht in April 1713, Philip V renounced his claim to the French throne and was recognized as King of Spain by most of the allies. France kept Alsace and Strasbourg. In return Louis ceded Hudson Bay and Gibraltar to England and agreed to disown poor James III.

Although he had brought his kingdom close to ruin, he had won a brilliant triumph, demonstrating the strength of the state which he had created: France would not be invaded again till the Revolution. With his usual realism, Louis now began negotiations for an alliance with Vienna. The Habsburg encirclement had been broken for ever. Sainte-Beuve says patronizingly, 'Louis had nothing more than good sense, but he had plenty of it.' One may think that the old King had more than good sense—he anticipated a realignment in European diplomacy by thirty years.

In May 1714 Louis suffered yet another tragedy, when his third and last grandson, the Duc de Berry, died after a fall from his horse. Berry's children had all died in infancy so (apart from Philip of Spain, who was not eligible) the King's only heir was his great-grandson, the frail, four-year-old Duc d'Anjou. The

heir presumptive was Monsieur's son, the disreputable Philippe d'Orléans. In August 1714 Louis went directly against the *loi fondamental* by forcing the Parlement to recognize the Duc du Maine and the Comte de Toulouse as Princes of the Blood, with the right of succession to the throne in the event of M d'Anjou's death. The education of the latter was to be entrusted to the Duc du Maine, who in these last days was the old King's favourite companion.

Louis was now nearer eighty than seventy. Yet his appetite for food continued to astonish observers—some believed that he had a gigantic tapeworm. It was still the appetite of which his sister-in-law had written, 'I have often seen the King drink four bowls of different sorts of soup and then eat an entire pheasant, a partridge, a large plate of salad, mutton with gravy or garlic, a dish of *patisserie* and after that fruit and hard-boiled eggs.' Large quantities of bread and cold meat with two bottles of wine were placed in his room every night in case he should feel hungry. Plenty of fruit and green vegetables seem to have saved him from any ill consequences. At this period he drank watered burgundy instead of champagne, usually Romanée St Vivant, which had originally been prescribed for him after his fistula operation by the surgeon, Fagon, who told him, 'Tonic and generous, it suits, Sire, a robust temperament such as yours.' He needed exercise as much as ever, walking in all weathers, and following the hunt in his little cart. He worked his customary hours. He still exhausted Mme de Maintenon with his demands and then 'slept like a child'. He kept his liking for Molière's comedies—especially *Le Bourgeois Gentilhomme*, *Georges Dandin* and *Le Coccu Imaginaire*—which were often performed at Versailles. In June 1715 he remarked, 'If I continue to eat with such a good appetite, I am going to ruin all those Englishmen who have wagered large sums that I will die by September.' But the English would win their bet.

Perhaps sensing that his end was not far off, he had grown steadily more devout in recent years. He listened dutifully to his new confessor, the sinister and fanatical Jesuit, Le Tellier. An old peasant who looked like a bird of prey, arrogant and illiterate and with burning eyes, Le Tellier has even been compared to Rasputin, such was his influence over Louis. The King was sincerely pious but he had a curiously underdeveloped religious

sense. On his deathbed he told Cardinal Rohan that in matters of religion he had only done what his bishops had advised him. 'It is you who will have to answer to God for everything that has been done . . . I have a clear conscience.'

The King enjoyed himself at Marly in the first few days of August 1715 and had a good stag hunt. Suddenly, on 10 August, he felt ill and returned to Versailles. Two days later sores broke out on his left leg. Although in pain, he worked as usual with his ministers, and interviewing ambassadors, and tried to soothe himself with frequent concerts. His leg began to smell foully and then turned black—it was gangrene. By 24 August, he knew he was dying. Next day he added a codicil to his will, nominating Philippe d'Orléans as chief of the Council of Regency.

He was already talking of 'the time when I was King'. He took a dignified farewell of his courtiers, thanking them for their service and asking their pardon for the bad example he had set them. At the end both he and they began to cry. 'I perceive that I am allowing my feelings to overcome me,' said Louis, 'and am making you do likewise. I beg your forgiveness for it. Farewell, gentlemen—I hope you will sometimes remember me.' Later, however, he rebuked two servants for weeping: 'Why do you shed tears? Did you think me immortal?'

He summoned his five-year-old great-grandson, who was placed on his bed. He told him, 'My child, you are about to become the greatest King in the world. Never forget your duty to God. Do not copy me in my taste for war. And try to relieve your people as much as you can, which I unhappily have not done because of the needs of the state . . . ' He then kissed the Dauphin, blessed him and burst into tears.

It was a long and agonizing death, which he suffered with dignity. He received the sacraments many times and prayed fervently. He told his wife, 'I thought it would be harder to die —I assure you it is not very terrible and does not seem difficult to me.' His last words were, 'Oh my God, come to my aid, make haste to succour me!' He died at a quarter to eight on the morning of Sunday 1 September 1715.

The whole country rejoiced. His coffin was hooted at on the way to Saint-Denis by a drunken mob, and Voltaire saw small booths set up along the route where people drank and sang. Saint-Simon says that the provinces leapt for joy. Both the

nobles and the lawyers felt that their deliverance had come. But the diarist also noted that no foreign court rejoiced—'all plumed themselves on praising and honouring his memory'.

Historians vary considerably in their judgement of Louis and, indeed, the motives for many of his actions remain as much a mystery now as they were to his contemporaries. On the whole, however, he is generally seen as a selfish megalomaniac, whose lust for glory ruined his people; whose demoralization of the French nobility made the Revolution inevitable; whose ruthlessness in personal relationships ruined the lives of his intimates. This picture owes a good deal to the almost hypnotic fascination of Saint-Simon's memoirs, and much to the impression made by the soulless bulk of Versailles. Yet Saint-Simon was biased to the point of derangement, while without its glittering courtiers, Versailles, essentially theatrical in conception, could never be more than a vast and deserted playhouse. The métier of absolute monarch was a demanding one which few human beings could perform without losing some of their humanity. None the less, Louis was a good father, a good son, a good brother and, for most of his married life, a good husband. If he made France suffer, he made her great. Napoleon, whose judgements it is always dangerous to ignore, once said, 'Louis XIV was a great King. He made France first among the nations. What French King since Charlemagne can be compared with him?'

'The Well-Beloved'

LOUIS XV (1715–1774)

'If *I* were Lieutenant of Police, I would prohibit those Paris cabriolets'

The children and grandchildren of Louis XV

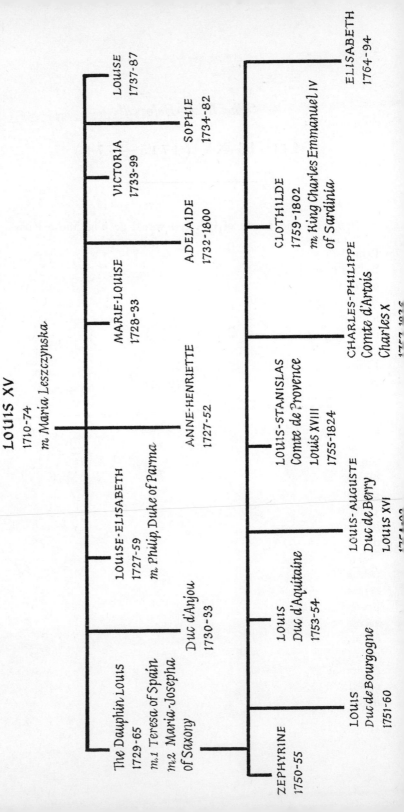

LOUIS XV
1710-74
m Maria Leszczynska

The Dauphin LOUIS
1729-65
m.1 Teresa of Spain
m.2 Maria-Josepha
of Saxony

LOUISE-ELISABETH
1727-59
m Philip, Duke of Parma

ANNE-HENRIETTE
1727-52

MARIE-LOUISE
1728-33

ADELAIDE
1732-1800

VICTORIA
1733-99

SOPHIE
1734-82

LOUISE
1737-87

ZEPHYRINE
1750-55

LOUIS
Duc de Bourgogne
1751-60

Duc d'Anjou
1730-33

LOUIS
Duc d'Aquitaine
1753-54

LOUIS-AUGUSTE
Duc de Berry
LOUIS XVI

LOUIS-STANISLAS
Comte de Provence
LOUIS XVIII
1755-1824

CLOTHILDE
1759-1802
m King Charles Emmanuel IV
of Sardinia

CHARLES-PHILIPPE
Comte d'Artois
Charles X

ELISABETH
1764-94

Louis XV is the Hamlet of the Bourbons. Few Kings have baffled historians as he has done; to most he is a classic example of the man who is not up to his job, though a surprising number think he may have been seriously under-estimated. He was no less of a mystery to his contemporaries. The shyest and most reserved of all his dynasty, his interest lies in his strange yet curiously attractive character and in its tragic inadequacy. For Louis XV, the eighteenth century was always the age of the Rococo, not of the Enlightenment.

He was born on 15 February 1710, the third and youngest son of the Duc de Bourgogne and Marie Adelaide of Savoy, and was soon after created Duc d'Anjou. One brother had already predeceased him; his remaining brother died in the same epidemic which carried off their parents. It has already been related how he was saved by the good sense of his governess, the Duchesse de Ventadour. She continued to be his governess for the first two years of his reign, taking the place of his mother; on his death-bed Louis XIV told the little boy to obey her, and he remained devoted to her for the rest of his life, calling her *Maman*.

The young King, a frail but beautiful child, was the idol of his people. Michelet recaptures their veneration: 'He, the only remains of so great a family, saved like the infant Joash, is preserved apparently that he himself may save others.' At his accession the crowd joined with wild and tearful emotion in crying *'Vive le Roi!'* Once again France was afflicted with a minority, but unlike his predecessors Louis XV had no mother to act as Regent. Nor did the nobility make any attempt at rebellion; it has been said that while during Louis XIII's minority they waged civil war and during Louis XIV's joined

in the Fronde, in the minority of Louis XV they were only capable of writing memoirs.

The new ruler of France was the King's 'wicked uncle', his cousin Philippe d'Orléans, a plump, short-sighted little man with a cynical grin. He quickly set aside Louis XIV's will—which had given considerable powers to the Duc du Maine—telling the Parlement firmly, 'I have been proclaimed Regent and during the minority I must have a King's authority.' Indeed, Orléans became King in everything but name, as heir presumptive to a sickly boy, whom everyone expected would soon make way for 'Philippe VII'; the eight years of his regency amounted to a reign on which he stamped his own scandalous, pleasure-loving character. Amiable, humane, tolerant, sceptical but open-minded, the Regent seems surprisingly modern. Yet he looked backward rather than forward, consciously modelling himself on his great-grandfather, Henri IV, whom he really believed he resembled. Alas, he took after him only in being amusing, loose-living and wearing spectacles. He was an insatiable womanizer, with more than a hundred mistresses (famous for their ugliness), and a drunkard with a weak head, who consumed bottle upon bottle of the new sparkling champagne.

Despite his hopes of the throne, the Regent was obviously very fond of his little cousin. He treated him exactly as he had treated Louis XIV—with deep respect. There is a charming portrait of them together; the Regent is seated at his work table, gesturing amiably and deferentially towards the little King who stands in the foreground, dressed in the height of grown-up fashion, wearing the star and sash of the Saint-Esprit. He adored the Regent, insisting that he sat down to dinner with him, contrary to all etiquette. At the end of 1715 Louis and his governess were sent to the old château of Vincennes, where long country walks improved his health. After a year the Regent had him brought to Paris to take up residence in the refurbished Tuileries. Soon he began to attend Council meetings, holding his favourite cat, but remaining tongue-tied; the ministers called the King's cat his 'cher collègue'.

In 1717 Peter the Great of Russia visited Paris. Observers were fascinated to see the gigantic Tsar—six foot eight inches

tall—take the tiny King under both arms, hoist him up and kiss him again and again; Louis showed no fear, while Peter was charmed with him; Saint-Simon says that the Tsar's gentleness was very moving. Despite his barbaric manners Peter was fêted enthusiastically by the French; the Regent took him to the opera (which he does not seem to have enjoyed, leaving early). He even visited the Sorbonne where he saw a statue of Richelieu; seizing it with both hands the Tsar cried, 'Great man, I would give half my kingdom to learn from you how to govern the rest!' None the less, during his stay Peter also foretold that the French lords would ruin themselves by their luxury.

Louis's childhood was not always happy. The same year that he met Peter, he had to part tearfully from his governess and was handed over to a Governor, Marshal de Villeroy, an old soldier courtier in his seventies; the King, who was only seven, refused to eat or even speak for several days. Villeroy was not altogether satisfactory. He told Louis that in dealing with ministers he must 'hold a chamber pot over their heads when they're in office, and pour it over them when they are out. He made him attend endless parades and receptions, which caused him to dislike appearing in public for the rest of his life; having to dance in ballets—'a pleasure for which he was far too young' —increased this dislike. When the King was eleven, a Turkish envoy reported that during an audience the senile Marshal had made Louis walk up and down: 'Come, walk about a little and show us how you move—walk a little faster to show the ambassador how light you are on your feet.' As a result he became abnormally reserved. The Regent's mother thought the King an ill-natured child: 'He loves no one but his old Governess, dislikes people for no reason at all and enjoys making cutting remarks.' Certainly he showed a cruel streak; when his cat Charlotte had kittens, he teased three of them to death, although devoted to cats (throughout his life, Versailles was full of them); he also shot a pet white deer.

Even so, Louis was deeply attached to his tutor, kindly old Bishop Fleury of Fréjus, who did more than merely see that the child received a good education. He encouraged him to make use of a toy printing press and played cards with him when he was bored. Fleury's shrewd understanding of small boys is

125

vividly preserved in the beautiful model warships (now in the Musée Marine) which he had made for the young King; Louis always retained a keen interest in the French navy.

To begin with the Regent seemed breathtakingly liberal. Prison doors opened, galley slaves were unmanacled, Huguenots and Jansenists were set free. He even thought of re-enacting the Edict of Nantes. He had Fénélon's *Télémaque*—an allegory criticizing Absolutism—reprinted. For a short time he replaced Louis XIV's bourgeois bureaucracy with a system of councils staffed by noblemen. He gave back to the Parlement of Paris its ancient right of refusing to register any royal edict of which they disapproved. (Louis behaved with precocious dignity during the wearisome *lit de justice* which followed his accession.) Orléans delighted the Parisians by bringing the court back to Paris, he himself governing from his town house, the Palais Royal. He allied with England, a country which he much admired; the alliance was joined by the Habsburgs and all three fought together against Spain in the war of 1719; the French army marched on its King's uncle, Philip V, storming Fuentarrabia. Yet if the Regent's policies were a complete reversal of those of Louis XIV, he was still not prepared to summon the States General and use it as an English Parliament, as his friend Saint-Simon suggested.

It was a time of great elegance. The Regent—whose paintings included works by Raphael, Titian, del Sarto, Veronese and Poussin—made Watteau painter to the King, an ethereal genius whose idealized, fantastic scenes of court life imply that there was more than debauchery to the Regency. Even the furniture—for example, that by Charles Cressent—seemed gayer and freer than that of the old King's reign.

In 1716, always open to new ideas, the Regent introduced a system of national credit finance invented by a Scots gambler, John Law; it was based on the principle that the country's economy would benefit if more money were in circulation, and that this could be achieved by issuing paper currency guaranteed by a state bank. Law, who was made Controller-General, also formed the *Compagnie du Mississippi* which quickly took over all the other state trading companies. There was a wave of frenzied speculation, during which great fortunes were made. Then dissatisfied investors began to sell shares; to save the

company Law incorporated it into the bank which was flourishing, but there were not sufficient assets. The public lost confidence in the new bank notes. In the summer of 1720 both bank and company collapsed, ruining large numbers of investors; many committed suicide. The Regent incurred considerable unpopularity for his part in this French South Sea Bubble; which unpopularity, most unfairly, was increased by a dreadful plague at Marseilles.

He was now on bad terms with the Parlement which had begun to compare itself with the British Parliament, in what Saint-Simon calls 'a mad career of infinite presumption, pride and arrogance'. Seeking better relations with Rome, the Regent forced the Parlement to register the Papal Bull against the Jansenists; the latter's supporters retaliated with a flood of scurrilous pamphlets accusing him of tyranny and even alleging that he was trying to murder the King. When the boy fell ill, the fishwives of Paris gathered under the Tuileries' windows, screaming 'to hell with the Regent'. In 1722 Louis was taken back to Versailles and moved into his great-grandfather's old rooms.

Orléans's approaches to Rome were partly dictated by a wish to secure a Red Hat for the Abbé Dubois, his old tutor who was now his secretary and *éminence grise*. Popular rumour credited this unsavoury cleric with being responsible for the Regent's debauched tastes. Saint-Simon described him as 'a little, wizened, herring-gutted man in a flaxen wig, with a weasel's face brightened by some small intellect. Within, every vice fought for precedence. Avarice, debauchery, ambition were his gods; perfidy, flattery and bootlicking his methods.' He had some strange hold over his former pupil, who on occasion addressed him as 'you shark'. Unwillingly, Philippe gave way to the man's shameless pleading and made him Archbishop of Cambrai. According to Saint-Simon, 'an appalling scandal' resulted which embarrassed even M le Duc d'Orléans. In fact, although indisputably vicious and greedy, Dubois was not without ability; he was the architect of the English alliance, receiving a fat English pension, and also worked for a *rapprochement* with Spain. In 1722 the Regent made him First Minister.

However, Dubois died in August 1723. The King had come

of age the previous February (thirteen was still the legal age of royal majority), so to retain his power Orléans—who had ceased automatically to be regent—had himself appointed First Minister in Dubois's place.

The King had been crowned at Rheims on 25 October 1722. A painting by Jean Baptiste Martin shows an awkward, boyish figure, crowned and holding the sceptre and *main de justice*. M d'Argenson wrote in his journal, 'How like Cupid he seemed in his long robes . . . our eyes filled with tears at the sight of this poor young prince.' The sacrament made a profound impression upon Louis; throughout his life he never doubted the divine origin of his authority. Oddly enough, however, it seems to have done little to increase his self-confidence.

For all that Fleury could do, Louis was growing up to be shy and unsure of himself. His chief indulgence was over-eating—especially game and cakes. Ironically in view of his later life, at this age he was frightened of women and rather prudish; he actually ordered a loose lady to leave Versailles. Reassuringly, he had the family passion for hunting and enjoyed shooting: his other amusements were cards and gambling, which helped to distract him from his chronic boredom and melancholia. There were surprising affinities between the young Louis XV and his great-great-grandfather, Louis XIII.

He was even involved in a mild homosexual scandal in 1722 when a group of young courtiers near him, including Villeroy's grandson were found indulging in sodomy. They were hastily banished; the King was told that they were being punished 'for pulling up the pallisades in the gardens'. Shortly afterwards the aged Marshal followed, protesting shrilly. Louis wept from fear rather than regret; the old man, anxious to keep his place, had told the poor child that he would undoubtedly be murdered if Villeroy left court. The King's too-enthusiastic friendship for the young Duc de La Trémouille, the first nobleman of the bedchamber, who was famed for his embroidery, also gave cause for alarm. Such fears were natural in the case of so beautiful a boy as Louis, but proved groundless.

In 1721 the Regent announced the King's engagement to his first cousin, the Infanta Maria of Spain. On learning of his betrothal Louis burst into tears. Recovering, he told an unmarried courtier, 'I am more experienced than you—I have a

wife and child.' For the Infanta was only four years old, and arrived in Paris sitting on Mme de Ventadour's lap and playing with her doll. The monarch (who had just passed his twelfth birthday) greeted her gravely, 'I am very glad, Madame, that you have reached France in such excellent health.' Overcome with embarrassment, he then refused to address another word to her, although she persisted in following him everywhere. Sighing, the little girl told Mme de Ventadour, 'He will never love me.' There is a most attractive painting of the engaged couple in the Pitti in Florence.

The scandal of Orléans's seraglio and of the 'daily filthiness and impiety' of the wild supper parties in the Palais Royal was noised abroad everywhere. It was even rumoured that the Duke slept with his favourite daughter, the widowed Duchesse de Berry, an utterly depraved creature who drank so much that she vomited over the company and rolled on the carpet. Her death at only twenty-four—worn out by a combination of drink and giving birth to an illegitimate child—was a severe blow to Orléans. He was also saddened by the death in 1722 of his grim old mother, Liselotte, to whom, more edifyingly, he had been devoted—he wept bitterly. He himself was growing iller every day, 'a man with a hanging head, a purple complexion and a heavy stupid look', although he was not yet fifty. He and everyone else knew that he was a dead man if he continued his debauchery, but he had lost all control. On 22 December 1723, discussing the ludicrous concept of final damnation with a mistress, Mme de Falaris, he suddenly fell against her, unconscious; it was an apoplexy. When a lackey tried to bleed him, another lady screamed, 'No! You'll kill him—he has just lain with a whore.' He was dead within two hours.

Philippe d'Orléans is generally regarded as a failure. None the less, Voltaire could write that the Regent's only faults were too much love of pleasure and too much love of novelty, and that of all the descendants of Henri IV, he most resembled him 'in his courage, kindliness, frankness, gaiety, lack of pomposity and deep culture'. Even that ferocious republican, Michelet, calls him 'the good' Duc d'Orléans, and claims that he used to say, 'If I were a subject I would certainly revolt.' Louis mourned him deeply, and spoke of him affectionately as long as he lived.

The Duc de Bourbon, who was the grandson of the great

Condé and a senior Prince of the Blood, demanded and obtained the post of First Minister. *Monsieur le Duc*, as he was known at court, was scarcely less debauched than Orléans, and far less able. In his early thirties, 'tall, bowed, thin as a rake, legs like a stork and a body like a spider, with two eyes so red that the bad one is difficult to distinguish from the good' (old Liselotte's description), Bourbon was hardly a charmer. He was already heartily disliked for having made a fortune out of Law's *Système*. Soon he had made his administration thoroughly unpopular by harrying the Jansenists. His most maladroit piece of work was the King's marriage.

The English were nervous at the prospect of a French *rapprochement* with Spain. Bourbon's mistress, the beautiful, nymph-like Mme de Prie—whom an exiled Jacobite called 'the most corrupt and ambitious jade alive'—was in receipt of an English pension and came out strongly against the Spanish match. Then in 1725 Louis fell dangerously ill, after which Bourbon lived in constant dread of the throne being inherited by the heir presumptive, the new Duc d'Orléans. 'What will become of me?' muttered Bourbon. He wanted a tractable, biddable Queen who would bear a Dauphin as soon as possible. The little Infanta was therefore sent back to Madrid. The Spanish ambassador cried out, 'All the blood of Spain would not suffice to wipe away the shame which France has caused my master!' (However, the Infanta was obviously delighted to go home—she said that she was very glad that she was not going to be married after all. In the end she married King Joao of Portugal.)

Europe was still more amazed by Bourbon's choice of a Queen, Marie Leszczynska. She was the daughter of King Stanislas Leszczynski, a once dashing and glamorous figure now living in seedy retirement in Alsace as a pensioner of France; he had even been forced to pawn his wife's jewels. Count of Lesno, he had been elected to the throne of the Polish Republic in 1704 when only in his twenties, and since losing it in 1709 had led a strange, adventurous life, pursued by assassins and living on charity; by now he had lost all hope of recouping his fortunes. When he heard the news of the French marriage, he shouted to his wife and daughter, 'Down on our knees to give thanks to God!' Unfortunately Marie was singularly lacking in Polish

allure, though not the web-footed monster of French popular gossip; she was nearly seven years older than her future husband and, while pleasant-looking, had hardly the beauty which one may expect of a Cinderella; she was good, pious, unaffected, sweet-natured and boring, her favourite occupation being the embroidering of altar cloths. Lack of any other suitable bride was the real reason for Bourbon's choice of 'the Princess of Poland', whom he no doubt hoped would be suitably grateful.

A marriage by proxy took place at Strasbourg Cathedral in August 1725, the Duc d'Orléans representing Louis; the bride wore a dress of silver brocade ornamented with roses and trimmed with silver lace. The King, for once amiable and at ease, married her for a second time in the chapel at Fontainebleau, after which there was a magnificent wedding banquet, presentations, a play, and supper amid dazzling fireworks. That first night Louis made love to his wife no less than seven times.

The King was fifteen when he consummated his marriage and was the father of five children by the time he was twenty. He was to have ten in all; in 1727 Marie presented him with twin daughters, Mmes Elisabeth and Henriette (known as Mme Première and Mme Seconde); another daughter in 1728 who died very young; the Dauphin Louis in 1729; the Duc d'Anjou in 1730 who died three years later; Mme Adelaide in 1732; Mme Victoire in 1733; Mme Sophie in 1734; Mme Félicité in 1736; and Mme Louise in 1737 (popularly known as Mme Dernière). It is said that all were begotten on the poor Queen without a single word from her husband.

To begin with, the marriage seemed happy enough, although Marie is credited with complaining that her life was nothing but, *'toujours coucher, toujours grossesse, toujours accoucher'*. At first she was overcome by the unaccustomed luxury and plenty; shortly after her wedding she fell so ill that she was given the last sacraments; according to her father, Marie's illness was due to eating nine dozen oysters, washed down with four flagons of beer, at a single sitting. Although many Frenchmen blamed Bourbon for such a *mésalliance*, her friendliness and lack of conceit won most hearts.

Ironically, Marie ruined her benefactors, Bourbon and Mme

de Prie. At their bidding she tried to persuade the King to dismiss Fleury, who had been telling him of the appalling state of the country, that inflation and famine were widespread; that there were food riots in the provinces and even in Paris starving men were breaking into bakeries. The Duke persuaded Marie to invite Louis to her apartments where he might see him alone, without fear of interruption. He presented the King with a letter from Cardinal de Polignac which contained a savage attack on Fleury. 'What do you think of this letter?' asked Bourbon. 'Nothing,' replied Louis. 'Your Majesty wishes to give a command?' 'Things will remain just as they are.' 'I have displeased Your Majesty?' asked Bourbon nervously. 'Yes.' Cunningly, Fleury had already left Versailles, leaving an affectionate letter of farewell. At the news Louis burst into tears and ordered Bourbon to bring him back. Shortly afterwards the Duke was banished to his estates. Mme de Prie was also banished; within a year, driven crazy by boredom, she had poisoned herself. Fleury took control of the government in June 1726 and was created a Cardinal before the year was out.

If Cardinal Fleury was hardly another Richelieu, he could at least claim to be a French Walpole. His programme was a simple one—peace and prosperity. War must be avoided at all costs and the economy came before everything else. In 1728 he and an excellent Controller-General, Philibert d'Orry—a true heir of Colbert—having fixed the ratio of gold to silver and of bank notes to coin, established the livre at twenty-four to the gold *louis d'or* (or six livres to the silver crown), a rate which remained until the Revolution. Stricter controls were imposed on tax farmers and government expenditure was cut; some taxes were even reduced. An excellent system of state roads was begun and *bureaux de commerce* were founded to encourage trade. Abroad, Orry reorganized the *Compagnie des Indes*—the French East India Company—and encouraged trade with the Spanish and Portuguese Americas. In 1739 Fleury's administration succeeded in balancing the budget for the first time since 1672 (and also for the last until the budget of the restored Bourbon government in 1815).

The King was perfectly happy to leave all power in the hands of an aged cleric. Pink-faced, beaming like an old cherub, the Cardinal was so powerful that all France was ready to attend the

little ceremony when he went to bed. M d'Argenson writes scornfully how ridiculous it was to see the old man folding his breeches, putting on a threadbare nightshirt and combing his four white hairs. But elsewhere the diarist also writes how Fleury 'loves the King and the realm and is honest and sincere'.

The Cardinal's greatest cross were the Jansenists. He tried to enforce the Papal condemnation, imprisoning a number of priests and even a bishop and dismissing Jansenist professors from the Sorbonne (including the great historian Rollin). By now the sect had almost hysterical popular support in Paris; miracles were reported to have taken place at Jansenist graves, notably at the church of Saint-Médard. Predictably the Parlements took up so popular a cause, refusing to register a royal decree against Jansenists in March 1730. Louis summoned the lawyers to Versailles, where they were told that the law and its interpretation came from the King, not from Parlement; 'Do not force me to show you that I am your master,' he threatened, clutching his whip. At one point during the struggle over a hundred magistrates were exiled. In the end Fleury gave way and recalled them. The alliance of Parlementaires and Jansenists would cause trouble later in the reign.

Even the Queen was anxious to keep on good terms with Fleury. He made Louis send her a letter which said, 'I beg you, Madame, and if need be, order you to do everything that the Bishop of Fréjus asks you, just as though it came from me.' Marie addressed the Cardinal almost obsequiously, while he treated her with cold respect.

However, even Fleury could not resist public pressure to go to war on behalf of Marie's father in 1733. Augustus II, Elector of Saxony and King of Poland, died in February. Stanislas Leszczynski hurried home to be elected King by his enthusiastic countrymen. Unfortunately Augustus III of Saxony was supported by the Habsburgs and by the Russians. The latter, a new factor in European politics, sent an army into Poland; Augustus was crowned at Cracow while Stanislas took refuge in Danzig, besieged by the Russians. Despite his frantic appeals, the French only sent 1,500 men under the Breton Comte de Plélo. Plélo made a heroic sortie but he was mortally wounded and his little force was wiped out. Just before Danzig fell, King Stanislas managed to escape, disguised as a sailor.

French prestige had to be redeemed, though Fleury grumbled that he did not want to ruin the King for the sake of his father-in-law. One French army attacked Augustus's Austrian allies in the Rhineland, while another attacked them in Italy. In Germany, after advancing triumphantly, the Marshal Duke of Berwick (James II's son by Arabella Churchill) had his head taken off by a cannonball; in Italy, after capturing Milan, gallant old Marshal Villars died, aged eighty-one. Having restored her reputation, France made peace in 1735. She recognized Augustus III as King of Poland, but in return Duke Charles of Lorraine—who had married the Emperor's heiress, Maria Theresa—gave up his duchy to Stanislas with remainder to France. The old adventurer reigned happily at Luneville as 'King of Lorraine' for the rest of his life, holding elegant court and patronizing Montesquieu and Voltaire; the latter wrote that it was impossible to be a better King or a better man. By 1740, due to Fleury's excellent diplomacy, France dominated Europe.

In 1740, when the Cardinal was ill, M d'Argenson confided to his diary that Louis was 'a King of thirty, very well informed', and had shown that he knew how to rule for himself. Later, d'Argenson—when his ambitions had been frustrated—claimed to despise Louis, but at this time even he succumbed to his charm. The young King was tall and magnificently built, and wonderfully handsome—huge, sad eyes, and a delicate Roman nose over a generous mouth redeemed from any femininity by a strong blue chin. Extremely shy, his reserve added to his fascination; he spoke little, but always in a pleasing, oddly husky voice. His haughty manner, which came from lack of self-confidence, intrigued rather than repelled. In addition, Nancy Mitford discerns 'a sexy moodiness of manner irresistible to women'.

So limited a personality as Queen Marie could not hope to hold him. She refused to let him into her bed on certain saints' days, and when she did she smothered him with blankets. Even her own father described Marie and her mother as 'the two most boring queens I ever met'. Marie once gave it as her opinion that the best way of dispelling *ennui* was eating—she herself sometimes ate a twenty-nine course dinner. In any case she had lost her figure and was ageing fast. Louis was a man of

violent appetites, a mighty trencherman and *gros buveur*, and by the late 1730s discreet valets were regularly procuring whores for him. Every ambitious young woman at court watched the King with greedy, fascinated eyes.

At Easter 1739, Louis refused to take Communion. During one of his little dinner parties at La Muette he had already toasted 'that unknown she'. The previous autumn d'Argenson had noted that the King had taken one of the Queen's ladies-in-waiting for his mistress, the Comtesse de Mailly; the diarist describes her as 'well built but ugly, a big mouth with good teeth which gives her rather a stupid look. She is of small intelligence and has no ideas about anything'; later he says that 'her ugliness scandalizes foreigners who expect a King's mistress to at least have a pretty face'. (Perhaps surprisingly, Mme de Mailly once boasted that sixteen artists had painted her portrait!) None the less, as an experienced married woman of twenty-seven—she was nicknamed 'the widow'—Louise-Julie de Mailly knew just how to put the shy King at his ease, flattering him with little attentions, such as making him a dressing-gown with her own hands and leaving it on his dressing-table. She was invited to the supper parties at La Muette and installed in a flat at Versailles. The Queen accepted the situation with surprising common sense and even humour—she may have been glad of the rest. When Mme de Mailly asked for leave to go to Compiègne where Louis was, the Queen replied, 'Do what you like—you're the mistress.' La Mailly did not have a particularly enjoyable reign—the King was constantly betraying her with other ladies. However, she no doubt felt safe in introducing him to her sister, Félicité de Vintimille (whom an enemy described as having 'the face of a grenadier, the neck of a stork and the smell of a monkey'.) As early as June 1739 the sisters were dining together with the King; he took them hunting and boating.

By 1740 Mme de Vintimille had supplanted her sister—the King even offered her Fleury's flat. Félicité was a big, bold woman with a rough tongue which somehow amused Louis. But even he was irritated by her outbursts of bad temper; on one occasion he told her, 'I know just how to cure you of your ill nature, Mme la Comtesse—to cut off your head; it wouldn't altogether be a bad idea as you have such a long neck.' In the

autumn of 1740 she gave birth to a son (the Comte du Luc—who grew up so like the King that he was called the *Demi-Louis* all his life). But La Vintimille developed puerperal fever and died of it. Louis was so miserable that he took to his bed, had a death mask made of her face, and then retired to Rambouillet almost by himself. When he returned to the court, it was to the forgiving arms of Mme de Mailly.

Unfortunately she was so unwise as to introduce him to her fat and even uglier sister, Adelaide, who took her turn as mistress, although she did not last very long. It is even possible that he slept with a fourth sister, Hortense. By this time lewd songs were being sung in Paris about the King's weakness for the family.

Mme de Mailly never learnt. In 1742 she presented her youngest sister, Marie-Anne de la Tournelle, who was beautiful, intelligent and thoroughly nasty. At her insistence Mme de Mailly was banished four leagues from court, 'with a harshness inexplicable in a Most Christian King', as d'Argenson comments. 'You bore me,' Louis told the poor woman. He created Marie-Anne Duchesse de Châteauroux, gave her the official title of *maîtresse en titre*, a flat at Versailles over his own, a house in Paris and a country estate; he also agreed to legitimize any children born to her. Success went to Marie-Anne's head and she was viciously rude to the poor Queen.

More responsible courtiers were alarmed by the King's immaturity and irresponsibility. D'Argenson observes that the monarch, 'rises at eleven and leads a useless life. He allows only one hour for work amid all his frivolous amusements; his Councils can scarcely be called work, as he lets his ministers do everything, merely listening or repeating what they say parrot fashion. He is still a child.' The new Duchesse de Châteauroux tried to make Louis devote more time to affairs of state and advised him to join his army, but he only moaned, 'Madame, you will kill me.'

France had been at war since 1741. It was a war which Louis had wanted to leave to other countries, but Marshal de Belle-Isle convinced him that he would be unworthy of his war-like forebears if he did not seize this chance of overawing Europe. He had allied with Prussia to deprive Maria Theresa of her succession to the Habsburg domains, but Frederick the Great

had quickly made peace after conquering Silesia. Fleury's foreign policy was in ruins; not only was France at war, but England emerged from the diplomatic isolation which the Cardinal had so carefully encouraged over the last decade, and joined in on the side of the Austrians. A French army had to surrender in Bohemia. Yet old Fleury—he had been born in 1653—clung to office though he was quite past it; news of reverses in Italy 'made him dizzy'.

In 1740 d'Argenson had seen the Cardinal coming out of the King's room; 'More like a ghost than a man, the merest shadow of a dried up old monkey. He grows thinner before your very eyes, his legs and feet drag, he is only half alive and fast failing . . . indeed at this afternoon's session the King's Council needed Extreme Unction rather than refreshments.' During the same year a bad harvest and rising prices had caused hunger riots all over the country, even in Paris; old hags seized the bridle of Fleury's coach and screamed through the windows, 'We're dying of hunger!'

None the less, totally deaf and growing blind, the Cardinal toiled on, working at his papers from six in the morning until six at night. He rouged his cheeks and joked that old age was a disability which he did not want to cure just yet. When at last he died, at the end of January 1743, his pupil wrote to his uncle, Philip V of Spain, 'I owe everything to him and always felt that he took the place of my parents.'

Louis presided over the first Council after the Cardinal's death. *'Messieurs, me voilà Premier Ministre!'* There is something faintly frivolous about the announcement; within two months d'Argenson was commenting bitterly that the King was simply not interested in how the realm was governed. It was now however that Mme de Châteauroux persuaded her royal lover to join his troops.

France's military situation had seriously deteriorated. Marshal de Noailles had received a bloody repulse at Dettingen in 1743, the French army falling back down the Rhine. The troops' morale had to be restored; it was felt that the appearance of the King at their head would have the desired effect. Louis marched into the Low Countries in April 1744 with a large force which included Mme de Châteauroux and one of her sisters (not Mme de Mailly). He was present when

Ypres and several other towns were taken. Then news came
that an Austrian army was advancing on Alsace and, together
with Noailles and 50,000 men, Louis went to meet it.

On the way he fell ill at Metz. It was a fever which failed to
respond to the normal purges and bleedings. Within a few days
everyone, including the King himself, believed he was dying.
The news alarmed the entire country. Michelet quotes a contemporary account: 'The people leapt from their beds, rushed
out in a tumult without knowing whither. The churches were
thrown open in the middle of the night. Men assembled in the
cross-roads, accosted, and asked questions without knowing
each other. In several churches the priest who announced the
prayer for the recovery of the King interrupted the chanting
with his sobs, and the people responded by their cries and
tears.'

The Bishop of Soissons, the Royal Almoner, refused to give
Louis the last sacraments unless Mme de Châteauroux was sent
away. Terrified, the King dismissed his mistress, made a
tearful confession and summoned the Queen. Marie came at
once—he embraced her and begged forgiveness. 'Only God has
been offended,' replied his pious consort. The Bishop also made
him make a full public confession, to be read in every parish
church; the citizens of Metz were privileged to hear Louis read
the confession in person. (M de Soissons would never again
receive preferment.) Prayers were said throughout the kingdom, even in the humblest village church.

Then a Dr du Moulin prescribed a powerful emetic. Suddenly
the King began to recover. He was quickly on his feet again and
the cure was termed a miracle. What was truly miraculous,
however, was the extraordinary outburst of popular rejoicing;
all over France the people danced and sang and lit bonfires in
the streets; Voltaire wrote some sycophantic verses which
compared Louis to the ever-glorious Henri IV, and which were
enthusiastically applauded. It was now that the King received
the name '*Le Bien-Aimé*'. He rejoined the army, then went home
to Versailles. Mme de Châteauroux, who had been hooted in
the streets and was ill, waited for her recall; the longed-for
message came and she rose from her bed, to be suddenly
stricken down with peritonitis; she was dead in two days, only
twenty-seven years old. Louis, from being euphoric after a

triumphant welcome into his capital, was prostrate; very unfairly he expressed his grief by ignoring the Queen.

However, he preserved sufficient decorum to attend the festivities which celebrated the marriage of the Dauphin to yet another Spanish Infanta, in February 1745. The culmination was a masked ball in the Gallery of Mirrors at Versailles—the famous Hall of the Clipped Yews—which was open to anyone who could afford a ticket. Here, disguised as a yew tree, he danced in the crowd with a delicious brunette who was dressed as Diana; when she removed her mask he recognized Mme Le Normant d'Etioles, whom he had noticed driving in a pink phaeton in the forest of Sénart where he sometimes hunted. A few days later there was another masked ball, at the Hôtel de Ville. Louis looked in briefly at yet another ball at the Opéra and then took a public cabriolet to the Hôtel de Ville where he had supper with Mme d'Etioles; they left discreetly, taking a cab to her house where they spent the night together. The court was quickly aware that there was a new *maîtresse en titre*. Soon Mme d'Etioles moved into Mme de Mailly's old flat at Versailles. She was a most beautiful young lady, tall, chestnut-haired, with exquisite eyes and teeth, a perfect complexion, and a lively, vivacious manner—she had a particularly delightful laugh.

As Jeanne-Antoinette Poisson, she had been born in 1721. Her father, who began life as a ship's steward, had made money as an army contractor but was then charged with embezzlement and fled abroad, whereupon her mother went to live with her rich friend, the tax farmer M Le Normant. The girl received the best education that money could buy, no less a person than Boucher being her art master. (Sainte-Beuve says 'she had been instructed in everything save morals which might have embarrassed her.') At nineteen she married the nephew of her mother's protector. Young Mme d'Etioles (the name of an estate purchased by her husband's family) belonged unmistakably to the new *arriviste* nobility, but though she could hardly expect to be invited to the best houses, she was generally recognized as one of the prettiest girls in Paris and considered to have surprisingly good manners. She had all the boundless social ambition of her class, reinforced by a fortune-teller's prophecy (when she was only nine) that she would grow up 'a

dish for a King', since when her mother had called her 'Reinette'
—little Queen. Like most people, Reinette was the oddest
mixture of good and bad qualities; she never saw her heartbroken husband again, yet she showed herself a loyal and loving
daughter to her disreputable old father. Intelligent, tactful,
sensitive to his slightest change of mood, she would love Louis
very genuinely and give him that soothing feminine companionship which held him far more closely than any physical ties.

Meanwhile the war dragged on, France being forced to continue fighting merely to obtain a reasonable peace settlement.
Louis was persuaded to take the field again and to accompany
Marshal Saxe. The King enjoyed the campaign thoroughly,
sleeping in barns on straw, telling dirty stories (received with
acclaim), and singing marching songs in a high, cracked voice.
Tournai had been besieged by the French, and an Anglo-
Hanoverian and Austrian army of some 46,000 men, commanded by the twenty-two-year-old Duke of Cumberland,
marched to relieve it. Saxe intercepted them at Fontenoy with
52,000 troops. He took up a strong defensive position; a
triangle based on the village of Fontenoy where his centre was,
his right at another village, and his left protected by a wood, the
entire position being criss-crossed with redoubts; his troops
included Parisian skirmishers imaginatively equipped with
crossbows (who later routed General Lord Ingoldsby). The
Marshal was incapacitated by dropsy and had to be driven
round the field in a light wickerwork carriage.

Cumberland's cavalry attacked the French from 6.00 am
onwards, but was driven back again and again. Finally, the
Duke changed his tactics, massed his infantry into a single
column, and then battered his way straight up hill into the
French centre. Louis, wearing a gold-laced coat and the
Cordon Bleu, watched through a telescope. It was now that,
after declining the Comte d'Auteroches's invitation to fire
first, the English mowed down 400 men of the *Regiment du Roi*
with a single volley. The entire front line of the French centre
disintegrated. It was midday. Cumberland's massive column
prepared to bludgeon the second line out of existence. The only
four French cannon available blazed away at the English, who
stood firm and then beat off charge after charge by the *Maison
du Roi*, the King's household cavalry. Louis put on his cuirass,

hoping to charge with them; he and the Dauphin were watching from a hillock. Noailles, who thought the battle lost, now advised the King to leave the field.

Suddenly Saxe drove up. When informed of the advice, he bellowed, 'What poltroon told you that?' He felt completely in control of the situation, explaining, 'Our Irish troops remain.' Shortly after, at about 2.00 am, the Irish Brigade—Clare's Dragoons, Dillon's, Lally's and all the other Wild Geese—charged up hill into the British, roaring in Gaelic, 'Remember Saxon treachery!' The enemy, which included the Grenadier and Coldstream Guards, had already suffered many casualties. Their mighty column faltered, then broke; the total allied losses were over 10,000 men, the Coldstream losing a colour.

Louis embraced Saxe on the field of victory and even wrote to the Queen. Tournai fell the following month and *Te Deums* were sung all over France. The King and his Marshal were the heroes of the nation; everywhere he was acclaimed with shouts of *Vive le Roi*. Yet Louis never went to war again; he had ridden over the battlefield of Fontenoy after it was all over, and had been horrified by the corpses and the bleeding, groaning wounded.

Had Louis XV been killed at Fontenoy he would have gone down to history as one of France's better Kings, and certainly as one of the most popular. His subjects all but worshipped him. His charm and good looks were the admiration of all (even the humblest peasant was familiar with the Adonis-like profile on the coinage). For nearly twenty years Fleury had given the country unusual prosperity, while a French army had now won a glorious victory.

Yet despite the victory, France's fight for an honourable peace dragged on for three more weary years. In Scotland, the rising of Prince Charles Edward, at first brilliantly successful, was crushed in 1746. In Italy, the French were defeated in the Milanese and in Piedmont. However, an Austrian invasion of Provence was swiftly repulsed by Marshal Belle-Isle, while in the north Marshal Saxe won two more great victories at Raucaux and Laffeldt, occupied almost the entire Austrian Low Countries and went on to invade Holland. But in 1747 Russia joined the enemies of France, who now stood alone. Across the Atlantic in New France, Louisburg fell to the English and also

Cap Breton Island, which commanded the mouth of the St Lawrence, despite the gallant *coureurs des bois* and their Iroquois blood-brothers. France was exceedingly lucky to obtain such a favourable treaty as that signed at Aix-la-Chapelle in April 1748; it was a mutual agreement that each government should restore its territorial gains.

During the Fontenoy campaign, Louis had written every day to Mme d'Etioles; one letter contained the patent creating her Marquise de Pompadour. Meanwhile the Abbé de Bernis, a man of fashion, was instructing her in the mysteries of court etiquette. (Though many years later, Talleyrand heard that she never quite lost her 'vulgar accent and gauche manner'.) Upon the King's triumphant return to Versailles in September 1745 she was presented to the Queen by the Princesse de Conti (in return for the payment of her gambling debts), in Louis's presence—he was red with embarrassment. The Queen greeted the new favourite with unexpected kindness. Mme de Pompadour was so agitated that, when taking her glove off, she broke her bracelet. Overcome, she told her lover's wife with deep emotion that she would do her best to please her.

The favourite certainly succeeded in pleasing Louis. Besides organizing every sort of party and diversion, she kept him amused with such toys as private theatricals. A minute playhouse, with room for only fourteen spectators, was erected at Versailles, the first performance taking place in 1747; the play was Molière's *Tartuffe*, which Louis thoroughly enjoyed. Later, the theatre was enlarged to hold over forty. More than sixty plays and operas were presented by the *Théatre des Petits Cabinets* before its creator brought it to an end in 1752, including works by such fashionable writers as Voltaire and Crébillon. The favourite chose the plays with great care, the King having a peculiar dislike of tragedies, preferring comedies with happy endings. The operas were those of Lully, Rameau and de Campra. There were also performances of sacred works— *motets* by Lalet and Mondonville. On one occasion Louis was so pleased by the little orchestra that he gave the musicians gold snuff boxes bearing his portrait. In the plays, however, the actors were all amateurs, consisting of Mme de Pompadour and her friends. Only very favoured members of the court were invited to the theatre.

Later, long after Mme de Pompadour's death, Louis commissioned his favourite architect, Jacques Ange Gabriel, to build a full-sized theatre at Versailles; it was known as Gabriel's Opéra. Less well known, perhaps, is another of the King's commissions, the cathedral at Versailles which was begun by Mansard de Sagonne in 1743. In addition Louis slowly converted Versailles to suit his passionate desire for privacy, constructing the famous *petits appartements* on the upper floors of the right wing, overlooking the Marble Courtyard, and reached by secret staircases; the palace became a 'rat's nest' of little flats. But at the same time he also redecorated the salons and great state rooms in the new Rococo style, supervising the redecoration, with almost unbelievably graceful results. His alterations at Fontainebleau were even more drastic. The Ecole Militaire and the Place de la Concorde (both by J A Gabriel) are also his creations—originally the latter was the Place Louis XV.

His mistress shared the King's mania for building, landscape gardening and the decorative arts. She has been described as 'undoubtedly the key to an understanding of French taste in the first half of the eighteenth century. She gave it just that exquisitely graceful and feminine touch which still fascinates us today.' Her houses were fabled for their elegance and beauty—notably the châteaux of La Celle, and of Bellevue, and the Hôtel d'Evreux (now the Elysée and the home of the Presidents of France); she also built 'hermitages' at Versailles and Fontainebleau. The prosperity of the state porcelain factory at Sèvres owed a good deal to her influence. Nancy Mitford wrote of her, 'Few human beings since the world began can have owned so many beautiful things.' Perhaps the most fitting monument to the friendship—one might almost say partnership—between Louis XV and Mme de Pompadour is the delicious little palace which he built for her in the gardens of Versailles, but which she did not live to see completed—the *Petit Trianon*.

Mme de Pompadour made the King aware of a new world of intellectuals, bringing him into contact with men like her doctor, François Quesnay, who was a pioneer economist and founder of the Physiocrats. She admired the period's leading thinkers, the *Philosophes*, who returned her admiration; when she died, d'Alembert said, 'She was one of us,' and Voltaire

went into mourning. But she failed to make a *Philosophe* of Louis XV, who although not without intellectual tastes—he amassed a fine library of scientific books, collected rare manuscripts, and spent much time in his laboratory—did not care for the new ideas. None the less, he cannot have objected to her patronage of men like Rameau.

One must not overlook the King's own patronage. He jealously protected his Academie des Beaux Arts, giving the best pupils bursaries to study in Rome at the French Academy in the Palazzo Mancini. He also attended the annual exhibitions in the Salon Carée of the Louvre. As a leading authority on eighteenth-century French art (Alvar Gonzalez Palacios in *Il Luigi XV*, Milan 1966) tells us, 'Louis XV himself could always recognize what was best in the art of his time. He could see talent even when it was accompanied by impertinence, as in the case of the painter Quentin La Tour' [who was rude and half-crazy]. The King also took special pains to help Boucher whose paintings still convey so much of the reign's atmosphere. Louis commissioned furniture from such masters as Oeben and Riesener, taking a keen interest in its manufacture, which sometimes took years. In addition he watched with pleasure the progress of the new state porcelain factory which had been founded in 1738 (at Vincennes—later it moved to Sèvres) as a rival to Meissen.

Mme de Pompadour was not strong, and after some years began to find Louis's physical demands exhausting. She tried such aphrodisiacs as hot rooms, chocolate and truffles, and even celery soup, but to no avail; her lover said unkindly that she was 'as cold as a coot'. In 1752 she therefore took the dangerous step of ceasing to sleep with him, relying on the indispensability of her companionship. She knew that so long as the King had his 'Deer Park' he would bed with illiterate girls who only interested him with their bodies, and ought therefore to be immune from the charms of any lady of the court. She had nothing to do with the Park, but prudently did nothing to discourage Louis in his use of it. Most unjustly it earned her the epitaph,

> *Ci-git qui fut vingt ans pucelle,*
> *Quinze ans catin, sept ans maquerelle.*

(Here lies a maid for twenty years, a whore for fifteen and a procuress for seven.)

The *Parc aux Cerfs* has given rise to pleasurable legends of naked young women being hunted through the woods by the King and his hounds. Carlyle writes zestfully of, 'a fabulous Griffin, devouring the works of men, daily dragging virgins into thy cave', Michelet of 'an infamous seraglio of children whom he bought'. In reality, the Park was a modest house in the town of Versailles which discreetly procured healthy young women of the people for His Most Christian Majesty's pleasure; many wealthy men of the period kept similar private brothels. The girls were engaged by Louis's valet, Lebel, and brought to a little flat in the palace known as the 'Bird Trap'; if they gave satisfaction they were then boarded—seldom more than one at a time—at the Park under the supervision of the house-keeper, Mme Bertrand. They were nearly always professional prostitutes with only their youth and beauty (and health) to recommend them. The most famous was Louise O'Murphy, whose posterior was immortalized by Boucher; she stayed at the Park for four years until she was dismissed for making an impertinent remark about Mme de Pompadour; the King arranged a good marriage for her. Before going to bed, Louis would sometimes make his little whores kneel down with him and they would say their prayers. Rumours about the establishment spread all over Paris and it was said that just as every man descends from Adam, so every Frenchman would descend from King Louis XV. Probably Louis sired no more than twenty bastards at most.

Otherwise, the King's private amusements were far from sordid. It was the world of *fêtes champêtres* and *commedia dell' arte* revels of the sort painted by Boucher and Fragonard, of picnics in Elysian parks, of Venetian carnivals, of parties on the water in gondolas, of balls in lamplit woodland glades where the court wore masks and dominoes and dressed as Pan and Flora, as Pierrot and Columbine. Louis loved music and adored dancing—pleasure has never been more elegant than it was in his reign. One bitter winter Mme de Pompadour had her flower-beds filled with porcelain flowers while the air was sprayed with summer scents.

None the less, life at court was still stately and much of court

etiquette remained unchanged until the Revolution. Even so, Louis XV's timetable was very different from that of Louis XIV. Although he slept in his great-grandfather's bed, instead of rising at the same hour every day he often slept long, telling his valet when to wake him; alternately he rose very early, before the servants, and lit his own fire. Having washed, shaved and dressed—he was scrupulously clean—he breakfasted on fruit and black coffee. He no longer used a *chaise percée* in public but had a modern, private *cabinet* with one of the new English water-closets. Council meetings, audiences and Mass occupied the morning, until he dined in public, by himself at a square table; unlike Louis XIV he ate with a knife and fork. He drank copiously but not heavily; his wines were usually burgundy or champagne (as Governor of Guyenne, the Duc de Richelieu once brought him the finest bordeaux obtainable, but the King merely sipped it, muttering 'drinkable', and never touched it again).

In the afternoon Louis hunted or shot; out of season he walked or went for a hard gallop. He killed on average over 200 stags a year, besides many wolves and wild boar, frequently exhausting his huntsmen and grooms. Violent physical exercise was essential to his wellbeing, though another reason why he, and indeed all Bourbons, were so passionately addicted to hunting may have been that it offered a chance of being by oneself and behaving naturally. There was a softer side to hunting which is often overlooked—ladies following the hounds down woodland rides in fast little phaetons, and the delightful hunt breakfasts painted by van Loo. Perhaps the greatest of all French sporting artists was discovered by Louis—Jean Baptiste Oudry, from whom the King commissioned a dazzling series of tapestries, 'The Royal Hunts of Louis XV'.

Like most Bourbons, Louis liked working with his hands. Sometimes he would spend a whole day toiling with his gardeners. He was an expert silversmith and at Marly in 1738 made a pair of candlesticks. He also turned ivory.

In the evening the King joined the Queen and the Royal family at supper, after which—having a true Bourbon appetite—he would often slip away and eat a second supper with his mistress. Then he might drive to Paris to go to the opera, to dance masked at one of the public balls, or to visit a brothel.

Louis XV by Quentin La Tour

Jean Antoinette Poisson, Marquise de Pompadour, by Boucher, 1759

Sometimes he stayed at home, giving little supper parties, playing cards and making coffee into the small hours of the morning; frequently his pages fell asleep on his bed waiting for the *Coucher*. As soon as they had left him, Louis, who did not even bother to undress, would jump out of the state bed and join his mistress by a secret staircase.

Frequently the King was away from Versailles. He spent much time at Compiègne, Marly, Rambouillet, La Muette, Fontainebleau, moving about to escape from his awful boredom. When he went to inspect the fleet at Le Havre in 1749, he travelled all night and hunted all day, exhausting his entourage. He was always escorted by his hunt staff and by a special body-guard of the Black and the Grey Musketeers; at Rambouillet 500 persons had to be housed on each visit. Louis understood little about money; once, hearing that the poor were starving, he sacked eighty gardeners, but took them back when it was explained to him that as a result they too would starve.

Although the King far preferred women's company, he had his male cronies, some being lifelong friends. Among them were the Duc d'Ayen (a Noailles and a soldier) and the Comte de Coigny, who was killed in a duel over a card dispute in 1749. From his youth these two accompanied Louis everywhere, were invariably invited to his little supper parties, and escorted him on the nocturnal expeditions. Other men friends were the Duc de Vallière (one of the better French soldiers of the reign and a gunnery expert), and the rather silly Duc de Penthièvre, a bastard Bourbon who was Grand Huntsman of France, and whose lovely château of Saint Leger was frequently borrowed by the King. Ayen, Vallière and Penthièvre all had the misfortune of outliving their master and of surviving until the Revolution.

An outsize member of his little circle was that illiterate *condottiere*, Maurice de Saxe. One of the 365 children of Augustus II—'The Strong'—of Saxony-Poland (Stanislas Leszczynski's supplanter), Marshal Saxe had been a soldier since the age of twelve, entering the French service in 1720. Louis rewarded his many victories by creating him Marshal General of France and giving him the château of Chambord. Saxe had strange and colourful ambitions; after losing his delightful little Grand Duchy of Courland on the Baltic, he dreamt of making himself King of Madagascar. A huge,

corpulent man, dropsical and stone-deaf, the Marshal was a glutton and a womanizer but his eccentricities were gladly suffered. He had an embarrassingly coarse wit; once, seeing Louis and Mme de Pompadour out walking together, he bellowed, 'There go the King's sword and the King's scabbard.' Saxe died in 1750, of over-exerting himself with a lady of pleasure.

The one member of the circle who dared to be openly hostile to Mme de Pompadour was the infamous Richelieu. Armand du Plessis, Duc de Richelieu and a great-nephew of the Cardinal, had been born in 1696 and was First Gentleman of the Bed-chamber (and therefore in charge of all court entertainments) for more than half a century. A brave and skilful soldier—he captured Minorca from the English in 1757—he was also almost unbelievably venal and unscrupulous; once he offered to sell the frontier town of Bayonne to the Spaniards, while during the Seven Years War his soldiers nicknamed him *Papa la Maraude* (Daddy Plunder). A creature of exquisite elegance and breathtaking extravagance who gave wonderful parties, the Duke also had intellectual pretensions; he was elected to the Academie Française, was the friend and patron of Voltaire, and was a notorious free-thinker. However, Richelieu's chief claim to fame was as a Don Juan; he was a sexual athlete whose uncanny gift of attracting women was attributed to super-natural powers; when he died at ninety-four, letters were found in his pocket from four ladies, who each begged for an hour in his bed. Countless scandals enveloped this insatiable debauchee and intriguer—he had been in the Bastille three times. Richelieu was really rather a horrible man, but the King, like most people, never tired of his disreputable, amusing company. Mme de Pompadour had the good taste to dislike him.

It is curious, even taking into account that war was the only occupation fit for a nobleman, that almost all Louis's closest friends were distinguished generals. Ironically, in view of his distaste for bloodshed, the King was surrounded by soldiers. The guardsmen of the *Maison du Roi* numbered no less than 10,000, including such specialized troops as the 150 Horse Grenadiers (reputedly the finest-looking men in France). Even when he went to Mass he arrived to martial music from a fife and drum band.

The portraits of Louis XV by Nattier, van Loo and Quentin La Tour give some idea of his good looks. Those who knew the King were even more struck by his charm and beautiful manners; by now a unique and fascinating compound of majesty and simplicity, he could be delightfully gay and talkative, though only in private. Manners had relaxed generally, the *honnête homme* giving place to the *bon compagnon* as the pattern for gentlemanly behaviour, and sometimes Louis was the best of companions. The Prince de Croy tells us of little dinner parties (so informal that sometimes the gentlemen dined in their shirtsleeves); there were no servants in the small room under the eaves, everyone helping himself and the King making the coffee. The Prince says, 'Often I felt more at ease with him than with almost anyone else—his kindness is engraved on my heart.' In public he was a very different person, shy and stiff. 'One could see that he wanted desperately to say something but the words died in his mouth', observes a courtier. The King could be rude too, sulky and scowling, especially when his dreadful melancholy was upon him, though according to Croy 'he never grumbled or shouted'. Savage things are said of Louis XV by other contemporaries who also knew him well, but these were invariably frustrated men whom he had dismissed from their posts.

His was a strange temperament. In his melancholy moods the King often showed a morbid obsession with death, which may have been due to his parents' untimely fate; like the Prince of Denmark he sought for his noble father in the dust; on occasion he was very like Hamlet in the churchyard—once, passing a cemetery, he sent a groom to find out if there were any newly-dug graves. At court he frequently inquired about dangerous operations and serious illnesses, asking people where they would like to be buried and even foretelling their demise. For although Louis literally lived for pleasure, he knew little happiness. His entire character and intellect were vitiated by pessimism. Even if the hostile d'Argenson could admit that the King 'gave orders like a master and discussed business like a minister', at Council meetings his suggestions were too easily over-ruled by his ministers, while he would agree to policies which his innate shrewdness told him were misguided. His hopeless lack of purpose is illustrated by the immortal remark

149

(made famous by Carlyle), 'If *I* were Lieutenant of Police, I would prohibit those Paris cabriolets.'

Yet with all his frivolity and dissipation, Louis—like all Bourbons—was a deeply religious man. He never missed Mass, walked tirelessly in processions, had an expert knowledge of the liturgy, and prayed with real devotion; he once said naively, 'I do not regret my rheumatism—it is in expiation of my sins.' He was also like all his family in being in no way an intellectual. He found the ideas of the *Philosophes*—*ces gens là* as he scornfully termed them—quite incomprehensible; their excessive rationality did not appeal to a doubting mind which knew very well that men are fools by nature. The King was old-fashioned too in his complete conviction that he had received absolute authority from God—he believed it no less firmly than had Louis XIV. For all his Rococo tastes, Louis XV was more a man of the seventeenth than of the eighteenth century.

Unlike Louis XIV, the King did not enjoy the company of men of letters. None the less his reign was the silver age of French classical literature. It saw the publication of *Candide*, *Manon Lescaut*, *Gil Blas*, *Emile* and the *Nouvelle Héloïse*, of Buffon's natural history and Vauvenargues's maxims, to name only masterpieces.

Unfortunately for Louis XV, his prime coincided with the age of the 'Enlightenment'. This was a climate of ideas, almost amounting to a new religious and political philosophy, which was largely derived from the thoughts of Newton and Spinoza, partly from the example of English freedom, and partly from the dissatisfaction of under-privileged bourgeois intellectuals. It was disseminated by Montesquieu, Diderot, Voltaire and a host of others, broadcast everywhere in France by means of a new encyclopaedia of knowledge which claimed to deal with every aspect of human activity. Later the Enlightenment was reinforced by Rousseau, though his pernicious ideas about equality and a return to nature were hardly compatible with reason. By the end of the reign, most literate Frenchmen had consulted the *Encyclopédie*, which could be obtained through the new Masonic lodges or at the public reading rooms despite every attempt at censorship. However, the *Philosophes* really wanted reform, not revolution. Their aim was to eradicate Diderot's 'artificial man', the man of tradition, which meant

putting an end to religious and intellectual intolerance (of which the Jesuits were a symbol, 'fanaticism's grenadiers' as d'Alembert called them); humanizing the country's barbarous mediaeval code; and setting the state on a sound economic basis. They were quite content with the *Ancien Régime*, so long as it could be brought up to date and made to function efficiently. They did not wish to destroy privilege, but merely to rationalize it, as—so they thought—had been done in England.

Louis disliked most new ideas, but eventually allowed the *Encyclopédie* to be published when *'sincère et tendre Pompadour'* (Voltaire's name for her) intervened in its favour. She tried to turn him into a 'Benevolent Despot' of the sort to be seen at Vienna or Berlin, but—predictably—was unsuccessful. None the less, he was not averse to his ministers holding fashionable views and actually made Voltaire his Historiographer Royal and a Gentleman of the Bedchamber.

Poor Queen Marie, prematurely aged, had become duller and dowdier than ever. Her dreadful red velvet bonnets were a constant cause for merriment. She painted execrable little pictures, performed dismally on the guitar, harpsichord and hurdy-gurdy, and worked day in, day out at her tapestry; her sole indulgences were gluttony and some mild gambling on a peculiarly dreary card game. Her religious duties were scrupulously observed—she frequently overspent her allowance on charities. The Queen was a frump, but a most dignified one— her stateliness put some in mind of the old court of Louis XIV— and everyone, including the King, respected her deeply. She had a cosy little circle of dull friends, most of whom joined with her in abominating all *Philosophes* and free-thinkers, in abhorring Jansenists and in cherishing Jesuits.

The Dauphin Louis, small-eyed and black-haired, resembled the King hardly at all. He was another Duc de Bourgogne, of whom some contemporaries had excessive hopes. Like his sainted grandfather, he had been an evil-tempered child who frequently struck his servants, but whose personality had completely changed when he was about fourteen; like his grandfather he became lethargic and taciturn, perhaps as a consequence of having grown unnaturally fat; he may well have suffered from a glandular affliction. Henceforward he was

disturbingly pious; his intimate friends were fanatic priests and, to the alarm of all Enlightened courtiers, he would throw himself flat on his face at the Elevation of the Host. His preferred occupation was 'vegetating'—his own name for it. His habitual rudeness, even boorishness, did not arouse affection. D'Argenson writes, 'If there really *is* some spark in him, it is a dying one, extinguished by fat and bigotry.' None the less, at sixteen he showed at Fontenoy that for all his lethargy he had plenty of courage, begging to lead a charge.

In 1745 the Dauphin married yet another Spanish Infanta, the red-haired Marie Theresa (sister of his father's former betrothed) with whom he quickly fell in love, but the poor girl soon died. The young husband was prostrate. In 1748 he was forced to take a second bride, the fifteen-year-old Marie Joséphine, straw-haired and sapphire-eyed, who was shy and plain (although the sour d'Argenson thought her 'a pretty child'). Despite bad teeth and a flat nose, she grew up high-spirited and surprisingly attractive, and the Dauphin fell in love again, becoming an uxurious husband; the pair shared a mutual love of religion and music, withdrawing into a secret world of their own. Five sons were born to them; the short-lived Ducs d'Aquitaine and de Bourgogne, and the Duc de Berry and the Comtes de Provence and d'Artois—the last three becoming Louis XVI, Louis XVIII and Charles X. There were also two daughters, Mesdames Clothilde and Elisabeth.

Louis had mixed feelings about the Dauphin. 'My son is lazy, quick-tempered and moody. He is not interested in hunting, women or pleasure. But he really does love goodness, he is genuinely virtuous, and he is not without intelligence'; this seems to have been the King's considered verdict. He cannot have been too pleased with the Dauphin's calculated rudeness to poor Mme de Pompadour, to whom he could not even bring himself to speak; he referred to her father as 'that gallows Bird'. Nor was Louis above sneering at him, especially at his plumpness—he once asked, 'Do I not have a well-fed son?' None the less, when the Dauphin was dangerously ill with small-pox in 1752, the King spent whole days and nights in his room.

Portraits of the Dauphin Louis show a not ill-looking face, a curious compound of sharpness and femininity. He undoubtedly had a stronger character than his father, and during a brief

regency when the King was ill in 1757, showed himself both firm and able. It was not easy to overrule him—later he defended the Jesuits to the bitter end—and he had no illusions about the growing weakness of the monarchy; he wrote that the realm's financial disorders must be attended to before anything else, that 'the monarch is nothing but the steward of the state revenues'. In his personal life he was civilized enough, collecting books and pictures, and playing the organ, the harpsichord and the violin; surprisingly, he was an admirer of Rousseau's *Contrat Social*. However, the Dauphin was no lover of the *Philosophes*, who—probably with reason—dreaded his accession and feared that the reign of 'Louis the Fat' would be a reign of bigotry and intellectual intolerance.

Another source of opposition to the Enlightenment were the King's daughters. He had six who grew to womanhood, and although they were not particularly beautiful he adored them all (to the extent of holding their hands when their teeth were drawn). The two he loved best predeceased him; these were the twins, Mme Henriette who died very young; and Mme Elisabeth, Infanta of Spain and later Duchess of Parma, who despite her marriage had frequently returned to Versailles. Croy says that Mme Henriette's death literally paralysed Louis, who was 'in a frightful state'. The twins' place in his affections was taken by the boyish, hot-tempered Mme Adelaide, who as a very pretty little girl had refused to leave him and be educated in a convent; she and the rather colourless Mmes Victoire—amiable and pretty—and Sophie—ugly and sly—never married, Adelaide and Victoire surviving the Revolution and dying only in 1800. The most unusual of the six was the youngest, the tiny, hump-backed Mme Louise. Brought up by the nuns of Fontevrault, from her girlhood Louise wished to take the veil. When she was over thirty her wish was granted and she entered the enclosed convent of the Carmelites at Saint-Denis, where she was blissfully happy praying for her sinful father. Until his death the King came to see her at least once a month, when she would bitterly attack the debauchery of the court and new ideas (later she was a critic of poor, giddy Marie Antoinette). 'Soeur Sainte-Thérèse de Saint-Augustin' was lucky enough to die just before the Revolution, in 1787. All Louis's daughters were loyal supporters of the Jesuits.

By 1750 Louis was at last growing unpopular. Ridiculously, he was suspected of speculating in the grain trade and forcing up the price of bread. When a new road was being built from Versailles to Compiègne, he had it re-routed to by-pass Paris, explaining, 'I do not see why I should go where people call me Herod.' (This was a reference to a popular scare that the government were abducting children to send to the colonies; according to Michelet there were even rumours that Louis bathed daily in children's blood 'to renew his exhausted frame'.) The fact that taxation had not been decreased after the end of the war in 1748 did not endear him to his subjects. However, the principal reason for the King's unpopularity was his association with Mme de Pompadour who had incurred the traditional hatred for all royal mistresses. Her bourgeois origins irritated the court—she was the first commoner to be *maîtresse en titre*—while everyone disliked her connection with a tax-farmer's family. Increases in taxation were invariably blamed on her extravagance (and admittedly she spent over a million and a half of the King's money, reckoned in English pounds of the period, in the course of her career). Savage pamphlets, the *Poissonades*, circulated, lampooning the poor woman without mercy. It was common knowledge that she ruled Louis. After meeting her, the Prince de Ligne described Mme de Pompadour as 'a second Queen', and M d'Argenson says in 1756, 'She is more the First Minister than ever.'

Oddly enough, France was more prosperous than ever before. As Pierre Gaxotte says, the reign of Louis XV was truly 'an era of agriculturists, bankers, ironmasters, shipwrights and planners'. For, after Orry's stabilization of the currency in 1726, a period of really remarkable economic expansion had set in and lasted for the rest of the reign. Admittedly the peasantry in many areas were often near starvation when there was a bad harvest, but on the whole agriculture flourished, though there were very few 'improving' landlords. There was also an industrial revolution, with an impressive increase in the number of mines and foundries. In addition, there was a marked growth in trade with the colonies. Sugar, rum, tobacco and coffee flowed into the great French seaports, much of it to be re-exported, bringing economic wealth and capturing a considerable part of the European market from the English.

Machault—Orry's successor as Controller-General—tried to introduce a new and equitable tax system, the *vingtième*, in 1749–51. This was to be a five per cent wealth tax on real property and capital, which would replace the old system with its inefficiency and injustices; under the new scheme everyone— noble and priest, bourgeois and peasant farmer—would pay, except tenant farmers or wage earners who were to be exempt. The scheme was quickly killed by the privileged classes— notably the clergy in general assembly and the Parlements.

The Parlements were challenging the monarchy once more. These powerful legal corporations, exclusive, rich and noble, had become bastions of reaction and privilege. The *noblesse de l'épée* were incapable of mounting another Fronde, and the mantle of rebellion had fallen on the Parlementaires who, once bourgeois and loyal, had with increasing exclusiveness grown feudal and fractious. By 'liberty' this judicial aristocracy meant a kind of legal neo-feudalism; in 1734 they burnt Voltaire's *Lettres Philosophiques*, and they resisted any attempt to reform their archaic and often cruel statutes. They claimed to be the custodians of the law with supreme jurisdiction, and as such to constitute a 'Senate of the Nation' which spoke for France. Although entirely selfish and reactionary, they none the less managed to attract popular support in their self-styled rôle of 'Fathers of the People'. Louis was not far wrong in describing the Parlement of Paris as 'an assembly of republicans'. They were also the greatest single obstacle to reforming the *Ancien Régime*.

In the 1750s the Parlementaires derived considerable strength from their support of the Jansenists. Although by then this sect had its mindless fanatics, it did not derive its support from mere popular superstition alone, as is too often suggested; whole monasteries adopted the theology of Port Royal—in the middle of the eighteenth century an entire Carthusian community fled from Paris to join the Jansenists in Utrecht. Jansenists were popular because of their defiance of the Pope, they enlisted qualified support from the *Philosophes* in their feud with the Jesuits, and they inspired respect by their piety. (In the next century even Stendhal admired their survivors, in *Le Rouge et Le Noir*.) By their reliance on the lower clergy in their battle with the bishops, the Jansenists undermined authority and helped spread republican ideas.

In 1752, the Archbishop of Paris forbade his clergy to give the last rites to dying men who could not produce a certificate proving that they had been shriven by a non-Jansenist priest. The Parlement thereupon ordered his pastoral letters to be burnt by the public hangman. The Crown intervened and a furious quarrel ensued, a number of magistrates being banished. Although the Jansenist conflict died down briefly in 1757— thanks to intervention by Rome—the Parlement of Paris then tried to unite with the provincial Parlements to form a single body which would work towards obtaining the powers of the English Parliament. Louis angrily ordered them to confine themselves to their normal business.

The King was keenly aware that the monarchy was in danger. 'At least it will last my time,' he muttered grimly to a friend. For his authority was under ceaseless attack from the privileged classes. In this context one should no longer distinguish between nobility of the sword and nobility of the robe; by the late 1750s some of the Dukes and Peers—'obscure men of illustrious origin' as Michelet calls them—were beginning to side with the Parlementaires. An aristocratic counter-revolution was taking place; as Tocqueville first recognized, the nobles were becoming a closed caste. Louis XIV had carefully excluded the nobility from the councils of state, but by the mid-eighteenth century they occupied almost all government posts, even those of the *Intendants*; the higher clergy were exclusively noble; the Parlements refused to admit lawyers who could not show four quarterings; and the army was becoming steadily more patrician.

Louis XV understood very well that the state's financial machinery was inadequate and that corruption was spreading. Unfortunately his pessimism made him reluctant to act—as C P Gooch says, 'for him all evils were incurable.' Furthermore, the growth of literacy and the new critical climate introduced by the Enlightenment made it difficult for an eighteenth-century King of France to act in the way that Louis XIV had done—this was the age of Voltaire, no longer of Bossuet.

Louis XV's unpopularity was made known to him in a peculiarly unpleasant fashion in January 1757. Ironically, he had already predicted that he would die like Henri IV. One snowy afternoon, as he was descending the Dogs' Staircase at

Versailles, an out-of-work serving man called Damiens stabbed
him with a little pen-knife. At first Louis thought he had merely
been hit. But touching his ribs he found them covered in blood,
and cried, 'Arrest that man, but don't hurt him!' Then he
muttered, 'Why do they want to kill me? I've harmed no one.'
He walked upstairs without assistance, but then fainted—from
shock rather than loss of blood. Reviving, he demanded a doctor
and confessor—above all he feared to die unshriven. Summoning
his family, he informed the Queen, 'I have been assassinated',
and told the Daulphin, 'Govern better than I have done', after
which he asked their pardon for his scandalous life. When the
priest came, after an hour and a half's confession, he begged for
the last rites.

Yet the assassin's 'weapon' had had to penetrate a fur overcoat, a velvet jacket and two shirts. The wound was hardly
more than a scratch, but Louis insisted, 'I shall not recover.'
Eventually his huntsman, deeply trusted, managed to convince
him that the wound was not mortal. Even so, the King refused
to emerge from behind his curtains for over a week. He would
not see Mme de Pompadour who feared that her reign was over;
for some it was a day of Dupes; M d'Argenson refused to
censor the royal post for her and was dismissed as soon as
Louis was in circulation again.

At Fontenoy, in killing many dangerous stags with the
sword, and in nursing the Dauphin's smallpox, Louis XV had
shown that he was no coward. To say that his behaviour on this
occasion was due to his obsessive fear of damnation—he was
not frightened of death—is only part of the explanation. His
terror has an uncanny resemblance to the mood of Henri IV on
the eve of his own assassination. In fact Louis showed many
symptoms of a manic-depressive state. Revealingly, he told his
doctor, 'My body is all right, but this is bad and won't heal',
pointing to his forehead. It is only fair to add that Damiens's
peculiarly horrible torture and execution—he suffered all the
barbarous penalties for regicide—were imposed by the
Parlement and not by the King.

The Seven Years War had begun in the previous year, 1756.
Already the English, jealous of French colonial prosperity, had
ordered its navy to board French merchantmen and even men-
of-war. Meanwhile, France had realized that her traditional foe,

Austria, was no longer her real enemy. At the same time the English, determined that the war should be fought on land as well as at sea, subsidized Frederick of Prussia, who was alarmed by the new Franco–Austrian alliance. He swiftly invaded and conquered Saxony, an ally of Austria, and won a series of victories in Bohemia.

The French army was in a parlous condition. Undeterred by terrible punishments, thousands deserted the colours every year, while since Saxe's death there were no great commanders; the rank of Marshal of France had become a mere court perquisite instead of a victor's accolade. Louis XV's one positive contribution was the foundation of the Ecole Militaire in 1752, an officer-cadet school for the sons of country gentlemen. French troops have seldom been so badly led as they were during the Seven Years War.

To begin with, the French offensive went well enough. Marshal d'Estrées defeated the English and occupied Hanover; however Richelieu threw away the victory by allowing the Duke of Cumberland to escape. In 1757 there took place one of the most terrible disasters ever suffered by a French army. It was commanded by a brave and elegant friend of Mme de Pompadour, Charles de Rohan, Prince de Soubise, who marched into Saxony with 50,000 men, to attack Frederick who had only 20,000. But Richelieu and the allied generals had, with criminal incompetence, omitted to provide food for the French troops; they had not eaten for three days and were scarcely able to walk when they arrived at the little village of Rosbach where Frederick was waiting for them. None the less, the French marched doggedly towards the enemy. Suddenly they were mown down by hidden artillery, and then their unprotected right flank was overwhelmed by General von Seydlitz's cavalry. The Prussians lost 165 men; 3,000 Frenchmen were killed, 7,000 taken prisoner. Soubise, the descendant of so many Huguenot paladins, wrote to the King, 'I write to Your Majesty in an agony of despair. Your army has been totally routed; I cannot tell you how many of your officers were killed or captured or are missing.' France was so horrified that the Dauphin begged to be sent to the front, without success. Next year, at Krefeld, Frederick again defeated the French.

Meanwhile the French navy was being annihilated. Thirty-

seven ships of the line and fifty-six frigates were sunk by the English, the remnant of the fleets being finally destroyed by Admiral Hawke at Quiberon Bay in 1759. The enemy blockaded every French port, raiding Normandy and Brittany, and put the entire French coast in a stage of siege—any sorties were blown out of the water. It was impossible to send aid to the colonies. There were only 5,000 troops in Canada, badly short of ammunition and provisions; in 1759 Quebec fell to an English army of 40,000. Most of the French possessions in the Caribbean were overrun, in India Pondicherry fell and even in Africa Senegal was occupied. It was the most disastrous war which France had known for a hundred and fifty years.

Contemporaries tended to blame poor Mme de Pompadour. Undoubtedly she meddled in politics, making and unmaking ministers—she had had the excellent Orry dismissed in 1745, to please her tax-farmer friends. For her, politics was a matter of personalities—Bernis said she judged affairs of state like a child —and she chose people for amiable qualities rather than abilities. Between 1755 and 1763 no less than twenty-five ministers were appointed and dismissed, 'falling one after the other like the figures in a magic lantern', said Voltaire. D'Argenson commented, '*C'est la vide qui règne.*' Nor was France able to make peace when Frederick openly laughed at '*Cotillon* (Petticoat) II' and named one of his bitch puppies 'Pompadour'.

Even if the idea of a woman prime minister does not seem so outrageous nowadays, it is difficult to find an explanation, let alone an excuse, for Louis XV's trust in his mistress's political judgement. Yet the twenty-five ministers were only peripheral; the key men were sound enough throughout the war, for the 'harlotocracy'—Carlyle's cruel definition—secured the appointment of Bernis and then Choiseul.

The Abbé François Joachim de Bernis had attached himself to Mme de Pompadour even before her meeting with the King, in poverty-stricken days when his highest ambition had been a garret under the eaves of Versailles. He was a light-weight, timid, hypochondriacal, an amateur of flowery verse, essentially a man of pleasure and fashion whose chief talents were those of the drawing-room. But, although he lacked the character to give them force, his political views were shrewd and sensible—he was a pioneer advocate of the Austrian alliance. The court did

not take the fat little Abbé very seriously. However, Mme de Pompadour had him appointed Ambassador to Venice, where he did so well that, in 1755, he was made Minister of Foreign Affairs and charged with negotiating the new alliance with Austria. He was wise enough to see that any continuation of the war would benefit only England, a defeatist attitude which was too pessimistic even for Louis. Despairingly, the Abbé wrote, 'I feel myself to be the Minister of Foreign Affairs for Limbo.' He resigned in December, consoled with a Red Hat.

Bernis had carefully prepared the way for his friend Choiseul to succeed him. Etienne François, Duc de Choiseul, was a big, pug-faced nobleman with red hair and sharp blue eyes. Not yet forty, the scion of an ancient family from Lorraine, he had begun life as a penniless army officer but had made his fortune by marrying the daughter of a rich army contractor ('manuring his lands', as the court termed such an alliance). Choiseul eventually managed to squander all her vast wealth and went bankrupt. Although no less ruttish in his private life than the King, he was intelligent and amusing and succeeded in charming Mme de Pompadour (who came from much the same sort of background as his wife); he knew just how to please her—when he sent her a large opal from Rome, she made Louis give him the *Cordon Bleu*. It was she who had him appointed Ambassador to the Holy See, where he got on wonderfully well with the amiable Benedict XIV, before going on to Vienna. Energetic and even dynamic, Choiseul was quite sure that he knew what was best for France. To the post of Minister of Foreign Affairs he soon added those of Minister for War and Minister for the Marine and Post-Master General. From 1758 to 1770 he was First Minister in all but name.

As Foreign Minister, Choiseul's skill inspired Catherine of Russia to call him 'the coachman of Europe'. He achieved a major triumph with his Family Compact. This famous treaty, which was signed in August 1761, was an alliance between all the Bourbon sovereigns—the Kings of France, Spain and the Two Sicilies, and the Duke of Parma and Piacenza. This immediately procured for France the services of the Spanish navy, which if not particularly effective, did at least divert the attentions of the English. But not even Choiseul, a former Lieutenant-General, could win the war, though at least he ensured that England too

fought to a standstill. Everyone wanted peace, and the war came to an end with the Treaties of Paris and Hubertusburg. For France, the price was her colonial empire—the English took Canada and half of Louisiana (the rest being given to Spain). She retained most of her rich West Indian possessions, but her ambitions on the Indian sub-continent were halted for ever.

Few Frenchmen seem to have regretted the loss of Canada, which Voltaire actually dismissed as 'a mere few acres of snow'. Louis himself was more interested in power in Europe than in power overseas. Like most contemporary monarchs, he operated his own secret service. His main objectives were to save Poland from Russia and to weaken England. In the first he was unsuccessful, Poland being partitioned at the end of his reign, despite tireless work by his agents; the King was one of the few Frenchmen to recognize the full might of the Russian menace. After the Treaty of Paris he concentrated on M de Broglie's scheme for invading England; later he allowed the plans to be shown to Choiseul who was impressed, and also sent an Irish officer to investigate a possible invasion of Ireland. The *Secret du Roi* achieved little but Louis regarded it as essentially a safeguard against any weakening of his authority. He once said, 'At my own court I enjoy less power than some lawyer at the Chatelet, over my armies less power than a Colonel. It is through the *Secret* that I can recover what I've lost.'

Choiseul was the French Pitt. He toiled feverishly to restore his country's position in the world. He handled the King brilliantly, never boring him with excessive details. Abroad he maintained the alliance with Austria and the Family Compact, besides detaching Portugal and Holland from England. The purchase and conquest of Corsica took place in 1768–9, an accession of territory which was a marvellous tonic for French pride, already soothed by the acquisition of Lorraine on the death of Louis's father-in-law in 1766. As Minister for the Marine, he reorganized the ports and the navy, building over sixty ships of the line and fifty frigates with the King's enthusiastic encouragement. At the same time, as Minister for War, he improved the army; the artillery was reorganized, training camps were set up, a serious attempt was made to raise the quality of non-commissioned officers, and colonels were no

longer allowed to appoint their own junior officers. His ultimate objective, too, was the invasion of England.

At home Choiseul was less effective. Money was needed to pay for the debts of the Seven Years War and for the new navy, and further taxes could only be obtained with the agreement of the Parlements. Not only did the Duke have little understanding of national finances, but he was not prepared to risk a complete confrontation with the lawyers. Accordingly he tried to buy their support by sacrificing the Jesuits who, as Ultramontanes and the Jansenists' arch-enemies, were hated by the Parlement-aires. As one who sympathized with the *Philosophes*, Choiseul himself had little love for the Order. In 1761 the Jesuit administrator of the Fathers' sugar plantations in the West Indies went bankrupt for a large sum (as a result of British privateering); the courts ordered the Order to pay, whereupon it unwisely appealed to the Parlement of Paris, who promptly accused the Fathers of seeking to undermine public morals and the fundamental law. Much against his will, Louis was eventually persuaded by Choiseul to banish the Jesuits from France and to close their schools; the King had done everything possible to save them. Later the Vatican was cajoled into suppressing the entire Order.

Unfortunately, far from being grateful, the Parlementaires remained as intractable as ever. In 1764 Louis summoned the leading members of the Paris Parlement to Versailles and threatened them, without effect. In 1766, in the Palais de Justice, at the famous *Séance de la Flagellation*—so called on account of the tremendous tongue-lashing which he gave them— the King told the Paris Parlement that 'the courts depend for their very existence on me alone . . . to me alone belongs the legislative power'. But the lawyers remained unabashed. In 1768 he again had to force them to register new taxes by a *lit de justice*. Despite threats and banishment, they continued to obstruct the Government's financial policy whenever possible. Choiseul was incapable of envisaging any solution.

Paradoxically, the Parlements who challenged absolutism were among the most repressive institutions in what was still an age of brutal intolerance and ferocious punishment. Admittedly, a knock on the door at night and the production of a royal *lettre de cachet* meant arbitrary incarceration in the Bastille or

Vincennes, but Louis XV was comparatively sparing in his use of this weapon. On the other hand the lawyers enforced their statutes with the utmost severity, especially on Protestants. When—ten years after the last Huguenot rising of 1752—some Protestant noblemen attempted to rescue their pastor who was being hanged, they were condemned and beheaded forthwith. The Calas affair (in which the Huguenot father of a young suicide was falsely accused by the Toulouse Parlement of murdering him for turning Catholic, found guilty and then barbarously executed) outraged public opinion; after a brilliant campaign of protest conducted by Voltaire, the King forced the Toulouse Parlement to make what reparation it could to the unfortunate man's family.

By the 1760s Mme de Pompadour had grown old and plump. Her position was much more secure since being made a lady-in-waiting to the Queen in 1756. None the less, in recent years her sway had been far from unquestioned. Her best friend, Mme d'Estrades, the mistress of M d'Argenson, had plotted to discredit her with the King, while there had been a number of take-over bids by Mme de Choiseul-Romanet and by the bewitchingly pretty Marquise de Coislin (who was known as 'Proud Vashti' and who tried to extort vast sums of money). In 1763 the King had an affair with young Mlle de Romans, whose beautiful black hair and satin skin were admired by no less a connoisseur than Casanova. Mlle de Romans, who had ambitions, might have been a really formidable rival; Louis set her up in a house at Passy where she bore him a son and he created her Baronne de Meilly-Coulongé; but her conceit put him off, luckily for Mme de Pompadour.

Since 1756, poor Mme de Pompadour, already weakened by miscarriages, had suffered from tuberculosis, coughing blood with pitiful regularity; she was also afflicted with insomnia, bronchitis and breathlessness, hiding her ravaged face with more and more cosmetics and an unfailing smile. D'Argenson noted sweetly, 'the bottom of her countenance is yellow and withered; as for her bosom it is kinder not to mention it.' None the less, she continued to work at her patronage like some hard-pressed man of affairs, writing as many as sixty letters a day. The disasters of the Seven Years War hurt her deeply for she was a true patriot—she commented, 'If I die it will be from

grief.' Eventually she found her position almost unbearable. According to her maid, she spent any time alone in tears; in 1763 she complained, 'My life is like that of the early Christians —a perpetual struggle.' She turned to religion—commissioning a Book of Hours illuminated by Boucher—and even considered returning to her husband. By now she was so short of breath that she had to move into a ground-floor flat. The poor woman was worn out, and when she contracted a bad inflammation of the lungs in February 1764 she sensed that her end was near. Louis went to Choisy to stay with her and then brought her back to Versailles, visiting her every day. Despite his soothing care, she grew steadily worse. The King now spent all his time in her room. Eventually they had to say good-bye, when the moment had come for her to receive the last rites. Mme de Pompadour died on 7 April 1764, with a courage which even the Dauphin admired. Louis could not attend her funeral, but watched from his study as the cortège left Versailles. He muttered, 'a friend for twenty years', and two tears fell from his eyes—he said to his servant Champlost, 'Those are the only tributes I can pay her.'

In the autumn of 1765 Horace Walpole, visiting the French court, noticed that the Dauphin was ailing—'He is a spectre and cannot live these three months', he wrote. The poor Dauphin, coughing and spitting blood, had indeed lost all his plumpness and, despite devoted nursing on the part of his wife— every day he told her, 'How I love you!'—died of tuberculosis on 20 December 1765. He was only thirty-four. The King was inconsolable, writing of 'a terrible blow for me', and of how he could have suffered 'no greater loss'. Louis now displayed the better side of his nature. He had liked the Dauphine, Marie Joséphine from the very first; they frequently wrote affectionate letters to each other. He was ready with the kindest and most understanding sympathy—the young widow wrote that in her misery, his kindness had been her only comfort. But in 1767 Mme la Dauphine died too, of tuberculosis.

On 24 June 1768, Queen Marie Leszczynska died; she had long been suffering from a tumour. While she lay dying the King spent more time with her than he had for many years— perhaps even he felt a little guilty. For several weeks after her death he showed the most edifying signs of grief and remorse,

though he also seemed somewhat preoccupied. The princesses, who fancied that he might remarry, suddenly realized with fury that the preoccupation was with a new mistress. At least the Queen was spared the news.

Since Mme de Pompadour's death Louis had been lonely, and there had been several volunteers for the post of *maîtresse en titre*. Some time in 1768—it is not known exactly when—he met the Comtesse du Barry; it is even possible that the King's valet brought her to the 'Bird Trap'. Jeanne Bécu was born in 1743, the illegitimate daughter of a dressmaker; her father seems to have been a friar, Frère Ange. She first came to Paris at the age of five, when her mother found employment as a cook in the house of a rich contractor. This employer was a kindly man who paid for the pretty little girl to be educated at an excellent convent. Leaving school at fifteen, Jeanne was by turn a hairdresser, a companion to an old lady, and a shop girl in a milliner's establishment where her lustrous dark eyes, radiant complexion and splendid bosom attracted both lovers and custom. She was taken up by M Jean Baptiste du Barry, a professional gambler and pimp, who peddled her services to various smart rakes. She lived with him for five years, calling herself Mme du Barry (although his wife was still alive) and meeting many noblemen from whom, despite being illiterate, she managed to acquire surprisingly polished manners. If she never actually worked in a brothel, she was none the less no better than a very high-class prostitute, albeit selective and at the top of her profession.

A singularly beautiful woman, far lovelier than Mme de Pompadour, she was nearly twenty-five when she first met the King. Choiseul privately thought that so low born a creature could only be a passing fancy. However, Jeanne had not been a prostitute for nothing; Louis told M d'Ayen that he was experiencing 'sensual pleasure of an entirely new kind', and M de Richelieu that 'she is the only woman in France who can make me forget I am nearly sixty' (the Duc de Noailles gave it as his opinion that this was because the King had never patronized a really good brothel). To make her respectable, M du Barry—who saw golden possibilities—hastily married her to his bachelor brother, a retired naval officer, who received a large down payment in cash and a magnificent pension before being

sent back to the country. By November 1768 she was living at Compiègne next to Mme de Pompadour's old flat, waited on by footmen in splendid livery; edifyingly, she attended the King's Mass on Sundays and feast days.

Soon she had her own château at Louveciennes, with marble pillars and lapis lazuli chimney pieces, supervised by her Bengali page, Zamor. (Years later Zamor would testify against her when she was being tried for her life.) In April 1769, Mme du Barry made her official entrance to court where, wearing a dress of virginal white, her hair snowily powdered and blazing with diamonds, she was presented to the indignant princesses and the little Dauphin. Although nervous, she carried off the ordeal with some style. The King, with his arm in a sling—he had broken it in a hunting accident—watched admiringly. He was quite enslaved and soon afterwards closed the *Parc aux Cerfs*, no doubt for excellent reasons.

In May 1770 the Dauphin—Louis-Auguste, Duc de Berry—was married at Versailles to an Austrian Archduchess. Louis-Auguste was sixteen, a fat lethargic youth who was irritated at having to miss his hunting on a day of such glorious weather. (Even Mme du Barry called him 'the fat, ill-bred boy'.) The Archduchess Maria Antonia—Marie Antoinette, as the French christened her—was a pink-faced little blonde of fifteen, dressed all in white. Among those who signed the register was the Dauphin's cousin, the Duc de Chartres, who, as 'Philippe Egalité', would vote for Louis-Auguste's execution nearly a quarter of a century later. A violent thunderstorm marred the evening and spoilt the firework display. At the great supper in the Versailles opera house—specially built for the occasion—the Dauphin, enjoying himself for the first time during that long, boring day, fell on the food with his customary voracious appetite. Poor Marie Antoinette merely picked at hers. The King whispered to his grandson, 'You mustn't have too heavy a stomach for tonight.' 'Why not?' answered the Dauphin, 'I always sleep much better after plenty to eat.' Sure enough, almost as soon as he was in the nuptial bed, Louis-Auguste fell into a deep sleep.

There then began a fierce feud between the little Dauphine and la du Barry. When Marie Antoinette first inquired just what was that beautiful lady's function, Mme de Noailles

replied cryptically, 'To make the King enjoy himself.' On learning the exact nature of Mme du Barry's employment, the Dauphine was horrified and refused to address a single word to her; soon the ladies of the court were supporting one side or the other, and fighting like cats. King Louis became irritated. News of his displeasure reached Vienna; the Empress Maria Theresa wrote to her daughter that she really must try to be polite to la du Barry, if only to please the King, and must feign ignorance of any squalid relationship. Finally, after nearly two years of ignoring her, the Dauphine at last acknowledged Mme du Barry's presence at court by saying coldly to her, '*Il y a beaucoup de monde aujourd'hui à Versailles.*' (There are lots of people at Versailles today.) Louis was delighted and sent beautiful gifts to Marie Antoinette. But the feud went on just the same.

Choiseul was silly enough to resent Mme du Barry, joking about her in public. The new favourite, who was very good-natured, did her best to make friends, but to no avail, and she ended by hating him. She then spared no opportunity of making spiteful remarks to him, especially during the King's little supper parties. In December 1770 Louis dismissed him. Horace Walpole wrote, 'Choiseul has lost his power ridiculously, by braving a *fille de joie* to humour two women—his sister and his wife.' In his retirement Choiseul wrote vitriolic memoirs, in which his gibes at the King suggest that there was something a little unstable about the Duke.

Indeed, there was much more to Choiseul's dismissal than the new favourite's hostility. He had all but plunged France into a new war with England by his excessive support of Spain's claim to the Falkland Islands. Nor was he the right man to cope with the Parlements. He was replaced by the *Triumvirat*—the Duc d'Aiguillon, the Chancellor Maupeou and the Controller-General Terray.

Louis's choice of d'Aiguillon is often dismissed as sheer bad judgement. Admittedly the Duke, another courtier soldier, was mediocre. Yet it is probable that the King chose him for sound reasons. D'Aiguillon was the one public figure who was a declared enemy of the Parlements; as Governor of Brittany he had been harried for years by the Parlement of Rennes, while the Parlement of Paris had only recently failed in an attempt to

try him for misgovernment. And unlike Choiseul, he could be relied on not to plunge the country into a war which she could not afford.

By now the Parlementaires had become an obstacle to national government. From obstructing taxes they had gone on to attacking the King's officials. To make their point they frequently refused to allow any legal business to be transacted, thus bringing the courts to a standstill. Even Voltaire recognized that 'this astonishing anarchy could not be allowed to continue. The Crown had to regain its authority or else the Parlement would have triumphed.' After Louis had stopped the proceedings against M d'Aiguillon by a *lit de justice*, they adopted their usual strike tactics. On the night of 19 January 1771, musketeers ordered them to resume their duties; they refused. Next day all 700 magistrates were exiled, after being informed that their offices had been abolished. The Parlements were dissolved all over France.

The Chancellor Maupeou set up new courts. Though these 'Maupeou Parlements' were laughed at, and even though they may have sometimes been corrupt, they were a step in the right direction—a blow against the most formidable obstacles to financial and even political reform.

Now that the Parlements were out of the way it was possible to introduce new taxes. Those envisaged were revolutionary, constituting an attack on wealth and privilege of almost twentieth-century proportions. The bad qualities of the Abbé Joseph Marie Terray—cynicism, avarice and lack of pity— made him an excellent Controller-General. He repudiated many of the government's more questionable financial obligations, delayed repayment of loans, reduced the income from *rentes*, converted *tontines* into life annuities, and abolished a number of court pensions and reduced others. He introduced a swingeing five per cent tax on real property as well as on income, and planned to bring in an entirely new system of taxation. He set up a board to control the grain trade, taxing it but also regulating it to meet supply and demand. To every complaint, Terray —known as the Vulture—answered, 'The King is master and necessity knows no laws.' At the same time he did his best to persuade his master to economize on the royal household.

The work of the *Triumvirat*, who governed France for the

rest of the reign, has some pretensions to be considered as a revolution. It has not received proper recognition because it came to an end prematurely; had it lasted, the Crown might well have succeeded in enforcing radical economies and political reforms in the teeth of the nobility's counter-revolution. The *coup d'état* of 1770 against the Parlementaires needed real courage, as did Terray's reforms. It is to Louis's credit that for the remainder of his life he gave these strong ministers unqualified support.

No doubt France was in decline, but the decline was not apparent to contemporaries. She was still the richest, most populous country in Europe. French had consolidated its position as the universal language; in the Holy Roman Empire rulers and nobility alike spoke it in preference to their native German. Copies of Versailles continued to be built by kings and princes throughout the Western world. And, to give some substance to the illusion, France went on making remarkable economic and industrial progress until the late 1770s.

Louis was sixty-four in 1774, still the handsomest man at court. Michelet paints a compelling picture of these last years. 'The god of flesh abdicated every vestige of mind. Avoiding Paris, shunning his people, ever shut up at Versailles, he finds even there too many people, too much daylight. He wants a shadowy retreat, the wood, the chase, the secret lodge of the Trianon.' By now he was thoroughly unpopular, 'Louis the well-hated' as the Parisians sang. Yet Mme du Barry was making him surprisingly happy. It was a very intimate relationship. Despite a brilliant superficial polish, the Countess retained some of the inelegant ways of her youth. Once, when Louis was preparing breakfast at the Trianon, she told him, 'France, you're making a muck of the coffee.'

However, during Lent they were badly frightened by a sermon which closed with the words, 'Forty days more and Nineveh will be destroyed.' At the end of April, after spending the night with Mme du Barry at the Petit Trianon, the King woke up feeling feverish, but hunted as usual. The next night he felt ill again and was taken back to Versailles. Then he developed a rash. Mirrors were kept from him but he was suspicious, complaining to the doctors, 'You tell me I'm not

ill and will soon be well again, but you don't believe a word of it—you should tell me the truth.' In fact the doctors thought he had already had smallpox and was immune; they were mistaken. Meanwhile his daughters and Mme du Barry nursed him devotedly—the former by day, the latter by night. At last he saw the spots on his hands and asked for a mirror. 'This is smallpox,' he gasped; 'at my age one doesn't recover!' Next day he sent Mme du Barry away—'Had I known earlier, you would not have entered the room. Now I must arrange matters with God.' He wept when he learnt she had gone—'so soon?' On 7 May he confessed, received Communion, and then asked the Grand Almoner to tell his gentlemen that he begged their forgiveness, and that of his people, for any scandal he might have given. His face was black and swollen, his body suppurating with sores and stinking; he told Adelaide that he felt neither happier nor calmer. The Prince de Croÿ writes, 'During his illness Louis XV has shown a courage both heroic and simple, gentle and unassuming.' Croÿ was a truthful man, yet the 'Enlightened' Duc de La Rochefoucauld-Liancourt tells us that the King lay dying 'in inconceivable fear and pusillanimity'. Louis died painfully at three o'clock on the afternoon of 10 May 1774.

Suddenly 'a terrible noise, just like thunder' was heard in the ante-chamber where the Dauphin and Marie Antoinette were praying. It was the court running to acclaim their new sovereign. Meanwhile the late King's body was in such a state of putrescence that his doctors dared not embalm him. He was therefore sealed in a lead coffin filled with quicklime and camphorated spirit, and taken by night to Saint-Denis. (So horrible were the rotting remains that one of the workmen paid to place them in their box is said to have died from uncontrollable vomiting.) As the cortège passed by, lit by flaring torches, the crowd jeered and cried, 'Tally-ho!' in mockery of Louis's well-known holloa; others shouted, 'There goes the ladies' pleasure.' In the words of Michelet, 'That dead man was Old France, and that bier the coffin of the Old Monarchy.'

With his secrecy, his Shakespearean gloom and indecision, and his passion for elegant pleasures, Louis is very hard to

assess—both as a man and a ruler. Carlyle's sneers and the late C P Gooch's subtler condemnation are fairly wide of the mark, but so too are the attempts at rehabilitation by right-wing French writers like Pierre Gaxotte. Louis was undoubtedly weak and apathetic; he was also shrewd and determined in the successful defence of his authority. On her deathbed Mme de Pompadour admitted that she found his personality *indéchiffrable* (indecipherable), and she had known and loved him for twenty years. In the end, Louis XV remains an enigma.

'The Suicide of France'

LOUIS XVI (1774–1793)

'I should like to be known as "Louis the Serious" '

The children of Louis XVI

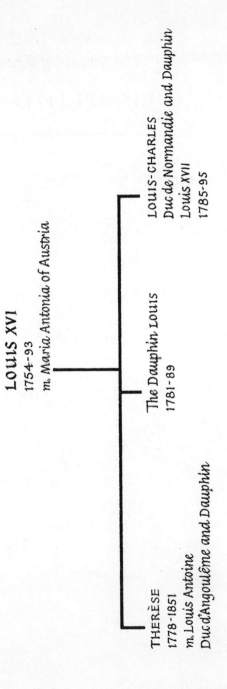

LOUIS XVI
1754-93
m. Maria Antonia of Austria

THERÈSE
1778-1851
m. Louis Antoine
Duc d'Angoulême and Dauphin

The Dauphin LOUIS
1781-89

LOUIS-CHARLES
Duc de Normandie and Dauphin
Louis XVII
1785-95

No king has been more unfortunate than Louis XVI. Yet had he reigned happily and prosperously, he would probably have been regarded as the dullest and most commonplace monarch in all French history. As it was, his tragic destiny showed him to be in some ways one of the noblest, if not one of the wisest, men who has ever tried to rule France.

Louis's personality is inextricably involved with the French Revolution. As it approaches, there is a steadily increasing note of drama in his story; at the end, the constantly changing attitude of his subjects towards him is terrifying. Unfortunately, in a book of this size one can only offer a brief and superficial account of the Revolution. Perhaps this is not altogether a handicap, for Louis as a human being is so often lost sight of amid the cataclysm; most studies concentrate on the perplexed, doomed ruler of 1789–93 and tend to neglect the odd young King of the 1770s and 1780s.

Louis XVI was born at Versailles on 27 August 1754, the third son of the Dauphin Louis and Marie Joséphine of Saxony, christened Louis-Auguste and created Duc de Berry. His childhood was no less overshadowed by death than that of Louis XV. His eldest brother, the Duc d'Aquitaine, died long before Louis-Auguste was born and the second, the Duc de Bourgogne, died in 1761; his father died in 1765 and his mother in 1768; by the time he was fourteen he was an orphan. Unfortunately, unlike his grandfather, there was no Mme de Ventadour to take the place of his mother, while the old King although fond of him —Louis-Auguste called him 'Papa Roi'—seems to have kept his distance.

His earliest memories were of his precociously brilliant elder

brother boasting how he would conquer England, and then dying painfully at ten of lymphatic glanditis—scrofula, the King's Evil itself. Louis-Auguste himself fell ill with the same tuberculosis at the age of seven, and, like Henri IV, was sent to the country where he acquired his iron health. His governor was M de Vauguyon, a pedantic Breton Duke whose piety had impressed his father; Louis-Auguste was rather frightened of him. The boy was oddly inarticulate and unselfconfident. His younger brothers, the sly and clever Provence and the handsome, lively Artois, made him feel inferior; he once said 'I love no one because no one loves me'. His usual companions were grooms and stable-boys. His aunts felt sorry for the lonely, gloomy child, particularly Adelaide who used to say, 'My poor Berry, you must make yourself at home with me—make a noise, shout, break things—but do something!'

Vauguyon instilled an almost excessive piety into him. Louis-Auguste was good at his Latin, learnt to speak German, and memorized much history even if he had small power of analysing it. Geography was the chief joy of his studies—he drew maps to perfection. He also read English with surprising ease, especially English history. With his tutor's help he translated Walpole's essay on Richard III. The Civil War fascinated him—he said that had he been Charles I he would never have made war on his people. When he was ten Louis-Auguste wrote a book of reflections on his conversations with his tutor. There is a pathetic and revealing entry; 'My greatest fault is my sluggishness of mind which makes all mental effort tiresome and painful for me; I am determined to overcome this fault . . . ' He was terrified when his father died; not only was he deeply upset but he dreaded his future responsibilities. In the two years left to her, his mother did her best to give him some confidence. A lady asked the earnest boy by what name he would like to go down to history: 'I should like to be known as "Louis the Serious" ,' was the touching reply.

The new Dauphin had his own printing press and produced a small book of Fénélon's political and moral maxims, much to Louis XV's irritation—he found the selection dangerously liberal and ordered his grandson to stop printing. However, Louis-Auguste had other pleasures—he was good with all tools and particularly interested in locks and machinery. Predictably,

he loved hunting and was a crack shot, shooting until his face was black with powder.

When he married Marie Antoinette, the Dauphin was a fat, clumsy youth—he had a pot belly by the time he was twenty—whose countenance, according to the Austrian ambassador, gave promise of 'only a very limited intelligence, little comeliness and no sensitivity'. The Neapolitan Ambassador thought he 'looked as if he had been brought up in the woods'. He could not dance, in an age when social accomplishments were everything. But Louis-Auguste's appearance was deceptive. When, during his wedding celebrations, a stampede caused by exploding fireworks killed hundreds in the Place Louis XV (now the Place de la Concorde) he sent his entire monthly allowance to the Lieutenant of Police, writing to the Lieutenant: 'I have learnt of the misfortune which happened in Paris because of me and am deeply distressed. I have just received the sum which the King gives me each month for personal expenses; I have nothing else but send it to you. Help those most in need. I have, Monsieur, much esteem for you.'

Indeed, in some ways the new monarch was a caricature of those much lamented paragons, his father the Dauphin and his great-grandfather the Duc de Bourgogne; he was certainly like them in being fat, pious and lethargic; and there was even a closer resemblance to that prototype of all fat Bourbons, the Grand Dauphin. Yet underneath the slack podgy face, the bone structure was surprisingly handsome; it appears in the profile on some early portrait medallions and in occasional drawings. The nose was unmistakably the great eagle's beak of the Bourbons, the short-sighted eyes—he used a lorgnette—large, mournful and kindly. He had an unusually pleasing voice. Eventually, despite obesity and shyness, contemporaries would recognize a most regal dignity in Louis XVI. If he thought slowly and was slow to make up his mind, he was none the less intelligent enough in his own way, but he did not care to talk about his interests. His worst fault was that terrible lack of self-confidence.

He was unfortunate in not having a wife who understood him, as Marie Joséphine had understood his father. At his wedding his grandfather had commented, characteristically, 'Marriages are never happy, but occasionally they are pleasant; let us hope that this one will be so.' Maria Antonia—Marie Antoinette—

was one year younger than her husband and they had not a single taste in common. Despite the influence of that wonderful and delightful woman, her mother the Empress Maria Theresa, she had grown up shallow and superficial; a French tutor said that trying to teach her was almost impossible—'she could only apply herself to what amused her.' She was essentially Germanic (even though French was her first language and her father had once been Duke of Lorraine) possessing all the German vices and virtues, and being a bouncing, sentimental girl, who rode astride, noisy and aggressive, very like the heroine of a Mozart opera or a Viennese operetta. (As a child she had played harpsichord duets with Mozart.) An ash-blonde, 'a head taller than all her ladies', she had a high, slightly bulging forehead, the jutting, unsightly Habsburg lower lip, and big blue eyes. None the less, it was generally conceded that Marie Antoinette, if not exactly pretty, was sublimely attractive. Her complexion was exquisite, her skin translucent. Not only was she elegant in her every movement, but she had a noble, queenly air; a man who knew her said, 'One would have offered her a throne without thinking, in the way one would offer any other woman a chair.' At first the French adored her but, quite soon after Louis's accession, the mood changed and many began to hate her. She was a kindly, warm-hearted person, cheerful and impetuous, but she was also tactless and arrogant. It may well have been her Germanic qualities which awoke aversion among Frenchmen.

The new Queen's character must have suffered from her physical relations—or the lack of them—with her husband. It is generally accepted that Louis suffered from phimosis—an irretractable foreskin—which made it impossible for him to accomplish the sexual act. He was so shy that it is likely that his wife attributed his lack of desire to sheer disinclination. To some extent she took refuge in pornography, reading erotic novels.

Every mistake which the poor girl made was immediately reported to Vienna by the Imperial ambassador, Count Florimond de Mercy. This suave and cynical Lorrainer wrote with gloomy relish, but he was not a liar, as has recently been suggested. Both Maria Theresa and Joseph II were far too discerning to retain a dishonest ambassador for twenty years in the world's most important capital.

At first the new King and his Queen were wildly popular. He

Louis XVI, by Duplessis

Marie Antoinette and her children, by Mme Vigée-Lebrun

declared solemnly, 'I want to be loved.' He announced that he would forgo his *joyeux avènement*, a heavy tax which each monarch traditionally levied on his accession; similarly, Marie Antoinette relinquished her *Ceinture de Reine*—the 'Queen's Girdle' tax which in times past had always accompanied the 'joyful event'. She wrote to her mother how much she was touched by the demonstrative affection of the people in the streets. Porcelain medallions were made at Sèvres, bearing the optimistic legend *Louis le Populaire*. In June 1775 Louis was crowned and anointed at Rheims Cathedral by the Archbishop-Duke, who was assisted by nine archbishops and twenty other prelates. The service was so moving that Marie Antoinette was reduced to tears. But when the crown was placed reverently on his head the King complained that it hurt him—not a good omen. Next day he pardoned all the inmates of Rheims prison, after first touching for the Evil. Yet, despite his deep religious faith, Louis lacked the confidence of his grandfather in his authority, in his Divine Right.

Louis's next step was even more popular than his relinquishment of the *joyeux avènement*. He recalled the aged Maurepas and sacked the *Triumvirat*. Maurepas was on the list of reliable men bequeathed to him by his father the Dauphin, and was furthermore recommended by Mme Adelaide as not being a Jansenist (like the far more capable Machault); the young King felt safe with old men. Maurepas, seventy-three years old but still vain and foppish, was intoxicated by the prospect of returning to Versailles and power, and his sole aim was to win applause. Accordingly, he supported Maupeou's replacement as Chancellor by Miromesnil, who ended the Maupeou courts and brought back the Parlements.

The King was none the less determined to be a reformer. He never forgot the advice given to him by his father on his death-bed. The Dauphin had told the clumsy, terrified boy that two strong reigns in succession were necessary, 'one to root out the evils and the next to prevent their recurrence'. In fact, this fat, slow, gentle creature, infinitely well-intentioned, never had the slightest chance of success. Looking back, Barnave (a prominent figure during the Revolution) said that even in 1774 the Crown's only hope of survival had been to become either a constitutional monarchy or else a military dictatorship. Louis possessed neither

the imagination nor the character to bring about the former, while he was hardly equipped to be a French Frederick the Great.

None the less, Louis did his best. To the delight of the intellectuals, he appointed as Controller-General the Baron Turgot de l'Aulne, a brilliant but charmless *Philosophe* in his forties, whose views were well known from his writings. He was a former *Intendant* of Limoges where his land register and new system of tax assessment—and tax collection—had made him thoroughly unpopular. The King nursed great hopes of this paragon. Maurepas had slyly filled Louis with horror at Terray's exactions, implying that M Turgot would dispell the people's discontent. Turgot himself possessed no such illusions; he wrote to the King, whom he naively cast in the rôle of Enlightened Despot, 'I shall be feared and hated by most of the court and by everyone who sells or seeks for pensions.' The new Controller-General was a difficult man, ill equipped to please. He announced that he intended to economize on expenditure, to do without borrowing more money. A French precursor of Adam Smith and Free Trade, who believed in a 'natural wage scale' and *laisser faire*, Turgot at once abandoned Terray's policy of attempting to regulate the grain and wine trades, abolishing many internal customs dues. He began to cut the tax-farmers' profits and investigated ways of making the fiscal system reasonably efficient. He even managed to persuade Louis to slash pensions. All these new measures were explained to the people during Mass on Sundays in every parish church in France. Unfortunately most courtiers were not interested in reform—they depended on pensions for their own expensive existence.

A much more popular new minister was Charles Gravier, Comte de Vergennes, whom Louis put in charge of foreign affairs. In his mid-fifties, Vergennes was an experienced diplomat, a former ambassador to Sweden and Turkey, and very unlike Turgot—beautifully dressed, impassive-faced and with all the amiable and excessively reassuring manners of his kind. Like Choiseul before him, he hated England, but unlike Choiseul he also had little love for Austria. However, like the King, Vergennes loathed the idea of war and always hoped for peace, though his judgement was erratic. The future President of the

United States of America, Mr Thomas Jefferson, when US ambassador to France, considered M de Vergennes a stimulating person 'to do business with', but incapable of understanding American institutions. 'It is impossible to have a clearer, better organized head, but age has chilled his heart.'

Perhaps the most interesting appointment was Malesherbes, also in his fifties, who was made minister in charge of the royal household, much to the Queen's irritation. This amiable and distinguished Parlementaire was a former President of the *Cour des Aides* who had defended the Parlement against Louis XV; he was also a celebrated liberal and friend to the *Philosophes*, the man whose tolerance as official censor had made possible the publication of the *Encyclopédie*. He was a character of Johnsonian proportions; a jolly, untidy figure in an old, snuff-stained brown suit, his wig askew, perpetually sucking a pipe and gesturing with a thick stick, whose hobbies were literature and botany. A keen reformer, Malesherbes would have liked France to have been given a constitution on the English model, although—as he would one day prove with his life—he was a most faithful servant of the Crown. His popularity made him a valuable ally for Turgot.

Within a year, largely through sacking useless officials, the Controller-General had reduced government expenditure by 66,200,000 livres (well over two and a half million pounds in contemporary English money). Unfortunately, his abandonment of controls on the grain trade sent wheat prices soaring and there were bread riots, even in Paris, popularly known as 'The Flour War'. As he had predicted, he outraged the privileged classes, including the clergy, and the party of religion at court soon turned the Queen against him; she did her best to discredit the Controller-General with the King. None the less, Turgot clung grimly to office, and Louis continued to support him, though more and more doubtfully. In 1776 the Controller-General introduced his famous Six Edicts—his programme for reform. The opposition took particular exception to the proposed abolition of the *corvée* (the peasants' duty work on the roads) and its replacement by a road tax on local landowners. Louis, rather surprisingly, forced the Parlement to register the edicts with the *lit de justice*.

But by now Marie Antoinette was really angry. Turgot had

insisted on recalling one of her protégés from London—the Duc de Guisnes (of Mozart's *Guisnes Concerto*)—where he was ambassador, on the grounds of incompetence. Turgot's position was weakened still further when Malesherbes resigned. He then terrified the King with a scheme for a national assembly, following it with an extraordinarily tactless letter—'Never forget Sire, that weakness put Charles I's head on the block.' He was dismissed in May 1776, after being Controller-General for only twenty months. Many historians believe that Turgot's dismissal marked the final doom of the old monarchy.

Louis, in his dealings with Turgot, had eventually shown all his own worst qualities—a fear of unpopularity, and a slowness of thought which invariably grew into irresolution. Added to this was his pathological terror of being dominated by any one minister. Yet the King was thoroughly honest and kind-hearted, and still hoped to make his people love him by good government. In the twentieth century he would have been an excellent constitutional monarch.

None the less, whatever his vices or virtues, Louis XVI was undeniably an oddity. He indulged in orgies of gluttony, frequently preparing the meals himself and then gorging and swilling until he was carried almost insensible to his bed, emitting *'un bruit très suspect'*. Certain disloyal courtiers called him 'the fat pig', while the naturalist Buffon, who saw him dining with his accustomed enthusiasm, was put in mind of a big monkey feeding at the zoo. One of the royal breakfasts consisted of four chops, a plump chicken, a thick slice of ham and six baked eggs, washed down by a bottle and a half of champagne; the same day he ate a gargantuan dinner. Indeed, the Austrian ambassador reported that the King's return from hunting was followed by meals so enormous 'that they deprive him of reason'. Plump even as a youth, he became inordinately fat (though in part this may have been due to glandular trouble.) Probably because of his hunting, his health did not suffer, apart from the occasional hangover, and he was famous for his strength; he could pick up a page standing on a heavy shovel and carry him round the room. The worst effects of the monarch's gorging were his primitive humour (consisting of the simplest practical jokes), a tendency to foul language and an almost Bohemian slovenliness; the Swedish King, the elegant Gustav III, was received by Louis

with hair uncombed and wearing a dressing-gown and odd shoes. It is only fair to add that he fasted rigorously throughout Lent.

Like so many of his dynasty, Louis XVI was never so happy as when working with tools. He enjoyed making clocks and locks; a smithy with two forges was attached to his library and a locksmith was in permanent attendance; he made a metal table which he gave to Vergennes. Mme de Campans says that the King's hands were often filthy—on at least one occasion the Queen screamed at him for being so dirty (though he took daily baths). He had a telescope room at Versailles, equipped with the most modern instruments through which he scanned his visitors, together with model warships and even small James Watt steam engines. Masonry was another relaxation and he built several walls with his own hands. Nor did he disdain chopping wood. Sometimes he was almost frivolous, indulging in backgammon or going to the play—Molière was a particular favourite.

However, unlike almost all Bourbons, Louis XVI had small interest in patronizing the arts. Nor was he a builder. He was equally untypical in his intellectual curiosity. His library was filled with works in Latin, German and English (he began a translation of Gibbon's *Decline and Fall of the Roman Empire*, which was later incorporated by Guizot into his own translation). He read Shakespeare, Fielding and Defoe—notably *Robinson Crusoe*—and glanced at most of the leading European newspapers and the English *Annual Register*—he was acquainted with all the more famous debates in the English Parliament. The King also owned many books on travel, science and geography and, in particular, history—especially naval and English. In fact he was very much a man of the Enlightenment. Unfortunately, he far preferred reading in his library to government business.

No wife could have been less suited to him than Queen Marie Antoinette. She had no intellectual interests whatsoever and her taste was inferior even to that of Mme du Barry (who had been sent to a convent for a dreadful, but mercifully brief, period of penance). Apart from ordering some good furniture from Riesener and Jacob, the Queen's one essay in patronage was to make Paris learn to like the music of her old music-master, Gluck—and his *Iphigénie* in particular. Her chief joys were

having her hair fantastically styled by her beloved coiffeur, Léonard, ordering extravagant if deceptively simple clothes from the great dressmaker Rose Bertin, and playing at being a dairymaid at her 'hamlet' next to the Petit Trianon (known as her 'Little Vienna'), where she kept cows and goats with ribbons round their necks, milking them daily. She was also a compulsive gambler, playing all night and every night. Desperately frustrated, she found a certain relief in emotional friendships with young favourites like the delightful Princesse de Lamballe, a honey-blonde widow of eighteen, whom Mme de Campan described as 'looking like spring peeping out from beneath sable and ermine'; and the beautiful but greedy Comtesse de Polignac, with whom Marie Antoinette was eternally arm-in-arm, and whose relations all sponged on her. There were undoubtedly sapphic undertones to these friendships. Soon the Queen's allowance had to be doubled—partly because of vast sums lost at the gaming table or spent on diamonds, partly for pensions for her friends.

Marie Antoinette also flirted much too much, with men like the middle-aged roué, Baron de Besenval, who commanded the Swiss Guards, and the impertinent but amusing Duc de Lauzun, whom eventually she had to snub. Her profligate young brother-in-law, Charles of Artois, presided over her gay supper parties at the Petit Trianon and took her racing; there were rumours that Artois was her lover, and he was undoubtedly too familiar—he was actually seen to pinch her. (Their friendship cooled after her children were born, an indication that it was innocent, if indiscreet.) There were also rumours that she slept with the Duc de Coigny, the Swedish Count Fersen (Colonel of the Royal Swedish Regiment) and the Franco-Irishman, Count Édouard Dillon; these slanders were largely circulated by the Duc de Chartres (later Orléans) who bragged vilely that he had had to rebuff the Queen's advances. Then there were stories that her bedroom was hung with diamond-studded tapestries, lit by a thousand candles, and had a bed with black satin sheets. Indeed, the poor woman was accused in countless filthy pamphlets of every known vice, including both Lesbian revels and Messalina-like orgies.

Within a few years Marie Antoinette was detested by almost all sections of society, who referred to her as 'The Austrian' and

expressed deep pity for the King. She had made herself thoroughly unpopular with the nobility by her rudeness, her breezy simplifying of etiquette, and her favouritism and preju-dice—throughout the reign she attacked her husband's ministers for the most frivolous reasons. Nor did her jokes about Louis, whom she spoke of as 'that poor fellow', endear her; referring to his blacksmith's forge, she once wrote that she had no desire 'to play Venus to his Vulcan'. The alarmed Austrian ambassador reported to Vienna as early as 1776 that, 'Each day fewer and fewer people come to Versailles and the situation will go from bad to worse if the Queen cannot make up her mind to conduct her court in a more sober and orderly fashion.' Maria Theresa sent dreadful letters to her daughter. The Empress told 'Madame my dear daughter' that she was behaving like a Pompadour or a du Barry rather than a Queen, and that the news of her amusements and ridiculously affected hair-styles— 'like an actress'—made her mother tremble. Marie Antoinette's lack of respect for the King was shocking. Furthermore, 'It is rumoured that you do not pay your country's noblemen the respect due to them and don't even talk to them, but chatter instead with your young ladies and play all sorts of silly games.'

In 1777 the Queen's brother, the Emperor Joseph II—a Viennese of the dour sort—visited France incognito to see just how bad things were. His considered view of his brother-in-law after meeting him was that Louis was 'a little weak but no fool', though curiously apathetic in mind and body. As for his sister, whom he reduced to tears, Joseph wrote grimly that she thought only of her pleasures and 'fulfills neither the duties of a wife or a Queen'. It was all to no avail, and Marie Antoinette remained one of the monarchy's greatest liabilities.

Nor were the rest of the Royal Family exactly an asset. Even *Mesdames Tantes'* were unpopular because of their bigotry. Horace Walpole saw them, and was as catty as only his sort of Englishman can be: 'The Four Mesdames, who are clumsy, plump old wenches with a bad likeness to their father, stand in a bedchamber in a row, with black cloaks and knitting bags, looking good humoured, not knowing what to say, and wriggling as if they wanted to make water.'

Monsieur (Provence) was sensible enough, but he was unattractive in appearance and had an icily cold manner. Artois

was worst of all, disastrously fond of wine, women and song, and gambling too—his debts were astronomical, twenty-one million livres by 1781, much to the fury of the taxpayers. Strikingly handsome, charming when he felt like it, he was often drunk and violently rude. One of his boon companions was the awful Chartres.

Philippe, Duc d'Orléans (known as Duc de Chartres until he became Orléans on his father's death in 1785) was considered a member of the Royal Family, though privately he saw himself as head of a rival dynasty, rather than a junior Prince of the Blood. Like so many of his line, the Duke was a byword for debauchery. Although smaller and older—he had been born in 1747—and beautifully dressed, he resembled King Louis in appearance, but his face was blotched purple from hard drinking and ravaged by the pox. He led a life of the utmost futility, drinking, whoring and gambling, proud of his skill at card tricks and throwing dice—on one occasion he is said to have offered to run stark naked through Paris for a bet. Like some of Balzac's villains, Orléans combined avarice with debauchery. When his losses at the gaming-table grew out of hand, he more than recouped them by building three arcades of shops round the gardens of the Palais Royal, which he turned into a public pleasure park; the arcades were soon filled with cafés, restaurants, hairdressers and jewellers' shops, and also casinos and smart brothels. He was already enormously rich, and the venture made him King of Paris, with the Palais Royal for his Versailles. The debauched little Duke hated his cousins, but was too ineffectual to do them much damage.

In 1776 Jacques Necker, a brilliant Swiss banker and writer on economics, was appointed 'Director of Finances'. (In practice he was Controller-General in everything but name, but it was considered unfitting that so prestigious a title should be given to a foreigner and Protestant.) A self-made man who had bought a French title, Necker was a plump, pot-bellied, yellow-faced bourgeois with awkward, oily manners, but extremely vain and socially ambitious. Through his wife's somewhat louche salon and his promiscuous blue-stocking daughter (the future Mme de Staël), he had made many useful friends whom he had no wish to upset by introducing new taxes. Although as a *Philosophe* Necker introduced a number of minor reforms—he

abolished 2,000 minor court posts—he was hardly another Turgot. In any case, the country's finances were soon completely out of control because of French intervention in the American Revolution; as Turgot had predicted, France was ruined from the moment the first shot was fired. Without war, Necker might have preserved some semblance of solvency—as it was, faced by impossible demands for money, all he did was borrow long-term loans at ruinous interest and then produce a reassuring booklet on the national finances, the *Compte rendu au Roi*; in fact, the *Compte rendu* was a massive cooking of the books.

From the very beginning, the French had shown remarkable sympathy for the Americans in their Revolution. No doubt some of this enthusiasm was a legacy from the Seven Years War, a determination to be revenged for the humiliations which England had inflicted on France. However, Frenchmen of the period undoubtedly felt genuine admiration for the colonists. Lord Stormont, the English ambassador, reported sardonically of the Parisians that, 'Our Wits, Philosophers and Coffee House Politicians . . . are all to a Man warm Americans, affecting to consider them as a brave People struggling for its Natural Rights and endeavouring to rescue those Rights out of the Hands of violent and wanton Oppression.' Indeed, the Declaration of Independence reflected all the most hallowed ideals of the French Enlightenment, and there was a popular clamour to join in and help these colonial heroes against the traditional enemy.

One person who definitely did not want war was the King. Although he understood little about finance, he must have shuddered at Turgot's warning. Louis hated bloodshed, and had small inclination to encourage rebellion against a fellow monarch; if he ever read it, he would certainly have agreed with a contemporary English pamphlet which cautioned him that the same spirit which had begun the American Revolution might well be preparing a revolution in France. However, the Americans were brilliantly successful in fanning the enthusiasm which so many Frenchmen felt for their cause; their ambassador, Benjamin Franklin, with his quaint (and carefully contrived) charm and his reputation as a scientist and man of letters, conquered both Versailles and Paris; he was popularly known as *l'ambassadeur électrique*. Only Louis disliked him. In addition, the

Americans had the writer Pierre Caron de Beaumarchais on their side; the future author of *Le Mariage de Figaro* pestered Vergennes ceaselessly. Eventually that cautious diplomat, too clever by half, was persuaded that an American victory would win back for France and Spain everything which they had lost during the Seven Years War. Maurepas and most of the other ministers agreed with him. Louis, always irresolute, gave way reluctantly; many years afterwards he told M de Molleville, his naval secretary, 'I never think of the American affair without regret—I was young then and advantage was taken of my youth, but now we have to suffer the consequences.'

Vergennes led the King by easy steps. First he obtained his permission to send a secret agent to Philadelphia, the pleasantly named Chevalier de Bonvouloir, to make contact with the revolutionary government. He then persuaded Louis to supply the rebels secretly with money, arms and uniforms, avoiding open war. The English raged but the French government blandly insisted that if any French supplies were reaching the colonists, it could only be the work of smugglers. The aid amounted to millions of pounds. In February 1778 France recognized the United States, signing a treaty of friendship and commerce, together with a secret treaty of military alliance. England at once declared war on France. Next year Spain joined in, on the side of France.

Many French volunteers had been fighting in America before 8,000 royal troops, including the Marquis de Lafayette, a red-haired, chinless wonder of nineteen, landed in 1780 to save the Revolution. Louis followed their campaigns with the keenest enthusiasm, poring over maps. At sea, Choiseul's new navy proved its worth under men like Estaing and Rochambeau, destroying the legend that Britannia rules the waves. The Comte de Grasse prevented reinforcements reaching General Cornwallis at Yorktown, forcing him to surrender with 7,000 men, a feat which made ultimate American victory certain, while the fat old Bailli de Suffren (who had learnt his seamanship with the Knights of Malta) terrorized the English navy in the Indian Ocean, winning four shattering victories in 1782 alone. Nearer home, the Duc de Crillon captured Minorca again, though the English just managed to hold Gibraltar against a furiously determined siege by the French and the Spaniards. However, a

massive invasion of England had to be called off because the crews were found to be scurvy-ridden.

Throughout the war, Necker, horrified at the expense, had been trying to make peace behind Vergennes's back, but George III's government refused to do so until France stopped helping the rebels. Most ungratefully, the Americans cynically concluded a separate peace with the English at the end of 1782, obtaining complete independence. None the less, the Treaty of Versailles which France signed with England on 3 September 1783 was ample revenge for the Seven Years War. In the West Indies she regained St Lucia and Tobago, in India most of her trading posts (including Pondicherry), and in Africa Senegal, besides many valuable trading concessions. England was humiliated, losing colonies of far greater worth than any which had been taken from France after the previous war. It was the last great triumph of the French monarchy.

France's prestige, at its highest for many years, was reflected in diplomacy during the remainder of the 1780s. Already she had prevented war breaking out between Prussia and Austria over Bavaria (in 1779) by tactful mediation. By subsidizing Gustav III, she was able to use Sweden as an instrument for exercising at least some small restraint on Prussian ambitions. In 1786 France signed a commercial treaty with England which lowered tariff walls, while the following year a treaty with Russia opened up hitherto unknown areas of trade. Culturally, the entire Western world was still in thrall to Francomania.

At home, Ernest Semichon claims that during Louis XVI's reign 'nearly every political, religious and judicial problem was investigated and in many cases solved'. If exaggerated, this claim is still not entirely without substance. Even Tocqueville admits that, 'During his entire reign Louis XVI was always talking about reform, and there were few institutions whose destruction he did not contemplate before the Revolution broke out and made an end of them.' He tried to improve conditions in prisons and hospitals, and ordered free treatment for sufferers from venereal disease. He abolished the death penalty for desertion. It was the King, not Necker, who was responsible for abolishing the 'Preparatory Question' (torture by water or the boot to extract a confession after arrest) in 1780, but the Parlements prevented him from abolishing torture before execution.

Louis also put an end to serfdom on Crown lands, though it was retained on the estates of the clergy and nobility. As will be seen, he envisaged legal reforms which would have swept away the Parlements.

New canals were dug between the greatest French rivers, while the naval harbour at Cherbourg was protected by an impressive sea wall. A Royal Society of Medicine was founded, together with a Veterinary College and a School of Mines, and the Academy of Sciences was expanded to include agriculture, biology, mechanical sciences and mineralogy. An institution for deaf mutes was established and also an institution for the blind. The world of European science was dominated by such Frenchmen as Lavoisier—'the father of modern chemistry'—and the agriculturalist Parmentier, who, with the King's encouragement, popularized the potato. Most dramatic of all, the brothers Montgolfier were making their first ascents in hot air balloons. It was not only for reasons of sycophancy that statues of Louis were erected all over the country with inscriptions like 'Servitude abolished', 'The Navy restored', and 'Commerce protected'. If it had not been for 'the unfortunate reality of the deficit', as he described the monetary crisis, Louis XVI might have bumbled happily on for the rest of his natural life.

It was a bad time for anyone to be poor. About 1778 France entered into a long depression, both agricultural and industrial. The rural economy, which was in any case backward enough, was severely damaged by a steep decline in grain prices and an even more catastrophic drop in the price of wine; as a result peasants could not make a living from their produce. The repercussions affected the hitherto advancing economy of the towns, where production fell disastrously in such industries as the cloth trade, and many workers were laid off. There was poverty and unemployment throughout the entire country, in painful contrast to the comparative affluence of Louis XV's reign. All classes found themselves short of money. Unfortunately, the recession coincided with a crisis in the national finances.

Tocqueville was perfectly correct in claiming that 'France was ruined before she ceased to be victorious'. It has been calculated that the American War may have cost the French government as much as 2,000,000,000 livres (well over £80 million). When Necker was dismissed in 1781, he had only avoided state bank-

ruptcy by massive borrowing, and during his last year of office, the annual deficit—the gap between revenue and expenditure— was at least 50 million livres (more than £2 million), quite apart from the hundreds of million livres of national debt. But the wily banker had concealed the full horror of the situation by his *Compte rendu*.

Necker was dismissed largely because old Maurepas had grown jealous of him, and had made the aristocratic party fearful of the half-hearted reforms which the Director of Finances had been trying to introduce. The opposition was led by the Duc d'Orléans, his son Chartres, Monsieur (the Comte de Provence) and the Comte Artois; characteristically, the latter called Necker 'a fornicating foreign bastard'. As soon as the Director had gone, a number of reactionary measures were brought in— four proofs of nobility (ie to show that all four grandparents had been noble) now became necessary for any candidate for a commission in the army. None the less, Louis insisted that bourgeois sailors should have the chance of becoming naval officers.

Despite Louis's good intentions, to survive a minister had to keep both the Queen and all the Princes on his side. Maurepas (who died at the end of 1781) understood this very well and would go to almost any lengths to ensure their support. During Marie Antoinette's first pregnancy, when she was unable to go to a ball and a torchlight charade was staged by the court to divert her, the venerable and all but octogenarian minister— who had been famed even as a young man for his impotence— appeared in pink silk as Cupid.

For Louis, the 1780s were probably the happiest years of his life. In 1777 he had at last consented to the very minor operation which made it possible for him to have normal relations with his wife. On 30 August of that year, Marie Antoinette wrote to her mother, 'I am so deeply happy . . . my marriage was perfectly consummated a week ago.' (The tone of her letter indicates that much of her objectional behaviour hitherto may well have been due to frustration.) Ingenuously, the King told *Mesdames Tantes* that the physical pleasure was even greater than he had anticipated. Nevertheless, he still did not sleep with the Queen as much as she would have liked, despite her 'tormenting him to come more often', and Maria Theresa remained sceptical

about any hopes of a pregnancy. However, in December 1778 Marie Antoinette at last gave birth to a child, the Princess Marie Thérèse—Madame Royale. (This grave little girl was later known as *Mousseline la sérieuse*, on account of her old-fashioned expression.)

Louis was overjoyed, as indeed was the entire country; when the Queen went to Nôtre Dame for her churching, she was cheered by the crowd. An exception to the general rejoicing was Monsieur who, at the christening, asked sourly who was the father. On 21 October 1781 Marie Antoinette had a second child, the Dauphin Louis-Joseph; the King was so overcome that he wept and stammered. Again gossips, led by Monsieur, said that the real father was Artois. It was a delicate creature, tormented by rickets and bone tuberculosis, whose health gave cause for alarm from the very beginning. But another son was born in 1785, Louis-Charles, Duc de Normandie—the future Louis XVII. There was also a fourth child, the Princess Sophie Béatrice, who did not reach her second year. Now that she had children the Queen led a much quieter life. Despite occasional squabbles, she and the King had always been good friends, and now fell genuinely in love with each other. She too grew fatter, with a bust measurement of forty-four inches (according to her dressmaker's order book).

Louis was extremely popular, especially with those who came into contact with him. Artois's Scots gardener, Thomas Blaikie, obviously liked what he saw; 'The King was dressed almost like a country farmer, a good rough stout man about twenty-five.' At thirty he was even fatter, as a consequence of hunting a little less and of reading rather more while continuing to indulge his extraordinary appetite. But the French have never blamed anyone for enjoying their food. When he visited the new naval base at Cherbourg in 1786, although the expense of the trip was sharply criticized in Paris, the King had a personal triumph; peasants lined the roads to cheer him as he passed. Louis was noticeably moved, kissing the girls and shouting back, '*Vive mon bon peuple!*' when the crowd cried '*Vive le Roi!*' Indeed most Frenchmen still felt an extraordinary reverence for the King—what the normally unsentimental Tocqueville defines as 'both the natural love of children for their father and the awe properly due to God alone'. Foreigners were astonished by the

passionate interest which the French took in the person of their sovereign. The Scot John Moore, who visited France in 1779, noted that Louis's slightest illness alarmed the entire country: 'Did he cough?—Yes, by Gad! And strongly—I am in despair.' This reverence continued right up to the Revolution. His subjects did not blame the deficit and the hard times on the King—it was all the fault of his advisers and that 'Austrian bitch' of a wife.

Many years later, the Comte de Hézecques, a royal page from 1786–92, gave a fascinating portrait of the King he had served. 'When seated on the throne Louis XVI looked well enough, but it has to be confessed that he walked with an unpleasant waddle . . . He dressed very plainly in grey or brown coats, with a steel or silver sword, though on Sundays and feast days he wore white velvet.' Hézecques adds, 'I spent nearly six years at court and I never once saw the King act rudely, even in the slightest way to any one of all his servants.' He also emphasizes that Louis had no favourites.

The basic ritual of Louis XIV's court was still observed, with *Lever* and *Coucher*, daily Mass and dining in public. Everything that the King ate, even in private or between meals, was tasted by an 'Officer of the Goblet' for fear of poison. Hézecques tells us that though only very ancient noblemen bowed to the State Bed when Louis was not in it, even the youngest and most modern courtiers backed to the wall when he approached, shuffling their feet in the hope of attracting their sovereign's attention. Even those on intimate terms could only address him in the third person: 'Has the King had good sport today?' 'Has the King caught a cold?'

Yet fewer and fewer people bothered to go to court. This was largely the fault of the Queen, who had no use for anybody outside her own set. The Duc de Lévis remembered that, 'Except for a few favourites, chosen by caprice or intrigue, everyone was shut out; rank, service, interest, high birth, were no longer sufficient to procure admission to the royal family's circle.' In consequence many noblemen began to consider presentation at court a waste of time. The Duke tells us that Versailles became 'no more than a little provincial town which one visited reluctantly and left as quickly as possible'. Even so, the pomp and ceremony remained as splendid as ever—Châteaubriand

says that those who did not know Versailles before 1789 have no conception of true magnificence.

According to the Comte de Ségur, by the 1780s, 'from one end of the kingdom to the other, opposition had become a point of honour.' Opposition meant different things to different people, even if the vast majority of educated Frenchmen subscribed to the Enlightenment and considered the *Ancien Régime* ruinously inadequate. Noblemen envied the power which the English ruling class had gained after their 'Glorious Revolution' of 1688 and, for all their love of Rousseau, had little taste for equality. Unfortunately for them, *égalité* was to be one of the French Revolution's great slogans; by Louis XVI's reign the sharp difference which once existed between the classes had been eroded; many an *haut bourgeois* was infinitely richer and more polished than some titled country booby squire, but the law denied him the status, privileges and opportunities which belonged to nobility alone. There was also the psychological factor, that artificial gap between noble and bourgeois, which gave rise to deep resentment. At the same time, because of the aristocratic counter-revolution, social mobility was far less in the later eighteenth century than it had been during its early years.

The dissatisfied bourgeois—businessmen, doctors, architects, lesser lawyers, minor civil servants and all the other professional people—had small concern for the miserable lot of the peasants. Throughout the countryside, hatred of the nobility was growing. Because of the economic depression, landowners were increasingly short of money in the 1780s and resorted to what has been called 'the seigniorial reaction'; not only were long-forgotten feudal dues exacted once again and the *corvée* extended, but common land was expropriated. Lawyers busily disinterred old title deeds and terrorized peasants with their documents. In consequence there was a vast increase in the already large numbers of indigent rural poor, while bad harvests drove even the most stolid peasant into a fury of resentment at the lord of the manor's greed.

Yet, despite all Michelet's horror-stories about the Bastille, the government was far from harsh. Someone asked the nona-genarian Duc de Richelieu—he did not die until 1788—if life had changed. The Duke replied that under Louis XIV people

had not dared to even speak, that under Louis XV they had whispered, and that now they spoke out loud. As Tocqueville points out, Beaumarchais's brief imprisonment shocked Paris far more than the persecution of the Huguenots in the previous century.

When Louis first read Beaumarchais's *Le Mariage de Figaro* in 1781—he read it aloud to Marie Antoinette—he cried out 'Detestable', complaining that, 'That man makes fun of everything which should be respected', and forbade the play's performance. For two years Beaumarchais campaigned to save his play, giving readings and enlisting support from very important personages like Artois. The play tells how a *grand seigneur*, Count Almaviva, plots the seduction of a servant girl and how her fiancé—his valet, Figaro—joins with the Countess in thwarting the Count's attempt to revive the *droit de seigneur*. Throughout, the valet's superiority over the nobleman is emphasized, and the unfairness of the social order—'You nobles merely take the trouble to be born', Figaro tells the Count. Eventually the King gave way to the popular clamour, and the play's first night on 13 June 1783 was a *succès de scandale*, cheered to the echo by the glittering audience whom the author ridiculed so subtly; some spectators realized its implications, but the fashionable world ignored them. Beaumarchais at once published a mocking pamphlet, whereupon he was arrested and sent to the St Lazare prison; the public outcry was so enormous that he was released after only twenty-four hours. The Queen had *Le Mariage de Figaro* put on at the Petit Trianon's little theatre, to a musical accompaniment composed by Paesiello—Figaro was played by Artois, Almaviva by M de Vaudreuil (Artois's crony) and the Countess by Marie Antoinette herself.

Talleyrand's claim that anyone who had not lived under the *Ancien Régime* did not know how sweet life could be, has often been questioned. Nevertheless he seems to be born out by Tocqueville. 'France in those days was a nation of pleasure seekers, all for the joy of life . . . The upper classes were far more interested in living beautifully than in comfort, in making a name for themselves than in making money.' It was not only the world of Beaumarchais but of Mozart too, of Gluck and Grétry. Of its popular songs, *Plaisir d'Amour*, with its bitter-

sweet yet simple elegance, conveys perfectly the spirit of the times. Stateliness went hand in hand with simplicity—at court, French country dances alternated with minuets. The fashionable painters, perhaps a little too relaxed, were Mme Vigée Le Brun, Greuze and '*L'aimable Frago*' (as Fragonard liked to be called), though Neo-classical giants were emerging—the sensation of the Salon of 1785 was Louis David's 'Oath of the Horatii'. The period's delightful furniture was also Neo-classical, made by Reisener, Weisweiller, Molitor, Schichtig, and Jacob. Under the influence of Rousseau, clothes were becoming simpler, though no less elegant; men no longer wore wigs but powdered their hair and often wore riding boots and English hunting coats and breeches. Women tried to look like shepherdesses. Furthermore, the eighteenth century had invented the café and the restaurant—by 1785 there were 600 cafés in Paris alone. Even the life of the poorer classes could be surprisingly gay, to judge from the novels of Restif de la Bretonne, who writes not only of the debaucheries of underworld Paris, but also of the joyous life of the well-to-do peasant household.

In 1783 Yolande de Polignac coaxed Marie Antoinette into persuading the King to appoint Charles-Alexandre de Calonne as Controller-General. He was a most agreeable man in his late forties, handsome, always beautifully dressed and invariably charming, with exquisite taste in pictures (he owned ten Titians), furniture and mistresses: the Duc de Lévis said that he was the only member of the *noblesse de la robe* who knew how to behave like a gentleman. He had had an impressive career in administration, having been an *Intendant* for nearly twenty years, and he was hailed as a new Colbert. Calonne always lived above his means and on being appointed he joked, 'The finances of France are in a deplorable state and I would never have accepted responsibility for them if my own were not in an equally shaky condition.' His policy was original, to say the least. He believed, 'A man who wants to borrow must appear to be rich; to seem rich one has to impress by lavish expenditure.' Calonne had no problems with Marie Antoinette, who was enchanted by him (whatever her loyal Mme de Campan may say to the contrary). When the Queen made one of her demands for an enormous sum of ready cash, he replied, 'If it is possible, Madame, it is already done; if it is impossible it shall be done.'

He levied no new taxes. His method was the same as Necker's—
simply to borrow.

Yet outside matters of finance, Calonne was surprisingly
imaginative. He tried to encourage a French industrial revolution on the English model, and—with Louis's support—suggested to a number of rich noblemen that they invest in mines
and factories. But like his master, the Controller-General had
no understanding of the way in which Pitt in England was able
to dispose of a national debt far larger than the French deficit,
by means of a sinking fund.

Two years after Calonne's appointment, the monarchy was
badly shaken by the comic opera affair of the Queen's necklace.
A seedy young adventuress (and occasional prostitute), the
Comtesse de la Motte-Valois, had been 'befriended' by the
Cardinal de Rohan, Prince-Bishop of the fabulously rich see of
Strasbourg and Grand Almoner of France. This ornament of the
boudoirs was a handsome, womanizing fop in his forties, straight
out of *Les Liaisons Dangereuses*, whose boundless conceit was
matched only by his fatuity. His conduct as French ambassador
in Vienna had been so scandalous that the Empress Maria
Theresa had actually asked for his recall; later, as a friend of
Mme du Barry, he had offended the Queen. However, Louis de
Rohan had ambitions of becoming a second Richelieu, and was
convinced that only Marie Antoinette's disfavour stood between
him and the highest office. Somehow Mme de la Motte persuaded the Cardinal that she had the Queen's ear; the Countess
arranged an 'interview', in the park at Versailles on a moonless
night, Marie Antoinette being impersonated by a young prostitute from the Palais Royal, dressed in white, who bore a
striking resemblance to her and who gave him a rose. Rohan
was completely taken in. His pliability was in part due to the
influence of the self-styled alchemist, magician and prophet,
Count Cagliostro, who had thoroughly bemused this useful
patron and had 'foreseen' a woman in white transforming the
Cardinal's life.

It was popular gossip that the Queen had been offered a
wonderful diamond necklace by her jewellers at an astronomical
price. Mme de la Motte informed the Cardinal that the Queen
wanted him to buy the necklace for her discreetly—the commission was confirmed by forged letters. With staggering

credulity, Rohan fetched the necklace from the jewellers, telling them that they would be paid in due course, and gave it to the Countess to take to Versailles—her husband speedily sold the stones in London. The theft came to light when the jewellers demanded payment from the Queen, and in August 1785 the Cardinal was arrested at Versailles as he was proceeding, vested for Mass, down the Hall of Mirrors to the Chapel Royal.

Next year Mme de la Motte was sentenced to be branded, but Rohan was acquitted by the Parlement of Paris; his acquittal was seen as a slur on the Queen and also as an example of social injustice. Louis, who was furious, banished the Cardinal to the country, thus heaping even more odium on poor Marie Antoinette, who was entirely innocent. (Later Rohan reformed, spending his last years in something very like sanctity.) Popular suspicions about the Queen's frivolity—and also her spitefulness —deepened. 'A nice little smear of dirt on both crown and crozier', commented an 'Enlightened' councillor of the Parlement. None the less, the affair helped to forge an alliance between the clergy and the lawyers who had saved the Cardinal. Mme de Campan, a lady-in-waiting whose memoirs are sometimes a little unreliable, spoke the truth when she said that the Affair of the Necklace marked 'the end of happy times'. Indeed Napoleon actually considered it to be a partial cause of the Revolution.

By 1786 even Calonne had to realize that a policy of pure optimism alone could no longer suffice. There was an annual deficit which he estimated at 112 million livres. He explained to the hapless King, who had no inkling that things were so desperate, that monies borrowed over the last ten years amounted to the then almost incredible sum of 1,250 million livres (well over £50 million in English money of the period). But for all his frivolity, the Controller-General could be both clear-headed and courageous. He proposed a programme of radical reform, derived partly from Turgot, which included a land tax from which no one, not even the clergy, would be exempt. Hoping to obtain as much support as possible, he persuaded Louis to call an Assembly of Notables, which met at Versailles in February 1787. It consisted of 144 persons, but had only twenty-seven representatives from the Tiers Etat (or Commons).

Unfortunately, the Notables were already convinced that the deficit was entirely due to the government's mismanagement

and that the solution was to force the King to share his power with the nobility, who would run things properly. Admittedly, of the 400,000 persons of noble birth in France at that time, most were small country gentlemen with minute incomes (in one case as little as £26 a year). But they felt as one with Dukes who possessed annual revenues in excess of £100,000 in their determination not to pay taxes.

When the Assembly met, the Controller-General addressed it with admirable frankness. Explaining that there was no way of remedying the deficit other than by taxing the privileged orders, he stressed that most of their rights and privileges would be untouched. The Franco–Irish Archbishop Dillon of Narbonne protested, 'M de Calonne wants to bleed France; and he is asking the Notables' advice on whether to bleed her in the foot, the arm or the jugular vein.' The Assembly demanded to see detailed accounts of national expenditure. The debates became bogged down in a welter of recrimination. Calonne, whom over-work had driven to the verge of collapse, forgot his manners for once and told the Notables that the King would introduce the reforms whether they liked them or not. He enraged the Assembly still further by a clumsy attempt to recruit public support, circulating a pamphlet which attacked the privileged orders and their refusal to pay their fair share of taxes; he asked the King to arrest twenty of the more outspoken Notables. Louis thought he had gone mad, lamenting that Vergennes was no longer alive to help him, and he dismissed Calonne at the end of April. Later, when the Notables informed him that the ex-Controller-General had concealed the true magnitude of the deficit, the King smashed a chair in his rage and roared that he should have had him hanged. Nevertheless, when the Parlement attempted to try Calonne, Louis stopped the proceedings. The former minister fled to England, to live in elegant exile.

For a time the King retreated to Versailles. He was so over-whelmed by the problem of the deficit that he spent whole days cursing and weeping. However, the Assembly of Notables was still there, and in a rebellious mood. Eventually Louis chose a new Controller-General. Archbishop Loménie de Brienne was the last ecclesiastical statesman of France. He was a no less colourful figure than Calonne and, like him, had been recom-mended by the Queen. A true child of the Enlightenment, the

Archbishop collected books, works of art and women (he suffered from secondary syphilis). A Deist rather than an atheist, he had no real Christian beliefs and had only entered the Church to restore the fortunes of his ancient but impoverished family.

Although Brienne revised Calonne's new tax to make it more palatable, his proposals were rejected out of hand by the Notables. He therefore dismissed them and, without much hope, had recourse to the Parlement of Paris, who promptly rejected both a proposed stamp tax and a property tax, and demanded the publication of the national accounts, and—menacingly—the summoning of the States General. In August 1787, perched on the purple velvet cushions of the *lit de justice*, Louis forced them to register the new taxes, whereupon the Parlementaires declared the taxes illegal; they were banished to Troyes where they continued to demand a States General. The *révolte nobilaire* dragged on. At one point Philippe d'Orléans told Louis publicly, in his timid, stuttering voice, that he was breaking the law of the land; the Duke was banished to the country, becoming a popular hero. Poor Marie Antoinette, whose extravagances were insignificant compared with those of Orléans, was christened '*La Reine Déficit*' and hissed at the Opera. In May 1788 Louis XVI copied his grandfather and took away most of the Parlements' powers, replacing them by forty-seven new courts, together with a plenary court (whose membership was to resemble that of the English House of Lords) for the registration of royal edicts. The King also abolished all remaining use of torture in legal proceedings.

But the deficit remained. Brienne tried desperately to reduce the expenses of the royal household, dismissing half the staff, such as the falconers, selling the wolfhounds and boarhounds, while a number of royal châteaux were sold or demolished to avoid the cost of maintenance, and pensions were slashed. But it was not enough. The Archbishop turned desperately to the Church, as a last resort. In Tocqueville's view, 'There has probably never been a clergy more praiseworthy than that of Catholic France just before the Revolution'; but among the few failings which he discerned was 'an instinctive, sometimes unjustified attachment to the rights of their corporation'. Brienne begged them to pay higher taxes. Their answer was, 'No, the people of France are not taxable at pleasure.' The final crisis

came in August 1788 when the Archbishop discovered that the treasury was bankrupt. He suspended all payments, raised a little money from floating bonds and appropriated the funds of the Invalides, the Théatre Française and the Opéra. He then resigned, thankfully (for as long as he lived, Brienne could never afterwards speak of his time as Controller-General without shaking).

Meanwhile, the royal authority was breaking down all over France. There had been riots in favour of the Parlements; and very nearly civil war in Grenoble in June, on 'The Day of the Tiles', when troops refused to fire on the mob. Louis capitulated. Amid wide rejoicing, he recalled the perennially popular Necker, who swiftly borrowed sufficient funds. The King dissolved the new courts and brought back the Parlements. On 24 September 1788 the Parlement of Paris registered the royal edict that the States General would be summoned in January of the following year.

In every bailiwick and parish solemn little councils met, not only to elect a representative but also to draw up a *Cahier des Doléances* (List of Grievances). It must be explained that the States General had never been an established legislative assembly; by tradition it was an extraordinary body which the King only summoned in times of crisis or national dissatisfaction. (As recently as the mid-1950s, a large group of French deputies, the Poujadistes, were demanding the calling of a States General.) Its members had always represented the 'estates' or classes, rather than the country. Now, however, the Third Estate was determined to speak for the nation as a whole.

The Parlementaires had assumed that the coming assembly would be modelled on that of 1614. But the middle classes insisted furiously that the Tiers Etat must be doubled, to take account of the increased numbers of the bourgeoisie, and that the Three Estates should vote together instead of separately. Their proposals meant that the Tiers Etat would dominate the States General. The Parlementaires rejected these presumptuous demands, and were then amazed to find themselves hooted in the streets—their popularity had vanished overnight. No one had anticipated such a development. Calonne wrote to Louis from London, 'I was unaware of the degree to which a division had developed between the nobility and the Third Estate in many

provinces of the kingdom. I tremble to hear of it.' Necker supported the Tiers Etat and the King gave way, announcing that their representation would be doubled. Marie Antoinette, who seemed to be learning a little political sense, declared that she was the 'Queen of the Third Estate'. Alas, Louis's insistence that the Estates vote separately lost him any support he might have hoped to gain from this concession.

The French Revolution was not a foregone conclusion. It is true, as Tocqueville says, 'that if it had not taken place the old social structure would still have collapsed everywhere, here sooner, here later, except that it would have continued to crumble piecemeal.' But by insisting on summoning the States General, the ruling classes had brought about the very thing they had sought to avoid—the loss of their privileges. The Third Estate alone were united, in their determination to secure radical changes; both the clergy and the nobility were divided among themselves; country priests were against the rich prelates, while the little hedge squires from the backwoods resented the great courtier lords and the Parlementaires. The privileged orders had made a revolution of which they were to be the first victims.

The situation was made even more explosive by the economic troubles. For all the new ideas, the country's economy still depended almost completely on grain production and there was a disastrous harvest in 1788; all the poorer classes, artisans and peasants alike, suffered miserably from a catastrophic rise in the price of bread. The winter of 1788–89 was one of the worst France had ever known. In the countryside brigands roamed unchecked.

Yet in Paris, despite feverish talk of reform and the occasional riot, the atmosphere was one not only of optimism but of gaiety. And the people were as fond of Louis as ever. A German traveller, von Vitzin, who visited France in 1788, wrote that love of monarchy was ingrained in the French—'the humblest chimney-sweep is enraptured with joy when he sees his sovereign.' Throughout all the recent storms and troubles Louis had never lost his popularity. In the provinces he was still applauded; at Arras a local notary, M de Robespierre, told people to thank God for their King.

The States General met at Versailles in the *Salle des Menus*

Plaisirs ('The Hall of Lesser Pleasures') on the morning of
4 May 1789. In the procession to its opening, the Host was
carried before the King, fittingly, for this was to be the last
great ceremonial appearance of the most sacred temporal
institution in Western Europe. Louis, wearing the purple hat of
state, walked under a canopy, followed by the Princes of the
Blood. The deputies were led by the 291 members of the First
Estate, the clergy, in their robes; after whom walked the 270
deputies of the Second Estate, the nobility, with swords,
plumed hats and gold-braided cloaks. The 578 deputies of the
Third Estate, the bourgeois, were in ridiculously old-fashioned
black suits, a humiliation which made them all the more touchy;
at the Mass in the church of Saint-Louis they insisted on occupying the front seats. None the less, a few noblemen had chosen to
walk with them, including M d'Orléans and a certain Comte de
Mirabeau.

Despite bickering between the three estates, the King was
treated with the utmost respect. The hall rang with repeated
shouts of *'Vive le Roi!'* and clapping, even during his address.
Surprisingly, Marie Antoinette was also acclaimed with cries of
'Vive la Reine!' which she acknowledged by curtseying to the
assembly—redoubled cheers won another, even deeper curtsey.

However, during these crucial days the King and Queen were
overwhelmed by a heart-breaking domestic tragedy. The
Dauphin Louis-Joseph had been dying since the last months of
1788; his deformed spine protruded, while one lung had been
almost destroyed by tuberculosis—Hézecques tells us that by
the beginning of 1789 his face had become distorted with pain.
A feverishly precocious child, abnormally intelligent for his
years, the Dauphin bore his sufferings with touching bravery;
he watched the opening procession of the States General from a
balcony, lying on a day-bed. When he died in June 1789, Louis
collapsed and was in tears for weeks, while Marie Antoinette's
hair went grey. To observe the customary mourning, the court
went to Marly. When some representatives of the Third
Estate insisted on seeing him and forced their way in, the King
muttered, 'Is there not a father among them?'

Unfortunately, in his broken mood Louis was easily swayed
by Artois, who begged him not to abandon the aristocracy.
Unlike Louis XIV, nearly everyone whom Louis XVI knew

belonged to the nobility or to the higher clergy; even his servants—at any rate, those with whom he came into contact—were gentlemen. The King was not sufficiently ruthless to throw his entire circle of friends and acquaintances to the wolves. Certainly he wanted the nobility to pay taxes, but he had no wish to ruin them. It never entered his head that the monarchy's only hope was an alliance with the bourgeoisie.

While Louis was away from Versailles the Third Estate seized the initiative. They proclaimed themselves a national Constituent Assembly and persuaded the clergy to join them. When the *Salle des Menus Plaisirs* was barred to them on 20 June, they met in a tennis court where they took the famous oath not to disperse until France had a new constitution. The King ordered them to end their Assembly and debate separately. They refused. M de Mirabeau, a dissolute idealist who had the makings of a French Charles James Fox, shouted at the youthful official who brought Louis's order, 'Monsieur, go and tell your master that we are here by the will of the people and will only leave at the point of the bayonet!' Some days later the Assembly was joined by a large group of liberal noblemen led by Orléans, who by now had hopes of succeeding his cousin on the throne. Although advised to break it up with troops, the King muttered weakly, '*Foutre!* If they don't want to go, leave them alone.' Necker said that he could see nothing against a national Assembly replacing the States General. However, bewildered and undecided, Louis then ordered up 30,000 troops from the provinces to Paris—mainly regiments of foreign mercenaries. On 11 July he dismissed Necker.

Uproar broke out, culminating three days later in the storming of the Bastille, the French Tower of London. (Ironically, Louis had already approved plans for its demolition.) The triumphant mob rampaged through the streets, joined by mutinous troops. The British ambassador, the cricketer Duke of Dorset, reported to his Secretary of State in London, 'Thus, my Lord, was accomplished the greatest revolution recorded in history, and, relatively speaking, considering the importance of the results, one which has been achieved with very little bloodshed.' Henceforward, one can only summarize the progress of the French Revolution, concentrating on the unfortunate Louis whenever his head can be seen in the maelstrom.

On 16 July 1789 Artois, the acknowledged leader of the privileged orders, left France, and many great nobles followed him. Necker was hastily recalled from Brussels. Before the month was over the American ambassador, Gouverneur Morris, was reporting to President Washington that the King had lost all authority. A National Guard was formed to protect the Assembly and placed under the command of that popular idol, the Marquis de Lafayette; they adopted a red, white and blue uniform and cockade—red and blue being the colours of Paris, white the colour of the monarchy. Orléans had himself painted in the new tricolour uniform. On 4 August liberal nobles voted enthusiastically for the abolition of their privileges; fuedalism vanished overnight—in theory at any rate. By 26 August the Constituent Assembly had published its Declaration of the Rights of Man (based on the American Declaration), which a historian has called 'the death certificate of the *Ancien Régime*'.

Meanwhile there was uproar in the countryside. Unemployment, the soaring price of bread, and general misery had all contributed to 'The Great Fear of 1789', triggered off by rumours that the nobility were about to seize Paris and then subdue the rest of the kingdom with an army of mercenaries; the brigands who already roamed France were regarded as their agents. In July and August mobs of panic-stricken peasants took up scythes and muskets to attack manor houses and abbeys; what they were really after were title deeds to their lands, and everywhere archives went up in flames; often the lord of the manor was forced to sign a document renouncing his dues. The Englishman Arthur Young heard in Besançon at the end of July that, 'Many châteaux have been burnt, others plundered, the *seigneurs* hunted down like wild beasts, their wives and daughters ravished . . . '

Many of the Assembly now considered that the revolution had gone quite far enough. A conservative party of *monarchiens* emerged, who hoped to give back to the King much of his power and to create a limited monarchy with an upper and lower house on the English model. Unfortunately, this only served to bewilder Louis still more. Marie Antoinette persuaded him to summon the reliable Flanders Regiment to Paris, despite Mirabeau's warnings. The Parisians, already suspicious that a counter-revolutionary plot was brewing, learnt on 2 October

that the day before the King's Bodyguard had given a dinner party for the officers of the Flanders Regiment, drinking loyal toast after loyal toast and singing emotionally Grétry's poignant aria, *O Richard, O mon Roy, l'univers t'abandonne*; the King and Queen had paid a brief visit to the party, where they had been cheered wildly. This news was embellished by tales that the health of the French nobility had been drunk and the tricolour cockade trampled underfoot.

Clamour overwhelmed the capital, fanned by a mad and evil journalist, Marat. It was rumoured that the King was about to seize Paris by force, that he was going to dismiss the Assembly; but it was the news of the banquet itself which enraged the women, for there had been a bread famine for months. On 5 October an armed rabble 5,000 strong—mainly women, and some of them well-to-do *bourgeoises*—set out from Paris to march the ten miles to Versailles; as they marched through the pouring rain they shouted, 'Bread! Bread!' or screamed what they would do to Marie Antoinette—'We'll cut off her head . . . rip her heart out . . . fry her liver . . . make her guts into ribbons.' The popular story that Marie Antoinette, when told of the bread famine, had cruelly said, 'Let them eat cake!' shows how deeply she was hated by the people.

At Versailles a delegation was allowed in to see the King. Its spokesman, a seventeen-year-old female art student, Louison Chabry, said simply, 'Bread, Sire' and then fainted. When she revived Louis kissed her on both cheeks and promised to do something about the famine. But the mob outside remained, throughout the wet night, despite the fact that the palace was patrolled by Lafayette and his National Guard. Early next morning, in Lafayette's absence, the crowd managed to break in through an unlocked door, killing and then decapitating two of the Bodyguard. Marie Antoinette barely had time to reach the King's apartments. Luckily Lafayette arrived and calmed the crowd by promising that Louis would speak to them. The King appeared on the balcony, but was too overwrought to say anything. With remarkable bravery the Queen took his place. The crowd, waving their axes and the heads of guardsmen on pikes, howled in derision, but when Lafayette kissed her hand they began to shout, '*Vive la Reine!*'

They also yelled, 'To Paris! To Paris!' The minister for the

royal household, M de Saint Priest, advised the King to flee to Rouen and raise an army to restore law and order, but Necker told him that such a step would be tantamount to abdication. Accordingly, Louis appeared on the balcony again and said, '*Mes enfants*, you want me to come with you to Paris. I consent, but only on condition that I shall never be parted from my wife and children.' He also demanded safe conduct for his Bodyguard. Shortly after midday an extraordinary procession set out for the capital, headed by a gloating, uproarious mob, and including the miserable men of the Flanders Regiment and of the Bodyguard who had all been disarmed and now wore the Revolutionary cockade in their hats. The same day the royal family was installed in the Tuileries, which they found dirty and dilapidated, and with only a few sticks of old-fashioned furniture; the Dauphin was frightened by its gloom.

The Assembly was unwise enough to follow the King to Paris, where it found itself at the mercy of the mob. It decided to change Louis's title—from being 'by the grace of God King of France and Navarre', he became 'by the grace of God and the constitutional law of the state, King of the French'. Daily, crowds flocked to the Tuileries to see their Parisian King and Queen.

Mirabeau, leader of what were now the moderates in the Assembly, submitted a secret memorandum to Louis urging him to flee to Normandy and from there offer the country a workable democratic constitution. (Louis had made his only clever move during the entire Revolution, by offering to pay Mirabeau's debts in return for his advice.) But Marie Antoinette did not trust Mirabeau, whose pock-marked face—like a diseased lion—and reputation for vice and atheism obscured his very real patriotism and political genius. In any case, the King was determined not to start a civil war. He had read Clarendon's *History of the Great Rebellion* and it had impressed him deeply— he was convinced that so long as he did not oppose the revolution by force of arms in the way Charles I had done, everything would turn out right. Ironically, he gave it as his opinion that, 'The Frenchman is incapable of regicide.' Such beliefs suited his lethargic nature—he had always hated having to make decisions. And to anyone so politically naive as Louis XVI the situation seemed far from hopeless; he remained extremely popular, and

medals and statues of him were still being inscribed 'Restorer of Liberty'. In February 1790, addressing the Assembly, he declared himself to be King of the Revolution.

Indeed, life at the Tuileries, which had been refurnished, was not so very different from what it had been at Versailles. Count Fersen, visiting Marie Antoinette in February 1792, was staggered by the splendour of her apartments. Though Louis was no longer able to hunt, he went riding in the Bois, unescorted and plainly dressed as befitted a citizen King, where he was sometimes cheered by workmen. His new position as a constitutional monarch was curiously modern. Men like the Comte de Narbonne and the Vicomte de Noailles really believed that the new constitution would work—even Louis himself thought so at times.

The King co-operated with the Assembly throughout 1790. On 14 July, the first anniversary of the storming of the Bastille, there was a great ceremony in the Champs de Mars, which some saw as a revolutionary coronation, a 'dispelling of Gothick mists'. Talleyrand, Bishop of Autun, said Mass (for the last time). Louis made a most successful speech to the huge crowd and then took the Civic Oath: 'I, the King of the French, do swear and declare that I will use all the powers delegated to me by the constitutional law of the state, to maintain the constitution decreed by the National Assembly and accepted by me.' Marie Antoinette, watching from a balcony of the Ecole Militaire, lifted up the six-year-old Dauphin to present him to the crowd, who cheered them emotionally. Most people thought that the revolution was over.

Unfortunately, the government, having abolished the traditional taxes, had to look for money elsewhere. On Talleyrand's advice it seized all church property; henceforward the state would pay the clergy's stipends. The government insisted that bishops and parish priests must be appointed by the state through the local authorities, and they were now required to swear an oath of obedience to the nation; the vast majority of French churchmen refused to take such an oath, which implicitly denied Papal supremacy, so 'Down went the old Church of France with all its pomp and wealth'. As a man of rigid religious principles, the King was horrified by the government's action. He still possessed the veto and refused to accept edicts against

non-juring clergy. It was the veto which eventually destroyed him.

The break with Rome did not come until the Pope denounced the oath in April 1791. By then France was hopelessly divided. The lesser nobility, many of whom had been mildly liberal, turned against the Revolution when titles and the traditional law of inheritance were abolished in June 1790. They followed the *grands seigneurs* into exile, and among them were a large number of army officers and naval men. Many of these *émigrés* waited in the Rhineland towns just over the frontier, hoping for civil war or armed intervention by the great powers. Marie Antoinette was no longer 'Madame Déficit' but 'Madame Veto'. Frantically she begged her brothers (the Emperors Joseph II, Leopold II and Francis II, who succeeded each other in turn) to invade France and save her. To Artois she wrote despairingly that Louis could not see his danger. At home, the constitutional-ists were steadily losing ground to the extremist republicans of the political clubs. In September 1790 even Necker had resigned and fled to Switzerland. The streets rang with that gayest, catchiest and most sinister of all revolutionary songs, *Ça Ira*. Curiously, it had been composed by Couperin.

Hitherto the King had roundly cursed anyone who spoke to him of flight or of conspiring against the Revolution. But by the autumn of 1790 he had had to realize that in Paris he was a mere prisoner and, after being threatened on a number of occasions, almost at the mercy of the mob. In November he therefore com-missioned M de Breteuil to negotiate secretly with foreign courts for help 'to re-establish my lawful authority and my people's happiness'. Shortly afterwards, the Assembly bullied him into signing an edict dismissing priests who would not take the oath. *Mesdames Tantes*, the Princesses Adelaide and Victoire, were sent to take refuge with old Cardinal de Bernis at the French embassy in Rome. Mirabeau, Louis's one really able adviser, died in March 1791, lamenting that he had unwittingly helped to pull down the monarchy. Paris became more and more suspicious of the King, especially after the flight of his aunts. Jacobin extremists attacked him in the Assembly and in the gutter press. They were not without provocation. Nearly 400 pugnacious noblemen haunted the Tuileries, swaggering and boastful and known as the *Chevaliers du Poignard*—Knights of

the Dagger. Their loose talk gave rise to rumours of conspiracy. One day, when they met at the Palace, they were arrested by a detachment of the National Guard—though only after a pitched battle—and dragged off to prison. Louis was so upset that he took to his bed. His Revolutionary subjects' worst suspicions were confirmed. At Easter 1791, when the royal family tried to visit Saint-Cloud, they were prevented by a howling mob who seized their horses' bridles. Louis commented, 'They want to murder me like Henri IV.' He realized that he had to get out of Paris at all costs.

The flight to Varennes was one of the worst-organized escape attempts in history. On the night of 20 June 1791 the King disguised in a brown wig, Marie Antoinette swathed in a voluminous black cloak, and the Dauphin dressed as a girl, together with Madame Royale and Louis's sister Mme Elisabeth, climbed into a small carriage driven by Count Fersen. As soon as they were outside Paris they exchanged it for an enormous green and yellow coach which made disguise superfluous—it even had the royal arms on the door. Most unfortunately, one of the detachments of loyal Hussars who were supposed to meet them *en route*, failed to make contact. At Varennes the Dragoons were waiting for them on the wrong side of the river. When they arrived there at midnight, the royal family were met by some Hussars, but too few of them. Suddenly the entire party was surrounded by a large and excited detachment of National Guardsmen. Louis, with his almost superstitious dread of shedding French blood, ordered the Hussars not to resist.

The coach and its dejected occupants were driven back to the capital, a melancholy and terrifying journey which took nearly four days, during which they were frequently stoned. When they reached Paris they drove to the Tuileries through silent crowds—placards warned, 'Whoever cheers the King will be flogged: Whoever boos him will be hanged.' Soldiers reversed arms as though at a funeral parade. The National Assembly suspended Louis until a committee of investigation reported diplomatically that he had been kidnapped and was therefore innocent. But as Gouverneur Morris, a good friend to the monarchy, reported to President Washington, 'It would not be surprising if such a dolt as this were to lose his throne.' Even

though the Assembly resisted an outcry for his deposition from Jacobins like Danton and Robespierre, the King was doomed. He had lost his last asset, his popularity.

Even now, however, his situation seemed far from desperate. In July a great anti-monarchist demonstration in the Champs de Mars was broken up by the National Guard, who opened fire and killed over sixty demonstrators; many Jacobin extremists went into hiding, Danton actually fleeing across the Channel. On 3 September 1791 the Constituent Assembly completed its work and introduced a definitive Constitution. The King retained his functions, but had to swear yet another oath, pledging his loyalty to all the provisions of the new Constitution. He did so publicly before the Assembly, with considerable aplomb; while he was taking the oath the Deputies rudely sat down, whereupon Louis sat down himself and continued. In private he was miserably dejected and wept, groaning, 'It's all over.' Marie Antoinette was furious with him. Reading his speech, which had been carefully prepared for him by the Assembly, she cried angrily, 'That's hardly the speech of a King deeply resentful of his ill treatment!' Louis simply shrugged his shoulders. But Paris was *en fête*—for a second time people thought that the Revolution was over. Poor simple Marie de Lamballe came home to her beloved Queen.

The Constituent Assembly had naively forbidden the re-election of any of its members. As a result, the new Legislative Assembly was far more to the left, though a minority were still convinced supporters of Louis XVI. At once egalitarian debates began as to whether he should still be addressed as Sire and Majesty. Emperor Leopold II and King Frederick William of Prussia had issued a declaration, in August, that it was in the interests of every European sovereign that the King of France should recover all his powers. In November 1791, at the Assembly's prompting, Louis issued a declaration to the effect that France was ready to fight in defence of its new constitution and laws; he also asked his fellow sovereigns to withdraw their troops from the French borders. In addition, he issued an open letter to his brother Artois, who was busy organizing an *émigré* army, inviting him to come home. On 20 April 1792 the King went to the Legislative Assembly and asked it to declare war on the new Emperor, Francis II.

Quite rightly, many people suspected Louis of playing a double game. Both he and the Queen believed that a war would be their salvation—6,000 out of 9,000 army officers had left the country and it was reasonable to assume that an undisciplined rabble would be speedily defeated. In fact, his open letter to his brother was a calculated lie—for many months he had been sending money to the *émigrés*, and to Artois in particular. He had already vetoed laws against them (to confiscate their property and make them liable to the death penalty if ever they returned to France), despite the Assembly's remonstrances. Ironically, he was now behaving exactly like his *bête noire*, Charles I, negotiating with both sides.

To begin with, the war went badly for France. A French attack in the Low Countries failed disastrously, largely because the men did not trust their officers. At home the new paper currency of *assignats* collapsed, resulting in savage inflation and food riots. In the panic, the Assembly began to lose control— on 20 June it was invaded by a savage mob who ordered the deputies to force Louis to sign an edict deporting priests who would not take the oath, and which he had been resisting for over a month.

At the same time, an enraged rabble stormed its way into the Tuileries to force the King to sign the edict. They made him don the red cap of Liberty—they tried to put one on Marie Antoinette but she promptly placed it on the Dauphin. Threatened with a bayonet, the King invited a soldier to feel his heart 'to see if I'm afraid'. He cheerfully drank from a bottle offered to him, and then appeared on the balcony, wearing his cap; but he none the less remained firm in his refusal to sign the edict. A young gunner officer who was watching outside asked a friend, 'Why on earth did they let in that scum? If a few hundred had been mown down by cannon, the others would still be running.' The officer's name was Captain Bonaparte. Nevertheless, the King's coolness and amiability impressed the mob, who withdrew, and aroused a certain admiration in most spectators. Moderate men were indignant and Lafayette prepared a counter-attack on the political clubs who had arranged the demonstration, but his plans were deliberately betrayed to the Mayor of Paris on the orders of Marie Antoinette, whose personal dislikes always overruled her judgement. By now the

royal palace of the Tuileries had an atmosphere 'like that of a wrecked ship in a storm'.

On 26 July the Duke of Brunswick, the general commanding the Prussian army, issued a proclamation which threatened that, if the Royal Family were harmed, Paris would be sacked and its inhabitants placed before firing squads; the Duke also announced that he was going to restore Louis XVI to his rightful powers. The French went almost mad with rage. Even moderates began to accuse the King of conspiring with the enemy—with justification Marie Antoinette was suspected of being an Austrian spy who was sending information to her brother the Emperor. The Assembly was inundated with letters and petitions demanding Louis's deposition.

The Paris Commune, which was now controlled by extremists, carefully organized a final assault on the Tuileries, arming the mob from the Faubourg Saint-Antoine and reinforcing it with like-minded National Guardsmen. In the early hours of 10 August they took up their position on the Place du Carrousel, in front of the palace, to the sound of ceaseless drum rolls and accompanied by twelve cannon. The Tuileries were defended by 900 red-coated Swiss Guards, 2,500 National Guardsmen, and 200 noblemen (including gallant old Malesherbes, well over seventy, who had brought his court sword). Unfortunately there was no one to lead them, as the National Guard officer commanding the palace had been lured away and murdered. Louis, as heedless of reality as ever, took a morning stroll in the garden, driving the mob outside the railings into a frenzy. The gates collapsed and the rabble swept in. But the King had already left, just in time, although the Queen wanted him to stay and die—he hoped to defuse the situation by taking refuge at the Manège (the royal riding school) where the Assembly were sitting. Unfortunately he forgot to tell the Swiss to withdraw. They and the armed gentlemen fired steadily into the mob until the courtyard was heaped with dead and dying *sans-culottes*. The mob had been all but beaten off when a message arrived from Louis ordering the Swiss to lay down their arms; they obeyed, whereupon they were hacked and clubbed to death, their severed heads being thrown into the air to be caught on pike points—over 800 died. Years afterwards Napoleon, who was not exactly a stranger to bloodshed, said

that he had never seen such carnage. A few Swiss got away through the gardens, while many of the nobles—including Malesherbes—escaped through secret passages.

After a miserably uncomfortable confinement in the minute writers' gallery at the Manège, the royal family were temporarily imprisoned in the former monastery of the Feuillants nearby. Louis had been quickly suspended from his functions by the Assembly, whose members were terrified by the mob outside howling 'Down with the tyrant!' Finally, the royal family were sent to the grim Tower of the Temple, a thirteenth-century building which until recently had been the headquarters of the Knights of Malta (it had been built by the Knights Templar). The prisoners' quarters were on two floors, dungeon-like rooms which they found in a filthy, verminous condition and almost without furniture. Louis's only comment was to remove a pornographic picture hanging on the wall, muttering, 'I can't allow such things to be seen by my daughter.' Soon, however, the rooms were swept out and furnished, humbly but adequately. A single servant, Cléry, the King's valet, waited on them. The Queen, Mme Elisabeth, the Dauphin and Madame Royale slept on the lower floor, Louis on the floor above. They met at breakfast, in the King's room which served as a sitting-room, and spent the day together. In the morning Louis, Marie Antoinette and Mme Elisabeth gave lessons to the children—Latin, history, geography and arithmetic—and at one o'clock went for a walk in the grounds before lunching at two. The King slept afterwards and then there was reading aloud. Mme Elisabeth mended their clothes. The food and wine seem to have been excellent and the archivist's fine library was available—after saying goodnight to his family at nine, Louis always read till midnight. The most unpleasant feature were the guards, two of whom were always in the sitting-room in case of any attempt at escape or to communicate with the outside world.

Outside, the terrified Assembly had dissolved itself and had been succeeded by the Convention, who proclaimed a republic and set about concocting yet another constitution. The Revolution was fighting for its life. Brunswick, having taken Longwy and Verdun, marched on Paris. On 20 November he was halted at Valmy by devastating fire from the French artillery (which was commanded by pre-1789 officers); to the amazement of all

Europe, Brunswick withdrew and then began a general retreat. Goethe, who was a spectator at the 'Cannonade of Valmy', prophesied that a new era of history had begun. Meanwhile, in Paris the extremists, determined to cow any opposition, had instigated the dreadful 'September Massacres', butchering more than 1,200 prisoners in the Paris jails. Although the royal family had no means of knowing what was happening, they were sometimes stoned and screamed at during their walks. One day a mob paraded outside, waving a pike bearing a beautiful blonde head which the Queen suddenly realized was that of her faithful friend, Marie de Lamballe; the *sans-culottes* tried to storm the Temple but were stopped by an official; a deputation was allowed in, one of them holding a piece of bleeding flesh which he claimed was the heart of Mme de Lamballe—Marie Antoinette fainted. The guards were increasingly insolent, addressing Louis as 'Capet'. One took particular pleasure in blowing tobacco smoke into the King's face. Some drew cartoons on the walls, of their prisoners hanging from gibbets— inscribed 'Louis taking an air bath' or 'Marie Antoinette dances'. But others were impressed by the King's dignity and simplicity—one remarked, 'A man who loves his children like that cannot have done all the evil that they say.'

The extremists demanded that 'Citizen Capet' be tried. Probably a majority of the Convention was against it. But on 20 November François Gamain, the locksmith who had once been a pampered favourite of the King's, showed the authorities a secret iron safe which he had built for him at the Tuileries; it was opened and found to contain hundreds of documents which revealed that Louis had been subsidizing *émigrés* and begging foreign powers to invade France and save him. On 11 December he was summoned before the Convention to be accused of treason. His appearance was not helped by his being unshaven (his razors had been confiscated), yet although stripped of the trappings of royalty, his dignity was overwhelming—even Marat observed, 'If he were not a King I would have said that he was a great man.' Everyone present was haunted by the recollection of Charles I's trial. Louis denied all charges and was allowed to choose counsel to defend him. The seventy-two-year-old Malesherbes came to the Temple and requested the honour. The King, in tears, embraced him but warned him that

he was risking his neck. 'Yours is a far greater sacrifice, because you are putting your own life in danger when you cannot even save mine.' Louis had no doubt as to the verdict and made his will. During his trial he was not allowed to see his family—for Louis an almost unbearable hardship.

The Jacobins, whipped up by Marat, bullied the Convention into deciding both guilt and sentence by a public vote. The Girondins, republicans but not murderers, tried to save the King by vainly demanding a referendum—it was refused, as the extremists knew that the country would acquit him. Tom Paine, the English revolutionary, proposed that the King be exiled to America. But fanatics howled for Louis's head, referring to him as 'that fat pig who cost us so much' or 'the snoring rhinoceros'. Yet even the most savage Jacobin was shocked by the behaviour of Orléans—now known as Citizen Philippe Egalité—who voted for his cousin's death (probably, like many others, he did so to save his own life). However, although a large majority found Louis guilty of conspiring against the state, a much smaller majority voted for execution—a single vote less, and he would have been saved. Malesherbes brought the verdict to Louis, falling at his feet. After comforting Malesherbes, the King told his valet to fetch a volume of history containing an account of the execution of Charles I. What hurt the simple creature most was that Orléans had voted for his death. The order for Capet's execution was issued on 19 January. Even the ferocious Carnot, the architect of the republic's victories, wept when he signed the death-warrant.

On Sunday 20 January 1793 a deputation called at the Temple to inform the King that he was to be executed within twenty-four hours. They refused his request for the sentence to be deferred for three days so that he could prepare his soul, but agreed to send him a non-juring priest. After a last evening with his family, he said goodbye. Marie Antoinette wanted to spend the night with him but he refused, promising to see everyone in the morning. They all insisted, 'You promise!' 'Yes, I promise.' The priest, the Franco–Irish Abbé Edgeworth, had supper with Louis who ate an excellent meal and then slept soundly.

Drums and trumpets sounded continuously throughout Paris from five am. The King's first words on waking were to ask Cléry to draw the curtains. 'I need daylight—yesterday's

business tired me.' After having his hair dressed so that his neck would be ready for the guillotine, Louis heard Mass and communicated. Making what possessions remained to him into small parcels, and asking Cléry to give his wedding-ring to Marie Antoinette, he told the valet, 'Tell the Queen, and my dear sister and my beloved children that I beg their pardon for not having allowed them to come upstairs—I wanted to spare them the pain of a cruel parting.' At eight-thirty am Louis, wearing a black cocked hat and a brown overcoat, and the Abbé Edgeworth were driven in the Mayor of Paris's carriage to the Place de la Révolution (now the Place de la Concorde). The square was packed with 20,000 troops, though the streets were deserted. On the way, the King read the Psalms from Edgeworth's breviary. When they arrived drums rolled, and as he climbed the steps of the scaffold the King shouted to the drummers, 'Keep quiet!'—they ceased. He loosened his shirt, taking off his cravat with an almost unnatural calm. He demurred a little when the executioners wanted to tie his hands, but then agreed. As he was about to lie on the board beneath the knife he cried, 'Frenchmen, I die innocent!' The drums began to roll. His last words were, 'May my blood strengthen the happiness of the Fr . . . ' As the knife fell, the Abbé Edgeworth prayed aloud, 'Son of Saint Louis, ascend to Heaven.'

However weak and indecisive Louis XVI may have been, no more honourable or decent man ever sat upon a throne. He could have escaped his fate many times over, if he had not been so determined to avoid shedding his people's blood. Ernest Renan saw his killing as self-murder, 'the suicide of France'.

'The Child in the Temple'

LOUIS XVII (1793–1795)

'Always alone—my mother stays in the other tower'

There is no episode in French history more painful than the
'reign' of Louis XVII. These two years, the last of his short
life, were years of utter misery; the boy who had been born to
the highest position in the world was systematically brutalized
and degraded, and then deliberately neglected until he died.
None the less, for a moment at least he knew that he was King of
France when, after his father's execution, his mother knelt
before him in homage.

Louis XVII—Louis-Charles—was born at Versailles on
Holy Saturday 1785, and at once created Duc de Normandie.
Marie Antoinette first learnt his sex when the child was shown
to her wearing the *cordon bleu* of the Saint-Esprit—the traditional way of informing a Queen that she had given birth to a
Son of France. In contrast to his brother, the Dauphin Louis-
Joseph, he began life as a healthy, lively boy, soon very talkative, with striking, somewhat girlish good looks, set off by his
long fair hair, but marred (according to contemporaries) by
excessively thick lips—though these are not apparent in the
many beautiful portraits of him. Hézecques tells us that he was a
noticeably sweet-natured child. He was only four when he succeeded his brother as Dauphin, too young to realize his new
importance. In a letter, written in that sad summer of 1789,
Marie Antoinette says that though healthy he is much too
nervous—'the slightest unusual noise has an extraordinary
effect on him.' He had to have as much fresh air as possible;
fortunately he loved flowers and gardening. The Queen herself
read him Perrault's fairy tales and La Fontaine's fables. She
noticed with concern that her son was bad at his lessons, owing
to lack of application rather than stupidity. However, she was

satisfied that he had the best governess possible in Yolande de Polignac.

Louis-Charles could remember little of the early days of the Revolution. He was obviously upset by the dreadful leave-taking of Versailles in October 1789; when the harridans screamed threats at the Queen on the way to Paris, he put his head out of the coach window and begged 'Forgive Mummy' (*Grace pour Maman*). Although his first sight of the Tuileries, dusty and unfurnished, frightened him, he became happy enough there, and enjoyed playing in the palace gardens wearing the red, white and blue uniform of the National Guard. In July 1790 1,500 Bretons marched up to Paris to swear loyalty to the King. After Louis XVI had embraced their leader, the entire contingent was taken to see the Dauphin who was picking flowers on the terrace of the Tuileries. 'The pretty boy gave a flower as long as they lasted to every Breton', says an English eye-witness, 'and then gathered lilac leaves, and for fear they should not last, tore them in two, and gave half a leaf apiece to the rest.'

Probably his first lasting moment of fear was the flight to Varennes; having fallen asleep after leaving the Tuileries, he said later that he woke up on the way out of Paris, terrified and convinced that 'someone was coming to murder him'. Such a timid, sensitive child was horribly scared by the hostile demonstrations—the shouting and the stoning—and by his parents' dejection on the miserable drive back.

Louis-Charles's last year at the Tuileries must have been a time of constant terror, not only when the mob stormed into the palace on 20 June 1791, and made him wear the red cap of Liberty, but each day and every day. Though his mother and father did their best to conceal their own fear from him, he must have sensed the savage hostility of the mob outside the railings. According to Mme de Tourzel, one of his governesses, the Prince Royal (as he was called by the new Constitution) was obviously aware of his parents' alarm, however much they tried to hide it. After the mob's invasion of the Tuileries in June 1792, the royal family dared not set foot outside the palace, and Louis-Charles was even banished from his beloved gardens; when his mother attempted to take him for a walk there, there was nearly a riot by the red-capped *sans-culottes*, who screamed threats and

insults at them through the railings and howled *Ça Ira*. During the flight from the palace to the Manège his parents kept the full horror of their situation from him, and mercifully he dozed throughout much of the ordeal in the minute writers' box.

The months in the Temple with his father and mother were probably happy enough for Louis-Charles. Admittedly, the contrast between palatial luxury and the Tower's rough furniture—some of which can still be seen at the Musée Carnavalet—must have come as a shock, but at least his parents were able to spend more time with him. They were invariably soothing and reassuring, despite the guards' provocation. The King and Queen did not even show emotion when the commissioners came to tell them that the monarchy had been abolished, though the boy realized that secretly they were very distressed, and he learnt to fear the constant visits by committees from the Convention. Cléry, that heroic valet, was deeply impressed by the child's sweet nature and attempts to comfort his parents. Naturally quick and intelligent, he learnt to live with the insolent guards, to recognize which of them was biddable or at any rate not a nuisance; on one occasion he reported to his father, as a good sign, that a guard was reading Tacitus.

When Louis XVI knew that he had been condemned to death, he told the Dauphin never to forget his Catholic faith and never to take vengeance upon regicides, raising the boy's hand into the air to give more solemnity to the oath. Louis-Charles tried, unsuccessfully, to run out of the Temple, with a touching little plan of begging the soldiers to save his father. While the cannon roared to celebrate the execution and the royal prisoners were all in tears, Marie Antoinette (it is said) knelt solemnly before her son and acknowledged him as King. Almost certainly the majority of Frenchmen and Frenchwomen joined with her in spirit. Only extremists wanted the First Republic—everyone else was heartily sick of the bloodshed and anarchy, the soaring inflation, the revolutionary wars at home and abroad.

The prisoners were guarded with the utmost vigilance. One plan to escape—in which Louis was to have been hidden in a laundry-basket—was betrayed; another was foiled by sheer accident. For a time General Dumouriez who commanded the republican armies in the Low Countries, intended to march on

Paris and enthrone Louis XVII, but he was defeated by the Austrians at Neerwinden in the spring, and deserted. In March 1793 the royalists rose in the Vendée where, led by the Marquis de Rochejacquelein, the pious peasants—the dreaded *Chouans*, so called from their hooting like owls when signalling—waged a bestial little war on the Godless government. Other risings were to follow—at Caen, Lyons, Bordeaux, Marseilles. The French would soon be at each other's throats, White (royalist) against Blue (democrat). The newly-formed Committee of Public Safety (the ten extremists who terrorized the Convention and formed the country's real government) regarded Louis as the greatest internal danger—he was the focal point of every counter-revolutionary conspiracy. Even the crazy Hébert, whose extremism had degenerated into mania, had to admit that, 'For royalists and moderates the King never dies—he is in the Temple.' It was also obvious that his mother and aunt had every intention of escaping and of taking him with them. The last straw came in June 1793 when it was discovered, just in time, that the Franco–Irish General Dillon had been plotting a *coup d'état* to dismiss the Convention at the point of the bayonet and proclaim Louis XVII.

Accordingly on the night of 3 July 1793 six commissioners—mostly Paris tradesmen—suddenly arrived at the Temple and burst in on the Queen who was quietly sewing by the side of her sleeping son. They announced brusquely that 'Capet's son is to be separated from his mother and family'. For an hour Marie Antoinette clutched Louis, who was weeping hysterically, imploring and beseeching the men to have mercy, but her prayers were in vain. At last she dressed the sobbing child, telling him to go with the men but never to forget how much she loved him. As they dragged him away, the King of France and Navarre screamed piteously.

In place of his mother Louis XVII now had a 'tutor', a Member of the Paris Commune, Antoine Simon. This successor to the *grand seigneur* Governors of the Bourbon child monarchs was a failed cobbler of nearly sixty, from the Paris back streets, who was living off the savings of his charwoman wife. Illiterate —he could neither read nor write—dirty, foul-mouthed and evil-tempered, Simon had been chosen deliberately as being best qualified 'to turn an aristocrat into a democrat'. Though it has

sometimes been questioned, there is no reason to doubt the traditional assessment of Simon. The child cried for two days and two nights, refusing to eat and begging to be taken back to his mother; eventually he grew too frightened to weep. The old cobbler quickly taught the boy, who was only eight and naturally trusting, to sing popular revolutionary songs like the *Marseillaise* and the *Carmagnole,* and to swear, and made him wear the red bonnet of a *sans-culotte.* Meanwhile his distraught mother, who could hear him crying in the room below, stayed at her window for hours on end in the hope of catching a glimpse of him when he went to play in the garden. Later, she said, 'Nothing can hurt me any more.'

Simon was frequently drunk, and made Louis drink till he was tipsy too, although wine nauseated the boy. From her own room his horrified sister heard her brother's shrill treble echoing the old man's hoarse voice in bawdy catches. The cobbler made the King of France fetch and carry for him, cursing and shouting at him, and beating him especially when drunk. Hébert seems to have instructed Simon to degrade the boy physically—the old man taught him to masturbate, damaging one of his testicles in the process. Probably he was also instructed to bring prostitutes into his room, who, it was hoped—although he was too small to have intercourse with them—might infect him with the pox (this instruction does not seem to have been carried out). Every effort was made to terrify Louis, Simon bellowing that he would send him to the guillotine. Such treatment soon had an appalling effect on the sensitive little boy. Only a few weeks after being dragged from his mother, referring to his relatives in the room above him, he was heard to yell, '*Foutre,* haven't those damned whores been guillotined yet?'

By the summer of 1793 the Austrians and Prussians were beginning to capture French frontier towns, while the English occupied Toulon and the Spaniards invaded Roussillon. Within France, royalist risings were going from strength to strength— even the Protestant mountaineers of the Cévennes rose for the lily banner of the Kings who had treated them so ill. Only the most savage measures sustained the tottering Republic, the guillotine crashing down monotonously. Robespierre and Carnot saved their Revolution in an orgy of French blood.

Scapegoats were needed, the most sensational possible, and the Austrian bitch was the obvious candidate. The Committee of Public Safety wished to humiliate her as well as to destroy her.

On 6 October Hébert and a commission visited the Temple to obtain 'evidence' from 'Capet'. Louis signed statements, obviously drafted by Hébert, accusing his mother of counter-revolutionary activities, and of deliberately teaching him to masturbate for her amusement. Madame Royale was brought down to confirm the statements, which her brother repeated— he even accused her of not telling the truth. Weeping with indignation, the girl was removed to make way for Mme Elisabeth, to whom poor Louis again repeated his 'statements'. Her comment was *'Oh! Le monstre!'* But one of those present said that she was prompted by astonishment rather than revulsion, and that it was quite obvious that her nephew was repeating word for word a lesson which he did not understand.

His poor, proud, silly mother, prematurely aged—white-haired and half-blind—died magnificently on 16 October 1793. At her trial—she was indicted as 'the scourge and bloodsucker of France'—Hébert's disgusting allegations prompted the fine reply, 'I appeal to all mothers here today.' Shouts of feminine support from the gallery so alarmed Robespierre that he muttered, 'The fool. He will save the woman yet!' Unlike her husband, the 'Widow Capet' was taken to the guillotine in an open tumbril like a dung-cart. On the scaffold her courage was sublime; although nearly fainting, she showed not the slightest trace of fear—she even apologized to the headsman for treading on his foot. Napoleon described Marie Antoinette's killing as 'something even worse than regicide', and the splendour of her bearing throughout her trial and execution, and the countless humiliations which accompanied them, disenchanted many of her former enemies with their new masters. For reasons of policy or from sheer indifference—one cannot believe from humanity—her death was kept a secret from her son, who for the rest of his short life always believed that she was somewhere in the Temple.

Thousands perished in the Terror, royalists like gallant old Malesherbes and his daughter and his grandchildren, together with republicans like André Chénier and Mme Roland—who

had once proclaimed, 'We can only be reborn through blood'—
and even the maniac Hébert. Some of the worst excesses took
place in the provinces—at Nantes 2,000 enemies of the state
were systematically drowned. Other casualties were the regicide
Philippe Egalité—characteristically, his speech from the scaffold
was 'one short, obscene word'—and Mme du Barry. On her way
to the guillotine, jolting over the cobbles in her tumbril, la du
Barry howled and shrieked, imploring a horrified crowd for
mercy; observers thought that if the French aristocracy had
behaved like her—instead of maintaining a silent, icy, dignity—
the Terror could never have taken place. As it was, in May 1794
Louis's aunt, Mme Elisabeth, was accused of 'planning to
massacre the people, to make away with freedom and restore
tyranny'; after the execution her headless body was thrown
naked into a common grave. Now only Louis's sister remained
in the Temple, though he never saw her again.

Everything associated with the monarchy had been demolished. Street names had been changed, statues pulled down.
Saint-Denis, the most sacred shrine of French royalty, had been
sacked in August 1793; the tombs of the Kings were broken
open and their remains dragged out and thrown into a limepit—
their embalmed hearts were sold as curiosities (years later the
painter Saint-Martin returned those of Louis XIII and
Louis XIV, practically undamaged, to Louis XVIII). The phial
containing the coronation chrism was smashed—nobody
noticed a monk in plain clothes stealing away with several
drops on a shard of the shattered *sainte ampoule*. But for all the
tearing down, the Convention could never forget that there was
still a King of France in the Temple.

For the last months of 1793 Louis remained with the Simons,
who seem to have grown quite fond of him; the old man had a
pigeon loft built for him and even had a toy singing canary,
which he had found, repaired and installed in the boy's room.
Some of the better-natured guards used to play draughts and
bowls with him. When they were drunk, it was a different
story; on one occasion they were found throwing 'Capet' round
the room, and blowing smoke into his face, while Simon kept on
pulling his long hair and threatening to kill him because he
refused to sing yet another filthy song. Later, old Mme Simon
too admitted that she had hit the child on a number of occasions.

But in January 1794 the Simons decided that the job entailed too much responsibility and resigned their post.

In the months to come, Louis may even have missed the dirty old cobbler's company. For the Committee of Public Safety decided that more extreme measures were necessary to guard against 'Charles Capet's' escape—people among the Paris mob could be heard referring to 'The King' or to 'Louis XVII'. Accordingly, a guard of four commissioners was appointed, to be relieved daily. There is no detailed account of what took place during the following months, but it seems that orders were given for the boy to be literally walled up on 19 January; apparently his door was nailed to the frame and further secured by great iron plates; his food was pushed in to him on a turn-box inserted in the door, while a small grating at the top of the door enabled the guards to peer in to see if he was still alive. No lamps or candles were allowed, a particularly cruel order as the one window was nailed and shuttered and the child was terrified of the dark—partly because of the rats which constantly scurried across the floor, and under, and sometimes over, his bed. Nobody entered that dark, airless room for six months, an eternity for an eight-year-old, and nobody spoke to him— except occasionally to shout at him through the grating.

In May 1794 Robespierre came to inspect Madame Royale, and it is more than likely that he peered through the grating at the dim form of his rightful King. The Princess, a spirited fifteen-year-old, had obviously learnt something of her brother's condition from the guards, and remembered that when she had last seen him the previous October he had seemed unhealthily fat; the man who passed him his food through the turn-box said that he had to shout through the grill to make the boy realize that it was there. She handed a note to 'the Sea-Green Incorruptible', demanding that a doctor should see her brother. Naturally, the enemy of tyrants ignored her request.

On 27 July 1794 Robespierre was deposed, to be beheaded shortly afterwards in circumstances of great agony and humiliation. (He fell because practically the entire Convention went in fear of their lives.) Next day the *ci-devant* Vicomte de Barras, who had organized the coup, visited Louis at the Temple. We know what he found from a report by later visitors. The room was almost unimaginably filthy and foul-smelling; the King of

France had had no means of washing and lay in his excrement on a urine-soaked invalid's cradle, covered with bugs and lice, surrounded by the rotting remains of uneaten food which the rats gnawed at will. At first Barras thought that the nightmare apparition with matted hair and huge finger-nails was asleep, but then he saw that it had woken and was watching him. Attempts to make Louis get up from his bed of filth failed—if picked up he collapsed as soon as he was released. In response to questions, he said he had no complaints about his guards. The guards told Barras that the child ate nothing and did not even seem to sleep much.

Barras, horrified, gave orders that Louis should receive medical attention at once and that the revolting room should be washed down immediately. He also recommended that he should be allowed to play in the garden with his sister, and that two women should be appointed to look after him. The Convention ignored his recommendations. Admittedly a new guardian, a young Creole 'democrat' from Martinique called Christophe Laurent, was appointed. But for a further two months, during the heat of summer, the child remained immured with his filth and his misery.

At last, on 1 September 1794, Laurent and two assistants unbarred the door. Asked why he had not eaten—there was an untouched meal on the table—Louis replied simply that he wanted to die. He was carried out and brought into another room, where he was bathed and deloused, and then a doctor saw him. He realized at once that the child was seriously ill, covered in sores and tumours—a skin condition made it torment for him to remove his breeches.

Louis's room was cleaned out and he was given toys, cards and writing materials, and taken each day to the top of the Tower for a breath of fresh air. One day he picked some flowers growing on the battlements and dropped them outside a door on the way down; it was the door of his mother's old room and he may have remembered how he had once brought her flowers from his own garden at the Tuileries—obviously he thought she was still there.

But the improvement was very slight. He was still not allowed to play in the garden, not to see his sister and not to have a light at night (although the guards managed to kill the rats in his

bedroom, with arsenic). However, in November Laurent acquired a more agreeable, if somewhat ineffectual assistant, one Gomin, who was timid but imaginative. He brought Louis flowers and even a lamp, and took him into another room. It was some weeks before the child trusted him sufficiently to speak. Suddenly Louis said, 'You're the man who gave me the flowers —I haven't forgotten.'

Just before Christmas 1794 commissioners again came to inspect the prisoner, whom certain members of the Convention had recently been referring to as 'a rallying point for aristocrats' —and also as 'the Capet foetus'. The commissioners' leader, Harmand, described the visit twenty years later (some months before he himself died of want and starvation). They found the King in a bare, scantily-furnished, but clean, set of rooms, playing with a pack of cards. Louis, dressed in a neat, slate-coloured sailor suit, looked extraordinary, with thin elongated limbs, a disproportionately small torso and chest, and curiously rounded shoulders, though 'the head was very handsome, with long fine hair which was well kept and light brown in colour'. Harmand found livid swellings on his arms and legs, which he attributed to rickets. What struck him most, however, was the child's refusal to speak or to answer questions, almost as though deaf and dumb; he did not even respond to offers of toys and sweets. Harmand was also shocked by the royal diet—a coarse bowl of blackish soup, some equally black beef, a platter of lentils, half a dozen burnt chestnuts, and no wine. He ordered grapes for the prisoner, who ate them without saying a word.

In January 1795 'Capet' had the honour of being the subject of a debate by the Convention, who discussed whether he and his sister should be exiled or remain in prison. A lawyer called Cambacères argued that 'the exile of a tyrant has always been the first step in his return to power', and cited the case of Tarquin and the Romans. The Convention voted to keep the children in prison. The only power which tried to save them was Spain; to his eternal honour, Charles IV—otherwise a pitiful degenerate, and immortalized as such by Goya—insisted on the release of his young cousins as a pre-requisite condition for any peace between the two countries.

Gomin knew something of what the 'tyrant' suffered. When the guard told yet another commissioner that Louis was ill, the

man replied, 'There are many children worth just as much as he, who are far iller—and many of the ones who die are worth a good deal more.' Gomin remembered that the prisoner repeated the words to himself. Another commissioner told Gomin in front of Louis, 'In six weeks time that child will either be an idiot or dead.'

His health worsened—tumours appeared on his knees and elbows which made any movement an agony. Ironically he was suffering from the King's Evil, a tuberculosis which sometimes attacks the bones as well as the lymph glands. Gomin did his best, bringing the child toys, playing draughts with him and fetching books from the Temple library for him to read. One evening he looked beseechingly at Gomin, whom he obviously thought understood him, and then looked at the door. 'Let me see her once before I die,' he begged. Gomin had not the heart to tell him that his mother was dead; he said awkwardly that it was impossible, whereupon the prisoner cried piteously.

Indeed by now there was no hope for King Louis XVII. On 16 March 1795 a royalist agent, M de Frotté, wrote to an adventurous Irishwoman, Lady Atkyns (who had wild dreams of rescuing 'the King') to tell her what he had heard from a member of the Convention: 'Under Robespierre they so debased the unfortunate child, physically and morally, that he cannot live . . . you have no idea of the degeneration and brutishness of the little creature.' If Louis was far from brutish, it was none the less true that his health was broken—he was increasingly attacked by fevers.

Laurent left the Temple that March, to be replaced by Etienne Lasne, a house-painter who had once been a soldier and had seen Louis at the Tuileries. A tough but kind-hearted character, the old soldier tried to make the boy as comfortable as possible, cleaning out his room meticulously. Accompanied by Gomin on the violin, he sang to him—sometimes marching songs of the royal guard, which they hoped the boy might remember—played cards with him and read to him. When Louis grew too weak to climb the stairs, Lasne would carry him to the top of the Tower where he could breathe fresher air.

At the beginning of May 1795, a tradesman managed to catch a glimpse of Louis XVII at the Temple, his face covered with ulcers and pimples, his body weirdly deformed—'the most

pitiable creature that ever was seen'—and barely able to sit up. It was plain that he was seriously ill and from 6 May doctors, supervised by commissioners, made regular visits, prescribing medicine and diet. Once, when the doctor was about to leave, Louis clung to him and—referring to the commissioners— begged, 'Don't leave me alone with those wicked men!'

He was growing weaker every day. Moved to a room which overlooked the Temple garden, he was barely able to look out of the window at the summer. Lasne and Gomin, who were really a very decent pair, did their best to cheer him, and Gomin brought him flowers assiduously. Then, on 6 June, Louis fainted and his guards suspected that he was failing. On the evening of 7 June, Gomin found him crying; asked if he was in pain, the prisoner sobbed, *'Toujours seul—ma mère est restée dans l'autre tour.'* He died during the night of 7–8 June 1795, with his arms round Lasne's neck. He was ten years old. He was buried secretly, by night, in a common grave at the cemetery of the church of Sainte-Marguerite; it is probable that the sexton later re-buried his remains nearer the church wall.

Many attempts were made to show that Louis XVII did not die in the Temple, and more than thirty claimants have tried to prove that they were Louis, or one of his descendants. Admittedly, the silent, rickety little wreck of 1795 bore small resemblance to the talkative, charming, intelligent child of 1793; and there may well have been a plot to rescue him, to substitute a deaf and dumb inmate of the Invalides hospital in his place. But all the evidence supports the traditional—and generally accepted—belief that the boy who died in the Temple was indeed Louis XVII.

Few will disagree with the Comte d'Hézecques's opinion that the little King had been given 'a course of poison more horrible and protracted than any dose of laudanum'. The Count adds, 'The saddest thing for France is that every member of the Convention was responsible for the infamy of his long martyrdom.'

'Tartuffe'

LOUIS XVIII (1795-1824)

'Unite—and forget'

The Bourbons did not die with the *Ancien Régime*. One of the least known of French Kings, Louis XVIII was also one of the ablest. Had he succeeded to the throne before his elder brother, Louis XVI, this unpleasant but interesting man might well have saved the monarchy.

Louis-Stanislas was born at Versailles on 17 November 1755, the fourth son of the Dauphin Louis, and given the ancient title of Comte de Provence. Like his brothers, his education was entrusted to the pious Duc de Vauguyon, whose repressive regime may have been responsible for his lukewarm attitude towards religion. From a very early age he showed unusual intelligence, aided by a phenomenal memory. Delicate, with deformed hips which made it difficult for him to ride a horse, he was studious and developed a taste for history and literature which lasted throughout his life. He particularly enjoyed Voltaire, and the writings of the *Encyclopédistes*. Naturally malicious, he was apt to sneer at his clumsy brother, Berry (the future Louis XVI), who was only a year older, mocking his bad grammar—'A Prince should at least know his own language.'

Berry gave him a revealing nickname—*Tartuffe*. This is the title-role of one of Molière's greatest plays, a study of a sanctimonious hypocrite who covets both his benefactor's wife and his benefactor's goods. As a Voltairean, Louis-Stanislas was not exactly sanctimonious, while he was to be a very restrained adulterer (at any rate by the standards of his brother Artois, or of his grandfather). But in secret he always coveted his brother's crown, and undoubtedly he resembled Tartuffe in his cynicism and cunning, in his cruel wit and in his icy selfishness. Probably the quality which most of all prompted his unenviable nickname was his false *bonhommie*.

When Berry ascended the throne in 1774, Louis-Stanislas was given the traditional style of *Monsieur Frère du Roi*. He was Heir Presumptive until the birth of the Dauphin Louis-Joseph in 1781, and no one was ever more conscious of the majesty of the French monarchy than Monsieur. Although only eighteen, he remonstrated angrily with his brother when he brought back the Parlements in 1774; 'France will soon have republican senators like those in Genoa, Venice or Berne and the King will be nothing more than a Doge.' But his brother told him that they were both too young to rely on their own judgement. Indeed, as a young man Monsieur was a thorough-going reactionary in every way. He voted against Turgot's Six Edicts and, while delighting in them himself, urged the King to suppress any works of the *Encyclopédistes* which might encourage sedition. He regarded the American Revolution as 'a punishable rebellion'.

Monsieur enjoyed pomp and circumstance. Despite his inability to ride, he kept one of the largest stables in France and his regiment of Carabineers was superbly mounted. As Grand Master of the Knights of St Lazarus, he restricted membership of that ancient hospitaller order to great noblemen. Everything about him was designed to enhance his pride and ostentation. Short, fat and swarthy, he overdressed in diamond-studded suits, and adopted a repellently haughty manner. Yet a gouache of Monsieur in his early twenties, by Moitte, shows a surprisingly attractive face, with the Bourbon nose but an amused grin.

The birth of Louis XVI's first child in 1778, Madame Royale, was a bitter blow to Monsieur. At the christening, when Cardinal Rohan asked what names would be given to the child, he was heard to mutter, 'But the first thing is to know who are the father and mother'; later, he seems to have tried to imply that the father was Artois. The birth of a Dauphin in 1781 must have been even more galling.

Monsieur had himself married in 1772, when he was only fifteen, but, despite boasting how he would outdo his brother, failed to beget children; it was rumoured that his impotency drove his wife to drink, though in fact he only became impotent much later in life. 'Madame' was Maria Giuseppina of Savoy, daughter of the King of Sardinia. She was small, dark, ugly,

insignificant, and bad-tempered, coarse-natured, and dirty in her person—Louis XV begged her parents to persuade her to wash her neck and clean her teeth. Mme de Campan says that the only thing worth mentioning about her was a 'pair of tolerably fine eyes'. Madame's favourite occupation was catching thrushes in nets and having them made into soup. (Monsieur was fond of food too, but with more elegance—he created a dish which consisted of a partridge stuffed with an ortolan, which in turn was stuffed with foie gras.) Their flat was in the left wing at Versailles on the side near the Orangery, Monsieur and Madame occupying separate floors.

Monsieur became a patron of literature, supporting a whole host of writers at his palace of the Luxembourg. He earned himself a name for wit and *bon mots*—it was he who coined the aphorism 'Punctuality is the politeness of Princes'. He wrote elegant light verse, ferocious political satire and libretti for two operas—*La Caravane du Caire* and *Panurge dans l'Ile des Lanternes*. Some of his verse he sent under assumed names to the *Mercure* and other newspapers. He read voraciously, his letters being filled with quotations ranging from Virgil to Voltaire.

When Emperor Joseph II paid his famous visit to Paris in 1778, he reported to his mother that Monsieur was 'an inscrutable creature, better-looking than the King, but mortally cold'. None the less, Louis-Stanislas got on well enough with Marie Antoinette—his sly jokes made her laugh; Mme de Campan says that the fête which he gave for the Queen at his château of Brunoy was the most magnificent ever given to her, a combination of masque and tournament.

Monsieur constantly intrigued against the government, writing numerous and often savage pamphlets. One described Turgot as 'a despot' and Louis XVI as 'the leading dummy in the kingdom'. He printed and circulated Necker's secret memorandum, a ruse which led to the minister's downfall (Necker had incurred his enmity by refusing to pay him a million livres which Louis-Stanislas claimed had been left to him by his parents). During the Assembly of Notables he presided over one of its committees and opposed most of Calonne's reforms.

Somewhat surprisingly in view of his ugliness, timidity and

ill-defined sexuality, Louis-Stanislas acquired a glittering young mistress, the high-spirited Mme de Balbi, who was one of Madame's ladies. Anne-Jacobé Caumont La Force had been born in 1759, the daughter of a distinguished member of Monsieur's household. Admired by all for her elegance and dashing appearance, she married the Comte de Balbi, grandson of a Genoese Doge, but he turned out to be insane; in 1780 violent behaviour culminated in his beating his wife with his cane after finding her *en galanterie*, and he was confined in a madhouse (some said with Monsieur's connivance). What appealed to Louis-Stanislas about la Balbi was not so much her physical charms, and certainly not her promiscuity, as her literary tastes and mordant wit; though it is likely that they slept together, for at this date he was not yet impotent. He installed her in a flat above his own at Versailles, Madame continuing to live below. In Paris Anne-Jacobé held court at the Petit Luxembourg, where she entertained the literary men whose company her lover enjoyed so much. Her extravagance on clothes, jewellery and gambling reached such heights that Monsieur soon found himself in serious financial difficulty.

Hézecques, who obviously disliked him intensely, gives an unflattering portrait of Monsieur in the late 1780s and early 1790s. 'Monsieur was very fat, but it was not the fatness which goes with strength and vigour, like Louis XVI. He had an unhealthy constitution and even as a boy took medicine to help his circulation and cure fits of giddiness, and this unhealthiness was made worse by lack of exercise. . . . No Prince was ever more ungainly than Monsieur; he had the waddle of the Bourbons in its most extreme form and all his fine clothes could not conceal his bad figure.'

Louis-Stanislas's real calibre first appeared after the decision to summon the States General. He encouraged the King to agree to double the Third Estate; in his brother's place he would have extracted the maximum popularity from such a concession. He saw no purpose in leaving Paris in 1789 and persuaded Louis XVI not to abandon his capital; only with hindsight does this advice appear disastrous; at the time, it seemed sound sense. Nor was he shaken by the storming of Versailles or by being dragged to the Tuileries in the King's wake in October 1789.

By 1790, however, Louis-Stanislas was having second thoughts. The Marquis de Favras, a professional adventurer and mercenary soldier, proposed rescuing the King and taking him to Péronne on the frontier; it seems, though there is no proof, that Monsieur borrowed two million livres to finance the operation. But Favras was denounced by a fellow plotter; it was rumoured that he had meant to raise 30,000 men and assassinate Lafayette. He was hanged but luckily incriminated none of the Royal Family.

Monsieur far preferred the idea of being a constitutional monarch to having no throne at all. He would have had no qualms about taking Louis XVI's place on the throne. However, after Favras, he was too cautious to intrigue during such dangerous times, but he hung on at the Luxembourg till the last possible moment, playing endless whist at the Tuileries with his dear brother (while grumbling about him behind his back; he told Mirabeau that the King's weakness and indecision were beyond belief, comparing his character to 'oiled ivory balls which one tries in vain to hold together'). Mirabeau contemplated forming a cabinet in which Monsieur would have been First Minister, but seems to have decided he was too nervous; probably Louis-Stanislas was hedging his bets.

With his usual astuteness he realized when the situation was finally out of control. During the Royal family's flight to Varennes, while Louis XVI trundled towards disaster, Monsieur, Madame and Mme de Balbi, equipped with false passports, left Paris by the Pont Neuf and drove to Le Bourget, driving from thence to Soissons, Laon and La Capelle, and crossing the Belgian frontier without incident.

Monsieur now set up a government in exile at Coblenz, where Artois and the Prince de Condé had each gathered an army of *émigrés*. He assumed the title of Regent on the grounds that the King had lost his freedom of action. He kept impressive state, entertaining regally, sent ambassadors to the European sovereigns in the hope of persuading them to invade France, and issued threatening proclamations which gravely embarrassed his brother in Paris. Calonne came over from England to be his Prime Minister.

Mme de Balbi's sway over Monsieur reached its zenith at Coblenz, where she was known as the 'Queen of the Emigration'

and aspired to a political rôle. Her promiscuity made Louis-Stanislas a laughing-stock. When he moved to Hamm, she went to Brussels instead, though with every intention of rejoining him later. However, Monsieur then learnt that it was common gossip that she had had twins by a youthful lover, and was so furious that he never saw her again.

After la Balbi's fall, the focus of Monsieur's affections was the Captain of his Bodyguard. Antoine-Louis-François de Bestiade, Comte d'Avaray, was thirty-four and a career soldier whose skilful organization of his master's escape to Coblenz had won him his master's confidence; later the infatuated Louis-Stanislas gave him the right to bear the royal arms of France on his own with the motto *Vicit iter durum pietas* (loyalty finds a way over even the stoniest road). Henceforward, until his death, he only left Monsieur when sent on special missions. The two men had no secrets from each other, Avaray's one fault in Monsieur's eyes being that he had no Latin. Indeed it is probable, though there is no actual proof, that Monsieur was a repressed homosexual. Significantly, Hézecques compares his character with those of Henri III and Monsieur, brother of Louis XIV (though admittedly he does not speak of common sexual tastes). Undoubtedly, Louis-Stanislas found full emotional satisfaction in male friendships, even if these were platonic because of his low sexual drive. Like Louis XIII, he sought the perfect friend.

During the campaign before Valmy, Monsieur was irritated by the bragging of the Prussian commander, the Duke of Brunswick. 'Be careful, Duke,' he warned him, 'I know that the French will defend their country—they are not always beaten.' As a result of the ensuing débâcle, by the end of 1792 Monsieur was living in a small wooden house at Hamm in Westphalia, short of food and heating. The exploits of the *Chouans* raised his hopes, but by the end of 1793, even they had been crushed, only M de La Rochejacquelin holding out in his Breton woods. Monsieur moved to Verona. Here, as King Louis XVIII—he assumed the title on his nephew's death—he issued what some *émigrés* termed the 'criminal' Proclamation of Verona; this promised that Absolutism would be restored and savage penalties inflicted when the King came home; it even listed those who would be quartered, those who would be broken on the

wheel (Talleyrand was among these), those who would be hanged, and those who would be sent to the galleys.

In December 1795 his niece, Madame Royale, was rescued from the Temple. The Austrians exchanged a number of important French prisoners for her and sent her to Vienna, from whence she was brought to the King. She received the warmest welcome of which his cold nature was capable and betrothed to her cousin, Louis d'Angoulême, Artois's son. Sadly, her experiences had ruined her nature and, 'The orphan of the Temple' was a sour bitter woman for the remainder of her long life (she did not die until 1851). Even so, a strong, sentimental attachment sprang up between her and the King; she was undoubtedly his favourite member of the royal family.

It must be remembered that a Bourbon restoration seemed almost inevitable until Napoleon was firmly established. The French people had more than a suspicion that *égalité* was killing *liberté* and *fraternité*, and the newspapers were full of royalist propaganda. Most Frenchmen longed for a return to the rule of law. Unfortunately, Louis, encouraged by reports from his agents in Paris, failed to realize that what France wanted was not the monarchy of 1789 but the constitutional monarchy of 1791. The bourgeoisie had no wish for the return of privilege; the peasants feared the re-introduction of feudal dues; and everyone who had bought *émigré* land dreaded confiscation. Nevertheless, by 1797 Royalist deputies had almost obtained control of the central government and Louis thought his restoration was imminent. But the army was still republican. On 4 September 1797—18 Fructidor, Year V, in the Revolutionary calendar—General Augereau staged a *coup d'état* and fifty-three Royalist deputies were condemned to deportation to Cayenne.

Meanwhile, the King was leading an odd, wandering life. He had left Verona for a brief spell with Condé's army at Blanckenberg in Brunswick, before settling at Mittau in the Baltic Duchy of Courland—now part of Soviet Latvia, a coastal land famed for its beauty. From here he watched General Bonaparte's rise to power with a mixture of hope and apprehension—was he Cromwell or was he General Monk? Before 18 Fructidor he offered him the Vice-royalty of Corsica and the title of Marshal of France if he would restore him. In 1800, when Bonaparte was

First Consul, the King wrote to him: 'You are taking a long time to give me back my throne; there is a danger that you may miss the opportunity. Without me you cannot make France happy, while without you I can do nothing for France. So be quick and let me know what positions and dignities will satisfy you and your friends.' Bonaparte replied, 'I have received Your Royal Highness's letter. I have always taken a keen interest in your misfortunes and in those of your family. But you must not think of returning to France—you cannot do so without marching over a hundred thousand dead bodies.' In 1803 Bonaparte sent an envoy to Mittau to propose that Louis and his family should surrender all claims to the French throne in return for independent principalities in Italy. The King wrote in reply, 'I do not confuse M Bonaparte with those who preceded him. I respect his bravery and military genius. . . . But he is mistaken if he supposes my rights can be made the subject of bargain or compromise.'

However, Bonaparte gave the French everything which they had thought could only be supplied by a Bourbon restoration. Not only did he bring back the Church and build wonderful roads and schools, but he restored the rule of law (besides introducing the *Code Napoléon*, one of the world's outstanding legal codes and one which could be understood by everybody, he even revived some of the courts of the old Parlement of Paris). When Napoleon assumed the title of Emperor in 1804, the King travelled to Sweden to join Artois—whom he had not seen for a decade—and issued a formal protest. But the Empire had a disquietingly permanent appearance.

Louis was forced to leave Mittau by the Tsar in 1807, whereupon he followed Artois's example and settled in England. Although the British government gave him £7,000 a year, they would not let him stay in London, so he established his shabby court at Gosfield Hall in Essex, moving in 1809 to Hartwell House in Buckinghamshire. The diarist Charles Greville, accompanied by his father, visited Louis at Hartwell the following year. Greville says that there were so many people in the house—nearly 150—that the place resembled 'a small rising colony' and that he had never seen so many Dukes in his life. The King received them in his private closet, so small that it seemed like a ship's cabin; the elder Greville said the way Louis

Louis XVII, by Kucharski

Louis XVIII, by Gerard

heaved his huge bulk backwards and forwards made him feel seasick. He gave them a very modest dinner, carving himself; the only wines served were port and sherry. They spent the evening playing whist at threepence a point. The atmosphere was a compound of privation, hopelessness and ridiculously pompous etiquette. The diarist noted with amusement that the local yokels referred disrespectfully to their august neighbour as 'old bungy Louis'.

The King was in constant touch with the professional adventurers and spies who were the only people in France still to take an active interest in the Bourbon cause. Most were of dubious reliability—one double agent even tried to persuade Louis to make a secret trip to Paris. Savary, Napoleon's Minister of Police, paid the Duc d'Aumont £1,000 a year to send him two letters a month reporting what went on at Hartwell. (At the Restoration the King told Savary with relish, 'You see, Monsieur, how little one can trust people. He [Aumont] always told me he was only paid £500—no doubt he didn't want to pay me my royalties, as I drafted the letters myself!) However, there was a genuine traitor at Hartwell who has never been identified, probably an *émigré* courtier; he or she was responsible for the capture and death of many royal agents.

For all his undoubted probity, Avaray, the King's favourite companion, inspired jealousy and even hatred. He particularly irritated conservative *émigrés* by speaking English and dressing like an Englishman. In 1808 a Vendéen veteran, General de Puisaye, accused Avaray of trying to have him assassinated. The scandal reached such proportions that Louis issued a public defence of 'the most feeling of friends' and appointed a committee of twenty-four noblemen who quickly declared Avaray innocent. The favourite at once challenged Puisaye to a duel, but the King had him arrested by the English authorities to prevent him fighting. As a mark of his esteem he then made Avaray a Duke. However, the favourite's health was collapsing —he seems to have been tubercular—and he had to leave England for a warmer climate at the end of 1810.

Louis's Queen, Maria Giuseppina, who despite their incompatibility had stayed with him, died the same year. The British government gave her a state funeral in Westminster Abbey, after which her body was sent home to Turin. The King was by

now in his late fifties, gout-ridden, cripplingly overweight and with a digestion which must have suffered dreadfully from his love of good food. He was prostrate when news came in 1811 that Avaray had died in Madeira.

Luckily, Louis quickly found a new dear friend, one who had been recommended by Avaray himself. Pierre-Louis-Jean-Casimir de Blacas, Comte d'Aulps, had been born in 1771 of an ancient family of Provence. Like his predecessor, he was a career soldier, a former dragoon captain. He had joined Louis's household at Verona and had stayed with him ever since. A quixotic figure who modelled himself on the heroes of French chivalry, he insisted on regarding his gouty master as the reincarnation of Saint Louis and Henri IV. He knew Latin, and soon Louis was devoted to him. As Blacas said later, 'You don't know the King—he must have a favourite and he might as well have me as anyone else.'

After the débâcle of Napoleon's Russian campaign, Louis was optimistic enough to send an envoy to Charles XIV of Sweden (the former Marshal Bernadotte) and the Tsar, but the envoy found little encouragement, the Tsar being positively hostile. Then in October 1813 Napoleon was defeated at Leipzig. The King refused to attend a triumphal banquet in London, commenting, 'I don't know if the disasters overtaking the French army are a means by which providence intends to restore legitimate authority, but neither I nor the Princes of my family can rejoice at events which are such a sorrow to our country.' None the less, Leipzig had transformed his situation. On 13 March 1814 Bordeaux hoisted the white flag of the Bourbons. To his amusement, Louis was invited by the Prince Regent to attend a ball at Carlton House for the first time; the walls were hung with draperies covered in fleurs-de-lis and the rooms filled with *émigrés* in hired court dress.

Yet the allies were still thinking of a settlement with Napoleon and even after the Marshals deserted him in April discussed such alternatives as Bernadotte and the Duc d'Orléans. Finally a demonstration in the Paris streets in favour of King Louis—carefully organized by Talleyrand and M de Vitrolles, Artois's agent—decided them in favour of the Bourbons.

Napoleon abdicated on 6 April 1814 and departed to Elba.

Under the skilful management of Talleyrand (whom Louis had once promised to break on the wheel), the Imperial Senate deposed the two-year-old Napoleon II and proclaimed Louis XVIII. Artois, who had been on the frontier of northern France since February, entered Paris on 12 April 1814 in his capacity as Lieutenant-General (Regent). He delighted the French by quickly negotiating what France wanted most of all—the evacuation of the occupying allied armies in return for withdrawing the French troops who were cut off in Italy and Germany. France kept the frontiers of 1792, including that of the Rhine.

At Hartwell, King Louis's carriage began its triumphal progress on 20 April, drawn by Englishmen instead of horses. The Prince Regent had come to fetch him, and in London the King was cheered by what seemed to be the entire capital and serenaded by brass bands outside his hotel in Albemarle Street. He dined at Carlton House with the Regent and the Archbishop of Canterbury; Louis bestowed the *Cordon Bleu* on his host, who reciprocated with the Garter (later the Regent said that buckling it on had been like putting a girdle round the waist of a stoutish woman). The King set sail for France on 24 April, on board the *Royal Sovereign*.

His Most Christian Majesty drove into 'his good city of Paris' through the Porte Saint-Denis on 3 May 1814—it was almost twenty-two years since he had seen his capital and he was in tears. With him in his carriage was the Duchesse d'Angoulême, whose last roof in Paris had been the Temple prison, and the aged Prince de Condé, the once redoubtable White general who was now blind and wandering in his wits. The 'royal invalid', as Chateaubriand lovingly called Louis XVIII, was received with all the martial splendour of the Grande Armée; Chateaubriand (in his somewhat unreliable, but always elegant, memoirs) noted that the Old Guard were shaking with rage when they presented arms. On the whole, however, most Frenchmen agreed with Talleyrand that without the ancient dynasty's prestige, France would have been 'either enslaved or partitioned'.

The King was certainly very different from the Emperor. His legs were swollen by gout and the great family nose now presided over a cascade of chins. He wore his hair in the fashion

of 1789—powdered white, combed into 'pigeons' wings' and a pigtail tied with a bow. His snuff-stained clothes were even more antiquated; he wore knee-breeches and red velvet gaiters and carried a three-cornered hat. Yet this fat, antediluvian little creature, with its preposterous dress, high shrill voice and pedantic jokes, somehow possessed a most regal dignity. Chateaubriand tells us that Louis XVIII never forgot for one moment that he was the King, and that Napoleon's Marshals 'were more intimidated when in the presence of this impotent old man than they had ever been in that of the terrible master who commanded them in a hundred battles.'

Even before entering Paris, Louis had granted a constitution, by the Declaration of Saint-Ouen on 2 May 1814. He had thus avoided having to accept that prepared by Talleyrand and the Imperial Senate and, by granting rather than accepting, safeguarded the monarchic principle. The Charter, as the constitution was known, consisted of a hereditary monarchy and two chambers on the model of the English Parliament—an upper house of Peers and a lower of Deputies who were elected by less than a hundred thousand voters. The King also promised freedom of worship and of the press, guaranteed property rights for those who had purchased *émigré* land, and undertook to maintain Napoleonic titles and the Légion d'Honneur.

The two Chambers constituted a system no less representative than the contemporary English Parliament. During his time at Hartwell Louis may well have taken an interest in English politics, but unfortunately he had no first-hand knowledge of how the system worked. His dear friend Blacas, who looked back to 1689 rather than to 1789 and who as Minister for the Household was the nearest thing to a Prime Minister, was disastrously ineffectual; as in 1790–92 ministers worked directly to the King without any proper co-ordination or cabinet.

The one area in which the regime of 1814–15 took positive action, the military, was especially unfortunate. Old *émigré* officers from the armies of Coblenz and the Vendée were given half pay and then promoted, while most of the Imperial Army was summarily retired; 14,000 veteran officers, many of them young men, were condemned to rot; Lady Morgan mentions a Captain reduced to working as a waggoner. At court, Marshals

were snubbed and reminded of their humble origins. What angered the army above all was the revival of the *Maison du Roi*, 6,000 strong, complete with Bodyguards, Horse Grenadiers, Musketeers and even the Hundred Swiss, which only noblemen could join. (Among them were two young poets—Alphonse de Lamartine and Alfred de Vigny.) Soldiers began to refer to the King as 'The Pig'.

When Napoleon landed near Fréjus on 1 March 1815 it was therefore hardly surprising that the army rallied to him. Some Marshals were canny enough to remain loyal to Louis XVIII, but most officers behaved like Ney, 'Bravest of the Brave', who first swore undying fidelity to the King, promising to bring the usurper back in a cage, and who then turned his coat.

The news reached the Tuileries on Sunday 5 March. Louis, his hands crippled by gout, had difficulty opening the envelope which contained the telegram. After reading it, he put his head in his hands and then said, 'It is the Revolution all over again.' Blacas protested that Napoleon was mad and that there was little danger. The King interrupted him impatiently: 'Blacas, *mon ami*, you are a very pleasant fellow but that's not quite enough. You have been wrong many times before and I am afraid that you are deluding yourself again.' None the less Louis started to wear the Légion d'Honneur and solemnly asked the Chamber of Deputies, 'How can I, at the age of sixty end my life better than by dying in defence of my country?' But the army was going over to the Corsican *en masse*. On 19 March Louis XVIII left Paris—at midnight, in his carpet slippers. Napoleon re-entered the Tuileries the very next day.

Ghent was the new Coblenz, Louis installing his court at a house lent by the King of the Netherlands. Here Guizot first saw Louis XVIII who 'gave me the impression of a rational, liberal-minded man, elegantly superficial, courteous to everyone, careful about appearances, not particularly interested in probing to the bottom of things, and as incapable of making the sort of mistakes which ruin a dynasty as he was of ensuring a dynasty's survival.' Fortunately, the allies, who had not demobilized their armies, at once announced their intention of crushing the Emperor. Significantly, Talleyrand remained loyal to the Bourbons, though he wrote from Vienna that the Congress blamed the King in large part for Bonaparte's return.

Meanwhile, the people of Ghent were astounded by the immense number of dishes and bottles consumed by their venerable guest, though he also impressed them by his calm during the panic caused by conflicting reports of the outcome of Waterloo.

Louis XVIII returned to the Tuileries on 8 July 1815, in a closed carriage. Parisians scowled at the fat old man forced on them by the enemy troops who swaggered through their city. The Emperors of Austria and Russia and the King of Prussia held parades on the Champs de Mars, treating the King of France with open contempt. The peace terms were an indemnity of £28 million; occupation for five years by an allied army of 150,000 troops; the surrender of French Savoy to Sardinia; and handing over the Saar to Prussia (which meant the final abandonment of the Rhine frontier). French pride was shattered. People muttered, 'The allies gave us the Bourbons but it was Frenchmen who gave us the Bonapartes.'

In fact it was a Frenchman, Talleyrand, who had given France the Bourbons. He was made Prime Minister as well as Foreign Minister by the King, who sent Blacas off to Naples as ambassador. Louis XVIII knew very well that Talleyrand had twice set the crown of France on his head and keenly resented the fact that all Europe knew it too. Although personally he despised the man, in 1814 he had greeted him with the most honeyed flattery. 'Our families date from the same epoch. But my ancestors were cleverer; if yours had been, it is you who would be inviting me to sit down now.' (In fact the King insisted in private that the Talleyrands only dated from the twelfth century.) For a period after the Hundred Days Louis could not do without him. Nor could he do without Fouché, the regicide Minister of the Interior. Having seen the pair go in together to kiss hands, Chateaubriand wrote, 'All at once the door opened and there entered, in total silence, Vice supported by Crime—that is to say M de Talleyrand on the arm of M Fouché.' Fouché was soon thrown to the wolves, but the King needed Talleyrand's genius to obtain a favourable peace settlement. However, Tsar Alexander then told Louis that Talleyrand was unacceptable; if the King would replace him by the Duc de Richelieu, whom the Russians knew and respected, the Tsar would see that France received good terms. Greatly to

Louis's relief, Talleyrand resigned at the end of September 1815.

The King has often been criticized for not making more use of Talleyrand, but he was totally unacceptable, not only to Ultras but to many moderates. Furthermore, he had betrayed Napoleon and might well betray the Bourbons. Louis would not willingly employ such a dangerous man, but he tried to mollify him with a shower of honours—Grand Chamberlain in 1815, a Duchy in 1817, the *cordon bleu* in 1820—and ignored his frequent attacks on royal ministers. Talleyrand once paid a grudging compliment—'All Bourbons are idiots except Louis XVIII.'

Meanwhile, a White Terror raged throughout France, in which nearly 300 people died. Everyone dreaded the royalist bands, the *Miquelets* and the *Verdets*, who settled old scores and plundered and looted, murder gangs equipped with pocket pistols, knives and sword-sticks, often working in collusion with the local police. At Nîmes Protestants, including women, were publicly humiliated and beaten solely on account of their religion. Marshal Brune was lynched at Avignon, General Ramel assassinated at Toulouse, General Lagarde murdered at Nîmes. Nor was the government less restrained; Marshal Ney was shot for desertion, as were young General de la Bedoyère, and four other generals. The King dared not intervene, while the rest of the royal family cheered on the Whites; Artois's son, M de Berry, joked, 'We are going Marshal hunting.' Great ladies, the *tricoteuses des salons*, raged against Imperialists and Liberals, as did many of the clergy. Special Provosts' Courts sat for three years, executions continuing well into 1816. Both police and terrorists were deliberately encouraged by the new Chamber of Deputies elected in August 1815, so fiercely royalist that Louis called it the *Chambre Introuvable*—the 'Nonesuch Chamber'. Its slogan was 'Time for an end to clemency'; when the King resisted its more savage decrees, it openly called him a Revolutionary, a 'crowned Jacobin'. Louis groaned, 'They are relentless', adding that if the Deputies could have their way 'they would purge me too'. It was later popularly said, 'If you have not lived through 1815, you do not know what hatred is.'

If 1815 was one of the most terrible years in French history,

1816 was scarcely better. Amid continuing anarchy, heavy rain caused a bad harvest and a cattle plague broke out; there was widespread famine. Already France was exhausted by years of warfare, years in which she had lost a million men, had been crushed by backbreaking taxes, and had had her trade crippled by the British blockade. Yet she had to find the money to pay for the indemnity and the army of occupation.

Furthermore, France was woefully disunited. Of 402 Deputies, the majority were Ultras who organized themselves into something like a political party; the Faubourg Saint-Germain formed its hard core, but its ranks were made up of small country squires and even of bourgeois and new men with landed interests. It included the *Purs*, the party's extremists who were often Vendéens or returned *émigrés*, ghosts of the *Ancien Régime*, crying for vengeance on its murderers. On the left sat a motley collection of Liberals who, to begin with, were only united in their loathing of the new regime; most came from the *haute bourgeoisie* and the *parvenu* Napoleonic nobility, both deeply resentful of the old aristocracy. Among this opposition were indestructibles like the novelist Benjamin Constant and Lafayette—'less a politician than a flag'.

However, when discussing Restoration parliaments, one should speak of groups of partisans rather than political parties. The groups which the King preferred were those of the Centre, sometimes known as Constitutionalists. They included Liberals who believed that France's best hope lay in observing the Charter, and also a tiny band of intellectuals called the *Doctrinaires*—Royer-Collard, the historian Guizot, and a French Whig, the Duc de Broglie—whose basic principle was that the rights of crown and country were indistinguishable. But most Constitutionalists were simply moderate Royalists. Louis XVIII believed that the Restoration's one chance of survival was to let such people govern France. Through them he intended to find a middle ground, adopting policies which would upset neither the old aristocracy nor the new rich of the Empire; ultimately he hoped to forge an alliance between both classes. As Balzac puts it, 'After every revolution genius in government consists of effecting a fusion, which is what Napoleon and Louis XVIII did, both being men of true genius.'

The King's motto, which he repeated over and over again, was 'Unite—and forget'.

The fact that Artois was the Ultras' acknowledged leader did not help Louis. The King was fond of his brother, or at least felt as sentimental about him as his cold nature allowed. Artois genuinely loved Louis but felt that his policies were misguided; he, Monsieur, knew what was best for France, and the Pavillon de Marsan (his wing of the Tuileries and one of the few parts which survived the fire of 1871) was the Ultras' chief meeting-place.

Indeed, apart from the King, the entire royal family were Ultras. Artois's eldest son, the ferret-eyed, long-nosed Louis, Duc d'Angoulême, was a gauche nonentity, as ill mannered as he was timid, without brains or character; he was said to be impotent. The childless Mme d'Angoulême, stiff, sour and red-faced, was the 'Orphan of the Temple' whose horrible experiences had so embittered her that she was dreaded by the entire court; she often reduced ladies-in-waiting to tears (though Fanny Burney found her charming). Artois's younger son, Charles-Ferdinand, Duc de Berry, had an ungovernable temper—sometimes he struck officers on the parade ground— which was almost as embarrassing as his attempts to ape Napoleon. In *Le Rouge et Le Noir* Stendhal gives what may well be a portrait of the Duke—'He was short and thick-set, with a florid complexion and gleaming eyes without any expression save the vicious ferocity of a wild boar.' Yet Berry was not entirely unattractive. He could be extraordinarily generous, frequently giving money to tramps, and was democratic enough to treat the merchant banker Greffulhe as a personal friend. He played the flute, was a discerning collector of pictures, and genuinely loved the opera and the theatre—he was a keen admirer of Talma. In 1816 the Duke married a beautiful madcap Bourbon cousin from Naples to whom, though he loved her, he was frequently unfaithful. They lived in Mme de Pompadour's old residence, the Elysée. Caroline de Berry was a small, lively blonde, with large blue eyes, and just a little too high-spirited. She joined her dour sister-in-law in constantly criticizing the weakness and foolishness of the King's policies.

There was a Duc d'Orléans in the Palais Royal once more, although the King would not allow him to style himself 'Royal

Highness'. Louis Philippe was the son of the regicide Egalité. Before emigrating he had fought with the army of the Revolution at Valmy in 1792, and he was regarded with some suspicion by the court. A sly, watchful man, Orléans was avaricious to the point of rapacity, working ceaselessly to regain all his father's vast estates.

The only other Prince of the Blood was the Prince de Condé, last of his line. His gallant old father had died in 1818 and the new master of Chantilly was a very different personality. He doted almost pathologically on his English mistress, Sophy Dawes, a fisherman's daughter from the Isle of Wight and a former maid-servant, whom he had married to the Baron de Feuchères; the Baron, at first under the impression that Miss Dawes was the Prince's illegitimate daughter, was enraged when he discovered the truth. Sophy returned to Condé and not only persuaded him to give her enormous presents but to bequeath Chantilly to the Orléans family, who had ingratiated themselves with her. The Prince does not seem to have derived much pleasure from his generosity—he hanged himself in 1830.

As Guizot puts it, 'King Louis XVIII had a cold heart and a liberal mind. His family's anger and irritation had little effect, once he decided not to let it bother him. It was his pride and joy to think himself clearer headed and shrewder, and to act according to his own judgement.' Chateaubriand is even more plainly-spoken: 'An egoist without principle, Louis XVIII wanted peace at any price. He supported his ministers for just as long as they could command a majority.'

As has been said, the Duc de Richelieu replaced Talleyrand as both Prime Minister and Foreign Minister at the end of 1815. This *grand seigneur*—'the very personification of nobility', Lady Morgan calls him—had made a career for himself in Russia during the emigration, becoming a Lieutenant-General and founding the town of Odessa. Hence Talleyrand's gibe when he was appointed his successor—'What a perfect choice, he knows the Crimea better than any man in France.' But for all Talleyrand's sneers, the Duke persuaded his friend the Tsar to reduce the indemnity and the allies to end their occupation in 1818, two years earlier than stipulated (some Ultras were horrified, and begged Wellington to stay). In

addition, Richelieu rebuilt the country's finances. Two former Napoleonic ministers worked a miracle for him—one an unfrocked priest, Baron Louis, and the other a Genoese, Count Corvetto. Their basic principle was that if a government wants credit, it must pay for it; accordingly they guaranteed all financial liabilities incurred by the Emperor. Stringent economies were made in the public service, civil servants being persuaded to draw only half their salaries for a six-year period. In 1817 a carefully calculated loan was negotiated from the English bankers, Messrs Baring. As a result of such measures, including an insistence that every minister must present annual accounts, the budget was balanced for the first time since 1739, while the indemnity was paid off by 1818. When Richelieu resigned that year, the Chambers voted him a pension of 50,000 francs in token of the country's gratitude.

One reason for the survival of Richelieu's ministry was the fact that its Minister of the Interior was M Elie Decazes. This dark-haired, fine-featured Gascon lawyer in his early thirties, the son of a little notary in the Gironde, had replaced Blacas as the King's dear friend. Of his appearance Talleyrand said— knowing that his words would be reported to Louis—'He resembles a moderately good-looking hairdresser's assistant.' Minister of Police during the First Restoration, Decazes had won his master's confidence by following him to Ghent, and then endeared himself by retailing malicious gossip about the country's leading figures, which he gleaned from police files. He never bored the King with tiresome detail but took care that he was informed of anything of genuine importance. In addition he was of a literary turn of mind, and an excellent listener who enjoyed Louis's stories. Soon the King was infatuated, addressing him as '*mon fils*' and writing to him three times a day— 'Come to receive the tenderest embraces of thy friend, thy father, thy Louis.' He even gave his adorable minister English lessons, and was amazed by his progress; in fact Decazes was discreetly visiting the best tutor in Paris after each lesson. The King said of 'his darling child' that, 'I will raise him so high that the greatest lords will envy him.' Again, one's mind goes back to Louis XIII.

The new favourite described his policy as 'to nationalize royalism and to royalize nationalism'. It was Decazes who

persuaded the King to dissolve the *Chambre Introuvable* in autumn 1816, obtaining a much more workable majority, and who was responsible for relaxing the press laws in 1817. The same year Louis approved a revision of the electoral laws, which gave the government more control of the *Chambre des Députés*. They were able to bring in the famous 'law' of Marshal Gouvion Saint-Cyr, which decided the structure of the French army until the Third Republic. Gouvion believed that while the monarchy could not trust the old Imperial army, it must none the less have reliable troops if France was to be a great power again. Henceforward the French army was recruited by a limited method of conscription which was infinitely less onerous than the universal conscription of Napoleon. Not only were many Imperial officers reinstated, but a third of all commissions were reserved for promotions from the ranks.

For all his moderate policies, there was almost excessive pomp and ceremony at the court of Louis XVIII. Balzac jokes that the King's drawing-rooms were so full of powdered heads 'that seen from above they gave the impression of a carpet of snow'. So conscious was Louis of protocol that when one day he fell over and lay helpless on the floor of the Tuileries and a junior officer named Nogent tried to help him to his feet, the King cried out, '*Non, O non, M de Nogent!*' and insisted on remaining on the ground till the Captain of the Guard arrived. Duchesses still sat on *tabourets* (stools) while lesser ladies stood. There were still royal cup-bearers and the Hundred Swiss still mounted guard. Louis observed a monotonous routine, rising at seven o'clock, when he was wakened by the First Gentleman of the Bedchamber. The King's daily council lasted from nine until he breakfasted at ten with his household—he retained the English hours of eating which he had known at Hartwell. From eleven till midday he gave audiences; the usual place for these in the Tuileries was a small study with an arched window, which had been Napoleon's favourite room; here Louis worked at an English walnut table from Hartwell. At midday the old Voltairean attended Mass, despite certain suspicions as to his sincerity—Guizot speaks of 'the freethinker's imagination which his grandfather had bequeathed him'—after which he received his ministers or held a weekly *Conseil du Roi*. He was too unfit to hunt, so instead he was taken for carriage exercise

every afternoon, always at full gallop as he loved speed; sometimes 300 horses were used in relays.

Another relaxation was conversation; Louis XVIII was a most amusing *raconteur* with a choice collection of anecdotes and dirty jokes; even Talleyrand admitted that, 'His conversation never flags and is always interesting.' The King sometimes gave delightful little dinner parties where he was the most convivial of hosts. He could disarm critics with his wit and seeming friendliness; one gambit, when communicating something known to the entire court, was to begin, 'Let me tell you in the strictest confidence . . .'

Usually, however, Louis dined at six with the royal family, a meal which was probably the chief pleasure of his life, for he remained a gourmet until the very end (Lady Morgan was told that he ate enough for four, though, added her devoutly royalist informant, '*C'est un appétit charmant, charmant*'). Finally, he received a few privileged friends before retiring to bed shortly after nine o'clock.

One long-forgotten pleasure was the French theatre. At the end of 1814 the King attended Racine's *Britannicus* at the Comédie Française, and the great Talma's performance reduced him to tears, bringing him to his feet in homage. He told the actor, 'I have a right to consider myself a critic, M Talma, as I saw Lekain' (the French Garrick, who had died in 1778). Soon Louis was going to the play once a week, either to the Comédie, or to his own theatre in the Tuileries. Although Talma was a protégé of Napoleon—royalists joked that the tyrant had taken lessons in deportment from the tragedian—and always remained a declared Bonapartist, the King none the less confirmed his pension. Nor did he blame him for performing before the Emperor during the Hundred Days, and later awarded him an additional pension of 30,000 francs (£1,200) from his own privy purse. He never lost his love of Talma's acting, for all its innovations, and particularly enjoyed his interpretation of Corneille's *Cid*. Talma was not the only actor whom Louis helped. He gave the equally great Mme Mars an annual pension of 20,000 francs, and when a priest refused to bury Mme Raucourt, an earlier ornament of the Comédie Française, sent one of his own chaplains to conduct the service.

Louis eventually acquired a certain popularity. His oddities

amused the French. The arrival of his wheel-chair at the theatre caused a hilarity which verged on affection. Wits called him '*Louis deux fois neuf*', referring to his two restorations, and joked that 'The King is one part old woman, one part capon, one part Son of France and one part bookworm.'

Indeed, superficially Louis XVIII may seem a rather endearing figure. In reality he was the least likeable of his dynasty, cold, calculating and selfish, with little kindness or sympathy. Chateaubriand thought that, 'Without being cruel, the King was hardly human, so insensitive was he to other people's misfortunes.' Talleyrand (of all people) once observed, 'Egotistical, insensitive, epicurean and ungrateful, that is what I have always found Louis XVIII.'

Louis's curious character intrigued contemporary novelists. Dumas has a peculiarly convincing portrait of him in *The Count of Monte Cristo*, hearing the news of Napoleon's return 'while making a note in a volume of Horace, Gryphius's edition, which was much indebted to the sagacious philosophical observations of His Majesty.' Balzac's picture of Louis in *Le Bal de Sceaux* carries no less conviction. The '*auguste littérateur*' relishes a polished turn of phrase or a *bon mot*; his own conversation—he has 'a sharp, thin little voice'—is full of puns, epigrams and allusions to the classics, and he is invariably mocking and malicious. That vulgar but perceptive woman, Lady Morgan, wrote in her travel diary in 1816, 'The King's character and constitution, his tastes and his habits, all tend to repose. He is false, not ferocious, and having permitted Ultra vengeance to glut itself during the first period of his Restoration, he now resumes habitudes nourished in his long exile. A fine gentleman, an elegant scholar; graceful (if not grateful), as the Bourbons always are; gracious, as the French princes always have been, even when their courtesies meant nothing—he owes much to the privacy and privation of Hartwell. . . . Sensual and sentimental, he applies the *bonhommie* of the old court to the courtiers of the present. He has his *petit mot galant* for the ladies.' However, the lady novelist is a little confused by his attitude towards Decazes. 'He *affiches* his innocent passion for the sister of the Duc de Decazes, and his friendship for her brother (his Prime Minister), by throwing his arms around his

neck *en bon Papa.*' None the less, Lady Morgan knew enough to recognize Louis's 'inherent falseness'.

The Restoration is not a popular period with French historians. It seems tame compared to the Revolution and the Empire; even at the time Chateaubriand grumbled, 'I have seen Louis XVI and Bonaparte die; after that it is a bad joke to live longer.' Furthermore, feelings of social inferiority and resentment engendered during that Indian summer of the French aristocracy may well have bequeathed an atavistic distaste for the Restoration. Yet it was in many ways a French equivalent of the English Regency, with a noticeably full-blooded style. It was very much a young man's world, the world of Balzac's heroes, Eugène de Rastignac and Lucien de Rubempré, and of Stendhal's Julien Sorel, trying to make their fortunes in a Paris which, although still without boulevards, had many of its modern landmarks, like the Bourse and the Madeleine, the Place Vendôme and the rue de Rivoli. It was gas-lit and by the end of the period it even had omnibuses. Nor was it merely the world of the rich dandies and adventurers who thronged the Opéra and the casinos, Tortoni's restaurant, the hôtels of the Faubourg Saint-Germain and the bankers' palaces in the Chaussée d'Antin. This was the time when Paris first became Bohemian and when the Latin Quarter became famous; the Left Bank was full of young writers, painters and law students of the sort depicted in Murger's *Scenes de la Vie de Bohème*, with their weird clothes and hand-to-mouth existence .

Culturally, it was a wonderful time. Freed from the censorship of the Napoleonic police state, Paris became the literary, artistic and musical centre of the world, full of enthusiasm and new ideas. In 1819 Lamartine published his *Méditations*, and Vigny brought out his first poems in 1822. Prosper Merimée, Dumas, Balzac, Stendhal, Sainte-Beuve and Alfred de Musset all published their first works during the Restoration. Few regimes have enjoyed such gratifying support from contemporary writers. Victor Hugo produced his own first book of verse in 1822, and its inspiration was so profoundly royalist that Louis XVIII awarded him a pension of 1,000 francs. And if the classical tradition of French painting was majestically continued by Ingres, such Romantic giants emerged as Delacroix and Géricault. As for music, Berlioz performed his first Mass

in 1825 and composed his *Romeo et Juliette* three years later; while everyone enjoyed Ahber's cheerful operas. Even if French Romanticism did not reach its full bloom until the 1830s, its beginnings must unquestionably be sought under the Restoration.

The government took a laudably constructive part in the nation's intellectual life. The Academie Française was given back the predominance of which it had been deprived by Napoleon. The Ecole des Chartes was founded in 1821, the Ecole des Arts et Manufactures in 1828 and the Ecole des Beaux Arts in 1830.

The Restoration tried hard to fill the vacuum left by the departure of Emperor-worship, with a cult of Henri IV, who was officially elevated to 'best and favourite King' (Nancy Mitford's words). His statue was re-erected on the Pont Neuf—Victor Hugo wrote an ecstatic ode to celebrate the event—and other statues were set up all over France, while his bust or his portrait presided in every town hall. The *Vert Galant*'s head also replaced that of Napoleon on the cross of the Légion d'Honneur. Instead of the Imperialist *Chant du Départ*, the national anthem became *Vive Henri Quatre*; its cheerful tune was supported by other royalist airs associated with Henri, notably *Charmante Gabrielle*. There were even free performances for the poor of Collé's *La Partie de Chasse de Henri IV*, a play which glorified the monarch. The official court painter, Baron Gérard, constantly produced 'scenes' from the great King's life. Rather touchingly, Louis wore a little white heron's feather in his hat in imitation of his ancestor's famous white plume. Nothing could have shown more plainly how effete and worn out was the dynasty than these reminders of Henri IV.

A cult of the martyred Louis XVI and his Queen and of Louis XVII was also encouraged. Their remains were discovered and identified—Chateaubriand could still recognize Marie Antoinette's features—and then reburied at Saint-Denis. All the other bones thrown out of the abbey in 1793 were dug up and re-interred in two vaults. One vault bore the inscription, 'Here lie the mortal remains of eighteen Kings, from Dagobert to Henri III; ten Queens, from Nantilde, wife of Dagobert, to Marguerite de Valois, first wife of Henri IV; twenty-four Dauphins, Princes and Princesses, Children and Grandchildren

of France.' The inscription on the other vault read, 'Here lie the mortal remains of seven Kings, from Charles V to Louis XV; seven Queens, from Jeanne de Bourbon, wife of Charles V, to Marie Leszczynska, wife of Louis XV; Dauphins and Dauphinesses, Princes and Princesses, Children and Grand-children of France, to the number of forty-seven, from the second son of Henri IV to the Dauphin, eldest son of Louis XVI'. But the magic had gone for ever. As the twentieth-century Royalist Bernanos made his curé say, despairingly, 'What force could have been capable of re-imposing the yoke?'

Despite a furious outcry from Artois and the Ultras, when Richelieu resigned in December 1818 after quarrelling with Decazes, Louis appointed a still more moderate Prime Minister, General Augustin Dessoles, though the new government's real leader was Decazes. The King cried all day at not being able to keep Richelieu; even if he was not particularly attached to him as a man, he recognized his worth. Decazes introduced new and surprisingly tolerant press laws, which were blocked by the upper Chamber, so Louis created nearly seventy new Peers, enabling the government virtually to abolish censorship. Even Liberals began to applaud the King. The Charter had become a kind of Edict of Nantes, which both protected liberties and strengthened the monarchy. The bourgeoisie and the peasants began to accept the regime, soothed by its conciliatory attitude and by the return of peace and prosperity.

Unfortunately, in the elections of 1819 the Constitutionalists were beaten by both the Liberals and the Ultras, the Centre commanding only a handful of votes in the lower Chamber. Among 90 Liberals out of 430 Deputies was the Abbé Grégoire, a former member of the Convention who had actually voted for the abolition of the monarchy in 1792; he had once observed publicly that 'Kings are in the moral order what monsters are in the physical'; special legislation was brought in to annul his election. But the Charter stipulated that one-fifth of the Chamber of Deputies had to be re-elected every year, and Dessoles and Decazes were increasingly worried by the signs of growing Liberal strength and the consequent drift of moderate Royalists into the Ultra camp. In November 1819, Dessoles resigned and Louis appointed his beloved Elie Prime Minister.

Decazes offered concessions to the Ultras, a stick-and-carrot policy which had some chance of success.

But on the night of 13 February 1820, the Duc de Berry, leaving the Opera with his wife by a side door, was stabbed by a Bonapartist fanatic, a saddler from the royal stables called Louvel, who had tracked him for four years—'a little weasel-faced mongrel, a snarling lone wolf'. The Duke did not die until six the next morning, but he did so with unexpected dignity, asking mercy for the assassin (who in the event was guillotined) and apologizing to the King for waking him. 'Don't worry,' replied the cold old man, 'I haven't lost any sleep.' The nobility of Berry's end was somewhat marred by his insistence on seeing his two children by his English mistress, Amy Brown. None the less, the Vicomte Hugo's inevitable ode hymned the Duke's '*Mort sublime*'.

Berry had left the Duchess pregnant, and to the joy of the Ultras, who feared the eventual accession of M d'Orléans (on whose face Chateaubriand saw barely-concealed triumph as he left the deathbed), she gave birth to a boy on 29 September 1820. This was the Duc de Bordeaux, the future Henri V. The news was announced that evening, and quickly spread throughout Paris; in the theatres audiences rose to their feet and sang emotionally *Vive Henri Quatre*. Crowds flocked to the Tuileries and danced *farandoles* in the streets; there was a lavish distribution of free wine in the Champs-Elysées—a hundred barrels at the King's expense. Victor Hugo was again inspired, writing not only an ode on the Duke's birth but another on the baptism of '*l'enfant sublime*'. A public subscription was organized, and, partly by strong-arm methods, raised so much money that the château of Chambord was purchased and presented to the '*Enfant de Miracle*'. Louis carefully copied King Henri d'Albret's behaviour at the birth of Henri IV, rubbing the baby's lips with garlic and giving him a sip of Jurançon wine. He was so overjoyed that he gave Talleyrand the *Cordon Bleu*. M d'Orléans was so infuriated that when he visited Mme de Berry his remarks about the baby's ugliness reduced the lady-in-waiting holding him to tears.

Berry's assassination brought down Decazes. At the Duke's deathbed his widow pointed at the Minister and screamed, 'There is the man who is the real murderer,' implying that his

attacks on the Ultras had stirred up the Jacobins. Chateaubriand wrote, with a lack of taste unusual in him, 'His feet have slipped in blood and he has fallen.' In the Chamber of Deputies a motion was proposed which actually accused the Minister of being an accomplice. At first the King stood firm—'The wolves ask nothing of the shepherd but to get rid of the dog,' he sneered. The entire royal family begged Louis to dismiss him. When Mme d'Angoulême warned the King that Decazes's weak government would endanger his life, Louis replied sarcastically, 'I will risk the knives and daggers.' He added, 'I have never known a heart more open nor one endowed with more sensibility than that of Count Decazes.' But eventually he yielded, and after giving Decazes a Dukedom sent him to London as ambassador, where Greville heard that he was being literally bombarded by the King with 'verses and literary scraps'. It is difficult to imagine a more dismal and frustrating sexual condition than that of the impotent homosexual; the loss of yet another 'dear friend' was a dreadful prospect for poor Louis.

Richelieu returned as Prime Minister but had little hope of implementing moderate policies. In the summer of 1820 new electoral laws, to give the government more control over the voters, plunged the country into a really dangerous crisis. For a moment the Liberals seem to have thought that their only hope lay in a *coup d'état*. Riots broke out in Paris; there were cavalry charges by *cuirassiers* and *gendarmes*, the students fighting back with sticks and stones. The police discovered an army plot to restore Napoleon (who did not die until the following year). But the rioters were ridden down and the plotters were shot. So great was the alarm that the Ultras increased their majority —at the end of 1820 there were only fifteen Liberal Deputies.

As Blacas had said, Louis XVIII had to have a favourite. This time he chose, rather surprisingly, a woman. Zoe Talon, Comtesse du Cayla, was the daughter of an old Parlementaire family, now in her mid-thirties and an exceptionally beautiful and amusing lady. She produced a letter from her dead mother-in-law imploring the King to protect Mme du Cayla from her cruel husband who wanted to take her children away. Louis was so overcome that, referring to Decazes, he cried, 'I too, Madame—they want to take away my child.' The King had

never known such a wonderful listener. In fact she had been put deliberately in Louis's way by the royal family, as she had Ultra sympathies and would make him forget 'darling Elie'. Soon the King was writing to her three times a day, and although there could be nothing sexual, they played chess together every Wednesday behind locked doors. Mme du Cayla became literally the last of the *maîtresses en titre*. He heaped gifts on 'his dear daughter', including substantial sums of money. He had built a magnificent château at Saint-Ouen (to commemorate his granting of the Charter) and gave it to her, being obsessed with the morbid fancy that from its windows she would one day look out and see Saint-Denis where he would lie buried. Paris was full of coarse jokes about la Cayla.

The liberal Duchesse de Broglie—Mme de Staël's daughter —saw Louis at the Tuileries in September 1821. 'The King was wheeled in, in his armchair. He is most unusual looking. In spite of his obesity he has considerable dignity and, for all his fat red face, a truly regal air. There is a perpetual smile on his lips, but his eyes are hard and unsmiling.'

Richelieu finally fell in December 1821, brought down by both Ultras and Liberals. Reluctantly the King sent for the Minister of Finance, M de Villèle, the leader of the Ultras. It was the end of Louis's gallant attempt to govern with a moderate administration and to unite France. As he himself had said in 1818 (long before Disraeli borrowed the phrase for English consumption) he did not want to be 'the King of two nations', but in the face of a seemingly invincible Ultra majority in the Chambers, and exposed to the blandishments of Mme du Cayla and unceasing pressure from his family, he gave up. Confined to his wheel-chair, he was growing older and iller every day. He stopped fighting his brother—'the two brothers have embraced,' wrote Comte Molé, 'and Louis XVIII has made way for Charles X.'

Joseph de Villèle was a crop-headed country gentleman from Languedoc, nearly fifty, who had had an unusually varied career. He had been a midshipman in Louis XVI's navy, but after nearly losing his life in the Terror, had left France for the West Indies, where he had made his fortune; there were rumours that he had dabbled in the slave trade. He belonged not to the Faubourg Saint-Germain but to the provincial

nobility—his town house was in Toulouse. Although a shy man, reserved to the point of dullness, he was a fine public speaker and the Ultras's most formidable spokesman. He was also a natural administrator who soon succeeded in putting his country's finances on so sound a footing that they remained stable for the rest of the century.

As an Ultra, Villèle was determined to improve the position of the Church, which had already made a remarkable recovery. Ultras and clergy joined in recognizing the ideas of the Enlightenment as a root cause of the Revolution, and the Church began a campaign to control education which culminated in 1824 with the appointment of Mgr de Frayssinous as Minister of Education. There were sinister rumours of the *Congrégation* (immortalized in Stendhal's *Le Rouge et Le Noir*), in reality no more than a zealous missionary organization; the actual substance behind these rumours were the *Chevaliers de la Foi*, a secret society of Royalist fanatics dedicated to restoring the Church to its old dominance, whose existence remained unknown until 1949. Understandably anti-clericalism grew apace. The Church was suspected of hoping to regain the estates it had lost during the Revolution, while Liberals regarded its bid to take over education as a real threat to human progress; Stendhal told his readers, 'Ever since the days of Voltaire the Church in France seems to have realized that its chief enemies are books.'

Villèle's foreign policy was one of caution. But he was saddled with no less incongruous a Foreign Minister than the Vicomte René de Chateaubriand, who decided that France must intervene in Spain and save Ferdinand VII from his new Liberal masters; many Ultras saw the situation in Madrid as a Spanish 1789 which might well turn into a Spanish 1793. In 1823 100,000 French troops, nominally commanded by M d'Angoulême, marched into Spain under the White Flag. As they crossed the River Bidassoa, a band of French Liberals met them, waving the *Tricolore*—the troops fired on them without hesitation. Angoulême's advisers, who had learnt from Napoleon's mistakes, forbade looting and bribed the Spanish peasants handsomely, and the French army occupied Madrid almost without resistance. Only at the siege of the Trocadero fortress outside Cadiz, where the Liberal government had taken

refuge, did the Spaniards show just enough fight for the French to claim a glorious victory. The monarchy's prestige was enormously enhanced, both at home and abroad, though King Ferdinand refused to pay any of the alarmingly expensive costs of the expedition.

Villèle dismissed his Foreign Minister thankfully, on a pretext of not co-operating on financial matters. 'Sacked like a servant', wrote the outraged Chateaubriand. It was a sad mistake to make an enemy of the last of the Frondeurs. For the remainder of the Restoration Chateaubriand led the Ultra opposition to the government in the Chamber of Peers, delivering beautiful and wounding speeches.

On 12 October 1823 *Te Deum* was sung at Nôtre-Dame for the victory in Spain. During the service the King dropped his prayerbook repeatedly and looked round him with the air of not knowing where he was. His gout, his varicose veins and all his other maladies had gradually pulled him down. Now he grew dropsical; it was rumoured that poor Louis was in such a state of decay that when his valets removed his socks one day, they found a loose toe. The obese old man became a frightful skeleton. None the less, he tried bravely to live up to his maxim that 'a King may die but he may never be ill'. Artois soon took over his duties of state; when consulted on ministerial appointments Louis would say, 'I'm old and wouldn't like to decide without knowing Monsieur's views—show him the list.'

In August 1824 the King collapsed during dinner and was carried to his bed. Soon he was unable to sit up and could not even raise his head, though he remained perfectly alert; on 12 September he told his confessor that he was well enough not to need a priest. Mme du Cayla made what was to be her final visit; she coaxed Louis into signing an order buying her the Hôtel de Montmorency. But by the night of 15 September it was obvious that the King was dying. He revived a little and Artois stayed by his bed, kneeling in prayer. Typically, Louis had time for a last joke, a pun, *'Allez-vous en, charlatans'*— dismissal for the doctors whom he despised and a summons for Charles d'Artois to draw near. He died at four am on the morning of 16 September 1824.

It was no small feat to be the only sovereign to die in possession of the throne during the last century of monarchical

government in France. Louis XVIII gave the French their first workable parliamentary system and was justified in seeing it as a truly great achievement. A character no less subtle than Talleyrand, he remained a pragmatist and an opportunist during an age of extremists. Quite unembittered by the Revolution, always able to judge what was possible and what was not, in his case it is palpably untrue to say that the Bourbons 'learnt nothing and forgot nothing'. He was beyond question the shrewdest royal statesman of his day. Indeed, Gambetta considered Louis XVIII 'the greatest King of France after Henri IV'.

'A Submissive Bigot'

CHARLES X (1824–1830)

'I would rather earn my bread than reign like the King of
England'

The children and grand-children of Charles X

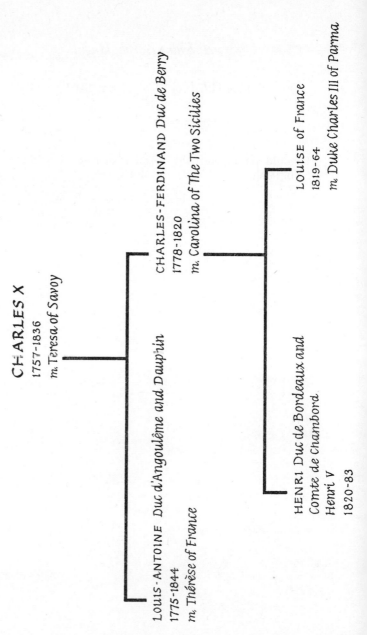

CHARLES X
1757-1836
m. Teresa of Savoy

LOUIS-ANTOINE Duc d'Angoulême and Dauphin
1775-1844
m. Thérèse of France

CHARLES-FERDINAND Duc de Berry
1778-1820
m. Carolina of The Two Sicilies

HENRI Duc de Bordeaux and
Comte de Chambord
Henri V
1820-83

LOUISE of France
1819-64
m. Duke Charles III of Parma

Until recently history books have dismissed Charles X—'an impossible monarch for the nineteenth century . . . a typical Bourbon, unable either to learn or to forget'. In reality Charles was much more a creature of the nineteenth century than Louis XVIII, while in many ways he was not the least attractive member of his dynasty. The tragedy of this honourable, kindly and friendly man lies in the contrast between his personality and his political ineptitude—in public life he nearly always acted with almost childlike *naïveté*.

He was born on 9 October 1757 at Versailles, christened Charles-Philippe and given the title of Comte d'Artois, which had once belonged to Saint Louis's brother. Artois's father, the Dauphin Louis, died when he was eight and his mother shortly after, so there was little discipline in his childhood; the Duc de Vauguyon, who made Louis XVI's early years such misery, could do little with his youngest brother, a naturally cheerful and unruly little boy and the one genuinely normal member of the family.

Charles grew into a handsome young man, tall, slim and broad-shouldered, with a fine, rather small head, very well set, with large brown eyes, black hair and the Bourbon nose. When he was only sixteen he was married to an equally juvenile Princess of Sardinia, Maria Theresa, daughter of Victor Amadeus III and sister to Madame. She was a dwarf, four foot high, with a grotesquely long nose, and completely characterless. They had two sons, Louis, Duc d'Angoulême, born in 1775, and Charles-Ferdinand, Duc de Berry, born in 1778; there were also two daughters who died young. But it was never more than a marriage of state.

269

The one responsible post given to Artois was that of Colonel-General of the Swiss Guards, and when he was seventeen he began to drill them. Maurepas, Minister for the Royal Household, rebuked him. 'You have acquired a liking for drill, Monseigneur. That does not become a Prince. Run up debts and we will pay them.' Charles thought this an excellent suggestion. He introduced English horse racing to France, importing English mounts and jockeys, and also started cabriolet racing, an early form of trotting in which he sometimes competed himself. The fashionable world flocked to his race meetings in the Bois de Boulogne. Charles bet heavily, but always seemed to lose, losses equalled by his card debts. In addition, he inherited the Bourbon mania for field sports; in 1785 he spent fifty-three days hunting boar, running down and personally dispatching eighty-nine animals (for a loss of eleven hounds killed and nearly 200 wounded). As might be expected, he was soon in debt, despite an income of almost £150,000; by 1781 it was reported that he owed 21 million livres—nearly £900,000. When he needed money he simply went to his brother, swearing and shouting until the King gave in.

According to the Austrian ambassador, the young Artois was frequently drunk and often violently rude. If there were spectators when he played tennis, he shouted insults until they left the court; once, after ordering 'all Jews and bastards' to leave, he noticed a single officer sitting calmly on the bench; asked angrily why he had not left with the others, the officer replied that he was neither a Jew nor a bastard. Charles surpassed himself at a masked ball in Paris in March 1778. He was escorting Mme Canillac, a lady of the town, when they met the Duchesse de Bourbon. After exchanging a few words, the irritated Duchess reached up and snatched off his mask whereupon he pulled her nose so hard and painfully that she wept. Her husband promptly challenged him to a duel; they met early one morning in the Bois de Boulogne, the fight being stopped after the Duke wounded Charles in the hand. Shortly afterwards, when the Bourbons went to the play they were received with such enthusiastic cheers that the Duchess again dissolved into tears.

Artois had the pathological sensuality of his house. Not only did he run through all the most famous prostitutes in Paris, but

he seduced many court ladies including the Duchesse de Guiche whom, so Hézecques tells us, 'the public long looked upon as one of his easiest conquests'. Hézecques also explains how Charles possessed 'that fashionable ease and light amiability which please women. One can well believe the rumours that few beauties could be cruel to him.'

It was to please a woman who was a friend and not a mistress that in 1779 Artois built the Bagatelle in the Bois de Boulogne. He had bet the Queen 100,000 livres that he could build and furnish a palace within nine weeks, and with the architect Bélanger and a thousand workmen he won his bet. The tiny white palace in the Etruscan style reveals another side of Charles besides mere extravagance; he was the only member of the Royal Family in his generation to have more than a casual interest in the arts; the Bagatelle is a perfect example of Neo-Classical art, and with its furniture and decoration is one of the most representative ensembles of the period.

Charles's rudeness was only a passing phase and he became a rather popular figure. Hézecques claims that before the Revolution 'the Comte d'Artois was adored by the people as he was affable to everyone and had our nation's cheerful temperament. His habit of driving about Paris and even his extravagance contributed to his popularity.' Mme de Campan confirms this, saying that 'the Parisians showed real affection for him'.

His one public-spirited action was to join the French army at the siege of Gibraltar in 1779. He was accompanied by his bosom friend, the Créole Marquis de Vaudreuil, and by M de Bourbon with whom he had been reconciled. They travelled in some comfort, their baggage and servants filling thirty-five carriages. He spent two months in the trenches, his visit being the routine morale-boosting tour of royalty visiting troops in the field—an affair of parades and dinner parties rather than fighting. Nevertheless Paris welcomed him home as a hero.

Otherwise Artois led a life of uninterrupted frivolity. He was fond of theatricals, acting many times in Marie Antoinette's little theatre at the Petit Trianon, notably as Figaro. He also gave an epic performance walking the tightrope. He had become the Queen's *chevalier servant*, escorting her to all the smart Paris plays and balls.

Ironically, it was through his membership of the Queen's set

that in 1785 Charles met the woman who reformed him, Mme de Polastron, the sister-in-law of Yolande de Polignac. Louise de Lussan d'Esparbés, Vicomtesse de Polastron, was only twenty-one, a delicate, nervous ash-blonde with china-blue eyes, a wonderfully sweet smile and a low voice; Lamartine describes her as 'the perfection of tenderness'. Charles and Louise fell completely and unreservedly in love. Even Hézecques admits that 'the passion of Mme de Polastron for the Comte d'Artois was as unconcealed as it was genuine, for heartfelt affection was their only bond'. Charles confided to one of Louise's friends, the Marquise de Lage, 'It's really true—in all the world I live for her alone. Never, no never, was Heaven pleased to form two hearts, two beings better suited to each other. I truly believe it, I even dare be sure of it, and you can have no idea how proud the very idea makes me. But if I deserve your friend, if my heart is worthy of making her happy, it is to her alone that I owe it. It is her advice, still more her sentiments, which have purified my soul and renewed it. Think what I owe her for teaching me how to be happy!'

Louise made Charles more responsible and he began to take a disastrous interest in public life. During the Assembly of Notables in 1787, he displayed an obvious distaste for reform, even if he did not support the *révolte nobilaire*. Calonne was a friend who had paid his debts twice, but when he was gone Charles attacked Loménie de Brienne, just as formerly he had attacked Necker, 'the fornicating foreign bastard'. He then resisted the doubling of the *Tiers Etat*'s representation in the States General, warned the King that the country was in the throes of a dangerous revolution (though agreeing that the tax burden must be shared more fairly) and opposed Necker's recall. By 1789 Artois was the acknowledged leader of the court party.

He had also again become one of the most unpopular men in France. It was known that he had done his best to stop the King making any concessions and the mob shouted abuse at him in the streets. The evening after the Bastille fell he tried to enlist support among the troops, buying them wine; he had a scheme for marching on the Assembly and arresting its members. Next day Louis was shown a pamphlet listing 'enemies of the people'; Artois's name came first. Seriously alarmed for his brother's safety, the King ordered him to leave France.

That night Charles escaped from his flat at Versailles, through a secret door. He rode to Chantilly where he borrowed a carriage from his cousin Condé, then drove to Valenciennes and crossed the Belgian frontier. A tutor followed with his sons, whom he sent to their grandfather at Turin, but their mother stayed at Versailles. Charles, who expected to be out of France for three months at most, was soon joined by Condé, and by the Polignacs and other members of the Queen's set (this flight by Artois and his friends later became known as 'The First Emigration').

The Emperor Joseph II made it plain that M d'Artois was not welcome in the Austrian Netherlands. So, after a delightful month with Louise in Switzerland, Charles presented himself to his father-in-law at Turin, where he was joined by his wife. King Victor Amadeus gave them a palace and an allowance but Charles had to be on his best behaviour, attending Mass daily and, so it was said, even sleeping with his wife; he did not dare see his mistress. In the end he informed the new Emperor—Leopold II, Marie Antoinette's second brother, who had succeeded Joseph in 1790—that life at Turin had become unbearable. Leopold told Charles to go to Coblenz which belonged to their cousin, the Elector Clement Wenceslas of Trier. Accompanied by sixty followers, Charles arrived there in June 1791 and was given the Castle of Schonbornslust for his residence.

Louise's friend, Mme de Lage, witnessed Artois's entry into Coblenz. 'Everyone was saying, "There he is, our Prince, our hope, the scion of Henri IV." They crowded round, all wanting to touch him. He possessed the sort of charm which bewitches the French and a way of looking at you like Louis XV, or so elderly people said.' Charles told the *émigré* troops that success was certain, even if not quite as near as he had hoped. Louise joined him and gave her entire fortune to help the White army.

The defeat at Valmy stunned the *émigrés*. On 19 November 1792 Artois wrote, 'One needs the pen of a Jeremiah, my dear Vaudreuil, to give you a picture of the situation since you left . . . everything is falling to pieces and we are all starving to death.' He hints that he might commit suicide 'were I not attached to life by a bond which every day grows dearer, more

precious and more essential . . . Thank God that at least my friend [Louise] is well.'

After two miserable months at Hamm, Charles set off to ask Catherine the Great for help. The Russian Empress, never indifferent to a handsome man, gave him a million francs and advised him to join the *Chouans*. 'You are one of Europe's great Princes,' Catherine told him, 'but there are times when you should forget it.' His self-esteem restored, he left St Petersburg in excellent spirits that spring, in a Russian warship bound for England, where he landed at Hull in May 1793. But the English government did not respond to a letter which he brought from the Empress, suggesting that they send troops to the Vendée.

Instead of joining the *Chouans*, Artois idled away his time at Hamm with Louise who, terrified, held him back when a gamble might have saved the Royalist cause. At the end of 1794, at the Duke of York's invitation, he joined the staff of the British expeditionary force in Holland, spending the winter with them at Arnhem. When the British were driven back, he wandered from Rotterdam to Osnabruck and then to Bremen in a most unprincely way; little is known of his movements at that date but it is said poverty forced him to eat in the cheapest and most squalid inns, at the public table. Finally, in July 1795, a British warship arrived at Hamburg to take him to England.

Already English and *émigré* troops had landed at Quiberon Bay, and had been swiftly routed by General Hoche, who shot all Royalist prisoners. The British government decided to try again, and to make use of Artois whom Louis XVIII had appointed Lieutenant-General of France. At the end of September Charles and a new expeditionary force of 4,000 men sailed from Portsmouth to land at Port-Breton on the Ile d'Yeu, just off the Vendéen coast. He contacted the *Chouan* leader, Charette de la Contrie, asking where he should join him on the mainland. Unfortunately Charette was cut off by General Hoche, who concentrated 50,000 men opposite the Ile d'Yeu. Frightful weather and an almost complete lack of supplies demoralized the Royalists, as more and more Republican troops arrived every day. On 18 November Artois took his expedition back to England. He was not cut out to be a Bonnie Prince Charlie.

He dared not land at Portsmouth, where he faced arrest for

Charles X in robes of state, by Gerard

Henri V, Comte de
Chambord

Comtesse de Chambord

debts contracted in equipping the *émigré* armies. Eventually arrangements were made for him to travel secretly to Edinburgh, where he moved into Holyrood House in January 1796; as a royal palace Holyrood conferred immunity from arrest, but he was only able to venture outside its grounds on Sundays. The gloomy palace, in the dark and squalid Old Town which better-class people had long since abandoned, was a crumbling ruin with few habitable rooms. Much of Charles's allowance of £7,000 was spent in providing for indigent courtiers who, for lack of accommodation in the palace, were forced to take wretched lodgings in the Old Town. However he was comforted by the arrival of Louise. (He had completely lost contact with his wife, who eventually died in Austria in 1808.) For all the discomfort of Edinburgh, he had had quite enough of adventures. In 1797 he forbade another Vendéen rising. He wrote, 'I refuse to authorize an insurrection in the Western Provinces—I cannot let myself be responsible for the useless shedding of blood.'

In August 1799, Charles at last reached an arrangement with his creditors and left Edinburgh for London, where he rented a house, 46 Baker Street. Louise de Polastron found a little house just round the corner, 18 Thayer Street, which still exists; here Charles spent most of his time playing whist; he regarded failure to call on Louise as a personal insult. He also went into English society, Lady Harrington's being a favourite drawing-room, where he often met the Prince of Wales. Mme de Boigne saw them both there, and says of Charles that 'though his face was not so handsome as the Englishman's, he had more grace and dignity while his bearing and way of dressing and manner of entering and leaving a room were incomparable.' Not that Charles neglected the *émigré* community. He received once a week and gave three annual dinners—on New Year's Day, St Louis's Day and St Charles's Day. He also made a point of visiting *émigré* schools, contributing to their maintenance. He even found time to be kind to the young Duc d'Orléans, Egalité's son, who was shunned by most *émigrés*.

Mme de Polastron had developed tuberculosis. It was aggravated by the foggy Edinburgh climate, and then by her cold damp bedroom in Thayer Street; in addition, her spirits were worn down by a nagging conscience—a devout Catholic,

she never ceased to worry about the irregularity of her relationship with Charles. Everyone else saw a deterioration in her appearance, but he was too much in love to notice. Finally friends called in George III's personal physician, Sir Henry Halford. His diagnosis was: 'The patient is in the last stage of consumption, and I fear that it is already too late to stop it.' On his instructions, Charles at once moved her into a stable, then an accepted cure for tuberculosis, in Brompton Grove (now Ovington Square). But it was obvious that Louise was failing, so she was taken back to Thayer Street, where Charles's chaplain, Père Latil, forbade her to see her lover and made her prepare her soul. She died on 27 March 1804, aged forty.

Louise's final moments are described by the Duchesse de Gontaut, who was nursing her. Charles had at last been let in, to say goodbye. 'She raised her hands to heaven and said, "A favour, Monsieur, grant me one request—give yourself to God, surrender yourself entirely to Him!" He fell on his knees and said, "As God is my witness, I swear it!" She repeated "Entirely to God!" Her head fell against my shoulder; that word was the last she uttered—she had ceased to breathe. Monsieur threw up his arms and uttered a dreadful scream.' Charles confessed and communicated the same day, receiving the sacraments from Latil. Henceforward he was a changed man, who heard Mass daily and spent long hours in prayer.

1804 was altogether a wretched year for him. In March the last serious Royalist plot against Napoleon failed; of its leaders, the Chouan Cadoudal was shot and General Moreau exiled, while General Pichegru committed suicide. Axel Fersen met Charles that autumn and says in his memoirs, 'He was kind enough to read me the entire account of the recent conspiracy involving Pichegru and Moreau. The whole plan had been his idea.' In May Bonaparte proclaimed himself 'Napoleon I, Emperor of the French'. The King had written from Mittau to condole with Artois on Louise's death, and at the King's suggestion he joined him in Sweden in October; they had not met for ten years and fell into each other's arms in tears. Together they issued a formal protest at Bonaparte's usurpation. But nobody took the Bourbons seriously any more.

Charles went back to Baker Street and his whist parties. Later he moved in with the King at Hartwell. His sons lived

there too, though Berry spent most of his time with Amy Brown and their children (there were even rumours of a secret marriage which had later to be annulled by the Pope). However, Angoulême, that ugly and ungracious little man, did not stray— his wife ruled him with an iron hand. It was said that Artois looked the *grand seigneur* as much as his sons behaved like plebeians. None the less, London society lionized them.

Hope revived in 1813, when Napoleon's reverses became serious. In January 1814 Artois sailed from Yarmouth, landing in Holland, and eventually entered Franche Comté by Switzerland. But most Frenchmen had forgotten the Bourbons, while the allies, who were still thinking of coming to terms with Napoleon, ignored him. However, everything changed when, on 6 April, the French Senate offered the crown to Louis XVIII.

On the morning of 12 April 1814 Artois, in his capacity of Lieutenant-General and escorted by Napoleonic Marshals, rode into Paris on a white horse, wearing the blue and silver uniform of the National Guard. Still a strikingly handsome man at fifty-seven, he made a most felicitous speech, ending with the words, 'Nothing is changed, save that there is one more Frenchman.' The streets rang with shouts of '*Vive les Bourbons! Vive le Roi! Vive Monsieur!*' as he rode to Nôtre-Dame to give thanks. Some people actually embraced his knees. When Charles entered the Tuileries he was asked if he was tired; he replied, 'Why should I be tired? This is the first happy day I have known for thirty years.'

He was ruler of France for nearly three weeks. But while he charmed the Marshals' wives, his liking for gentlemen of the *Ancien Régime* and open contempt for the achievements of the past twenty years made many people uneasy. He seems to have expected to remain in power, with his brother as a mere figurehead; his motive being not so much ambition as a profound distrust of Louis's moderate policies. But Louis XVIII, who entered Paris on 3 May, was determined to reign. The Duc de Duras asked him whether the crown was truly re-established. Louis replied, 'It will stay in our hands if I outlive my brother. But if he outlives me, then I guarantee nothing.'

When the Hundred Days came, Charles went to the provinces to try and rally support. On hearing that the King had fled, he gave up hope and, escorted by 300 picked cavalry, rode to

Belgium where he joined his brother. During the uncertain days at Ghent, he was obviously convinced that Louis's moderation was responsible for their misfortunes. He had always considered that a show of firmness could have stopped the Revolution in 1789; now he believed that the concessions made to the Revolution had paved the way for Napoleon's return.

After the royal family came back to Paris in 1815, Artois steadily opposed Louis XVIII's moderate policies, though never in public. But everybody knew Monsieur's real opinions, that he was encouraging the White Terror. However, the dissolution of the *Chambre Introuvable* in 1816 put an end to the Ultra majority and diminished his political influence.

Artois was not quite so foolish as is generally assumed. The Ultras were much more than a mere mob of blimpish backwoodsmen; they intended to rebuild, rather than resurrect, the *Ancien Régime*, and their political ideas were so far removed from pre-1789 attitudes as to constitute a Revolution of the Right. They were not only men of the Emigration, but also the heirs of the Notables and Parlementaires of the *revolte nobilaire* of 1787; they accepted Parliamentary government readily, as a means of controlling the King and of perpetuating their own power. And Charles, far from being an Absolutist, believed that a strong monarchy in partnership with a strong ruling class offered the best hope of a lasting Restoration.

The Ultras possessed two formidable political thinkers in Louis de Bonald and Joseph de Maistre, the 'Prophets of the Past'. Bonald, arguing that the traditional social order had been divinely revealed, proposed an alliance of 'Throne and Altar'. The Comte de Maistre regarded the ideas of the Enlightenment and the Revolution as Satanic in origin; because of Original Sin men could not be made good simply by restructuring society; the only solution was a rigidly hierarchical society based on ultramontane Catholicism. His belief that 'Spiritual absolutism is the sole principle of stability and continuity' has something of Orwell's 1984 about it, as does his grim *Eulogy of the Executioner*—'take away from the world that incomparable agent and in a moment order becomes chaos.' Bonald and de Maistre were supported by translations of Burke's *Reflections on the French Revolution*, while Romanticism and the emotional Christianity of Chateaubriand supplied the enthusiasm. To be a true Ultra,

one had to be a pious Catholic; as a modern historian has written, 'Gone was the frivolous, Godless aristocracy of *Ancien Régime* France; in its place was a spiritually and politically regenerated caste.'

Charles was unmistakably a man of the nineteenth century, in contrast to Louis XVIII who always remained one of the eighteenth. He readily adopted the new political ideas, corresponding with de Maistre while still in exile. If he did not share his brother's literary tastes, one need not believe that 'he never read a book'; we know he was familiar with both de Maistre's and Bonald's political writings and with Scott's novels. His weakness came not from stupidity—although admittedly he was only of mediocre intelligence—but from invariably seeing things as he wished them to be. Unfortunately this was a fault common to almost his entire circle of friends and advisers. Lady Morgan observed in 1816, 'There appears, indeed, among these ardent royalists a resolute determination to see every object through the medium of their own wishes.'

Throughout Louis's reign, Charles vehemently opposed any policy of compromise with the Liberals. On one occasion he threatened to leave the Tuileries with his sons, whereupon the infuriated King screamed that there were still prisons for rebellious princes. In 1818 Charles actually begged Wellington to stay with his army of occupation. In the summer of that year there were rumours that he was plotting to seize the throne, the so called 'Conspiracy of the Water's Edge', but so desperate a course was out of character, though he considered the policies of Richelieu and Decazes disastrous—'a programme which includes persecution of the King's friends and of those of the realm and contempt for monarchical institutions.'

If he was unhappy about his brother's government, Charles was content with his family. He quickly took to his new daughter-in-law, Caroline de Berry. After the sadness of a grandson and a grand-daughter dying in infancy, he was overjoyed at the birth of a healthy child in September 1819, Louise-Marie-Thérèse. She was given the ancient title of 'Mademoiselle'.

Charles was heartbroken by Berry's murder in 1820. He also realized that the dynasty faced extinction; Angoulême was impotent, while even *Purs* admitted that he seemed unfitted to be King, with no thoughts beyond his hounds and his chess. In

tears, Charles actually discussed the possibility of remarrying with his friend Vitrolles, who suggested the sister of Ferdinand VII of Spain, the widowed Duchess of Lucca; he was sufficiently interested to ask Vitrolles what she looked like, but abandoned the idea when Caroline de Berry gave birth to her miraculous son.

His grandson became the most important person in Charles's life. Young Henri and Mademoiselle watched constantly from the windows of the Élysée, where they lived, for the arrival of his fast little phaeton and then ran eagerly to greet '*Bon-papa*' who was more like a father than a grandfather. He let them do literally what they wanted; when Sir Thomas Lawrence was painting his portrait, Charles refused to send his grandchildren out of the room, although they were tormenting both Sir Thomas and himself.

As a result of Berry's murder the Ultras came to power. Although Artois asked Richelieu to take Decazes's place as Prime Minister, he soon engineered his resignation. It was this which made the King complain angrily of Charles, 'He conspired against Louis XVI, he conspires against me and one day he will probably conspire against himself.' What really irritated the King was that with Villèle's appointment as chief minister, Charles had all but taken over the government.

Artois deserves some credit for supporting Villèle; even if he was generally acknowledged by the Ultras as their leader, Villèle's charmlessness, caution and lack of enthusiasm can hardly have appealed to Charles. Villèle was one of the most gifted finance ministers in French history, who not only put public accounting on a lastingly regular basis but directly contributed to the increase in banking, and encouraged his friend Baron Jacques de Rothschild to settle in Paris. For almost every year of his administration the budget showed a surplus. Prosperity was evident in industrial development throughout the 1820s. New coal mines were dug, the canal system was lengthened, a steamboat service was started on the Loire, and a French locomotive was constructed in 1827. Roads began to be macadamed. In Paris, the first pavements were built and omnibus services were introduced; gas lighting spread throughout the entire capital.

Prosperity was one of the two planks of Artois's simple

scheme for strengthening the monarchy. The other was glory. He shared the indignation of most Frenchmen at losing the 'natural' frontiers of 1792; he too had been humiliated by Waterloo, even if it had saved the Bourbons. The triumph of the French army in Spain exceeded his wildest hopes. In December 1823, at an official dinner at the Hôtel de Ville, he saluted 'the glory of French arms'; the applause was so great that he was overcome by emotion and could not finish his speech.

The discord between Artois and the King vanished as Louis's health deteriorated. Charles was genuinely grief-stricken at his brother's deathbed, so much so that he did not realize Louis had gone until the Baron de Damas whispered, 'Sire, the King is dead.' Charles bent and kissed Louis's cold hand. Then Damas flung open the doors to announce to the waiting courtiers, 'Messieurs, the King is dead. The King, Messieurs.'

Next day Charles told his grandchildren, who were puzzled by the violet coat he wore in mourning, that although he was King now he would see them just as much as ever, and nothing would part them from him. Mademoiselle, who was only five, was very worried, murmuring, 'King—that's not the worst of it'; her governess, Mme de Gontaut, suspected the little girl thought her grandfather would henceforth be confined to a wheel-chair like poor old Louis.

According to custom, Charles was not present at Louis XVIII's funeral when Saint-Denis, hung with black velvet but ablaze with candles, saw the ancient rites for the last time, complete even to the laying-up of the King's helmet and spurs. Later Charles congratulated old Marquis de Dreux-Brézé, Grand Master of the Ceremonies of France, on his conduct of the service. The Grand Master apologized for any mistakes; 'Next time we will do better.' 'Thank you, Brézé, but I am in no hurry,' replied the King.

Charles X made his *joyeuse entrée* into his capital on Monday 27 September 1824. He refused to take precautions against assassination. 'Why should I? They can't hate me without knowing me and I'm quite sure that when they do know me they won't hate me.' It was raining, but at the barrier at the Etoile the King mounted a magnificent Arab horse, as a hundred and one guns boomed out in salute, and then began his triumphal

way to Nôtre-Dame, down the Champs-Elysées and along the rue du Faubourg Saint-Honoré. At the Elysée he insisted on riding out of the procession to greet his grandchildren who were waving from one of the windows. The crowd were delirious; even that sour republican, Benjamin Constant, found himself shouting, *'Vive le Roi'*—'Aha, I have captured you at last,' laughed the King who heard him. When he came home at last to the Tuileries, Charles was asked if he was weary; he answered happily, 'No, joy never tires one.' The cheers were even louder three days later when he reviewed his army on the Champs de Mars. The King's popularity owed something to an ordinance abolishing press censorship, but more to his undeniable charm.

Even at sixty-seven, Louis XVI's youngest brother was the glamorous sort of Bourbon. Although his hair was white, he had the physique and bearing of a man twenty years younger and looked especially impressive on horseback. His friendliness could be overwhelming. Comte de Puymaigre says, 'If one had been awed by Louis XVIII's imposing manner, the same could not be said of Charles X; when strolling with him one had constantly to remind oneself that one was talking to the King of France.' He received persons of plebeian origin in exactly the same way as he received Dukes. Indeed, Charles X deserved the title of 'First Gentleman in Europe' far more than George IV; his character was infinitely more honourable than that of the fat hedonist across the Channel. There were no greedy mistresses, no scandals, no ruinous extravagance.

Lamartine, who often met him, analysed the character of King Charles. 'He had a typically French temperament—light, quick, spontaneous, always ready with an amusing reply, a friendly smile, a frank look, a hand extended, thoroughly amiable in manner; always wanting to please and be liked, a person one could confide in, with a loyalty in friendship rare in a King, genuinely modest, anxiously seeking the best advice, scrupulously conscientious and hard on himself while indulgent to others.' But the founder of the Second Republic also saw much to criticize; he considered that—in modern terms—Charles was essentially a lightweight without the brains or the character necessary for a ruler in his circumstances. 'Looking at him, we were attracted by the man but distrusted the monarch.'

Charles X was crowned at Rheims on Sunday 29 May 1825. A spectator, Comte d'Haussonville, noted with amusement that the King's distinguished bearing 'evoked a thousand little cries of ecstasy from my lady neighbours'. Clad only in a crimson satin shirt, Charles lay full length at the feet of the Archbishop-Duke, once the humble Père Latil, to be anointed with the chrism of Clovis; enough oil had been saved from the breaking of the *sainte ampoule* at the Revolution to suffice for just one coronation. (Louis XVIII had refused to be crowned, pleading ill-health.) The service was attended by many leading intellectuals including Chateaubriand, Lamartine who wrote a *Chant du Sacre*, and Victor Hugo who produced his regulation ode ('O God! Keep always this King whom a people adore'). Hugo recalls that it was a radiant day, and how the long clear windows (the stained glass had been broken during the Revolution) let dazzling daylight into the cathedral. 'All the light of May was in that church,' says Hugo, 'gilding the Archbishop and the altar with its rays.' Doves were released, to fly in the luminous cloud of incense which filled the nave. When he had been crowned and enthroned, the cathedral doors were thrown open and the people acclaimed the Most Christian King in his diamond crown, roaring cannon and trumpets salutes, heralds throwing gold and silver medals into the crowd. Afterwards he banqueted on a dais, still wearing his crown, with the Dauphin and the Dukes of Bourbon and Orléans in their coronets. Next day he held a chapter of the Knights of the Saint-Esprit, and the day after rode on a white horse to the Hospital of Saint-Marcoul where he touched one hundred and twenty-four sufferers for the Evil.

There was a distinct lack of enthusiasm in the crowd's welcome when Charles returned to Paris. Yet far from being an ill-considered revival, the coronation of 1825 was well suited to the prevailing mood of historical Romanticism. The period's Liberals were inspired by a creed far more fantastic than that of the Ultras; they saw the Revolution as the culmination of a 1,300-year-old struggle by the Gallo-Romans against Frankish oppressors, whose latter-day representatives were the nobility.

The Ultras may be forgiven for thinking, in the age of Metternich and pre-Reform Bill England, that the times seemed ripe for putting their ideas into practice. The enactment of the dramatic law of sacrilege in 1825—condemning those who stole

communion vessels containing the consecrated Host to lose both hand and head—was a sign and token of the new alliance between throne and altar. It was never enforced.

The law had the King's fervent support. Guizot, a Protestant, calls Charles 'a submissive bigot to his fingertips', and the royal enthusiasm for taking part in religious processions—he was constantly walking round Nôtre-Dame under a canopy—might seem to confirm Guizot's opinion. Nothing damaged Charles more than being identified with the aggressive clergy of the period; he was even suspected of being a secret Jesuit. Yet in private life he was an unusually tolerant man, who never criticized any of his courtiers for a lack of belief.

An attempt in 1826 to restore primogeniture (and end the break-up of great estates) aroused such fury throughout the entire country, even among noble families, that Villèle desisted. However, the government did succeed in indemnifying the *émigrés*. A thousand million francs (£40 million) was raised by lowering the interest on government bonds by two per cent. As over four-fifths of those indemnified belonged to the nobility and clergy, and as the majority of bond holders were bourgeois, the measure naturally outraged the middle-class. But it brought security to everyone who had purchased confiscated *émigré* property during the Revolution.

Charles was very fashionable in his Romantic Philhellenism. When the English Foreign Secretary, George Canning, visited Paris with his wife in 1826, the King took them to a play in the theatre at Saint-Cloud; Canning was even invited to dinner with the Royal Family at the Tuileries (it was the first time Charles had sat at the same table as a commoner since becoming King). What Charles wanted was English co-operation in working for Greek independence. He got it. In October 1827, in Navarrino Bay, a combined Anglo–French fleet sank the Turkish navy, while the following year General Maison threw the Pasha of Egypt and his troops out of the Morea.

Unlike Louis XVIII, Charles presided over all cabinet meetings. He hunted only two days a week, although so fond of his sport that Parisians nicknamed him '*Robin des Bois*'. The King's favourite time of the year was October, when he went to Compiègne for a fortnight devoted entirely to hunting. Lamartine says that 'a love of horses, a taste for the greenwood, the

music of hounds, the thrill of following stag and roebuck, the stirring gone-away and *hallali* sounded on the braying horns, always excited him, just as a brave man responds to the smell of battle.' He adds that hounds and horses were a way of life for Charles. The old King loved the open air and all its pleasures, even to just lying on his back on the grass at Saint-Cloud.

While Charles did not have favourites, he had a little circle of close friends—the Duc de Montmorency, the Duc de Doudeauville, the Duc de Blacas, the Prince de Polignac and the Baron de Damas. Their amusements were rather limited, being restricted to innumerable whist parties. Indeed, apart from cards and hunting, the King's one indulgence was a certain love of display; the smallsword which he wore on ceremonial occasions had its hilt encrusted with diamonds (today it may be seen at the Louvre in the Galerie d'Appollon). Even this was only because he thought his subjects expected it of him. In fact he had so little time for luxury that M de Doudeauville had to remonstrate with him about the shabbiness of his bedroom.

Sometimes the King went out into society, as when he attended the Mary Stuart ball organized by Mme de Berry at the Pavillon de Marsan for the carnival of 1829. He particularly enjoyed going to the Opéra.

Charles had a pleasant taste in music. Rossini's comic opera, *Il Viaggio di Rheims*, in honour of the coronation, won the composer the posts of Master of the King's Music and *Inspecteur Général du Chant en France*. After the triumphant success of *Le Comte Ory* in 1828, the government offered Rossini an annual pension in return for six operas; Charles, who deeply admired his work, personally signed the contract. It quickly resulted in *William Tell* which took Paris by storm in 1829—the King awarded Rossini the Légion d'Honneur only four days after the first performance. Charles also commissioned an opera from Meyerbeer, *Robert le Diable*.

In February 1830 Charles gave further proof of his tolerance of new fashions. Victor Hugo's *Hernani*, a play which broke every rule of French classical drama, had been put on at the Odéon and caused a pitched battle between traditionalists and Romantics. Six outraged representatives of the Académie Française waited on the King, imploring him to stop the production. To their horror he refused, laughing and saying, 'In

matters of comedy, gentlemen, I am only one of the audience.'
In the event, *Hernani* heralded the triumph of French Romanticism and transformed French drama.

By this time Charles was politically in very deep waters.
There had been too many unpopular measures; attempts at
election rigging, the total surrender of education into clerical
hands, the sacking of large numbers of Imperial officers, and a
new and heavy-handed press censorship. In any case the
bourgeoisie resented being ruled by men who were, like
Stendhal's Marquis de la Mole, despising anyone not descended from 'people who had ridden in the royal carriages'.
Still more unsettling was the economic depression of 1826
whose effects lasted for several years. When the King reviewed
the National Guard on the Champs de Mars one beautiful spring
Sunday in 1827, they booed him so loudly that his horse shied
and nearly threw him. To yells of *'A bas les ministres! A bas
les Jésuites!'* he answered, 'I came here to receive homage, not
to be given advice.' With his usual elegance Charles—who was
now seventy—continued his inspection, riding along the ranks,
gracefully acknowledging cheers and ignoring insults. Next day
the National Guard was disbanded, on Villèle's advice.

To the King's surprise, Villèle lost the election of November
1827. The number of Liberal and government deputies was
roughly the same, about 175 each; dissident Ultras amounted to
75. Despite everything Charles could do to dissuade him,
Villèle insisted on resigning. With his customary gaucheness,
the Dauphin explained to him, 'You're too unpopular.' The
former Prime Minister answered the silly little man, 'I hope to
God I'm the only one who has become unpopular.' The
Dauphin's wife, Mme d'Angoulême, warned the King that in
letting Villèle go 'you have just taken the first step down from
your throne'.

Villèle's successor was the Vicomte de Martignac, a lawyer
from Bordeaux. He was an Ultra, though of a much more
moderate kind than his predecessor. Charles disliked his anticlericalism, and had no real confidence in him, but let him try.
Like Richelieu, Martignac wooed the centre, relaxing press
censorship and placing the educational activities of the Jesuits
under restraint, gestures which earned his government some
slight popularity. When the King toured Alsace in autumn 1828,

he was cheered so enthusiastically that he exclaimed, 'Had I known how much I was liked, I would have kept Villèle.' The poor man believed from now on that outside Paris his people really did 'adore' him. Meanwhile Martignac's supporters drifted away steadily throughout 1829.

Although Charles read all the Liberal newspapers conscientiously, he could never understand that the opposition to the Ultras was social and anti-clerical, rather than political. Neither he nor any of his narrow circle realized that the vast mass of articulate Frenchmen detested being dictated to by haughty *émigrés* and overbearing priests. He now chose to appoint a chief minister who was a grand seigneur, and whose mentality he found more congenial than that of petty provincial nobles like Martignac and Villèle.

In August 1829 a new government was formed with Prince Jules de Polignac as its leader. 'Dear Jules', who had been born in 1780, may not have been Charles's son, as has sometimes been suggested, but with his charm and his piety and his vagueness, he undoubtedly had a good deal in common with the King. In politics, Polignac was a *Pur* of *Purs* who believed that God had chosen him to save France from atheism and revolution—he had visions like Jeanne d'Arc. His appointment was the biggest mistake of Charles's entire life. Yet the simple old King was not the only person to be deceived; the great Duke of Wellington thought Polignac to be the ablest man that France had had since the Restoration. As for a hard line policy, even Villèle wrote to tell the King that he did not believe that the royal authority could be maintained by making concessions and 'by looking for support to those who want to tear it down'.

There was general astonishment at the new ministry. Mme d'Angoulême told the King, 'This is an adventure and I don't like adventures—they've never brought us luck.' Talleyrand foresaw the end of the Restoration, and M d'Orléans began to see interesting prospects, concealing his pleasure when the young Adolphe Thiers suggested in a Liberal newspaper that the older branch of the Bourbons should be replaced by the younger; Charles had always been kind to him, even granting him the coveted 'Royal Highness', which Louis XVIII had withheld, but Louis Philippe was not noted for gratitude. The opposition to Polignac in the press, the salons and the cafés

grew frenzied, while that in the Chambers was so violent that Greville heard that 'the King does nothing but cry'. Charles could never realize that, by employing Polignac as his chief minister, he had made himself the embodiment of vengeful reaction, and he was deeply distressed by the lack of cheering when he rode through the Paris streets.

Naively, the King believed that all would be well if sufficient military glory were forthcoming. The unrest among the Catholic Belgians, who hated their new Dutch masters, gave Charles and Polignac an intoxicating vision of regaining the Rhine frontier and even the whole of Belgium; the dream was dissipated by Prussian opposition. Luckily Dey Hussein of Algiers struck the French Consul with his fan, which was a good enough excuse to invade the pirates' lair. In May 1830 a fleet of 469 merchantmen, escorted by 100 warships, took 38,000 troops and 4,500 horses to Africa. The army, commanded by the Minister for War, General de Bourmont (the 'traitor of Waterloo') entered the city of Algiers on 5 July 1830 and hoisted the Lilies over the Kasbah. The cost of the entire expedition was paid for by the Dey's treasure.

Meanwhile at the opening of the Chambers in March 1830, Charles more or less threatened, in an extraordinary speech from the throne, that if necessary he would use force to keep his ministers. The opposition replied with an Address to the King, demanding that he appoint his ministers from the majority in the lower chamber—the Charter had never made clear how they were to be chosen. But if Charles were to accept the will of the majority, he would surrender the government of France to men who were hostile to the Bourbons and to the whole concept of the restored monarchy. Charles, believing as he did in a strong monarchy, had once exclaimed, 'I would rather earn my bread than reign like the King of England!' He therefore ordered new elections to take place in June and July; in a proclamation he explained to the electors that to maintain the Charter, 'I must be able to use freely the sacred rights which are the prerogative of my crown', ending rather pathetically, 'It is your King who asks you, it is a father who calls on you.' But the electorate were unmoved; out of 428 deputies returned, 274 were supporters of the Address.

As Charles saw it, in his simplicity, he now had only one

course—to change the electoral system. Strictly speaking, there was provision for this in the Charter. The King told his cabinet that the men of the Left were trying to pull down the monarchy, and he reminded them how weakness had destroyed Louis XVI. 'I remember very well what happened. The first concession made by my brother was the signal for his destruction . . . rather than be carted to the scaffold we will fight and they will have to kill us in the saddle.' In his blindness, Charles saw his measures as essentially legal and in no way a *coup d'état*. 'Dear Jules', who was acting as Minister for War in Bourmont's absence, assured him that there would be no trouble and that in 1830 Frenchmen cared more for prosperity than politics. On 26 July the King therefore issued his 'Four Ordinances of Saint-Cloud'; these dissolved the new Chamber of Deputies before it had even met, restricted the franchise to 10,000 land-owners, and called fresh elections; they also imposed the first really rigorous press censorship since the Empire.

That day Charles went hunting. As he was about to leave Saint-Cloud, Mme de Berry ran up, waving the *Moniteur* in which the ordinances had been published. She cried, 'You are a real King at last! My son will owe his crown to you and his mother thanks you deeply.'

Chateaubriand wrote sadly, 'Yet another government hurling itself down from Nôtre-Dame.' By that evening, a Monday, the mob was in the streets and stoning ministers. On the next day the army had to be called out; most of the troops were in Algeria or on the Belgian frontier, and the effective garrison of Paris was down to 9,000 men. Polignac concealed the gravity of the situation from Charles, who was still at Saint-Cloud, telling him it was nothing but a riot, and that were he mistaken 'I shall give Your Majesty my head in atonement'—he also spoke of a reassuring vision he had had of Our Lady. Meanwhile barricades were going up, arsenals being stormed. By Thursday 29 July the mob—mainly *petit bourgeois* rather than working-class, and led by Napoleonic veterans—had taken the Louvre and the Tuileries, and the army was retreating, many men deserting to the rebels. Yet few deputies had any wish to depose Charles X; they only wanted to be rid of Polignac. If the King had been at the Tuileries in the centre of Paris, instead of outside at Saint-Cloud, a compromise would have been reached.

At last, from the terrace at Saint-Cloud, through a spy glass, poor Charles saw the *tricolore* flying from Nôtre-Dame. He sent an emissary, promising to dismiss Polignac and withdraw the ordinances, and appointed the Duc de Mortemart as Prime Minister. But it was too late. Soon the situation at Saint-Cloud became so dangerous that the King had to move to the Grand Trianon, and then to Rambouillet. Throughout, the old monarch displayed his habitual dignity. Each time the cannon were heard, he gently flicked the cloth of his card-table as though he had seen a spot of dust. Later, with his usual simplicity, he told Mme de Gontaut that he had only tried to appear calm because it seemed the best thing to do. The Duchess says she cried when she saw his sad, resigned face and knew that he realized it was all over.

On 1 August Charles appointed the Duc d'Orléans Lieutenant-General of France. On 2 August 1830, at Rambouillet, he abdicated; for a brief moment there was a Louis XIX until the Dauphin also signed an act of abdication. Then Charles saluted his grandson as King, and presented the ten-year-old Henri V to his guards. Orléans cunningly pretended that he had no authority until the Chambers had debated the abdication; as he expected, the deputies refused to accept the boy. On 7 August Orléans, produced 'like a rabbit out of a hat' by the Liberals, was proclaimed 'Louis Philippe, King of the French'.

Charles had waited trustingly at Rambouillet for the Lieutenant-General to proclaim Henri V. On 3 August, however, hearing that an armed rabble was approaching (some by the new omnibuses), he decided to leave France, although he could have cut them to ribbons. Indeed, as Chateaubriand points out, had Charles fallen back on Chartres or Tours, the monarchy would have survived, as most of the army was loyal. However, like his martyred brother, the old King was not prepared to shed French blood.

But he did not depart like Napoleon, cowering in a closed carriage, or like Louis Philippe in 1848, disguised as an English tourist. Even the sternest critics of Charles X admit that the dignity of his exit had something of the old grandeur of the House of France. Accompanied by cavalry, artillery and infantry of the guard, he marched to Cherbourg beneath the Lilies, insisting on the observance of every detail of etiquette

as though he were still King. French monarchs always dined alone at a square table, and when only a round one could be found, he ordered it to be cut square. At Cherbourg, on 16 August, after saying goodbye to his guards, he boarded a ship bound for England. He wept as it set sail.

Charles landed at Weymouth, staying briefly at Lulworth Castle nearby before travelling to Holyrood which had once more been made available. To his relief, he discovered that nearly £500,000 in gold had been deposited in a London bank by Louis XVIII, in 1814, for just such an emergency. He spent two years in Edinburgh, much more agreeably than before as he was able to leave Holyrood and shoot with the Scots nobility; a great walker, he enjoyed strolling through the Edinburgh streets, when he was usually followed by a large and friendly crowd.

In the summer of 1832, without Charles's permission, Caroline de Berry tried to raise the Vendée for her son. The little rising was easily crushed, and later she was captured. She was then discovered to be pregnant, and Louis Philippe arranged for her delivery to be witnessed by government officials. It was hastily explained that the Duchess had secretly married her secretary the year before, but she was completely discredited. Charles never saw her again.

In September 1832 the King left Scotland for Bohemia, where he found a suitably regal residence in the Gothic Hradschin at Prague. Chateaubriand visited him there, to be shown in by the ever-faithful Blacas, and was much moved. He wrote, 'Charles X, if he distressed me as a monarch, always endeared himself to me as a man.' The King still thought that he had been right to act as he had. 'I wanted to leave my grandson a throne more secure than mine was.' With his unquenchable optimism the old man was certain that one day the French would call Henri back, nor was his instinct entirely wrong. Meanwhile he was as charming as ever, shot a little, played cards and said his prayers.

In the autumn of 1836 a cholera epidemic made the King move his little court from Prague to Gorizia in north-eastern Italy, not far from Trieste. On the morning of 5 November it was realized that he had contracted the dreaded disease. He died the following day and, shrouded in the habit of a Franciscan, was buried in the friary of Castagnavizza, where he still lies.

Chateaubriand comments that, when the thirty-fifth successor of Hugues Capet died, 'an entire era of the world's history went with him'.

'Poor Charles X is dead', King Leopold of the Belgians told his niece, the English Princess Victoria. (Leopold's letter is often quoted, but is too important to omit.) 'History will state that Louis XVIII was a most liberal monarch, reigning with great mildness and justice to his end, but that his brother, from his despotic and harsh disposition, upset all the other had done and lost the throne. Louis XVIII was a clever, hard-hearted man, shackled by no principle, very proud and false. Charles X an honest man, a kind friend, an honourable master, sincere in his opinions and inclined to do everything that is right.'

Indeed, in a simpler political climate Charles might have had a peaceful and prosperous reign. It is not true, as is so often alleged, that he tried to restore the *Ancien Régime*; never for one moment did he attempt to destroy the legal and administrative institutions which his brother had inherited in 1814, and even in 1830 he believed that he was acting constitutionally. He was particularly unfortunate in his choice of Polignac—almost anyone else could have avoided the storm. A contemporary wrote, 'A time will come when, secretly or openly, half the French people will regret the departure of that old man and that child and will say, "If the 1830 Revolution was to be tried all over again, it would not succeed." ' The writer was Balzac.

The Third Restoration

HENRI V (1830 – 1883)

'Henri V will never abandon the flag of Henri IV'

There are some kings who never reigned, whom history none the less calls King. James III of England and Louis XVII are familiar enough. Henri V is less well known.

Many contemporaries saw the Revolution of 1830 as a French version of the English Revolution of 1688, equating the Bourbons with the Stuarts, and in many ways Legitimism, the creed of those loyal to the Bourbon dynasty, was a kind of French Jacobitism. Its supporters included every Frenchman who loved the old kings and the old religion, while it had all the poignant romance common to great lost causes of the Right. But for many years Legitimism was very far from being a lost cause. For France did not finally make up her mind what sort of government she really wanted until the very end of the nineteenth century. In 1830, even Liberals like Stendhal thought a republic 'a horrible condition anywhere else than in America—'tis the real cholera morbus'; and without Louis Philippe and the division among Royalists, France would almost certainly have remained a monarchy into the present century. Fervent Legitimists believed that Heaven would not allow the Orleanists—'the regicide dynasty'—to keep the throne they had stolen, and all good Catholics prayed hopefully for a Third Restoration.

Furthermore, besides the simple creed of the Dukes and country squires, there was also an intellectual Legitimism. Balzac, Vigny, Gustave Doré and later Taine, Renan and even Pasteur, were all Legitimists. Taine and Renan, who were 'scientific' historians, launched a powerfully argued attack on the entire philosophy of the Revolution and on the whole cult of reason and democracy (which had been accepted by Orléanism).

Henri - Charles - Ferdinand - Marie - Dieudonné d'Artois de Bourbon, Duc de Bordeaux, styled Comte de Chambord and known to his followers as King Henri V, had been born in 1820, the son of the murdered Berry. Fatherless, forbidden to see his mother after her disgrace in 1832, deprived of his adored grandfather in 1836, Henri spent his youth in Austria in the midst of fanatical Ultra exiles. His aunt d'Angoulême filled him with tales of her martyred parents, while Jesuit tutors—archreactionaries in the nineteenth century—instilled an uncompromising piety into the boy, as well as some rather slanted history. He grew up unused to being contradicted, for his courtiers still followed the old etiquette, and it is hardly surprising that he acquired too much faith in his own judgement. The old King had been a father rather than a grandfather to him, and fundamentally Henri's political convictions were those of Charles X: later he derided 'sterile parliamentary confrontations from which the sovereign usually emerges so weakened as to be all but powerless'. Above all, he grew up to be a Catholic of the penitential sort, expecting affliction rather than mercy from his God; his natural haughtiness was tempered by genuine humility. He was devout to the point of mysticism, a faithful husband and a loyal friend. Of all his dynasty, he resembled most his great-grandfather—the Dauphin Louis, son of Louis XV.

In appearance, Henri V was the short, stout sort of Bourbon, his face that of a man of sorrows, mournful and austere. Apart from brilliant, piercing eyes, a heavy beard and a curious hairiness, his chief characteristic was a pronounced limp due to a riding accident when he was twenty-one. In manner he was unmistakably regal, though reserved and silent. He undoubtedly possessed what is nowadays known as 'charisma'.

In 1843 the King set out on a long European tour, arriving in England later that year, much to Queen Victoria's emotion. He stayed in Belgrave Square, from where he issued a manifesto: Legitimists sang *Vive Henri Quatre* under his window while he received their leaders. In 1846—after a sad little romance with a Russian Grand Duchess, broken off by order of the Tsar—he married a Habsburg, Archduchess Marie Theresa, daughter of the Duke of Modena. She was a tall, angular old maid, three years older than he, soured by premature deafness, arrogant

and blindly reactionary in her political and religious views, and with a deep distrust of the pagan French (whose language she spoke with a peculiarly ugly accent). They were to be childless.

Henri's sister, Mademoiselle, had left him the year before to marry their cousin, the future Charles III of Parma. The young Duke was assassinated in 1854, whereupon Mademoiselle became Regent for her six-year-old son, Robert I. But in 1860 even Parma was lost to the Bourbons, when the *Risorgimento* swept Robert off his throne and incorporated the Duchy into the new Kingdom of Italy. Poor battered Mademoiselle died four years later.

After the 'Revolution of Contempt' had ejected Louis Philippe and his Bourgeois Monarchy in 1848, and during the subsequent reaction, the majority in the French Assembly was divided between Legitimist and Orleanist deputies. A group of the former went to meet Henri at Wiesbaden to discuss the situation with him, but no positive policy emerged. Legitimist officers planned a *coup d'état* for 1849, but it never took place. In the event, Louis Napoleon took advantage of the Royalists' disunity to give the French the strong monarchy which they sought and set himself up as Napoleon III. But the tawdry *Opèra Bouffe* world of the Second Empire, with its crowned adventurer, its flash court and its foreign business barons, thoroughly disgusted the Legitimists, and indeed many other Frenchmen as well.

The Legitimist party was both well supported and well organized. There were three sorts of Legitimist. First, men of action like the Duc des Cars and General de Saint-Priest, who would have liked a *coup d'état*. Then the parliamentarians, such as Pierre-Antoine Berryer, a golden-voiced lawyer from Lorraine who was called 'the tribune of the monarchy'. Although of bourgeois origin, he was the idol of the French nobility on account of his wonderful speeches: Emile Olivier (Napoleon III's 'liberal' prime minister) said, 'He who has never heard Berryer speaking on one of his good days, does not know what oratory is.' Berryer hoped for a decentralized constitutional monarchy. Decentralization—and hatred of Paris—was one of the inspirations of the third group, the populist Legitimists, who tried to forge a kind of radical Tory alliance with the Republicans; they were led by the Marquis de Rochejacquelein, who advocated

universal suffrage. Some of these democratic noblemen even went so far as to argue that true virtue was to be found only in peasants.

These three Legitimist groupings were co-ordinated by a high command in Paris which was appointed by the King. The *Bureau du Roi* consisted of twelve devoted noblemen who met once a week under the chairmanship of the Duc de Lévis or the Duc des Cars—or later, the Marquis de Dreux-Brézé (one meets again all the old names so familiar under the *Ancien Régime* and during the Restoration). Besides laying down guide-lines for policy, the Bureau also organized fund-raising, with gratifying results: despite their lamentations, the upper ranks of the French nobility had remained surprisingly wealthy. At local level there was a network of clubs and secret societies: in some instances, Freemasons' Lodges were actually taken over. There was even a Legitimist news agency, founded in 1848 by a M de Saint-Chéron; the *Correspondance Saint-Chéron* sent out well-composed press releases to newspapers all over France.

From the 1840s to the 1870s, the Legitimist party was probably the best organized and best disciplined political opposition in French history. Another Louis XVIII would have regained his throne easily in 1849 or after 1870. Alas, Henri V was incapable of being a politician. In a sense he was not even a Legitimist—to himself and to his more deluded followers he was simply the re-incarnation of *la vieille France*, a formula which was hardly an election winner. Legitimist leaders complained respectfully but bitterly of their King's lack of leadership.

Henri lived happily enough in his castle at Frohsdorf (in Upper Austria, near Salzburg) with a little court of devoted friends headed by Blacas's son, where he was treated with simple yet impressive etiquette. He hunted and shot and played his whist and attended Mass, just as his grandfather had done, his chief pleasure being his beautiful grey horses. He was fond of his charmless, sterile wife, who loved him deeply. A romantic whose favourite authors were Dumas and Chateaubriand, his fantasies of Old France were far preferable to the reality. Only if the country which had beheaded his great-uncle, rejected his grandfather, murdered his father and disgraced his mother, begged him humbly to return, would he contemplate ascending the throne of his ancestors. He wanted no *coups*

d'état, no Vendées, no counter-revolutions; everything must be left to Divine Providence. With his Wagnerian isolation, dreaming medieval dreams in his lonely turrets, he has been compared to the Bavarian Ludwig II at Neuschwanstein.

The extraordinarily unreal atmosphere of his court was typified by the elder Blacas. When the old Duke died in 1839, he left instructions for his body to be buried at the feet of Charles X, in the best traditions of thirteenth-century French chivalry. This mock-medievalism was to be the ruin of the Legitimist cause.

However, Henri made a political move in 1859, when the *Risorgimento* threatened the Papal States. He announced that he was ready to 'pay with his blood for a cause which was that of France, the Church and God'. There was an enthusiastic response to his appeal. Legitimist volunteers flocked to the Pope's army to become the redoubtable *Zouaves Pontificales*, who fought beneath the Bourbon Lilies; a detachment from the Vendée was only dissuaded with difficulty from wearing the Crusaders' cross.

Then, unexpectedly, Napoleon III was utterly defeated by the Prussians at Sédan on 2 September 1870, and a provisional republic was proclaimed two days later. In the general election of February the following year, the Right triumphed—180 Legitimists were returned, together with over 200 Orleanists and 30 Bonapartists, to be faced by only 200 Republicans who were split into moderates and extremists. The Left were thrown into even more disorder in the spring by the Communards' Revolution in Paris, and by its savage repression. All that stood in the way of a restoration was the President, Adolphe Thiers, who had been prominent in bringing down Henri's grandfather and who believed that a republic 'would divide Frenchmen least'; and the disunity of the monarchists.

One should not forget how alarming the idea of a republic must have seemed to many Frenchmen in 1871. The only European republic which then existed was Switzerland, while memories of the Revolution and of 1848 and its riots, and the recent and bloody experience of the Commune, did not inspire confidence among moderates. Furthermore, conservatism was strengthened by the current Catholic revival, a kind of moral rearmament which expressed itself in huge pilgrimages and in

building a great basilica at Montmartre to atone for the sins of France.

The law which exiled the Bourbons was repealed. Henri returned briefly to France in 1871, spending three days at his château of Chambord. Here he issued a proclamation declaring that, while he would never abandon the Lilies—'I will not let the standard of Henri IV, of François I, of Jeanne d'Arc, be torn from my hands'—he was ready to accept parliamentary government. He then left France. The Orleanists tried desperately to persuade him to make way for the Comte de Paris, but in January 1872 Henri issued a second proclamation, refusing to abdicate; in February he held a monster rally at Antwerp. The impasse between Legitimists and Orleanists lasted for another year.

On 24 May 1873 Thiers fell, manœuvred into resigning by the Right. His successor was the Franco-Irish Marshal, Patrice de MacMahon, Duc de Magente; a convinced Legitimist, he only accepted the Presidency to pave the way for a Restoration. The real power behind this honourable but simple old soldier were three Orleanist Dukes: the Duc de Broglie, Prime Minister; the Duc d'Audiffret-Pasquier, President of the Assembly; and the Duc Decazes, Foreign Minister (and the son of Louis XVIII's darling Elie). Then the Whigs turned Jacobite: the government, 'the Republic of Dukes', determined to forge an alliance with the Legitimists. The latter were nearly all noblemen, a wonderfully picturesque collection from the Faubourg Saint-Germain and the depths of the countryside; some were quite ready for another White Terror, like the fanatical *Chevaux-Légers* or 'Light Horse', but there were also those like the Comte de Falloux who believed in constitutional monarchy and accepted the *Tricolore*. Moderate Legitimists were prepared to bargain with the Orleanists—the fact that that mainly bourgeois party was now led by Dukes facilitated negotiations—on the basis that the childless Henri should reign so long as he lived and then be succeeded by the Orleanist Pretender, who in any case was his heir presumptive. (Louis-Philippe-Albert's descendant is the present French Pretender, Henri, Comte de Paris.)

The army was willing to support the Restoration; an officer who protested publicly was summarily retired, and there were

plenty of Legitimist generals like the Marquis de Gallifet (familiar to readers of Proust) who had slaughtered the Communards with such cruel zest. Opposition was expected in many parts of France from peasants who believed that not only would tithes and feudal dues return, but that Henri V was going to bring back the legendary *droit de seigneur*—the nobleman's right to every peasant girl on her wedding night. None the less, even that great Republican Gambetta thought that as a whole France was too tired of bloodshed to resist; if the peasants did rise, the troops would crush them and the government would then be congratulated for crushing anarchy.

On 5 August 1873, two distinguished visitors arrived unexpectedly at Frohsdorf. They were Louis-Philippe-Albert, Comte de Paris and Head of the House of Orleans (he was the usurper's grandson), and his uncle the Prince de Joinville. It was a difficult moment—Henri's consort was known to bear a hatred for the Orleans amounting to mania. The Count, who looked more like a German professor than a French nobleman, hesitated when Henri V entered the room, then bowed and greeted his cousin as his King. Henri embraced him. 'You were quite right to come here privately like this without waiting,' he said. 'The *Bon Dieu* will reward you.' The Count, whom he now acknowledged as Dauphin, was in his mid-thirties and had as much practical ability as the King possessed idealism and honour—he had even studied English trade unionism. Shortly after his visit to Frohsdorf, the Comte de Paris publicly recognized Henri as 'the sole representative of the monarchic principle in France'.

On the evening of 14 October a delegation headed by the Legitimist M Pierre Chesnelong—not a nobleman oddly enough, but a successful draper—met their King in a little pavilion in the garden of a hotel at Salzburg. During a pleasant dinner party, full agreement was reached on universal suffrage and ministerial responsibility. But then Henri announced grimly, 'I will never abandon the White Flag,' M Chesnelong, a glib Gascon, made his famous reply, 'Your Majesty must allow me not to have heard those words.' After an hour's argument, the King reluctantly agreed that the *Tricolore* could remain the flag of France until after the Restoration, when he would refer the matter to the Assembly. Chesnelong returned in triumph with

the wonderful news that an agreement had been reached, not only on the constitution but on the flag.

Everyone was now convinced that the King would have his own again. The President of the Assembly, the Duc d'Audiffret-Pasquier, declared triumphantly on 18 October, 'In three weeks the national, hereditary and constitutional monarchy will be established.' The Faubourg Saint-Germain ordered court dress, while coaches prepared for the Most Christian King's *joyeuse entrée* into 'his good city of Paris' may still be seen at Chambord. Daniel Halévy writes of 'an amazing rally of *la vieille France*, of the old nobles, of Dukes and country squires, of priests and heralds'. It was the French nobility's final fling.

On 31 October 1873, on Henri's orders, the Legitimist newspaper *L'Union* published a letter which he had written to M Chesnelong. The King could not abandon the White Flag. 'I cannot agree to open a strong and healing reign by an act of weakness,' he explained. 'It is the fashion to contrast the stubbornness of Henri V with the flexibility of Henry IV . . . but I wish to remain just what I am.'

As a boy, Henri had seen the French army march off under the White Flag to conquer Algiers. With his contempt for Bonapartism, he was incapable of understanding that a new military tradition had grown up since he had left France, based on glorious victories in Italy and the Crimea, in Africa, China and Mexico, and on heroism in defeat during the martyrdom of 1870. All these campaigns had been fought under the *Tricolore*.

Marshal MacMahon, who had served beneath the Lilies as a young man, was thunderstruck by Henri's decision. He said that if the army was forced to fly the White Flag, 'the *chassepots* [rifles] would go off by themselves!' Broglie decided that the only thing left was to introduce a bill extending the Marshal-President's powers for seven years, the *Septennat*, in the hope of at least saving conservative government. The Third Restoration was over. As the Pope, Pio Nono, wryly observed, 'Whoever heard of a man giving up a throne for a napkin?'

Then followed an incident as romantic as anything in those novels by Alexandre Dumas which the King enjoyed so much. The Assembly sat at Versailles, and there Henri arrived secretly on 10 November, accompanied only by his valet, to stay at a small house in the rue Saint-Louis. (He had to bring

his valet, as he had never learnt how to tie his own tie cravat.) His faithful gentlemen, the Duc de Blacas and the Marquis de Dreux-Brézé, joined him and were informed of an amazing scheme. He would appeal to MacMahon as a French nobleman, tell him to bring a cavalry brigade, then together, arm-in-arm *à la Française*, they would go into the Assembly, who would proclaim Henri King. Poor Blacas went to the Marshal with the preposterous plan, asking him to call on his master, by night if necessary, and leaving the key of the house in the rue Saint-Louis; obviously a King could not call on a subject. But MacMahon had taken an oath to the Assembly, and his honour would not let him break it. Henri waited in vain, before saying sadly, 'I expected a Constable of France but I find only a Chief of Police.' On 19 November, the Assembly voted for the *Septennat*—a tacit rejection of the monarchy. There is a legend that, disguised in a voluminous cloak, the King waited during a grey and misty afternoon in front of the palace, by the pedestal of Louis XIV's statue, to hear the result.

Later a Legitimist general said, 'If only we had known!' But the King had left France for ever on that night of 19 November 1873, to return to his dreaming in Upper Austria. In June 1874 the Duc de La Rochefoucauld, as a last desperate step, proposed to the Assembly that the monarchy be restored; his motion was defeated by 272 notes to 79. On 30 January 1875, France became a Republic—by one vote.

King Henri, fortified by the rites of Holy Church, died at Frohsdorf on 24 August 1883 after a long and painful illness borne with much courage. He was never a bitter man, and one may guess that his last years were happier than they would have been had the Third Restoration succeeded. It is easy to blame him for throwing away the crown of France. Yet, as the late Sir Denis Brogan (hardly an admirer) writes, Henri V 'had made, not by cowardice but by pride and dignity, the great refusal'. Professor Cobban even goes so far as to say of Henri that 'trained as he said himself to expect nothing from God and nothing from man, free from worldly ambition or knowledge, lame, isolated, living in and for the past', he was 'perhaps the noblest of his line'.

It was fitting that Henri V should die childless. However magnificent in their days of glory, the Bourbons, like the

dinosaurs, could not adapt to a new and alien environment. Theirs was the first great monarchy to fall before democracy, never to be restored. The failure of the Third Restoration announced the doom of all hereditary monarchies of the crowned and anointed sort, not only in Europe but throughout the entire world.

SELECT BIBLIOGRAPHY

Princes of the Blood

P. de Bourdeille de Brantôme: *Oeuvres Completes* . . . ., Paris 1864–82
G. Dodu: *Les Valois*, Paris 1934
R. Fawtier: *Les Capétiens et la France*, Paris 1941
C. V. Langlois: *St. Louis—Philippe le Bel—Les derniers Capétiens directs (1226–1328), in Histoire de France depuis les origines jusqu'à la Révolution*, ed. E. Lavisse, vol III, pt ii, Paris 1900–11
A. de Ruble: *Antoine de Bourbon et Jeanne d'Albret*, Paris 1881–6
H. Vrignault: *Genéalogie de la maison de Bourbon*, Paris 1957

Henri IV

T. A. d'Aubigné: *Memoires de la vie de T. A. d'Aubigné*, Amsterdam 1731
S. Beguin: *L'Ecole de Fontainebleau—le Manièrisme à la cour de France*, Paris 1960
P. de Bourdeille de Brantôme: *op. cit.*
Sir Anthony Blunt: *Art and Architecture in France 1500–1700*, Penguin 1953
Sir George Carew: *A Relation of the State of France, An Historical View of the Negotiations between the Courts of England, France and Brussells from the year 1592 to 1617*, ed. T. Birch, London 1749
Marguerite de Valois: *Les Mémoires de la roine Marguerite*, Paris 1628
J. H. Mariéjol: *La Reforme et La Ligue: l'Edit de Nantes 1559–98*, in Lavisse, vol VI, pt. i
J. H. Mariéjol: *Henri IV et Louis XIII 1598–1643*, in ibid pt. ii
R. Mousnier: *The Assassination of Henri IV*, trans J. Spencer, Faber and Faber 1973
Sir John Neale: *The Age of Catherine de Medici*, Jonathan Cape 1957 (new edn.)
R. Ritter: *Henri IV lui-même: l'Homme*, Paris 1944

D. Seward: *The first Bourbon: Henri IV of France and Navarre*, Constable 1971

F. C. Spooner: *The Economy of Europe 1559–1610* in *The New Cambridge Modern History* vol. III Cup. 1968

M. de Béthune, Duc de Sully: *Memoires*, Amsterdam and Paris 1638–63. Rearranged by the abbé de L'Ecluse, London 1747

P. de Vaissière: *Henri IV*, Paris 1928

C. H. Wilson: *Trade, Society and the State*, in *The Cambridge Economic History of Europe*, vol. IV, Cup. 1967

J. Berger de Xivrey: *Recueil des Lettres Missives de Henri IV*, Paris 1843–76

Louis XIII

L. Batiffol: *Le Roi Louis XIII à vingt ans*, Paris 1910

Sir A. Blunt: *op. cit.*

C. J. Burckhardt: *Richelieu*, Allen & Unwin 1940 and 1968

P. Erlanger: *Louis XIII*, Paris 1946

P. Erlanger: *Cinq Mars*, Paris 1962

J. Howell: *Lustra Ludovici*, London 1646

F. De Montglat: *Mémoires de Montglat*, Paris 1850

Mme de la Motteville: *Mémoires de Motteville sur Anne d'Autriche et sa cour*, Paris 1886

J. Levron: *La Vie Quotidienne à la cour de Versailles*, Paris 1965

J. Lough: *An Introduction to Seventeenth Century France*, Longmans, Green & Co. 1954

J. Mariéjol: *op. cit.*

D. P. O'Connell: *Richelieu*, Weidenfeld & Nicolson 1968

C. Romain: *Louis XIII, un grand roi méconnu*, Paris 1934

Duc de Saint-Simon: *Mémoires*, Paris 1879–1930

G. Tallemant des Réaux: *Les Historiettes de Tallemant des Réaux*, Paris 1854–60

V. C. Tapié: *La France de Louis XIII et de Richelieu*, Paris 1952

L. Vaunois: *Vie de Louis XIII*, Paris 1936

C. V. Wedgwood: *The Thirty Years War*

C. V. Wedgwood: *Richelieu and the French Monarchy*, English University Press 1949

C. H. Wilson: *op. cit.*

Louis XIV

Lord Acton: *History of Freedom and other Essays*, London 1907

Select Bibliography

Sir A. Blunt: *op. cit.*

Marquis de Dangeau: *Mémoires du Marquis de Dangeau*, Paris and London 1817

Elisabeth Charlotte, Princesse de Bavière, *Correspondance complète de Madame, Duchesse d'Orleans*, Paris 1904

P. Erlanger: *Louis XIV*, Paris 1960

C. Haldane: *Mme de Maintenon*, Constable 1970

R. M. Hatton: *Louis XIV and his world*, Thames and Hudson 1972

E. Lavisse: *Louis XIV: La Fronde: Le Roi: Colbert (1643–85)*, in Lavisse *op. cit.* vol. 7 pt. i

E. Lavisse: *Louis XIV: La Réligion: Les Lettres et les Arts: La Guerre (1643–85)*, in ibid, vol. 7 pt. ii

J. Levron: *op. cit.*

W. H. Lewis: *The Sunset of the Splendid Century*, Eyre & Spottiswoode 1955

J. Lough: *op. cit.*

Louis XIV: *Mémoires*, Paris 1927

D. Maland: *Culture and Society in Seventeenth Century France*, Batsford 1970

N. Mitford: *The Sun King*, Hamish Hamilton 1966

C. de Montesquieu: *Lettres Persanes*, Paris 1721

D. Ogg: *Louis XIV*, Oxford 1967

Cardinal de Retz: *Oeuvres*, Paris 1870–1920

A. de Saint-Léger, A. Rébelliau, P. Sagnac and E. Lavisse: *La Fin du Règne (1685–1715)*, in Lavisse *op. cit.*, vol. 8 pt. i

Saint-Simon: *op. cit.*

Mme de Sevigné: *Lettres*, Paris 1862–6

E. Spanheim: *Relation de la cour de France en 1690*, Paris 1909

V. L. Tapié: *Baroque et Classicisme*, Paris 1957

Voltaire: *The Age of Louis XIV*, Dent 1958

C. H. Wilson: *op. cit.*

J. B. Wolf: *Louis XIV*, New York 1968

G. Ziegler: *Les Coulisses de Versailles. Le Regne de Louis XIV*, Paris 1963

Louis XV

Marquis D'Argenson: *Memoires et Journal* . . . Paris 1857–58

T. Bainville: *Histoire de France*, Paris 1924

T. Carlyle: *The French Revolution*, London 1837

H. Carré: *Le Règne de Louis XV*, in Lavisse *op. cit.* vol. 8 pt. ii

Duc de Croÿ: *Journal Inédit du Duc de Croÿ 1718–84*, Paris 1906

P. Gaxotte: *Le Siècle de Louis XV*, Paris 1933

Select Bibliography

A. Gonzalez Palacios: *Il Luigi XV*, Milan 1966
G. P. Gooch: *Louis XV. The Monarchy in Decline*, Longmans, Green & Co. 1956
C. J. F. Henault: *Mémoires*, Paris 1911
J. Lough: *An Introduction to Eighteenth Century France*, Longmans 1960
Duc de Luynes: *Mémoires du Duc de Luynes sur la cour de Louis XV 1735–58*, Paris 1860–65
J. Michelet: *Histoire de France*, Paris 1876–78
N. Mitford: *Mme de Pompadour*, Hamish Hamilton 1954
D. Ogg: *Europe of the Ancien Régime 1715–1783*, Collins 1965
H. Walpole: *The Letters of Horace Walpole*, O.U.P. 1905

Louis XVI

C. A. Behrens: *The Ancien Régime*, Thames & Hudson 1967
E. Burke: *Reflections on the Revolution in France*, London 1790
Mme de Campan: *Mémoires sur la Vie Privée de la Reine Marie Antoinette*, Paris 1823
T. Carlyle: *op. cit.*
H. Carré, P. Sagnac and E. Lavisse: *La Règne de Louis XVI* (1774–8), in Lavisse *op. cit.*, vol. 9 pt. i
Vicomte F. A. R. de Chateaubriand: *Mémoires d'Outre Tombe*
A. Cobban: *A History of Modern France*, Jonathan Cape 1962–5
A. Dumas: *La Route de Varennes*, Paris 1889
B. Faÿ: *Louis XVI, ou le Fin d'un Monde*, Paris 1961
A. Gonzalez Palacios: *Il Luigi XVI*, Milan 1966
Comte d'Hézecques: *Mémoires*
G. Lewis: *Life in Revolutionary France*, Thames & Hudson 1972
J. Michelet: *op. cit.*
F. A. Mignet: *Histoire de la Révolution Francaise 1789–1814*, Paris 1898
G. Morris: *A Diary of the French Revolution 1789–1793*, Houghton Mifflin 1939
Napoleon: *Correspondance de Napoléon I*, Paris 1858–69
S. K. Padover: *The Life and Death of Louis XVI*, New York 1939
G. Pernoud and S. Flaissier: *La Révolution*, Paris 1959
G. Rudé: *The Crowd in the French Revolution*, Oxford 1959
Comte de Ségur: *Histoire et Mémoires par le Général Comte de Ségur*, Paris 1873
J. M. Thompson: *English Witnesses of the French Revolution*, Blackwell 1938

308

Select Bibliography

J. M. Thompson: *The French Revolution*, Blackwell 1944
A. de Tocqueville: *L'Ancien Régime et la Révolution*, Paris 1877

Louis XVII

A. de Beauchesne: *Louis XVII, sa vie, son agonie, sa mort*, Paris 1852
A. Castelot: *Louis XVII*, Paris 1960
Comte d'Hezécques: *Mémoires*
G. Lenotre: *Le Roi Louis XVII et l'énigme du Temple*, Paris 1927
J. B. Morton: *The Dauphin (Louis XVII)*, Longmans 1937
Thomson: *op. cit.*

Louis XVIII

F. B. Artz: *France under the Bourbon Restoration 1814–1830*, Harvard
    University Press 1931
H. de Balzac: *Le Bal de Sceaux*, Paris 1967
V. W. Beach: *Charles X of France*, Colorado 1971
C. A. de Bertier de Sauvigny: *La Restauration*, Paris 1953
J. F. Bertrand: *Talleyrand*, Putnams 1973
Comte Beugnot: *Mémoires du Comte Beugnot 1783–1818*, Paris 1868
F. Burney: *The Diary of Fanny Burney*, Dent 1950
Sir Denis Brogan: *The French Nation from Napoleon to Pétain 1714–
    1940*, Hamish Hamilton 1957
J. P. T. Bury: *France 1814–1940*, Methuen 1949
Mme de Campan: *op. cit.*
Chateaubriand: *op. cit.*
A. Cobban: *A History of Modern France*
H. F. Collins: *Talma*, Faber & Faber 1964
A. Dumas: *Les Blancs et les Bleus*, Paris 1890
A. Dumas: *Le Comte de Monte-Cristo*, Paris 1850
Duchesse de Gontaut: *Mémoires de Madame la Duchesse de Gontaut,
    gouvernante des Enfants de France pendant la Restauration 1777–
    1836*, Paris 1892
C. C. F. Greville: *The Greville Memoirs 1814–60* (ed. L. Strachey and
    R. Fulford), MacMillan 1938
Comte d'Hézecques: *Mémoires*
A. L. Imbert de Saint-Armand: *The Duchesse of Angoulême and the Two
    Restorations*, London 1892

Select Bibliography

A. L. Imbert de Saint-Armand: *La Duchesse de Berry et la cour de Louis XVIII*, Paris 1887

A. de Lamartine: *Oeuvres*, Paris 1849

G. Lefebvre: *Napoléon*, Paris 1936

G. Lewis: *op. cit.*

J. Lucas-Dubreton: *Louis XVIII*, Paris 1925

Lady Morgan: *Lady Morgan in France* (ed. E. Suddaby and R. J. Yarrow), Oriel Press 1971

Napoleon: *Correspondance*

E. Saunders: *The Hundred Days*, Longmans 1964

Comte de Villèle: *Mémoires et correspondance du Comte de Villèle*, Paris 1888–1904

M. Weiner: *The French Exiles 1789–1815*, John Murray 1964

Charles X

F. B. Artz: *op. cit.*

F. B. Artz: *Reaction and Revolution 1814–1832*, Harper Crow (New York) 1963

V. W. Beach: *Charles X of France*, Colorado 1971

J. F. Bertrand: *op. cit.*

G. de Bertier de Sauvigny: *op. cit.*

Sir Denis Brogan: *op. cit.*

Duc de Broglie: *Mémoires*

J. P. T. Bury: *op. cit.*

Mme de Campan: *Mémoires*

Vicomte F. A. R. de Chateaubriand: *op. cit.*

Vicomte F. A. R. de Chateaubriand: *Mémoires*

R. Cobb: *A Second Identity: essays on France and French History*, O.U.P. 1969

A. Cobban: *op. cit.*

Duchesse de Gontaut: *Mémoires*

A. Gonzalez Palacios: *Il Luigi XVI*, Milan 1966

C. F. C. Greville: *op. cit.*

Comte d'Hézeques: *Mémoires*

V. Hugo: *Choses Vues*, Paris 1887

A. L. Imbert de Saint Amand: *The Duchesse of Berry and the court of Charles X*, London 1893

A. L. Imbert de Saint Amand: *op. cit.*

A. L. Imbert de Saint Amand: *op. cit.*

D. Johnson: *Guizot: Aspects of French History 1787–1874*, Routledge and Kegan Paul 1963

Select Bibliography

A. de Lamartine: *Mémoires*

G. Lewis: *op. cit.*

A. Maurois: *Promethée, on la Vie de Balzac*, Paris 1965

Lady Morgan: *op. cit.*

Napoleon: *Correspondance*

Stendal: *To the Happy Few (selected letters translated by N. Cameron)*, John Lehman 1952

A. de Tocqueville: *Souvenirs d'Alexis de Tocqueville*, Paris 1944

Comte de Vaudreuil: *Correspondance intime du Comte de Vaudreuil et du Comte D'Arrtois pendant l'Emigration 1789–1815*, Paris 1889

Comte de Villeule: *Memoires et correspondance*

M. Weiner: *op. cit.*

Henry V

Sir Denis Brogan: *The Development of Modern France 1870–1939*, 1940

M. L. Brown: *The Comte de Chambord: The Third Republic's Uncompromising King*, Duke University Press 1967

Comte de Chambord: *Mes Idées*, 1872

Comte de Chambord: *Correspondance de 1841 à 1879*, Paris 1880

Vicomte F. A. R. de Chateaubriand: *Mémoires*

A. Cobban: *op. cit.*

Baron M. de Damas: *Mémoires 1785–1862*, Paris 1922

Comte de Falloux: *Mémoires d'un Royaliste*, Paris 1888

D. Halévy: *La république des ducs*, Paris 1937

Baron J. G. Hyde de Neuville, *Mémoires et Souvenirs*, Paris 1892

P. de Luz: *Henri V*, Paris 1931

S. Osgood: *French Royalism under the Third and Fourth Republics*, The Hague 1960

T. Zeldin: *France 1848–1945*, O.U.P. 1973

INDEX

313

Index

Index

Index

Index

327

Index

328

Index

Spanish Netherlands, 23, 53, 61, 105; see also Dutch
Spanish Succession, War of the (1701–1713), 107, 110–16
Spannheim, Ezekiel, 98, 104
Spinoza, 150
Staël, Mme de, 33, 186, 262
Stanislas Leszczynski (ex-King of Poland), 130, 133–4, 147
States General, 126, 272 (1614) 38–9, 201; (1789) 200, 201–3, 204, 238
Steinkirk, battle of (1692), 107
Stendhal, (Henri Beyle), 155, 251, 257, 263, 286, 295
Stormont, Lord, 187
Strasbourg, 105, 107, 116, 131
Suffren, Bailli de, 188
Sully, Maximilien de Béthune, Duc de (Baron de Rosny), 18, 21, 23, 24, 25–6, 27, 29, 30, 31, 32, 33, 38, 54
Sweden, 72, 92–3, 105, 180, 189, 242, 276
Swiss Guards, 213–14, 224, 247, 254, 270
Swiss Republic, 299

taille (property tax), 25, 83
Taine, Hippolyte, 295
Tallard, Marshal, 111, 113
Talleyrand-Perigord, Charles Maurice de Prince de, 142, 195, 208, 241, 244, 245, 246, 247, 248–9, 252, 253, 255, 256, 260, 265, 287
Talma, François Joseph, actor, 251, 255
Talon, Omar, 71
Tartuffe (Molière), 89, 142, 235
taxation, 23, 25, 54, 55, 74, 75, 83, 84, 132, 154, 155, 162, 168, 179, 181, 199, 200, 208, 250
Télémaque (Fénelon), 126
Temple, imprisonment of royal family in (1792–5), 214–17, 223–32, 241, 245
Terray, Joseph Marie, 167, 168, 169, 180
the Terror (1793–4), 226–7
theatre, 87, 117, 142–3, 195, 255, 271
Théâtre des Petits Cabinets, Versailles, 142
Théâtre Français, 201
Thiers, Adolphe, 287, 299, 300
Thirty Years War, 59, 72
Thou, François-Auguste de, 65
Thou, Jacques Auguste de, 29
Tiers Etat (Commoners), 198, 201–2, 203, 204, 238, 272
Tiers Parti, 19
Tocqueville, Alexis de, xiv, 156, 189, 190, 192, 195, 200, 202
Torcy, Marquis de, 114
Toulon, 84, 113, 225

Toulouse, 45, 53, 163, 249, 263
Toulouse, Comte de (Louis XIV's son), 99, 117
Tournai, siege of, 140, 141
Tourzel, Mme de (Louis XVII's governess), 222
Treaty of Aix-la-Chapelle (1748), 142
Treaty of Hubertusburg (1763), 161
Treaty of Paris (1763), 161
Treaty of Ryswick (1697), 107
Treaty of Utrecht (1713), 116
Treaty of Versailles (1783), 189
Triple Alliance (England, Sweden and United Provinces), 92–3
Triumvirat, 167–9, 179
Trocadero, siege of (1823), 263–4
Tuileries, Paris, 28, 46, 82, 89, 238, 239, 247, 248, 255, 260, 262, 277, 282, 284, 289; Louis XV takes up residence in, 124, 127; Louis XVI's enforced residence during Revolution in, 207, 208, 209–10; and *sans-culottes'* storming of, 212, 213–14, 222; Louis XVII's childhood in, 222–3; and Artois's residence in Pavillon de Marsan, 251, 279, 285; occupation by Parisiens (1830), 289
Turennes, Henri de la Tour d'-Auvergne, Vicomte de, 76–7, 78, 93, 94
Turgot de l'Aulne, Anne-Robert-Jacques, Baron, 180, 181–2, 187, 198, 236, 237
Turin, 65, 106, 243, 273
Turkey, 26, 103, 180, 284

Ultras (during Restoration), 249, 250, 251, 252, 256, 259–60, 261, 262–3, 264, 278–9, 280, 283, 286–7, 296
L'Union (Legitimist paper), 302
United Provinces *see* Dutch
Unton, Sir Henry, 18, 19

Vallière, Duc de, 147
Valmy, battle of (1792), 214–15, 240, 252, 275
van Loo, painter, 146, 149
Varennes, Royal flight to (1791), 210, 222, 239
Vauban, Sebastien de, Marshal, 92, 105
Vaudreuil, Marquis de, 195, 271, 273
Vauguyon, Duc de, 176, 235, 269
Vauvenargues, Luc de Clapiers, Marquis de, 150
Vaux-le-Vicomte, Fouquet's château at, 82–3
Vendée, Vendéens, 224, 246, 250, 274, 275, 291, 299
Vendôme, Antoine, Duc de *see* Antoine de Bourbon

331

Index